W9-BYJ-510

KOVELS'
Guide to Selling, Buying, and Fixing Your Antiques and Collectibles

BOOKS BY RALPH AND TERRY KOVEL

American Country Furniture 1780–1875

Dictionary of Marks—Pottery & Porcelain

A Directory of American Silver, Pewter and Silver Plate

Kovels' Advertising Collectibles Price List

Kovels' American Silver Marks

Kovels' Antiques & Collectibles Price List

Kovels' Antiques & Collectibles Fix-It Source Book

Kovels' Book of Antique Labels

Kovels' Bottle Price List

Kovels' American Art Pottery:
   The Collector's Guide to Makers, Marks, and Factory Histories

Kovels' Collector's Guide to American Art Pottery

Kovels' Collector's Source Book

Kovels' Depression Glass & American Dinnerware Price List

Kovels' Guide to Selling Your Antiques & Collectibles

Kovels' Illustrated Price Guide to Royal Doulton

Kovels' Know Your Antiques

Kovels' Know Your Collectibles

Kovels' New Dictionary of Marks—Pottery & Porcelain

Kovels' Organizer for Collectors

Kovels' Price Guide for Collector Plates, Figurines,
   Paperweights, and Other Limited Editions

KOVELS'

Guide to Selling, Buying, and Fixing Your Antiques and Collectibles

Ralph & Terry Kovel

Crown Trade Paperbacks
New York

Copyright © 1995 by Ralph and Terry Kovel

All rights reserved. No part of this book may be reproduced or transmitted
in any form or by any means, electronic or mechanical, including photocopying, recording, or by any information storage and retrieval system,
without permission in writing from the publisher.

Published by Crown Trade Paperbacks, 201 East 50th Street, New York,
New York 10022. Member of the Crown Publishing Group.

Portions of this book were previously published in *Kovels' Antiques
& Collectibles Fix-It Source Book* and *Kovels' Guide to Selling Your
Antiques & Collectibles*.

Random House, Inc. New York, Toronto, London, Sydney, Auckland

CROWN TRADE PAPERBACKS and colophon are trademarks of Crown
Publishers, Inc.

Manufactured in the United States of America

DESIGN BY DEBORAH KERNER

Library of Congress Cataloging-in-Publication Data
Kovel, Ralph M.
[Guide to selling, buying, and fixing your antiques & collectibles]
Kovels' guide to selling, buying, and fixing your antiques & collectibles /
Ralph and Terry Kovel.
Includes bibliographical references and index.
1. Antiques—United States—Marketing.   2. Antiques—Conservation
and restoration—United States.   I. Kovel, Terry H.   II. Title.
NK1125.K643   1995
745.1′068′8—dc20   94-27289
CIP
ISBN 0-517-88313-9

10 9 8 7 6 5 4 3 2 1

First Edition

This book is dedicated to the collectors, dealers, restorers, and just plain folks who took the time to tell us what they do that would help other collectors. It was only with their help that we could complete this book.

Contents

Part II
General Information and Source Lists   261

Part III
Loving Care for Your Collectibles   305

Acknowledgments

Collecting the information, names, and current addresses for this book was an almost impossible job. Gay Hunter was the coordinator. She converted all of the lists of names and books into a huge data-base file and kept it up to date for over two years. We sent more than 3,300 letters to find the up-to-date information on over 2,500 publications and companies listed here. The last corrections went into the book a week before it was printed.

Amy Garvey helped to edit copy, and Robyn Smigel worked on the extensive bibliographies and proofread many of the lists. Marcia Goldberg proofread the chapter copy. Cherrie and Edie Smrekar and others in our office who usually work on Kovel newsletters or books were also drafted into service as deadlines neared.

Sharon Squibb, our Crown editor, set the tone, edited the pages of copy, directed the projects, and did all those other things a good editor does that no one knows about. Thanks also go to Pamela Stinson, production editor, Deborah Kerner, designer, Ken Sansone, art director, and Bill Peabody, production manager.

We know our name is the one that appears on the cover, but we also know all too well that we couldn't have done it alone. We thank all of the people who have been involved in producing this book and then give extra, extra thanks to Gay and her computer.

Read This First

*E*veryone has something to sell or fix. Maybe the table your mother gave you twenty years ago that she said was "very old and valuable," or the broken chair that rattles, or the baseball card collection from your childhood that is taking up needed space and could be worth thousands of dollars. Newspapers are always reporting stories of unsuspected treasures that have been sold at auction. A woman bought a blackened metal coffeepot for $75 at a Pennsylvania yard sale. After polishing it and checking the mark, she realized that she had a rare and valuable eighteenth-century chocolate pot and sold it at auction for $110,000. An American tourist in England bought an oil painting of two hummingbirds for $3 at a flea market, realized it was valuable, and took it to be auctioned. It sold for $96,000. An auctioneer, while checking items from an estate, noticed a carved walking stick in a corner of the basement. The owner said her husband had received a group of the sticks in payment for roof repairs. She was going to put them in a garage sale, but instead the eight folk-art canes by Milton

Boshaw, a Chippewa Indian from Michigan, were auctioned for $44,000.

This book will tell you where you can get the information about what, when, where, and how to sell or fix your collectibles. It is based on thirty-five years of knowledge and information we have gathered for reporting antiques prices and writing about the antiques and collectibles market. *Kovels' Antiques & Collectibles Price List* is a best-seller found in almost every library and bookstore. Over 1.5 million copies have been sold. Our newspaper column, "Kovels: Antiques and Collecting," appears in hundreds of news-papers. We read thousands of letters each month, many of them filled with questions about what to sell, how to sell, and what is it worth. There have been so many questions that over twenty years ago we started a monthly newsletter, *Kovels on Antiques and Collectibles*, a subscription publication for those who collect or actively buy and sell antiques. To fill the need for information about other collectibles, we have authored special price books about bottles, advertising collectibles, Depression glass, Royal Doulton, collector plates, and more. We have written reference books on art pottery, country furniture, pottery and porcelain marks, and silver marks. And we have written several books filled with information for beginning collectors. Our television shows about collecting, including prices, have been seen on The Discovery Channel and public television channels in many cities.

Have you ever thought about your Barbie or Shirley Temple doll, your glass dishes from the 1930s, your silver candlesticks, or Great-grandmother's dishes? If you wanted to, could you sell them for the best possible price? Barbie doll dresses have sold for as much as $800 each, but her boyfriend's clothes are priced even higher. Wouldn't you like to get $1,000 for Ken's tuxedo? One sold for that price in 1989. Would you ever dream of asking thousands of dollars for a pink Mayfair Federal–pattern Depression glass shaker when other shakers sell for under $50? If you ask the right questions and sell in the right places, you can get top dollar for your items.

"What is my antique worth?" "Where can I sell it?" "How do I know if I am being cheated?" "Should I sell my things to a collector or a dealer?" All these questions arise when you decide to try to sell an antique or collectible that is no longer of interest to you. The dealers know the answers to these questions because they make money buying and selling antiques. You should know the answers before you lose money by selling foolishly. This book has been written to help you dispose of a few items or a houseful of treasures accumulated over the years. It will warn you about the legal and ethical pitfalls. (For example, it is illegal to sell any form of firearm, even a World War I souvenir, without a special license. It is bad form to sell an American flag; it should be given away.)

Usually an antique should be sold "as is," with no restoration or repairs. But sometimes, a repair will help you to get the most money for the antique. This book lists antiques and collectibles by type and suggests how to price them and who might buy them. Be sure to use the Index to find the special instructions for selling the type of collectible you own. Part II at the end of the book lists current price books, general research sources, auction houses, appraisal associations, matching services, and other important information on where to sell, how to price, and how to care for a collection. We have written an entire book giving up-to-date prices, *Kovels' Antiques & Collectibles Price List*, so we have not listed many actual prices here. Our price book helps identify and price collectibles, but there are many other sources, too. All these are included in Part II.

All the books listed here can be found, but some are privately printed or out of print, and it may take extra effort. Ask at your local bookstore or library. A bookstore can order books if they are still in print, and we have included all the necessary information about publisher and source in our lists, even for privately printed books. The full address information for well-known publishers of books listed can be obtained from your local library or bookstore.

If your library does not have the book, it can find out where it is available for loan. Ask the librarian to locate the book through an interlibrary loan. The smallest library can make interlibrary loan arrangements. Don't ignore the libraries in museums and historical societies. Only current price books less than two years old are listed here.

We wrote to or called every club and publication listed to verify the address and other information. Clubs and publications that did not respond are not listed. We felt if they did not respond to our letter, they would not answer you. The list is accurate as of January 1995.

The abbreviations used are: MAG for magazine, NP for newspaper, and NL for newsletter. The listing is alphabetical by name or title. First we list clubs with the names of their publications. Then we list publications that are not connected to a club.

When writing to the companies listed here, be sure to send a long SASE (self-addressed, stamped envelope) for the literature. When calling, remember the time zones and call at the appropriate time. Noon in New York is nine o'clock in the morning in California. It may be useful to consult *The Official Museum Directory,* published by the National Register Publishing Company, 3004 Glenview Road, Wilmette, Illinois 60091. A copy should be in your library. The register lists many types of museums that may be able to help you identify pieces. When trying to repair or replace collectibles, don't forget that many manufacturers have old parts available, will sometimes restore their older machines, and sometimes remake old pieces that can be useful to you.

Ralph Kovel,
Accredited Senior Appraiser,
American Society of Appraisers

Terry Kovel,
Accredited Senior Appraiser,
American Society of Appraisers

At first glance this book seems to be about selling and repairing antiques. But a careful reading will show you how to *buy*. All of the information about how repairs affect value translate into how condition determines what you should pay for an item. All of the reference books tell what you should be looking for when buying. Many of the publications are filled with buying and selling ads that are a good source of antiques or collectibles that are of special interest to you. Buying a toy? Be sure to notice that many restorers offer parts like tires, headlights, decals, or even missing figures to improve a damaged piece. It might pay to buy a broken toy and have it fixed. It might pay to look carefully at the toy you plan to buy to be sure it has not been repaired. Black light proof restorations on glass or pottery are now offered. It means there is a new problem for buyers of expensive pieces. Send for the restoration catalogs to keep tabs on the reproductions that you may find at a show. And be sure to learn the proper way to care for the antiques and collectibles you do buy. Don't inadvertently lower the value by using an improper cleaning method or storage area.

How to Sell Your Antiques & Collectibles

HOW TO SELL THE CONTENTS OF A HOUSE

*I*f you plan to empty an entire house, be methodical. Keep the house locked and do not allow anyone inside without an escort. This includes relatives, friends, and lawyers who may be handling the estate.

Don't throw away or dispose of anything before you check on its value. Everything can be sold, from old magazines to half-filled bottles or broken toys. The biggest mistake you can make is to throw away items before you offer them for sale. We once helped settle an estate of a recluse. The family cleaned the house before we were called. We noticed a shelf of stamp-collecting books and asked to see the collection. "The only stamps we saw were on some old letters and postcards. We threw them away." They also burned fifty years of old magazines (probably worth over $2 an issue) because the basement was too crowded. Another, wiser family had a well-advertised house sale after they found their elderly aunt had saved clothes. They found over 2,000 dresses (which were sold for $5 to $20 each), 500 hats ($4 each), 25 plastic purses ($12 each), and hundreds of scarves, bolts of fabric, belts, gloves, etc. The clothing stored in the closets and attic brought more money than the furniture, china, and silver.

You must first sort the merchandise. Empty every cupboard, trunk, drawer, and closet. Try to sort everything into the separate categories used in this book; put the pottery and porcelain in one place and the clothes in another. You may have to borrow or rent tables. Then your job is to decide on a fair price and the best place to sell the items. If there are records of purchase prices through the years, or insurance covering major items, try to look for these lists.

If you are still buying antiques and plan to sell them someday, start keeping the proper records now. Buy a notebook, a card file, a computer inventory program, or an inventory book, and record each item with a description including size, color, marks, condition, price paid, where purchased, any history, and the date. You will need this for proof of loss in case of fire or theft, and it will help you set a selling price in later years. Keep all labels, stickers, auction catalogs, and original boxes. They all add to the selling price of the antique. A toy car from the 1940s with a box is worth 25 percent more than the toy without the box. If the antique belonged to a famous person, try to get a letter from the seller with any of the history. It will also add to the resale value. If you reframe, restore, or repair your antique, be sure to list all costs in your inventory. Proper restoration can often add to the value. Improper restoration will lower the value.

After you have sorted through your objects for sale, assemble your tools: a ruler, magnet, magnifying glass, marking crayon (one that can be used on porcelains), paper tags (that can be pinned on clothing), small sheets of paper for notes to be placed with items, colored dot stickers, pencil, pen, loose-leaf notebook with lined paper, a price book (we suggest the latest edition of *Kovels' Antiques & Collectibles Price List*), and a flashlight.

Examine all the items, and make notes about any of the marks, labels, breaks, or family history. Measure all large pieces of furniture you want to sell. Check to see whether the metal pieces are bronze, brass, or iron (a magnet will stick to iron), and see if the clocks, toys, and musical items work. If you decide you do not want to sell an object, try to move it to another area. Put your notes on the small pieces of paper, and put the paper in or on the object.

If you have friends who are collectors or even flea market and house sale buffs, you might ask for advice. This can be complicated because they may be your best customers later. Explain that you are in the investigative stages and will not sell anything yet. Put a colored dot on anything you might later want to give or sell to your advisers.

Otherwise you might forget it, and you could possibly lose a friend.

When you have enough knowledge and information, use a price book to look up the retail prices of your antiques. Include these in your notes. There will be many pieces that you will not be able to identify or price at this time. Do not be discouraged. Remember, the more you know about antiques and collectibles, the higher the price you can ask. We have a friend with a very rare prisoner-of-war ship model made in about 1820. We tried to determine the price for months. Prices for these models range from $1,000 to $25,000. We learned an ivory model is more valuable than a wooden one, and the original glass case and straw mat almost double the value. The question was, should our friend ask $5,000 from a dealer and see what happens, or should he sell it at auction where it could fetch as little as $1,000, or possibly much more than $5,000? We asked many dealers at shows about this model and one day a collector called from another city. He had been told about the model and offered $2,500 for it. This seemed fair, so the model was sold.

HOW TO SET PRICES

One of the most difficult aspects of selling an antique is determining the price. If you have a salable item, everyone wants it. Dealers will offer to buy, but they will almost always insist that you set the price. Friends and relatives may want the antique, but will either expect it as a gift or will tend to offer less than the top price you might get from a stranger.

Your old Christmas ornaments are worth more to a collector of ornaments than to anyone else. And you would probably think an ornament shaped like an angel is worth more than one that looks like a potato. It isn't. (An old potato ornament is very rare and is currently worth over $100.) The problem is that you must know what categories of collectibles are in demand and who wants them, and you must learn the requirements of the serious collector. For example, an out-of-production Cabbage Patch doll in used condition is worth about 20 percent of its original price. That Cabbage Patch doll in mint condition is worth about 80 percent of its original price. The same doll in mint condition with the original box in mint condition is worth about 30 percent more than the original price. This is true of most collectibles; the original finish, box, labels, and directions add to the value. Poor condition, flaked paint, chips, dents, or missing parts may make a collectible almost worthless. Repairs may add or detract. A good repair to an old, usable nineteenth-century country chair will add to the price you can ask, but a new coat of paint on an old tin toy will lower the price by 80 percent. The toy would be worth more with the old, flaking paint.

Watch for these price-increasing features:

- Original box.
- Mint condition.
- Provenance. Absolute proof that the item belonged to someone of historical importance—from rock stars to authors to Civil War generals. Proof must be a letter or photograph linking the person to the item. Family gossip doesn't count.
- Maker's label.
- Direction book that might have come with the item.
- Miniature version of a normally full-sized item.

- Event-related objects, such as souvenirs of World's Fairs, coronations, or political campaigns.
- Brands or makers that are especially popular, such as Avon, Hummel, Coca-Cola, R.S. Prussia, or Lalique.
- Anything that pictures a railroad, streetcar, train, or sport.
- A pair is worth more than two items sold as singles; a full set is worth more than the sum of the parts.
- Occupation-related objects like medical instruments.
- Documents or objects related to local or national history.
- Objects related to the history of the women's movement or to black history.
- The "naughty factor." We first heard this term from an auctioneer with a prestigious New York City gallery. He said the rule was, "The more erotic the piece, the higher the price." Collectors seem to pay higher prices for anything connected to tobacco, alcohol, gambling, drugs, or sex.

There is not always one correct price. You must decide whether you want to set a low price in order to sell the item quickly. In general, the more work you do studying the antique or collectible and who might want to buy it, the higher the price you will get. This takes time, but it can also be fun, especially if you buy low and sell high.

These are the only five places to learn the correct price for an antique or collectible.

Please note that there are advantages and disadvantages to each source.

1. A knowledgeable collector friend. Your friend's advice is free, but as the old saying goes, "You get what you pay for," and it could be wrong.

2. A price book. Price books come in all qualities. Bad ones are inaccurate and may misinform you. Good ones tell prices, but often you must know a lot about the subject to be able to locate the exact item and its price in these guides, and this takes time. There is a current list of general price books in Part II at the back of this book. Specialized price books are listed with each category.

3. The antiques publications (see Part II) are filled with "for sale" ads with descriptions and sometimes pictures. Some items, like Depression glass or common toys, appear over and over in the ads. You can try to confirm your prices by reading these ads. Your sale price to a dealer will be a third to a half of the advertised price. If you decide to try selling through the mail yourself, you should ask for the full price.

4. Visits to shops, shows, auctions, flea markets, and house sales. Your observations, although free-of-charge, can be time-consuming, but they may help you to understand why one chair is worth more than another. Don't be insistent or demanding because you may want a favor. Talk to the dealer. If the dealer isn't busy, you can get an abundance of information.

5. A formal appraisal. An appraisal is usually expensive. Appraisers are like doctors. They sell their expertise and training, and their time is valuable. The average big-city appraisal costs about $150 an hour or more. Never get an appraisal for a few inexpensive items; however, jewelry, sterling silver, or large collections of coins, stamps, or other specialties probably should be appraised if you do not plan to sell at auction. There is no reason to have an appraisal if you sell at auction. The estimate placed on the item by the auction house is the appraised value. You may want to put a reserve on the piece at auction to ensure that, through bad weather or other factors, you do not risk your item being sold well below value.

There are other points to remember about appraisals. *Never* hire an appraiser who sets charges based on a percentage of the value of the items. Never expect the person who appraises your antiques to buy them. If your appraiser offers to buy at the appraised value, *beware!* Do not expect a dealer to be a free appraiser. The dealer is trying to buy at the lowest possible price and will not want to tell you what your antiques are worth unless you are paying for that information. A dealer will often ask to be permitted to buy (at the price you set) rather than take the job of appraising for a fee.

All of this "dancing around" by dealers is frustrating to those who know very little and wish to sell some antiques or collectibles, but that is how the market works. Dealers are selling antiques to make a living and not to make you happy. The better they buy, the more they make; but the more they buy, the more they have for sale.

There is a list of national appraisal associations in Part II. Other appraisers can usually be found in the Yellow Pages of your telephone book under "Appraisers." Most auction galleries will appraise. Many antiques dealers and household liquidators can appraise average items. Information about specialized appraisers is listed in the appropriate categories.

Sneaky Ways to Get Prices

There are a few tricks to learning prices that may help. Some types of antiques and collectibles are purchased because they are inexpensive, attractive substitutes for new department-store furniture and tableware. If you are trying to sell dishes, silver flatware, furniture, or even linens, you should always check on the price of comparable new ones at your local gift or department store. Your old furniture and dishes will sell quickly at a third to a half the price of the new, so that should be the lowest price you should ask. They could be worth more than the new. Old, used linens usually sell for 20 to 30 percent less than new ones, unless they have hand embroidery or lace, a design that's characteristic of an era like free-form design 1950s tablecloths, or are in very unusual, hard-to-find sizes, like a five-yard tablecloth.

There are auction galleries in some cities that give free appraisals. They need merchandise to sell, and this is one of their forms of advertising. Check in the Yellow Pages of the phone book for auction houses. Watch the antiques section of want ads in your newspaper for special announcements of free appraisal days by out-of-town galleries.

It is possible to send a picture and description (include size, condition, history, and marks) of a seemingly valuable item to an out-of-town auction gallery and ask what it would bring at auction. Some galleries will write an answer to this type of inquiry. They are under no obligation to answer your inquiries, and you are under no obligation to sell your antique through the gallery, although you may later decide it is the best way to sell it. You should include a self-addressed, stamped envelope to encourage an answer and the return of your pictures.

All dealers and matching services buy as well as sell. A matching service buys old pieces of silver, glass, or china and resells them to customers who are trying to complete old sets. This solves the constant problem of what to do when you chip the twelfth cup or grind up Grandma's silver teaspoon in the garbage disposal. If you are trying to sell a standard item like Depression glass, silver flatware, or Haviland china, you can check the retail prices of these items at the shows or through the mail-order listings. You should be able to sell your pieces to these or other dealers for about a third to half of the quoted prices.

How Prices Work in the Antiques Market

Once you have learned the correct retail price for an antique, you must still be concerned about how to price your item. No matter which method of selling you use, you are not selling from a retail store. An antiques dealer must at least double the cost of an item when selling it. This is considered a fair business practice because the dealer must pay rent, advance money to buy stock, pay expenses to move the item, and store it until it is sold. In addition, an item might have to be restored. The dealer must meet a payroll, pay taxes, advertise, and cover the other expenses of a small business. If you have your own garage or flea market sale, you will learn that dealers usually expect at least a 20 percent discount for buying more than one item. Collectors are often given this 20 percent "dealer discount" at shops, sales, and shows if they ask for it. There is also a quantity discount. Dealers and collectors expect a "lump sum" price for ten items to be less than the sum of the ten prices. Let's take some examples.

• An antiques dealer buys a rare French paperweight for $1. It is offered for sale in the shop for $1,000, which might be the appropriate price for such a rarity. That markup would be based on expert knowledge of the actual value of the item, rather than on its cost.

• A dealer buys a spindle-back oak chair at a flea market for $40. He does minor refinishing and prices it at $79, which is roughly a 100 percent markup. It would not be priced at $80, because the psychology of pricing for antiques is much like that at a grocery store. A $79 item sells much faster than an $80 one. He puts the chair in the shop. At the next sale he sees an identical chair for $60. He purchases it at 20 percent dealer's discount and returns to the shop where he prices the pair of chairs at $225. (A pair is usually worth more than two singles.) His cost for the two chairs is $88, and now his markup for the two is about 155 percent. If another dealer comes to the shop to buy the chairs, the selling price might have to be $180 (that 20 percent "dealer's discount" has to be considered). This means the chairs only cost $88 and were sold for $180, a profit of $92 with a markup of about 105 percent. Usually the dealer who is buying is getting a large number of items or is a good customer, so a discount is a form of promotion for the shop.

• A dealer has a customer for a large oak dining-room table. While bidding at an auction, the dealer sees a table that is just what the customer wants and bids $350. She moves it to the shop at a cost of $25, calls the customer, and offers the table for $500, which was the top price the customer seemed prepared to pay. The markup from a cost of $375 to a sale price of $500 is only 33 percent. A quick sale with a low profit margin is sometimes a good idea when you are not sure when a better deal might come along.

• A "picker" buys a tin toy for $5 at a church rummage sale and sells it for $10 to a flea market dealer, who then sells it to a toy dealer for $18. The toy dealer goes to a toy show in Ohio and sells the toy to another dealer for $35. It is sold again to another dealer from California for $70. A customer in California walks into the shop and eagerly buys the toy for $175. (It sometimes happens this way.) We always joke that if the dealers ever stopped buying from each other, there would be no antiques business. An item is often bought and sold four or five times before it reaches the ultimate collector. Each time there is an increase in price. This is not too different from the food business. A farmer sells peas to a processor who sells to a distributor who sells to a grocery store who sells to the consumer. Each time the price rises.

How does all of this affect the price of the collectible you are selling to a dealer? You should be warned that prices in the antiques business are based on supply and demand. The closer you can get to selling it to the ultimate collector, the higher the price you can ask. The general rule is that a dealer's gross profit margin should be 100 percent of the antique's cost. A dealer usually charges double what he pays you. This means that when you look in *Kovels' Antiques & Collectibles Price List* and see a doll worth $100, you should plan on selling yours to a dealer for half, or about $50. You must also remember that most of the prices listed in price books are those found in retail shops, not from small flea market dealers or yard sales. We often hear people complaining that they sold an antique to a dealer and later saw it in the shop at a much higher price. Of course! The dealer must make a profit! No one complains that a dress shop buys new clothes for $10 and often sells them for $30, tripling their money. Many other shops sell this way. There are few that sell for less than a 100 percent markup, which is the typical pricing formula for the antiques dealer.

If You Sell Through an Auction Gallery

Auction galleries sell for a commission that usually ranges from 10 to 25 percent of the sale price, so you receive less than the announced sale price. If your dresser sells at auction for $150, you will get from $135 to $112.50, depending on the commission you contracted for. If the dresser sells for $300, you get from $270 to $225, depending on the commission rate. If you have given the auction gallery instructions not to sell the dresser for less than $150 and no one bids high enough, you will still owe the auctioneer a fee for trying to sell it, probably 5 percent, or $7.50.

Sometimes it is far more profitable to donate your items to a charity than it is to sell them. The tax deduction for charitable contributions can be valuable if you are in a high tax bracket. There may be a fee to pay for an appraisal if the item is worth more than $5,000 (part of the new tax law). Some things are very valuable to a museum but very hard to sell elsewhere because of limited interest. We once appraised a donation of annotated sheet music that was used in a landmark-status burlesque house, which for historic reasons was of great value to the music section of a large library. Architects' drawings, old photographs of local scenes,

historical documents, and old maps are often worth much more as a donation. The tax laws seem to change each year, so if you are considering a large gift, consult your accountant or the local Internal Revenue Service office.

WHERE TO SELL

There are only eight ways to sell your antiques and collectibles. Each of these methods requires some work. The more you work, the more money you will probably be able to keep after the sale. You get your cash immediately by some methods, while others can take months. Each of these methods is successful only if you learn the rules and secrets of others who sell antiques and collectibles. Remember that the usual rules of credit apply. Get cash or assure yourself that the check offered will be good. You don't know the customer, and once in a while there are problems with checks or credit. Don't let anything leave your possession until you have cash, a check, or a written agreement about the sale.

Sell to an Antiques Dealer, Friend, or Acquaintance

The easiest way to sell an antique or collectible is to call a dealer and sell anything you can for whatever price is offered. This might be a good method if you are from out of town, have inherited a few large pieces, and must move them as soon as possible. The dealer will probably not set the price, so if your asking price isn't low enough, your item won't sell. The dealer's travel time counts, so try the closest dealers for best and quickest results. Find a list in the Yellow Pages of the phone book or in the antiques publications listed in Part II in the back of this book.

Never let anyone in the house when you are not there. If possible, make sure at least two people are in the house when a potential buyer arrives. The antiques business is never run on credit: Be sure you get the money when the collectibles are taken. If you or your relative bought the antique you are trying to sell from a dealer, try to sell it back to the same dealer. The dealer knows the piece, liked it before, and knows how it will sell, so usually the original dealer will offer the highest price.

Sometimes friends and relatives want to buy from you. Offer the antique to them first, at the price you plan to ask the dealer. Tell them that if the dealer refuses at that price, you will offer it to them again at a lower price. Would you give your friend a $100 bill? Then don't give away your antiques for lower-than-wholesale prices. If you want to give an antique to a friend, don't charge anything. Sometimes it is best to avoid even offering to sell to friends and relatives. It can become a source of friction that can last for years.

If you have a few antiques and a lot of time, you can look up your items, determine the best price a dealer can offer, and take the items or a picture of the items to nearby dealers.

Sell at a Garage or House Sale

*I*f you have a house full of goods, you can call one of the local house sale (tag sale)

firms or auctioneers. Look in the Yellow Pages of the phone book under "Liquidators" or in your newspaper's weekly listing of sales. The entire sale (advertising, pricing, security, permits, staff, and special problems) can be handled by these people. You pay them a percentage on all items sold. Be very sure that you check references for the people you hire. They will be handling your money, and the money you receive is based on their records. Before anything is started, you must have a written contract, which should list your responsibilities and the seller's responsibilities and fees. Be sure the seller is insured in case of serious damage or loss. Many of us are emotionally involved with our personal items. If you are, do not attend the sale. You may be upset and may even interfere with the sale and discourage a potential customer. If you are fond of some pieces, set a price and tell the staff not to sell below that price without your approval. It is always best to cut prices on the last day so that you can sell whatever is left. Arrange in advance (put it in the contract) that the unsold pieces should be sent to your favorite charity and the house should be left "broom clean." If you have only a few items to sell, the dealer might be able to place them in someone else's sale. This is illegal in some cities, but silver, jewelry, and furs are often sold in this way.

You can join a group of friends and arrange a big garage or house sale. Choose the most prestigious address. It helps if it is near parking and a main road. Go over the methods of bookkeeping and payment very carefully beforehand. There is often confusion about who owned the items sold. Price your own items, and be sure everyone knows all the rules about cutting prices. This works best if at least one member of the group has had experience with this type of sale.

Anyone can run a garage or house sale; there are books about how to do it in most libraries. Before making any arrangements, check with the local police to learn about permits for sales, parking, signs, sales tax, and other problems. Some apartment buildings and complexes and towns do not allow sales. It is important to check with the police about other local sales laws: in some states it is illegal to sell guns, alcoholic beverages, endangered-animal parts, used mattresses, bedding, some Indian relics, gambling devices, and other objects.

Try going to some local sales, and take note of their setup for the sale, their security precautions, their tagging and pricing, and even their price reduction policy, if possible. Your local newspaper may offer a free garage sale kit, including directions and signs. Advertising is always important. Place your ad in the weekly or daily paper for your neighborhood on the day that all the garage sale ads appear.

THEFT IS THE BIGGEST PROBLEM FOR A NOVICE RUNNING A HOUSE SALE

Watch out for large open bags, pocketbooks, large unbuttoned raincoats, or any sort of box or bag that is brought into your sale. If possible, have shoppers check all large items and coats at the door. If you are having a garage sale, never let anyone in your house. If you are having a house sale, always have one salesperson in each open room, so they can watch and discuss prices. Be sure each sales slip is written by your salesperson in the room with that particular item. For example,

have one sales helper in charge of all linens and clothes, and put all of these items in one room. Keep small, valuable items like jewelry in a special closed case near the cashier. All money should be paid in one place, preferably on a table that faces the exit door, and the money box should be watched at all times. If it is a very large sale, it might be advisable to hire an off-duty policeman. Be sure all other exit doors are locked, and tape shut any doors to cabinets that do not contain merchandise for sale. Before leaving at night, check all window and door locks. Burglars have been known to visit a sale, open a window, and return later that night for "free" antiques, knowing the house is unoccupied. Thieves might even take sinks, radiators, and copper plumbing. It is sensible to inform your local police of the sale, so they can put an extra watch on the house at night. After all, you did place an ad in the paper telling everyone that there is an empty house filled with merchandise.

Expect to have some losses. We have heard stories from professional house-sale staffs that are hard to believe. Price tags are often switched. Boxes are filled with unpaid-for items. A two-foot-high vase disappeared from a room that was guarded by a policeman. One saleslady even lost her lunch because she had brought it in a fancy department-store bag.

Take Your Items to a Consignment Shop

Most cities have consignment shops. These stores sell other people's merchandise and charge a commission. Some antiques shops will take merchandise on consignment for sale with their own antiques. Look in the Yellow Pages of the phone book for "Consignment Shops." Visit the stores to see if your collectibles will fit in with the other items on sale. Ask antiques dealers if consignment is possible in their shops or at shows. Be sure to get a signed copy of the consignment agreement, which should include all charges, how long your money is held, and how the items are insured while in the shop. You, in turn, will probably have to sign an agreement with the shop and you should retain a copy. On the consignment agreement, write a full description of the objects including the words "dented" or "flaked paint" or any other indication of wear. If your item doesn't sell and you take it back, you want to be sure that it has not been damaged in the store. The shop or dealer is probably best able to set the price. Visit the shop after a few weeks to see if your item has sold. If it has not, you should discuss reducing the price.

Sell Through an Auction Gallery

Most major collections, important paintings, sculptures, and large antique furniture pieces are sold through auction galleries. These pieces require a special buyer who is either a professional antiques dealer or a knowledgeable collector. The gallery should mail announcements of the sale to these people, advertise in national antiques publications and local papers, and handle all the problems of the sale. Everything is negotiable at an auction gallery if you have enough items to consign. The printed rates usually say the consignor must pay 10 to 25 percent commission. Some auction galleries

charge the buyer 10 to 15 percent of the purchase price—a "buyer's premium"—and then charge 10 to 25 percent to the seller.

Always try to get the best rate. With negotiation, many of the extras, such as charges for shipping, pictures in the catalog, etc., could be free. You can ask for extra advertising, a catalog, even a preview party. No demand is unreasonable if your items are important enough to be a major sale for the gallery. Of course, a major sale in New York City is very different from a major sale in a small town.

If you permit the auctioneer to use your name in the advertising, it may mean higher prices at the sale. Collectors like to buy "fresh" antiques; these are pieces that have not been sold and resold in shops recently. Be sure to get a written contract from the auctioneer stating the terms, the approximate date the pieces will be sold, the time of payment to you, extra charges, and details regarding the advertising that is to be placed. Make sure the gallery has fire and theft insurance. If you are unfamiliar with the auction house, ask for references, and find out whether the money for your items is kept in a separate escrow account. This helps protect you from loss if the gallery has financial problems.

Check the credit rating of the auctioneer. Should the auctioneer go bankrupt, you have very little chance of getting your money for items that were sold. You may even have trouble proving that you own the unsold but consigned pieces.

Discuss the "reserve." Sometimes you decide you do not wish to sell below a certain price. This is the reserve price. If no bid is made above this reserve, you must usually pay a fee of approximately 5 percent of the agreed reserve price to the auctioneer. Do not place a high reserve on a piece. If you want too much, it will not sell, and you should not be auctioning it at all. Some major auction houses and many small auctioneers prefer only sales without reserves. If your antique does not sell above the reserve price, you can decide if you want to take your item back or have the auction gallery "sell it out the back door." In other words, if your antique fails to sell, the auctioneer can often sell it privately after the auction for a lower price. The usual commission rates apply for this kind of sale.

If you go to the auction, remember that it is not only in poor taste but also illegal in some states to bid on your items. If you bid the item up, you are a "shill." If you end up with the high bid, you would still owe the gallery the buyer's premium plus your charges.

Sell at a Country Auction

At a country auction, which is very different from an auction gallery, the auctioneer usually goes to the house or farm and sells the items on the site. There is very limited advertising, no catalog, and often no chairs for the buyers. There are rarely reserves, the seller's commission may be lower, and there is almost never a buyer's premium. This is a very successful method of emptying a small-town or rural house filled with the accumulation of a lifetime. If there are valuable pieces of antique furniture, the major dealers somehow seem to find out and pay good prices. If there are no major items, just typical seventy-five-year-old things, you will be pleased at the prices you can get for some items that an auction gallery would sell in box lots or not at all. The half sets of dishes, basement tools, old lawn mower, and even torn magazines and rolls of chicken wire will sell to someone.

Go to a Flea Market or Show and Offer Your Items to a Dealer

A slightly sneaky way to sell antiques and collectibles is to sell to dealers or even customers at shows and flea markets, although this is discouraged at most big shows. Take clear photographs of anything you want to sell. Record the size, marks, and any other interesting history on the back of the picture. You might also include a price, but write it in code so only you can read it. (The easiest code uses letters. Pick a special word or words of ten different letters. Try "my antiques." In that code, m = 1, y = 2, etc. The letters "aqm" are the code for $371.) Check in the local newspapers for dates and go to a major antiques show. Put the small antiques in the trunk of your car and take the photographs with you. Find a dealer at the show who sells items similar to yours, and wait until the booth is empty. Never start a selling discussion when a dealer has a customer. Ask the dealer if he is interested in buying, then show your pictures. Dealers are usually interested because it is harder to buy than to sell. Most dealers will ask you to set the price. Add 20 percent to the lowest price you will accept and negotiate from there. If you ask too much, the dealer will just say no. Remember, the dealer should be able to sell the piece for twice what you ask. Sometimes a dealer will not want your items but can suggest a customer, possibly another dealer or a collector, who is attending the show. Be discreet. Don't bring big objects into the show. The dealer has paid for the exhibit space. If you are selling in competition with the dealers, you might be asked to leave. Don't expect a free appraisal. You must know the value of your antique to be able to sell it.

TAKE YOUR ITEMS AND SET UP YOUR OWN BOOTH AT A FLEA MARKET

If you have time, enjoy crowds, and don't mind packing and unpacking, you can set up your own booth at a flea market. Look in the local newspaper or an antiques paper in your area (see Part II). Flea markets will be listed. Visit a few, talk to the dealers, and get information about how to rent space. Sometimes a table for the day is under $10. Notice how the tables are arranged and what to do in case of rain. It is also important to know whether to bring lunch, or if there is a lunch stand on the premises. Always ask how early you can set up. Dress for all types of weather: Bring umbrellas or sunshades, sweaters or heavy boots. Bring a chair. Bring a closed box to hold money, and newspapers and bags for wrapping. Try to take an assistant. You may want to eat, go to the rest room, or visit other booths, and you should never leave your booth unattended. You must stay for the full day, even if it rains. You must price the items, keep records, give receipts. It is almost the same as having your own garage sale. Learn the state sales tax regulations. You may need a resale license. Flea markets are often checked by state inspectors. Remember that in some states it is illegal to sell items like guns, slot machines, liquor, endangered species' pelts or parts, and a few other things. Watch out for theft, too.

Place an Ad and Sell by Mail

Specialized collections of small items, like political campaign material, buttonhooks, or souvenir spoons, can be sold by mail. The best pieces to sell this way are well-known, easy-to-describe pieces like Royal Doulton figurines, carnival glass, beer cans, or Depression glass. Large items are difficult. Furniture is almost impossible unless it will be picked up by the buyer. Check the ads in the antiques papers. Anyone selling antiques may be buying antiques, so anyone offering to sell an item like yours is a prospective customer. There are also "antiques wanted" ads that can give you leads.

When you place an ad for your antiques, be sure to request a self-addressed, stamped envelope (SASE) from anyone asking for more information. Otherwise you may find you have to pay for first-class postage on each letter to answer queries, and that can add up. A United States resident should ask for a check payable in U.S. funds on a U.S. bank, because a Canadian bank check will cost you a fee to deposit. International sales are easiest by credit card. If you are selling between the United States and Canada, be sure to specify the currency expected and the exchange rate.

You may want to send out a numbered list of the objects, with a full description of each, including size, marks, and condition. Include every defect, and set a price. If possible, take pictures or make photocopies and add these to the list. Make photocopies of the list and send it with a letter of explanation. Include your name and address, zip code, and phone number, including the area code. Enclose a self-addressed, stamped envelope (SASE) for the return of your list and pictures. Don't try to sell damaged items by mail.

You will have to pack and ship the items. Breakage is your problem, so wrap carefully and always insure all packages. Ask for a payment before you ship the antique and be sure the check or credit card is good. Offer the pieces with geography in mind. Some items sell for higher prices in the West than in the East. Get a return receipt to show that the package arrived. It should be understood that there are full return privileges and that the antique may be returned to you for a refund. The buyer pays the return postage or shipping.

If you place an ad in the local paper or the antiques papers to sell your items, study the format of other ads for ideas in composing your own. Include a full description and either a phone number or address, and ask for an SASE for inquiries. Security may be a problem, so don't use your address if you live alone. Consider renting a post-office box. Make appointments to show the antiques, but always have someone else with you for security. In the antiques papers it is best to include the price. In your local paper it is not necessary. A local ad is best for large items like a dining room set.

Find a Customer by Writing or Calling

A few special pieces might be sold to a particular customer who is nationally known. For example, The Hoover Company has a collection of vacuum cleaners. They might want one that is not in their collection. Write to that customer or the appropriate museum, enclosing a picture, description, price, your phone number, and an SASE. Museum collections are listed in *The Official Museum Directory,* the American Association of Museums, 1994 (National Register Publishing Co., Wilmette, IL 60091). The annual directory can be found in your local library or perhaps at your local historical society or art museum.

How to Fix Your Antiques & Collectibles

*I*t's beautiful. It's valuable. But it's broken. If you want to preserve the value of your antiques by keeping them in top condition or if you want to restore them properly, read on. But remember it is not usually a good idea to repair an item to sell it. Fix it if you want to keep it. Listed are hard-to-find repair shops and sources for replacement parts located in all parts of the country.

More than sixty different types of collections are discussed here. A short paragraph tells what flaws should be repaired, how repairs affect value, and other tips. Craftsmen, supply sources, informative books, and other material related to restoring antiques are listed. If you are missing the wheel on a toy truck, need a glass liner for your silver mustard pot, or a restorer for your Tiffany lamp, a source is listed.

At the end of the book (in Part II) are lists of those who repair and refinish many different types of antiques, sources of supply for conservation materials, and ways to display collections. This is where you will find places to buy acid-free paper, special waxes, products for wood graining, gold leafing, and the like. We also list auction houses, appraisal groups, clubs, publications, and matching services.

We have tried to make this book easy to use, but we realize that many subjects overlap. If you are restoring or selling a piece of furniture, start with the Furniture section, but also look under Wicker, Rattan & Basketry, Hardware, Metals, Textiles, and other headings. You will find helpful comments like "See also Metals" in the Fireplace Equipment section. There is also an index at the end of the book.

Many useful books, leaflets, videotapes, or computer programs are included. We have also listed available reprints of original instruction books. Although most of the books are in print and can be found at a bookstore or library, a few are harder to locate. These can be ordered at your library through an interlibrary loan. Ask the librarian to help you.

To assemble the names in this book, we wrote to the thousands of suppliers, restorers, and repair services we had heard about. Only those who replied are included. We felt that if we could not get an answer to an offer to give a free listing, you would have trouble getting mail-order repair information or service. There are many other reliable repair services and conservators we have not yet heard about and we welcome any suggestions for additions or corrections in future editions. We have not used the services of everyone listed in this book, and inclusion here should not be considered an endorsement of any kind. You will find local restorers' names in the Yellow Pages of the phone book.

Each listing in this book includes the address and phone number. If you write, send an SASE (self-addressed, stamped envelope) or an LSASE (long self-addressed, stamped envelope). If you telephone, don't forget that the time listed is the time in the area where the restorer lives, not necessarily the time where you live. The listings are alphabetized by computer so that all names of companies and individuals appear in alphabetical order by first word.

Always contact the company by phone or letter before sending anything. The firm will tell you the best way to ship: postal service, delivery service company like UPS or Federal Express, or motor freight. Insure your piece when sending it. If using the post office, send it registered, with a return receipt requested. Other delivery services can track the package from your receipt number.

When we list a company as doing repairs by "mail order," that does not necessarily mean that it is only by mail. If you live nearby, you may be able to take the piece into the shop. Many places that do a primarily walk-in business will send you a part by mail if you pay in advance. We have found that a good craftsman will try to fix out-of-the-ordinary items if the challenge and pay are appropriate. It doesn't hurt to inquire about difficult repairs.

The last corrections were made to the lists in this book in January 1995. Some firms may have had a change of location or phone number since then.

To assemble the names in this book, we wrote to the thousands of suppliers, restorers, and repair services we had heard about. Only those who replied are included. We felt that if we could not get an answer to an offer to give a free listing, you would have trouble getting mail-order repair information or service. There are many other reliable repair services and conservators we have not yet heard about and we welcome any suggestions for additions or corrections in future editions. We have not used the services of everyone listed in this book, and inclusion here should not be considered an endorsement of any kind. You will find local restorers' names in the Yellow Pages of the phone book.

PART I

The Collectibles

Advertising & Country Store Collectibles

The country store and its contents have delighted collectors for years. Around 1950 the first serious collectors of advertising materials began searching for signs, containers, bottles, store bins, and other objects found in an old country store. It became the vogue to decorate restaurants, homes, and shops with nostalgic collectibles from old stores, and prices rose as supplies dwindled. By the 1990s, prices went as high as $93,500 for a tin sign showing a flag made of Campbell's Soup cans.

There are collectors clubs for people who specialize in everything from bottle openers to tin containers. The nostalgia craze in restaurant decorating and the "country look" for homes have made unusual items with interesting graphics and company names into prize pieces. There are clubs for collectors interested in brands like Planters Peanuts or Coca-Cola, for collectors of tin containers, sugar packets, or bottles, and for collectors fond of fast-food restaurants. Publications for many of the clubs accept advertisements, and these are the best places to offer your items for sale. You can also write to dealers to advise them you are selling items, or you can place an ad. Ads in general-interest publications also sell items. A visit to dealers at mall shows, flea markets, or antiques shows where advertising pieces are sold will help you locate a possible buyer. Highest prices are paid at special advertising shows held during the year. These shows are announced in the general publications for collectors.

Tin containers with lithographed designs, signs, bottles, boxes, giveaways, cut-out magazine ads, or any advertisement can be sold. Neon signs, cash registers, calendars, lunch boxes with brand names or attractive graphics, gas-pump globes, or any other auto-related, brand-marked items sell quickly. If your advertising collectible pictures a train, automobile, airplane, flag, bottle, a black person, or partially clad female, it is worth a premium, up to 50 percent more. If it includes the name COCA-COLA, PLANTERS PEANUTS, MOXIE, CRACKER JACK, HEINZ, or JELL-O, it is worth two to ten times as much as a similar item for a less popular brand. If it is an ad for whiskey, beer, cigarettes, or a drug-related product, it will sell quickly. A tin sign is worth ten times as much as the same sign on paper. If you have a set of old roly-poly tins or a Coca-Cola item dating before 1900, it could be worth thousands of dollars. Beer can collectors have their own clubs, publications, and shows. They trade cans rather than buy them. Only the very unusual or the old cone-top cans sell well. For more information, see the Beer section.

Large items like a saloon bar, counters, floor-standing coffee grinders, and popcorn wagons are expensive, but there are dealers who specialize in them. Look for ads in special publications, or talk to dealers at the shows. These items often sell through an ad in the local newspaper.

You may think you own a piece of advertising art, but an auction gallery may consider it folk art. Folk art brings higher prices. If you have a handmade wooden piece, a very large figure, or an unusual clock, it might bring the highest money at an auction gallery that usually would not sell advertising collectibles. Advertising clocks sell to both advertising collectors and clock collectors, so check publications and shows for both groups.

All types of labels can be sold: cigar box labels, fruit crate labels, food can labels, labels for luggage, beer bottles, tobacco pouches, and brooms. Most labels you find offered by dealers were found in old print shops or canneries. Thousands of a single design were found, then resold in small groups to dealers, often for less then 5 cents each. They were eventually sold as single labels to the collector. All sales and resales included markups, so if you are buying common labels, you pay far more than twice the amount you will get if you are selling common labels. If you are fortunate enough to find an attic filled with the remains of your grandfather's label company, you have a treasure that should be sold to dealers at the wholesale level. If you have a few orange crate labels that were framed and hung in your kitchen, you sell them to a collector friend or at a flea market.

There has been a lot of hype in the selling of "stone-lithographed cigar box labels" as rare and valuable art. Some labels are rare, but most were found in bundles of a thousand and are not rare. Framed, matted examples found in gift shops are priced as decorative pictures and do not have the resale value you would hope for in the antiques market. Cigar box and fruit crate labels are the best known, the largest, and the most decorative, and so sell the highest. Other labels, from broom handle to beer bottle, are often traded or sold for a few cents.

Many companies publish books on their history that will serve as visual guides to help with restoration of old materials. These are available from the companies, many listed in this book. Reproductions of decals and other details of trademarked pieces are available. It is also possible to buy old parts through ads in collectors' publications.

Beware of reproductions. Many lithographed tin and paper items originally made for the gift shop trade are now found at flea markets. New belt buckles and watch fobs with brand names have been made in old styles. One dealer boasts that he has sold over 130,000 new printed tin signs—some copies of old ones, some "concoctions" made with the help of art from old magazine ads.

When restoring old advertising, less is best. Don't repaint tin or paper unless the defect is glaring. Frame all paper items with appropriate nonacid mounts.

Old brass cash registers are now wanted by both collector and shopkeeper. Many are in use in stores that feature nostalgia. The machines made by National Cash Register or other companies still in business can often be restored by the company. National Cash Register was recently bought by AT&T, but someone in the business community may know where the machines can be repaired. A call to the local sales representative is a quick way to find out. Parts are available for some models. Remember, inflation has had a great impact; early machines register only to $10 or perhaps $100, not the high numbers seen today.

For other helpful information, see Coin-operated, Paper, Pottery & Porcelain. Some repair information is found under other headings, such as Paper, Metals, Glass, Dolls, or Clocks.

Price Books

Advertising Antiques, Tony Curtis (Lyle Publications, Glenmayne, Galashiels, Scotland, © 1993).

Antique Tins, Fred Dodge (Collector Books, Paducah, KY, © 1995).

Collector's Guide to Trading Cards, Robert Reed (Collector Books, Paducah, KY, © 1993).

Encyclopedia of Antique Advertising, 8th edition, Ray Klug (L-W Books, PO Box 69, Gas City, IN 46933, © 1993).

Gas Pump Globes, Scott Benjamin and Wayne Henderson (Motorbooks International, PO Box 1, 729 Prospect Ave., Osceola, WI 54020, © 1993).

Gas Station Collectibles, Mitch Stenzler and Rick Pease (Schiffer, Atglen, PA, © 1993).

General Store Collectibles, David L. Wilson (Collector Books, Paducah, KY, © 1994).

Hake's Guide to Advertising Collectibles, Ted Hake (Wallace-Homestead, Radnor, PA, © 1992).

Huxford's Collectible Advertising, Sharon and Bob Huxford (Collector Books, Paducah, KY, © 1995).

An Introductory Guide to Collecting Advertising Trade Cards, booklet (Trade Card Collectors Assoc., Box 284, Marlton, NJ 08053).

McCollecting: The Illustrated Price Guide to McDonald's Collectibles, Gary Henriques and Audre DuVall (Piedmont, PO Box 730218, San Jose, CA 95173, © 1992).

Overstreet Premium Ring Price Guide, annual, Robert M. Overstreet (Gemstone Publishing, 1966 Greenspring Dr., Timonium, MD 21093).

Pat Jacobsen's First International Price Guide to Fruit Crate Labels and *Pat Jacobsen's Collector's Guide to Fruit Crate Labels*, Thomas Patrick Jacobsen (Patco Enterprise, 437 Minton Court, Pleasant Hill, CA 94523, © 1994).

Pepsi-Cola Collectibles, Everette and Mary Lloyd (Schiffer, Atglen, PA, © 1993).

Pepsi-Cola Collectibles, Vol. 3, Bill Vehling and Michael Hunt (L-W Books, Box 69, Gas City, IN 46933, © 1993).

Petretti's Coca-Cola Collectibles Price Guide, 9th Edition, Allan Petretti (Nostalgia Publications, Inc., 21 South Lake Drive, Hackensack, NJ 07601, © 1994).

Tobacco Tins: A Collector's Guide, Douglas Congdon-Martin (Schiffer, Atglen, PA, © 1992).

Tomart's Price Guide to McDonald's Happy Meal Collectibles, Meredith Williams (Tomart Publications, 3300 Encrete Ln., Dayton, OH 45439, © 1992).

Value Guide to Advertising Memorabilia, B.J. Summers (Collector Books, Paducah, KY, © 1994).

Wilson's Coca-Cola Price Guide, Helen and Al Wilson (Schiffer, Atglen, PA, © 1994).

Archives & Museums

American Advertising Museum, 9 NW Second Ave., Portland, OR 97209. 503-AAM-0000.

Coca-Cola Company Archives, PO Drawer 1734, Atlanta, GA 30301. 404-676-2121.

Dr Pepper Company Archives, PO Box 655086, Dallas, TX 75265-5086. 800-527-7096.

Historical Society of Western Pennsylvania, 4338 Bigelow Blvd., Pittsburgh, PA 15213, 412-681-5533. H. J. Heinz Company history.

McDonald's Archives, Dept. 159, 2010 E. Higgins Rd., Elk Grove Village, IL 60007, 708-952-2348.

Nabisco Food Group, Public Relations Plaza, Floor 3, Parsippany, NJ 07054, 800-NABISCO. Att.: David R. Stivers, Archivist.

Clubs & Publications

Advertising Cup and Mug Collectors of America, *The Cupletter* (NL), Box 680, Solon, IA 52333.

Antique Advertising Association of America, *Past Times* (NL), PO Box 1121, Morton Grove, IL 60053.

Citrus Label Society, *Citrus Peal* (NL), Noel Gilbert, sec. treas., 131 Miramonte Dr., Fullerton, CA 92635.

Coca-Cola Collectors Club International, *Coca-Cola Collectors News* (NL), PO Box 49166, Atlanta, GA 30359-1166.

Dr Pepper Collectors Club, *Lion's Roar* (NL), PO Box 153221, Irving, TX 75015.

Florida Citrus Labels Collectors Association, PO Box 547636, Orlando, FL 32854-7636.

International Swizzle Stick Collectors Association, *Swizzle Stick News* (NL), PO Box 1117, Bellingham, WA 98227-1117.

McDonald's Collector Club, *Newsletter of the McDonald's Collectors Club* (NL), 5407 W. Berenice Ave., Chicago, IL 60641 (send LSASE for information).

National Association of Paper and Advertising Collectors, *P.A.C.* (NP), PO Box 500, Mount Joy, PA 17552.

Peanut Pals, *Peanut Papers* (NL), 804 Hickory Grade Rd., Bridgeville, PA 15017 (Planters Peanuts).

Pepsi-Cola Collectors Club, *Pepsi-Cola Collectors Club Newsletter* (NL), PO Box 1275, Covina, CA 91722.

Trade Card Collector's Association, *Advertising Trade Card Quarterly* (NL), Box 284, Marlton, NJ 08053.

Advertising Collectors Express (NL), Fast Food Collectors Express (NL), Box 221, Mayview, MO 64071 (all ads).

Antique Amusements, Slot Machine & Jukebox Gazette (NP), 909 26th St. NW, Washington, DC 20037.

Card Times (MAG), 70 Winifred Ln., Aughton, Ormskirk, Lancashire, U.K. L39 5DL (cigarette cards, trading cards, sports and nonsports cards, phone cards, printed ephemera, etc.).

Collecting Tips Newsletter (NL), Box 633, Joplin, MO 64802 (McDonald's items).

Flake: The Breakfast Nostalgia Magazine (MAG), Box 481, Cambridge, MA 02140 (cereal boxes).

Let's Talk Tin (NL), 1 S. Beaver Ln., Greenville, SC 29605.

Neon News (NL), PO Box 668, Volcano, HI 96785 (neon art and signs).

The Premium Watch Watch (NL), 24 San Rafael Dr., Rochester, NY 14618 (watches available as premiums).

Tin Fax (NL), 205 Brolley Woods Dr., Woodstock, GA 30188 (modern tins).

Tin Type (NL), PO Box 440101, Aurora, CO 80044 (tins).

World of Fast Food Collectibles (NL), PO Box 64, Dept. DM, Powder Springs, GA 30073.

Repairs, Parts & Supplies

Chuck Kovacic, 14383 #B Nordhoff St., Panorama City, CA 91402, 818-891-4069, 8:00 A.M.–8:00 P.M.; fax: 818-891-4069. Restoration of antique advertising: paper, cardboard, metal, porcelain, tins, and trays.

Hickory Bend Antiques and Collectibles, Bill Heuring, 2995 Drake Hill Rd., Jasper, NY 14855, 607-792-3343; fax: 607-792-3309. Brass cash register parts, supplies, repair, and restoration. Mail order worldwide. Send SASE for free catalog.

Past Gas Company, 308 Willard St., Cocoa, FL 32922, 407-636-0449, Mon.–Fri. 8:00 A.M.–5:00 P.M.; fax: 407-636-1006. Restoration of gas pumps from 1920s to 1950s, Coke machines, barber poles, neon, and clocks. Gas pump parts catalog $1.

Play It Again Sam's Inc., 5310 W. Devon,

Chicago, IL 60646, 312-763-1771, Mon.–Sat. 9:00 A.M.–5:00 P.M.; fax: 312-763-1772. Service, restoration, parts for cash registers, barber poles, and wooden barber chairs. Send SASE for free brochure.

R.S. Pennyfield's, PO Box 1355, Waterloo, IA 50704, 319-233-9928; fax: 319-291-7136. Repair and restoration of antique advertising items, including glass and paper signs. Appraisals.

Tony Orlando, 6661 Norborne, Dearborn Heights, MI 48127-2076, 313-561-5072, business hours. Conservation and restoration of wooden cigar store figures.

Weber's Nostalgia Supermarket, 6611 Anglin Dr., Fort Worth, TX 76119, 817-534-6611, Mon.–Fri. 9:00 A.M.–5:00 P.M., Sat. 10:00 A.M.–5:00 P.M. Gas-pump globes, decals, hoses, nozzles, gaskets, bezels, and collectibles. Mail order worldwide. Catalog $4, free with order.

Wood 'n Wildlife, 9922 Bostwick Park Rd., Montrose, CO 81401, 303-249-5863, before 9:00 P.M. Restoration of cigar store figures and other objects. Send SASE for more information.

Architectural Antiques

*T*he tops of stone pillars, pieces of carved wooden fretwork, doors, windows, stair railings, exterior tiles, wooden flooring, paneling, and other pieces of buildings are now bought and sold in the antiques market. Many of these items are large, heavy, and difficult to move, but there are specialists who deal in "architectural antiques." Sometimes they are salvage dealers who demolish buildings and remove any salable parts. If you have rights to a large building or an old house that is about to be destroyed, examine it carefully for valuable collectibles that can be saved. Not only the wood or stone carvings, but many other parts of a building can be sold. Any sort of ornamental ironwork is in demand, including elevator doors, radiator covers, ventilator grills, locks, handles, or hinges. Light fixtures, church pews, marble benches, anything decorative, is desirable. Even special wall coverings or carpeting can be sold.

Usually, the best way to sell architectural items is to place an ad in the paper and have the buyers come and take their pieces out of the building. (Don't be surprised or upset if they knock down the walls or floor to remove something.) If you own doors, phone booths, or a wrought-iron fence, you can sell them through an ad or by contacting an auctioneer or a dealer who sells this type of collectible. Most dealers are not interested because architectural pieces sell slowly.

There is added value if a building or house was designed by a well-known architect. To price architectural pieces, think of them in terms of use. A plain, used door should sell for less than a new door. A door with a carving sells for its decorative value.

REPAIR

Most cities now have dealers or specialists who have architectural pieces and can help you restore any pieces you might find. Marble yards and tombstone makers can help. Wrought-iron fence makers can often make the parts you need to reuse a radiator grille as a door or a gate as a wall ornament. Some cities are so concerned with saving the best of the past they have established government-run shops to recycle the architectural pieces found through urban renewal.

Books

Old-House Journal Restoration Directory, annual (2 Main St., Gloucester, MA 01930).

Victorian Homes Sourcebook, annual (106 Old Mill, Millers Falls, MA 01349).

Also refer to the chapter on General Clubs, Publications & Computer Programs in Part II.

Publications

Old-House Journal (MAG), 2 Main St., Gloucester, MA 01930.

Victorian Homes (MAG), PO Box 61, Millers Falls, MA 01349.

Repairs, Parts & Supplies

A. F. Schwerd Manufacturing Company, 3215 McClure Ave., Pittsburgh, PA 15212, 412-766-6322, 8:30 A.M.–5:00 P.M.; fax: 412-766-2262. Reproduction wood columns, standard styles or custom. Complete aluminum bases available for exterior. Free catalog.

AA Abingdon Affiliates, Inc., 2149 Utica Ave., Brooklyn, NY 11234, 718-258-8333, Mon.–Fri. 8:00 A.M.–4:00 P.M.; fax: 718-338-2739. Original Victorian and Art Deco metal ceiling and wall patterns. Brass, copper, mirror, or prepainted white. Brochure $1.

Antiquities, 5 Ordnance Mews, The Historic Dockyard, Chatham, Kent, U.K. ME4 4TE, 0634 818866; fax: 0634 818877. Water and oil gilding, interior and exterior.

Architectural Antiques Exchange, 709-15 N. Second St., Philadelphia, PA 19123, 215-922-3669, 10:00 A.M.–5:00 P.M. daily; fax: 215-922-3680. Architectural salvage. Antique and reproduction wood and marble mantels, doors, armoires, sideboards, leaded and beveled glass, pier and over-mantel mirrors, antique bars, etc. Free brochure.

Architectural Iron Company, PO Box 126, Schocopee Rd., Milford, PA 18337, 800-442-IRON; fax: 717-296-IRON, 8:00 A.M.–5:00 P.M. Restoration and reproduction of wrought and cast iron. Custom casting and stock patterns. Installation available in northeastern U.S.; shipping worldwide. Catalog.

Art Glass Studio Inc., 543 Union St., 3A, Brooklyn, NY 11215, 718-596-4353, Mon.–Fri. 9:30 A.M.–5:30 P.M.; fax: 718-596-4353. Restoration of leaded and stained-glass windows. Duplication of any stained-glass window. Church restorations.

B & G Antique Lighting, 28-05 Broadway (Rt. 4W), Fairlawn, NJ 07410, 201-791-6522, Mon.–Sat. 9:00 A.M.–5:00 P.M.; fax: 201-791-6545. Architectural metal work.

Bathroom Machineries, PO Box 1020, Murphys, CA 95247, 209-728-2031. Early American and Victorian bathroom fixtures and accessories; reproductions. Reproduction brass hardware. Restoration of antique plumbing fixtures; brass polishing. Victorian Hardware catalog $3; Bathroom Machineries catalog $3.

Botti Studio of Architectural Arts Inc., 919 Grove St., Evanston, IL 60201, 800-524-7211, 708-869-5933, 8:30 A.M.–4:30 P.M.; fax: 708-869-5996. Stained glass; beveled glass; etched, sandblasted, and bent glass; glass painting. Restoration, conservation, and consultation. Restoration of murals and sculptures, all mediums. Free brochure.

Bradbury & Bradbury, PO Box 155, Benicia, CA 94510, 707-746-1900, Mon.–Fri. 9:00 A.M.–5:00 P.M.; fax: 707-745-9417. New hand-printed Victorian and Edwardian wallpapers, borders, and ceiling papers. Catalog $10.

The Brass Knob, Architectural Antiques, 2311 18th St. NW, Washington, DC 20009, 202-332-3370, Mon.–Sat., 10:30 A.M.–6:00 P.M., Sun. 12:00 P.M.–5:00 P.M. Architectural antiques, specializing in restored lighting, hardware, fireplace mantels, ironwork, and decorative detail.

Chatham Glass Co., Jim Holmes and Deborah Doane, Box 522, North Chatham, MA 02650, 508-945-5547, Mon.–Sat. 10:00 A.M.–5:00 P.M. Bull's-eye windows blown to your exact size, from 4 × 4 inches to 12 × 12 inches. Call for prices.

Chatree's, 711 Eighth St., SE, Washington, DC 20003, 202-546-4950. Repair and reproduction of ornamental architectural forms; plaster molding; stonecasting.

Chelsea Decorative Metal Co., 9603 Moonlight Dr., Houston, TX 77096, 713-721-9200, 9:00 A.M.–5:00 P.M.; fax: 713-776-8661. Pressed-tin for ceilings and cornices, Art Deco to Victorian. Catalog $1.

Conner's Architectural Antiques, 701 P St., Lincoln, NE 68508, 402-435-3338. Architectural elements from old structures, including columns, doors, fireplace mantels, hardware, light fixtures, stairways, and windows. Stained, etched, and beveled glass windows.

Crawford's Old House Store, 550 Elizabeth, Room 92, Waukesha, WI 53186, 800-556-7878, 8:00 A.M.–5:00 P.M. Old-style turned hardwood corner protectors and door stops. Builders' hardware, Victorian bath fixtures, ceiling rosettes, etc.

Crossland Studio, 118 E. Kingston Ave., Charlotte, NC 28203, 704-332-3032, Mon.–Fri. 8:30 A.M.–6:00 P.M., Sat. 9:00 A.M.–4:00 P.M. Antique doors, mantels, stained and beveled glass, columns, balusters, newel posts, and stair rails.

Crown Corporation, NA, 1801 Wynkoop St., Suite 235, Denver, CO 80202, 800-442-2099, 9:00 A.M.–5:00 P.M.; fax: 303-292-1933. Architectural details. Polyurethane crown molding, ceiling medallions, chair rails, columns, pedestals, corbels. Reproductions of wallcoverings, 1850–1910. Catalog $2. Call for a dealer near you.

18th Century Design Associates, 397 Massey Rd., Springfield, VT 05156, 802-885-1122, Mon.–Sat. 9:00 A.M.–6:00 P.M. Architectural services, preservation consulting on antique houses and related structures, reproduction woodworking, historical research. Catalog $3.

Gold Leaf Studios, Inc., PO Box 50156, Washington, DC 20091, 202-638-4660, Mon.–Fri. 9:00 A.M.–5:30 P.M.; fax: 202-347-4569. Architectural gilding.

Grand Era Reproductions, PO Box 1026, Lapeer, MI 48446, 313-664-1756, 8:00 A.M.–5:00 P.M.; fax: 313-664-8957. Custom-order reproduction porch brackets, screen and storm doors, door hardware. Can reproduce missing brackets. Wooden items are custom made. Mail order worldwide. Catalog $2.

Hardware+Plus, Inc., 701 E. Kingsley Rd., Garland, TX 75041, 214-271-0319, technical assistance; 800-522-7336, order line; fax: 214-271-9726. Nostalgic plumbing fittings and fixtures, molded interior and exterior millwork and ornamentation, tin ceiling panels. Free brochure.

Helen Williams, 12643 Hortense St., Studio City, CA 91604, 818-761-2756, anytime. Antique Delft tiles, seventeenth-century Dutch firebacks. Send SASE for free brochure.

Hippo Hardware & Trading Co., 1040 E. Burnside, Portland, OR 97214, 503-231-1444, Mon.–Fri. 10:00 A.M.–5:00 P.M., Sat. 10:00 A.M.–6:00 P.M.; fax: 503-231-5708. Original hardware, lighting, plumbing, and house parts for restoration. Salvaged architectural pieces; remanufactured hardware and other old house parts. Victorian to Ozzie and Harriet periods. Send photo of items sought. Reproduction catalog $2.

Historic Homes Implementers, 1328 S. Brook St., Louisville, KY 40208, 502-637-7429; fax: 502-636-1372. Consulting and acquisition services for anything needed for mature or historic homes—exterior and interior. Contacts, sources, restoration techniques, and reproductions.

Linoleum City, Inc., Fred Stifter, 5657 Santa Monica Blvd., Hollywood, CA 90038, 213-469-0063, 8:30 A.M.–5:30 P.M.; fax: 213-465-5866. Loose-lay vinyl that simulates old felt-base linoleum rugs; cork floor and wall tiles, natural marbleized battleship linoleum; natural linoleum desktop; solid vinyl floor tiles; and other floor coverings. Shipped anywhere in the United States. Brochures available. Set of cork tile samples $5; marbleized linoleum samples or desktop linoleum samples, $5; loose lay rug samples $3.

Mad River Woodworks, 189 Taylor Way, PO Box 1067, Blue Lake, CA 95525, 707-668-5671, Mon.–Fri. 8:30 A.M.–5:00 P.M. Custom millwork, ornamental gingerbread moldings and turnings, balustrades, brackets, corbels, gable-top treatments, newels, post finials, redwood gutters, rosettes, screen doors, spandrels, and more. Custom made or order from catalog. Shipped nationwide. Free estimates. Catalog $3.

Master Woodcarver, 103 Corrine Dr., Pennington, NJ 08534, 609-737-9364 after 5:00 P.M. Hand carving for all period moldings, mantels, etc. Conservation.

McDan Woodworking, David Dannenberg and Michael McClintock, 374 E. Broad St., Gibbstown, NJ 08027, 609-423-5337, 7:00 A.M.–3:00 P.M.; fax: 609-224-0968. Will custom-make anything wooden. Architectural millwork, interior and exterior woodwork, historic replication.

Midwest Architectural Wood Products, 1051 S. Rolff St., Davenport, IA 52802, 319-323-4757, 8:00 A.M.–5:00 P.M.; fax: 319-323-1483. Custom wood windows for restoration projects. Sashes, storms, screens, and more. Catalog $2.

Old World Restorations, Inc., 347 Stanley Ave., Cincinnati, OH 45226, 800-878-1911, 513-321-1911, Mon.–Fri. 8:30 A.M.–5:30 P.M.; fax: 513-321-1914. Architectural restoration; murals, statuary, frescoes, marble, gold leaf, etc. Free brochure.

Ole Fashion Things, 402 SW Evangeline Thwy., Lafayette, LA 70501, 318-234-4800, 800-228-4967, Tues.–Sat. 10:00 A.M.–6:00 P.M. Architectural embellishments: fireplace mantels, plaster ceiling medallions, crown moldings, brackets, and appliqués. Catalog $5.

Original Woodworks, 360 N. Main St., Stillwater, MN 55082, 612-430-3622, Thurs.–Sat. noon–5:00 P.M. Architectural restorations. Stripping and refinishing mantels, doors, etc. Replacement carvings. Curved and specialty glass; faucets, knobs, locks, and other hardware.

R. Wayne Reynolds, Ltd., Wayne Reynolds, 3618 Falls Rd., Baltimore, MD 21211, 410-467-1800, 9:00 A.M.–5:30 P.M.; fax: 410-467-1205. On-site gilding on architectural ornamentation. Consulting services. Call for a statement of capabilities.

Remodelers & Renovators Supply, PO Box 45478, Boise, ID 83711, 208-322-6221, 9:00 A.M.–5:00 P.M. Plumbing supplies and hardware for vintage houses, available in brass; some chrome and glass. Catalog $3.

Renovation Source, Inc., 3512 N. Southport, Chicago, IL 60657, 312-327-1250, Tues.–Sat. 10:00 A.M.–6:00 P.M. Architectural antiques, repair and restoration. Door hardware, stained-glass windows, doors, fireplace mantels, and other decorative details of wood, stone, plaster, and iron.

Restoration Clinic, Inc., 2801 NW 55th Ct., Bldg. 8 W, Fort Lauderdale, FL 33309, 800-235-OLDY, anytime; fax: 305-486-4988. Conservation and restoration, including architectural, stone, wood, glass and metals. By appointment only. Send SASE for free leaflet *What to Do Until the Restorer Comes.*

The Restoration Place, 305 20th St., Rock Island, IL 61201, 309-786-0004, 9:30 A.M.–5:30 P.M.; fax: 309-786-5834. Resource center for restoration and renovation products and services, architectural pieces, period lighting, plumbing, and millwork. Building and furniture hardware, antique and reproduction. Free brochure. Catalog $8.

Roy Electric Co., Inc., 1054 Coney Island Ave., Brooklyn, NY 11230, 718-434-7002; fax: 718-421-4678. Antique and reproduction plumbing fixtures. Catalog $6, refundable with order.

Steptoe and Wife Antiques Ltd., 322 Geary Ave., Toronto, ON, Canada M6H 2C7, 416-530-4200. Mon–Fri. 9:00 A.M.–5:00 P.M.; fax: 416-530-4666. Architectural restoration products. Cast-iron spiral staircases, plaster architectural details, moldings, ceiling medallions, friezes, corbels. Catalog $3.

Stoneledge, Inc., 17 Robert St., Wharton, NJ 07885, 201-989-8800, Mon.–Fri. 9:00 A.M.–5:00 P.M.; fax: 201-361-6574. Conservation and restoration of architectural elements; wood, stone, metal, and other materials. Free brochure.

Traditional Line Ltd., 143 W. 21st St., New York, NY 10011, 212-627-3555, 8:30 A.M.–5:00 P.M.; 212-645-8158. Full-service architectural restoration in the New York metropolitan area. Hardware repair and reproduction.

Victorian Collectibles Ltd., 845 E. Glenbrook Rd., Milwaukee, WI 53217, 414-352-6971, 9:00 A.M.–5:00 P.M.; fax: 414-352-7290. Reproduction historic American wallpapers, 1850–1910.

Vintage Plumbing/Bathroom Antiques, 9645 Sylvia Ave., Northridge, CA 91324, 818-772-1721, anytime. Repairs antique bathroom fixtures, especially old lavatories and pull-chain toilets. Repairs or replicates faucet parts and waste parts.

Vintage Wood Works, Hwy. 34 S., PO Box R, #2557, Fredericksburg, TX 78624, 903-356-2158, 8:00 A.M.–4:30 P.M.; fax: 903-356-3023. Handcrafted reproductions of Victorian architectural details, including balusters, brackets, corbels, fittings, gables, posts, screen doors, stair parts. Mail order. Catalog $2.

Wrecking Bar, 292 Moreland Ave. NE, Atlanta, GA 30307, 404-525-0468, Mon.–Sat. 9:00 A.M.–5:00 P.M. Architectural components, including wood carvings, mantels, capitals, wrought iron, spindles, newels, doors, brass and copper hardware, and more. Brochure.

Autographs

Nineteenth-century autograph collectors wanted just the signatures of famous people. They cut names from the bottoms of letters or other documents, destroying much of their value. Today's collector prefers the entire letter or document. Never cut out a signature! If you find old books, letters, deeds, or even scribbled notes signed by an author or famous person, keep them intact. Never cut, erase, or repair anything. Torn pages are preferred to taped pages. Glue from the tape can eventually destroy the paper.

All correspondence can have a value. This includes letters from distant relatives describing a war, an old Western town, the food eaten for dinner, or many other everyday events. Content, condition, date, place written, signature, postmarks, and other factors all affect the value. Very high prices are paid for letters or diaries about American life, especially if they describe disasters, the Gold Rush, Indians, whaling, the Revolutionary or Civil wars, or pioneer life. Hand-drawn maps, sketches by artists, and inscribed or annotated books are all of value.

Very high prices are paid for letters and documents of presidents, signers of the Declaration of Independence, important political and military figures, composers, authors, or scientists. But many government documents were signed by secretaries or even by machines that reproduced a president's signature, and these are worth very little. Land grants, army discharges, and many other legal papers were signed with the president's name and not always hand-signed by the president. There are many of these, and their value is very low. Slave-related documents have become more valuable because of their historic value, and they sell best at black collectibles shows.

There is little interest in documents written in foreign languages, so you may find a letter written by a famous French statesman will sell for a high price in France but not in an English-speaking country. Some autograph dealers have international outlets and get good prices for foreign material.

Supply and demand is the key to pricing an autograph. Button Gwinnett and Thomas Lynch, Jr., signed the Declaration of Independence and died soon after. Because there is such great demand for a complete set of signatures of the Declaration's signers, these two autographs have a very, very high value. Other, more important men signed the Declaration, but there is an ample supply of their writings. This same pricing rule holds for more recent signatures, like those of James Dean or Marilyn Monroe.

Autographs and letters that are forgeries, copies, or reproductions have almost no resale value. You must own an original. Most libraries have excellent books about autograph collecting that offer many hints about what is valuable. Autographs can be sold to local antiques dealers or to local antiquarian book dealers, or coin or stamp dealers who also handle autographed materials. If no local dealers are to be found, you may be able to sell important material through an out-of-town auction gallery. There are galleries that specialize in autographs and historic material.

Out-of-town dealers who buy autographed materials will not buy from a description or photocopy. Carefully pack the material between pieces of cardboard, place it in a strong envelope, and seal with tape. Always get references before you send anything. Send the material first class, insured if it is worth under $300, or registered mail if it is worth more. Keep a photocopy for yourself as well as a list of what you sent. The dealer will usually send you a check. This is one of the very few areas of collecting where you are not expected to set the price.

REPAIR
Autographs that have been cut off documents have very little value. It is better to keep a complete damaged piece of paper than to trim any of it for a better appearance. If the damage is unsightly, frame the paper with acid-free mounts so only the perfect parts show.

Most of the repair and conservation information you need can be found in the section on Paper.

Price Book
Sanders' Price Guide to Autographs, George and Helen Sanders with Ralph Roberts (WorldComm, 65 Macedonia Rd., Alexander, NMC 28701, © 1994).

Clubs & Publications
Manuscript Society, *Manuscripts* (MAG), 350 N. Niagara St., Burbank, CA 91505.

Universal Autograph Collectors Club, *Pen and Quill* (MAG), PO Box 6181, Washington, DC 20044-6181.

Autograph Collectors & Collecting (MAG), 510-A S. Corona Mall, Corona, CA 91719.

Autograph Review (NL), c/o J.W. Morey, 305 Carlton Rd., Syracuse, NY 13207 (autographs of sports figures, entertainers, military figures).

Autograph Times (NP), 2303 N. 44th St., #225, Phoenix, AZ 85008.

Collector (MAG), Walter R. Benjamin Autographs, Inc., PO Box 255, Hunter, NY 12442.

Barbed Wire & Insulators

The first barbed wire was patented by Lucien Smith of Kent, Ohio, in 1867. More than 1,500 different varieties of barbed wire are known. Collectors prefer pieces that are eighteen inches in length.

Telephone and telegraph insulators have been collected since the 1960s by serious collectors who know the makers, use, and patent histories of the insulators. Never attempt to remove an insulator from a pole. There are often power lines on the poles and collectors have been electrocuted. You can sometimes find old insulators left by repairmen buried at the pole base.

R E P A I R

Insulators can be repaired by specialists and by those listed in other sections of this book who do glass and ceramic work.

Clubs & Publications

American Barbed Wire Collectors Society, *Wire Collector News* (NL), 1023 Baldwin Rd., Bakersfield, CA 93304.

New Mexico Barbed Wire Collectors Association, *Wire Barb & Nail* (NL), PO Box 102, Stanley, NM 87056.

Barbed Wire Collector (NL), 1322 Lark, Lewisville, TX 75067.

Canadian Insulator Collector (MAG), Mayne Island, BC, Canada V0N 2J0.

Crown Jewels of the Wire (MAG), PO Box 1003, St. Charles, IL 60174-1003 (insulators).

Rainbow Riders' Trading Post (MAG), PO Box 1423, Port Heuneme, CA 93044.

Barber Poles & Barber Collectibles

The barber pole is said to have been made to represent the blood-soaked rags wrapped around the pole in earlier days. The red-and-white-striped pole has been a symbol of the pharmacist or barber since the eighteenth century. Old barber poles are now considered folk art. Information about selling and repair can be found in the folk-art section.

Other barber antiques such as bottles, shaving mugs, or even old chairs have a value to special collectors. Look in the sections on Bottles, and Pottery and Porcelain, to learn more about selling and repairing these collectibles. Barber chairs have a very special market and sell best though an ad in the local paper or an antiques paper. Because they are heavy, few dealers will offer to buy. You must find a collector.

Club & Publication

National Shaving Mug Collectors Association, *Barber Shop Collectibles Newsletter* (NL), 11 Walton Ave., White Plains, NY 10606.

Repairs, Parts & Supplies

William Marvy Company, 1540 St. Clair Ave., St. Paul, MN 55105, 612-698-0726, 800-874-2651, Mon.–Fri. 8:00 A.M.–4:30 P.M., Sat. 9:00 A.M.–1:00 P.M.; fax: 612-698-4048. Barber pole parts. Free brochure.

Beer Cans & Breweriana

*T*here are many collectors of beer cans, but most cans are traded and not sold. The best way to get rid of a collection is to go to a show-and-swap meet for beer can collectors. The local papers and the beer can collectors publications will list them.

Cans are often sold in groups. Anyone who buys a six-pack has the start of a beer-can collection at almost no cost. Some can be traded for other cans, and there is no cost. If you sell some of the recent cans for anything, even 50 cents, you have a profit.

The best sellers are cone-top cans. They are old and not easily found. Collectors prefer cans that have been opened from the bottom. Rust, dents, and other damage destroy the value of a common can and lower the value of rare cans.

The way collectors of beer cans and breweriana organize themselves into special-interest factions with shows, publications, and clubs can be confusing. There are collectors of early tin beer signs who attend advertising shows. There are collectors of beer bottles who are bottle collectors and go to bottle shows. Beer can collectors usually buy at beer can shows or flea markets. Books about beer often discuss the cans as well as the bottles and all of the brewery history that is available under the broad term "breweriana."

Breweriana is anything related to beer and beer cans. This includes signs, labels, ads, coasters, glasses, hats, and the unpressed metal used to make cans. Breweriana will sell either at a beer-can collectors show or to the advertising collectors. For more information, see the section on Advertising Collectibles.

REPAIR

There is one clever restoration tip for crushed beer cans that you might want to try. Fill the dented can about one-third full with dry beans, then add water and seal the can. The pressure from the expanding beans will push outward and remove most of the dents.

Cone-top cans can be repaired by experts who solder new tops on the old cans. Repairing beer cans is almost the same as repairing any commercial tin container, including soft drink cans. More information about this can be found in the section on Metals.

Price Books

The Beer Tray Book, Volume I—1992/1993, Paul Burden (PO Box 218, Medfield, MA 02052, © 1992).

Contemporary Beer Neon Signs, Robert Swinnich (L-W Book Sales, Gas City, IN, © 1994).

Official Price Guide to Beer Cans, 5th edition, William E. Mugrage (House of Collectibles, New York, © 1993).

Reference Book

American Breweries, Donald Bull, Manfred Friedrich, and Robert Gottschalk (Bullworks, PO Box 106, Trumbull, CT 06611, © 1984).

Clubs & Publications

American Breweriana Association, Inc., *American Breweriana Journal* (MAG), PO Box 5, Friend, NE 68359-0005.

Beer Can Collectors of America, *Beer Cans & Brewery Collectibles* (MAG), 747 Merus Ct., Fenton, MO 63026-2092.

National Association of Breweriana Advertising, *Breweriana Collector* (NL), 2343 Met-To-Wee Ln., Wauwatosa, WI 53226.

National Pop Can Collectors, *Can-O-Gram* (NL), PO Box 7862, Rockford, IL 61126.

Black Collectibles

*A*nything that pictures a black person or is related to black culture is considered a "black collectible." This includes everything from early slave documents and photographs of life in earlier times to advertisements, figurines, and other stereotypical depictions. In a price book listing of black collectibles you will find items related to Aunt Jemima, the Cream of Wheat man, Amos 'n' Andy, a fast-food chain known as Coon Chicken Inns, and many nameless black people. There are several books about black items and several special shows every year.

Black collectibles are also bought and sold at advertising or general antiques show. Black rag dolls are classed as both folk art and collectible dolls and are sold by dealers in both of these specialties. Some of the black material is derogatory, and you may be concerned about the propriety of offering it for sale. Remember, that the majority of the dealers who specialize in black items and the majority of the collectors of black items are themselves black. They want the pieces as part of their heritage, and are eager to buy. Of great interest are any slave-related documents, pictures, or memorabilia.

Any item picturing a black person will sell at a good price. Amos 'n' Andy toys are worth 50 percent more than comparable toys showing white cartoon figures. Even small, dime-store "joke" figurines of past years are selling for over $50 each. Visit an antiques show and check prices on black collectibles before you try to sell yours. Many sell for far more than the amateur would believe.

Price Books

Black Dolls 1820–1991: An Identification and Value Guide, Myla Perkins (Collector Books, Paducah, KY, © 1993).

Black Memorabilia for the Kitchen: A Handbook & Price Guide, Jan Lindenberger (Schiffer, Atglen, PA, © 1992).

Black Memorabilia Around the House, Jan Lindenberger (Schiffer, Atglen, PA, © 1993).

Club & Publications

Black Memorabilia Collectors Association, *Collecting Our Culture* (NL), 2482 Devoe Terr., Bronx, NY 10468.

Black Antiquities Newsletter (NL), 12000 Edgewater Dr., Suite 1303, Lakewood, OH 44107 (includes bi-monthly mail-bid auctions).

Books & Bookplates

Selling books presents different problems from selling other types of collectibles. Age is one of the factors that determine price, but it is not as important as people believe. Some books written during the past twenty-five years are worth more than books that are 200 years old. The value of a book is determined by rarity, condition, edition, and age. It is also influenced by whether it has the original wrapping intact, who owned it, if there is a bookplate or a signature, who printed it, and the subject.

Books can be sold at house sales and auctions. They also can be sold to stores that carry used books and to antiquarian book dealers. It is necessary to think about a possible customer for your unusual books. For example, old local history books might be needed by a historical society library. You can also sell to private buyers if you are persistent and find the right customer.

If you have hundreds of books that were purchased over a period of time by an average book buyer, not a serious collector, you can sell the group at a house sale. You can call in a book dealer or friend to buy, but try to sell the entire collection. Otherwise you may find that the best books have been sold and the ones remaining have little value.

If you have a number of rare books, contact an antiquarian bookseller. They are listed in the Yellow Pages of the phone book or can be found selling books at one of the many antiquarian book fairs. *Buy Books Where—Sell Books Where* by Ruth Robinson and Daryush Farudi is an annual publication listing sellers of out-of-print books. Most book collectors specialize by type or subject, and Robinson's book may give you some ideas about what is valuable.

First editions of important books are often valuable. To determine if a book is a first edition, look at the copyright page to see if it says "First Edition." Look on the title page to see whether the date agrees with the copyright date. Some recently published books list the numerals 1 through 10 on the bottom of the page. If the 1 is still in the list, it is the first printing. When there is a second printing the 1 is removed. By the tenth printing only the 10 remains. Books printed by certain small private presses and special printings of books are very valuable. Book-of-the-Month Club editions, special collector editions made in quantity, or reissues of old books have little value. First editions by the best 1930s and 1940s mystery writers are popular, but the books must have original dust jackets for highest value.

Bibles, encyclopedias, dictionaries, and textbooks have very low value. McGuffey readers, disaster books (describing a flood or earthquake), and books made into movies are of little value unless they are first editions or related to *Gone With the Wind.* The first McGuffey, the first edition of an important movie book, or a rare disaster book does sell well. Old cookbooks, decorating books, catalogs, horticulture and flower arranging books, sports books, history books, and early books on science and medicine have value. Very early children's books and illustrated books in good condition are wanted.

Books with unusual photographs, engraved illustrations, or other attractive pictures are worth money. Unfortunately, the pictures are sometimes worth more out of the book than the entire book is worth. That is why many nineteenh-century books of flower prints have been taken apart. Look for illustrations by WALLACE NUTTING, N.C. WYETH, ROCKWELL KENT, MAXFIELD PARRISH, BESSIE PEASE GUTMANN, and ARTHUR RACKHAM.

"Association" books are collected. Any book with a signature by an important owner or author or with an inscription to an important person has the added value of its association with that person. Sometimes the autograph is more valuable than the book. Some bookplates are also very valuable; a Charles Dickens or Paul Revere plate is worth hundreds of dollars.

Covers are important; leather bindings, elaborate gold-decorated bindings, and paper dust covers of special interest add value. Fore-edge painting (pictures on the front edge of the page) and pop-up illustrations also bring higher prices.

Paperback books that are first editions in good condition sell well. You can tell age by the price printed on the book and sometimes by low numbers used by publishers for identification. If there is a bar code, the book was published after 1970. Some collectors specialize, buying only books with lurid covers or with art by well-known illustrators.

Worn paperbacks sell only to buyers who want a book to read at a very low price. Condition is important for all types of books. Would you want a chipped cup? A torn book is the chipped cup of the book business. Transparent-tape repairs lower value. If you mail a book to a buyer, wrap it in a padded book bag, and send it book rate, insured. Postage for books, magazines, and other printed materials is a bargain. Ask your post office.

REPAIR
Rebinding antique books reduces their value and should be avoided unless it is absolutely necessary. However, if you must, there are bookbinders in many cities. They are listed in the Yellow Pages under "Bookbinders" or you can learn about them from some of the better bookstores or decorating studios.

Bookplate collecting was a major hobby fifty years ago and many fine old books were mutilated by eager collectors who only wanted the bookplates. That is not recommended today. Unless the book is in very bad repair, it is worth more with the bookplate than a mutilated book and a cut-out bookplate. Little can be done to restore a bookplate outside of simple cleaning and pressing with an iron. Nothing can be done if old glue has stained the plate.

Keep bookplates, books, and all paper items in a controlled environment where they will not become too wet or dry or be attacked by insects, bookworms, or rodents. If you collect paper items, it would be wise to buy the necessary humidifier or dehumidifier for your home.

Price Books

Bookman's Price Index, annual (Gale Research, Detroit, MI).

Books Identification and Price Guide, Nancy Wright (Avon Books, New York, © 1993).

Collecting Little Golden Books, 2nd edition, Steve Santi (Books Americana, Florence, AL, © 1994).

Maud Humphrey: Her Permanent Imprint on American Illustration, Karen Choppa and Paul Humphrey (Schiffer, Atglen, PA, © 1993).

Official Price Guide to Old Books, Marie Tedford and Pat Goudey (House of Collectibles, New York, © 1994).

PBs at Auction, annual (International Paperback Collectors Society, 102 Joanne Dr., Holbrook, NY 11741).

Books on Repair

Binding and Repairing Books by Hand, David Muir (Arco Publishing Co., New York, © 1987).

Care of Fine Books, Jane Greenfield (Lyons & Burford Publishers, New York, © 1988).

Cleaning and Caring for Books, Robert L. Shep (Sheppard Press, London, © 1983).

Cleaning and Preserving Bindings and Related Materials, Carolyn Horton (American Library Association, 50 East Huron St., Chicago, IL 60611, © 1975).

Clubs & Publications

Alice in Wonderland Collector's Network, *Alice in Wonderland Collector's Network Newsletter* (NL), 2765 Shellingham Dr., Lisle, IL 60532.

American Society of Bookplate Collectors & Designers, *Bookplates in the News* (NL), *Year Book* (annual), 605 N. Stoneman Ave., #F, Alhambra, CA 91801.

Big Little Book Club of America, *Big Little Times* (NL), PO Box 1242, Danville, CA 94526.

Burgess Book Collectors, *Burgess Book Collectors' Bulletin* (NL), Thornton W. Burgess Society, 6 Discovery Hill Rd., East Sandwich, MA 02537.

Cook Book Collectors Club of America, Inc., *Cook Book Gossip* (NL), PO Box 56, St. James, MO 65559.

Harrison Fisher Society, *Harrison Fisher Newsletter* (NL), PO Box 8188, Redlands, CA 92375-9998.

Horatio Alger Society, *Newsboy* (NL), 585 St. Andrews Dr., Media, PA 19063.

International Paperback Collectors Society, *IPCS Journal* (NL), 21 Deer Ln., Wantagh, NY 11793 (collectible paperbacks).

International Society of Bible Collectors, *Bible Collectors' World* (MAG), 3909 Snow Creek Dr., Aledo, TX 76008.

International Wizard of Oz Club, *Baum Bugle* (NL), c/o Fred M. Meyer, 220 N. 11th St., Escanaba, MI 49829.

Kate Greenaway Society, *Under the Window* (NL), PO Box 8, Norwood, PA 19074.

AB Bookman's Weekly (MAG), PO Box AB, Clifton, NJ 07015 (all ads for out-of-print books).

Beyond the Rainbow Collector's Exchange (NL), PO Box 31672, St. Louis, MO 63131 (Wizard of Oz memorabilia).

Book Source Monthly (MAG), PO Box 567, Cazenovia, NY 13035-0567 (includes book auction calendar, book fair calendar, annual directory of private collectors, etc.).

Bookmark Collector (NL), 1002 W. 25th St., Erie, PA 16502.

Books Are Everything! (MAG), PO Box 5068, Richmond, KY 40475 (paperbacks).

Cookbook Collectors' Exchange (NL), PO Box 32369, San Jose, CA 95152-2369.

Dime Novel Round-Up (MAG), 87 School St., Fall River, MA 02720.

Illustrator Collector's News (NL), PO Box 1958, Sequim, WA 98382.

Joan Walsh Anglund Collectors News (NL), PO Box 105, Amherst, NH 03031.

Martha's KidLit Newsletter (NL), PO Box 1488, Ames, IA 50014 (out-of-print children's books).

Modern Library & Viking Portable Collector (NL), 340 Warren Ave., Cincinnati, OH 45220-1135.

Mystery & Adventure Series Review (MAG), PO Box 3488, Tucson, AZ 85722.

Paperback Parade (MAG), PO Box 209, Brooklyn, NY 11228-0209.

Yellowback Library (MAG), PO Box 36172, Des Moines, IA 50315 (for collectors of dime novels and related juvenile series literature).

Repairs, Parts & Supplies

Andrew Hurst, 2423 Amber St., Knoxville, TN 37917, 615-523-3498, 8:00 A.M.–7:00 P.M. Conservation and restoration of leather books and encapsulation of documents. Can stabilize red rot of leather.

Archival Conservation Center, Inc., 8225 Daly Rd., Cincinnati, OH 45231, 513-521-9858, 8:30 A.M.–3:30 P.M. Repair and restoration of works of art on paper, including family Bibles. Free brochure.

Cellar Stories Books, 190 Mathewson St., Providence, RI 02903, 401-521-2665, Mon.–Sat. 10:00 A.M.–6:00 P.M., machine after hours. Out-of-

print search service. Referral to person who does book binding and repair.

George Martin Cunha, 4 Tanglewood Dr., Lexington, KY 40505, 606-293-5703, 8:00 A.M.–5:00 P.M.; fax: 606-233-9425. Repair and restoration of rare and valuable books, manuscript materials, and works of art on paper. Preservation surveys for books and paper records, with recommendations for restoration, if required.

Harcourt Bindery, 51 Melcher St., Boston, MA 02210, 617-542-5858, 8:30 A.M.–4:00 P.M.; fax: 617-451-9058. Hand-binding and book repair services, cloth and leather, rare book restoration, worldwide. Protective boxes. On-site library surveys and refurbishing, nationwide. Free brochure.

James Macdonald Company, Inc., Jacques Desmonts, 25 Van Zant St., East Norwalk, CT 06855, 203-853-6076, 7:30 A.M.–4:30 P.M. Restoration of old and rare books. Full-cloth and quarter-leather slip cases. Cloth, quarter or full leather binding.

Linda A. Blaser, 9200 Hawkins Creamery Rd., Gaithersburg, MD 20882, 301-774-2267, before 8:00 P.M. Conservation of books and flat paper items.

Northeast Document Conservation Center, 100 Brickstone Sq., Andover, MA 01810-1494, 508-470-1010; fax: 508-475-6021. Nonprofit regional conservation center specializing in treatment of art and artifacts on paper, including books. Preservation microfilming, preservation planning surveys, disaster assistance, technical leaflets. Brochure.

Preservation Emporium, PO Box 226309, Dallas, TX 75222-6309, 214-630-1197, Mon.–Fri. 9:00 A.M.–5:00 P.M., Sat. 9:00 A.M.–4:00 P.M.; fax: 214-630-7805. Acid-free/lignin-free storage materials and conservation chemicals. Bookbinding and restoration. Full conservation treatments and restoration work. Paper deacidification, cleaning and treatment of leather bindings, repair or replacement of marbled end sheets.

Sandlin's Books & Bindery, 70 W. Lincolnway, Valparaiso, IN 46383-5522, 219-462-9922, Mon.–Sat. 9:00 A.M.–5:00 P.M. Antiquarian books, bookbinding, and restoration.

Scott K. Kellar, Bookbinding & Conservation, 2650 Montrose Ave., Chicago, IL 60618, 312-478-2825, Mon.–Fri. 9:00 A.M.–5:00 P.M. Repair and conservation of valuable books; rebinding and protective enclosures.

Bottles & Go-Withs

*B*ottles can be divided into two separate selling markets. Modern figural bottles like Jim Beam, Ezra Brooks, and Avon have been collected for the past twenty years; they are found at the liquor store or flea market, and there are several national collector clubs for them. Their market has gone up and down, and today some people have large collections that are worth less than their original cost. Old and antique bottles are favored by a very different group of people. They are serious collectors who dig for bottles, trade bottles, belong to antique bottle clubs, go to shows, and think of bottles as a part of the fun in their lives.

It is easy to price new bottles, but it is hard to sell them. The new figural bottles, including Avon and the liquor decanters, are listed with detailed descriptions and retail prices in the price guides such as *Kovels' Bottles Price List.* You will be fortunate to get 50 percent of that price if you have a new bottle in mint condition with original labels. There are many national clubs for modern bottle collectors. An ad in the publications for these clubs is often the best place to sell. Some states have active collectors and clubs that sponsor modern bottle shows, but in other areas there is little interest.

Make a list of your bottles. Only those in perfect condition sell. Damaged bottles are worth pennies at a garage sale. Determine the prices and offer to sell either to dealers or by mail to collectors who read the ads in the bottle and general publications. Bottles that picture trains, cars, or sporting events are going up in price because they sell well to sports memorabilia collectors or to train and car collectors. Find these groups in the sports collectibles and toy sections.

Old bottles, especially rare ones, sell best at bottle shows and bottle auctions. Highest prices are paid by serious dealers and collectors. Many of these bottles are listed in *Kovels' Bottles Price List.* The listed price is very close to the price you should ask from a collector. Dealers buy at 30 to 50 percent less. Many types of old bottles are collected, including milk bottles, canning jars, inks, inkwells, medicines, bitters, sodas, poisons, whiskeys, figurals, and most desirable of all, historical flasks.

Rare colors and markings indicate an old bottle worth thousands of dollars. Common bottles can sell for a few dollars. Aqua-colored glass with bubbles is common. Desirable colors are cobalt blue, dark purple, honey amber, clear green, yellow, and sometimes white milk glass.

A rough scar on the bottom of a bottle is called a pontil. This is usually an indication of a hand-blown bottle. Seam marks on the neck of the bottle usually indicate a newer, machine-made bottle. Old is usually more valuable than new.

Machine-made bottles with no redeeming features sell best at flea markets or house sales. Any type of perfume bottle and attractive figural bottles sell well at antique shows. Figural liquor bottles like those by Jim Beam sell for very little unless they are sports-related or feature cars, planes, or trains.

Warning! In some states it is against the law to sell bottles with liquor inside. It is illegal in every state to sell bottles that contain drugs such as opium or cocaine. These drugs sometimes remain in old bottles found in drugstores from the early 1900s, when the now-banned drugs were legal medicines.

Beginning collectors make several mistakes. Bottles are collected for their beauty and history. Years ago it was common to soak the labels off, but it is not being done today. Do not remove or destroy any paper labels, tax stamps, or other paper glued to a bottle or the original box, if available. The box and labels add to the value. Today advertising collectors and some specialty bottle collectors pay a premium for bottles with original paper labels, even if the labels are damaged. When regluing a label, be sure to use an adhesive that will not stain the paper.

Uninformed collectors sometimes misunderstand the marks embossed on bottles. Don't think that the date 1858 in raised numerals in the glass of your fruit jar means that it is either old or rare. The date is the year the screw-top jar was patented, and the number was used for many years after 1858.

Bubbles in the glass, "whittle marks," and pale aqua glass are not rare and are not indications of very expensive bottles. A nick or flaw is always significant in a rare bottle, and substantially lowers its value. Condition is important and a nick, scratch, or cloudy interior can lower the value by as much as 70 percent. A bottle that is less than fifty years old that is damaged is often worthless.

GO-WITHS

Anything that pictures a bottle or was used with a bottle is of interest to bottle collectors. This includes bottle openers, jar openers, milk bottle caps, canning jar rubber rings and tops, corkscrews, fancy bottle corks, ads, and pamphlets. These items can all be sold. The corkscrew and bottle-opener collectors have very specific wants, and the best place to sell good examples of these is through the collector clubs and ads.

Don't underestimate the value of old openers. The current record price for a corkscrew is over $1,000. Figural bottle openers often sell for over $50—and the record price is over $1,000.

REPAIR

An old privy or dump may not seem like the perfect vacation spot. To a collector of old bottles, it is heaven. Some of the best bottles are dug from old dumps or constructions sites, or are pulled from river bottoms. Many are in need of repairs. Local bottle clubs always welcome members and bottle shows are filled with collectors who delight in talking about their hobby, the bottles they have found, and possible restoration services.

There are all types of old bottles, including inkwells, flasks, bitters, medicines, poisons, and whiskeys. Many collectors search for recent bottles such as milk bottles, fruit jars, and modern figural whiskeys. Some manufacturers now have their own publications and books, which are usually available at bottle shows. Each group has special information about the correct appearance of the bottle, which could help with repairs.

The restoration rules for metal go-withs, such as openers, are the same as for other iron collectibles, like toys or doorstops. Never repaint; it lowers the value.

Beware of "sick" bottles. The cloudy effect inside the bottle is etched in the glass. If the bottle is for display, you can swish some clear mineral oil in the bottle, then seal the bottle. This temporarily covers the cloudy look. It is possible to polish the inside of a bottle, but it is very expensive, requires talent, and is a risky repair. Only the most expensive historic flasks or early bottles are usually restored in this manner.

Bottles can be repaired with the new plastics. Some of the repairs are invisible except under black light, but there is an even more expensive plastic that cannot be seen by black light.

See the section on Writing Utensils for inkwells, and the section on Glass.

Price Books

The Auction Price Report for Antique Bottles, William E. Brown (William E. Brown, 8251 N.W. 49th Ct., Coral Springs, FL 33067, © 1993).

Avon & C.P.C. Collector's Encyclopedia, 13th edition, Bud Hastin (PO Box 9868, Kansas City, MO 64134, © 1994).

Bottles Identification and Price Guide, Michael Polak (Avon Books, New York, © 1994).

The Collector's Price Guide to Bitters Bottles, Glenn A. Poch (215 Coventry, Mount Prospect, IL 60056, © 1992).

Kovels' Bottles Price List, biennial, Ralph and Terry Kovel (Crown, New York).

Mini Beer Update: A Supplement to Miniature Beer Bottles & Go-Withs, Robert E. Kay (216 N. Batavia Ave., Batavia, IL 60510, © 1989).

Museum

Seagram Museum, 57 Erb St. W., Waterloo, ON, Canada N2L 6C2. Exhibit and archives.

Clubs & Publications

American Collectors of Infant Feeders, *Keeping Abreast* (NL), 1849 Ebony Dr., York, PA 17402-4706.

Avon Times, *Avon Times* (NL), PO Box 9868, Kansas City, MO 64134.

Candy Container Collectors of America, *Candy Gram* (NL), PO Box 8708, Canton, OH 44711-8708.

Cow Observers Worldwide (C.O.W.), *MOOSletter* (NL), 240 Wahl Ave., Evans City, PA 16033 (cow collectibles).

Cream Separator Collectors Association, *Cream Separator & Dairy Newsletter* (NL), Rt. 3, Arcadia, WI 54612.

Crown Collectors Society International, *Crown Cappers' Exchange* (NL), 4300 San Juan Dr., Fairfax, VA 22030 (crown caps from beer and soda bottles).

Federation of Historical Bottle Collectors, *Federation Glass Works* (NL), Barbara A. Harms, Treasurer, PO Box 224, Dolton, IL 60419.

Figural Bottle Opener Collectors, *Opener* (NL), 117 Basin Hill Rd., Duncannon, PA 17020 (includes auctions).

International Association of Jim Beam Bottle and Specialties Clubs, *Beam Around the World* (NL), 2015 Burlington Ave., Kewanee, IL 61443.

International Chinese Snuff Bottle Society, *Journal* (MAG), 2601 N. Charles St., Baltimore, MD 21218.

International Perfume Bottle Association, *Perfume Bottle Quarterly* (NL), PO Box 529, Vienna, VA 22183.

Jelly Jammers, *Jelly Jammers Journal* (NL), 6086 W. Boggstown Rd., Boggstown, IN 46110.

Lilliputian Bottle Club, *Gulliver's Gazette* (NL), 54 Village Circle, Manhattan Beach, CA 90266-7222.

Midwest Antique Fruit Jar & Bottle Club, *Glass Chatter* (NL), PO Box 38, Flat Rock, IN 47234.

National Ski Country Decanter Club, *Ski Country Collector* (NL), 1224 Washington Ave., Golden, CO 80401.

Painted Soda Bottle Collectors Association, *Soda Net* (NL), 9418 Hilmer Dr., La Mesa, CA 91942.

Society of Inkwell Collectors, *Stained Finger* (NL), 5136 Thomas Ave. S., Minneapolis, MN 55410.

Tops & Bottoms Club, *T & B* (NL), PO Box 15555, Plantation, FL 33318 (nonprofit matching service for Lalique bottles and stoppers only).

Antique Bottle & Glass Collector (MAG), PO Box 180, 102 Jefferson St., East Greenville, PA 18041.

DECODING ADVERTISING COPY
When you read the ads for bottles, it might help to know these terms and abbreviations:

- ABM means automatic bottle machine.
- BIMAL means blown in mold, applied lip, open pontil.
- FB means free-blown.
- IP means iron pontil.
- ISP means inserted slug plate. Special names were sometimes embossed on a bottle, especially a milk bottle, with a special plate inserted in the mold.
- SC means sun-colored.
- SCA means sun-colored amethyst.
- OP means open pontil.

Bitters Report (NL), PO Box 1253, Bunnell, FL 32110.

Bottles & Bygones (MAG), 30 Brabant Rd., Cheadle Hulme, Cheadle, Cheshire, England SK8 7AU.

Bottles and Extras (MAG), PO Box 154, Happy Camp, CA 96039.

British Bottle Review (MAG), 5 Ironworks Row, Elsecar Project, Wath Rd., Elsecar, Barnsley, S. Yorkshire, England S74 8HJ.

Canadian Bottle & Stoneware Collector (MAG), 179 D Woodridge Cres., Nepean, ON Canada K2B 7T2.

Creamers (NL), PO Box 11, Lake Villa, IL 60046-0011 (individual glass advertising creamers).

Fruit Jar Newsletter (NL), 364 Gregory Ave., West Orange, NJ 07052-3743.

Just For Openers (NL), 3712 Sunningdale Way, Durham, NC 27707 (bottle openers and corkscrews).

Milk Route (NL), 4 Ox Bow Rd., Westport, CT 06880-2602.

Mini Beer Update: A Supplement to Miniature Beer Bottles & Go-Withs, Robert E. Kay (216 N. Batavia Ave., Batavia, IL 60510, © 1989).

Miniature Bottle Collector (MAG), PO Box 2161, Palos Verdes Peninsula, CA 90274.

Repairs, Parts & Supplies

Jar Doctor, R. Wayne Lowry, 2105 E. 250 St., Lebanon, IN 46052, 317-482-4033, evenings and weekends, or leave message. Cleaning machines and supplies for bottles, jars, insulators, and round glass items such as cruets, pitchers, and glasses. Jar and bottle cleaning and repair; etching and light scratches removed. Call about specific items. Most glass items can be cleaned.

Just Enterprises—Art & Antique Restoration, Gary & Susanne Gottfried, 2790 Sherwin Ave., #10, Ventura, CA 93003, 805-644-5837, 10:00 A.M.–noon, 2:00 P.M.–5:00 P.M. Restoration of glass, including perfume bottles, cameo glass, Lalique, and Steuben.

Lid Lady, Charles Bodiker, 7790 E. Ross Rd., New Carlisle, OH 45344, 513-845-1266. Lids for antique and new items, china to zinc. Send SASE for a reply.

Paradise & Co., 2902 Neal Rd., Paradise, CA 95969, 916-872-5020, anytime, answering machine; fax: 916-872-5020. Replacement parts for perfume atomizers. Send bottles for new replacement parts and removal of old parts if necessary. Replacement daubers, glass siphons, sprayer tops, collars, cords, balls and tassles. Send SASE for brochure.

Pop Shoppe Video Connection, Jim Millar, 2180 Ellery Ave., Clovis, CA 93611-0652, 209-298-7531, 6:00 P.M.–9:00 P.M. Cleaning kit for painted label (ACL) soda bottles, includes *Cleaning Secrets for ACL Soda Pop Bottles* and supplies. Free flyer.

Society of Inkwell Collectors, 5136 Thomas Ave. S., Minneapolis, MN 55410, 612-922-2792; fax: 612-920-7835. Glass inserts for inkwells. Can direct you to the appropriate source for repairs.

Appraiser

See the chapter on Auction Houses for specialty auction houses that appraise and auction bottles.

The Oriental Corner, 280 Main St., Los Altos, CA 94022, 415-941-3207, Tues.–Sat. 10:30 A.M.–5:00 P.M.; fax: 415-941-3297. Appraisers of Chinese snuff bottles.

Carousels, Carousel Figures & Amusement Park Collectibles

*T*he hand-carved, wooden charging horse or prancing pig that was part of the amusement park merry-go-round is now classed as "folk art" and sells for thousands of dollars. If it is possible to identify the makers of some of the animals, and if the name of the amusement park that owned the merry-go-round or the name of the artist can be determined, the value goes up 50 percent.

The most valuable carousel figures are the most unusual. Menagerie animals are rarer than horses and usually sell for thousands of dollars. Tigers, polar bears, pigs, ostriches, giraffes, goats, and other animals are most desirable. The quality of the carving, elaborate saddles and trappings, jeweled bridles, windblown manes, imaginative figures at the saddle cantles, and glass eyes add to the value.

The figures in the outside row on the carousel were seen by the public and had the most elaborate decoration, with the "lead" horse showing off the best work. American figures bring higher prices in this country than European figures. American horses are more highly decorated on the right side because the carousel goes in a counterclockwise direction; English carousels are the reverse. Horses are called either standers (three or four feet on the ground), prancers (back feet on the ground), or jumpers (no feet on the ground). All are equally valuable.

Any part of the carousel will sell to a folk art collector: the trim above the center section, the carved carriage sides, even the signs of the maker have a value. Metal carousel horses also sell, but for much lower prices. Because carousel figures and parts are large, they are most often sold through well-advertised auctions.

The market is nationwide. Buyers travel long distances to get a rare figure or a complete carousel, and they are not daunted by the problem of moving a large item.

There are many other carvings and decorations from amusement parks that are now wanted by collectors: the figures from the fun house; the painted canvas backdrops from the sideshow; carts, planes, cars, and other parts of rides; and penny-arcade equipment and gifts. If you are lucky enough to own any parts of a defunct amusement park, be sure to check with local auctioneers and shops.

Most antiques are less valuable if restored. Oil paintings, automobiles, and carousel figures may be the major exceptions to this rule. Newly painted, old carousel figures sell at auction for very high prices, often much higher than for similar figures with "park paint." This is one of the few types of collectibles that go up in value if the paint is new. Stripped figures are worth 25 percent less than park paint; repainted ones are worth 25 to 50 percent more.

REPAIR

The carousel has become an accepted part of American folk art. Museums and collectors are adding horses, carvings, cresting, chariots, and musical mechanisms to their collections. It is best to keep most of these wood carvings in unrestored condition unless the finish has deteriorated or been badly damaged. Some restorers remove the old finish and repaint the animals, or restore damaged wood and finish. Do not restore one of these figures yourself unless you are talented and trained. A poor restoration can destroy the resale value.

Be very careful if you plan to strip and paint a carousel figure. The tastes of collectors may change and the aged original paint may become the preferred finish. This has already happened with painted Shaker furniture: Unpainted, refinished pieces brought the highest prices in the early 1980s; now any piece with the original paint commands a premium price.

Catalog

Carousel Shopper, Box 47, Dept. K, Millwood, NY 10546 (catalog of resources, including restorers, supplies, books, and more).

Clubs & Publications

National Amusement Park Historical Association, *National Amusement Park Historical News* (NL), PO Box 83, Mt. Prospect, IL 60056.

National Carousel Association, *Merry-Go-Roundup* (MAG), PO Box 4333, Evansville, IN 47724-0333.

Carousel News & Trader (MAG), 87 Park Ave. W., Suite 206, Mansfield, OH 44902.

Repairs, Parts & Supplies

Alice Porter, 1149 J Ave., Ogden, IA 50212, 515-275-2716, 9:00 A.M.–5:00 P.M. Carousel restoration.

Amusement Arts, Bruce and Myrna Zubee, PO Box 1158, Burlington, CT 06013, 203-675-7653, daily 9:00 A.M.–8:00 P.M. Antique carved wooden carousel figures restored. Rounding boards, scenery panels, band organs, mirrors, and other carousel items are available. Identification and appraisals of antique figures given at no charge. Send photos of both sides of the figure.

Carousel Tails, R.D. 8 Box 272, Meadville, PA 16335, 814-333-9311, 9:00 A.M.–6:00 P.M. Tanned horse tails. Free brochure.

Carousel Works, Inc., 225 Central Ave., Mansfield, OH 44905, 419-522-7558, Mon.–Fri. 8:00 A.M.–4:00 P.M.; fax: 419-524-9603. Restoration of carousels and individual figures.

Carousel Workshop Inc., 218 S. High St., Deland, FL 32720, 904-728-4229, 9:00 A.M.–6:00 P.M. Restoration of carousel horses. Bases in cast iron and wood, horse tails, stirrups, bits, and reins. Call for appointment. Catalog $2.

Carrousel Care Consultants, Betty Brug Largent, 10009 N. Moore, Spokane, WA 99208, 509-466-3186, evenings. Carousel horse restoration. Will assist in information for operation, promotion, and maintenance of carousels.

Carv/Craft Carousel Animal Stands, Ray Jones, 417 Valley Rd., Madison, WI 53714, 608-222-1100, 8:00 A.M.–4:00 P.M. Cast-iron carousel animal display stands. Send SASE for brochure.

Custom Carving and Restoration, Marlene Irvin, PO Box 771331, Wichita, KS 67277, 316-722-1872, 9:00 A.M.–9:00 P.M., answering machine, will return calls. Restoration of carousel animals made of wood, fiberglass, and metal. Restoration of merry-go-round crestings, rounding boards, and ornate carving.

Daniel's Den, John Daniel, 720 Mission St., South Pasadena, CA 91030, 213-682-3557, 10:00 A.M.–4:00 P.M. Restoration of carousel figures. Parts, stands.

David Boyle, 36 Andrews Trace, New Castle, PA 16102, 412-656-8181, 8:00 A.M.–midnight; fax: 412-667-8598. Restoration of carousel animals. Custom-made display stands. Send SASE for brochure.

Erb Consulting Engineering, Alan S. Erb, 2318 Tahiti St., Hayward, CA 94545, 510-783-5068, 3:00 P.M.–12:00 P.M. Self-playing mechanical music machines, specializing in carousel organs and roll-playing pianos. Restoration.

Fabricon Carousel Co., Inc., Marvin Sylvor, 84-06 73rd Ave., Glendale, NY 11385, 718-326-7999, 9:30 A.M.–5:30 P.M.; fax: 718-326-9604. Carousel restorations, individual horses and full carousels.

Flying Tails, John and June Reely, 1209 Indiana Ave., South Pasadena, CA 91030, 213-256-8659, 9:00 A.M.–5:00 P.M. Carousel horses restored. Real horsehair tails. Send a double-stamped SASE for a brochure.

Great Canadian Nickelodeon Co. Ltd., RR #4, Mount Forest, ON Canada N0G 2L0, 519-323-3582, Mon.–Sat. 9:00 A.M.–6:00 P.M. Complete restoration or repairs of band and fairground organs. Custom-built parts. Brochure.

Hagy Sales, Bill Hagy, 754 E. Main St., Ephrata, PA 17522, 717-738-0366, 10:00 A.M.–9:00 P.M.; fax: 717-733-7100. Real horse tails in a variety of colors and sizes available for carousel horses. Send SASE and $1 for pictures.

Hawk's Eye Studio, Pamela Hessey, 145 Hillside Ln., Martinez, CA 94553, 510-228-7309, 8:30 A.M.–6:00 P.M. Conservation of carousel animals. Wood restoration and painting. Referrals to dealers and suppliers of eyes, tails, brass poles, and books. Studio visits by appointment. Call ahead. Crating and shipping for out-of-state collectors. References available upon request.

Horsing Around Ltd., Keith and Sarah Miller, 965 Hillwell Rd., Chesapeake, VA 23320, 804-482-7702, evenings, or leave message on machine. Full restoration services for wooden carousel horses from the late 1800s and early 1900s. Stands. Send SASE for catalog.

Hughes Carousel Restoration, Bill Hughes, 10325 Dougherty Ave., Morgan Hill, CA 95037, 408-778-5077. Wood restoration service for wooden carousel horses; brought to paint-ready finish.

Janet L. Berwin, 2111 Plattin Rd., Festus, MO 63028, 314-937-6998; fax: 314-894-8815. Glass mirrored jewels for restoration work. Glass eyes for carousel animals. Mail order worldwide. Send $2 for product list.

John & Nan's Carvings, John and Nancy Margraff, 3443 Ulman St., San Diego, CA 92106, 619-222-0790, anytime. Repair and restoration of carousel figures. Custom carving.

LCM Studio, Linda C. McDonald, 10243 York Ln., Bloomington, MN 55431, 612-830-1152. Carousel horse restoration.

Little Hawk Studio, Stan Hawkins, 2230 El Capitan, Arcadia, CA 91006, 818-445-3054, 6:00 P.M.–10:00 P.M. Major repair of any style carousel horses. Specializing in repair of P.T.C., Dentzel, and M. C. Illions figures.

Maureen Murphy Bluhm, 2519 Columbus Ave., Sandusky, OH 44870, 419-627-9749, 9:00 A.M.–6:00 P.M. Carousel restoration: horses and other animals, rounding boards, signature panels, scenery panels.

Melton's Carousel World, Roger and Carol Melton, 425 Pollasky, Old Town Clovis, CA 93612, 209-298-8930, 9:00 A.M.–5:00 P.M. Restoration of all forms of carousel art. Custom paint to client's need.

Merry-Go-Art, Don and Ruth Snider, 2606 Jefferson Street, Joplin, MO 64804, 417-624-7281, 9:00 A.M.–5:00 P.M. Restoration of wooden antique carousel horses and figures.

Merry-Go-Round Museum, PO Box 718, Sandusky, OH 44870, 419-626-6111, Mon., Wed.–Sat. 11:00 A.M.–5:00 P.M., Sun. noon–5:00 P.M. Restoration of carousels. Brochure. Located at the corner of W. Washington and Jackson streets.

Midwest Carousel Organization, Craig A. Swanson, 1952 Lake Dr., Independence, MO 64055, 816-833-3573, 8:00 A.M.–10:00 P.M., 816-860-7655 Voice Mail Service. Carousel animal restoration. Repair, painting, and replacement of missing parts. Written quote provided before work is begun. Shipping at owner's expense. Free delivery and pickup within 300 miles of Kansas City. Brochure $2 and SASE.

Morris Caroussell Works, Terri-Lee Morris, PO Box 786, Philadelphia, PA 19105, 215-383-1655. Antique carousel figures restored and refinished. Wooden bases for displaying carousel animals. Catalog $2.

Pride of the Midway, Robert Jeffery, 10827 Oro Vista, Sunland, CA 91040, 818-353-1786, after 6:00 P.M. Complete restorations of carousel animals. Roped tubing and finials available. Send SASE for lists.

Quarterhorse Investments, Inc., Sally L. Craig, 336 W. High St., Elizabethtown, PA 17022. Carousel horse restoration supplies; restoration consultation. Tanned horsehair tails for carousel horse and rocking horse restorations. Appraisals. Send SASE for brochure.

Quill Hair & Ferrule, Ltd., Peter and Ken Miller, PO Box 23927, Columbia, SC 29224, 800-421-7961, Mon.–Fri. 8:30 A.M.–4:30 P.M.; fax: 803-736-4731. Gold-leaf restoration and supplies; faux finishing supplies. Mail order. Catalog $5.

Restoration & Reproductions by Wolf, Steve and Kris Crescenze, 211 Gunston Rd., Welcome, MD 20693, 301-932-2734, Mon.–Fri. 5:00 P.M.–9:00 P.M., weekends 9:00 A.M.–9:00 P.M. Restorations of antique carousel horses. Send SASE for brochure.

Revisions, Thane Snider, 105 N. Gray, Joplin, MO 64801-2840, 417-782-8604, anytime. Restoration of antique carousel figures, single figures to complete carousels. Damaged and dry rotted wood replaced and recarved. Repainting. Send SASE and photos for estimate.

Rockinghorse Antiques, Bette Jeane Rutkowski, 111 St. Helena Ave., Dundalk, MD 21222, 410-285-0280, 8:00 A.M.–11:00 P.M. Restoration of carousel horses and related items. Appraisals, identification. Free brochure.

Rosa Ragan Restoration, Rosa P. Ragan, 100 Snow Ave., The Store, Raleigh, NC 27603, 919-829-1884, 8:30 A.M.–5:00 P.M. Complete restoration of carousel animals. Original paint specialist. Paint and wood restoration of antique band organ facades. Send SASE for information.

Sheild Art & Hobby Shop, Sandra H. Sheild, 4417 Danube Dr., King George, VA 22485-9374, 703-663-3711 anytime, leave message if no answer. Restoration of antique and new carousel figures. Free pick-up and delivery within 500-mile radius.

The Spirited Steeds Studio, 610 N. Alma School Rd., Suite 18, Dept. K, Chandler, AZ 85224, 602-786-6465, Mon.–Fri. 8:00 A.M.–5:00 P.M.; E-mail (Prodigy) FWXC07A. Antique carousel horse restoration services. Reproductions of carousel carvings. Allan Herschell specialists. Appointment required, address for mail only. Send clear photos for restoration estimate.

Tony Orlando, 6661 Norborne, Dearborn Heights, MI 48127-2076, 313-561-5072, business hours. Conservation and restoration of wooden carousel animals.

W. P. Wilcox, 2122 W. Midwood Ln., Anaheim, CA 92804, 714-635-0917, 9:00 A.M.–5:00 P.M. Repair and restoration of carousel animals.

Weaver's Antiques, Ken and Barbara Weaver, 7 Cooks Glen Rd., Spring City, PA 19745, 215-469-6331. Carousel figure restoration. Brass poles, jewels, eyes, etc. Send SASE for brochure.

William Stenning, RR 8, London, ON, Canada N6A 4C3, 519-453-0996, 9:00 A.M.–5:00 P.M. Parts for carousel animals. Will cast to your sample. Horseshoes, stirrup hangers, stirrups, belly plates, foot mounts, pole hooks, pig tails. Aluminum-alloy stand bases. Free brochure.

Wood 'n Wildlife, 9922 Bostwick Park Rd., Montrose, CO 81401, 303-249-5863, before 9:00 P.M. Restoration of carousel horses and other objects. Send SASE for more information.

Celebrity Memorabilia

Celebrity memorabilia is bought and sold in four major categories: items related to the movies; items related to TV, radio, and recording stars; comic-related items; and historic personality items. Each has a slightly different market.

TV, RADIO, AND RECORDING STARS

TV and radio materials are collected by fans and by those who are interested in old-time radio. Contact these collectors through the radio publications, at the special shops and shows, or at the large flea markets. *Star Trek* fans have special shows each year and buy and sell old scripts, tapes, and all sorts of memorabilia. Disneyana collectors are eager to buy Mouseketeers items. *M.A.S.H., Howdy Doody, The Man from U.N.C.L.E.,* and *The Honeymooners* also have special collector organizations. Old *TV Guides* and other magazines are also wanted.

Recording stars often appeared on TV or in movies, so there are several reasons their memorabilia would be collected. Try selling your items to dealers in records who also have "go-withs," or to the regular twentieth-century collectibles dealers. You should also check any local fan club members if you have some rarities or a large box of material.

HISTORIC PERSONALITIES

Charles Lindbergh, any prominent political figure, the astronauts, composers, scientists, explorers, notorious criminals, and many others with a claim to fame interest collectors today. Often the best place to sell "association" items, like a chair that belonged to Teddy Roosevelt or Queen Victoria's underdrawers, is through a national auction that specializes in autographs and historic items. Less important items can be sold through these same national sales, through some mail-order auctions, or to dealers or collectors. Look for other possibilities. An astronaut's autographed picture might interest a collector of space toys. Lindbergh and his flight have fascinated airplane lovers for many years, and there are so many collectors that these items even have a special section in *Kovels' Antiques & Collectibles Price List*.

If you are fortunate enough to be the descendant of an important person or have acquired a large collection of material about one person, you might offer it as a collection to the historical society that would be most interested, one in the hometown, state, or center of activity of the famous person. There may also be a Hall of Fame that would be interested; everything from aviation to rock and roll to football has a Hall of Fame.

A large collection should be sold as a unit to obtain the best price. In other words, the price for the whole is greater than the price for the sum of the parts. This means you must find a dealer or auctioneer who will take all of it. If you sell one or two important pieces you will lower the interest in the remaining collection.

See also the section on Movie Memorabilia, and the section on Phonographs & Records, Radios & Television Sets.

Price Books

British Royalty Commemoratives, Douglas H. Flynn & Alan H. Bolton (Schiffer, Atglen, PA, © 1994).

Collector's Guide to Hopalong Cassidy Memorabilia, Joseph J. Caro (L-W Books, PO Box 69, Gas City, IN 46933, © 1993).

Greenberg's Guide to Star Trek Collectibles, Vols. 1, 2 & 3, Christine Gentry and Sally Gibson-Downs (Kalmbach Publishing, PO Box 1612, Waukesha, WI 53187, © 1992).

KISS Collectibles Identification and Price Guide, Karen and John Lesniewski (Avon Books, New York, © 1993).

Official Price Guide to Frank Sinatra Records and CDs, Vito R. Marino and Anthony C. Furfero (House of Collectibles, New York, © 1993).

Clubs & Publications

Batman TV Series Fan Club, *Batman TV Series Fan Club* (NL), PO Box 553, Springdale, UT 84767.

C.A.L./N-X-211 Collectors Society, *Spirit of St. Louis Newsletter* (NL), 727 Younkin Pkwy. S., Columbus, OH 43207-4788 (Lindbergh memorabilia).

Dionne Quint Collectors, *Quint News* (NL), PO Box 2527, Woburn, MA 01888.

Doodyville Historical Society, *Howdy Doody Times* (NL), 8 Hunt Ct., Flemington, NJ 08822.

Friends of Hopalong Cassidy, *Hoppy Talk* (NL), 6310 Friendship Dr., New Concord, OH 43762-9708.

Galaxy Patrol Fan Club, *Galaxy Patrol Space-O-Gram* (NL), c/o Dale L. Ames, 22 Colton St., Worcester, MA 01610 (air and space heroes from radio and TV, Capt. Midnight, etc.).

Girl Groups Fan Club, *Girl Groups Gazette* (MAG), PO Box 69A04, Dept. K, West Hollywood, CA 90069.

International Al Jolson Society, Inc., *You Ain't Read Nothin' Yet!* (NL), 2981 Westmoor Dr., Columbus, OH 43204.

Marx Brotherhood, *Freedonia Gazette* (MAG), 335 Fieldstone Dr., New Hope, PA 18938-1012 (Marx Brothers).

Munsters & The Addams Family Fan Club, *Munsters & The Addams Family Reunion* (MAG), PO Box 69A04, Dept. K, West Hollywood, CA 90069.

Roy Rogers/Dale Evans Collectors Association, *Roy Rogers/Dale Evans Collectors Association Newsletter* (NL), PO Box 1166, Portsmouth, OH 45662.

Shirley Temple Collectors By The Sea, *Lollipop News* (NL), PO Box 6203, Oxnard, CA 93031.

Star Trek: The Official Fan Club, *Official Star Trek Magazine* (MAG), PO Box 111000, Aurora, CO 80042.

Beatlefan (MAG), PO Box 33515, Decatur, GA 30033.

Good Day Sunshine (MAG), 397 Edgewood Ave., New Haven, CT 06511-4013 (Beatles memorabilia).

Silver Bullet (NL), PO Box 553, Forks, WA 98331 (Lone Ranger memorabilia).

Strange New Worlds (MAG), PO Box 223, Tallevast, FL 34270 (science fiction collectibles).

Trek Collector: A Newsletter for Star Trek Fans and Collectors (NL), PO Box 2411, Venice, CA 90294-2411.

TV (Show) Collector (MAG), PO Box 1088, Easton, MA 02334 (shows and performers, not TV sets).

Under Western Skies (MAG), Rt. 3, Box 263H, Waynesville, NC 28786 (movie, TV, and radio Westerns).

Clocks & Watches

According to some collectors, a home without a ticking clock has no heart. Clocks that work always sell well. It does not seem to matter if they are old, new, Art Deco, or eighteenth-century French. One problem with pricing clocks is that two clocks that look the same to a novice may look very different to an expert. Years ago we ran a picture of a clock owned by a reader of our newspaper column. It was an 1880 wall clock with elaborate "gingerbread" trim. We gave a suggested value. The day after the column appeared, we started to receive phone calls and letters from readers. We got another, clearer picture of the clock, and when we examined the trim very carefully, we saw what our clock-expert readers had noticed. This was a rare version of the wall clock, worth in the thousands of dollars, not just the few hundred dollars we had suggested.

Our rule for pricing antiques is that if it moves or makes noise, it brings a premium price. This includes animated alarm clocks, grandfather clocks with chimes, and any other clock that makes noise or has moving parts other than the hands. Figural clocks of any age sell well. Look for LUX on the label and double the price.

To identify a watch, you must open it and look for names, labels, and construction features. If you can't do this yourself, ask a local jeweler to help. When you check the value in a watch price book, you must know the name on the dial or movement, the number of jewels, serial number, size of case, and if it is solid gold or plate. A clock must also be opened to see if there is a label and to check on the type of mechanism running the clock. If it winds, the key is important.

An old clock with replaced works is a "marriage" and is only worth 10 to 20 percent as much as an all-original clock. Grandfather or tall-case clocks are often found in an altered state. During the past 200 years, many owners will have repaired or glorified their clocks with additions or changes. If the feet or finials are new, subtract 10 percent. If the door is new, subtract 20 to 25 percent. If the base has been shortened, subtract 30 percent. If the case has been refinished badly or the carvings destroyed, deduct 25 percent or more.

A slightly restored painted dial or minor replacement of parts or case lowers the value by about 10 percent. If the dial is totally repainted, it lowers the value of the clock to the value of the case; the repainted dial is worthless. A restored, cracked, or damaged enameled dial lowers the value by up to 50 percent. If the face is old but a replacement, deduct 20 percent.

Wristwatches that look old-fashioned are in demand and are worn as jewelry even if they do not keep time because they have not been cleaned and repaired. Dealers who specialize in old watches or jewelry will buy them. Look for these dealers at the shows or in the Yellow Pages of the phone book under "Watch Repair" or "Jewelry."

Of course, solid-gold watches are far more valuable than gold-plated or chrome-plated ones. The names ROLEX, PATEK PHILIPPE, HAMILTON, VACHERON & CONSTANTIN, OMEGA, PIAGET, MOVADO, GRUEN, TIFFANY, LE COULTRE, and CARTIER add value. Diamond watches must be appraised by a qualified jeweler for the diamond and gold value. The wristwatch must sell for more than the "breakdown" value (see section on Jewelry).

Winding stems positioned out of sight in the back and triangular or other odd-shaped cases add value. So do calendars, stopwatches, chimes, and other special features. Look for the special buttons or levers that indicate these items on the watches. Unusual watches with psychedelic dials, moon dials, cartoon characters, moving figures, or slogans are considered novelties and can be sold, but they usually do not bring high dollars.

Pocket watches are wanted by watch collectors but not necessarily by a jewelry buyer. This is a special market, and the best prices are paid by the serious collector. A very low serial number adds to the value.

When pricing watches, be sure to determine the difference between the markings on gold-plated and solid-gold cases. The marks can be misleading: the words "Guaranteed 5 (10, 20, 30) Years" appear on cases that are gold filled or rolled gold, and the karat mark was used with the year guarantee until 1924. After that, the government required the cases to be marked "10K gold filled" or "10K rolled gold plate." A solid-gold case will probably be marked with the karat mark and the words "Warranted U.S. Assay," or in a few instances, marked with hallmarks. Contact a watch dealer or an auction gallery if you want to sell a good, solid-gold pocket watch.

Antique grandfather clocks, especially American examples, should be examined by a qualified appraiser. If unaltered, they are usually worth thousands of dollars and should be sold by a professional dealer or auction house with national exposure for the best price. Also, be sure to check carefully on the value of carriage clocks, chronometers, novelty clocks, and elaborate clocks with ormolu or porcelain decorations. Many of these are worth big money.

REPAIR

Repairing clockworks is a job for an expert. It is always best to have a specialist fix the inside of a broken clock unless you have the required talent. Clock face and dial repainting and reverse glass painting for clock doors require specialists, but refinishing a clock case can be done at home. Clocks with pendulums need special adjustments to keep accurate time and often must be leveled on a shelf or floor. A local clock repair service will do this, or you may be able to correct the swing by following the directions available in various books. Lowering the weight makes the clock go slower.

If you acquire an electric clock that is more than twenty years old, always have the wiring checked and replaced. Old wiring is a fire hazard.

When you buy an old clock or watch, take it to an expert first to see if it needs to be cleaned. This is usually the only restoration required. Old-style bands for wristwatches can be found at many jewelry stores.

Price Books

American Shelf and Wall Clocks, Robert W. D. Ball (Schiffer, Atglen, PA, © 1992).

Automatic Wristwatches from Switzerland, Heing Hampel (Schiffer, Atglen, PA 19310, © 1994).

Comic Character Timepieces: Seven Decades of Memories, Hy Brown (Schiffer, Atglen, PA, © 1992).

Complete Price Guide to Watches, Cooksey Shugart and Richard E. Gilbert (Collector Books, Paducah, KY, © 1993).

Wristwatches, Gilbert L. Brunner & Christian Pfeiffer-Belli (Schiffer, Atglen, PA, © 1993).

Books on Repair

Black Forest Clocks, E. John Tyler (NAG Press, London, © 1977).

Black Forest Cuckoo Clock, Karl Kochmann (Antique Clock Publishing, PO Box 21387, Concord, CA 94521, © 1976).

Clock Repairer's Handbook, Laurie Penman (Arco Publishing Co., New York, © 1985).

Clocks and Clock Repairing, Eric Smith (TAB Books, Div. of McGraw Hill, Blue Ridge Summit, PA, © 1990).

Essence of Clock Repair, Sean C. Monk (American Watchmakers Institute Press, 3700 Harrison Ave., PO Box 11011, Cincinnati, OH 45211, © 1983).

Grandfather Clock Maintenance Manual, John Vernon (Van Nostrand Reinhold Co., New York, © 1983).

Horological Hints and Helps, F. W. Britten (Antique Collectors' Club, Woodbridge, Suffolk, England, © 1977).

Illustrated Guide to House Clocks, Anthony Bird (Arco Publishing Co., New York, © 1973).

Making and Repairing Wooden Clock Cases, V. J. Taylor and H. A. Babb (David & Charles, North Pomfret, VT, © 1986).

Re-Covering Cuckoo Clock and Bird Cage Bellows, John J. Goggin (16 Jones Lane, Huntington, NY 11743, © 1986).

Repairing & Restoring Pendulum Clocks, John Plewes (Blandford Press, Poole, Dorset, England, © 1984).

Repairing Antique Clocks, Eric P. Smith (Sterling Publishing Co., New York, © 1993).

Repairing Old Clocks & Watches, Anthony J. Whiten (NAG Press, London, © 1979).

Striking and Chiming Clocks, Eric Smith (Arco Publishing Co., New York, © 1985).

Clubs & Publications

Antiquarian Horological Society, *Antiquarian Horology* (MAG), New House, High St., Ticehurst, East Sussex, England TN5 7AL.

National Association of Watch and Clock Collectors, Inc., *NAWCC Bulletin* (MAG), 514 Poplar St., Columbia, PA 17512-2130.

Swatch Collectors of Swatch, *Swatch World Journal* (NP), *Swatch Collectors of Swatch Times* (NL), PO Box 7400, Melville, NY 11747-7400.

Heritage Report on Antique Jewelry (NL), c/o JCK, Chilton Way, Radnor, PA 19080-9253 (antique and period jewelry and watches).

International Wrist Watch (MAG), 2001 W. Main St., Suite 100, Stamford, CT 06902.

The Premium Watch Watch, 24 San Rafael Dr., Rochester, NY 14618 (watches available as premiums).

Watch & Clock Review (MAG), 2403 Champa St., Denver, CO 80205.

Repairs, Parts & Supplies

Another Time Restorations, PO Box 42013, Portland, OR 97242-0013, 503-656-9757. Clock repair. Custom wood and metal work.

Armor Products, PO Box 445, E. Northport, NY 11731-0445, 516-462-6228, 9:00 A.M.–5:00 P.M.; fax: 516-462-5793. Clock movements, dials, numerals, hands, and accessories. Free catalog.

Barap Specialties, 835 Bellows, Frankfort, MI 49635, 800-322-7273, 9:00 A.M.–5:00 P.M. Clock parts, tools, finishing materials, etc. Catalog $1.

Brass Foundry Castings, The Old Wheelwright Shop, Brasted Forge, Brasted, Kent England TN16 1JL, 0959-563863, 9:00 A.M.–5:00 P.M.; fax: 0959-561262. Clock mounts and other fittings. Catalog £18.

Burt Dial Company, PO Box 774, Rt. 107N, Raymond, NH 03077, 603-895-2879, Mon.–Fri. 9:00 A.M.–5:00 P.M. Refinishing and restoration of antique clock dials and reverse glass paintings. Refinishing of silver and gilt hall clock dials and silver and brass dials. Free brochure.

Carl Rinker, 6226 Waterloo Rd., Box 38, Atwater, OH 44201, 216-947-2268, phone and fax, weekdays 6:00 P.M.–11:00 P.M., Sat. 7:00 A.M.–5:00 P.M. Parts for clocks made to order from sample or drawing. Mainsprings, gears, and pinions. Repairs. Catalog $3.

Clocks Etc., 3401 Mount Diablo Blvd., Lafayette, CA 94549, 510-284-4720, anytime; fax: 510-284-3677. Complete clock restoration.

Dial House, Martha and Richard Smallwood, Buchanan Hwy., Rt. 7, Box 532, Dallas, GA 30132, 404-445-2877, Mon.–Fri. 7:30 A.M.–9:00 P.M. Antique clock dials preserved, restored, or re-created. Free brochure.

Faire Harbour Ltd., 44 Captain Peirce Rd., Scituate, MA 02066, 617-545-2465, 8:30 A.M.–6:30 P.M. Antique clocks repaired.

Fendley's Antique Clocks, 2535 Himes St., Irving, TX 75060, 214-986-7698, 6:30 P.M.–10:00 P.M., Sat. 9:00 A.M.–4:30 P.M. Gerald Fendley C.M.C., Richard Cox C.M.C., C.M.B.H.I. Specializing in wheel and pinion cutting for antique clocks. Clock parts made, spring barrels repaired or made new. Free catalog.

Fred Catterall, 54 Short St., New Bedford, MA 02740, 508-997-8532, days, evenings until 9:00 P.M. Banjo clock replacement pictures, in original colors and sizes. Paper dials, prestained finials, top blocks, and pontils. Antique clocks repaired. Brochure and 5 × 7-inch color photo, $1.50.

Gordon S. Converse & Co., 1029 Lancaster Ave., Berwyn, PA 19312, 215-296-4932 or 215-296-4938, 9:00 A.M.–5:00 P.M.; fax: 215-964-1181. All kinds of antique clocks restored. Cases, mechanisms, and dials restored. Catalog describes restoration services, lists values of antique clocks, shows current stock of antique clocks for sale, available by subscription, $20.

Horton Brasses, PO Box 120Q, Nooks Hill Rd., Cromwell, CT 06416, 203-635-4400, 8:30 A.M.–4:00 P.M.; fax: 203-635-6473. Clock hardware. Finials, hinges, knobs, escutcheons. Parts, nails, books, and videos. Catalog $3.

Ingrid Sanborn & Daughter, 85 Church St., West Newbury, MA 01985, 508-363-2253, 9:00 A.M.–5:00 P.M., 7:00 P.M.–8:30 P.M. Restoration and reproduction of reverse paintings on glass. Restoration of original gilded surfaces and japanning.

J & K Curios, 4868 SW Southwind Ct., Dunnellon, FL 34431, 904-465-0756, Mon.–Fri. 9:00 A.M.–9:00 P.M. Porcelain clock housings and dials restored. Free estimates.

Jandi Goggin, Box 175, Huntington, NY 11743-0175. Complete or partial restoration of singing birdcages, boxes, and cuckoo bellows. Repair kit for do-it-yourselfers. Send LSASE for information.

Johnson Watch Repair, 2735 23rd St., Greeley, CO 80631, 303-330-5228, 9:00 A.M.–5:00 P.M. Repair and restoration of antique wrist and pocket watches.

Klockit, PO Box 636, Lake Geneva, WI 53147, 800-556-2548, 8:00 A.M.–8:00 P.M.; fax: 414-248-9899. Clock parts, including quartz and mechanical movements, dials, bezels, hardware, wood parts, plans, and kits. Free catalog.

Martines' Antiques, Margaret and Joseph Martines, 516 E. Washington, Chagrin Falls, OH 44022, 216-247-6421. Clock repair and appraisals. Open 11:00 A.M.–5:00 P.M.

Merritt's Antiques, Inc., 1860 Weavertown Rd., PO Box 277, Douglassville, PA 19518-0277, 215-689-9541, Mon.–Fri. 7:30 A.M.–5:00 P.M.; fax: 215-689-4538. Clock repair supplies, tools, book, and parts. Catalog $3.

Sal Provenzano, PO Box 843, Bronx, NY 10469, 718-655-7021. Singing birdcages, bird boxes, feathering on birds, music boxes, and animated figures repaired.

Simonson Clock Shop, 240 E. Washington St., Medina, OH 44256, 216-725-7056, shop, 10:00 A.M.–5:00 P.M., 216-647-5548, home. Clock restoration. In-home service on floor clocks. Free estimates. Appraisals. Shop hours Mon., Tues, Fri., Sat. 10:00 A.M.–5:00 P.M.; Thurs. 1:00 P.M.–8:00 P.M. Closed Sun. and Wed.

Swiss Watch Services, Inc., 1402 Third Ave., Suite 714, Seattle, WA 98101, 206-622-3643; fax: 206-622-7927. Restoration of antique watches, specializing in Swiss watches.

Tec Specialties, PO Box 909, Smyrna, GA 30081. Clock dials, decals, backboard labels, and day/month strips. Mail order only. Will ship worldwide. Discount prices. Free catalog.

Time Will Tell, 962 Madison Ave., New York, NY 10021, 212-861-2663, 10:00 A.M.–6:00 P.M.; fax: 212-288-4069. Complete overhaul and restoration of wristwatches and pocket watches, specializing in Patek Philippe, Audemars, Piguet, Vacheron & Constantin, Tiffany, Cartier, Breguet, and Rolex. Appraisals of wrist and pocket watches. Catalog.

Timesavers, 7745 E. Redfield, #500, Scottsdale, AZ 85260, 800-552-1520, 8:00 A.M.–4:00 P.M.; fax: 800-552-1522. Clock repair parts and supplies. Keys, bobs, cuckoo material, bushings, mainsprings, glass, dials, hands, watch materials, movements, batteries, books, tools, and display items. Catalog $3.

Van Dyke's, Box 278, Woonsocket, SD 57385, 605-796-4425, 800-843-3320, orders only, 8:00 A.M.–6:00 P.M.; fax: 605-796-4085. Clock parts. Catalog $1.

Venerable Classics, 645 Fourth St., Suite 208, Santa Rosa, CA 95404, 800-531-2891, 9:00 A.M.–5:00 P.M.; fax: 707-575-3626. Restoration of clocks. Shipping instructions and free brochure available on request.

Vod Varka Springs, U.S. Rt. 30, PO Box 170, Clinton, PA 15026-0170, 412-695-3268, 8:45 A.M.–4:30 P.M.; fax: 412-695-3268. Custom-made springs. Flat-type springs for clocks. Made to order per print or sample.

Yankee Drummer House of Time, Appletree Mall, PO Box 909, Londonderry, NH 03053, 603-437-2410, Mon.–Fri. 10:00 A.M.–8:00 P.M., Sat. 10:00 A.M.–10:00 P.M. Repair and restoration of clocks and watches. Some parts available. Can fabricate parts or find a source for any part for any timepiece. European clocks a specialty. Repair and shipping services worldwide.

Clothing & Accessories

*T*here are old clothes and there are vintage clothes. Styles change so quickly that today clothes twenty-five years old or more can be considered vintage. Anything that is wearable, in good condition, with no permanent stains or damaged fabric, can be sold. The silly hats of the 1940s, the bowling shirts and Hawaiian prints of the 1950s, and the plastic purses of the 1960s are in demand to be worn, not displayed. The white cotton petticoats and camisoles that were once underwear are now party dresses. Beaded flapper dresses or old lace wedding dresses are wanted for special occasions. Before you send old clothes to the local thrift shops, be sure they are not worth more money at a vintage clothing store.

Silk that is crumbling, fabric deteriorating under the arms, moth holes, and stains make a piece of clothing unwearable and unsalable. Only pieces in good condition are of value. Lace trim, buttons, even special embroidery, can be salvaged and sold separately. Vintage clothing with designer names can sell for thousands of dollars. Look for CHANEL, FORTUNY, WORTH, ADRIAN, CLAIRE McCARDELL, BONNIE CASHIN, and other important names.

Very small sizes are more difficult to sell because so few people can wear them. We often think our ancestors must have been tiny because so many dresses are size 6 or less. Remember, the waists were cinched, so an 18-inch waist was not unusual. It's easy to make a dress smaller, but more difficult to make it larger. Many dresses were remade for use by other family members, so each time a dress was altered, it was usually made for a smaller person.

Accessories, including men's and women's hats, purses, fur pieces, scarves, and neckties, sell well. Cashmere sweaters and coats, for men and women, sell quickly. Very old Levi's and other jeans sell in some parts of the country. Most are exported to Japan. Ordinary men's clothes do not sell at vintage clothing stores; shoes are also difficult to sell. Give them to charity.

FASHION ACCESSORIES

*C*ombs, buckles, purses, canes, compacts, and other accessories are avidly collected. These items sell through the major antiques shows and dealers. Beaded purses have long been popular as both decorations to hang on a wall and as useful purses. Now collectors buy leather arts and crafts purses, needlepoint and petitpoint, plastic, hand-painted wooden, and other unusual-looking pocketbooks dating from before 1980.

REPAIR

Collecting vintage clothing is a fairly recent hobby. Many cities have shops that specialize in old clothing that can be worn every day. There is usually someone at these shops who can repair old clothing or furnish the trim and material needed for repairs. A few bridal and antiques shops also sell old fabrics, lace, or dresses. Check the Yellow Pages of the telephone book under "Clothing Bought & Sold" or "Second Hand Stores" to locate the dealers who sell and repair old clothes.

Dirt and sunlight do more harm to old fabrics than cleaning. Most fabrics can be gently washed in pure soap, not detergent, or they can be carefully dry-cleaned. The rules for old fabrics are the same as those for modern ones. Some stains may be permanent, but the overall soil should be cleaned away. Repairs to rips should be made before the pieces are cleaned. This avoids more damage. Loose beading and lace trim should be repaired as soon as damage is noticed.

See also the section on Textiles.

Price Books

The Art of Fashion Accessories, Joanne Dubbs Ball and Dorothy Hehl Torem (Schiffer, Atglen, PA, © 1993).

Canes from the Seventeenth to the Twentieth Century, Jeffrey B. Snyder (Schiffer, Atglen, PA, © 1993).

A Century of Handbags, Kate Dooner (Schiffer, Atglen, PA, © 1993).

Collecting Antique Linens & Lace Needlework: Identification, Restoration and Prices, Frances Johnson (Wallace-Homestead Book Company, Radnor, PA, © 1991).

Collector's Encyclopedia of Compacts, Carryalls & Face Powder Boxes, Laura M. Mueller (Collector Books, Paducah, KY, © 1994).

Plastic Handbags: Sculpture to Wear, Kate E. Dooner (Schiffer, Atglen, PA, © 1992).

Vintage Vanity Bags & Purses, Roselyn Gerson (Collector Books, Paducah, KY © 1994).

Clubs & Publications

Antique Comb Collectors Club, *Antique Comb Collectors Club Newsletter* (NL), 4901 Grandview, Ypsilanti, MI 48197.

Buttonhook Society, *Boutonneur* (NL), 4017 Pinedale Dr., Baltimore, MD 21236-1612.

Compact Collectors Club, *Powder Puff* (NL), PO Box S, Lynbrook, NY 11563.

Costume Society of America, *Dress* (MAG), *CSA News* (NL), 55 Edgewater Dr., PO Box 73, Earleville, MD 21919.

Fan Association of North America, *Quarterly of the Fan Association of North America* (MAG), 505 Peachtree Rd., Orlando, FL 32804 (hand-held fans).

Fan Circle International, *Fans* (NL), Cronk-Y-Voddy, Rectory Rd., Coltishall, Norwich, England NR12 7HF (hand-held fans).

National Button Society, *National Button Bulletin* (NL), 2733 Juno Pl., Akron, OH 44333-4137.

Basically Buckles (MAG), HC 2 Box 5, La Moure, ND 58458 (new commemorative buckles).

Cane Collector's Chronicle (NL), c/o Linda Beeman, 99 Ludlam Crescent, Lower Hutt, Wellington, NZ.

Lady's Gallery (MAG), PO Box 1761, Independence, MO 64055 (vintage fashions, culture, antiques).

Vintage Lill's Newsletter on Vintage Clothing (NL), 19 Jamestown Dr., Cincinnati, OH 45241.

Repairs, Parts & Supplies

Cereus Inc., 31 Brook Ln., Cortlandt Manor, NY 10566, 914-737-3769, anytime; fax: 924-737-4333. Conservation, cleaning, repair, and stabilization of folding fans: seventeenth to twentieth centuries; paper and vellum, wood, ivory, mother-of-pearl, painting, carving, and fabric repairs. Price quotation before work is done.

Lane Conservation Associates, Nan Lane Terry, Director, 9 Station St., Brookline, MA 02146, 617-738-1126, 10:00 A.M.–6:00 P.M. Conservation of textiles and costumes. Consultations on proper storage and display. Collection surveys.

The Laundry at Linens Limited, Inc., 240 N. Milwaukee St., Milwaukee, WI 53202, 800-637-6334, 414-223-1123, Mon.–Fri. 8:00 A.M.–4:00 P.M.; fax: 414-223-1126. Laundering and restoration of bed, bath, and table linens; wedding dresses, christening gowns, and other clothing; needlepoint and some other special items. Free brochure.

Ledgewood Studio, 6000 Ledgewood Dr., Forest Park, GA 30050-3228, 404-361-6098, 10:00 A.M.–4:00 P.M.; fax: 404-361-5030. General costuming supplies. Fabrics, trims, buttons, lace, and sewing supplies for costumers and restorers. Mail order and shows only. Catalog $2 plus a triple-stamped LSASE.

Uncle Sam Umbrella Shop, 161 West 57th Street, New York, NY 10019, 212-582-1976, 212-582-1977, Mon.–Fri. 9:30 A.M.–6:15 P.M., Sat. 10 A.M.–5:00 P.M.; fax: 212-717-5460. Restoration of all types of umbrellas and canes. If the customer has only the handles, the shop can supply the umbrella and/or the shaft.

Unique Art Lace Cleaners, 5926 Delmar Blvd., St. Louis, MO 63112, 314-725-2900, 9:00 A.M.–4:00 P.M. Cleaning and repairing of fine wedding veils, wedding gowns, and antique clothing. Send items for price quotation and consultation. Fee $25, applied to bill if work is performed.

Coin-Operated Machines, Jukeboxes & Slot Machines

*T*here is a corollary to the joke among antiques dealers that anything that moves or makes noise has a value. They say that there is even more value to anything with a money slot. This includes most types of music-making machines, from nineteenth-century Swiss boxes to 1950s jukeboxes. Slot machines, gum-ball machines, and the myriad gamelike machines known as "trade stimulators" or amusement park coin-ops are included in the valued, "it moves and makes money" antiques.

The granny fortune-teller, horse-race games, claw-digger steam-shovel games, love testers, and Kinetoscopes (movie machines), among many others, all sell well. Collectors are more interested in the item's "gimmick" value than in its age. A moving figure, an unusual configuration, or very elaborate case will add value. Even perfume dispensers, match, cigarette, gum-ball, or sandwich machines, and all types of games of chance, sell well. Be sure the machine works with U.S. coins. Some English games have been imported; their value is much lower.

"Trade stimulators" were games that encouraged the sale of cigarettes, cigars, drinks, and other products or services. A slot machine was made to pay out money from the machine, while the trade stimulator rewarded the player with products or free games. It was an easier machine to make but often had many of the other features of a slot machine.

Jukeboxes gained favor as collectibles during the 1970s. The general rule is that the more neon lights and Art Deco trim there is on a jukebox, the more it will be in demand, and the higher the price.

The highest prices paid for slot machines and coin-operated games are paid by the dealers and auctioneers who specialize in them. Contact these people at the appropriate shows or sales, which are listed in the antiques trading papers and in the magazines written for collectors in this area. If you are selling any type of slot machine or gambling device, be sure to check the laws in your state, since the sale of these items is illegal in some places.

The easiest way to sell a large game or jukebox is through pictures and descriptions. Buyers won't travel to your house if the machine doesn't seem to be a good one. You must make the effort to take pictures and write letters, place ads, or talk to dealers, or you will get very little for the machine. A neighbor may think it would be a nice toy for the basement, but only a real collector will pay a top price.

The make, model, serial number, patent dates, address of the manufacturer, and other important information can be found on an identification plate under or behind the machine. A dealer or serious collector can identify a jukebox from a picture. (So can you, if you get the right books from the library.) Even arcade games and pinball machines can be identified from clear photographs. Take a picture of the top playing area and another of the back glass area so all details show well.

REPAIR

Any broken machine that moves or makes noise is worth less than half its value in working condition. Some types of machines are so difficult to repair that they are only worth about 20 percent if broken, but remember that many of these machines sell for thousands of dollars if perfect. Buying parts for any of the coin-operated machines requires some ingenuity. Machines can be found in special shops and shows, but some of the best buys are made by smart collectors who follow their local newspaper's classified section. A machine in very poor condition is still useful for parts that can be used to repair other machines. There are specialists who fix slot machines and jukeboxes.

There are several good books that give the history of jukeboxes and list the models and stores that sell parts or repair existing machines. Reprints of some of the original instruction books can also be found.

Price Books

Classic Soda Machines, Jeff Walters (Memory Lane Publishing, PO Box 6239, Laguna Niguel, CA 92607, © 1992).

Jukeboxes, 1900–1902, Volume I , Frank Adams (AMR Publishing Company, PO Box 3007, Arlington, WA 98223, © 1992).

The Jukebox Bluebook, 2nd edition, edited by Ben C. Humphries (Jukebox Ventures, Inc., 5213 Mohawk Dr., Suite 1-R, Knoxville, TN 37914, © 1993).

Reference Book

American Premium Guide to Coin Operated Machines, Jerry Ayliffe (Crown Publishers, New York, © 1981).

Publications

Always Jukin (NP), 221 Yesler Way, Seattle, WA 98104.

Antique Amusements, Slot Machine & Jukebox Gazette (NP), 909 26th St. NW, Washington, DC 20037.

Coin Drop International (NP), 5815 W. 52nd Ave., Denver, CO 80212.

Coin Machine Trader (NL), Box 602, Huron, SD 57350.

Coin Slot (MAG), 4401 Zephyr St., Wheatridge, CO 80033.

Coin-Op Classics (MAG), 17844 Toiyabe St., Fountain Valley, CA 92708.

Coin-Op Newsletter (NL), 909 26 St. NW, Washington, DC 20037.

Gameroom Magazine (MAG), 1014 Mt. Tabor Rd., New Albany, IN 47150 (arcade games, carousels, Coca-Cola collectibles, music boxes, neon, radios, slots, and more).

Jukebox Collector (MAG), 2545 SE 60th Ct. #110, Des Moines, IA 50317-5099.

Loose Change (MAG), 1515 S. Commerce St., Las Vegas, NV 89102.

pinGame journal (MAG), 31937 Olde Franklin Dr., Farmington Hills, MI 48334.

Scopitone Newsletter (NL), 810 Courtland Dr., Manchester, MO 63021 (film jukeboxes).

Repairs, Parts & Supplies

Ancient Slots and Antiques, 3127 Industrial Rd., Las Vegas, NV 89109, 702-796-7779, 8:30 A.M.–5:00 P.M.; fax: 702-796-4389. Restoration of antique slot machines. Parts. Free brochure.

Antone's Buy & Sell Shop, 735 Harlem Rd., West Seneca, NY 14224, 716-649-6285, 9:00 A.M.–9:00 P.M. Slot machine repair and restoration. Original parts for mechanical slots, all makes.

Bernie Berten, 9420 S. Trumbull Ave., Chicago, IL 60642, 708-499-0688, 8:00 A.M.–9:00 P.M.; fax: 708-499-5979. Slot machine repair and restoration. Complete parts service. Reproduction reel strips, award cards, and castings. Nickle and chrome plating. Send two first-class stamps for 32-page catalog.

Bob Nelson's Gameroom Warehouse, 826 W. Douglas, Wichita, KS 67203, 316-263-1848, 10:00 A.M.–6:00 P.M. Repair and restoration of coin-operated machines. Parts and schematics for most coin-operated machines; balls and cabinets for Pachinkos. Will ship worldwide. Send $2 for list of schematics and operating instructions.

Boston Juke Box Co., 311 Needham St., Newton, MA 02164, 617-964-2036, phone and fax, Mon.–Sat. 9:30 A.M.–5:00 P.M. Antique jukeboxes restored. Diner parts.

C & C Electronic Restorations, Enos Crum, 143R Edwards Rd., Johnstown, OH 43031, 614-967-3573, Mon.–Fri. 9:00 A.M.–6:00 P.M., Sat. 10:00 A.M.–5:00 P.M.; fax: 614-967-3573. Service and restoration for jukeboxes.

Charles Maier, Jukebox Service, 3016 Derry Terr., Philadelphia, PA 19154-2519, 215-637-2869, 9:00 A.M.–9:00 P.M. Jukebox parts and repair service. Blank title strips. Reprints of service manuals and brochures. Catalog of manuals and books $3.

CSSK Amusements, Chuck Martin, Box 6214, York, PA 17406, 800-PINBALL, 717-757-3740, evenings: fax: 717-840-HELP. Pinball parts and service. Reconditioning and restoration. Send SASE for list.

Cupertino Jukebox Co., 1142 Scotland Dr., Cupertino, CA 95014, 408-255-9178, 2:00 P.M.–9:00 P.M. Restoration parts for jukeboxes. Send SASE for list of parts and supplies.

Daniel's Den, John Daniel, 720 Mission St., South Pasadena, CA 91030, 213-682-3557, 10:00 A.M.–4:00 P.M. Restoration of automatic musical instruments. Parts.

Donal Murphy, c/o E.W.I., 2015 N. Kolmar Ave., Chicago, IL 60639, 312-235-3360, 9:00 A.M.–5:00 P.M.; fax: 312-235-3370. Pinball parts: coils, caps, drop targets, flipper bushings, rollovers, doors, front moldings, backglasses, playfields, plastic shield sets, flippers, etc. Free brochure.

Donnie Kueller, 841 Robinwood Rd., Washington Township, Westwood, NJ 07675-4244,

201-664-1928, 9:00 A.M.–5:00 P.M.; fax: 201-664-1928. Jukebox restoration, service, and parts. Catalog $1 plus 32 cents postage.

Evans and Frink, 2977 Eager, Howell, MI 48843. Reproduction reel strips and award cards for slot machines. Send six first-class postage stamps for catalog.

Funtiques, PO Box 825, Tucker, GA 30085-0825, 404-564-1775, 9:00 A.M.–5:00 P.M.; fax: 404-279-2791 anytime. Vintage jukebox and amusement parts and supplies; tubes, needles, cartridges, obsolete parts, and reproduction parts.

George Bursor, 977 Kings Rd., Schenectady, NY 12303, 518-346-3713, 8:30 A.M.–11:00 P.M. Jukebox amplifier repair, specializing in Wurlitzer and Rock-Ola. Seeburg '50s jukebox restoration. Original jukebox parts for sale. Send SASE for free brochure.

Great Canadian Nickelodeon Co. Ltd., RR #4, Mount Forest, ON Canada N0G 2L0, 519-323-3582, Mon.–Sat. 9:00 A.M.–6:00 P.M. Complete restoration or repairs of all automated music machines: player pianos, pipe organs, monkey organs, music boxes, nickelodeons, orchestrions, jukeboxes, band and fairground organs, etc. Custom-built parts. Brochure.

Home Arcade Corp., 1108 Front St., Lisle, IL 60532, 708-964-2555, Mon.–Sat. 9:00 A.M.–5:00 P.M.; fax: 708-964-9367. Reproduction parts and decals for Coke machines. Mail order. Catalog $3, refundable with order.

Jack Suarez, 34 Edgewood Ave., Albany, NY 12203, 518-489-1450. Jukebox parts.

Jim & Nadiene Farago, 4017 42nd Ave. S., Minneapolis, MN 55406-3528, 612-722-0708, anytime. Jukebox service manuals, originals and reprints, 1930–1975. Rebuilding of jukebox amplifiers, tube types only. Amplifiers only, no mechanism parts or cosmetic parts, no complete jukebox restoration. Call or write for shipping, packing details, costs, etc.

John Durfee's Coin-op Restoration, 57 S. Main St., Orange, MA 01364, 508-544-3800, Mon.–Fri. 10:30 A.M.–4:30 P.M.; fax: 508-544-8250. Parts and restoration. Grain painting, cabinet repair and finishing, mechanical restorations, rebuilding. House-call services available. Shipping worldwide. Send SASE for free brochure.

Joseph S. Jancuska, 619 Miller St., Luzerne, PA 18709, 717-287-3478, after 6:00 P.M. Restoration and appraisals of slot machines, nut and gum machines, and arcade machines. Literature on coin-operated machines.

Jukebox Junction, Inc., PO Box 1081, Des Moines, IA 50311, 515-981-4019, 8:30 A.M.–5:00 P.M.; fax: 515-981-4657. Reproduction jukebox parts. Restorations.

Jukebox Media, 8795-K Corvus St., San Diego, CA 92126-1920, 619-271-8294. Jukebox amplifiers and antique electronics repaired and restored. How-to video tapes on jukebox restoration.

Just Slots, 46 Ellerker Rise, Willerby, Hull, England HU10 6EY, 0482 655504, 0836 767575, 10:00 A.M.–8:00 P.M. Spares, repairs, and restorations for vintage one-armed bandits, slot machines, arcade collectibles, and other old coin-operated machines.

Ken Durham, 909 26th St. NW, Washington, DC 20037, 202-338-1342, 10:00 A.M.–10:00 P.M. Jukebox service manuals. Books and price guides on slot machines and other coin-operated machines. Send SASE for book list. Sales list of countertop coin machines and parts $2.

Lloyd's Jukeboxes, 22900 Shaw Rd. #106, Sterling, VA 20166, 703-834-6699, Mon.–Sat. 10:00 A.M.–6:00 P.M.; fax: 703-834-9083. Restoration of antique jukeboxes. Video game, pinball, AMP, and jukebox repair service available in their shop or your home. Parts. Appraisals.

Mayfair Amusement Company, 60-41 Woodbine St., Ridgewood, NY 11365, 718-417-5050, 10:00 A.M.–5:00 P.M.; fax: 718-386-9049.

Pinball parts, backglasses, and service. Circuit board repair. Vintage parts for electromechanical and solid-state pinball machines. Large selection of pinball backglasses. Schematics and manuals. Free brochure.

Memory Lane Sodaware, PO Box 6239, Laguna Niguel, CA 92607, 714-348-1822, 8:00 A.M.–5:00 P.M.; fax: 714-348-8105. Restoration parts for classic soda machines; decals to doorliners. Mail order worldwide. Catalog $2.

New England Jukebox & Amusement Co., 77 Tolland Turnpike, Manchester, CT 06040, 203-646-1533, Mon.–Thurs. 10:00 A.M.–6:00 P.M., Fri. 10:00 A.M.–9:00 P.M., Sat. 10:00 A.M.–4:00 P.M.; fax: 203-646-1533 after hours. Complete restoration of jukeboxes. New and used jukebox parts. Reproduction parts for 1940s and 1950s Coke and Pepsi machines. Showroom and warehouse open to the public.

Nostalgic Collector, Kim Gutzke, 7134 15th Ave. S., Minneapolis, MN 55423, 612-866-6183, anytime. Restoration of light-up jukeboxes, Coke machines, slot machines, arcade games, and other coin-operated machines. Jukebox parts, including shiny embossed foils, pilaster extrusions, grille screens, kickplates, shrouds, and decals. Send SASE for free brochure.

Obsolete Electronics, Bill Bickers, 1304 Tenth St., Cochran, GA 31014, 912-934-4900, Mon.–Sat. 9:00 A.M.–6:00 P.M. Repair of jukebox amplifiers and selection receivers. Parts, including tubes.

Paul's Chrome Plating Inc., 341 Mars-Valencia Rd., Mars, PA 16046, 412-625-3135, Mon.–Fri. 8:00 A.M.–5:00 P.M., plus Wed. 7:00 P.M.–8:30 P.M.; fax: 412-625-3060. Copper, nickel, and chrome plating. Polishing stainless steel and aluminum. Specializing in the restoration of jukeboxes.

Paul's Pinball, Paul M. Kunik, 470 Glen Rd., Berkshire, NY 13736, 607-657-8097, evenings. Repair and reconditioning of coin-operated amusement machines. Specializing in electro-mechanical pinball machines. Will also repair other arcade-type amusements: bowling machines, shooting galleries, etc. Upstate–Central New York area.

Pinball Paramedic, Tony Miklos, 1372 Tagart Rd., East Greenville, PA 18041, 215-541-4167, 9:00 A.M.–7:00 P.M. Repair and restoration of coin-operated amusement devices, including jukeboxes, pinball machines, and slot machines.

The Pinball Resource, Steve Young, 37 Velie Rd., LaGrangeville, NY 12540-5512, 914-223-5613, 8:00 A.M.–11:00 P.M.; fax: 914-223-7365. Parts, supplies, restoration information, reproduction parts, repairs, literature, and parts catalogs for pinball machines from 1930 to the present. Mail and telephone orders worldwide. Telephone inquiries encouraged for repair information and values. Free catalog.

Pinball Wizard, Chance and Elaine Tess, 21934 John R. Rd., Hazel Park, MI 48030, 313-399-6438, 10:00 A.M.–10:00 P.M. Specializing in the service and restoration of all makes and models of pinball machines; 1950s Seeburg jukeboxes; 1940s, '50s, and '60s Wurlitzer jukeboxes. Sells new 45 RPM records for jukeboxes. Record catalog $2.

R. S. Pennyfield's, PO Box 1355, Waterloo, IA 50704, 319-233-9928; fax: 319-291-7136. Repair and restoration of early coin-operated machines and gambling machines. Appraisals.

Saint Louis Slot Machine Co., Tom Kolbrener, 2111 S. Brentwood Blvd., St. Louis, MO 63144, 314-961-4612, Mon.–Fri. 9:00 A.M.–5:00 P.M., Sat. 9:00 A.M.–2:00 P.M. Repair and restoration of antique slot machines and soda machines. Parts available.

Sound Remedy, 331 Virginia Ave., Collingswood, NJ 08108, 609-869-0238, 9:00 A.M.–6:00 P.M. Jukebox loudspeakers repaired. Free price list.

Speed & Sport Chrome Plating, 404 Broadway, Houston, TX 77012, 713-921-0235, 8:00 A.M.–5:00 P.M. Chrome, nickel, and gold plating of jukeboxes, Coke machines, etc. Mail order throughout the U.S.

Ted Salveson, PO Box 602, Huron, SD 57350, 605-352-3870, 8:00 A.M.–6:00 P.M. Service manuals, books, and other literature on coin-operated machines. Pool cloth, pinball legs, locks, needles, all-purpose coin machine cleaner, and other supplies. Newsletter. Appraisal service. Catalog $4.

Tim Nabours Novelty, 8510 County Rd. 6 NW, Annandale, MN 55302, 612-963-5953, Mon.–Fri. 8:30 A.M.–5:00 P.M., Sat. 10:00 A.M.–3:00 P.M. Parts and accessories for pinball games, jukeboxes, and all related amusement devices. Free brochure.

Vern Tisdale, 8402 N. 18th Ave., Phoenix, AZ 85021, 602-944-8444, 7:00 A.M.–9:00 P.M.; fax: 602-997-6376. Parts for repairing old jukeboxes. Amplifiers rebuilt. Free advice. Will refer you to other sources if he doesn't have what you need. Shipping worldwide.

Vic-Clar Antique Juke Boxes, 9313 Rose St., Bellflower, CA 90706, 310-866-7107, 8:30 A.M.–8:00 P.M. Jukebox restoration and refurbishing.

Victory Glass Company, 3260 Ute Ave., Waukee, IA 50263, 515-987-5765, 9:00 A.M.–5:00 P.M.; fax: 515-987-5762. Reproduction parts for Wurlitzer, Seeburg, and Rock-Ola jukeboxes of the 1930s through 1950s. Service manuals, needles, and cartridges; 45 and 78 RPM record sets. Free catalog.

Wiesner Radio & Electronics, 149 Hunter Ave., Albany, NY 12206, 518-438-2801, 9:00 A.M.–5:00 P.M. Repair of obsolete electronic equipment, including jukebox amplifiers.

Videos

TroubleShooting the Seeburg Selectomatic 100, **Jukebox Media,** 8795-K Corvus St., San Diego, CA 92126-1920, 619-271-8294. Step-by-step, how-to restoration tape, covers 1940s to 1950s Seeburgs. 90 minutes, $39.95. *Seeburg Engineering Manual,* a booklet on the theory of operation, $14.95.

TroubleShooting the Seeburg Tormat Selection System, **Mike Zuccaro,** 8795-K Corvus St., San Diego, CA 92126-1920, 619-271-8294. Restoration

video covering Seeburgs made from 1955 to 1965. 45 minutes, $24.95.

Coins, Tokens & Credit Cards

*D*o you remember going to the bank for rolls of pennies so you could search for the rare dates? Have you kept a box of foreign coins brought by traveling relatives? Collections of this sort, even those started by grandpa as a boy, have less value than imagined because of the poor condition of the coins. However, you can never be sure there is not a treasure hiding in with the ordinary, so you must examine coin collections carefully.

If you have inherited a properly stored, serious collection of coins in good to mint condition, you have even more reason to be careful about selling. We remember appraising an estate that had a library full of coin books. We asked about the coins, and the almost unbelievable answer was, "Oh, there were lots of old coins. I took them to the bank and deposited them into the savings account." That is exactly the wrong thing to do.

You will find many books in the public library about coin values and the buying and selling of coins. The prices given are the going retail prices, not what you will get for your coins from a dealer, who will probably offer half of the listed price. The books picture coins and indicate prices for coins in all grades or conditions. They refer to coins in proof (PRF), uncirculated (UNC or MS), extremely fine (EF or EX), very fine (VF), fine (F), very good (VG), good (G), or poor (PR) condition. Each book has a slightly different code. Beware! It takes an expert to know the condition of a coin. All you can do is learn the range of prices for your coin if it seems to be in excellent condition. That means it has the bright, shiny finish of a new coin, no scratches, no nicks, no overall wear.

Never clean a coin! That lowers the value. The bright finish must be the original one. Remember, an old coin or bill is almost always worth at least the face value. Check the meltdown value of silver coins. When silver prices were high in the 1970s, coins were worth much more than face value or even coin collectors' values. Many coins in poor condition were melted and sold as silver.

The most obvious place to sell coins is to a coin dealer. There is a listing of "Coin Dealers" in the Yellow Pages of the telephone book, which will also list those large department stores that have coin departments. Anyone who sells coins, buys coins. Auctioneers sell good quality coins, local antiques auction galleries may have special sales for coins or include them in regular sales, and then there are also some nationally known coin auction houses. Some of the latter are listed in Part II and others can be found through the advertisements in any of the coin publications.

If you send your coins to be auctioned, be sure to ask who pays for insurance for the coins while at the gallery, photography of coins for the catalog, and any advertising.

You must pay a fee to the auctioneer, and you should ask what percentage of the sale price that will be, get a signed contract or agreement, and send the coins by insured mail and with a full inventory list.

Information about coins and coin prices can often be obtained by telephone. An accurately described coin can be researched in the current editions of any of the price books, and an approximate value can be given by phone. Some dealers will give the approximate price they will pay by phone.

If you inherit what appears to be a good collection, it might be advisable to contact a coin appraiser. They will be listed in the Yellow Pages under either "Coin" or "Appraiser." The probate court must use appraisers to determine the value of coins in an estate, and the names of these appraisers are known to the lawyers and judges in your city. A qualified appraiser should belong to some of the national numismatic organizations. The appraiser can also arrange for the sale of your coins. Be sure to ask the charge for appraisal or for disposing of the collection. We have found that an amateur does not do well trying to sell a collection of rare coins. It takes a professional auctioneer or appraiser to watch out for your interests.

Coins and paper money can often be sold to friends, to dealers at coin shows, or to jewelers who advertise for pieces for meltdown. We caution you to be sure that you do *not* have a very rare coin before you sell by this method. It takes an expert to understand the difference in value between a coin with a mint mark and one without it, and any of the other details that determine great rarity and value.

Although many coin dealers routinely buy and sell by mail or through ads in the numismatic publications, we urge caution in these dealings. Most publications try to screen the dealers, but sometimes a dishonest person may offer to buy at fair prices for months before problems surface. If you plan to sell to an unknown person, try to get references. Ask how long you must wait for your money and include a full list of the coins you want to sell. If possible, have someone, perhaps a local collector, help you determine the condition of your coins. You could be wrong, and a fine-looking coin may only be extra good or an unscrupulous dealer could tell you that your coin is in worse condition than it really is. Sometimes you may have to wait too long for your money from the sale of your coins. Send the coins registered mail. Postal fraud is a crime, and even dishonest dealers try to avoid it.

There are many special categories for coins. You must learn what mint set, proof set, reissue, restrike, type set, and other words mean. If you have sets or rolls of coins, sell them as a unit, do not break them up.

Tokens and any other types of "money" also have a value to a coin collector. Some specialize in store tokens, odd types of money that are not metal coins, mis-struck coins, and error coins. Even canceled and blank checks are wanted. A relatively new collectible that can be sold is a credit card. The first paper American Express card in good condition is worth $500. Telephone cards and store charge cards and tokens are also collected. Paper bills are very popular, and these should be researched and sold in the same way as coins.

Almost every type of "money," from wooden nickels to gold coins, has a value. If the money is an unfamiliar-looking American coin or bill, it is even more important to check the value. Medals are sold through coin dealers. Even jewelry made from coins can be sold through coin dealers.

Solid-gold coins present a special problem. They can be sold for the gold content or for the numismatic value. In recent years many investors have started to buy gold coins. The value changes daily with the price of gold. Look for nicks in the edges that indicate bits of the gold have been removed. This lowers both values. Coins mounted in bezels as jewelry retain numismatic value if they can be removed with no damage to the coin. Of course, the coin may be scratched from wear. Coins mounted as jewelry with soldered links have lost the numismatic value even if the link is removed. The solder will damage the edge of the coin. Gold coins in good condition sell for the highest prices at coin shops and auctions.

REPAIR

The value of rare coins, perhaps more than for any other type of collectible, is determined by condition as well as rarity, beauty, and history. For this reason, coin collectors are particularly careful about handling, storing, or cleaning coins.

The perspiration from a hand will eventually damage a coin. It should always be handled with gloves or by the edges. Never store coins in bags where they might rub against each other. Try storing them in an area where they will not tarnish. Keep them away from damp places, too much direct sunlight, off floors, and away from rubber bands, tape, metal, and cardboard. The sulfur in the rubber or cardboard will eventually damage the coins. There are many types of holders with spaces for specific coins, or envelopes and filing boxes that are made for coin storage.

Never clean your coins. If it must be done, consult an expert. There are dips, cleaning cloths, and other products made to clean coins, but they may cause damage if not used correctly.

Never clean a token or a medal; it lowers the value. Handle the pieces as little as possible and wear white cotton gloves. The perspiration from your hand can mark the metal.

Checks and credit cards should be stored or restored in the same way as any paper or plastic items.

Price Books

Auction Prices Realized, U.S. Coins, annual, edited by Bob Wilhite and Tom Michael (Krause, Iola, WI).

Commemorative Coins of the United States Identification and Price Guide, Anthony Swiatek (Avon Books, New York, © 1993).

Guidebook of U.S. Coins, annual, R. S. Yeoman (Western Publishing, Inc., Racine, WI).

Coin World Guide to U.S. Coins, Prices & Value Trends, annual, William T. Gibbs (Coin World, PO Box 150, Sidney, OH 45365).

The Official 1995 Blackbook Price Guide of United States Coins, 33rd edition, Marc Hudgeons (Random House, New York, © 1994).

The Official 1995 Blackbook Price Guide of United States Papery Money, 27th edition, Marc Hudgeons (Random House, New York, © 1994).

Standard Catalog of U.S. Tokens 1700–1900, Russell Rulau (Krause, Iola, WI, © 1994).

Standard Catalog of World Coins, annual, Chester L. Krause and Clifford Mishler (Krause, Iola, WI).

Standard Catalog of World Paper Money, 7th edition, Albert Pick (Krause, Iola, WI, © 1994)

Standard Guide to Small-Sized Paper Money, Dean Oakes (Krause, Iola, WI, © 1994).

Standard Catalogue of World Coins, annual, Chester Krause and Clifford Mishler (Krause, Iola, WI).

Krause also publishes several other books on coins, paper money, and related collectibles.

Clubs & Publications

Active Token Collectors Organization, *ATCO* (MAG), PO Box 1573, Sioux Falls, SD 57101.

American Numismatic Association, *Numismatist* (MAG), 818 N. Cascade Ave., Colorado Springs, CO 80903-3279.

American Credit Piece Collectors Association, *Journal of the American Credit Piece Collectors Association* (NL), PO Box 2465, Midland, MI 48640 (charge coins, charga-plates, credit cards, affinity cards, ATM cards, etc.).

American Society of Check Collectors, *Check Collector* (MAG), PO Box 577, Garrett Park, MD 20896.

American Vecturist Association, *Fare Box* (NL), PO Box 1204, Boston, MA 02104-1204.

Canadian Numismatic Association, *Canadian Numismatic Journal* (MAG), PO Box 226, Barrie, ON, Canada L4M 4T2.

Casino Chip & Gaming Token Collectors Club, *Casino Chip & Token News* (NL), 5410 Banbury Dr., Columbus, OH 43235.

The Elongated Collectors, *TEC News* (NL), 203 S. Gladolins, Momence, IL 60954-1709.

International Bank Note Society, *International Bank Note Society Journal* (MAG), *Inside IBNS* (NL), PO Box 1642, Racine, WI 53401.

International Organization of Wooden Money Collectors, *Bunyan's Chips* (NL), 413 Delaware Ave., Elkton, MD 21921-6604.

Latin American Paper Money Society, *LANSA* (NL), 3304 Milford Mill Rd., Baltimore, MD 21244.

Liberty Seated Collectors Club, *Gobrecht Journal* (MAG), 5718 King Arthur Dr., Kettering, OH 45429 (Liberty Seated coins).

Love Token Society, *Love Letter* (NL), 3200 Ella Ln., Manhattan, KS 66502.

National Scrip Collectors Association, *Scrip Talk* (NL), Box 67, Sophia, WV 25921.

Orders & Medals Society of America, *Journal of the Orders & Medals Society of America* (MAG), PO Box 484, Glassboro, NJ 08028.

Society of Lincoln Cent Collectors, *Lincoln Sense* (NL), 13515 Magnolia Blvd., Sherman Oaks, CA 91423.

Society of Paper Money Collectors, *Paper Money* (MAG), Box 2999, Leslie, MO 63056.

Society of Philatelists and Numismatists (SPAN), *Ex-SPAN-sion* (NL), 1929 Millis St., Montebello, CA 90640-4533 (specializing in philatelic-numismatic combinations).

World Proof Numismatic Association (W.P.N.A.), *Proof Collectors Corner* (MAG), PO Box 4094, Pittsburgh, PA 15201.

Bank Note Reporter (NP), *Coin Prices* (MAG), *COINS Magazine* (MAG), *Numismatic News* (NP), *World Coin News* (MAG), 700 E. State St., Iola, WI 54990.

Celator (NP), PO Box 123, Lodi, WI 53555 (ancient numismatics and antiquities).

Coin World (NP), PO Box 150, Sidney, OH 45365.

Credit Card Collector (NL), PO Box 460247, Houston, TX 77056.

Error Trends Coin Magazine (MAG), PO Box 158, Oceanside, NY 11572-0158.

Jakira Journal (MAG), PO Box 022785, Brooklyn, NY 11202-0057.

Lin Overholt's Card Trader (NL), PO Box 8481, Madeira Beach, FL 33738 (credit cards, telephone cards, charge coins, charga-plates, and telephone tokens).

Moneycard Collector (MAG), PO Box 783, Sidney, OH 45365.

Premier Telecard Magazine (MAG), PO Box 2297, Paso Robles, CA 93447.

Rare Coin Review (MAG), *The Coin Collector* (NP), Bowers and Merena Galleries, Inc., Box 1224, Wolfeboro, NH 03894.

Supplies

Lin Terry, 59 E. Madison Ave., Dumont, NJ 07628, 201-385-4706; fax: 201-385-0306. Coin holders, mounts, tubes, currency holders, supplies, and books.

Videos

Building a Coin Collection from Pocket Change, 46 minutes, $29.95; *Collecting Credit Cards,* 48 minutes, $29.95; *Collecting U.S. Paper Money,* 37 minutes, $29.95, **Advision Incorporated,** 3100 Arrowwood Ln., Boulder, Co 80303-2419, 800-876-2320. Write for complete list of videos available.

Comic Art

*A*ction Comics No. 1 was the first superhero comic. In June 1938, this comic book introduced Superman. In fine condition, the comic now sells for over $19,000. A copy of *Marvel Comics No. 1,* Oct.–Nov. 1939, in mint condition, sold in 1984 for $35,000. In 1991, a collector paid $55,000 for Detective 27, the first comic book in which Batman appeared. Most of the high-priced comics contain superheroes.

Age alone does not determine the value of a collectible comic. Comic strips started in 1896 with the introduction of the "Yellow Kid." The first monthly comic book was the 10-cent "Famous Funnies," which appeared in July 1934. Comics were popular with children, young adults, and especially servicemen during the 1940s. After the war, there was a movement to censor comics, to remove the violence and sex, and many comic books were burned. The paper drives of the war and the reformation movement after the war mean few of the old copies remain. The newsprint used for comics is easily damaged by heat, light, and moisture.

Those comics that were not destroyed by a series of young readers were often preserved until a tidy mother decided they were no longer worth saving. It is the lucky collector who finds a box of well-preserved, old comic books in an attic where they avoided house-cleaning days. Comic books are wanted by young collectors who specialize in superheroes, Westerns, funny animals, jungle, SF (science fiction), or special issues or full years of favored comics. They are also purchased by serious older collectors who have more money and more expensive desires.

Comic collecting became an organized pastime in about 1960. Several magazines and newspapers were started that discussed the history of comics, reported on new comics, and, of course, included buy and sell ads. Today there are comic shops and comic shows in most major cities. Reprints, price books, and research materials are available. Most comic collectors are not children; they are affluent, educated adult males.

The easiest place to find old comic books is at the special comic book stores. You may be able to find one nearby. If there is no shop listed in the Yellow Pages of the telephone book, you could try selling at a comic show, a mall show, or a store that sells used books. Check the local papers or ask your friends' children. If you find a large collection of comic books, you should go to a comics convention. Trading takes place at the convention and in the rooms of the hotel during the convention days and nights. The standard comic price guides, including the original one, *The Overstreet Comic Book Price Guide,* by Robert Overstreet, list almost every title and issue. The prices are high retail, and dealers at a comic show often start out offering to sell you a comic at half the Overstreet price. You will get even less for your comics, though very rare editions usually hold their value.

Condition is very important. A serious collector stores the comics in special plastic bags to protect them from added tears, cover bends, or spine damage. When pricing comics, remember to check condition. This is one field of collecting where finding a retail price is as simple as reading a price guide that is available in every library and most bookstores. The comic must be in original, unrestored condition. It should not be repaired by gluing, restapling, recoloring, trimming, or bleaching. Rusty staples, bad printing, creases, even yellow paper, will lower the value. Mint copies have almost-white pages and glossy covers. A good copy has only suffered from average use, slight soil, possible creases or minor tears, but has no tape or missing pages.

It is not only comic books that are collected but also comic strips from newspapers, the original art from comics and cartoons, and even the original celluloid drawings used to make animated movie cartoons. The Disney cels were offered for sale to tourists at Disneyland when it first opened. The framed cel was sold for about $15. Each cel was marked on the back with a short history of celluloids. Other cels were sold earlier by Courvoisier Art Galleries in San Francisco and each was marked on the mat framing the cel and on the back. A scene from Snow White showing the evil queen as a hag dipping the apple into a pot of poison sold in 1986 for $30,800. Other original comic art used for posters or publicity also sells for thousands of dollars.

The original art for comic books and comic strips was so undervalued before 1970 that it was often burned by the newspaper syndicates. The artists of the comics you read now usually own their art and either give it to special friends or sell it. A single strip is worth over $100 if it is the work of a popular artist, and under $25 if it's by a forgotten artist. The subject matter makes the difference in the price. Old political cartoons and sports cartoons for local papers are of minimal value. Any strip for PRINCE VALIANT, LI'L ABNER, or YELLOW KID is of value. All types of comic art sell at comic book shows.

It is easy to sell good comics by mail. Buyers look for comic books through the ads in the comic collector publications.

REPAIR

Collectors have become serious about comic art. Most of these materials are now of enough historic importance to be found in universities and museums. The strips and "cels" (celluloid pictures used for movie cartoons) were not made to be permanent, and they fade and deteriorate easily. Watch out for excessive light, heat, or humidity, which quickly damage the materials. There are restorers for many of these items, but the restoration is expensive.

COMIC-RELATED MATERIALS

Little Lulu dolls, posters of Spiderman, lunch boxes printed with pictures of the Flintstones, cookie jars, and anything else that shows a cartoon character are all collected by someone. The best place to sell these items is to the comic book and comic art collectors. (See the above section on Comic Art.) Dealers at flea markets and shopping mall antiques shows are always looking for these items.

See also the sections on Movie Memorabilia, Paper Collectibles, and Photographs.

Price Books

Cartoon Friends of the Baby Boom Era, Bill Bruegman (Cap'n Penny Productions, 137 Casterton Ave., Akron, OH 44303, © 1993).

Comic Buyer's Guide 1994 Annual, 3rd edition (Krause, Iola, WI, © 1993).

Hake's Guide to Comic Character Collectibles, Ted Hake (Hake's Americana, PO Box 1444, York, PA 17405, © 1993).

Original Comic Art Identification and Price Guide, Jerry West (Avon Books, New York, © 1992).

The Overstreet Comic Book Price Guide, annual, Robert M. Overstreet (Avon Books, New York).

Archives

Walt Disney Productions, 500 S. Buena Vista St., Burbank, CA 91521, 818-972-3302 (will help with research).

Clubs & Publications

Animation Art Guild, *Update* (NL), 330 W. 45th St., Suite 9-D, New York, NY 10036.

Don Manina's Button Club, *Pin & Button Club News* (NL), Box 2774, Seal Beach, CA 90740 (Disneyana buttons and pins).

Caniff Fan Club, *Caniffites* (NL), Box 632, Manitou Springs, CO 80829-0632. (Milton Caniff comics).

Imagunation Guild, *ImagunEars* (NL), PO Box 907, Boulder Creek, CA 95006 (Disneyana).

National Fantasy Fan Club for Disneyana Collectors & Enthusiasts, *Dispatch* (MAG), *Fantasy Line* (MAG), PO Box 19212, Irvine, CA 92713.

Peanuts Collector Club, *Peanuts Collector* (NL), 539 Sudden Valley, Bellingham, WA 98226.

Pogo Fan Club, *Fort Mudge Most* (NL), Spring Hollow Books, 6908 Wentworth Ave. S., Richfield, MN 55423.

R. F. Outcault Society, *R. F. Outcault Reader* (NL), 103 Doubloon Dr., Slidell, LA 70461 (Yellow Kid, Pore Li'l Mose, Buster Brown, etc.).

Smurf Collectors Club, *Smurf Collectors Club Newsletter* (NL), 24 K Cabot Rd. W., Massapequa, NY 11758.

Animation Magazine (MAG), 5889 Kanan Rd., #317, Agoura Hills, CA 91301.

Card & Comic Trader (MAG), 410 Mare Blvd., Suite 406, Tampa, FL, 33619 (free publication distributed at Florida card and comic shows).

Comics Buyer's Guide (NP), 700 E. State St., Iola, WI 54990.

Duckburg Times (MAG), 3010 Wilshire Blvd., #362, Los Angeles, CA 90010 (Donald Duck and other Disneyana).

FCA & ME TOO! (NL), 301 E. Buena Vista Ave., North Augusta, SC 29841 (Fawcett collectors).

In Toon! (NL), PO Box 217, Gracie Station, New York, NY 10028 (animation art).

Mouse Rap Monthly (MAG), PO Box 1064, Ojai, CA 93024 (Disneyana).

Tomart's Disneyana Update (MAG), 3300 Encrete Ln., Dayton, OH 45439-1944 (Disney merchandise).

Repairs, Parts & Supplies

Northeast Document Conservation Center, 100 Brickstone Sq., Andover, MA 01810-1494, 508-470-1010; fax: 508-475-6021. Nonprofit, regional conservation center specializing in treatment of cartoon cels. Preservation planning surveys, disaster assistance, technical leaflets. Brochure.

The Restoration Lab, Susan Cicconi, Conservator of Ephemera, PO Box 632, New Town Branch, Boston, MA 02258, 617-924-4297.

Comic book restoration, including stain removal, tape removal, invisible mending, dry cleaning, spine rebuilding, missing piece replacement, deacidification, color in-painting, and flattening wrinkles and creases. Work done on books worth $1,000 or more in present condition. Send for more information, requirements, and rates.

Restorations, PO Box 2000, Nevada City, CA 95959, 916-477-5527. Restoration supplies for repairing comic books. Standard Repair Pak, spine repair kit, reglossing spray, tape removal kit, stain removal kit, lightening solution, and more. Mylar bags. Brochure.

Video

The Bob Cook Yellow Kid Collection, **Richard Olson,** 103 Doubloon Dr., Slidell, LA 70461, 504-641-5173. A video catalog of over 350 Yellow Kid collectibles. $19.95.

*D*olls

*D*olls are easy to sell, but hard to price. Rare old French and German dolls from the nineteenth century bring thousands of dollars and should be sold to a top doll dealer or through an auction gallery. Several galleries have sales devoted just to dolls. The major collectors, with the most money and the best dolls, go to these auctions and pay high prices. Some sales even include lots of doll bodies, legs, arms, and eyes from old dolls, which are valued for repairs. We have seen a headless body sell for over $100.

Collectors divide dolls into several general categories: antique dolls are seventy-five years old or older, collectible dolls are from twenty-five to seventy-five years old, and modern dolls are those made during the past twenty-five years. Contemporary dolls are those still being made. The general rule is that it takes twenty years for a doll to start to go up in value, so the dolls whose prices are rising today are Barbie and other dolls of the 1960s. The most valuable Barbie is the first model, which has holes in the feet because it was made to fit on pegs on a stand.

If your dolls are not rare and over seventy-five years old, they will probably sell well in shops that deal in dolls. The collectible foreign dolls of the 1930s to 1950s were difficult to sell for any price until the 1970s. Now they are found at most shops and doll sales. Stuffed cloth dolls, advertising and comic figures, composition dolls like Shirley Temple dolls, dolls that are replicas of famous people, characters from literature or movies, and, of course, the teenage dolls sell quickly if they are priced properly. These are moderately priced dolls although a few, like a mint original Shirley Temple or Barbie, will be worth over $1,000.

Many dolls are marked by the manufacturer. Look at the back of the neck, on the shoulders, or on the head of a hard porcelain or composition doll. Sometimes there are labels on the bottom of the feet, on the chest, in the clothes, or on extra tags. A few dolls can be accurately identified by the shape of eyes, face, feet, hands, or other parts, or by some peculiarity of construction. A doll expert can easily recognize these features.

Look for twentieth-century dolls marked MATTEL, MADAME ALEXANDER, RAVCA, STEIFF, SCHOENHUT, LENCI, VOGUE, and STORYBOOK. Any KEWPIE or RAGGEDY ANN is worth money. Earlier dolls are often marked with initials or symbols. Look these up at your library in the two-volume *Collector's Encyclopedia of Dolls* by Dorothy S., Elizabeth A., and Evelyn J. Coleman.

Save all the boxes and hang tags that come with the doll. They add to the value. Always save all the accessories. The tiny pair of ice skates or the straw hat can add much to the value. If you should find the printed fabric that was sold to be made into a stuffed doll, don't cut and stuff it. It is worth more uncut. Paper dolls are worth more uncut.

Don't restore any damaged dolls unless that is your business. A collector prefers to see the doll before restoration. A dealer can have the restoration done at a lower price, so the economies of the market make it smarter to sell a doll "as is."

Doll accessories sell well. Old clothing, doll carriages, chairs, and even old photographs of children with old dolls sell quickly. The celluloid pin found on the original Shirley Temple doll is so important that it has been reproduced. Barbie's clothes, including shoes, purse, and sunglasses, are valuable, and so are her accessories—the phonograph, her cars, airplane, or house.

If you have an antique doll or a collection of 1930s dolls, you have a valuable asset, but you must set the price to sell it. Dolls that are to be sold through a major doll auction need no formal appraisal. Just photograph the doll dressed and undressed. The pictures should show details of construction, a close-up of the face, and any marks or damage. Send the pictures and a description to a doll auction house.

If you want an appraisal so you can sell the doll to a dealer or friend, you can pay for one from a local doll dealer or doll hospital. Some of the doll auction galleries will do appraisals by mail for a fee. Local members of the major appraisal societies (listed in Part II) should be able to tell you the value of your dolls. Doll appraisal clinics are held in many parts of the country in conjunction with sales where professional advice is available either for a small fee or free, and some doll shows also give verbal appraisals for a small fee.

There are several good books that give doll prices listed here; your bookstore or library will have them. Study these books carefully. You will usually find a doll similar to yours, but you will rarely find exactly the same doll. Even so, the prices provide a guide.

Condition is important. Even minor cracks and repaints lower the value of pre-1920 dolls by 50 to 75 percent. Although original clothes are preferred, replacements that are old retain much of the value. Once you have a general idea of the value of your doll, you can sell it through an auction, to an antiques or doll dealer, in a shop, at a special doll show, at a house sale, or by any of the other methods discussed in the Introduction. There seems to be an emotional "something" that influences buyers of dolls and toys, so pricing is sometimes best set by determining how "lovable" your toy might be.

A word of caution! If you send your doll to a dealer on consignment or to an auction, always be sure to keep a complete pictorial record and a written description. Have the dealer sign and return your record after examining the doll. Set dates for payment or the return of any unsold dolls.

REPAIR

Doll collectors judge their collections by beauty, rarity, age, and condition. Examine your old doll carefully. Has it been repainted? Is the body original? Are the arms and legs undamaged? Is the surface of the face uncracked? Doll heads can be professionally mended. Many of the same restorers who mend porcelains will repair a china-headed doll (see the section on Pottery & Porcelain).

Bodies can be restored or replaced. Old and new clothing is available, as are patterns for period doll dresses. A restored doll is worth more than a damaged doll, but much less than an all-original one. Too often there is an argument later about the doll's condition if the doll is returned because it couldn't be sold.

There is a classic horror story told by doll collectors about the doll that went to a doll hospital to be repaired. When it was returned, it appeared to be a totally different doll, with a new head, new body and arms. The doll hospital insisted that it was the old doll, repaired. The collector was certain that the old doll was so valuable that the dishonest repairer switched the parts. This is a legend, but there is the possibility of a misunderstanding anytime you give your valuable items to another person.

Repairs, new parts, and replacements sometimes seem to "appear." It is like hanging new curtains in a room. The room looked fine before, but after fresh, bright curtains are added, the woodwork and walls look nicked, smudged, and in need of paint and the carpet seems faded.

The sound mechanisms of old dolls and stuffed animals can be repaired, but the restoration is expensive. To replace the voice in a "talking Barbie," the entire head must be removed and split, the voice mechanism's

DECODING ADVERTISING COPY

When reading the ads for dolls, it might help to know these terms and abbreviations:

Alex. - Madame Alexander
A.M. - Armand Marseille
Amer. Char. - American character
b - back
bj body - ball-jointed body
bk - bent knees
bl - blue, blond, or blown
br - brown
c - circumference
cell. - celluloid
cl - cloth or closed
cl m - closed mouth
comp - composition
dh - dollhouse
dk - dark
EJ - Emile Jumeau
ex - excellent
f - front
gc - good condition
gl - glass
h - high
hd mk - head mark
hh - human hair
hp - hard plastic
IDMA - International Doll Makers Association
incl - included
jcb - jointed composition body
JDK - Johannes Daniel Kestner
jtd - jointed
K&R - Kammer and Reinhardt
l - long; luster, leather, or lower
l.t. - lower teeth
m - mohair
mib - mint in box

mk - mark
mld hair - molded hair
mtd - mounted
NIADA - National Institute of American Doll Artists
NRFB - never removed from box
O.CL.M. or o/c - open-closed mouth (open lips parted but no opening in bisque)
ODACA - Original Doll Artists Council of America
oilcl - oilcloth
om - open mouth
orig - original
p - pierced
PD - Petit & Dumontier
pm - papier-mâché
pr - pair
pt - paint or part
ptd - painted
pw eyes - paperweight eyes
RD - Rabery & Delphieu
redr - redressed
rep - repair
repl - replacement
rt - right
S&H - Simon & Halbig
SFBJ - Societé Française de Fabrication de Bébés et Jouets (a group of French dollmakers)
sh pl - shoulder plate
sl - sleeping
stat - stationary
sw. n. - swivel neck
syn. - synthetic
tc - terra-cotta
UFDC - United Federation of Doll Clubs
undr - undressed
u.t. - upper teeth
vgc - very good condition
w - wash

rubber parts replaced, the head reglued, and the joint repainted. It is sometimes less expensive to buy a new doll, but there are times when emotional attachment to a doll makes restoration a good idea.

If you are taking a doll to be repaired, there are a few rules that must be followed to assure you and the doll hospital a happy transaction. Photograph the doll and the damaged parts. Take pictures of the marks, body, hair, and clothes. Get a written estimate of the cost of the repair and the work that is to be done before agreeing to the work. It is often easy to remember an old doll as more glamorous than it actually was, and sometimes when the restored doll is returned it appears unfamiliar. We often hear complaints that a head or body was replaced or that the repairs were more extensive than expected. The pictures and estimate will help solve these problems.

Price Books

Barbie Rarities, Florence Theriault (Gold Horse Publishing, 2148 Renard Ct., Annapolis, MD 21401, © 1992).

Black Dolls Book II, Myla Perkins (Collector Books, Paducah, KY, © 1995).

Black Dolls 1820–1991: An Identification and Value Guide, Myla Perkins (Collector Books, Paducah, KY, © 1993).

Blue Book of Dolls & Values, 11th edition, Jan Foulke (Hobby House Press, Grantsville, MD, © 1993).

Chatty Cathy Dolls, An Identification and Value Guide by Kathy and Don Lewis (Collector Books, Paducah, KY, © 1994).

Collector's Guide to Ideal Dolls, Judith Izen (Collector Books, Paducah, KY, © 1994).

Doll Collector's Price Guide (MAG), PO Box 420235, Palm Coast, FL 32142.

Doll Fashion Anthology & Price Guide, 4th

edition, A. Glenn Mandeville (Hobby House, Grantsville, MD 21536, © 1994).

Madame Alexander Dolls Value Guide, A. Glenn Mandeville (Hobby House, Grantsville, MD 21536, © 1994).

Modern Collector's Dolls, Sixth Series, Patricia R. Smith (Collector Books, Paducah, KY, © 1994).

The Price & Identification Guide to Old Magazine Paperdolls, 3rd edition, booklet, Denis C. Jackson (TICN, PO Box 1958, Sequim, WA 98382, © 1994).

Reference Books

Collector's Encyclopedia of Dolls, Dorothy S., Elizabeth A., and Evelyn J. Coleman (Crown, New York, NY, © 1968).

Collector's Encyclopedia of Dolls, Volume Two, Dorothy S., Elizabeth A., and Evelyn J. Coleman (Crown, New York, NY, © 1986).

How to Collect French Bébé Dolls and *How to Collect French Fashion Dolls,* Mildred and Vernon Seeley (HP Books, PO Box 5367, Tucson, AZ 85703, © 1985).

Clubs & Publications

Cabbage Patch Kids® Collectors Club, *Limited Edition™* (NL), PO Box 714, Cleveland, GA 30528.

Chatty Cathy Collectors Club, *Chatty News* (NL), 2610 Dover St., Piscataway, NJ 08854-4437.

Ideal Collector's Club, *Ideal Collector's Newsletter* (NL), PO Box 623, Lexington, MA 02173.

International Rose O'Neill Club, *Kewpiesta Kourier* (NP), PO Box 668, Branson, MO 65616.

Madame Alexander Doll Club, *Review* (NL), PO Box 330, Mundelein, IL 60060.

Modern Doll Club, *Modern Doll Journal* (NL), 305 W. Beacon Rd., Lakeland, FL 33803.

Original Paper Doll Artists Guild (OPDAG), *OPDAG News* (NL), PO Box 14, Kingfield, ME 04947.

Toy Store's Collectors Club of Steiff, *Collectors Life* (NL), PO Box 798, Holland, OH 43528.

United Federation of Doll Clubs, *Doll News* (NL), 10920 N. Ambassador Dr., Suite 130,

Kansas City, MO 64153 (information packet available).

Antique Doll World (MAG), 225 Main St., Suite 300, Northport, NY 11768.

Barbie Bazaar (MAG), 5617 Sixth Ave., Kenosha, WI 53140.

Cabbage Line (NL), 8500 CR 21, Clyde, OH 43410 (Cabbage Patch dolls).

Celebrity Doll Journal (MAG), 5 Court Pl., Puyallup, WA 98372.

Collectors United (NP), PO Box 1160, Chatsworth, GA 30705 (buy-sell-trade ads).

Contemporary Doll Collector (MAG), *Doll Crafter* (MAG), 30595 Eight Mile, Livonia, MI 48152-1798.

Doll Castle News (MAG), PO Box 247, Washington, NJ 07882.

Doll Designs (MAG), PO Box 420452, Palm Coast, FL 32142-9841.

Doll Reader (MAG), PO Box 467, Mt. Morris, IL 61054-7896.

Doll Times (NP), 218 W. Woodin, Dallas, TX 75224.

Doll World (MAG), PO Box 420077, Palm Coast, FL 32142-9895.

Dolls—The Collector's Magazine (MAG), PO Box 1972, Marion, OH 43305.

Joan Walsh Anglund Collectors News (NL), PO Box 105, Amherst, NH 03031.

Midwest Paper Dolls & Toys Quarterly (NL), Box 131, Galesburg, KS 66740.

Miller's Barbie ® Collector (NL), W. One Sumner #1, Spokane, WA 99204 (featuring Barbie dolls, fashions, and accessories).

Nancy Ann Clearinghouse (NL), 2054 Pioneer Blvd., Grand Island, NE 68801.

Northern Lights Paperdoll News, PO Box 871189, Wasilla, AK 99687.

Paper Doll News (NL), PO Box 807, Vivian, LA 71082.

Paperdoll Review (MAG), Box 584, Princeton, IN 47670.

Patsy & Friends Newsletter (NL), 8915 S. Orange, Fresno, CA 93725.

Rags (NL), PO Box 823, Atlanta, GA 30301 (Raggedy Ann and Andy dolls).

Teddy Bear and Friends (MAG), 900 Frederick St., Cumberland, MD 21502.

Teddy Bear Review (MAG), PO Box 1948, Marion, OH 43306-2048.

Repairs, Parts & Supplies

A. Ludwig Klein & Son, Inc., PO Box 145, Harleysville, PA 19438, 215-256-9004, Tues.–Fri. 10:00 A.M.–5:00 P.M. Doll restoration. Appraisals and insurance claims by appointment. Free brochure.

Carolyn's Doll Fantasy, 331 Wolfs Bridge Rd., Carlisle, PA 17013, 717-243-0861, Mon.–Sat. 9:00 A.M.–6:00 P.M. Antique doll restoration. Composition dolls restored.

Chili Doll Hospital & Victorian Doll Museum, Linda Greenfield, 4332 Buffalo Rd., North Chili, NY 14514, 716-247-0130, Tues.–Sat. 10:00 A.M.–4:30 P.M. Restoration services, specializing in antique doll repair. Wigs, costumes, and stands available. Send SASE for brochure.

Christensen Doll Hospital, 1226 W. Fifth St., Santa Ana, CA 92703, 714-647-0294, 9:00 A.M.–3:00 P.M.; fax: 714-647-0418. Services for Barbie and friends. Talking mechanisms fixed, hair redone, faces painted, eye mechanisms repaired. Knees, hips, arms, and necks repaired. Cuts, chews, and scrapes restored. Free appraisals only on dolls sent by mail; appraisals are not given over the phone. Send LSASE for order form and price list.

Cobwebs, Herbert A. Elion, Sheila Thall, 1850 Union St., #1480, San Francisco, CA 94123, 415-474-6899, 9:00 A.M.–4:00 P.M.; fax: 415-474-7699. Bisque doll repair. Doll parts search. Antique doll clothing.

Collectible Doll Company, 1421 N. 34th St., Seattle, WA 98103, 206-634-3131, 800-468-3655, order desk, 9:00 A.M.–5:00 P.M.; fax: 206-632-2848. Doll-making supplies. Molds for doll bodies and parts, mohair doll wigs, china paint, patterns, how-to videos on repro painting and on wig making. Toy museum. Catalog $6.

Create-A-Doll, 146 E. Chubbuck Rd., Chubbuck, ID 83202, 208-238-0433, 10:00 A.M.–5:00 P.M., except Sun. Leather and imitation leather doll bodies. Reproduction of French and German styles, 8 inches to 30 inches. Brochure $1.50.

D & J Glass Clinic, 40658 267th St., Sioux Falls, SD 57106, 605-361-7524, 9:00 A.M.–5:00 P.M.; fax: 605-361-7216. Doll restoration; composition, bisque, eyes, wigs, etc.

Dean's China Restoration, 131 Elmwood Dr., Cheshire, CT 06410, 800-669-1327, Mon.–Fri. 9:00 A.M.–5:00 P.M. Repair and restoration of china figurines and dolls. Invisible repairs. Mail order worldwide. Free brochure.

Dempsey & Baxter, Sherri and Jack Dempsey, 1009 E. 38th, Erie, PA 16504, 814-825-7690, Mon.–Fri. 10:00 A.M.–5:00 P.M. Antique (pre-1925) doll restoration.

Doll Cellar, Gloria McCarty, 2337 46th Ave. SW, Seattle, WA 98116, 206-938-4446, 8:00 A.M.–10:00 P.M. Doll stands and accessories. Send large SASE and 50 cents for illustrated list.

Doll City U.S.A.®, 2080 S. Harbor Blvd., Anaheim, CA 92802, 714-750-3585, 10:00 A.M.–6:00 P.M.; fax: 714-750-3584. Doll eyes, wigs, stands, and accessories. Catalog $2.

Doll Connection, 117 Market St., Portsmouth, NH 03801, 603-431-5030. Doll parts, supplies, clothes, and restoration. Wed.–Sat. 10:00 A.M.–4:00 P.M. or by appointment.

Doll Heaven, 502 Broadway, New Haven, IN 46774, 219-493-6428, Tues.–Fri. 10:00 A.M.–4:00 P.M., Sat. 10:00 A.M.–2:00 P.M. Doll repair and restoration, specializing in broken bisque and composition dolls. Wigs, bodies, stands, shoes and socks, custom sewing for all dolls.

Doll Hospital, 419 Gentry St. #102, Spring, TX 77373, 713-350-6722, Tues.–Sat. 10:00 A.M.–5:00 P.M.; Sun. 1:00 P.M.–6:00 P.M.; fax: 713-446-3353. Doll repair and restoration, including work on dolls damaged by fire, smoke, or flood. Period costuming. Doll appraisals for insurance purposes.

Doll House, Nanci Zigler, 1263 N. Parker Dr., Janesville, WI 53545, 608-752-7986, afternoons and evenings. Custom-made leather and cloth bodies for antique doll heads. Custom leather parts for antique bodies: lower and upper legs, upper arms, torsos, leather arms with hand-stitched fingers. General antique doll restoration and authentic period dressing. Mail order. Brochure $4.

Doll Lady Doll Hospital, 94 Pent Rd., Branford, CT 06405, 203-488-6193, Mon.–Fri. anytime. Composition ball-jointed doll bodies and parts, china limbs, ceramic bisque parts and bodies, dollhouse doll kits and parts. Doll repairs. Custom-made clothes and leather shoes. Catalog $2.50.

Doll World, Cynthia Bows, 1014-B Oak Hill Rd., Lafayette, CA 94549, 510-283-2299 days, 510-827-5540 evenings. Doll repairs and doll clothes.

Doll'tor Jean's Doll Hospital, RR 2, Box 573, Chadbourne Ridge Road, West Buxton, ME 04093, 207-727-5385, Mon.–Fri. 11:00 A.M.–4:00 P.M., after 7:00 P.M., or leave message. Complete antique and modern doll restoration and repair. Call before sending doll for free estimate so that shipping instructions can be given.

Freda's Doll Repair & Supplies, 6204 Monterey Dr., Klamath Falls, OR 97603, 503-882-2204, 8:00 A.M.–10:00 A.M., answering machine other times. Doll accessories and repairs. Shoes, socks, wigs, hats, some bodies, eyes, and outfits. By appointment.

G. Schoepfer Inc., 138 W. 31st St., New York, NY 10001, 203-250-7794, 9:00 A.M.–5:00 P.M.; fax: 203-250-7796. Glass and plastic eyes for dolls, teddy bears, mechanical banks, etc.

Hamilton Eye Warehouse, Box 450, Moorpark, CA 93021, 805-529-5900, 8:00 A.M.–5:30 P.M. Specializing in doll eyes: paperweights, hollow-blown glass, acrylic, dollhouse doll eyes, 2 mm to 30 mm, 15 colors. Color catalog $1.

I.P.G.R., Inc., PO Box 205, Kulpsville, PA 19443, 800-869-5633 orders only; 215-256-9015, Tues.–Fri. 9:30 A.M.–4:30 P.M., Sat. 9:30 A.M.–1:30 P.M.; fax: 215-256-9644. Complete line of restoration materials for dolls. Catalog $3, refundable with first order.

International Doll Restoration Artists Association, Lavonne Lutterman, Rt. 2, Box 6, Worthington, MN 56187, 507-372-2717, anytime. Workshops for those interested in the restoration of ceramic ware as a career. Workshops on porcelain dolls. Arrangements by telephone only.

J & H China Repairs, 8296 St. George St., Vancouver, BC Canada V5X 3C5, 604-321-1093, 7:30 A.M.–2:00 P.M. Restoration of porcelain, figurines, and dolls.

J & K Curios, 4868 SW Southwind Ct., Dunnellon, FL 34431, 904-465-0756, Mon.–Fri. 9:00 A.M.–9:00 P.M. Porcelain and composition dolls restored. Restoration of mechanical characters, but not the mechanism. Free estimates.

Joyce's Doll House of Parts, 20188 Williamson, Clinton Twp., MI 48035-4091, 810-791-0469, weekdays only till 4:00 P.M. Replacement limbs for antique dolls. Porcelain bisque and china arms and legs for all-bisque dolls; china heads. Wigs, shoes, and other supplies for doll makers.

Kais, Inc., 11943 Discovery Ct., Moorpark, CA 93021, 805-523-8985; fax: 805-523-9170. Dollmaking supplies, including eyes, mohair wigs, synthetic wigs, porcelain slip, china paint, shoes, etc.

Kandyland Dolls, 7600 Birch Ave., PO Box 146, Grand Ronde, OR 97347, 503-879-5153, 8:00 A.M.–6:00 P.M. Restoration of antique dolls. Clothes renewed and copied. Custom sewing. By appointment only.

L. Hulphers, 3153 W. 110th St., Inglewood, CA 90303, 213-678-1957, noon–9:00 P.M., seven days a week. Replacement doll bodies made of composition, leather, cloth, and bisque. All sizes, styles, and shapes.

Lamp Lady and Dolls, Lois M. Beckerdite, 623 Charwood Dr., Cincinnati, OH 45244, 513-528-5628, 10:00 A.M.–10:00 P.M. Doll restoration. Bisque, porcelain, china, composition, hard plastic, cloth, and others. Restringing, wigs, sleep eyes, reproduction head and body parts. Mail order worldwide. Send SASE for free brochure.

Ledgewood Studio, 6000 Ledgewood Dr., Forest Park, GA 30050-3228, 404-361-6098, 10:00 A.M.–4:00 P.M.; fax: 404-361-5030. Specialty doll costuming supplies. Fabrics, trims, buttons, lace, and sewing supplies for costumers and restorers. Mail order and shows only. Catalog $2 plus a long, triple-stamped self-addressed envelope.

MacDowell Laboratories, Robert MacDowell, Rt. 1, PO Box 15A, Aldie, VA 22001, 703-777-6644, Mon.–Fri. mornings, answering machine other times. Restoration of antique dolls; bisque, china, papier-mâché, Schoenhut. Restoration taught on an individual basis. Brochure on restoration classes available.

Madelene Sansom, 5838 Huntington Ave., Richmond, CA 94804, 510-526-0171, 9:00 A.M.–5:00 P.M. Old, out-of-print knit and crochet doll clothes patterns dating back to the turn-of-the-century. Mail order only. Catalog $2.

Manhattan Doll Hospital, 176 Ninth Ave., New York, NY 10011, 212-989-5220, Mon.–Fri. 11:00 A.M.–5:45 P.M. Doll repair.

Mini-Magic, 3675 Reed Rd., Columbus, OH 43220, 614-457-3687, Mon.–Fri., 1:00 P.M.–5:00 P.M. Silks, wools, and cottons useful in costume restoration. Museum washing paste, oxygen bleach for fabric restoration and conservation. Acid-free boxes, tissue. Will answer questions over the phone, letters if an SASE is enclosed with a request.

Morgan's Collectibles, 831 SE 170th Dr., Portland, OR 97233, 503-252-3343, 9:00 A.M.–9:00 P.M. Doll restoration seminars. Send LSASE for free brochure.

New York Doll Hospital, Inc., 787 Lexington Ave., New York, NY 10021, 212-838-7527, 10:00 A.M.–6:00 P.M., except Sunday. Repairs, restorations, and appraisals of antiques dolls and animals. Work performed on all dolls and animals, including battery driven and pull string. Doll wigs, antique doll parts, doll clothes made to order. Mechanical toys repaired. Send item for estimate.

Royal-T Cleaners, 17942 Magnolia, Fountain Valley, CA 92708, 714-963-6110; fax: 714-836-9239. Doll clothes cleaned professionally. Will pre-spot, clean, and ship to you in acid-free tissue paper. Work guaranteed. Call or write for information.

Seeley's Ceramic Service, Inc., PO Box 669, Oneonta, NY 13820-0669, 607-433-1240, Mon.–Fri. 8:00 A.M.–5:00 P.M.; fax: 607-432-2042. Reproduction composition bodies; German, French, lady, baby, and toddler models. Mohair wigs, unstyled, and mohair locks for wig making. Parts for composition bodies, painted in several colors; doll eyes; patterns for dolls. Catalog $9.50.

Speak-Up! Rick Lehman, Mike Vollaro, 25 Stratler Dr., Shirley, NY 11967, 516-924-6256. Chatty Cathy and Mattel talkers repaired. Talk boxes and neck flanges repaired or replaced. Broken torso pieces cold bonded. Dolls and clothing cleaned and mended, hair washed and set, stuffing disinfected.

Viv's Ribbons & Laces, 212 Virginia Hills Dr., Martinez, CA 94553, 510-933-7758, 10:00 A.M.–5:00 P.M. Ribbons, braids, trims, Swiss hat straw, buckles, jewelry findings, and more. Mail order. Wholesale or retail catalog $3.50.

Wilders Doll Center, 350 E. Walton Blvd., Pontiac, MI 48340, 313-334-1177, 9:00 A.M.–9:00 P.M. Repairs, replacement parts for old dolls, wholesale and retail doll supplies, doll clothing,

original patterns, and doll molds.

Wood 'N Wildlife, 9922 Bostwick Park Rd., Montrose, CO 81401, 303-249-5863, before 9:00 P.M. Restoration of papier-mâché dolls, toys, and other objects. Send SASE for more information.

Yesteryears Doll Museum, PO Box 609, Sandwich, MA 02563, 508-888-1711, Mon.–Sat. 10:00 A.M.–4:00 P.M., May 15–Oct. 31. Doll hospital and doll restoration services. Restorations done year-round. Antique doll and miniature museum closed in winter. Appraisals.

Sheryl Garcia, 11 N. Beverly Ave., Youngstown, OH 44515, 216-792-0549. Reproduction of old and new doll clothes. Can copy from photos. Period costuming. Doll underwear. Catalog $3.

Videos

The Art of Doll Repair and Restoration, **Concept Videos,** PO Box 30408, Bethesda, MD 20824, 800-333-8252. 94 minutes. $39.95.

Colemans on Doll Collecting, **Concept Videos,** PO Box 30408, Bethesda, MD 20824, 800-333-8252. 72 minutes. $29.95.

Joe Blitman's Oh, You Beautiful Doll! Featuring Barbie, **Joe Blitman,** 5163 Franklin Ave., Los Angeles, CA 90027, 213-953-6490, 8:00 A.M.–10:00 P.M.; fax: 213-953-0888. Includes a review of Barbie dolls from 1959 to 1993, how to identify specific Barbies, how to clean and restore dolls and clothes, which dolls to invest in, how to buy and sell Barbie dolls. 60 minutes. $24.95 plus $3.50 postage. European format VHS $34.95 plus $7.00 postage.

The Coronation Story, an Alexander Masterpiece, **Sirocco Productions, Inc.,** 5660 E. Virginia Beach Blvd., Suite 105, Norfolk, VA 23502, 804-461-8987; fax: 804-461-4669. Third in the Siroco Historical Doll Series. 90 minutes. $49.95.

Dionne Quintuplet Dolls, an Alexander Exclusive, 1934–1939, **Sirocco Productions, Inc.,** 5660 E. Virginia Beach Blvd., Suite 105, Norfolk, VA 23502, 804-461-8987; fax: 804-461-4669. Second video in the Sirocco Historical Doll Series. 84 minutes. $49.95.

Dolls of the Golden Age, 1880–1915, **Sirocco Productions, Inc.,** 5660 E. Virginia Beach Blvd., Suite 105, Norfolk, VA 23502, 804-461-8987; fax: 804-461-4669. Fourth video in the Sirocco Historical Doll Series. The Colemans present the history of French, German, and American dolls. Informative; great pictures. 60 minutes. $49.95. A future video will cover American dolls up to World War II.

Scarlett Dolls, an Alexander Tradition, 1937–1991, **Sirocco Productions, Inc.,** 5660 E. Virginia Beach Blvd., Suite 105, Norfolk, VA 23502, 804-461-8987; fax: 804-461-4669. 72 minutes. $49.95.

Shirley Temple Dolls & Memorabilia, A Video History of an American Icon, **Sirocco Productions, Inc.,** 5660 E. Virginia Beach Blvd., Suite 105, Norfolk, VA 23502, 804-461-8987, fax: 804-461-4669. 90 minutes. $49.95.

Firearms, Knives & Military Memorabilia

*C*ollectors of military memorabilia search for everything from toy soldiers to working guns. Many of these souvenirs are dangerous, and any gun, hand grenade, or other military object that might hold explosives should be checked by local police or other experts. If you have children in a home with military memorabilia, be sure the guns and knives are safely locked up. Old guns should have the barrels filled so it is impossible to accidentally discharge the guns. Old rifles may be unsafe to shoot, and often even safe antiques have a recoil that will surprise the inexperienced.

Never attempt to sell firearms, swords, dangerous war souvenirs, or other weapons before checking with local police about your city and state laws. The laws concerning the sale of guns are very strict. You could be subject to a fine or jail sentence, or even be held responsible for any death caused by a gun you sold illegally. Don't sell or trade firearms or weapons to friends or other collectors before you know the law.

The safest way to dispose of a gun, rifle, or perhaps an eighteenth-century blunderbuss is to have it auctioned or sold by a reputable firearms dealer. They will be listed in the Yellow Pages of the phone book under "Guns" along with antique gun appraisers. It pays to check on the value of any large collection before offering it for sale.

War souvenirs sell well, especially medals, books, historic documents, photographs, uniform caps and insignias, foreign flags, small firearms, and knives. Be very careful, some types of knives are illegal and should not be sold as anything but collector's items. Knife collecting includes everything from penknives to daggers, regardless of their age. Don't try setting up a table at a garage sale or flea market without knowing the law. Grenades, bullets, and other explosive objects are dangerous, and many become unstable with age. Never handle old explosives before you talk to the local bomb removal squad. It is amazing how often an old box of souvenirs has a dangerous grenade in it.

Never let children near any of these items.

There are many serious collectors of firearms and weapons. Early swords, especially decorated Japanese ceremonial pieces, military dress uniform swords, or any good sword made before 1850, command high prices. Kentucky rifles, muskets, Civil War weapons, dueling pistols, and even World War I and II guns are in demand. Well-made military knives can also be sold to collectors of weapons.

The buyers for these items are not usually found at the average antiques show. Some flea markets have a few tables of dealers who specialize in war materials. Ask the collectors and dealers in your area who sell weapons. They can tell you about the clubs, the shows, and the auctions that are the best for you.

Once or twice a year some Japanese dealers travel from city to city looking for old Japanese swords and other weapons that might have been taken to the United States after World War II. They advertise and set up a buying office in a local hotel. Be sure you check on the value of your war souvenirs before you sell. Few Americans understand the great value of certain ceremonial swords. A local museum expert might be able to tell you the age or rarity of your pieces.

REPAIRS

Repairs to any sort of weapon should only be done by an expert. Many shops that sell modern firearms have staff members who can repair old guns. Other restorers can be located through the publications listed below. Because of the legal problems of shipping guns, repair work must be done locally.

Repairs on knives can be done by companies that repair or sell modern knives, or by specialists in military or hunting equipment.

Price Books

American Premium Guide to Pocket Knives & Razors, 3rd edition, Jim Sargent (Books Americana, Florence, AL, © 1992).

Official Price Guide to Antique and Modern Firearms, 7th edition, Robert H. Balderson (House of Collectibles, New York, © 1994).

Price Guide to Pocket Knives 1890–1970, Jacob N. Jarrett (L-W Books, PO Box 69, Gas City, IN 46933, © 1993).

Standard Catalog of Firearms, 5th edition, Ned Schwing and Herbert Houze (Krause, Iola, WI, © 1995).

Standard Knife Collector's Guide, Roy Ritchie and Ron Stewart (Collector Books, Paducah, KY, © 1993).

Clubs & Publications

American Blade Collectors, *Blade* (MAG), *Edges: The Journal of American Blade Collectors* (NL), 700 E. State St., Iola, WI 54990.

American Edge Collectors Association, *A.E.C.A.* (NL), PO Box 2565, Country Club Hills, IL 60478.

American Society of Military Insignia Collectors, *Trading Post* (MAG), *Newsletter* (NL), 526 Lafayette Ave., Palmerton, PA 18071-1621.

Association of American Military Uniform Collectors (AAMUC), *Footlocker* (NL), PO Box 1876, Elyria, OH 44036.

Japanese Sword Society of the United States, *Japanese Sword Society of the United States Newsletter/ Bulletin* (NL), PO Box 712, Breckenridge, TX 76424.

Napoleonic Society of America, *Member's Bulletin* (NL), 1115 Ponce de Leon Blvd., Clearwater, FL 34616.

National Knife Collectors Association, *National Knife Magazine* (MAG), PO Box 21070, Chattanooga, TN 37421-0070.

Winchester Arms Collectors Association, Inc., *Winchester Collector* (NL), PO Box 6754, Great Falls, MT 59406.

Airgun Ads (NP), Box 33, Hamilton, MT 59840.

Blue & Gray Magazine (MAG), 522 Norton Rd., Columbus, OH 43228 (Civil War memorabilia).

Courier (MAG), 2503 Delaware Ave., Buffalo, NY 14216 (buy, sell, trade Civil War items).

Gun List (NP), *Gun Show Calendar* (MAG), 700 E. State St., Iola, WI 54990.

Gun Report (MAG), PO Box 38, Aledo, IL 61231-0038.

Knife World (NP), PO Box 3395, Knoxville, TN 37927.

Man at Arms (MAG), PO Box 460, Lincoln, RI 02865.

Military Collector Magazine (MAG), PO Box 245, Lyon Station, PA 19536 (annual).

Military Images Magazine (MAG), R.D. 1, Box 99A, Henryville, PA 18332 (military photographs, 1839–1900).

Military Trader (MAG), PO Box 1050, Dubuque, IA 52004-1050.

North South Trader's Civil War Magazine (MAG), PO Drawer 631, Orange, VA 22960 (Civil War memorabilia).

Repairs, Parts & Supplies

Carl "Frank" Funes, 57 Maplewood Ave., Hempstead, NY 11550, 516-481-0147, 7:00 P.M.–9:00 P.M. Restoration of arms, armor, and artifacts; rust removed from weapons. Free brochure.

Dilliott Gunsmithing, Inc., 657 Scarlett Rd., Dandridge, TN 37725, 615-397-9204, Mon.–Fri. 9:00 A.M.–5:00 P.M. Repair and restoration of antique and obsolete firearms. Will make unavailable or obsolete parts. Call or write for shipping and estimate information.

M. W. Dulin, 353 Lambert Dr., Asheboro, NC 27203, 910-625-0643, 9:00 A.M.–9:00 P.M. Repair and restoration of antique swords, antique firearms (flint and percussion), and other weaponry. For an estimate of cost, write describing object and work needed.

Videos

Bowie Knives: 1820–1879, **Marill Productions,** PO Box 460820, San Francisco, CA 94146-0820, 415-282-3844. Knives from the collections of Robert Berryman and Charles Shreiner II, auctioned at Butterfield & Butterfield in 1992. 45 minutes. $39.95 plus $3.50 shipping and handling. Also available, *With Compliments of Colonel Colt,* Colt presentation revolvers and longarms. 55 minutes. $39.95 plus $3.50 shipping and handling. Special price for both videos, $59.95.

Appraisers

Antique Village Museum, Larry Donley, 8512 S. Union Rd., Union, IL 60180, 815-923-9000, anytime; fax: 815-923-2253. Military relic appraisal service. All wars, all nations.

Carl A. Robin, PO Box 30244, Raleigh, NC 27622, 919-787-0206; fax: 919-782-1718. Appraisals of firearms and militaria. Authentication, expert witness testimony, litigation support, consultancy to museums and collectors.

Larry Donley, **Antique Village Museum,** 8512 S. Union Rd., Union, IL 60180, 815-923-9000; fax: 815-923-2253. Military relic appraisal service. All wars, all nations.

Fireplace Equipment

An old fireplace had many pieces of equipment: a set of tools, fireback, andirons, coal basket, fender, and such aids as bellows or match holders. All are considered collectibles and enjoy tremendous popularity.

Some imagination is needed to repair these items. Look in your local phone book for firms that make iron fences or decorative metal pieces. Companies that replate metal often repair. See also Metals.

Repairs, Parts & Supplies

The Brass Knob, Architectural Antiques, 2311 18th St. NW, Washington, DC 20009, 202-332-3370, Mon.–Sat., 10:30 A.M.–6:00 P.M., Sun. 12:00 P.M.–5:00 P.M. Architectural antiques, specializing in restored fireplace mantels, ironwork, and other decorative detail. Warehouse, The Brass Knob, Back Doors, at 1701A Kalorama Rd. NW, Washington, DC 20009. Catalog.

Country Iron Foundry, PO Box 600, Dept. X93, Paoli, PA 19301, 215-353-5542, Mon.–Fri. 9:00 A.M.–5:00 P.M.; fax: 215-644-0367. Cast-iron firebacks, antique and contemporary designs. A fireback will protect the back of the fireplace from heat damage, while radiating more heat into the house. Catalog $3.

Lemee's Fireplace Equipment, 815 Bedford St., Bridgewater, MA 02324, 508-697-2672.

Fireplace cranes, all kinds of fireplace equipment. Catalog $2.

New England Firebacks, PO Box 162, Woodbury, CT 06798, 203-263-5737, 8:00 A.M.–5:00 P.M. Firebacks in Early American designs. Shipped worldwide. Brochure $1.

Pine & Palette Studio, 63 Ventura Dr., Danielson, CT 06239, 203-774-5058; fax: 203-774-3990. Handcrafted fireplace bellows. Repairs, using leather and brass. Free brochure.

Sleepy Hollow Chimney Supply Co., 85 Emjay Blvd., Brentwood, NY 11717, 800-553-5322, 8:00 A.M.–6:00 P.M. Manufacturer and distributor of rigid and flexible stainless flue liners and high temperature ceramic insulation. Manufacturer of Bellfires® refractory fireplace, retrofit to old fireplaces. Catalog $2. Free brochure.

Thomas Loose, Blacksmith-Whitesmith, Rt. 2, Box 2410, Leesport, PA 19533, 215-926-4849, 9:00 A.M.–4:00 P.M. Seventeenth- and eighteenth-century reproduction iron fireplace cooking accessories. Hooks and hardware.

Folk Art

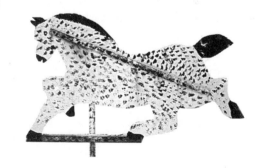

There is an ongoing argument among experts over what is folk art. For the purposes of this book, folk art is whatever is called folk art by some experts. It may have been made in the eighteenth, nineteenth, or twentieth century. It may be naive art by an untrained artist, or an old advertisement, or carnival figure. This is one collecting field with few hard and fast rules of quality, condition, and age. Beauty is in the eye of the beholder, and what seems primitive to one may be considered superior by another. Some collectors prefer pieces with worn paint and rough wooden edges; others want pristine paint. Don't do any restoration unless the piece is so badly damaged that it would be useless without restoration. If you think your folk art piece is of value, be sure to ask an expert before any work is done.

The meaning of the term "folk art" has changed. In the 1950s it referred to stiff, formal American portraits done by itinerant painters of the seventeenth and eighteenth centuries, ships' carved figureheads, cigar store figures, weather vanes, and a few other large signs and carvings. In the 1970s an important book on folk sculpture was written, and folk art took on a new meaning. Large carvings that were often exaggerated or bizarre, duck decoys, quilts, paintings in the Grandma Moses style, commercial weather vanes, carousel horses, and even printed advertising tins all became defined as folk art. (Carousel horses and paintings are in their own chapters in this book; tins are listed in Advertising & Country Store Collectibles; quilts are in Textiles.)

The experts still debate the meaning of the words "folk art," but for you, the seller, folk art is what the customer wants to call folk art. Age is of little importance. Decorative value, humor, the artist's fame, and some "hype" determine the value. We watched a prestigious dealer sell an 1890s iron-bladed lawn mower for several thousand dollars at a folk art show. It had a "sculptural quality." Another dealer was selling a thirty-year-old five-foot figure made of bottle caps for $35,000.

Look at what you want to sell. If it is primitive, colorful, attractive, or very unusual, it will be purchased. Price is arbitrary for most items. There are listed prices for decoys, carousel figures, cigar store figures, quilts, and paintings by known artists or from known schools of painting. These pieces should be researched because treasures do indeed look like trash to the uninformed in this market. There is almost no way to set a price by comparison on a hand-carved bird cage, a cemetery statue, a wooden maypole, or a cast-cement urn. It is one price at a flea market, and quite another if anointed as "art" by a prestigious dealer. (There is growing concern about tombstones and statues removed from cemeteries. It is illegal to own or sell them.)

Look at the folk art books in your library. Visit folk art exhibits. Talk to the dealers and collectors at shows. If your object is large, colorful, and strange, price it a little higher than you might have thought possible. A collection of intricate carvings made by your grandfather or a group of nineteenth-century paintings by a distant relative should possibly be offered for sale through an auction gallery. It is the public who sets the price, and the gallery will show the pieces to more prospective buyers than you could. An appraisal of the collection will only be as good as your appraiser, and most appraisers who are not in the larger cities might not understand the market for unique folk art pieces.

An unusual piece of folk art will sell quickly. We were once offered a large cut-out tin sign of a black boy advertising a store in a small Ohio town. In two months it had been sold and resold to dealers five times until it finally appeared in an ad for a New York folk art gallery at twenty times the price we had originally seen. You will not be able to get the very top price for your folk art, but you should get a third of its retail value in the best shops. Don't ignore commercial items that might attract folk art buyers. Side-show banners and other circus memorabilia, chalk (plaster) figures, birdhouses, garden ornaments, fraternal-order carvings and banners, even religious paintings, prints, and figures are considered folk art.

Duck decoys have attracted a special group of collectors for many years. But in the 1980s the fish decoy was "discovered." Carved wooden fish used by fishermen were eagerly bought as examples of folk art. They became so popular that new ones appeared, and today both duck decoys and fish decoys are being made for the gift shop trade to be sold as new folk art decorations.

In 1993 a duck decoy sold for $192,500, but many decoys also sold for around $25. Most were sold for prices in between these two amounts. Because decoys are collected as art, the most expensive are not necessarily the oldest. The quality of carving and decoration and the fame of the maker determine the price.

Average working decoys in poor condition sell quickly if they are reasonably priced. They should be offered through the normal antiques channels and shown to dealers, collectors, auctioneers, and friends. What is difficult is deciding if your decoys are just average or are "stars."

Once again we suggest you try doing serious research at a library. There are many books that picture decoys and tell about the important makers. Try to identify your decoys. Remember, the decoy was originally made to lure a bird, and your decoy should be an identifiable fowl. The nondescript, rough silhouette of a bird is not a valuable decoy although it will sell as a decorative piece of folk art.

If your decoys seem to be valuable, you should take them to an appraiser or auction gallery to get an expert opinion. If you live in an area with no decoy appraisers nearby, you should be able to get enough information by sending a clear photograph to one of the auction galleries that regularly sells decoys. The most successful decoy auctions have been on the East Coast.

Decoy collectors are a special group with their own clubs, publications, and events. It is not easy to learn about them. Talk to local collectors to learn about events in your area. Those who make modern decoys can often restore old ones. Many decoys are included in shows and sales that interest the folk art and "country look" collectors.

REPAIR

Collectors of hunting decoys are often as interested in modern decoys of top quality as they are in older, used ones. Waterfowl decoys are the most popular, and many collectors also want fish decoys. Restoration should be done by a craftsman in the appropriate field. A painted figure might be restored by a carousel-figure expert or a furniture-restoration firm. Paper, glass, or metal pieces require other specialists. We once had a tin chimney replaced on a folk art house by the man putting metal heat ducts in our room addition, and painted by the house painter who worked on the walls.

Clubs & Publications

Folk Art Society of America, *Folk Art Messenger* (NL), PO Box 17041, Richmond, VA 23226 (nonprofit organization that studies folk art).

Great Lakes Fish Decoy Collectors & Carvers Association, *Thru the Shanty Hole* (NL), 35824 W. Chicago, Livonia, MI 48150.

Decoy Hunter Magazine (MAG), 901 N. 9th St., Clinton, IN 47842.

Decoy Magazine (MAG), PO Box 277, Burtonsville, MD 20866.

Folk Art (MAG), Museum of American Folk Art, 61 W. 62nd St., New York, NY 10023.

Folk Art Finder (NL), 117 N. Main St., Essex, CT 06426.

Appraiser

Salt & Chestnut Weathervanes, 651 Rt. 6A at Maple St., West Barnstable, MA 02668, 508-362-6085, 11:00 A.M.–5:00 P.M.; fax: 508-362-3012. Weather vanes appraised.

Furniture

*T*he largest antiques you will have to sell are probably pieces of furniture. They are also among the most valuable, though the size creates special problems and limits your methods of sale. "Antique" furniture, which includes anything made before 1960, has a market value that can be determined from price books, auctions, and shop sales. You will hear about chairs that sell for $150,000 each, even one that brought $2.75 million,

but these are the great rarities of the eighteenth century. You have less valuable pieces.

Any usable piece of furniture has a resale value. Higher prices are paid for pieces in fine condition. Because new furniture is made with staples, glue, and veneers, well-constructed older pieces, even those in poor condition, can be sold. Study the price books and the reference books in the library to find out about your furniture. If you have an antique-collecting friend, ask for an opinion about the pieces.

If you own furniture that is exceptionally large (for example, a large bed, a grandfather clock that is over eight feet tall, or a very wide desk), be sure to determine how it can be removed from the room—maybe there is a removable finial or top cresting—and note this for the prospective buyer since wise collectors have learned the hazards. A seven-foot-eleven-inch piece will sell for a better price than an eight-foot-one-inch piece because most of today's homes have eight-foot ceilings. Deduct 50 percent from the value if a bookcase, desk, grandfather clock, or bed is over eight feet high or is too wide to go through an average door.

If you have any information about the furniture (old bills, where and when the pieces were bought, maker's labels, type of wood, pictures of the piece before you restored it, or written family history), present it to the prospective buyer with the furniture. A label adds to the value by 10 to 100 percent if the piece is worth less than $30,000. On the superstars of the furniture world, the pieces worth over $30,000, a label can increase the price four to five times. The fame of the maker determines how much value is added.

If you inherited the pieces from elderly relatives, search all seat cushions for hidden valuables. Look for hidden compartments in desks. Look underneath drawers or inside the furniture. Carefully slit the backing on framed pictures and mirrors and look for valuable papers or money.

If you think there are some pieces of furniture over fifty years old, contact a local auctioneer and talk about the possible value at auction. The auction will advertise good antiques and get a higher price than you could through your own ads. If you are selling the entire contents of a house, a house sale might be best. The furniture may not bring top prices, but it will bring buyers, including antiques dealers, to the sale, and the other small items will sell for more. Do not invite a dealer in to pick out a few items if you are trying to sell the entire contents of the house. A smart dealer will buy the few good pieces, and you will have trouble getting anyone to come to see the remaining ones.

If you advertise a sale, you need a few fast-selling items, like a rolltop desk or large dining room set, to entice dealers and collectors. Auctioneers will want the entire contents of the house only if there are some choice pieces. Price your pieces for your local market. It takes an expert to determine the age of a piece in a period style. A Chippendale chair dating from the eighteenth century is worth $1,500 to $150,000; a Chippendale-style chair from the nineteenth century is worth $2,000 to $3,000; a twentieth-century copy is worth $200 to $500. If you have good reason to believe that your furniture is antique and may not bring a good price at a local auction, write to an out-of-town auction gallery about selling it. Send photographs of the front, back, and bottom construction. Oak furniture sells best in the West, elaborate Victorian in the South, and Art Deco in the East and southern Florida.

For period or old reproduction chairs of average quality: A pair is worth three times as much as a single; a set of four is worth six to seven times as much as a single. Six chairs are worth ten to twelve times as much as a single. A set of eight chairs is worth twelve to fifteen times the price of one chair. A set of twelve chairs including two armchairs is worth twenty times the price of one chair.

Dining-room table and chair sets should be sold as a unit. The breakfronts and buffets may be sold separately for better overall prices. A bedroom set usually brings the highest price when sold as a unit. Don't split the set so a friend can have the dresser. Offer the full set, but take bids on the individual pieces in case you can't sell the full set at a high enough price. Sell a piano to a local piano store, or place an ad to sell it from the house. Unless they are top quality, pianos are very difficult to sell. The old square pianos do not stay in tune, sell low, and are usually purchased to be made into desks.

Serious collectors searching for pre-1875 painted furniture in original condition will pay a premium. Choice, painted furniture in good condition is worth 50 percent more than an unpainted similar piece. The paint was not as durable as polished wood; in poor condition it has to be sold at a lower price. Black ebonized Victorian furniture used to be worth 30 percent less than a similar piece with an unpainted finish, but sometime in 1992, collectors started to pay a premium for good ebonized pieces. It is very difficult to restore. If the original finish on a chair or table was painted and the piece has been stripped to natural wood, deduct 75 percent. In other words, a painted piece that is stripped is worth less than a similar piece that was originally made with a natural wood finish. Painted furniture made after 1900 is not rare and not yet in great demand.

Wicker, twig, cast-iron, and horn pieces are back in style and sell well. Furniture from the 1950s by important makers brings good prices at auction or from Art Moderne dealers. Some pieces from the 1960s are gaining in value. Names of makers from the 1850s to 1950s such as WOOTON, HERMAN MILLER, GUSTAV STICKLEY, LARKIN, HUNZINGER, POTIER AND STYMUS, HERTER, ROUX, NOGUCHI, and RUSSEL WRIGHT add value.

Do not worry too much about how to move heavy antique furniture. There are always local movers listed in the telephone book. There are also some long-distance moving companies that specialize in moving uncrated antique pieces. Ask any local antiques dealer for the name of someone in your area.

Most of the furniture that is bought and sold in America is English or American in design and manufacture. Other, less easily recognized types are also in demand. Pictures of all these types of furniture can be found in books at your library. Identify your piece from the pictures, then check in the price books for values.

FURNITURE STYLES LIST

IMPORTED

Oriental (eighteenth–twentieth centuries). Dark woods, often teak or rosewood, oriental designs. Made in China, Japan, Korea, or India. Later pieces have elaborate carvings, lacquer, stone inlay. Some pieces were made in European shapes but with oriental woods and decorations. All-wooden armchairs, screens, plant stands, large display cabinets.

Scandinavian (eighteenth–nineteenth centuries). Brightly painted peasant designs cover much of the wood. Blue and red preferred. Large cupboards, lift-top blanket chests, carved wooden chairs.

Dutch (eighteenth–nineteenth centuries). Traditional European shapes in Chippendale through Victorian styles covered with elaborate inlay in small designs. Chairs, tables, chests of drawers, cabinets.

French (eighteenth–nineteenth centuries). Louis XV style, rococo flowing lines, ornate curves, cabriole legs, asymmetrical; and Louis XVI style, dainty, neoclassical, straight legs.

Fantasy Furniture (1800–present). Carved shell chairs, Egyptian, Greek, Persian-inspired accessories, Bugatti designs.

AMERICAN

Late Empire (1825–1850). Heavy; pillar and scroll design. Mahogany, cherry, maple, solid or veneer. Chests of drawers, round wooden knobs. Scroll-arm, rolltop sofas, lyre-base tables, sleigh beds, wooden-back chairs.

Victorian Gothic Revival (1830–1850). Designs resemble gothic church arches; carvings, little upholstery. Walnut, rosewood, mahogany, maple. Straight-back chairs with carved high backs, settees, armchairs, washstands.

Victorian Rococo Revival (1845–1865). French-looking, ornamented, curved, carved fruit and flowers. Rosewood, mahogany. Curved sofas, parlor sets, marble-topped tables, slipper chairs.

Eastlake Victorian (1870–1900). Rectangular furniture, contrasting color woods, incised lines. Walnut, burl, maple, veneer, oak. High-back beds, washstands, chairs, chests, and mirror dressers.

Colonial Revival or Centennial (1876–1950). Copies of the eighteenth- and early nineteenth-century William and Mary, Chippendale, Sheraton, Empire, and other designs.

Golden Oak (1880–1920). Mass-produced, heavy, dark or light oak, ash. Asymmetrical cabinets, chests of drawers, rolltop desks, claw-foot or pedestal dining tables, press-back chairs.

Cottage (1890–1920). Painted Eastlake adaptations, marbleized or solid color paint, trimmed with lines, flowers, pictorial medallions. Bedroom sets, small tables, chairs.

Mission (1900–1920). Straight lines, solid wood—usually oak, no ornamentation, smooth surface. Rectangular tables, chairs, sofas, bookcases.

Office Furniture (1900–1930). Mission-inspired working pieces made for the office. Filing cabinets, large rolltop desks, lift-up glass-front stacked bookcases, captain's chairs, children's school desks.

Art Deco (1910–1930). Straight lines, geometric. Light-colored wood or black lacquer finish, mirrored surfaces. Square pedestal tables, bedroom sets.

Twig or Rustic (1890–1930). Bark-covered branches joined together to form chairs, tables, beds, plant stands, smoking stands. Animal horns, antlers, other natural materials used regionally.

Country (1700–1950). A "look," unsophisticated, worn, simple, handmade, solid wood, faded paint. Tables, large cupboards and shelf units, wooden chairs, stools.

Waterfall (1930s). Patterned veneer on cabinet doors, tabletops, or bed backs placed to make V-shaped design. Rounded corners, round mirrors. Base woods are poplar or ash. Bedroom and dining room sets.

"Costume" (1930s). Copies of earlier brass and ormolu-trimmed furniture, especially French Louis XV and XVI. The name comes from costume jewelry, inexpensive copies of real jewelry.

Moderne (1930–1950s). Sometimes called Hollywood Art Deco. The theatrical, modern-looking furniture seen in movies. Art Deco–inspired but a bit less severe and more dramatic. Coffee tables, dressing tables, glass-topped tables, rounded upholstered chairs.

Mid-Century Modern (1950s). Organically shaped, new materials and technology. Plastic, plywood, chrome, aluminum, steel. Interchangeable units and stacked chairs, coffee tables, wall-mounted shelf units. Blond "Scandinavian" sets.

Wicker (1850–1930). Victorian and Art Deco style pieces made of wicker or wicker-like twisted paper. Sometimes painted.

Brass and Iron Beds (1900–1920). Victorian to Deco styles. Solid brass or brass plated.

REPAIRS

Repairs seriously change the value of an antique or collectible. The rarer the piece, the more acceptable a repair. An eighteenth-century American table can have replaced casters, a spliced foot, or even a restored edge, with no great loss in value. A twentieth-century table should be in pristine condition. The supply is greater and a perfect table probably exists, so a repaired piece loses value.

You should do easy repairs before you try to sell a piece. Dust and wipe off dirt. Rub the edges of drawers with paraffin to make them open easily. Reglue any loose parts or veneer. Tighten knobs and glue any wobbly legs by forcing the appropriate glue into the joints. Polish brasses if they need it. A light rubbing with scratch polish will often improve the look of the surface.

Sometimes an accurate restoration is impossible because there is no model to follow. We saw a Goddard block-front desk that should have been worth over $200,000. Unfortunately, all of the legs had been cut off in the 1880s, and new feet were made. There is no way to know what the original legs looked like, so the desk is worth about $20,000.

Formulas for pricing are only a guide and not infallible. The formulas below are for pieces in attractive condition with almost invisible repairs.

Chest of drawers, good to excellent quality, pre-1850. If brasses are replacements, deduct 10 percent. If finish has been totally restored, deduct 10 percent. If one front foot has been replaced, deduct 10 percent. If two rear feet have been replaced, deduct 15 percent. If all feet have been replaced, deduct 70 percent. If important decorative carving has been replaced or if veneer is new, deduct 20 percent.

Chair, good quality, pre-1850. Look in a general price guide for a chair similar to yours. If the slip seat has been replaced, deduct nothing. If glued block braces (the structural supports under the chair) have been replaced, deduct nothing. If one or two leg brackets are restored, deduct nothing. If all leg brackets are restored, deduct 10 percent. If one leg is replaced, deduct 33 percent. If a splat or an important part of the chair back has been replaced, deduct 33 percent. If the top crest rail is replaced, deduct 10 to 15 percent.

Early nineteenth-century furniture with veneered fronts. If veneer is replaced, deduct 50 to 90 percent. Original veneer is an important part of the design of the furniture. A small, well-matched patch does not lower the value, but a totally new veneer surface cannot imitate the original appearance. Sometimes just one drawer has replaced veneer. If it is a well-matched piece of wood, deduct 50 percent. If all the veneer on the front of the piece is replaced, deduct 90 percent.

Eighteenth- or early nineteenth-century table, good quality. If top is replaced, deduct 50 percent. If one plain leg is replaced, deduct 20 percent. If all carved feet have been restored or replaced, deduct 90 percent. Watch out for "marriages," a top of one table put on the legs of another. Look underneath the top for signs of this. There will be unexpected screw holes or color variations.

Desk, pre–1900. If the interior compartments or drawers are missing, deduct 30 percent. If the interior compartments or drawers are accurately replaced, deduct 20 percent. If one interior drawer or drawer front is a replacement, deduct nothing. If the desk has been created from a reworked bookshelf cabinet (drawer removed, fall front added), deduct 75 percent.

Other. If the top of a table or chest is warped but can be fixed, deduct 20 percent. If the top of a table or chest is extremely warped or split, the sides split, or inlay or marquetry badly damaged, deduct 75 percent. If the top of a table or chest has been reworked, given rounded edges, extra trim or carving, deduct 50 percent. If the marble top of a Victorian table is badly cracked or damaged, deduct 50 percent.

Watch out for repairs that affect value on later pieces of furniture. Glass doors on secretary-desks are more desirable than wooden doors because they are preferred for display. Add 50 percent to the value for original glass, but if the glass is a replacement for a solid wooden door, subtract 50 percent.

Welsh cupboards with original spoon holders are worth 50 percent more than plain cupboards, but if the spoon holders have been newly added, price the cupboard like a plain one.

REFINISHING AND RESTORING

Refinishing and restoring furniture has been discussed in dozens of books. For precise information on what to do, how to do it, and what finishes are best, we suggest that you go to your local hardware or paint store or library, and study the products, books, and methods. Local experts are listed in the Yellow Pages of your telephone book. We have listed a few of the major books and included sources for many of the materials. You may find additional sources in the hardware section.

The general rule for refinishing an antique is "less is better." Never strip a piece that can be restored. Never remove a painted surface that can be saved. If you want furniture with a natural wood finish, don't buy an antique with an original painted finish. For many years, collectors used a polish made with boiled linseed oil, which has a finish that darkens with age and cannot be removed. Do not use it. Certain early paints made with buttermilk, blood, and other pigments are almost impossible to remove from wood pores. Many pieces of furniture are made of a variety of woods, so stripping and refinishing may result in a hodgepodge of colors.

Our ancestors seem to have delighted in surrounding themselves with chairs. Inventories of homes from the late eighteenth century list over a dozen chairs even in small bedrooms. We often wonder how they found room for all of them. Whatever the reason, the chair is still one of the most popular pieces of furniture in a home. An odd chair from a different period is often placed in a room as a special accent.

Refinishing and restoring chairs can be handled by most amateurs. Recaning, upholstering, and other more complicated parts of refinishing may require a few special lessons, but many adult education centers and schools offer this type of instruction. Libraries are filled with books that furnish detailed refinishing information. Most of these services are available through local decorating shops or services. Look in the Yellow Pages under "Caning," "Furniture Repairing & Refinishing," and "Upholsterers."

Sometimes a wooden chair needs minor "tightening." The glue has dried and the parts wobble. Special products found in hardware stores can solve this problem. Just squirt a bit of the special glue into the loose joints. If the parts are very loose, you may have to take the arm or leg off the chair, clean the pegs or posts and holes, and reglue them with modern wood glue.

Some people hesitate to buy antique beds because they worry about technical problems, such as special mattress sizes and special restoration techniques. The problems can be solved in various ways:

1. Measure an antique bed carefully before buying it. Make sure the bed is not too high for your ceiling, because surgery on bedposts reduces the bed's value.
2. Rope "springs" are satisfactory, but they must be properly laced and tightened periodically. A box spring can also be used if it is supported by metal brackets. Standard brackets can be screwed to the frame, but the best solution is to have six or eight hanging supports custom-made by an ornamental ironworker. They do not harm the frame or reduce the value of the bed. If the box spring combined with a standard mattress is too high, a thinner foam-rubber mattress can be substituted.
3. Odd-sized mattresses and box springs can be custom-made in most major cities or ordered by mail.

4. Antique-style bed hangings, canopies, and rope springs are also available.

It is best to be sure your bed is one of the standard sizes in use today if you plan to use readily available sheets and bedspreads. Brass beds require special care; restoration for these is discussed in the section on Metals.

Price Books

Collector's Encyclopedia of American Furniture, Volume 3, Robert W. and Harriett Swedberg (Collector Books, Paducah, KY, © 1994).

Colonial Revival Furniture, David P. Lindquist and Caroline C. Warren (Wallace-Homestead, Radnor, PA, © 1993).

Country Furniture, Ellen M. Plante (Wallace-Homestead, Radnor, PA, © 1993).

Furniture of the Arts & Crafts Period (L-W Books, PO Box 69, Gas City, IN 46933, © 1992).

The 1912 Quaint Furniture Catalog, edited by Peter A. Copeland and Janet H. Copeland, and *Price Guide 1993–1994 for Quaint Furniture.* Reprint of Stickley Brothers Company catalog with separate price guide that corresponds to original catalog (The Parchment Press, 321 Park Ave., Parchment, MI 49004, © 1993).

Warman's Furniture, Harry L. Rinker (Wallace-Homestead Books Co., Radnor, PA, © 1994).

Books and Leaflets on Repair

Art of Painted Finish for Furniture & Decoration, Isabel O'Neil (William Morrow & Co., New York, © 1971).

Collecting & Restoring Wicker Furniture, Richard Saunders (Crown Publishers, New York, © 1990).

Complete Book of Furniture Repair & Refinishing, Ralph Parsons Kinney (Charles Scribner's Sons, New York, © 1981).

Complete Book of Furniture Restoration, Tristan Salazar (St. Martin's Press, New York, © 1982).

Conservation and Restoration of Antique Furniture, Stan Learoyd (Sterling Publishing Co., New York, © 1983).

Early American Decoration, Esther Stevens Brazer (Pond-Ekberg Company, Springfield, MS, © 1961).

Emyl Jenkins' Appraisal Book, Emyl Jenkins (Crown Publishers, New York, © 1989).

Furniture Care and Conservation, 3rd edition, Robert F. McGiffin, Jr. (AASLH, 172 Second Avenue North, Suite 102, Nashville, TN 37201, © 1992).

How to Gold Leaf Antiques and Other Art Objects, Donald L. Chambers (Crown Publishers, New York, © 1973).

How-to Guide, leaflet, Savogran Company (259 Lenox Street, Norwood, MA 02062).

Keeping It All Together, Marc A. Williams (Ohio Antique Review, Inc., 12 East Stafford Avenue, Worthington, OH 43085, © 1988).

Knock on Wood, Bruce E. Johnson (G.P. Putnam's Sons, New York, © 1984).

Manual of Traditional Wood Carving, Paul N. Hasluck (Dover Publications, New York, © 1977).

Preserving Your Investment, Marc A. Williams (Furniture Conservation Services, 572 Washington Street, Haverhill, MA 01830, © 1983).

Windsor Chairmaking, Michael Dunbar (Hastings House Publishers, New York, © 1976).

Wood Polishing and Finishing Techniques, Aidan Walker (Little, Brown & Co., Boston, © 1985).

Woodframe Furniture Restoration, Alan Smith (Little, Brown & Co., Boston, © 1985).

Club & Publication

Wooton Desk Owners Society, *Wooton Desk Owners Society Newsletter* (NL), Box 128, Bayside, NY 11361.

Repair, Parts & Supplies

A Carolina Craftsman, 975 S. Avocado St., Anaheim, CA 92805, 714-776-7877, 8:00 A.M.–5:00

P.M.; fax: 714-533-0894. Catalog sales of antique replacement hardware for houses and furniture. Free literature on a specific item; complete catalog set $5, refundable with first order.

Able to Cane, 439 Main St., PO Box 429, Warren, ME 04864, 207-273-3747, anytime. Restoration of antique furniture. Caning and basketry supplies. Catalog $1.

Antique Restoration Co., 440 E. Centre Ave., Newtown, PA 18940, 215-958-2343, Tues.–Sat. 9:00 A.M.–5:00 P.M. Furniture stripping, repairs, and refinishing. Faux finishes. Brass and copper polishing, caning, rush, and split weave. Free brochure.

Antique Restoring Studio Inc., DBA Trefler & Sons, 99 Cabot St., Needham, MA 02194, 617-444-2685, Mon.–Fri. 9:00 A.M.–5:00 P.M., Sat. 10:00 A.M.–2:00 P.M.; fax: 617-444-0659. Restoration of furniture, including painted furniture and oriental lacquer. Repair breaks, replace missing parts and missing veneer and inlay, repair fire and water damage. Free brochure.

Artistic Finishers East, Wade Denson, 2350 E. Javelina Ave., Mesa, AZ 85204, 800-283-5323 anytime; fax: 914-368-1535. Gold- and metal-leaf supplies, tools, books, and instructional materials.

Barap Specialties, 835 Bellows, Frankfort, MI 49635, 800-322-7273, 9:00 A.M.–5:00 P.M. Chair cane, tools, finishing materials, hardware, etc. Catalog $1.

Bob Morgan Woodworking Supplies, 1123 Bardstown Rd., Louisville, KY 40204, 502-456-2545, 8:00 A.M.–4:30 P.M.; fax: 502-456-4752. Veneers, faces, 2 plys, flexibles, burls, exotics, thin hardwoods, chair repairing supplies, etc. Brochure $1.

Brass Foundry Castings, The Old Wheelwright Shop, Brasted Forge, Brasted, Kent England TN16 1JL, 0959-563863, 9:00 A.M.–5:00 P.M.; fax: 0959-561262. Furniture mounts, escutcheon pins, hand-cut nails, kidney bow keys, clock mounts, handmade brass chicken

wire, lead sheet, candle sconces, galleries, brass stringing, hinges, feet, castors, and other fittings. Repairs to vintage fittings. Catalog. Write for price and ordering information.

Broadnax Refinishing Products, Inc., 112 Carolina Forest, Chapel Hill, NC 27516, 919-967-1011; fax: 919-942-4686. Furniture care and refinishing products, including furniture refinisher, wood preservative, and furniture and household cleaners. Free flyer. *Good News for Antiques and Fine Furniture,* a book on refinishing, cleaning, and repairing furniture, is available for $7.50.

C & H Supply, 5431 Mountville Rd., Adamstown, MD 21710, 301-663-1812, Mon.–Fri. 9:00 A.M.–5:00 P.M.; fax: 301-874-2524. Reproduction brass hardware, wood and porcelain knobs, table parts, chair-caning supplies, replacement chair seats, short bed rails, cannonballs for iron and brass beds. Veneers, paint and varnish removers, stains and lacquers. Most orders shipped within 24 hours. Catalog $4.

Cane & Basket Supply Company, 1238 S. Cochran Ave., Los Angeles, CA 90019, 213-939-9644; fax: 213-939-7237. Chair caning supplies, rawhide, fiber rush, pressed fiber replacement seats, rubber webbing for modern chairs, Shaker tape, books, tools, and supplies. Mail order worldwide. Catalog $2.

Caning Shop, 926 Gilman St., Dept. KOV, Berkeley, CA 94710-1494, 510-527-5010, Tues.–Fri. 10:00 A.M.–6:00 P.M., Sat. 10:00 A.M.–2:00 P.M., answering machine after hours. Complete line of chair caning and basketry supplies, including cane, splint, reed, rush, sea grass, Shaker tape, pressed-fiber seats, books, and tools. Catalog $1, refundable with purchase.

Carter Canopies, Box 808, Troutman, NC 28166, 704-528-4071, 9:00 A.M.–5:00 P.M.; fax: 704-528-6437. Hand-tied fishnet canopies, valances and table overlays, custom dust ruffles, spreads, and coverlets. Mail order nationwide. Brochure $1.

The Chair & Uphostery Shop, Lawrence Nelson, 101 South St., Chagrin Falls, OH 44022, 216-247-2126, any day 10:00 A.M.–5:00 P.M. Open Friday and Saturday 10:00 A.M.–noon. Gluing, repair, finish restoration, upholstering. Cane, rush, splint, and Shaker tape weaving. Patio furniture strapping. Free brochure.

Chatree's, 711 Eighth St., SE, Washington, DC 20003, 202-546-4950. Furniture repaired and refinished. Caning, upholstering, marbleizing, wood graining, glazing, gilding, and faux finish.

Country Accents, PO Box 437, Montoursville, PA 17754, 717-478-4127, 9:00 A.M.–5:00 P.M. Handcrafted pierced metal panels in sixteen different types of metal. Custom work a specialty. Materials for the do-it-yourselfer, including piercing tools, blank metal stock, and patterns. Mail order U.S. and Canada. Catalog $5.

Craftsman Wood Service Company, 1735 W. Cortland Ct., Addison, IL 60101, 708-629-3100, 8:30 A.M.–5:00 P.M.; fax: 708-629-8292 for information; 800-543-9367 for orders. Over 4,000 items for the wood hobbyist, including cane and upholstery supplies, tools, finishes, and hard-to-find hardware. Mail order worldwide. Catalog $1.

Crossland Studio, 118 E. Kingston Ave., Charlotte, NC 28203, 704-332-3032, Mon.–Fri. 8:30 A.M.–6:00 P.M., Sat. 9:00 A.M.–4:00 P.M. Custom stripping, refinishing, and repair of antique furniture.

David Linker Ltd., 109 S. 5th St., 5th Floor, Brooklyn, NY 11211, 718-388-9443, Mon.–Fri. 9:00 A.M.–5:00 P.M. Conservation and restoration of antique furniture. Specialists in seventeenth- and eighteenth-century French furniture.

Dawson's Antiques, Tom Dawson, 512 N. Ave. B, Washington, IA 52353, 319-653-5043, 9:00 A.M.–5:00 P.M., answering machine other times. Antique furniture restored.

Deborah Bigelow Associates, Inc., 291 Main St., Beacon, NY 12508-2735, 914-838-3928, 10:00 A.M.–4:00 P.M. Furniture conservation and restoration. Upholstery conservation, collection surveys, necessary on-site treatment, care and maintenance recommendations, technical analysis, insurance estimates, illustrated talks on antique furniture conservation. Free brochure.

Deller Conservation Group Ltd., 2600 Keslinger Rd., Geneva, IL 60134, 708-232-1708, 8:00 A.M.–5:00 P.M. Specializing in the conservation of historic and artistic wooden artifacts and furniture. French polishing, preservation of polychrome surfaces and gilded surfaces, documentation, and analysis. Send LSASE for brochure.

Derby Desk Company, 140 Tremont St., Brighton, MA 02135, 617-787-2707, 10:30 A.M.–5:00 P.M. Restores antique desks made c.1860–1890.

Dotty McDaniel, 1900 Stoney Ridge Rd., Cumming, GA 30131, 404-887-8518, anytime. Chair caning. Laced cane, pressed cane, split oak, binder cane, fiber rush, natural rush, sea grass, Shaker tape, and Danish cord. Wicker restoration and repair.

18th Century Hardware Company, Inc., 131 E. Third St., Derry, PA 15627, 412-694-2708, 8:00 A.M.–4:30 P.M. Manufacturers of hardware for antique furniture. Can duplicate almost anything. Metal items cleaned, polished, and lacquered. Catalog $3.

Engelhard & Koenig Inc., 2 Jansen St., Danbury, CT 06810-7026, 203-778-1441, 8:00 A.M.–5:00 P.M.; fax: 203-778-1453. Furniture refinishing, antique furniture restoration, exact replica custom furniture. Free brochure.

Finishing Products, 8165 Big Bend, St. Louis, MO 63119, 314-962-7575, Mon.–Sat. 9:00 A.M.–5:00 P.M.; fax: 314-962-7785. Aniline stains, custom lacquers and coatings, strippers, heat guns, crackle paint, graining tools, glazes. Furniture hardware and caning supplies. Catalog.

Florentine Antiques & Restoration, Giordano Grazzini, 86 Regan Rd., Ridgefield, CT 06877, 205-431-8726, 9:00 A.M.–5:30 P.M.; fax: 201-431-8726. Antique furniture restoration, specializing in carving, gilding, turning, inlay, and French polish using traditional European techniques.

Floyd J. Rosini, Route 22 North, Millerton, NY 12546, 518-789-3582, 9:00 A.M.–5:00 P.M.; fax: 518-789-6386. Furniture repaired, restored, and reconditioned. French polishing. Furniture care products, including furniture and metal polish, touch-up markers, and other supplies. Appraisals of English and American furniture.

Formby's Workshop, 825 Crossover Ln. #240, Memphis, TN 38117, 800-367-6297, Mon.–Fri. noon–8:00 P.M., Sat. 10:00 A.M.–6:00 P.M. Removers, stains, clear finishes, accessories. Free brochure and hints booklet.

Furniture Library, 1009 N. Main St., High Point, NC 27262, 910-883-4011, 9:00 A.M.–5:00 P.M.; fax: 910-883-6579. Over 7,000 books on furniture and furniture-related subjects are available for research. Free catalog of books for sale.

Furniture Restoration Supply Co., 5498 Rt. 34, Oswego, IL 60543, 800-432-2745, 708-554-2745, Mon.–Fri. 8:00 A.M.–5:00 P.M., Sat. 8:00 A.M.–noon; fax: 708-554-1545, anytime. Upholstery supplies, caning and wicker repair supplies, stripping and refinishing supplies. Catalog $2, refundable with first purchase.

Galleria Hugo, 304 E. 76th St., New York, NY 10021, 212-288-8444, 9:00 A.M.–6:00 P.M. Restoration of furniture mounts and decorative arts. By mail or by appointment only.

George G. Whitmore Co., Inc., 311 Farm Hill Rd., Middletown, CT 06457, 203-346-3492, Mon.–Fri. 8:00 A.M.–4:30 P.M. Furniture restoration. Free brochure.

Gold Leaf Studios, Inc., PO Box 50156, Washington, DC 20091, 202-638-4660, Mon.–Fri. 9:00 A.M.–5:30 P.M.; fax: 202-347-4569. Conservation of gilded furniture.

GST Designs, 3 Russell Rd., Stratford, CT 06497, 203-375-3807, 6:00 P.M.–9:00 P.M. Wood turning. Can duplicate any type of spindle or finial, for modern or antique furniture, in hard or soft wood. Single items or production runs.

Gundula's & Peerless Rattan at the Wrap n Post, 624 S. Burnett Rd., Springfield, OH 45505, 513-323-0003, 513-323-7353. Retail and wholesale chair caning supplies. Hours: Mon.–Fri. 8:30 A.M.–5:30 P.M.; Sat. 8:30 A.M.–2:30 P.M. Orders may be left on answering machine. Phone orders shipped promptly. Free price list.

Handpainted Walls, Floors, Cloths & Furniture, Jacquelyn Sage, 2272 W. 29th Pl., Los Angeles, CA 90018, 213-733-5459, 11:00 A.M.–2:00 P.M. and 4:00 P.M.-6:00 P.M. Furniture glazed, decorated, finished, or unfinished.

Hardware+Plus, Inc., 701 E. Kingsley Rd., Garland, TX 75041, 214-271-0319, technical assistance; 800-522-7336, order line; fax: 214-271-9726. Period and reproduction furniture hardware and parts, including knobs, latches, hall tree hooks, assorted bed and trunk parts, Victorian and Eastlake hardware, pressed-fiber seats, and caning supplies. Free brochure. Hardware catalog $5.

Hope Co., Inc., PO Box 749, 12777 Pennridge Drive, Bridgeton, MO 63044, 314-739-7254, 8:00 A.M.-4:00 P.M.; fax: 314-739-7786. Hope's Furniture Refinisher, Tung Oil, Tung Oil Varnish, and Lemon Oil. Free brochure.

Howard Products, Inc., 411 W. Maple Ave., Monrovia, CA 91016, 818-357-9545, 800-266-9545, 7:30 A.M.-4:30 P.M.; fax: 818-359-6440. Wood care products: Restor-A-Finish restores existing finish; Feed-N-Wax feeds wood, Orange Oil cleans and polishes wood. Silver polish, copper and brass polish, and jewelry cleaner. Free information pack.

Image Maintenance Assurance, Inc., David Kummerow, PO Box 8407, Bartlett, IL 60103, 708-830-7965, 8:00 A.M.-7:00 P.M.; fax: 708-830-1458. Repair and restoration. Refabrication of parts, including glass, metal, and marble. Appraisals of art, furniture, and household goods. Will make house calls.

Ingrid Sanborn & Daughter, 85 Church St., West Newbury, MA 01985, 508-363-2253, 9:00 A.M.–5:00 P.M., 7:00 P.M.–8:30 P.M. Restoration and reproduction of reverse paintings on glass. Restoration of painted furniture; color matching a specialty. Restoration of original gilded surfaces and japanning.

Joseph Biunno, 129 W. 29th St., 11th Floor, New York, NY 10001, 212-629-5630, 9:00 A.M.–5:00 P.M.; fax: 212-268-4577. Restoration and refinishing of fine furniture and antiques. Repair and restoration of antique locks and keys. Manufacturers of custom drapery hardware.

Leonardi, Leonard Rothblum, 5641 Lawton Dr., Sarasota, FL 34233, 813-922-1938, 9:00 A.M.–5:00 P.M. Furniture restoration. Refinishing, veneering, faux-finishing designs, gold leafing, wood carving, and wood turning.

Master Woodcarver, 103 Corrine Dr., Pennington, NJ 08534, 609-737-9364 after 5:00 P.M. Hand carving for all period furniture. Conservation.

Meeting House Furniture Restoration, Jonathan Schechtman, 11 Waterman Hill, Quechee, VT 05059, 802-295-1309, Mon.–Sat. 9:00 A.M.–5:00 P.M., answering machine other times. Restoration of antique furniture and wooden heirlooms. Repair and replacement of damaged veneers and inlays, reproduction of carved elements, and refinishing in traditional and comtemporary coating materials. Chair re-seating, brass and metal restoration. Specialists in the restoration of flood- and fire-damaged furniture.

Dr. Michael A. Taras, 215 S. Craggmore Dr., Salem, SC 29676, 803-944-0655, Mon.–Fri. 8:00 A.M.–5:00 P.M. Wood identification.

Minuteman Furniture Restoration, Jim Gauthier, 115 N. Monroe St., Waterloo, WI 53594, 800-733-1776, 8:00 A.M.–5:00 P.M.; fax: 414-478-3966. Furniture restoration products for stripping, refinishing, repairing, veneering, and faux finishing. Catalog $2.

National Association of Furniture Repair and Refinishing Specialists, John Rybski, 321 S. Houghton, Milford, MI 48381, 313-684-6411, 9:00 A.M.–9:00 P.M.; fax: 313-684-0224. Membership open to professionals and hobbyists. The main objective of the association is to promote the productivity, profitability, and professionalism of the members through sales and marketing advice, trade shows and training seminars, and a certification program. Can supply names of restorers in your area.

Nelson Dale, Restoration Services, 621 Main St., #3, Waltham, MA 02154, 617-647-9470, 9:00 A.M.–5:00 P.M. Furniture conservation, including finishes, veneer, marquetry, and gilding. Free brochure.

Nowell's, Inc., PO Box 295, 490 Gate 5 Rd., Sausalito, CA 94966, 415-332-4933. Nowell's Finish Restorer cleans and conditions marred, scratched, and dirty surfaces; cleans and preserves unscratched painted surfaces.

Original Mattress Factory, 4930 State Rd., Cleveland, OH 44134, 216-661-8388, 9:00 A.M.–8:00 P.M. weekdays, noon–5:00 P.M. weekends; fax: 216-661-BEDS. Custom-size mattresses and box springs for antique beds. Three-quarter-size and special custom sizes made and shipped in two weeks or less. Amish-built box springs. Innerspring or foam construction available.

Original Woodworks, 360 N. Main St., Stillwater, MN 55082, 612-430-3622, Thurs.–Sat. noon–5:00 P.M. Antique furniture restoration. Reconstruction and veneering. Color shading and matching of repairs are a specialty. Replacement parts, legs, turnings, carvings. Cane, rush, splint, leather seats, and supplies. Restoration hardware for furniture. Curved and specialty glass.

Paxton Hardware Ltd., PO Box 256, 7818 Bradshaw Rd., Upper Falls, MD 21156, 410-592-8505, 9:00 A.M.–5:00 P.M.; fax: 410-592-2224. Period brass furniture hardware, including ball feet, hinges, hooks, locks, pulls, supports, table and desk hardware. Caning materials, wood inlays and veneer, woodworking books, and restoration products. Free brochure. Catalog $4.

PECO Glass Bending (Pat's Etcetera Co., Inc.), PO Box 777, 810 E. First St., Smithville, TX 78957, 512-237-3600, 10:00 A.M.–3:00 P.M.

Pressed fiber replacement chair seats for turn-of-the-century pressed back chairs. Bent glass for antique china cabinets, secretary-bookcases, show cases, and other items. Standard radius and custom-bent glass. Shipped nationwide by UPS. Send SASE for brochure.

Phyllis Kennedy, 9256 Holyoke Ct., Indianapolis, IN 46268, 317-872-6366. Restoration hardware for antique furniture. Ball and claw feet, bed hardware, catches, chair parts, desk lid supports and locks, Duncan Phyfe caps, Eastlake hardware. Store located at 10663 Andrade Dr., Zionsville, IN 46077. Catalog $3.

Price House Antiques, 137 Cabot St., Beverly, MA 01915, 508-927-5595, daily 10:00 A.M.–5:00 P.M. Restoration of antique and other wicker furnishings. Caning, porch-weave seats, natural and fiber rush seat replacements. Furniture refinishing.

R. Bruce Hamilton, Antique Restoration, 551 Main St., PO Box 586, West Newbury, MA 01985, 508-363-2638, Tues.–Fri. 8:00 A.M.–5:30 P.M., Sat. 9:00 A.M.–noon. Restoration and conservation services. Leather and cloth surfaces replaced, missing parts duplicated. Specializing in preserving surface patina and making structural repairs.

R. Wagner Company, 205 NW 10th Ave., Portland, OR 97209, 503-224-7036, 9:00 A.M.–5:00 P.M.; fax: 503-274-1057. Restoration on European, Oriental, and American painted furniture.

R. Wayne Reynolds, Ltd., Wayne Reynolds, 3618 Falls Rd., Baltimore, MD 21211, 410-467-1800, 9:00 A.M.–5:30 P.M.; fax: 410-467-1205. Complete conservation treatment for gilded decorative art objects, including furniture, frames, and mirrors. On-site gilding on architectural ornamentation. Consulting services. Call for a statement of capabilities.

Raphael's Antique Furniture Restoration, Mark DeVito, owner, 655 Atlantic St., Stamford, CT 06902, 203-348-3079, Mon.–Fri. 8:30 A.M.–4:30 P.M., Sat. 9:00 A.M.-noon. Restoration of antique furniture. Gold-leaf application.

Renaissance Restorations, Ltd., Ted Mader, 27 Castle Hill Rd., Wilmington, VT 05363, 802-464-2343, after 4:00 P.M.; fax available when previously notified. Furniture repair and commissions, including iron and bronze blacksmithing. Classes in furniture repair. Call or write for details.

Restorers of America, RD 4, Box 382, Wynantskill, NY 12189, 407-364-8661, anytime. Restoration of furniture. Supplies, workshops, and seminars.

Richard Blaschke Cabinet Glass, 670 Lake Ave., Bristol, CT 06010, 203-584-2566, Mon.–Fri. 10:00 A.M.–5:00 P.M., Sat. and Sun. noon–5:00 P.M., closed Tues. Curved replacement glass for china closets and windows. Popular sizes in stock, or will cut to order. Will install. Free brochure.

Richmond Desk Leathers Inc., 9411 Derbyshire Rd., Richmond, VA 23229, 804-741-1680, anytime. Releathering of desk tops and other items. Hand gold tooling. Restoration and French polishing service. Mail order or on site. Free brochure. Leather color samples given on request.

Robinson's Antiques, 170 Kent St., Portland, MI 48875, 517-647-6155. Antique replacement hardware matching service. Furniture hardware, spindles, and furniture parts. No reproductions. Send photocopy of item required with SASE for reply. Restoration of period furniture through the early twentieth century. Stripping, refinishing, and repairs.

Shaker Workshops, PO Box 1028, Concord, MA 01742, 617-646-8985, Mon.–Fri. 9:00 A.M.–5:30 P.M.; fax: 617-648-8217, 24 hours a day. Replacement Shaker chair-seat tape, furniture kits, paints, and stains. Shaker furniture restored; seats rewoven. Catalog $1.

Sheffield Plains Antiques, Jeff Von Er, PO Box 598, S. Main St., Rt. 7, Sheffield, MA 02157, 413-229-0113, Wed.–Sun. 11:00 A.M.–4:00 P.M.; fax: 413-229-8914. Gold-leaf restoration, burnish gilding, reverse painting, églomisé panels.

Sheild Art & Hobby Shop, Sandra H. Sheild, 4417 Danube Dr., King George, VA 22485-9374, 703-663-3711 anytime, leave message if no answer. Furniture repaired. Missing carved pieces replaced.

SPNEA Conservation Center, 185 Lyman St., Waltham, MA 02154, 617-891-1985, Mon.–Fri. 9:00 A.M.–5:00 P.M.; fax: 617-893-7832. Furniture and upholstery conservation; nonabrasive hardware cleaning. Brochure available.

Stoneledge, Inc., 17 Robert St., Wharton, NJ 07885, 201-989-8800, Mon.–Fri. 9:00 A.M.–5:00 P.M.; fax: 201-361-6574. Furniture conservation and restoration. Free brochure.

Studio Workshop, Ltd., 22 Bushy Hill Rd., Simsbury, CT 06070, 203-658-6374, 9:00 A.M.–6:00 P.M. Restoration and repair of antique furniture.

Susan Riley, Seat Weaver, 1 Ireland St., West Chesterfield, MA 01084, 413-296-4061, 8:00 A.M.–4:00 P.M., 6:00 P.M.–8:00 P.M. Specializing in the replacement of natural rush seating. Also, splint and cane of all sorts, repairs and replacement of rails and/or turnings when necessary.

Traditional Line Ltd., 143 W. 21st St., New York, NY 10011, 212-627-3555, 8:30 A.M.–5:00 P.M.; 212-645-8158. Full-service furniture restoration. Restoration woodworking, fabrication of missing elements, hardware repair and reproduction.

USDA Forest Products Laboratory, One Gifford Pinchot, Madison, WI 53705, 608-231-9200; fax: 608-231-9508. Scientific analysis of wood to determine genus. Samples should be cut with the grain from an inconspicuous spot and should be about the size of a pencil eraser if of temperate wood, and larger if tropical wood. Call for more information. Up to five samples per year may be sent for free analysis. A list of consultants is available

Van Dyke's, Box 278, Woonsocket, SD 57385, 605-796-4425, 800-843-3320, orders only, 8:00 A.M.–6:00 P.M.; fax: 605-796-4085. Furniture components, including claw feet, table pedestals, legs, bentwood chair parts, reproduction pressed chair backs, seats, supports, leather desktop pieces, and

rolltop desk components. Brass hardware of all kinds, trunk parts, pie-safe tins, curved-glass china cabinet parts, isinglass for stove doors, cane, reed, veneer, upholstery supplies, tools, stains, varnishes, brushes, modeling compounds. Special parts designed to duplicate the original pieces. Mail order worldwide. Catalog $1.

Victor von Reventlow, 13 Bergen St., Brooklyn, NY 11201, 718-858-0721, 1:00 P.M.–midnight. Conservation and restoration of furniture, laminations, and inlays. Collection conservation surveys. Send SASE for flyer listing services.

Walter Raynes, 4900 Wetheredsville Rd., Baltimore, MD 21207, 410-448-3515, Mon.–Fri. 8:30 A.M.–4:30 P.M. Antique furniture restoration and conservation. Detailed carving and hardware repairs.

Wayne's Woods, Inc., 39 N. Plains Industrial Rd., Wallingford, CT 06492, 800-793-6208, 9:00 A.M.–5:00 P.M.; fax: 203-949-0769. Reproduction hardware, refinishing supplies, furniture restoration and refinishing. Free catalog.

Wicker Workshop, Larry Cryderman and Shoshana Enosh, 18744 Parthenia St. #1, Northridge, CA 91324, 818-886-4524, anytime; fax: 818-886-0115. Restoration and repair of wicker, caning, rushing, split reed, hickory, and splint. Spindles for chairs and rockers. Upholstering.

Williamstown Regional Art Conservation Laboratory, Inc., 225 South St., Williamstown, MA 01267, 413-458-5741, 8:30 A.M.–5:00 P.M.; fax: 413-458-2314. Conservation of historic furniture and gilded objects. Reproductions and facsimiles of wood and gilded objects made to order. Free brochure.

Wise Company, 6503 St. Claude, PO Box 118K, Arabi, LA 70032, 504-277-7551, 9:00 A.M.–5:00 P.M. Chair caning supplies. Antique reproduction brass and miscellaneous hardware. Catalog $4.00.

Wood & Leather Craft, 4921 Route 97, Callicoon, NY 12723-5032, 914-887-4241, 8:00 A.M.–6:00 P.M. Genuine leather tops, gold tooled period designs. Brown, green, red, or black finish. Send measurements for estimate and free samples.

Y & J Furniture Co., PO Box 1361, Durham, NC 27702, 919-682-6131, Mon.–Fri. 8:30 A.M.–5:30 P.M., Sat. 8:30 A.M.–noon. Restoration of fine furniture. Repair, refinishing, reupholstering. Can duplicate old pieces, replace missing table leaves, rebuild old beds to be standard size, replace missing pulls. Showroom: 1612 East Geer Street, Durham, NC 27704.

Videos

Traditional Gilding & Contemporary Metallics, Glass Gilding–Vol. I and Vol. II, **Art Essentials of New York, Ltd.,** 3 Cross St., Suffern, NY 10901-4601, 914-368-1100, 800-283-5323; fax: 914-368-1535.

Identification of Older & Antique Furniture, **ID Video,** c/o Fred Taylor, PO Box 10634, Tampa, FL 33679, 813-935-4088. Brief historical perspective on American furniture, details on construction techniques, materials, and style.

Chair Caning by Jane Nelson, 105 minutes. $39.95. *Chair Rushing with Jane Nelson,* 30 minutes. $24.95. **Nelson Video,** 117 Cottage Ave., Cashmere, WA 98815, 509-782-2644.

Refinishing Furniture with Bob Flexner, 60 minutes, illustrated booklet. $29.95. *Repairing Furniture with Bob Flexner,* 70 minutes, illustrated booklet. $29.95. *The Woodfinishing Video with Michael Dresdner,* 60 minutes. $34.95. Companion book available, **Taunton Press,** 63 S. Main St., Newtown, CT 06470, 800-888-8286. Other books on woodworking are also available.

Glass

Glass is one of the most difficult types of antiques to identify and price. Few pieces are marked, reproductions abound, and quality is not always the reason for a price. A novice will have great difficulty (some experts do, too) in identifying reproductions. It is a major task to learn the names of the many glasswares.

First, sort your glassware. Sets of goblets, plates, and cups and saucers should be put in one group. Vases, figurines, candlesticks, and other decorative items should be considered separately. We wrote *Kovels' Know Your Antiques* and *Kovels' Know Your Collectibles* for the beginner. There is a chapter on glass in each book, written to help make identifying the type of glass a less complicated task. The colored art glass of Victorian times is described in terms of color and design. The names Pomona, Peachblow, amberina, Quezal, and others will make more sense after you study a little. Go to a large antiques show and look for glassware that resembles yours; dealers will be glad to tell you what it is called. Then you can look up the prices in any of the books listed in here. Victorian glass has been reproduced and modern versions are made today. Milk glass, purple or blue slag glass (it resembles a marble cake), pressed glass, and many types of colored glass baskets, cruets, and plates are being made for the gift-shop trade. You probably can't tell the old from the new without expert help. If you know your glass vase belonged to a great-grandmother, you should research the value carefully. Some of the strangest-looking glass pieces are of great value. Almost all types of gold iridescent glass, one of the types made by L. C. TIFFANY, are very valuable. Any piece of glass that can be identified as being from the Tiffany workshops has a high value. The signature on a piece doubles the value. Also look for STEUBEN, DURAND, QUEZAL, KEW BLAS, WEBB, and small trademarks like the fleur-de-lis or initials that identify the makers.

Blown glass of the eighteenth and early nineteenth centuries is older than art glass, but seldom brings as high a price unless very rare. Although the English collectors eagerly buy goblets with blown and twisted stems and decanters with applied decorations, the American collectors have never been as interested. Many decanters from the 1820s sell for under $350. Early blown bottles are a whole different story. Very rare mold-blown whiskey flasks can sell for tens of thousands of dollars. Even common ones sell for hundreds. (See section on Bottles.)

Cut glass, especially the very elaborate pieces known as "brilliant cut," was not easy to sell until the 1970s. Suddenly, after over fifty years of being out of favor, it was back in demand. The cost of making the glass is high, so the antique pieces began to rise in value. Today, old cut glass is high priced, very much in demand, and, if in perfect condition, it sells very quickly. Small or large nicks lower value by 25 to 50 percent depending on rarity of the design. If the object is made of colored and clear glass, add 100 percent. If the glass is sick (cloudy) and does not seem to wash clean, deduct 40 percent.

If the glass is signed, add 25 percent. The signature can be difficult to find, but is usually on the smooth surface of the inside of a bowl. Because the marks are acid-etched, they are very faint and can only be seen if the bowl is turned to catch the light the right way. Ask an antiques dealer to show you a signature on a piece of cut glass and you will quickly learn how to find others. Only about one in ten pieces is signed.

There are several kinds of feet that could be put on a piece of cut glass. A round disc and short stem on a vase are common, but the same type of foot on a carafe, sugar or creamer, bowl, jug, decanter, or ice tub adds 15 percent. A tall foot on a compote is the rule, but the same tall foot on a berry bowl, spooner, cologne, sugar, or creamer adds 15 percent. If there are decorations on the feet, add 2 percent more. Peg feet on a vase, bowl, bucket, creamer, or sugar raise the value by 10 percent. Cut glass prices are listed in the general price books and in some specialized books. It is best to try to determine the name of the pattern by looking at the cut glass picture books in your library. Even without the pattern name, you can decide approximate value.

Cameo glass and Art Nouveau– and Art Deco–inspired glasswares are very popular and very high priced today. Quality and signature are important. Often a small piece that will fit on a breakfront shelf is preferred to a very large vase, since serious collectors run out of space. Cameo glass is made of several layers of glass of different colors. The design is made by cutting away the top color to make patterns. French cameo glass was inspired by the Art Nouveau tradition. GALLÉ, A. WALTER, DAUM NANCY, ARGY-

ROUSSEAU, MÜLLER FRERES, DE VEZ, DELATTE, and LEGRAS are names found on French cameo glass that add to the value. If cameo glass is signed by Gallé, add 100 percent. If the piece is signed by a less important maker, add 50 percent to the value of a similar unsigned piece. The best name of all, from a seller's viewpoint, is WOODALL. He was an English artist and his cameo glass vases are worth thousands of dollars. The American STEUBEN glassworks made an acid-cut, cameolike ware that also sells well. LALIQUE is another marketable name. Lalique glass is still being made. The older pieces, signed "R. Lalique," were made before 1945 and are worth 100 to 500 percent more than the newer ones. (The pieces made after 1945 are signed "Lalique.") The best pieces of Lalique are the more uncommon colored pieces. Most of the glass was made in frosted, clear, or opalescent glass.

Pressed glass, made in Victorian times, was a very popular collectible in the 1930s, but lost favor until the 1980s. It was inexpensive and easy to find, perhaps because the design was unfashionable or because almost undetectable reproductions were made. The prices remained low until collectors began to realize that the 1890 pressed-glass goblet now sold for the same price as a 1930s Depression glass piece, and bargain hunters began looking for pressed-glass sets again. To price these, you need a good book listing patterns. Learn the name of your pattern, then look in the latest edition of a price guide for a retail value. Only perfect pieces sell because the supply is plentiful. Pressed glass sells best at a general antiques show or through mail-order ads.

Carnival glass, an inexpensive iridescent glass popular in the early twentieth century, can be sold to the interested collector. The highest prices are for rare patterns and forms; punch bowls and certain pitchers and lamps sell well. Ordinary carnival glass is not high priced, so be realistic when you set your selling price. Check the carnival glass guides to see if you own a rare pattern or color. Most of the guides have sketches or photographs of each pattern. It is a bit complicated to understand how to identify the color of carnival glass. The color of the glass itself, not the color of the iridescence seen on the top, is the determining factor.

Depression glass began gaining favor with collectors during the 1970s. It was then that the pale pink or green lacy pattern pieces were first noticed. Sets were assembled from garage sales. A cup often cost a nickel and a plate a dime. Today there are many serious collectors of all types of Depression glass, from pastels to bright ruby, cobalt blue, or forest green. Hobnail, the Sandwich patterns, and even enamel-decorated pieces are wanted. The highest prices are paid at Depression glass shows. Try to find one in your area.

Another good place to sell your Depression glass is through the trade papers that specialize in glass. Prices are easily determined from the price books, in which patterns are pictured and priced. There are at least fifteen current price books on Depression glass. Reproductions of Depression glass have been made: Some are sets for everyday use; some are copies of the rarities, such as the pink Cherry Blossom cookie jar that sells for hundreds of dollars if original.

In the 1980s, a group of buyers appeared who were willing to pay good prices for the studio and art glass made from the 1950s on. VENINI, KOSTA, ORREFORS, HOLMEGAARD, AFORS, TOSO, BARBINI, and BODA are some of the most important foreign names. There are also American makers with names like EDRIS ECKHARDT, DOMINICK LABINO, BLENKO, ERICKSON, HIGGINS, and JIM LUNDBERG. In general, the more Art Moderne in appearance, the more abstract the forms and heavier the glass bodies, the higher the prices. Signatures are very important for these pieces.

One of the best-selling types of glass is that unnamed group made from the 1930s to the 1970s, sometimes called "elegant glass ware." Included are certain patterns by HEISEY, FENTON, FOSTORIA, CAMBRIDGE, IMPERIAL, and DUNCAN AND MILLER. These and a few other American companies made fine quality, cut-crystal goblets, wines, plates, and figurines for the gift-shop trade. Heisey is well known for both its decorated pieces and its heavy, modern, glass animal figures. Very high prices are paid for these figures and for the goblets with animal- or bird-shaped stems. Small is big with the animal figures; the small sizes sell for the most.

If your glass was inherited from parents or grandparents, you could easily have some of these pieces. They were sold in all parts of the country and were popular wedding gifts. The problem is identification. There is a Heisey glass museum in Newark, Ohio, and several clubs for the other types of glass. A clear photograph and letter to these groups may get you the information about age and pattern name that you need to determine a price using the price guides. There are books showing many of the patterns, but it is not a quick research project. A few of the pieces are signed with initials or insignia, but most are not. If you have this type of glass, go to the antiques shows and glass shows and ask questions to try to determine a price. Most small local auction galleries do very well with this type of glassware and get high prices for you. They should be able to identify it and tell you the approximate value. It is difficult to sell a partial set of drinking glasses, because the new owner will not be able to fill in the twelfth for a party. All other types of glass made after the 1930s can sell for surprisingly high prices. We have seen and purchased many pieces of unmarked Heisey for under $5 at garage sales, where they are often overlooked and underpriced by the amateur seller.

Glass candlesticks of any kind are now selling very well. They seem to have come back into fashion in the 1980s. Remember, even if your glass looks like dime-store junk to you, or like a misshapen ashtray made from a glob of glass, you are selling and not buying. To the trained eye, your glass dish may be a treasure, and you must train your eye enough to recognize the high-priced items.

REPAIR

Many glass replacement parts for doors and windows are included in this chapter. Reproductions of many of the glass products can be found, so be cautious when you buy. Publications and price guides often list the well-known reproductions. Fake glass marks are not uncommon, as it is simple to acid-stamp, etch, or sandblast a name on a less desirable piece of glass to raise the value of it for the unsuspecting buyer.

Glass should never be kept in a sunny window. Old glass (before 1900) was made of a slightly different mixture and may turn colors. Any glass can magnify the sun and cause scorch marks on furniture or carpets, or even start a fire.

Chipped glass can be ground down. A local glass-repair shop can be located through the Yellow Pages. New epoxy mixtures can be used to make repairs on glass that are almost impossible to detect without the use of a black light. This type of repair is expensive and only a few restorers offer the service. Any glass can be polished, including the insides of small-necked bottles. There is a danger of breakage and it is a very specialized job. Stained glass can be cleaned and restored. Look for a restorer in the Yellow Pages under "Glass, Stained & Leaded." Sets of glasses can be completed with the help of a matching service. Many are listed in Part II.

See Paperweights.

Price Books

Carnival Glass Auction Prices, Tom and Sharon Mordini (36 N. Mernitz Ave., Freeport, IL 61032, © 1994).

Collectible Glassware from the '40s, '50s, '60s, 2nd edition, Gene Florence (Collector Books, Paducah, KY, © 1994).

The Collector's Encyclopedia of Depression Glass, 11th edition, Gene Florence (Collector Books, Paducah, KY, © 1994).

The Collector's Guide to Old Fruit Jars, Red Book No. 7, Douglas M. Leybourne, Jr. (PO Box 5417, North Muskegon, MI 49445, © 1993).

Cruets, Cruets, Cruets, Vol. II, Elaine Ezell and George Newhouse (Antique Publications, PO Box 553, Marietta, OH, © 1993).

The Definitive Guide to Shot Glasses, Mark Pickvet (Antique Publications, Marietta, OH, © 1992).

Definitive Pictorial Guide to Westmoreland's Salt and Pepper Shakers (Over 75 Sets) and Salt Dips (Over 25) 1889–1984, Ruth Ann Grizel (WB Book Sales, PO Box 65, Solon, IA 52333, © 1992).

Depression Era Glassware Identification & Value Guide, 3rd edition, Carl F. Luckey (Books Americana, Florence, AL, © 1994).

Dugan/Diamond: The Story of Indiana, Pennsylvania, Glass, William Heacock, James Measell, and Berry Wiggins (Antique Publications, Marietta, OH, © 1993).

Elegant Glassware of the Depression Era, 5th edition, Gene Florence (Collector Books, Paducah, KY, © 1993).

Fifties Glass, Leslie Piña (Schiffer, Atglen, PA, © 1993).

Findlay Glass Price Guide, Virginia Motter and James Measell. Updated price list for Smith & Measell's *Findlay Glass: The Glass Tableware Manufacturers, 1886–1902* (Antique Publications, PO Box 553, Marietta, OH 45750, © 1993).

Fostoria American, A Complete Guide, Sidney P. Seligson (4510 Barbados, Wichita Falls, TX 76308).

Fostoria: An Identification and Value Guide of Pressed, Blown & Hand Molded Shapes, Ann Kerr (Collector Books, Paducah, KY, © 1994).

Glass Animals of the Depression Era, Lee Garmon and Dick Spencer (Collector Books, Paducah, KY, © 1993).

The Glass Collectors Handbook and Price Guide, William Friedberg (William Friedberg, 462 Hillcreek Rd., Shepherdsville, KY 40165, © 1992).

Glass of René Lalique at Auction, edited by Hugh D. Guinn (Guindex Publications, PO Box 4702, Tulsa, OK 74159, © 1992).

Imperial's Vintage Milk Glass, Myrna and Bob Garrison (Collector's Loot, 3816 Hastings Dr., Arlington, TX 76013, © 1992).

Made in Czechoslovakia, Book 2, Ruth A. Forsythe (Antique Publications, PO Box 553, Marietta, OH 45750, © 1993).

Mary Gregory Glassware, R. and D. Truitt (5120 White Flint Dr., Kensington, MD 20895, © 1992).

Price Survey, 4th edition, Kent G. Washburn (Kent Washburn Antiques, 8048 Midcrown, Suite 26, San Antonio, TX 78218-2334, © 1994).

PYREX by Corning, A Collector's Guide, Susan Tobier Rogove and Marcia Buan Steinhauer (Antique Publications, Marietta, OH, © 1993).

Standard Encyclopedia of Carnival Glass, 4th Edition, Bill Edwards (Collector Books, Paducah, KY, © 1994)

Toothpick Holders: China, Glass and Metal, The National Toothpick Holder Collector's Society (Antique Publications, Marietta, OH, © 1992).

Verlys of America Decorative Glass 1935–1951, Carole and Wayne McPeek (PO Box 1120, Newark, OH 43055, © 1992).

Very Rare Glassware of the Depression Years, 3rd series, Gene Florence (Collector Books, Paducah, KY, © 1993).

Warman's Glass, Ellen Tischbein Schroy (Wallace-Homestead, Radnor, PA, © 1992).

Warman's Pattern Glass edited by Ellen Tischbein Schroy (Wallace-Homestead, Radnor, PA, © 1993).

Westmoreland Glass: Our Children's Heirlooms, Ruth Ann Grizel (FSJ Publishing Co., PO Box 122, Iowa City, IA 52244, © 1993).

Wheeling Glass 1829–1939, Collection of the Oglebay Institute Glass Museum, edited by Gerald I. Reilly (Antique Publications, PO Box 553, Marietta, OH 45750, © 1994).

Clubs & Publications

Akro Agate Collectors' Club, *Clarksburg Crow* (NL), 10 Bailey St., Clarksburg, WV 26301-2524.

American Carnival Glass Association, *American Carnival Glass News* (NL), 9621 Springwater Ln., Miamisburg, OH 45342.

American Cut Glass Association, *Hobstar* (NL), PO Box 482, Ramona, CA 92065-0482.

Antique & Art Glass Salt Shaker Collectors Society, *Pioneer* (NL), 2832 Rapidan Tr., Maitland, FL 32751.

Candy Container Collectors of America, *Candy Gram* (NL), PO Box 8708, Canton, OH 44711-8708.

Collectible Carnival Glass Association, *Collectible Carnival Glass Association* (NL), 2360 N Old S.R. 9, Columbus, IN 47203.

Collectors of Findlay Glass, *Melting Pot* (NL), 10217 Stickle Rd., St. Louisville, OH 43071.

Fenton Art Glass Collectors of America, Inc., *Butterfly Net* (NL), PO Box 384, Williamstown, WV 26187.

Fostoria Glass Collectors, *Fostoria Reflections* (NL), 21901 Lassen St., #112, Chatsworth, CA 91311 (also includes information on other glass).

Fostoria Glass Society of America, Inc., *Facets of Fostoria* (NL), PO Box 826, Moundsville, WV 26041.

Glass Knife Collectors Club, *Cutting Edge* (NL), 711 Kelly Dr., Lebanon, TN 37087.

Heart of America Carnival Glass Association, *H.O.A.C.G.A. Bulletin* (NL), 3048 Tamarak Dr., Manhattan, KS 66502.

Heisey Collectors of America, *Heisey News* (NL), 169 W. Church St., Newark, OH 43055.

International Carnival Glass Association, *Carnival Pump* (NL), RR #1, Box 14, Mentone, IN 46534.

Lalique Society of America, *Lalique Magazine* (MAG), 400 Veterans Blvd., Carlstadt, NJ 07072.

Michiana Association of Candlewick Collectors, *MACC Spyglass* (NL), 17370 Battles Rd., South Bend, IN 46614.

Morgantown Collectors of America, *Morgantown Newscaster* (NL), 420 First Ave. NW, Plainview, MN 55964.

Mt. Washington Art Glass Society, *Mt. Washington Art Glass Society Newsletter* (NL), 5600 Meadowbrook Dr., Ft. Worth, TX 76112.

National Cambridge Collectors, Inc., *Cambridge Crystal Ball* (NL), PO Box 416, Cambridge, OH 43725-0416.

National Candlewick Collectors Club, *Candlewick Collector* (NL), 275 Milledge Terr., Athens, GA 30606.

National Depression Glass Association, *News & Views* (NL), PO Box 69843, Odessa, TX 79769.

National Duncan Glass Society, *National Duncan Glass Journal* (NL), PO Box 965, Washington, PA 15301-0965.

National Early American Glass Club, *Glass Club Bulletin* (MAG), *Glass Shards* (NL), Box 8489, Silver Spring, MD 20907.

National Fenton Glass Society, *Fenton Flyer* (NL), PO Box 4008, Marietta, OH 45750.

National Greentown Glass Association, *N.G.G.A. Newsletter* (NL), PO Box 107, Greentown, IN 46936.

National Imperial Glass Collectors Society, *Glasszette* (NL), PO Box 534, Bellaire, OH 43906.

National Milk Glass Collectors Society, *Opaque News* (NL), 1113 Birchwood Dr., Garland, TX 75043.

National Reamer Collectors Association, *National Reamer Collectors Association Quarterly Review* (NL), 405 Benson Rd. N., Frederic, WI 54837-8945.

National Toothpick Holder Collectors Society, *Toothpick Bulletin* (NL), Red Arrow Hwy., Box 246, Sawyer, MI 49125.

National Westmoreland Glass Collectors Club, *Towne Crier* (NL), Box 372, Export, PA 15632.

Old Morgantown Glass Collectors' Guild, *Topics* (NL), PO Box 894, Morgantown, WV 26507-0894.

Pairpoint Cup Plate Collectors of America, Inc., *Thistle* (MAG), *Mini-Thistle* (NL), Box 890052, Weymouth, MA 02189-0001.

Stretch Glass Society, *Stretch Glass Society Newsletter* (NL), PO Box 573, Hampshire, IL 60140.

Swan Seekers Network, *Swan Seekers News* (NL), *Swan Seekers Marketplace* (NL), 4118 E. Vernon Ave., Phoenix, AZ 85008-2333 (Swarovski crystal secondary market).

Tiffin Glass Collectors Club, *Tiffin Glassmasters* (NL), PO Box 554, Tiffin, OH 44883.

Whimsey Club, *Whimsical Notions* (NL), 4544 Cairo Dr., Whitehall, PA 18052 (glass whimsies).

Acorn (MAG), *Cullet* (NL), Sandwich Glass Museum, PO Box 103, 129 Main St., Sandwich, MA 02563.

Collector Glass News (NL), PO Box 308, Slippery Rock, PA 16057 (cartoon character, fast-food, and promotional glassware).

Daze (NP), 10271 State Rd., Box 57, Otisville, MI 48463 (Depression glass).

Glass Collector's Digest (MAG), PO Box 553, Marietta, OH 45750-9979.

Jody & Darrell's Glass Collectibles (NL), PO Box 180833, Arlington, TX 76096-0833 (secondary market for Boyd's Crystal Art Glass and other glass).

The Original Westmoreland Glass Collector's Newsletter (NL), PO Box 143, North Liberty, IA 52317.

Phoenix & Consolidated Glass Collectors News & Views (NL), Box 81974, Chicago, IL 60681-0974.

Salty Comments (NL), 401 Nottingham Rd., Newark, DE 19711 (open salts).

Repairs, Parts & Supplies

A. Ludwig Klein & Son, Inc., PO Box 145, Harleysville, PA 19438, 215-256-9004, Tues.–Fri. 10:00 A.M.–5:00 P.M. Restoration of glass. Appraisals, insurance claims by appointment. Free brochure.

Antique Restoration by Wiebold, 413 Terrace Pl., Terrace Park, OH 45174, 513-831-2541, Mon.–Fri. 9:00 A.M.–5:30 P.M., Sat. 10:00 A.M.–2:00 P.M.; fax: 513-831-2815. Restoration of opaque and clear glass. Chips ground, damaged or missing areas filled. Bent glass panels for lamp shades, beveled mirrors, chandelier parts. Free brochure.

Antique Restoring Studio Inc., DBA Trefler & Sons, 99 Cabot St., Needham, MA 02194, 617-444-2685, Mon.–Fri. 9:00 A.M.–5:00 P.M., Sat. 10:00 A.M.–2:00 P.M.; fax: 617-444-0659. Restoration of glass, including stained glass. Repair breaks, hide damage to colored glass, remove chips to crystal glasses. Chandeliers a specialty: cleaning, repairing broken arms, and rewiring. All types of enamels repaired. Free brochure.

Art Glass Studio Inc., 543 Union St., 3A, Brooklyn, NY 11215, 718-596-4353, Mon.–Fri. 9:30 A.M.–5:30 P.M.; fax: 718-596-4353. Restoration of leaded and stained-glass windows. Duplication of any stained-glass window. Church restorations.

Beaver Glass Restoration, 23 Hatton Pl., Edinburgh, Scotland EH9 1UB, 031-667 8996, 9:00 A.M.–5:00 P.M. U.K. Blue glass liners and decanter stoppers supplied and fitted. Glass repair, including grinding and polishing chipped crystal glasses, decanters, bowls, and vases; declouding decanters, glasses, etc.

Blenko Glass Company, Inc., PO Box 67, Milton, WV 25541, 304-743-9081. Hand-blown restoration glass. Bull's-eye panes, antique sheet glass, rondels, scrap glass, epoxy, and tools. Brochure.

Blue Crystal (Glass) Ltd., Unit 6-8, 21 Wren St., London, England WC1X 0HF, +44 71 578 0142, 8:15 A.M.–4:45 P.M. Blue glass inserts for antique silver. Reproduction crystal tableware cut to match or as specified. Bottles for cruet stands, claret bottle for silver mount, etc. Mail order worldwide.

Bob and Linda Keimig, 3016 Montrose Dr., Bartlesville, OK 74005, 918-335-3265, evenings or leave message on machine. Glass candy container replacement paper closures; tin and paper parts. Mail order worldwide. Send SASE for price list.

Botti Studio of Architectural Arts Inc., 919 Grove St., Evanston, IL 60201, 800-524-7211, 708-869-5933, 8:30 A.M.–4:30 P.M.; fax: 708-869-5996. Stained glass; beveled glass; etched, sandblasted, and bent glass; glass painting. Restoration, conservation, and consultation. Free brochure.

Burnham & LaRoche Associates, 441-43 Fulton St., Medford, MA 02155, 617-395-5047, 8:00 A.M.–4:30 P.M. Restoration of stained-glass lamp shades. Bent glass for Tiffany type lampshades. Restoration and repair of stained-glass windows.

Butterfly Shoppe, 637 Livernois, Ferndale, MI 48220, 313-541-2858, Mon.–Wed. 10:30 A.M.–4:00 P.M., Thurs. until 7:00 P.M. Chips removed from crystal goblets. Send item UPS for estimate.

Chatham Glass Co., Jim Holmes and Deborah Doane, Box 522, North Chatham, MA 02650, 508-945-5547, Mon.–Sat. 10:00 A.M.–5:00 P.M. Bull's-eye windows blown to your exact size, from 4 × 4 inches to 12 × 12 inches. Call for prices.

Chatree's, 711 Eighth St., SE, Washington, DC 20003, 202-546-4950. Glass repair; stained glass repair and replacement; chandeliers repaired.

Chaudron Glass & Mirror Co., Inc., Henry Chaudron, 1801 Lovegrove St., Baltimore, MD 21202, 410-685-1568, Mon.–Fri 8:00 A.M.–5:00 P.M., Thurs. to 8:00 P.M. Resilvering of mirrors, hand beveling, stone wheel engraving on flat glass.

Clear as Glass, PO Box 1209, Kingsport, TN 37660, 615-247-7643. Restoration of "sick" glass. Removal of the residue that causes the inside of a glass container to become cloudy.

Crystal Medic, Jon Kurtz & Carol Jasper, 3126 Fairview Street, Davenport, IA 52802, 319-322-5512. Conservators of crystal and glass. By appointment only.

Crystal Mountain Prisms, PO Box 31, Westfield, NY 14787, 716-326-3676, anytime. Replacement glass prisms for chandeliers and lamps. Glass chains, Czechoslovakian cut balls, pendalogues, bobeches. Mail order only.

Crystal Workshop, Edward D. Poore, PO Box 475, 794 Rt. 6A, Sagamore, MA 02561, 508-888-1621, Mon.–Fri. 8:00 A.M.–5:00 P.M. Glass engraving, pattern reproduction, restoration of glass paperweights, repair of antique and contemporary glass, glass liners made and fitted, stoppers fitted, custom glass work.

Curran Glass & Mirror Co., 30 N. Maple St., Florence, MA 01060, 413-584-5761, Mon.–Fri. 10:00 A.M.–4:00 P.M. Architectural, leaded, and etched glass restoration. Glass bending, beveled and slumped glass work.

D & J Glass Clinic, David Jasper, 40658 267th St., Sioux Falls, SD 57106, 605-361-7524, 9:00 A.M.–5:00

P.M.; fax: 605-361-7216. Glass and crystal repair. Chips removed, teeth reshaped, stoppers fitted or removed, collectible marbles polished. Free brochure.

David Wixon & Associates, Inc., 189 Kenilworth Ave., Glen Ellyn, IL 60137, 708-858-7618, Mon.–Sat., day and evenings; fax: 708-858-7623. Custom design, construction, repair, and restoration of stained and beveled glass. Historic residential and ecclesiastical glass a specialty. Commissions accepted nationwide. No charge for initial phone consultation. Brochure.

Dean's China Restoration, 131 Elmwood Dr., Cheshire, CT 06410, 800-669-1327, Mon.–Fri. 9:00 A.M.–5:00 P.M. Glass and crystal repair and restoration. Invisible repairs. Mail order worldwide. Free brochure.

Delphi Stained Glass, 2116 E. Michigan Ave., Lansing, MI 48912, 800-248-2048, Mon.–Fri. 9:00 A.M.–9:00 P.M., Sat. 9:00 A.M.–5:00 P.M.; fax: 517-482-4028. Hand-blown glass for window repairs. Color matching service for repairs of antique stained-glass windows. Glass etching and engraving supplies, stencils; stained-glass kits and supplies; beveled glass; books, and tools. Catalog $5.

Drehobl Brothers Art Glass Company, 2847 N. Lincoln Ave., Chicago, IL 60657, 312-281-2022, 9:00 A.M.–4:30 P.M. Leaded glass and Tiffany lampshades repaired. Bent glass panels, custom beveled glass designs.

Dunhill Restoration, c/o Lee Upholstery, 2309 Lee Rd., Cleveland Heights, OH 44118, 216-921-2932, Mon.–Sat. 9:00 A.M.–5:00 P.M. Conservators of antiques and collectibles. Chipped and broken glass repaired. Replacement of missing parts, such as finials, handles, etc.

Eastern Art Glass, PO Box 341, Wyckoff, NJ 07481, 201-847-0001, 9:00 A.M.–5:30 P.M.; fax: 201-847-0231. Glass etching and mirror decorating supplies, stencils, kits, video instructions, and accessories for the do-it-yourselfer. Glass engraving tools and courses. Mail order nationwide. Catalog $2, refundable with first order.

Ferguson's Cut Glass Works Inc., 4292 Pearl Rd., Cleveland, OH 44109, 216-459-2929, 9:00 A.M.–4:30 P.M. Crystal and glass repair. Beveled glass and mirrors. Chandelier restoration. Hand-cut and engraved door panels.

The Finishing Touch, Ned Guyette, 5128 W. Center St., Milwaukee, WI 53210, 414-444-4557. Repair and restoration of glass and crystal. Cracks and chips repaired.

Foster Art Restoration, 711 W. 17th St. C-12, Costa Mesa, CA 92627, 800-824-6967, 8:30 A.M.–5:00 P.M., 714-645-9953; fax: 714-645-8381. Repair of broken or otherwise damaged crystal and other art works and collectibles. Free brochure.

Glass Restoration by Dianne, 54 Hartford Turnpike, Piccadilly Square, Vernon, CT 06066, 203-647-7074, Tues.–Sat. 10:00 A.M.–5:30 P.M. Restoration of all types of glassware. Chips removed, broken pieces repaired. Pieces accepted via mail. Brochure.

Glass Studio, Thomas E. Matthews, PO Box 87, Lompoc, CA 93438, 805-736-1729, 7:00 A.M.–3:00 P.M. Cut and art glass repair; recutting to remove chips. Sick decanters and vases cleaned; stoppers supplied and fitted. Studio located at 4314 W. Ocean Ave., Lompoc, CA 93436.

Golden Age Glassworks, B. Arrindell, 339 Bellvale Rd., Warwick, NY 10990, 914-986-1487, 9:00 A.M.–9:00 P.M.; fax: 914-986-6147. Stained- and leaded-glass window restoration, custom design, and manufacture. Expansions and alterations of existing panels; framing. Residential and commercial. Mailing or shipping can be arranged.

Great Panes Glassworks, 2861 Walnut St., Denver, CO 80205-2235, 800-338-5408, Mon.–Fri. 8:30 A.M.–5:00 P.M.; fax: 303-294-0163. Historic restoration glass. Photo stenciled, sandblasted glass, stone, tile, brass, and stainless steel. Mail order and shipping worldwide. Free brochure.

Greg Monk Stained Glass 98-027 Hekaha St., Bldg. 3, Aiea, HI 96701, 808-488-9538, 10:00 A.M.–

6:00 P.M. Stained-glass supplies, instruction. Repairs to lamps and windows. Will ship worldwide.

H. W. Kopp, Glass Grinding, 26 State St., Skaneateles, NY 13152, 315-685-5073, mornings. Glass restoration, beveling, cutting, grinding, polishing, hole drilling. Bells made from stem glasses with broken bases. Chips removed.

Harry A. Eberhardt & Son, Inc., 2010 Walnut St., Philadelphia, PA 19103, 215-568-4144, Mon.–Fri. 9:00 A.M.–5:00 P.M. Restoration of glass, cloisonné, porcelains, Satsuma, and other objects of art.

Hess Restorations, 200 Park Ave. S., New York, NY 10003, 212-260-2255, 10:30 A.M.–4:00 P.M. Restoration of glass. Chips ground off glasses; replacement blue glass liners for silver salt dishes, sugar baskets, and condiment holders. Brochure.

Hoffer Glass, George J. Hoffer, 613 W. College Ave., Appleton, WI 54911, 800-236-2413 (Brian or Glenn), 8:00 A.M.–5:00 P.M.; fax: 414-731-8272. Double-strength curved glass for china cabinets. Most sizes in stock and available for immediate shipment. Convex and oval picture frame glass in stock. Send pattern or call with sizes for quote. Free brochure.

Hudson Glass Co. Inc., 219 N. Division St., Peekskill, NY 10566-2700, 914-737-2124, 800-431-2964, 9:00 A.M.–5:00 P.M.; fax: 914-737-4447, 800-999-3294. Bent glass for china cabinets, stained glass, tools, and supplies. No repairs. Catalog $3.

I.P.G.R., Inc., PO Box 205, Kulpsville, PA 19443, 800-869-5633 orders only; 215-256-9015, Tues.–Fri. 9:30 A.M.–4:30 P.M., Sat. 9:30 A.M.–1:30 P.M.; fax: 215-256-9644. Complete line of restoration materials. Catalog $3, refundable with first order.

J & K Curios, 4868 SW Southwind Ct., Dunnellon, FL 34431, 904-465-0756, Mon.–Fri. 9:00 A.M.–9:00 P.M. Art glass restored. Missing handles, arms, legs, and fragments reconstructed. Free estimates.

J. Peter Owen, 29 Murray St., Augusta, ME 04330, 207-622-3277, anytime. Replacement

bent slag glass panels and other stained-glass lamp shade repairs.

Jar Doctor, R. Wayne Lowry, 2105 E. 250 St., Lebanon, IN 46052, 317-482-4033, evenings and weekends, or leave message. Cleaning machines and supplies for bottles, jars, insulators, and round glass items such as cruets, pitchers, and glasses. Jar and bottle cleaning and repair; etching and light scratches removed. Call about specific items. Most glass items can be cleaned.

Jonathan Mark Gershen, 1463 Pennington Rd., Ewing Township, NJ 08618, 609-882-9417, Mon.–Fri. 10:00 A.M.–4:00 P.M. Repair and restoration of glass, porcelain, and pottery. Missing parts fabricated, shattered pieces restored, historically accurate reconstruction of decorative art objects. Send for information on how to ship your items to the studio for evaluation. Worldwide service.

Just Enterprises—Art & Antique Restoration, Gary and Susanne Gottfried, 2790 Sherwin Ave., #10, Ventura, CA 93003, 805-644-5837, 10:00 A.M.–noon, 2:00 P.M.–5:00 P.M. Restoration of glass, including perfume bottles, cameo glass, Lalique, and Steuben.

Lid Lady, Charles Bodiker, 7790 E. Ross Rd., New Carlisle, OH 45344, 513-845-1266. Lids for antique and new items, china to zinc. Send SASE for a reply.

Manor Art Glass, 20 Ridge Rd., Douglaston, NY 11363, 718-631-8029, 9:00 A.M.–5:00 P.M.; fax: 718-631-0308. Repair and restoration of stained glass. Leaded glass, etched, and carved glass. Custom-designed windows and doors.

Manufacturers Glass, Ltd., 650 Reed St., Santa Clara, CA 95050, 408-748-1806, Mon.–Fri. 8:30 A.M.–5:30 P.M.; fax: 408-748-0160. Repair of antique stained-glass items. Custom stained-glass windows; beveling and etching.

Melotte-Morse Stained Glass Inc., 213 South 6th, Springfield, IL 62701, 217-789-9515, 8:00 A.M.–5:00 P.M.; 217-789-9518. Repair and restoration of stained-glass lamps and windows.

Replication of decorative sandblasted designs. Free brochure.

Nelson Dale, Restoration Services, 621 Main St., #3, Waltham, MA 02154, 617-647-9470, 9:00 A.M.–5:00 P.M. Glass reconstruction, cracks and missing pieces. Free brochure.

Old World Restorations, Inc., 347 Stanley Ave., Cincinnati, OH 45226, 800-878-1911, 513-321-1911, Mon.–Fri. 8:30 A.M.–5:30 P.M.; fax: 513-321-1914. Restoration and conservation of art and antiques, including glass. Free brochure.

Origina Luster, Box 2092, Dept. K, Wilkes-Barre, PA 18703, 717-693-3624. Portable ultraviolet black light; Origina Luster restores transparency to "sick" glass.

Pairpoint Crystal Co., 851 Sandwich Rd., PO Box 515, Sagamore, MA 02561, 800-899-0953, 508-888-2344, Mon.–Fri. 8:30 A.M.–6:00 P.M.; fax: 508-888-3537. Handcrafted, full lead crystal liners for silver salts, vases, and more. Cobalt, amethyst, and ruby. Custom work available. Call for details. Will ship anywhere in the U.S. Reproduction catalog $4.

PECO Glass Bending (Pat's Etcetera Co., Inc.), PO Box 777, 810 E. First St., Smithville, TX 78957, 512-237-3600, 10:00 A.M.–3:00 P.M. Bent glass for antique china cabinets, secretary-bookcases, show cases, and other items. Standard radius and custom-bent glass: serpentine bends, S curves, J bends, and irregular curves. Convex glass for old picture frames. All shipped nationwide by UPS. Send SASE for brochure.

Peter's Antiques, 4113 Oechsli Ave., Louisville, KY 40207, 502-893-8498, business; 502-458-8498, residence. Glass repaired and restored.

Pleasant Valley Antique Restoration, Joe Howell, 1725 Reed Rd., Knoxville, MD 21758, 301-432-2721, 9:30 A.M.–9:00 P.M. Restoration of glass. Previous restorations detected and verified.

R & K Weenike Antiques, Roy H. Weenike, Rt. 7, Box 140, Ottumwa, IA 52501, 515-934-5427. Glass grinding and polishing, removal of nicks.

Ray Errett, 218 Chestnut Street, Corning, NY 14830, 607-962-6026, 1:00 P.M.–4:00 P.M. Glass repair and restorations, chips on glasses ground and polished. Consulting work on any glass problems.

Restorations By Linda, Linda M. Peet, 1759 Hemlock St., Fairfield, CA 94533, 707-422-6497. Crystal and cut glass repaired. Free estimates.

Restorite Systems, PO Box 7096-A, West Trenton, NJ 08628, 609-530-1526. Products for restoring glass. Repair kit for broken or chipped glass includes supplies necessary to mend dozens of pieces and illustrated instruction book. Mail order only. Free brochure.

RGS Glass & Frame Corp., Ron's Gallery Supply, 159 Duane St., New York, NY 10013, 800-735-7667; fax: 212-587-5957. Bent glass, custom shapes. Shipped worldwide.

Richard Blaschke Cabinet Glass, 670 Lake Ave., Bristol, CT 06010, 203-584-2566, Mon.-Fri. 10:00 A.M.–5:00 P.M., Sat. and Sun. noon–5:00 P.M., closed Tues. Curved replacement glass for china closets and windows. Popular sizes in stock, or will cut to order. Will install. Free brochure.

Rikki's Studio Inc., Gilbert Kerry Hall, 2809 Bird Ave., Coconut Grove, FL 33133, 305-446-2022, 305-446-2230, 9:00 A.M.–4:30 P.M.; fax: 305-446-6388. Restoration of crystal, including grinding and polishing. Lamps restored and rewired. Chandeliers repaired. Appraisals.

S. A. Bendheim Co., Inc., 61 Willet St., Passaic, NJ 07055, 800-221-7379, 201-473-1733 in New Jersey; fax: 201-471-3475. Restoration glass ™ using original cylinder method, available in two levels of distortion: Light and Full. Free brochure. Sample set of Light and Full Restoration Glass, $10.95.

Sharon Smith Abbott, Fine Wares Restorations, PO Box 753, Bridgton, ME 04009, 207-647-2093, 8:00 A.M.–5:00 P.M., answering machine after hours. Glass conservation services for museum and private collections. Treatments include cleaning, bonding, gap filling, and replacement by casting with appropriate resins. Written estimates and suggested treatment provided at no cost. Glass restoration a specialty.

Stained Glass Associates, PO Box 1531, Raleigh, NC 27602-1531, 919-266-2493, 8:00 A.M.–5:00 P.M. Manufacturing, repairing, and restoring stained-glass windows for churches, commercial and residential installations.

Studio Workshop, Ltd., 22 Bushy Hill Rd., Simsbury, CT 06070, 203-658-6374, 9:00 A.M.–6:00 P.M. Restoration and repair of stained-glass windows and panels.

Sunburst Stained Glass Co., Inc., 20 W. Jennings, Newburgh, IN 47630, 800-982-1521, 812-853-0460, Mon.–Fri. 9:00 A.M.–5:00 P.M. Sat. 10:00 A.M.–4:00 P.M. Stained, beveled, etched, and grooved glass. New and restoration. Painting and firing. Brochure $2.

Tops and Bottoms Club, Madeleine France, PO Box 15555, Plantation, FL 33318, 305-584-0009, 10:00 A.M.–5:00 P.M.; fax: 305-584-0014. Lalique perfume bottle matching service. Mail order.

Van Dyke's, Box 278, Woonsocket, SD 57385, 605-796-4425, 800-843-3320, orders only, 8:00 A.M.–6:00 P.M.; fax: 605-796-4085. Glass eyes for dolls and toys, pendulums and prisms, glass ball claw feet, curved-glass china cabinet parts, isinglass for stove doors. Special parts designed to duplicate the original pieces. Catalog $1.

Venerable Classics, 645 Fourth St., Suite 208, Santa Rosa, CA 95404, 800-531-2891, 9:00 A.M.–5:00 P.M.; fax: 707-575-3626. Restoration of crystal and other materials. Specializing in statuary, dolls, lamps, and clocks. Shipping instructions and free brochure available on request.

Victor Rothman for Stained Glass, 31 Gramatan Dr., Yonkers, NY 10701, 914-965-1196, anytime. Stained-glass restorations; windows, skylights, and lamps. Covering the entire U.S.

Vigues Art Studio, 54 Glanders Rd., Woodbury, CT 06798, 203-263-4088, 10:00 A.M.–5:00 P.M. Conservation and restoration of glass.

W. G. T. Burne (Antique Glass) Ltd., 11 Elystan S., London, England SW3 3NT, 071-589 6074, 9:00 A.M.–5:00 P.M.; fax: 081-944 1977. Repair and restoration of glass. Specialists in English and Irish eighteenth- and nineteenth-century glass tableware, decanters, chandeliers, lustres, candelabra, wall lights, and collectors pieces. Valuations.

Westminster Stained Glass, Laura S. Chaffee, 62 Westminster St., Springfield, MA 01109, 413-734-4382, 8:00 A.M.–6:00 P.M. Stained-glass windows and lamps repaired and restored. Custom work: new windows, panels, and lamps. By appointment only.

Whittemore-Durgin Glass Co., Box 2065 LT, Hanover, MA 02339, 800-262-1790, 617-871-1743, Mon.–Fri. 8:30 A.M.–4:30 P.M.; fax: 617-871-5597. Stained-glass supplies, repair parts, tools, books, and equipment. Lamp hardware; patterns for lampshades, windows, and panes; accessories for jewelry, boxes, and clocks. Catalog.

Wright's Stained Glass, 330 Winchester Ave., Martinsburg, WV 25401, 304-263-2502, Mon., Wed., Fri.–Sun., 10:00 A.M.–5:00 P.M.; fax: 304-267-2705. Custom designed stained glass. Reproduction stained glass to match existing glass. Old stained glass reframed. Repairs to all types of stained-glass objects. Mail order worldwide. Catalog $3.

Yesteryears Antiques, 123 Hedges Rd., Patchogue, NY 11772-5531, 800-782-9169, 9:00 A.M.–8:00 P.M. Curved china cabinet glass. Radius charts for curved glass $4.

Videos

American Art Glass: 1880–1930, Tiffany, Steuben, Mt. Washington, and Durand, identification, tips on collecting, 30 minutes, $29.95 plus $3 shipping; *European Art Glass: 1880–1939,* Daum Nancy, Gallé, Lalique, Loetz, Moser, Venetian art glass, and Webb, identification, tips on collecting, 30 minutes, $29.95 plus $3 shipping; *Lalique Glass,* adapted from the book *Lalique Glass* by Nicholas M. Dawes, includes sample auction prices, 35 minutes,

$29.95 plus $3 shipping. **Award Video & Film Distributors, Inc.,** 3520 Bayou Louise Ln., Sarasota, FL 34242, 813-955-1818; fax: 813-346-2583.

Dale Ender, PO Box 246, Sawyer, MI 49125, fax: 616-426-3832. Videos on toothpick holders. Royal Bayreuth, Heisey, all thirty-two known patterns shown.

A Tour Through the Westmoreland Glass Factory, $19.95. **FSJ Publishing Company,** PO Box 122, Iowa City, IA 52244, 319-626-2807. Other videos include: *The Glass Room Video* features Westmoreland and Imperial carnival glass, 90 minutes, $19.95. *1924: Westmoreland's First Full Color Catalog,* 65 minutes, $19.95; future release— *Westmoreland Revisited,* tour of factory today, $19.95.

American Art Glass, 1880–1930, 30 minutes, $29.95; *European Art Glass, 1880–1939,* 30 minutes, $29.95; **John A. Shuman, III,** PO Box 57, Pottstown, PA 19464, 215-469-9325.

European Glass, Investing in Glass, **National Early American Glass Club,** Box 8489, Silver Spring, MD 20907.

Candlewick, At Home in Any Home, Vols. 1 and 2, **National Imperial Glass Collectors' Society,** PO Box 534, Bellaire, OH 43906. Two-volume set from 1993 NIGCS convention show convention display, members-only auction, Imperial workers seminar, brief history of Imperial Glass Corporation, and a seminar on Candlewick. Vol. 1, 120 minutes; Vol. 2, 68 minutes. Two-volume set: members $44, non-members $49.

RegaloVetro, 1840 41st Ave. E., Seattle, WA 98112. Mail order sales of video tapes for collectors. Send SASE for list of tapes available.

Living Glass: Popular Patterns of the Depression Era, Vols. 1 and 2, **RoCliff Communicatons,** 8422 N. Park Ct., Kansas City, MO 64155, 800-762-5431. Vol. 1, 98 minutes, patterns from Hocking/Anchor-Hocking, Jeanette, and Hazel-Atlas, $34.95. Vol. 2, 91 minutes, Federal, MacBeth-Evans, Indiana, Imperial, and more, $34.95. Two-volume set, $54.90.

Fragile Art, **WBGU TV,** 245 Troup St., Bowling Green, OH 43403.

Early American Pressed Glass II, **Wisconsin Antiques Dealers Association Educational Film Committee,** c/o Sharron Cypher, 135 N. Main, Hartford, WI 53027, 414-673-2751. 30 minutes. $15.

Hardware

*L*ocks and keys have intrigued collectors since medieval times, and today collectors want everything from wrought-iron door locks to brass-tagged hotel keys. Wooden locks were used by the Egyptians about 2000 B.C. By the Middle Ages, huge metal locks were made to keep intruders out of the castle. Collectors divide locks into types and often specialize in categories such as railroad locks, trick locks, ball and chains, institutional locks, combination locks, padlocks, or locks made by special companies or for special events. A few locks have historical value because they can be traced to a maker or historic building.

Locks sell well in flea markets and antiques stores, in restored and in original condition. Missing keys are not a problem. The best prices are paid for locks with special features, those with unusual mechanisms or rare logos, and those in pristine condition with the original box and key.

Keys are priced by rarity, shape, and age. Old iron keys are best, but some collectors now buy brass hotel keys either tagged or with the name on the key. Look for the names YALE, VAN DORN IRON WORKS, and WINCHESTER.

REPAIR

Some collectors want examples of old doorknobs or iron latches to display as part of a collection, but most people want to use the old hardware. When using old doorknobs, you must be sure the measurements correspond to the thickness of your door. Old doors are sometimes thicker than newer doors.

Hardware for old furniture is difficult to match but relatively easy to replace. When possible, match existing hardware—some designs are still being made. A few companies will make a copy of your hardware from the sample you submit. If the hardware is not original or can't be matched, replace it with old or new pieces. Be sure to get hardware of the correct style and period.

When replacing hardware, try buying pieces that will cover the old screw holes. Special hardware for old refrigerators, trunks, doors, and windows can be found.

For more information, see Furniture, Metals, Pottery & Porcelain, and Trunks sections.

Price Books

Paracentric Guide to Key Collecting, 2nd edition, Don Stewart (Key Collectors International, PO Box 9397, Phoenix, AZ 85068, © 1993).

Poorman's Story & Ornamental Padlocks, 3rd edition, Don Stewart (Key Collectors International, PO Box 9397, Phoenix, AZ 85068, © 1992).

Treasure Chest Padlocks, 2nd edition, Don Stewart (Key Collectors International, PO Box 9397, Phoenix, AZ 85068, © 1993).

Clubs & Publications

American Lock Collectors Association, *American Lock Collectors Association* (NL), 36076 Grennada, Livonia, MI 48154.

Antique Doorknob Collectors of America, *Doorknob Collector* (NL), PO Box 126, Eola, IL 60519-0126.

West Coast Lock Collectors, *West Coast Lock Collectors Newsletter* (NL), 1427 Lincoln Blvd., Santa Monica, CA 90401.

Repairs, Parts & Supplies

A Carolina Craftsman, 975 S. Avocado St., Anaheim, CA 92805, 714-776-7877, 8:00 A.M.–5:00 P.M.; fax: 714-533-0894. Catalog sales of antique replacement hardware for houses and furniture. Free literature on a specific item; complete catalog set $5, refundable with first order.

Al Bar-Wilmette Platers, 127 Green Bay Rd., Wilmette, IL 60091, 708-251-0187, Mon.–Fri. 8:00 A.M.–5:00 P.M., Sat. 8:00 A.M.–3:00 P.M. Restoration of metal antiques from sterling silver pieces to brass light fixtures. Plating, polishing, repairing, lacquering. Door and window hardware polished and lacquered. Antique door hardware for sale. Will provide quotes from photos sent. Nationwide service. Daily UPS service. Please insure all shipments.

Albert Constantine & Son, Inc., 2050 Eastchester Rd., Bronx, NY 10461, 718-792-1600, Mon.–Sat. 8:00 A.M.–5:00 P.M. (May 1–Labor Day, Sat. until 1:00 P.M.), order line: 800-223-8087; fax: 800-253-WOOD. Hardware, tools, and supplies. Ice box hardware, cabinet hardware, trunk fittings, locks, specialty hinges, antique brass and porcelain pulls, box hardware, etc. Catalog $1.

Antique Bath and Kitchens, 2220 Carlton Way, Santa Barbara, CA 93109, 805-962-8598, noon–5:00 P.M. Old copper and brass sinks fabricated and repaired, old faucets repaired. Old toilet parts, shower conversion parts. Catalog $2.

Antique Hardware Store, 9730 Easton Rd., Kintnersville, PA 18930, 800-422-9982, daily, 9:00

A.M.–5:00 P.M.; fax: 215-847-5628. Old-style door, window, cabinet, and specialty hardware; claw-foot tub supplies, plumbing fittings, specialty lamp shades, floor grills, tin ceilings. Custom hardware and plumbing fixtures. Free catalog.

Arden Forge Co., 301 Brintons Bridge Rd., West Chester, PA 19382, 215-399-1530. Victorian and colonial hardware for architecture and furniture. Hinges, latches, slide bolts, shutter dogs, and other items. Original and reproduction hardware, iron, cast iron, steel, copper, tin, pewter, lead, and zinc. Antique lock repair. Write or telephone for availability and price.

Armor Products, PO Box 445, East Northport, NY 11731-0445, 516-462-6228, 9:00 A.M.–5:00 P.M.; fax: 516-462-5793. Furniture hinges, drawer pulls, composition overlays, lamp supplies, table hardware, box hardware, wood turnings, tools, and finishing supplies. Free catalog.

Barap Specialties, 835 Bellows, Frankfort, MI 49635, 800-322-7273, 9:00 A.M.–5:00 P.M. Lamp parts, tools, finishing materials, hardware, etc. Catalog $1.

Bathroom Machineries, PO Box 1020, Murphys, CA 95247, 209-728-2031. Reproduction brass hardware. Early American and Victorian bathroom fixtures and accessories; reproductions. Restoration of lighting fixtures and antique plumbing fixtures; brass polishing. Victorian Hardware catalog $3; Bathroom Machineries catalog $3.

Brass Foundry Castings, The Old Wheelwright Shop, Brasted Forge, Brasted, Kent England TN16 1JL, 0959-563863, 9:00 A.M.–5:00 P.M.; fax: 0959-561262. Furniture mounts, escutcheon pins, hand-cut nails, kidney bow keys, clock mounts, handmade brass chicken wire, lead sheet, candle sconces, galleries, brass stringing, hinges, feet, castors, and other fittings. Repairs to vintage fittings. Catalog £18.

The Brass Knob, Architectural Antiques, 2311 18th Street NW, Washington, DC 20009, 202-332-3370, Mon.–Sat., 10:30 A.M.–6:00 P.M., Sun. 12:00 P.M.–5:00 P.M. Architectural antiques, specializing in restored hardware, lighting, fireplace mantels, ironwork, and other decorative detail. Warehouse, The Brass Knob, Back Doors, at 1701A Kalorama Rd. NW, Washington, DC 20009. Catalog.

C & H Supply, 5431 Mountville Rd., Adamstown, MD 21710, 301-663-1812, Mon.–Fri. 9:00 A.M.–5:00 P.M.; fax: 301-874-2524. Reproduction brass hardware, wood and porcelain knobs, table parts, chair caning supplies, replacement chair seats, short bed rails, cannonballs for iron and brass beds, replacement trunk parts, pie-safe tins, ice box hardware, kitchen cabinet hardware, flour bins. Veneers, paint and varnish removers, stains and lacquers. Most orders shipped within 24 hours. Catalog $4.

Cirecast, Inc., 380 Seventh St., San Francisco, CA 94103, 415-863-8319, 8:30 A.M.–4:30 P.M.; fax: 415-863-7721. Victorian door and window hardware, replicated from customer's original product using the lost wax casting process. Brochure.

Classic Accents, 12869 Eureka, South Gate, MI 48195, 313-282-5525. Push-button light switches, decorative and plain cover plates, brass polishing paste, carbon filament Victorian light bulbs, hand-tied tassels. Free catalog.

Conner's Architectural Antiques, 701 P St., Lincoln, NE 68508, 402-435-3338. Old, original, and reproduction hardware. Plating and polishing.

Craftsman Wood Service Company, 1735 W. Cortland Ct., Addison, IL 60101, 708-629-3100, 8:30 A.M.–5:00 P.M.; fax: 708-629-8292 for information; 800-543-9367 for orders. Over 4,000 items for the wood hobbyist, including hard-to-find hardware. Mail order worldwide. Catalog $1.

Crawford's Old House Store, 550 Elizabeth, Room 92, Waukesha, WI 53186, 800-556-7878, 8:00 A.M.–5:00 P.M. Old-style turned hardwood corner protectors and door stops. Builders hardware, Victorian bath fixtures, ceiling rosettes, etc.

Crown City Hardware Co., 1047 N. Allen Ave., Pasadena, CA 91104, 818-794-1188, Mon.–Fri.

8:30 A.M.–5:00 P.M.; fax: 818-794-1439. Restoration hardware, all periods and styles. Decorative hardware for doors, windows, cabinets, and furniture, made of brass, iron, and crystal. Antique and custom-made hardware. Locks repaired and cleaned, keys made. Retail shop and mail order. Catalog $6.50.

D.C. Mitchell Reproductions, 1132 Powderhorn Dr., Newark, DE 19713, 302-998-1181, 8:00 A.M.–5:00 P.M.; fax: 302-994-0178. Hand-forged reproductions of period hardware in brass and iron. Knobs, pulls, hooks, handles, latches, box locks, shutter bolts, and several types of hinges. Free brochure.

Doug Poe Antiques, 4213W 500N, Huntington, IN 46750, 800-348-5004, 8:00 A.M.–5:00 P.M., except June–August, 7:00 A.M.–4:00 P.M. Antique restoration hardware. Cast brass pulls, die-cast brass knobs, stamped brass keyholes, keys, hooks, wood casters. Free flier.

18th Century Hardware Company, Inc., 131 E. Third St., Derry, PA 15627, 412-694-2708, 8:00 A.M.–4:30 P.M. Manufacturers of hardware for antique furniture. Can duplicate almost anything. Metal items cleaned, polished, and lacquered. Catalog $3.

Eugenia's Place, 3522 Broad St., Chamblee, GA 30341, 404-458-1677, 404-261-0394, 10:00 A.M.–9:00 P.M. Antique hardware. Door hardware, knockers, furniture hardware, twist bells. No reproduction hardware. Send for flyer.

Faneuil Furniture Hardware Company, Inc., 163 Main St., Salem, NH 03079, 603-898-7733, 8:00 A.M.–4:30 P.M.; fax: 603-898-7839. Solid brass reproduction pulls, knobs, hinges, escutcheons, casters, bed hardware, and other fittings for period furniture. Mail order worldwide. Catalog $3.

Farmerstown Hardware & Supplies, Junior and Robert Hershberger, 3155 S.R. 557, Dept. K, Baltic, OH 43804, 216-893-2464, Mon.–Fri. 8:00 A.M.–5:00 P.M. Door hardware, Hoosier cabinet parts, Aladdin lamp parts, wood carvings, spool cabinet decals,

antique telephone parts, glue, wax, and many hard-to-find items. Wholesale catalog $2.

Green Star Forge, Rear #4 Richard St., Raynham, MA 02767-1729, 508-824-3077, 7:00 A.M.–9:00 P.M. Reproduction hardware, custom and novelty hardware. Restoration. Send SASE for brochure.

Hardware+Plus, Inc., 701 E. Kingsley Rd., Garland, TX 75041, 214-271-0319, technical assistance; 800-522-7336, order line; fax: 214-271-9726. Period and reproduction furniture hardware and parts, including caning supplies. Door and window hardware, nostalgic plumbing fittings and fixtures, molded interior and exterior millwork and ornamentation, tin ceiling panels, and wax. Free brochure. Hardware catalog $5.

Hippo Hardware & Trading Co., 1040 E. Burnside, Portland, OR 97214, 503-231-1444, Mon.–Fri. 10:00 A.M.–5:00 P.M., Sat. 10:00 A.M.–6:00 P.M.; fax: 503-231-5708. Original hardware, lighting, plumbing, and house parts for restoration. Salvaged architectural pieces; remanufactured hardware and other old house parts. Victorian to Ozzie and Harriet periods. Send photo of items sought. Reproduction catalog $2.

Historic Housefitters Company, Farm to Market Rd., Dept. K, Brewster, NY 10509, 914-278-2427, 9:00 A.M.–5:30 P.M.; fax: 914-278-7726. Hand-forged eighteenth-century hardware for use in restoration or reproduction Colonial homes. All types of door hardware, including thumb latches, strap hinges, and H and HL hinges. Custom blacksmithing. Will ship worldwide. Catalog $3.

Horton Brasses, PO Box 120Q, Nooks Hill Rd., Cromwell, CT 06416, 203-635-4400, 8:30 A.M.–4:00 P.M.; fax: 203-635-6473. Solid brass reproduction furniture hardware. Drawer pulls, knobs, bed hardware, table hardware, hinges, porcelain knobs, and hand-forged black iron. Clock hardware. Parts, nails, polishes, books, and videos. Catalog $3.

Jim Leonard, Antique Hardware, 509 Tangle Dr., Jamestown, NC 27282, 919-454-3583, 6:00 P.M.–10:00 P.M. and weekends. eighteenth- and nineteenth-century wrought-iron door hardware and fireplace equipment. Thumb latches, elbow latches, slide bolts, strap hinges, ram's horn hinges, sawtooth trammel lighting device holders, cupboard and blanket chest hardware, etc. Send $2 for price list and photos of hardware available.

Joseph Biunno, 129 W. 29th St., 11th Floor, New York, NY 10001, 212-629-5630, 9:00 A.M.–5:00 P.M.; fax: 212-268-4577. Repair and restoration of antique locks and keys. Manufacturers of custom drapery hardware.

Kayne & Son Custom Forged Hardware, Steve Kayne, 76 Daniel Ridge Rd., Candler, NC 28715, 704-665-8868, 8:00 A.M.–11:00 P.M.; fax: 704-665-8303. Repair, restoration, and conservation of all metals, including pot metal and cast iron. Furniture hardware recast. Hand-forged hardware made to your design. Oven doors, Blake hardware, locks, parts, and unavailable pieces reproduced. Cast brass colonial hardware. Early American hardware in brass, antique, or black finish. Reproductions catalog $4.

Lehman Hardware, PO Box 41, 4779 Kidron Rd., Kidron, OH 44603-0041, 216-857-5441 Mon.-Sat. 7:00 A.M.–5:30 P.M., Thurs. 7:00 A.M.–9:00 P.M.; fax: 216-857-5785. Hardware, lamp parts, stove paint, stove door gaskets, tools, and more. Catalog $2.

Liz's Antique Hardware, 453 S. LaBrea, Los Angeles, CA 90036, 213-939-4403, 10:00 A.M.–6:30 P.M. daily; fax: 213-939-4387. 350,000 pieces of original antique hardware for doors, windows, furniture, curtains, lighting, and bath accessories. Mail order matching service. To match antique hardware by mail, send photo of item or items, template of sizes, quantity desired, and $10 handling fee. If not available, your request will be kept on file until located.

Marlborough Country Barn, N. Main St., Marlborough, CT 06447, 203-295-8231; in Connecticut, 800-852-8893; fax: 203-295-7424, Tues., Wed., Sat. 10:00 A.M.–5:30 P.M., Thurs. and Fri. 10:00 A.M.–8:00 P.M., Sun. noon–5:00 P.M. The Restoration Center features reproduction hardware, lighting, paints, stencils, and accessories.

Merit Metal Products Corp., Daryl Schaefer, 242 Valley Rd., Warrington, PA 18976, 215-343-2500, 8:30 A.M.–5:00 P.M.; fax: 215-343-4839. Manufacturers of solid brass restoration and renovation hardware. Cabinet and furniture hardware. Full refinishing capabilities. Catalog $10.

Michael J. Dotzel & Son, 402 E. 63rd St., New York, NY 10021, 212-838-2890, 8:00 A.M.–4:00 P.M. Hardware. Lacquering, silverplating, and chrome plating. Missing parts cast.

Monroe Coldren and Son, 723 E. Virginia Ave., West Chester, PA 19380, 215-692-5651, Mon.-Sat. 8:30 A.M.–5.00 P.M. Brass, copper, and iron work. Metal work repaired and custom crafted. Eighteenth- and nineteenth-century hardware, lighting, and fireplace accessories.

Muff's Antiques, 135 S. Glassell St., Orange, CA 92666, 714-997-0243, Tues.–Sat. 11:00 A.M.–5:00 P.M. Hard-to-find hardware for furniture, trunks, rolltop desks, ice boxes, and Hoosier cabinets. Kitchen jar lids, glass knobs, claw and ball feet, hooks, carvings, highchair trays, pressed-fiber seats, angle lamp bowls and chimneys, lamp parts, shades, and burners; phone parts. Keys made, locks repaired. Mail order worldwide. Hardware catalog $5.

Old and Elegant Distributing, 10203 Main St. Ln., Bellevue, WA 98004, 206-455-4660, Mon.-Sat. 9:00 A.M.–6:00 P.M., 9:00 P.M.–11:00 P.M.; fax: 206-455-0203. Hardware, bathroom sinks, lighting parts, architecturally carved wood, and other supplies.

Ole Fashion Things, 402 SW Evangeline Thwy., Lafayette, LA 70501, 318-234-4800, 800-228-4967, Tues.–Sat. 10:00 A.M.–6:00 P.M. Fancy plumbing fixtures, claw-foot bathtubs, pedestal lavatories,

Victorian-style washstands, drop-in basins, plumbing hardware. Catalog $5.

Paxton Hardware Ltd., PO Box 256, 7818 Bradshaw Rd., Upper Falls, MD 21156, 410-592-8505, 9:00 A.M.–5:00 P.M.; fax: 410-592-2224. Period brass furniture hardware, including hinges, hooks, locks, pulls, supports, table and desk hardware; campaign and box hardware; ice box and Hoosier hardware; miscellaneous hardware and framing supplies. Lamp replacement parts. Cleaning and restoration products. Free brochure. Catalog $4.

Phyllis Kennedy, 9256 Holyoke Ct., Indianapolis, IN 46268, 317-872-6366, 10:00 A.M.–5:00 P.M. Hardware and parts for antique furniture, Hoosier cabinets, and trunks. Specializing in parts for Hoosier cabinets, including flour bins, bread drawers, roll doors, wire racks, sugar jars, and more. Store located at 10663 Andrade Dr., Zionsville, IN 46077. Catalog $3.

Remodelers & Renovators Supply, PO Box 45478, Boise, ID 83711, 208-322-6221, 9:00 A.M.–5:00 P.M. Hardware and plumbing supplies for vintage houses, available in brass; some chrome and glass. Catalog $3.

Renovation Source, Inc., 3512 N. Southport, Chicago, IL 60657, 312-327-1250, Tues.–Sat. 10:00 A.M.–6:00 P.M. Door hardware, decorative architectural details of wood, stone, plaster, and iron. Repair and restoration.

The Restoration Place, 305 20th St., Rock Island, IL 61201, 3039-786-0004, 9:30 A.M.–5:30 P.M.; fax: 309-786-5834. Resource center for restoration and renovation products and services. Building and furniture hardware, antique and reproduction. Free brochure. Catalog $8.

Robinson's Antiques, 170 Kent St., Portland, MI 48875, 517-647-6155. Antique replacement hardware matching service. Furniture hardware, door knobs, fancy hinges. No reproductions. Send photocopy of item required with SASE for reply.

Steptoe and Wife Antiques Ltd., 322 Geary Ave., Toronto, ON Canada M6H 2C7, 416-530-4200. Mon.–Fri. 9:00 A.M.–5:00 P.M.; fax: 416-530-4666. Old-fashioned curtain rods and decorative drapery hardware. Cast-iron table bases. Free brochure.

Thomas Loose, Blacksmith-Whitesmith, Rt. 2, Box 2410, Leesport, PA 19533, 215-926-4849, 9:00 A.M.–4:00 P.M. Seventeenth- and eighteenth-century reproduction iron hardware, kitchen utensils, fireplace cooking accessories, hooks, candlesticks, and candlestands. Catalog $1.

Tremont Nail Company, PO Box 111, Dept. K-94, Wareham, MA 02571, 800-842-0560, 8:00 A.M.–4:30 P.M.; fax: 508-295-1365. Manufacturer of 20 different types of cut nails. Restoration hardware. Free brochure.

Van Dyke's, Box 278, Woonsocket, SD 57385, 605-796-4425, 800-843-3320, orders only, 8:00 A.M.–6:00 P.M.; fax: 605-796-4085. Brass hardware of all kinds, rolltop desk components, trunk parts, pie-safe tins, knobs, clock parts; porcelain, marble, glass and wood knobs. Special parts designed to duplicate the original pieces. Mail order worldwide. Catalog $1.

Wayne's Woods, Inc., 39 N. Plains Industrial Rd., Wallingford, CT 06492, 800-793-6208, 9:00 A.M.–5:00 P.M.; fax: 203-949-0769. Reproduction hardware, refinishing supplies, furniture restoration and refinishing. Free catalog.

Windy Hill Forge, 3824 Schroeder Ave., Perry Hall, MD 21128-9783, 410-256-5890, 8:00 A.M.–5:00 P.M. Custom and reproduction hardware for homes and furniture. Colonial box locks and latches, snow irons, shutter hold-backs, wall washers, cast brackets, restoration parts in iron, brass, lead, and sheet metal. Free brochure.

Wise Company, 6503 St. Claude, PO Box 118K, Arabi, LA 70032, 504-277-7551, 9:00 A.M.-5:00 P.M. Antique reproduction brass and miscellaneous hardware. Chair caning supplies. Catalog $4.

Wrecking Bar, 292 Moreland Ave. NE, Atlanta, GA 30307, 404-525-0468, Mon.–Sat. 9:00 A.M.–5:00 P.M. Brass and copper hardware. Brochure.

Yesteryears Antiques, 123 Hedges Rd., Patchogue, NY 11772-5531, 800-782-9169, 9:00 A.M.–8:00 P.M. Brass reproduction hardware for turn-of-the-century furniture, including wheels, oak carvings, brass bed balls, drawer pulls, knobs, escutcheons, Hoosier and ice box parts, etc.

*H*oliday *C*ollectibles

*I*f your attic has been used for storage for the past thirty years or more, it probably holds some valuable holiday collectibles. Christmas ornaments, light bulbs, tree holders, cards, tinsel, Halloween papier-mâché pumpkins, skeletons, costumes, candy containers, even Fourth of July banners, or fireworks package labels, are eagerly collected. The prices paid for old Christmas ornaments are astounding. Do your homework. Look at the books about holiday collectibles at your library. There are six or seven fine books with color pictures, descriptions, and some price information. There is also price information in the annual general price lists like *Kovels' Antiques & Collectibles Price List.*

Don't just put out a box of ornaments at your garage sale; you might be giving away money. If you do not have time to do the research, take the holiday memorabilia to a local auction gallery or to a dealer who is already selling this type of merchandise. These pieces sell best the month before the holiday, so be sure to talk to the dealers several months earlier. Sell Christmas ornaments by October 1, Halloween pumpkins by August.

In general, anything figural will sell well: Santa Claus, black cats, sleighs filled with toys, even bottles shaped like holiday symbols. Newer items are often made partially of plastic, so study anything you have that is made entirely of paper, iron, or tin. Early blown-glass ornaments are hard to date because they have been copied since the 1950s, but even relatively recent ones are worth money to the right person. Chains of bubble lights, working bubble light bulbs, or figural bulbs, working or not, and all sorts of old paper and tinsel ornaments can be surprisingly high-priced. The old chicken-feather Christmas trees are now classed as folk art and sell for hundreds of dollars even if they are only twelve inches high. Postcards and greeting cards sell as holiday items at regular shows and also do well at the specialty shows for paper items.

R E P A I R

Save the old metal caps from broken early glass ornaments. They are different from the new ones and can be used on other early glass ornaments that are missing them. It is possible to find new old-style tinsel, paper cutouts, and spun "clouds" when restoring old ornaments.

Many old glass ornaments are now being sold again; with a little ingenuity, you could find a new glass bird for your old glass-and-tinsel bird nest, or use other combinations of old and new to save treasured pieces.

Look in gift shops that sell stickers and fancy wrapping paper.

Many reprints of Victorian "scrap" figures are now available. Feather trees are being reproduced and there are a few craftsmen who can repair old trees. The old base is one of the clues to age, so don't repaint or remove it. If it is unsightly, cover it with a cloth.

Halloween pieces made of pressed cardboard or crepe paper will fade if kept in too sunny a spot. Never light a candle in the center of a cardboard pumpkin. It may be attractive, but it is a fire hazard. Many old jack-o'-lanterns had tissue-paper inserts for eyes. You can easily make a reproduction if you can find an old one to use as a pattern.

Easter eggs and candy containers should be carefully stored where the remains of food will not attract rodents and insects. Bits of paper lace used on some Easter pieces can be replaced by using parts of paper doilies found in stores that specialize in gourmet cooking supplies.

Specialized information can be found in the Glass, Paper, and Pottery & Porcelain sections.

Price Books

Christmas Collectibles, 2nd edition, Margaret and Kenn Whitmyer (Collector Books, Paducah, KY, © 1994).

Christmas Through the Decades, Robert Brenner (Schiffer, Atglen, PA, © 1993).

The Joy of Christmas Collecting, Chris Kirk (L-W Book Sales, PO Box 69, Gas City, IN 46933, © 1994).

1995 Price Guide on Hallmark Ornaments (Rosie Wells Enterprises, Inc., RR #1, Canton IL 61520, © 1994).

Ornamental & Figural Nutcrackers: An Identification & Value Guide, Judith A. Rittenhouse (Collector Books, Paducah, KY, © 1993).

Snow Babies, Santas and Elves: Collecting Christmas Bisque Figures, Mary Morrison (Schiffer, Atglen, PA, © 1993).

Clubs & Publications

California Ornament Collectors, *California Ornament Collectors Newsletter* (NL), PO Box 1431, Rohnert Park, CA 94927-1431.

National Valentine Collectors Association, *National Valentine Collectors Bulletin* (NL), PO Box 1404, Santa Ana, CA 92702 (includes mail auction of valentines).

Deck the Halls (MAG), PO Box 476879, Chicago, IL 60647.

Golden Glow of Christmas Past (NL), 6401 Winsdale St., Golden Valley, MN 55427.

I Love Christmas! (NL), 510 7th Ave., Coralville, IA 52241.

Joan Ketterer's Twelve Months of Christmas (NL), PO Box 97172, Pittsburgh, PA 15229.

Ornament Collector (MAG), R.R. #1, Canton, IL 61520.

Trick or Treat Trader (NL), PO Box 499, Winchester, NH 03470.

Repairs, Parts & Supplies

Jerry Arnold, 3520 Dellwood Rd., Cleveland Heights, OH 44118, 216-321-7418, 9:00 A.M.–9:00 P.M. Repair and restoration of belsnickles, Santas, papier-mâché items, fur beards, etc., on antique holiday items. Send photo for free estimate, SASE for brochure.

Ivory

*A*ll ivory does not come from elephant tusks. Ivory can also be from other animals, such as walruses, hippopotamuses, or whales. There is also "vegetable ivory." Some vegetable materials have a similar texture and density and look like ivory, but it is possible to see the growth rings on a large piece of an elephant's tusk. Some types of plastic look very much like ivory. Determining whether you have ivory or plastic may prove a problem. The standard test is to heat a needle red hot while holding it with pliers. Press the point of the needle into the bottom of the ivory piece. Plastic will melt, but ivory will not.

The value of ivory objects is determined by the quality of the carving and its condition. If the ivory is milk white because it was washed, deduct 30 percent. If the ivory is noticeably cracked, deduct 75 percent. Oriental ivory carvings, from large elephant tusks to tiny netsuke (Japanese buttons), sell quickly to friends and dealers. New ones are being made, but premium prices are paid for the old ones. A signature adds 50 percent or more.

If you suspect you have an old, top-quality ivory carving, make an appointment with the proper person at your local art museum. You should be able to learn the age and the quality, but do not ask the value. A museum cannot appraise for you. Once you know the age, it is not difficult to compare your carving with others of similar quality that you can find at good shops, shows, or auctions. Price guides list hundreds of ivory items under such headings as Ivory, Scrimshaw, Netsuke, Carving, Orientalia, or Jewelry.

Scrimshaw is ivory or ivorylike material decorated or carved by sailors or other artists. It is a very popular, high-priced form of folk art and sells to maritime collectors and folk art enthusiasts at important shows and auctions. If you have some old scrimshaw, a carved tooth, a small box, tool, or a whimsy, it should be appraised by an expert before it is sold. Beware! Imitation scrimshaw, especially carved teeth, has been made for the past twenty years or more. Some plastic reproductions are so realistic they have fooled auctioneers. Modern craftsmen make and sell "scrimshaw" made on plastic or fossilized walrus tusks. Even poor-quality, modern ivory carvings can be sold, but they have a low value, about half the retail price.

REPAIR

Ivory requires special care and cleaning. Never make the mistake that we made many years ago when we carefully washed our first ivory carving, leaving it an undesirable white color. It has been years since we erred and the carving has still not regained the yellow-brown tint or patina preferred by collectors. If a carving is handled, body oils and moisture will eventually help to age it, but that would take more than one lifetime. Artificial coloring is not satisfactory. Never wash old ivory. The proper steps for cleaning can be found in technical books on restoration.

Ivory can be repaired by experts. Minor breaks can be mended by using a good commercial glue. Thin slices of ivory for inlay replacement are available.

Repairs, Parts & Supplies

A. Ludwig Klein & Son, Inc., PO Box 145, Harleysville, PA 19438, 215-256-9004, Tues.–Fri. 10:00 A.M.–5:00 P.M. Ivory restoration. Statuary and monuments, appraisals, insurance claims by appointment. Free brochure.

Broken Art Restoration, Michelle and Bill Marhoefer, 1841 W. Chicago Ave., Chicago, IL 60622, 312-226-8200, Tues.–Fri., 9:00 A.M.–5:00 P.M. Ivory, pottery, porcelain, ceramics, wood, metal, and stone art objects restored. Missing parts replaced, invisible repairs made to almost any art object. Free brochure.

Carl "Frank" Funes, 57 Maplewood Avenue, Hempstead, NY 11550, 516-481-0147, 7:00 P.M.–9:00 P.M. Restoration of ivory and artifacts. Free brochure.

Ceramic Restorations, Inc., Jareth Holub, 161 West 61st Street, Apt. 9F, New York, NY 10023, 212-247-8657, 9:00 A.M.–6:00 P.M. Ivory repair and restoration. Free estimates.

D & J Glass Clinic, David Jasper, 40658 267th St., Sioux Falls, SD 57106, 605-361-7524, 9:00 A.M.–5:00 P.M.; fax: 605-361-7216. Restoration of ivory.

Dean's China Restoration, 131 Elmwood Drive, Cheshire, CT 06410, 800-669-1327, Mon.–Fri. 9:00 A.M.–5:00 P.M. Repair and restoration of ivory. Mail order worldwide. Free brochure.

Hess Restorations, 200 Park Avenue South, New York, NY 10003, 212-260-2255, 10:30 A.M.–4:00 P.M. Restoration of ivory. Brochure.

I.P.G.R., Inc., PO Box 205, Kulpsville, PA 19443, 800-869-5633 orders only; 215-256-9015, Tues.–Fri. 9:30 A.M.–4:30 P.M., Sat. 9:30 A.M.–1:30 P.M.; fax: 215-256-9644. Complete line of restoration materials. Catalog $3, refundable with first order.

John Edward Cunningham, 1525 East Berkeley, Springfield, MO 65804, 417-889-7702, Mon.–Sat. 9:00 A.M.–5:00 P.M. Ivory restored. Hand-carved genuine ivory replacement parts for Art Deco, Japanese figurines, jewelry, and inlays. Missing parts replaced. Mail order or by appointment. Send SASE for more information.

Just Enterprises—Art & Antique Restoration, Gary and Susanne Gottfried, 2790 Sherwin Avenue, #10, Ventura, CA 93003, 805-644-5837, 10:00 A.M.–noon, 2:00 P.M.–5:00 P.M. Restoration of ivory.

Loughlin's Restoration Studio, 749 Indian Beach Circle, Sarasota, FL 34234, 813-355-7318, Mon.–Fri. 9:00 A.M.–5:00 P.M. Restorers of ivory and jade.

Phoenix Restoration Inc., 5305 North 7th Street, Suite C, Phoenix, AZ 85014, 602-263-5178, 800-234-5178, 8:00 A.M.–6:00 P.M.; fax: 602-263-6009. Restoration and conservation of ivory.

Sano Studio, 767 Lexington Avenue at 60th Street, New York, NY 10021, 212-759-6131, 10:00 A.M.–5:00 P.M. Restoration of antique ivory.

T. S. Restoration, J. M. Denson, 2622 North Dobson Road, Chandler, AZ 85224. Restoration of ivory, by appointment. Mail order. Send LSASE for information.

Venerable Classics, 645 Fourth Street, Suite 208, Santa Rosa, CA 95404, 800-531-2891, 9:00 A.M.–5:00 P.M.; fax: 707-575-3626. Restoration of ivory, jade, and other materials. Specializing in statuary, dolls, lamps, and clocks. Shipping instructions and free brochure available on request.

Jewelry

*P*recious jewelry (costume jewelry is discussed at the end of this chapter) has a special monetary worth known in the trade as "meltdown." This is the value of the piece if it is totally destroyed and the wholesale price of the gold, silver, and gem is calculated. You must never sell for less than meltdown. It is like giving dollar bills away.

Great-grandmother left you her heirloom diamond pin, probably dating from about 1910. It is made of white metal and has many small diamonds set in the old-fashioned way. You might be able to take it to a local jeweler to learn the meltdown value. "Jewelry Buyers" are listed in the Yellow Pages of the phone book, and the ads indicate those who buy "estate" jewelry and scrap. These are the people to tell you the lowest price you should take. They will test the metal to see if it is white gold, silver, or platinum; they will check the diamonds and then tell you what they will pay. Sometimes there is a small fee for this service. Most do not take into consideration the artistic value of the piece or the antique interest. These dealers will buy old jewelry, broken watches, gold teeth, anything that is made of precious stones or metals. This is the place to sell damaged silverware and jewelry.

Now that you have a base price, you can determine what a jeweler who sells antique jewelry will pay, which includes the added dollars offered for the artistic value. Of course, you can also sell it to a friend, to an antiques dealer, or through an auction house. Some jewelers will take the pieces on consignment. Remember, styles in modern jewelry change and influence the value of antique pieces.

In recent years, large brooches have again become stylish. Bar pins, which were unsalable as wearable jewelry in the 1970s, are now in demand. Watch slide bracelets and charm bracelets gained favor in the 1990s. Large antique brooches have a low break-up value because the stones are usually small. The pins are especially attractive to the insurance-conscious, mugger-wary buyer, and they sell well. If you have decided it would be nice to make a modern pin using the old stones, be sure to check the prices carefully. It might be better to sell the old piece as an antique and buy a totally new one. The old stones are often of poor quality, and the expense of a new setting for the old stones may be more than the value of the finished, reworked piece.

Jewelry can easily be sold directly to a dealer. Often shops and jewelers who sell "estate jewelry" will make you an offer. Some large department stores sell estate or antique jewelry in a special department or at special sales several times a year. The buyers for these departments might want your jewelry. If you go to an antiques show and see dealers with pieces like yours, you can probably sell your items. Because most shops and dealers specialize, it is best to look for someone with jewelry like yours. A dealer who specializes in watches and gold chains may not want a small diamond pin.

One problem with selling antiques, especially jewelry, is proof of ownership. The buyer of your jewelry must be sure that you really own the piece and have a legal right to sell it. Many pieces of stolen jewelry are offered to dealers during the year. Have good personal identification with you and offer to show it. Don't send a teenager to sell jewelry. The dealers are fearful that even if the jewelry belongs in the family, the seller is not the true owner.

There are often marks on jewelry that add to the value. A known signature adds up to 100 percent or more. Although most marks are found on the back of the piece, be sure to check the catch on a necklace and the sides of a large piece. If it says FABERGÉ (ФАБЕРЖD), you have a piece worth thousands of dollars. If the name TIFFANY, LALIQUE, FOUQUET, MARCUS, CASTELLANI, OMAR RAMSDEN, MÜRRLE, BENNETT AND CO., or GIULIANNO appears, the piece is worth hundreds to thousands of dollars. If it is a piece of silver jewelry marked GEORG JENSEN, HA (Hector Aguilar), KALO, ARTHUR STONE, KEM WEBER, or CASTILLO, it is probably worth hundreds of dollars.

Use a magnifying glass. The hallmarks used on silver or gold are a series of small pictures like this ⬙⬙⬙⬙. Check the meaning in the appropriate books. Some marks indicate the country of origin, which may be important in setting the price. English, Danish and Mexican silver has an added value for collectors. Some marks indicate the makers. The names that add to the value, especially the names of important designers of the Art Nouveau and twentieth-century Arts and Crafts schools, can be found in books. The library will also have books on jewelry makers and on silver marks.

(Remember the words "silver plate" in an English publication mean solid silver, but in an American book they signify just a thin coating of silver over another metal.)

The words and symbols on jewelry can be confusing. Pure gold is 24 karat, but it is too soft to be useful for jewelry. Gold quality marks 14K (karat), 18K, 20K, and 22K indicate solid gold (not hollow). If it is 14 parts pure gold and 10 parts of another metal, it is 14/24 parts gold or 14 karat.

"Gold filled," "gold plated," "rolled gold," or "gold overlay" means your jewelry has limited meltdown value since it consists of only a layer of gold on another metal. Be careful, because sometimes the label is "14K gold filled," which probably means it is classed as "costume jewelry."

"Sterling," "coin," and "800" are desirable silver quality marks. Nickel silver and German silver are not silver at all. They are white metals similar to pewter. "Quadruple plate" and "triple plate" mean the pieces have only a thin layer of silver over another, less valuable metal.

Platinum may look like silver, but it is much more valuable. If it says "PLATINUM" in tiny letters on the back of the jewelry, take it to a jeweler for a professional appraisal before you sell it.

Prices are up for cultured pearls. Irregularly shaped freshwater pearls, baroque cultured pearls, and smooth, spherical pearls are in style. The graduated pearl necklace is temporarily out of style, and the best prices today are for strings of pearls of one size. Good pearls are always strung with a knot between each bead. There is a strange rule for drop-shaped natural pearls. If they are drilled end to end they are worth 40 percent less than if they are drilled at the top only.

A black (ultraviolet) light will tell if your pearls are cultured or fakes. When viewed by black light, cultured and real pearls look slightly fluorescent, but fake pearls glow a bright white. The glow produced by a black light will also show if stones are real or glass. If the setting is made of gold, have a jeweler check any large stones to see if they are good quality diamonds, sapphires, or rubies, or just plain glass. Even experts are being fooled by zirconium, a diamond substitute. Gemstones are usually cold to the touch and very hard; a stone with worn edges is probably just colored glass.

Some stones, old or new, are doublets or even triplets. That means a piece of the colored stone is joined with clear stone. Almost all gem-quality opals sold today are doublets or triplets. We once bought an emerald, complete with a Colombian government guarantee of authenticity, for a bargain price. It turned out to be a clear piece of the mineral beryl, called an "emerald" when it is green. Underneath the clear part was a dark green piece of glass. The top tested as an emerald; the green glass improved the color. By making it a doublet, the color was enhanced and the finished stone looked dark green, but it had no gem value.

There are some styles of very early Spanish, Hungarian, and English jewelry made with foil-backed stones. A piece of silver or colored foil is set behind a clear or colored stone to enhance the color. These are wanted by collectors as examples of a rare type of antique jewelry.

Some types of antique jewelry are not being made today. Mourning jewelry was often made of braided hair set with gold trim as a memorial to the departed. Enameled rings with images of funeral urns and special rings given as gifts at funerals are also among the best-known mourning jewelry. All these are wanted by collectors, although they are not considered as popular as wearable jewelry.

Berlin ironwork was made for a short time in the early nineteenth century. It was actually made of iron, instead of gold, during a time when gold was needed for the war effort against Napoleon. This is rare and valuable to serious collectors. So is gold jewelry set with feathers from China and jet or black beads made from composition material. Both were popular in the late nineteenth century. Hat pins, elaborate combs, watch-chain slides, studs, scarf rings, posy holders, cuff links, watch fobs, and other similar types of jewelry are not worn much today, but are wanted by special collectors.

The English made a special type of jewelry from carved quartz backed with a specially applied picture, often of a dog or horse. The finished stone looks like glass with a piece of paper behind it. It is actually a very valuable form, usually set in cuff links for men. The Chinese made clear quartz beads like miniature crystal balls set in loops of wire; they look like glass but are very valuable.

Cameos are of special interest. Agate or carnelian cameos have more value than shell cameos. The light pink and white shell cameos are easy to identify because the curve of the shell can always be seen. Stone cameos have flat backs. The quality of the carving and the setting help determine the value. The more detail, the better. Remember, beautiful women in the nineteenth century were chubby-faced and had full noses. Today's beauty is thin and pug-nosed. This helps to date a cameo.

Don't underestimate the value of old beads of amethyst, pink quartz, garnet, amber, or colored stones. It takes an expert to recognize the quality, so be sure to show them to a qualified appraiser before putting them in the junk box at your garage sale. Don't think that something you consider ugly, like lava stone (dirty gray), or a realistic bug pin, has no value. Gold pins and necklaces designed with snakes, beetles, and dragonflies are of extra value.

Some of the important early jewelry by innovative designers, such as RENÉ LALIQUE or many of the English Arts and Crafts artists, were deliberately made from inexpensive materials like glass, base metals, cut steel, moonstones, and enamels. The quality of workmanship can make these as valuable as gold and precious stone jewelry. Look carefully for a name.

American Indian jewelry has a special market. If you can trace the history of an Indian necklace, pin, or ring back over fifty years, it may be very valuable. Try to sell it to a collector of Indian artifacts, or through Western dealers.

Compacts, lipstick cases, money clips, cigarette cases, and cigarette lighters are sometimes made of precious metals and stones. These should be sold like any other type of precious jewelry or to the specialist collector. Those made of imitation gold and silver also have a resale value, and they should be sold to costume jewelry dealers or to specialists who favor compacts, lighters, and other "smalls."

COSTUME JEWELRY

Prices for top-quality costume jewelry are now higher than those for precious pieces. Old beads, rhinestones, marcasite, enameled Art Nouveau and Art Deco, and plastic pieces are all in vogue. The major auction houses have even had complete sales of the costume jewelry made since the 1920s. Names that add value to costume jewelry are EISENBERG, HOBÉ, SCHIAPARELLI, HATTIE CARNEGIE, KRAMER, MATISSE, WEISS, VOGUE, HOLLYCRAFT, JOSEFF, WIESNER, SARAH COVENTRY, REGENCY, VENDOME, FLORENZA, MONET, CORO, TRIFARI, NAPIER, and KENNETH LANE. Some are still working, but pre-1960 pieces by these companies bring premium prices.

Look at the new jewelry being offered in the department stores. Run-of-the-mill old pieces are worth about 60 percent of the cost of comparable new ones. Old rhinestones are probably worth more than new ones, because old rhinestones are of better quality. Two- or three-color Bakelite plastic pins and bracelets are worth more than new jewelry. So are many of the pieces with important makers' names.

Be very careful what prices you ask for costume jewelry you sell at house and garage sales. Dealers at flea markets, mall shows, vintage-clothing stores, and at the best antique stores get high prices for rhinestone and plastic costume jewelry and good Art Deco designs. The bigger and gaudier, the better.

FABLES TO IGNORE WHEN TRYING TO IDENTIFY JEWELRY

Opals are unlucky. We think they are lucky, but because of the superstition, ordinary opal jewelry sells at lower prices than similar pieces with other stones. Gem-quality opals sell at high prices.

Amber floats. Only a loose bead in salt water floats.

A fine setting will hold real stones. If no one has changed them.

Pearls improve with age. They absorb skin oils and cosmetics, change color, scratch, and even rot if stored incorrectly.

REPAIR

Antique jewelry has become very popular during the past few years, particularly Georgian, Victorian, Art Nouveau, Art Deco, costume, Mexican silver, and American Indian jewelry. Always be sure when buying old jewelry that you get an all-original piece. Many are changed or "married" (mismatched) or are modern copies.

Repairing old jewelry requires the greatest concern, because repairing or remodeling can destroy the antique value. Repairs should be made in the spirit of the original jewelry. Replace old gems or stones with old stones; if you put a modern cut diamond in a piece with old mine-cut diamonds, the new one will be too bright and look out of place. Replacing earring backs, safety catches, or pin backs or restringing beads does not affect the value of most old jewelry and will definitely help to prevent loss. Many artisans now make necklaces of old and new beads. They may also be able to restring your old beads. Many jewelers will restring pearls and other valued beads.

Many local jewelers know how to appraise and repair old jewelry, but they often consider old jewelry "scrap" and figure the value based on the meltdown of the elements. Be sure to go to someone who understands the problems of old pieces, old methods, and old stones.

Jewelry can and should be cleaned at home. Be particularly careful of pieces with pearls or opals. They can be damaged by incorrect care, oil, and temperature changes. Never store opals or pearls in an airtight bag or bank safe-deposit vault. Lack of air may dull the luster.

Price Books

The Buyer's Guide to Affordable Antique Jewelry, Anna M. Miller (Citadel Press, New York, © 1993).

Collecting Rhinestone & Colored Jewelry, leaflet, Maryanne Dolan (Books Americana, Florence, AL, © 1993).

Copper Art Jewelry: A Different Lustre, Matthew L. Burkholz and Linda Lichtenberg Kaplan (Schiffer, Atglen, PA, © 1992).

Costume Jewelry Identification and Price Guide, 2nd edition, Harrice Simons Miller (Avon Books, New York, © 1994).

Cuff Jewelry: A Historical Account For Collectors and Antique Dealer, Howard L. Bell, Jr. (Bell's, PO Box 11695, Raytown, MO 64138, © 1993).

Jewelry and Metalwork in the Arts and Crafts Tradition, Elyse Zorn Karlin (Schiffer, Atglen, PA, © 1993).

Clubs & Publications

American Hatpin Society, *American Hatpin Society Newsletter* (NL), 20 Monticello Dr., Rolling Hills Estates, CA 90274.

Chicago Midwest Bead Society, *Chicago Midwest Bead Society Newsletter* (NL), 1020 Davis, Evanston, IL 60201.

International Club for Collectors of Hatpins and Hatpin Holders, *Pictorial Journal* (MAG), *Points* (NL), 15237 Chanera Ave., Gardena, CA 90249.

International Watch Fob Association Inc., *International Watch Fob Association Newsletter* (NL), 11895 Hwy. 99, Burlington, IA 52601.

Midwest Watch Fob Association Inc., *Midwest Watch Fob Association Newsletter* (NL), 11895 Hwy. 99, Burlington, IA 52601.

National Cuff Link Society, *The Link* (NL), PO Box 346, Prospect, IL 60070 (cuff links and other garment fasteners, including tie bars, shirt studs, collar buttons, belt buckles, money clips, etc.).

Vintage Fashion & Costume Jewelry Club, *Vintage Fashion & Costume Jewelry Newsletter* (NL), PO Box 265, Glen Oaks, NY 11004.

Heritage Report on Antique Jewelry (NL), c/o JCK, Chilton Way, Radnor, PA 19080-9253 (antique and period jewelry and watches).

Margaretologist (NL), Center for Bead Research, 4 Essex St., Lake Placid, NY 12946.

Ornament (MAG), PO Box 2349, San Marcos, CA 92079-2349.

Repairs, Parts & Supplies

Boone Trading Company Inc., PO Box BB, 562 Coyote Rd., Brinnon, WA 98320, orders: 800-423-1945; customer service: 206-796-4330, Mon.–Fri. 8:00 A.M.–5:00 P.M.; fax: 206-796-4511. Beads, gemstones, ivory, bone, scrimshaw findings and supplies, ivory jewelry blanks, feathers, and artifacts. Catalog.

Dunhill Restoration, c/o Lee Upholstery, 2309 Lee Rd., Cleveland Heights, OH 44118, 216-921-2932, Mon.–Sat. 9:00 A.M.–5:00 P.M. Jewelry repaired.

Indian Jewelers Supply Company, PO Box 1774, Gallup, NM 87305, 800-545-6540, 505-722-4451; fax: 505-722-4172. Jewelry-making supplies, including beads, clasps, miscellaneous findings, squash-blossom necklace parts, and imitation claws; metalsmithing and lapidary tools and supplies, books, and tools. Catalog $3.

Lambert Holding Company, 807 Silom Rd., 4th Floor, Bangkok 10500, Thailand, 800-791-GEMS (U.S.), 662-236-4343 (Bangkok); Fax: 662-236-4810 (Thailand). Reproductions of antique and nonantique jewelry pieces from pictures or models. Will duplicate the lost half of a pair of cuff links, earrings, or other jewelry. Free catalog.

Myron Toback, Inc., 25 W. 47th St., New York, NY 10036, 212-398-8300, 8:00 A.M.–4:30 P.M.; fax: 212-869-0808. Hardware distributor for jewelry. Full stock in 14K, 18K, and silver. Jewelry findings in gold and silver; solders for repair; sheet and wire. Mail order worldwide. Catalog $3.

Old China Patterns Limited, 1560 Brimley Rd., Scarborough, ON Canada, M1P 3G9, 416-299-8880; fax: 416-299-4721. Flannel cotton storage pouches for jewelry. Custom sizes available.

T. B. Hagstoz & Son, Inc., 709 Sansom St., Philadelphia, PA 19106, 800-922-1006, 215-922-1627. Jewelry tools and supplies. Findings, solders, casting supplies, and many metals, including gold, sterling silver, pewter, copper, bronze, brass, and nickel silver.

Trail Blazer, 210 West Hill, Gallup, NM 87301, 505-722-5051, Mon.–Sat. 9:00 A.M.–5:30 P.M. Indian jewelry repaired.

Vogue & Vintage, 187-20 Union Turnpike, Jamaica Estates, NY 11366, fax: 718-454-1248, Mon.–Sat. 10:00 A.M.–5:00 P.M. Jewelry repaired and restored. Earrings converted from pierced to clip-on or clip-on to pierced.

WTC Associates, Inc., 2532 Regency Rd., Lexington, KY 40503, 800-535-4513, 10:00 A.M.–5:30 P.M.; fax: 606-277-5720. Silver plating, sterling repairs, missing parts reproduced. Brass, copper, nickle, and gold plating. Work on pot metal.

Videos

Hidden Treasures: A Collector's Guide to Antique and Vintage Jewelry of the 19th and 20th Centuries. How to identify the age, material, and value of an old piece of jewelry. 60 minutes, $24.95 plus $5.80 shipping & handling. **Venture Entertainment Group, Inc.,** 5350 White Oak, Suite 213, Encino, CA 91316, 818-981-7813.

Kitchen Paraphernalia

Anything that was ever used in a kitchen, from a wrought-iron kettle holder of the 1700s to a 1960s juicer or reamer to a chrome toaster, has a sale value. Most buyers want something nostalgic and decorative to put in a modern kitchen. Any unusual object will sell quickly at a house sale or flea market or to friends. Some antiques shops deal in utensils that were made before 1930 and dishes with the "country look." Very modern-looking equipment, preferably chrome, bright-colored pottery or plastic pitchers, toasters, canisters, and a few other objects with Art Deco designs are sold by a different group of dealers. The electric items of the past, such as old toasters, mixers, and waffle irons, have little value unless the design is very unusual and decorative. An electric toaster with a blue willow porcelain plaque or a leaf-decorated 1950s glass plaque on the side will sell for over $100. The same toaster without the attractive sides is worth almost nothing. A rare glass iron sells for hundreds of dollars; an electric metal iron is almost unwanted.

Think of the kitchen gadgets in terms of the question, "How will it look on a wall or shelf?" Anything with red and white or green and cream does well. These were the colors favored in the 1930s. Colored plastic handles add value to old eggbeaters and other utensils. Eggbeaters are very salable. The nineteenth-century ones are iron; by 1900 the eggbeater had an iron gear, but stainless-steel beaters. The beaters and gears soon were all stainless. Many eggbeaters have dates in raised numbers on the gears. Ice-cream dippers sell for much more money than seems possible. Check the price guides carefully. Almost any dipper manufactured before 1940 is worth over $50; many are worth much more. Juicers or reamers also sell for high prices. Favored are those with colored glass or figural shapes. All out-of-production cookie cutters, molds, nutcrackers, bottle openers, and apple peelers have value.

Mixing bowls of all kinds, pitchers, storage jars, and other ceramic kitchen items have a dual value. They are wanted by both the kitchen and the pottery collectors. (See section on Pottery & Porcelain.) Check the maker from the marks and look in both a general price guide and a kitchen price book.

Your mother's and grandmother's kitchens are still filled with treasures: scrapers, forks, funnels, dessert molds, ice-cream molds and pans, either purchased new or "borrowed" from an aging parent who no longer baked. Now that microwaves, electric burners, self-cleaning ovens, and dishwashers have changed the requirements, many old pots and bowls are out of favor with cooks. Don't throw anything away until you check on the value. Even molded-plastic string holders, clocks, and menu planners can have value. All salt and pepper sets, cookie jars, and stove or refrigerator sets are collected.

Don't ignore the old stove, refrigerator, vacuum cleaner, or washing machine. If decorative, they will sell, sometimes to an appliance store that needs one for a window display. Cookbooks and recipe pamphlets sell well, too. (See sections on Advertising; Books.)

In general, the oldest sells for the highest price. Items that are figural, especially those picturing blacks, sell well; so do plastic, brass, copper, and colorful pottery. Anything that moves, like an apple peeler, will sell. Aluminum and chrome in very modern styles are now of interest to collectors of 1950s items. Early wooden items are wanted by "country" collectors, but sometimes not-so-old, but well-worn, wooden cutting boards and knives are overvalued by novice collectors. Watch for the names DOVER and ENTERPRISE on metal kitchen gadgets.

REPAIR

Collectors should remember that while old items are fine for decorations, they are sometimes not safe to use for food preparation. Some types of pottery had a lead glaze that is poisonous. Copper molds and pots should never be used unless the tin lining is flawless. Companies that re-tin pots are listed in the Metals section. Chipped graniteware could add bits of crushed glass to your food. Woodenwares should only be treated with edible oils, not linseed oil. Iron skillets and baking pans should be seasoned. Coat an iron pot with edible cooking oil and bake it at 300 degrees for about two hours. Special dull black and rust-resistant paint is available if you want to repaint iron, but it must not be used on utensils that hold food.

Directions and supplies for the care of Glass, Metals, and Pottery & Porcelain are listed in those sections.

Price Books

Beat This: The Eggbeater Chronicles, Don Thornton (Off Beat Books, 1345 Poplar Ave., Sunnyvale, CA 94087-3770, © 1994).

Black Memorabilia for the Kitchen: A Handbook & Price Guide, Jan Lindenberger (Schiffer, Atglen, PA, © 1992).

The Collector's Encyclopedia of Granite Ware, Book 2, Helen Greguire (Collector Books, Paducah, KY, © 1993).

Collector's Guide to Wagner Ware and Other Companies (L-W Book Sales, PO Box 69, Gas City, IN 46933, © 1994).

Griswold, Volume 2, L-W Book Sales (PO Box 69, Gas City, IN 46933, © 1994).

Griswold Cast Iron, L-W Book Sales (L-W Books, PO Box 69, Gas City, IN 46933, © 1993).

Clubs & Publications

Cookie Cutter Collectors Club, *Cookie Crumbs* (NL), 1167 Teal Rd. SW, Dellroy, OH 44620.

KOOKS: Kollectors of Old Kitchen Stuff, *Kitchen Antiques & Collectibles News* (NL), 4645 Laurel Ridge Dr., Harrisburg, PA 17110.

Midwest Sad Iron Collectors Club, *Pressing News* (NL),11940 Lavida Ave., St. Louis, MO 63138.

National Graniteware Society, *National Graniteware Society Newsletter* (NL), PO Box 10013, Cedar Rapids, IA 52410.

National Reamer Collectors Association, *National Reamer Collectors Association Quarterly Review* (NL), 405 Benson Rd. N., Frederic, WI 54837-8945.

Around Ohio (NL), PO Box 14, Bloomingburg, OH 43106 (cookie cutters).

Cast Iron Cookware News (NL), 28 Angela Ave., San Anselmo, CA 94960 (3 volumes available).

Cookies (NL), 5426 27th St. NW, Washington, DC 20015 (cookie cutters).

Kettles 'n Cookware (NL), Drawer B, 11918 Second St., Perrysburg, NY 14129.

Repairs, Parts & Supplies

C & H Supply, 5431 Mountville Rd., Adamstown, MD 21710, 301-663-1812, Mon.–Fri.

9:00 A.M.–5:00 P.M.; fax: 301-874-2524. Flour bins for Hoosier cabinets, pie safe tins, ice box hardware, kitchen cabinet hardware. Veneers, paint and varnish removers, stains and lacquers. Most orders shipped within 24 hours. Catalog $4.

Farmerstown Hardware & Supplies, Junior and Robert Hershberger, 3155 S.R. 557, Dept. K, Baltic, OH 43804, 216-893-2464, Mon.–Fri. 8:00 A.M.–5:00 P.M. Hoosier cabinet parts. Wholesale catalog $2.

Hardware+Plus, Inc., 701 E. Kingsley Rd., Garland, TX 75041, 214-271-0319, technical assistance; 800-522-7336, order line; fax: 214-271-9726. Hoosier and kitchen hardware, bin pulls and handles, ice box hardware, assorted catches and hinges. Free brochure. Hardware catalog $5.

Horton Brasses, PO Box 120Q, Nooks Hill Rd., Cromwell, CT 06416, 203-635-4400, 8:30 A.M.–4:00 P.M.; fax: 203-635-6473. Kitchen bin pulls and other hardware. Catalog $3.

Lorrie Kitchen & Dan Tucker, 3905 Torrance, Toledo, OH 43612, 419-478-3815, 8:00 A.M.–10:00 P.M. Labels for Anchor Hocking and Owens Illinois kitchen canisters. Send a self-addressed stamped envelope for brochure.

Muff's Antiques, 135 S. Glassell St., Orange, CA 92666, 714-997-0243, Tues.–Sat. 11:00 A.M.–5:00 P.M. Hard-to-find hardware for ice boxes and Hoosier cabinets. Also kitchen jar lids, and glass knobs. Mail order worldwide. Hardware catalog $5.

Phyllis Kennedy, 9256 Holyoke Ct., Indianapolis, IN 46268, 317-872-6366, 10:00 A.M.–5:00 P.M. Specializing in parts for Hoosier cabinets, including flour bins, bread drawers, roll doors, wire racks, sugar jars, and more. Store located at 10663 Andrade Drive, Zionsville, IN 46077. Catalog $3.

Wm. A. Randle Restorations, 2706 Deerford St., Lakewood, CA 90712, 310-422-2424, noon–6:00 P.M. Vintage electric appliance restoration service, specializing in pre–World War II kitchen appliances, such as toasters, coffee mills, blenders, and waffle irons. Inventory of donor pieces for parts; cloth power cord, plugs, etc. Painting, metal finishing, fabricating, and electrical repair. Shipping worldwide.

Lamps & Lighting Devices

All types of lamps and lighting devices, including candlesticks, rushlight holders, and railroad lanterns, can be sold. Buyers purchase electric lamps to give light and to be decorative. Earlier forms of lighting are purchased either as part of a historic collection or as decorative pieces. To sell rushlights, old candlesticks, or even flashlights, you must find the proper collector. There are many who collect whale oil lamps, Sandwich-glass oil lamps, or some other specialty. These lighting devices are over 100 years old, and they sell well to dealers and at auctions. Judge the market by the device's appearance. Some belong in a "country look" home, while others are for the more sophisticated home filled with English nineteenth-century antiques or 1950s kitsch.

Lamp bases from the late nineteenth and twentieth centuries were often made by important glass, pottery, or metalworking firms. A Tiffany lamp has value as a lamp and because it is Tiffany. Consequently, it sells for many times more than a comparable lamp without the Tiffany mark. Spectacular Tiffany lamps can sell for hundreds of thousands of dollars. Cameo glass lamps by Gallé are also priced at least 100 percent more than common cameo lamps. The signature of a less important cameo glass maker adds only 50 percent. Sell these lamps and other special types of glass-shaded lamps to glass collectors.

A pottery lamp base made by an important pottery firm sometimes sells best as a lamp; occasionally, however, a lamp base is sold as a freestanding figurine or as a vase. If a hole for wiring is drilled in the bottom of a vase and the lamp is dismantled, the vase has a flaw. Factories like Rookwood or Van Briggle often made the base with the hole—the glaze even shows it is still in original condition—but the collector still pays half as much for a vase with a hole in the bottom. Figurines can usually be removed from the base with no indication of their original use. Lamps often have decorative metal bases that hide any indication of the maker of the pottery. It is a gamble to try to see if there is a mark.

In general, table lamps, unless by known makers, do not sell well. The highest prices are obtained at house sales or flea markets. Lamp shades have suddenly become of interest to decorators, and old fringed or parchment shades can be sold with or without the lamp. Brass floor lamps have become popular again, because many of the new ones are not made of solid brass. They can be refinished, rewired, and resold for a good price, so some dealers will buy a good metal floor lamp in any condition. Special types of lighting, like chandeliers, wall sconces, and torchères, have limited markets. Lamps that are in eccentric modern shapes, have moving parts like dancing hula girls, or have special effects like lava lamps or "moving water" reflected on the shade, sell well.

The highest-priced lamps have leaded or painted glass shades. If the maker can be identified from either design or signature, the lamp has added value. Thousands of dollars are paid for good lamps by HANDEL, TIFFANY, DIRK VAN ERP or PAIRPOINT. Lamps sell for hundreds to thousands of dollars if made by STEUBEN, BRADLEY AND HUBBARD, DUFFNER & KIMBERLEY, EMERALITE, or JEFFERSON. Be sure to check the Glass and Pottery & Porcelain sections of this book if your lamp is marked by a known glass or pottery company, and then look in the general price books for the maker's name. If it isn't listed, the maker was unimportant. Outstanding Art Deco or 1950s lamps sell for good prices no matter who made them; price is determined by the appeal.

REPAIR

Lamps and lighting devices are collected for many reasons, the most obvious being that they can light a room. If you are using old lamps in your home, be sure they are restored so they can be safely used. Oil and kerosene lamps have well-known hazards. Always check to be sure that all of the parts are working. Most early lamps can be converted to electricity. The original burner can be replaced with a new electric socket and cord. The unit will fit into the available space of the old lamp and can be removed or added with no damage to the antique value of the lamp. If you do electrify an old lamp, be sure to keep the old parts. The next owner may want an all-original lamp. The original brass fittings for Tiffany or Handel lamps are very important.

The light bulb was invented in 1879. That means that some electric lamps can be over 100 years old. If you are using any electric lamp that is more than 25 years old, be sure it is safe. The cord should not be frayed, and if it is an old-style silk-wrapped cord or a stiff rubber cord, it should be totally replaced. Local lamp shops can rewire any lamp. Look for them in the Yellow Pages of the telephone book under "Lamps—Mounting & Repairing." If the sockets or pull chains need repairing, ask the shop to use as many of the old pieces as possible. Old sockets were made of solid brass, but now most of them are plated. A serious collector will always want the original chain. Some pay extra to get old acorn-tipped pull chains.

Reproductions of almost all parts of old lamps are available: glass shades, lamp chimneys, sockets, hangers for chandeliers, and more. Old metal lamps can be cleaned or replated. Leaded shades can be repaired. Art glass shades are being reproduced or can be repaired.

The lamp shade and lamp finial can often make the difference between an attractive, period-look lamp and an unattractive hodgepodge. Finials with old pieces of jade or porcelain are being offered by decorating services and mail-order houses. More sources are in the Glass and Metals sections.

Price Books

Aladdin Collectors Manual & Price Guide #15, J. W. Courter (3935 Kelley Rd., Kevil, KY 42053, © 1994).

Aladdin Electric Lamps Collectors Manual & Price Guide #2, J. W. Courter (R-1, Simpson, IL 62985, © 1993).

Quality Electric Lamps: A Pictorial Price Guide (L-W Books, PO Box 69, Gas City, IN 46933, © 1992).

Student Lamps of the Victorian Era, Richard C. Miller and John F. Solverson (Antique Publications, Marietta, OH, © 1992).

Value Guide for Miniature Lamps, compiled by John F. Solverson. Price and rarity guide for lamps listed in Solverson's *Those Fascinating Little Lamps; Miniature Lamps* by Frank R. and Ruth E. Smith; and *Miniature Lamps II* by Ruth E. Smith (Antique Publications, Marietta, OH, © 1994).

Clubs & Publications

Aladdin Knights of the Mystic Light, *Mystic Light of the Aladdin Knights* (NL), 3935 Kelley Rd., Kevil, KY 42053.

Night Light: The Miniature Lamp Collectors' Club, *Night Light* (NL), 38619 Wakefield Ct., Northville, MI 48167.

Old Mine Lamp Collector's Society, *Underground Lamp Post* (NL), 4537 Quitman St., Denver, CO 80212.

Rushlight Club, Inc., *Rushlight* (MAG), *Flickerings* (NL), Suite 196, The Fairway, Jenkintown, PA 19046.

Coleman Collector (NL), Coleman Company, Inc., PO Box 1762, Wichita, KS 67201.

Light Revival (NL), 35 W. Elm Ave., Quincy, MA 02170.

Repairs, Parts & Supplies

A-Bit-of-Antiquity, Richard Dudley, 1412 Forest Ln., Woodbridge, VA 22191, 703-491-2878, 7:00 P.M.–10:00 P.M. Restoration, repair, deplating, and polishing of lamps. Specializing in oil lighting. Shades and burners for oil lamps.

Abercrombie & Co., 9159A Brookeville Rd., Silver Spring, MD 20910, 301-585-2385, anytime; fax: 301-587-5708. Lamp and lighting fixture repair. Metal repair, plating, and polishing. Custom matching of patinas and oxidized finishes.

Al Bar-Wilmette Platers, 127 Green Bay Rd., Wilmette, IL 60091, 708-251-0187, Mon.–Fri. 8:00 A.M.–5:00 P.M., Sat. 8:00 A.M.–3:00 P.M. Restoration of brass light fixtures. Plating, polishing, repairing, lacquering. Will provide quotes from photos sent. Nationwide service. Daily UPS service. Please insure all shipments.

American Period Showcase, 3004 Columbia Ave., Lancaster, PA 17603, 717-392-5649, 8:30 A.M.–5:00 P.M. Repair and reproductions of period lighting fixtures. The Period Candlstik, made from a formula containing beeswax, holds a 25-watt bulb and can be used in chandeliers and sconces. It is available in two sizes. Also located at 300 Old Dairy Rd., Wilmington, NC 28405. Brochure $2.50.

Antique & Colonial Lighting, 10626 Main St., Clarence, NY 14031, 716-759-2661, Mon,–Fri. 10:00 A.M.–5:00 P.M., Sat.–Sun. noon–5:00 P.M. Lighting restoration and polishing, specializing in antique lighting. Antique shades, lamps, and parts. Mail order worldwide.

Antique Lamp Parts & Service, E.W. Pyfer, 218 N. Foley Ave., Freeport, IL 61032-3943, 815-232-8968, 8:00 A.M.–8:00 P.M. Lamp repair and wiring, brass and metal refurbishing, replacement of missing parts. Old chandeliers restored, oil and gas lamps converted to electric. Parts and glass for old or new lamps. Old parts for antique kerosene, electric, and gas lamps; Aladdin lamp parts. By appointment only.

Antiquities, 5 Ordnance Mews, The Historic Dockyard, Chatham, Kent, U.K. ME4 4TE, 0634 818866; fax: 0634 818877. Restoration of antique lighting. Chandelier conservation, cleaning, and restoration products. Replacement glass drops, pins, wax-coated and glass candle sleeves, silk-covered lighting flex, candle bulbs, lamp fitments. Free brochure.

Armor Products, PO Box 445, East Northport, NY 11731-0445, 516-462-6228, 9:00 A.M.–5:00 P.M.; fax: 516-462-5793. Lamp supplies. Glass chimneys. Free catalog.

Asheville-Schoonmaker Mica Company, 900 Jefferson Ave., Newport News, VA 23607, 804-244-7311, Mon.–Fri. 8:00 A.M.–4:30 P.M.; fax: 804-245-5236. Built-up mica plate for restoration of lamp shades and other decorative purposes. Sample kit $20, rebated on first order.

B & G Antique Lighting, 28-05 Broadway (Rt. 4W), Fairlawn, NJ 07410, 201-791-6522, Mon.–Sat. 9:00 A.M.–5:00 P.M.; fax: 201-791-6545. Restoration. Lamps and other lighting cleaned, repaired, and rewired. Brass fixtures polished, crystal chandeliers taken apart and washed and rewired. Metal refinishing and plating. All work done in their shop.

B & P Lamp Supply Co., Inc., 843 Old Morrison Rd., McMinnville, TN 37110, 615-473-3016; fax: 615-473-3014. Manufacturer and wholesaler of lamp parts, including metal founts, oil burners, wicks, Aladdin-type burners, chimneys, smoke bells, lamp hardware, light bulbs, lamp-making kits, shades, finishing and cleaning supplies, and reproduction lamps. Catalog.

Barap Specialties, 835 Bellows, Frankfort, MI 49635, 800-322-7273, 9:00 A.M.–5:00 P.M. Lamp parts, tools, finishing materials, hardware, etc. Catalog $1.

Bathroom Machineries, PO Box 1020, Murphys, CA 95247, 209-728-2031. Restoration of lighting fixtures; brass polishing.

Bradford Consultants, PO Box 4020, Alameda, CA 94501, 510-523-1968; fax: 510-814-0481. Edison-type carbon filament light bulbs, twisted silk-covered lamp cord. Free brochure.

Brass & Copper Polishing Shop, Don Reedy, 13 S. Carroll St., Frederick MD 21701, 301-663-4240, Mon.–Fri. 8:00 A.M.–5:00 P.M. Antique and new lamp parts and supplies. Brass, copper, and silver polishing, repair, and lacquering.

Brass 'n Bounty, Richard Dermody and Maryanne Baiakian, 68 Front St., Marblehead, MA 01945, 617-631-3864. Restoration of chandeliers, floor lamps, and sconces, including gas, transitional gas and electric, and electric. Old shades used exclusively.

The Brass Knob, Architectural Antiques, 2311 18th St. NW, Washington, D.C. 20009, 202-332-3370, Mon.–Sat., 10:30 A.M.–6:00 P.M., Sun. 12:00 P.M.–5:00 P.M. Architectural antiques, specializing in restored lighting, hardware, fireplace mantels, ironwork, and other decorative detail. Warehouse, The Brass Knob, Back Doors, at 1701A Kalorama Rd. NW, Washington, DC 20009. Catalog.

Candle Snuffer, 28 Maple Root Rd., Coventry, RI 02816, 401-397-5565, Tues.–Sat. 9:00 A.M.–5:00 P.M. Lamp parts and supplies; restoration and refinishing. Glass and fabric lampshades.

Century House Antiques & Lamp Emporium, 46785 Rt. 18 W., Wellington, OH 44090, 216-647-4092, Mon.–Sat. 10:00 A.M.–5:00 P.M., Sun. noon–5:00 P.M., closed Thursdays. Lamp parts and supplies; restoration and refinishing. Shades, chimneys, burners, smoke bells, Aladdin parts. Custom cloth and paper shades. Shades painted to match Gone with the Wind bases. Metal stripping, polishing, lacquering, wiring. Send SASE for flyer.

Chatree's, 711 Eighth St., SE, Washington, DC 20003, 202-546-4950. Lamps, chandeliers, and other lighting fixtures repaired, rewired, and polished.

Classic Accents, 12869 Eureka, South Gate, MI 48195, 313-282-5525. Carbon filament Victorian light bulbs, push-button light switches, decorative and plain cover plates, brass polishing paste. Free catalog.

Conant Custom Brass, PO Box 1523A, 270 Pine St., Burlington, VT 05402, 802-658-4482, Mon.–Fri. 9:00 A.M.–5:00 P.M., Sat. 10:00 A.M.–5:00 P.M.; fax: 802-864-5914. Antique glass shades and lamp parts. Free brochure.

Conner's Architectural Antiques, 701 P St., Lincoln, NE 68508, 402-435-3338. Restoration of lighting fixtures; lamp parts. Old lighting fixtures and reproduction lighting.

The Copper House, RR 1, Box 4, Rt. 4, Epsom, NH 03234, 603-736-9798; 800-281-9798 (New Hampshire only). Beeswax candlecovers that fit 25-watt bulbs.

Country Fare, Rt. 188 South, 45 Quaker Farms Rd., Southbury, CT 06488, 203-264-7517, Wed.–Fri. 10:00 A.M.–5:00 P.M., Sat. 10:00

A.M.–3:00 P.M. Restoration of antique lamps. Custom work a specialty: mounting, rewiring, and restoration. Parts and supplies, glass replacements. Custom lamp shades: pierced, botonical, recovered, reproduced.

Crowfutt Art Brass, 94 Bethlehem Pike, Philadelphia, PA 19118, 215-242-8818, Tues.–Sat. 10:00 A.M.–6:00 P.M.; fax: 215-242-8846. Chandeliers and other lighting rewired. Antique metal restoration, refinishing, and repairing: brass, copper, iron. Brochure.

Crystal Mountain Prisms, PO Box 31, Westfield, NY 14787, 716-326-3676, anytime. Replacement glass prisms for chandeliers and lamps. Glass chains, Czechoslovakian cut balls, pendalogues, bobeches. Mail order only.

Curran Glass & Mirror Co., 30 N. Maple St., Florence, MA 01060, 413-584-5761, Mon.–Fri. 10:00 A.M.–4:00 P.M. Glass restoration, including bent glass lamp chandeliers. Leaded, etched, beveled, and slumped glass work.

D & J Glass Clinic, David Jasper, 40658 267th St., Sioux Falls, SD 57106, 605-361-7524, 9:00 A.M.–5:00 P.M.; fax: 605-361-7216. Lamp repair or conversion. Free brochure.

Dec-Art, Inc., 7731 Long Point Rd., Houston, TX 77055, 713-523-5267. Lamp repair and rewiring, metal polishing and plating, parts and accessories. Replacement lamp shades, custom-made lamps and shades.

Delphi Stained Glass, 2116 E. Michigan Ave., Lansing, MI 48912, 800-821-9450, help line; 800-248-2048, order line. Lamp hardware and fittings. Catalog $5.

Dunhill Restoration, c/o Lee Upholstery, 2309 Lee Rd., Cleveland Heights, OH 44118, 216-921-2932, Mon.–Sat. 9:00 A.M.–5:00 P.M. Conservators of antiques and collectibles, specializing in the repair of lamps, china, porcelain, and pottery.

Elcanco Ltd., PO Box 682, Westford, MA 01886, 508-392-0830, 800-423-3836, Mon.–Fri.

9:00 A.M.–5:00 P.M. Handcrafted electric wax candles, flamelike bulbs, 6-volt transformers, and beeswax candlecovers. Morelite electric wax candles. Brochure $2.

Faire Harbour Ltd., 44 Captain Peirce Rd., Scituate, MA 02066, 617-545-2465, 8:30 A.M.–6:30 P.M. Lamp parts, restoration, and repair. Specializing in Aladdin kerosene mantel lamps. Will search for customer's wants. Mail order. Catalog $2, refundable with $15 purchase.

Farmerstown Hardware & Supplies, Junior and Robert Hershberger, 3155 S.R. 557, Dept. K, Baltic, OH 43804, 216-893-2464, Mon.–Fri. 8:00 A.M.–5:00 P.M. Aladdin lamp parts. Wholesale catalog $2.

Ferguson's Cut Glass Works Inc., 4292 Pearl Rd., Cleveland, OH 44109, 216-459-2929, 9:00 A.M.–4:30 P.M. Chandelier restoration.

The Finishing Touch, Ned Guyette, 5128 W. Center St., Milwaukee, WI 53210, 414-444-4557. Repair and restoration of lamps. Cracks and chips repaired, missing parts reproduced.

Fred Kuntz, 47 Larchwood Dr., Painesville, OH 44077, 216-352-9630, evenings and weekends. Reproduction mica chimneys and some Pyrex globes, for Coleman and other makes of lanterns and lamps. Restoration work. Free information sheet on Coleman lantern chimneys.

Galleria Hugo, 304 E. 76th St., New York, NY 10021, 212-288-8444, 9:00 A.M.–6:00 P.M. Restoration of nineteenth-century metal lighting and decorative arts. Hand finishing only, no plating or stripping. Replacement shades for Argand mantel lamps. By mail or appointment only.

Glass Restoration by Dianne, 54 Hartford Turnpike, Piccadilly Square, Vernon, CT 06066, 203-647-7074, Tues.–Sat. 10:00 A.M.–5:30 P.M. Pinwork replacement for chandeliers and candelabra. Restoration of all types of glassware. Chips removed, broken pieces repaired. Brochure.

Greg Monk Stained Glass, 98-027 Hekaha St., Bldg. 3, Aiea, HI 96701, 808-488-9538, 10:00 A.M.–6:00 P.M. Hawaii. Stained-glass supplies,

instruction. Repairs to lamps and windows. Will ship worldwide.

Heart Enterprise, 149 Duranta St., Roseville, CA 95678, 916-783-4802, 8:00 A.M.–10:00 P.M. Custom designed Victorian lamp shades; original frames recovered; supplies for Victorian lamp shades. Videos on making and restoring lamp shades. Catalog $3.

Hexagram, 426 Third St., Eureka, CA 95501, 707-443-4334, 10:30 A.M.–5:00 P.M. Lighting repair and restoration. Specializing in Victorian lighting.

Hippo Hardware & Trading Co., 1040 E. Burnside, Portland, OR 97214, 503-231-1444, Mon.–Fri. 10:00 A.M.–5:00 P.M., Sat. 10:00 A.M.–6:00 P.M.; fax: 503-231-5708. Salvaged architectural pieces, including original lighting. Remanufactured hardware and other old house parts. Victorian to Ozzie and Harriet periods. Send photo of items sought. Reproduction catalog $2.

Historic Housefitters Company, Farm to Market Rd., Dept. K, Brewster, NY 10509, 914-278-2427, 9:00 A.M.–5:30 P.M.; fax: 914-278-7726. Hand-forged eighteenth-century lighting for use in restoration or reproduction Colonial homes. Custom blacksmithing. Mail order shipped worldwide. Catalog $3.

Historic Lighting Restoration Service & Sales, 10341 Jewell Lake Ct., Fenton, MI 48430, 313-629-4934, 8:00 A.M.–9:00 P.M. Restoration of old gas and electric lighting fixtures; brass polishing, lacquering, gas fixtures electrified. Specializing in restoration by mail.

John Kruesel's General Merchandise, 22 SW 3rd St., Rochester, MN 55902, 507-289-8049, 10:00 A.M.–5:00 P.M.; fax: 507-289-8602. Restoration of period lighting. Auctioneering: full service, appraisals.

J. Peter Owen, 29 Murray St., Augusta, ME 04330, 207-622-3277, anytime, leave message on machine. Replacement bent slag glass panels and other stained-glass lamp shade repairs.

Lamp Glass, 2230 Massachusetts Ave., Cambridge, MA 02140, 617-497-0770, Wed.–Sat. 10:00 A.M.–6:00 P.M.; fax: 617-497-2074. Replacement glass lamp shades and parts, including student shades, chimneys, Gone with the Wind globes, banker's lamp shades, prisms. Mail order to U.S., Canada, and Puerto Rico. Catalog $1.

Lamp Lady and Dolls, Lois M. Beckerdite, 623 Charwood Dr., Cincinnati, OH 45244, 513-528-5628, 10:00 A.M.–10:00 P.M. Lamp parts, supplies, rewiring, restoration. Reproduction hand-painted globes to match your antique base, kiln fired. Mail order worldwide. Send SASE for free brochure.

The Lamp Shade Lady, Mary Maxwell, 149 Duranta St., Roseville, CA 95678, 916-783-4802, 8:00 A.M.–8:00 P.M. Antique lamp shades recovered or reproduced. Custom designs, wire frames, beaded fringes, silk chiffon, thick rayon fringe, linings, lamp shade kits, and videos on making and restoring lamp shades. Catalog $3.

Lampshades of Antique, Dept. K, Dorothy Primo, PO Box 2, Medford, OR 97501, 503-826-9737, 8:00 A.M.–5:00 P.M. Design, manufacture, restoration, re-creation, and recovery of Victorian fringe fabric lamp shades. New and vintage fringe, fabric, and trim in stock. Catalog $4.

Leacock Coleman Center, John Lapp, 89 Old Leacock Rd., PO Box 307, Ronks, PA 17572, 717-768-7174, Mon., Wed., Thurs. 7:00 A.M.–5:00 P.M.; Tues., Fri. 7:00 A.M.–8:00 P.M., Sat. 7:00 A.M.–noon. Glass shades for old Coleman table lamps. Replacement parts for Coleman table lamps and lanterns. Lamps and lanterns repaired. Aladdin lamps, parts, and shades in stock. Send SASE for a brochure of Coleman-style shades available.

Lehman Hardware, PO Box 41, 4779 Kidron Rd., Kidron, OH 44603-0041, 216-857-5441, Mon.–Sat. 7:00 A.M.–5:30 P.M., Thurs. 7:00 A.M.–9:00 P.M.; fax: 216-857-5785. Lamp parts including cotton wicks, burners, chimneys, Aladdin replacement parts, Dietz lamp parts, etched glass shades for round-wick oil lamps,

Victorian lamp brackets, reflectors, gas light parts, stove paint, stove door gaskets, tools, and more. Catalog $2.

Lighting Elegance, 147 W. Badillo St., Covina, CA 91723, 818-339-7278, Mon.–Fri. 10:00 A.M.–6:00 P.M., Sat. 10:00 A.M.–5:00 P.M. Restoration and refinishing. Lamp repair. Hard-to-find chimneys, burners, and fixture glass. Reproduction glass shades, material shades, and shade recovering. Catalog $5.

Lundberg Studios, PO Box C, 131 Oldcoast Rd., Davenport, CA 95017, 403-423-2532, Mon.–Fri. 8:00 A.M.–4:00 P.M.; fax: 408-423-0436. Replacement lampshades for Tiffany and Handel lamps. Special overhead and 2¼-inch fitter shades. Photos available, $1.

McBuffer's, 20401 Roseland Ave., Euclid, OH 44117, 216-486-6696, Mon.–Fri. 9:00 A.M.–5:00 P.M., Sat. 9:30 A.M.–12:30 P.M. Lamps repaired and rewired. Metal refinished and repaired. Free brochure.

Melotte-Morse Stained Glass Inc., 213 S. 6th, Springfield, IL 62701, 217-789-9515, 8:00 A.M.–5:00 P.M.; 217-789-9518. Repair and restoration of stained-glass lamps. Free brochure.

Michael J. Dotzel & Son, 402 E. 63rd St., New York, NY 10021, 212-838-2890, 8:00 A.M.–4:00 P.M. Chandeliers rewired and polished. Lacquering. Missing parts cast.

Muff's Antiques, 135 S. Glassell St., Orange, CA 92666, 714-997-0243, Tues.–Sat. 11:00 A.M.–5:00 P.M. Lamp parts, shades, and burners; angle lamp bowls and chimneys. Mail order.

Museum Quality Restorations, PO Box 402, Palmyra, NJ 08065, 609-829-4615, 11:00 A.M.–7:00 P.M. Lighting restoration, reproduction globes, and brass castings. Restoration of finishes to nineteenth century fixtures. Catalog $3, free brochure with SASE.

N. Bucki, 7974 Rt. 98 S., Arcade, NY 14009, 716-492-0839. Reproduction globes. Will custom paint and fire glass copies of Gone with the Wind lamp tops. No repairs or metal parts. Send SASE for brochure.

Nowell's, Inc., PO Box 295, 490 Gate 5 Rd., Sausalito, CA 94966, 415-332-4933, Mon.–Sat. 9:30 A.M.–5:00 P.M.; fax: 415-332-4936. Parts for oil, gas, and electric antique lamps and fixtures. Restoration and repair of old lighting fixtures. Smokeless, odorless lamp oil, gas-type and electric-type glass fitter shades, clip-on paper shades. Catalog.

Old and Elegant Distributing, 10203 Main Street Ln., Bellevue, WA 98004, 206-455-4660, Mon.–Sat. 9:00 A.M.–6:00 P.M., 9:00 P.M.–11:00 P.M.; fax: 206-455-0203. Lighting parts and other supplies.

Old Lamplighter Shop, Musical Museum, Deansboro, NY 13328, 315-841-8774, 10:00 A.M.–4:00 P.M. Lamp parts, repair, and restoration; electrification. Metal lamp parts, burners, chimneys, frames, etc. Specializing in oil lamps of the 1890s. Glass shades painted to match bases, slag glass bent to fit your Tiffany type shade. Send photos for free advice. Free brochure.

Olde House Lighting, Daniel E. Hodges, 847 17th St., Des Moines, Iowa 50314, 515-288-7304, 5:00 P.M.–10:00 P.M. Refurbishing and restoration of antique lighting fixtures, gas, electric, and combination gas/electric. Conversion of gas fixtures to electric. Original and reproduction lighting parts available. Reproduction lamp shades.

Paxton Hardware Ltd., PO Box 256, 7818 Bradshaw Rd., Upper Falls, MD 21156, 410-592-8505, 9:00 A.M.–5:00 P.M.; fax: 410-592-2224. Lamp replacement parts, glass and fabric lamp shades. Free brochure. Catalog $4.

Rare & Beautiful Things, PO Box 6180, Annapolis, MD 21401, 410-263-2357. Appraisals and consultations on restoration. Gas and electric lighting fixtures and shades c.1870–1940. By appointment.

Restoration & Design Studio, Paul Karner, 249 E. 77th St., New York, NY 10021, 212-517-9742,

Mon–Fri. 10:00 A.M.–5:00 P.M., Wed. 1:00 P.M.–5:00 P.M. Lamps and lighting fixtures restored and rewired. Missing parts reproduced, patina restored.

Retinning & Copper Repair, Inc., Jamie Gibbons, 525 W. 26th St., New York, NY 10001, 212-244-4896, Mon.–Fri. 9:00 A.M.–5:00 P.M.; fax: 212-695-3058. Refinishing and repairing of metal objects, including lamps. Polishing and laquering of brass, copper, bronze, etc. Can help you find a repair service for a particular item. Free telephone help for the do-it-yourselfer. Pieces accepted via UPS or Parcel Post. Turnaround time generally one week.

Rikki's Studio Inc., Gilbert Kerry Hall, 2809 Bird Ave., Coconut Grove, FL 33133, 305-446-2022, 305-446-2230, 9:00 A.M.–4:30 P.M.; fax: 305-446-6388. Lamps restored and rewired. Chandeliers repaired. Appraisals.

Riverwalk Lighting, 401 S. Main St., Naperville, IL 60540, 708-357-0200, Mon.–Sat. 9:00 A.M.–5:00 P.M.; fax: 708-357-0317. Restoration lamp parts, antique and new. Antique lamp shades recovered.

Roy Electric Co., Inc., 1054 Coney Island Ave., Brooklyn, NY 11230, 718-434-7002; fax: 718-421-4678. Restoration of antique lighting. Replacement parts and glass shades. Antique and reproduction gas, oil, and electric lighting. Catalog $5, refundable with order. Free color brochure.

Rumplestiltskin Designs, 1714 Rees Rd., San Marcos, CA 92069, 619-743-5541, Mon.–Sat. 9:00 A.M.–6:00 P.M.; fax: 619-480-5539. Hand-beaded fringe in assorted patterns and colors. All glass or glass and plastic mix. Heavy rayon fringe. Antique metallic guimpe (braid) in bolts. Brochure $1 and SASE. Include resale number, letterhead, or business card and phone number for wholesale prices.

Saltbox, 500-B State St., Greensboro, NC 27405, 919-273-8758, 10:00 A.M.–5:00 P.M.; fax: 919-294-2683. Restoration of antique lighting. Handmade reproduction lighting in copper and brass. Tin rushlights, chandeliers, lanterns, etc. Catalog $3.50.

Shades of Yesteryear, Stephen Harper, 315 N. Lott Blvd., Gibson City, IL 60936, 217-784-4655. Restoration of antique lighting, specializing in early electric and gas lighting.

The Silk Shade, PO Box 243, Santa Monica, CA 90406, 310-395-6360, anytime. Turn-of-the-century Victorian lamp shades. Shipped anywhere. Send SASE and $2 for brochure.

Specialized Repair Service, 2406 W. Bryn Mawr Ave., Chicago, IL 60659, 312-784-2800, Mon.–Fri. 8:30 A.M.–5:00 P.M., Sat. 9:00 A.M.–1:00 P.M. Repair of metal items, including chandeliers and lamps.

St. Louis Antique Lighting Company, 801 N. Skinker Blvd., St. Louis, MO 63130, 314-863-1414, 8:00 A.M.–4:30 P.M.; fax: 314-863-6702. Restoration of antique lighting and architectural bronze work. Custom design and fabrication of antique lighting; exact reproduction of historic fixtures. Historic preservation consultation. Appraisals. Catalog $3.

Talas, Division of Technical Library Service, Inc., 213 W. 35th St., New York, NY 10001, 212-736-7744, Mon.–Fri. 9:00 A.M.–5:00 P.M.; fax: 212-465-8722. Vellum for lamp shades, archival storage materials and supplies, tools, and other items. Catalog $5.

Van Dyke's, Box 278, Woonsocket, SD 57385, 605-796-4425, 800-843-3320, orders only, 8:00 A.M.–6:00 P.M.; fax: 605-796-4085. Replacement parts for Aladdin and other oil lamps, glass pendulums and prisms. Special parts designed to duplicate the original pieces. Catalog $1.

Venerable Classics, 645 Fourth St., Suite 208, Santa Rosa, CA 95404, 800-531-2891, 9:00 A.M.–5:00 P.M.; fax: 707-575-3626. Restoration of lamps. Shipping instructions and free brochure available on request.

Washington House Reproductions, PO Box 246, Washington, VA 22747, 703-675-3385, 10:00 A.M.–6:00 P.M. Repair and restoration of old lighting devices. Refinishing, stripping of nickel plating, conversion to electricity.

Westminster Stained Glass, Laura S. Chaffee, 62 Westminster St., Springfield, MA 01109, 413-734-4382, 8:00 A.M.–6:00 P.M. Stained-glass lamps repaired and restored. Custom work. By appointment only.

Whittemore-Durgin Glass Co., Box 2065, Hanover, MA 02339, 800-262-1790, 617-871-1743, Mon.–Fri. 8:30 A.M.–4:30 P.M.; fax: 617-871-5597. Lamp hardware; patterns, forms, and accessories for lamp shades. Catalog.

William Spencer, Inc., 118 Creek Rd., Rancocas Woods, NJ 08054, 609-235-1830, 10:00 A.M.–5:00 pm.; fax: 609-235-8552. Lighting restoration and refinishing. Metal refinishing.

Yankee Barn Lighting, PO Box 95, Forestburgh, NY 12777, 914-794-7299, Mon.–Fri. 9:00 A.M.–5:30 P.M.; fax: 914-794-7549. Glass shades, bases, parts, and components for lighting restoration; refinishing; reproduction antique-style lighting.

Yesterday Once Again, Box 6773, Huntington Beach, CA 92615, 714-963-2472, Mon.–Fri. 6:00 A.M.–9:30 A.M., 4:30 P.M.–8:30 P.M., Sat. and Sun. after 11:30 A.M.; fax: 714-963-2105, Attn.: Yesterday Once Again. Carbon filament light bulbs, replicas of Edison's 1890 bulb. Victorian-style light bulbs suitable for use in glass chimney lamps. Mail order worldwide. Free catalog.

Yestershades, 4327 SE Hawthorne, Portland, OR 97214, 503-235-5645, 11:00 A.M.–6:00 P.M. Victorian lamp shades elaborately designed with silks, satins, antique laces, beads, and fringes. Lamp bases available. Wholesale and retail. Catalog $3.50.

Videos

How to Make Victorian Style Lamp Shades, 65 minutes, $48; *How to Restore Traditional Style Lamp Shades,* 68 minutes, $48, both videos $80. **The Lamp Shade Lady,** Mary Maxwell, 149 Duranta St., Roseville, CA 95678.

Leather Goods

Leather requires special care. Use only accepted leather cleaners and preservatives. Never use general-purpose waxes and polishes. Most department, furniture, and hardware stores sell suitable leather cleaners. Products such as neat's-foot oil and mink oil, sold in shoe stores, leather shops, and shoe repair shops, are made especially for use on leather. If the leather binding on your book is deteriorating into red crumbles, there is little that can be done. More leather-related sources can be found in the sections on Books and Furniture.

Repairs, Parts & Supplies

Joy Liotta Horvath, 1822 Stratfield Rd., Norwalk, CT 06432, 203-372-6011. Repair and restoration of handbags, belts, luggage, desktop accessories, jewelry boxes, and other small leather goods. Repair and restoration of alligator a specialty. Appraisals.

Wood & Leather Craft, 4921 Rt. 47, Callicoon, NY 12723-5032, 914-887-4241, 8:00 A.M.–6:00 P.M. Genuine leather tops, gold tooled period designs. Brown, green, red, or black finish. Send measurements for estimate and free samples.

Magazines

You may not be able to sell a book by its cover, but that is probably the best way to sell an old magazine. It is often the cover illustration that brings the money for old but not rare magazines. A picture of Marilyn Monroe on a *Life* magazine or a Norman Rockwell illustration on the cover of the *Saturday Evening Post* means there is more value than expected for the magazine. There are other parts of magazines that sell well: advertisements, paper dolls, and stories by famous authors. There is a moral dilemma here. Should you cut up the magazine and destroy it forever, or is it better to try to sell the parts? The whole magazine is often worth less money than the parts, but it does take time and extra research to know how to sell the individual pages. If you are selling the whole magazine, be sure that every page is still in your magazine. Missing pages lower the value dramatically. The first issue of any magazine has a value, even if the magazine is now unknown.

Collectors prize cover illustrations as well as inside story and advertising illustrations by known artists. Names to look for are JESSIE WILLCOX SMITH, ROLF ARMSTRONG, HOWARD CHANDLER CHRISTY, PALMER COX, ERTÉ, HARRISON FISHER, J. C.

LEYENDECKER, F. X. LEYENDECKER, CHARLES DANA GIBSON, JAMES MONTGOMERY FLAGG, KATE GREENAWAY, WINSLOW HOMER, THOMAS NAST, ROSE O'NEILL, MAXFIELD PARRISH, COLES PHILLIPS, ARTHUR RACKHAM, FREDERIC REMINGTON, PETTY, and NORMAN ROCKWELL.

The early hand-colored fashion illustrations from the nineteenth-century *Godey's Ladies Book* or *The Delineator* are often torn from the magazines and sold separately. The woodcuts by Winslow Homer and other important artists that appeared in *Harper's Weekly* are also cut and removed.

Photographic covers and illustrations by less well-known artists can have extra value. A *Life* magazine photograph by ALFRED STEIGLITZ or MARGARET BOURKE-WHITE, either inside or on the cover, adds value. Stories in *Life* about the Kennedys, Marilyn Monroe, sports figures, and some politicians and movie stars add value. A *Time* or *Newsweek* cover showing a baseball player, especially LOU GEHRIG, TY COBB, or BABE RUTH, a famous person from the 1920s through the 1940s, some World War II personalities such as ADOLF HITLER or GENERAL DOUGLAS MacARTHUR, or a famous movie star has added value. There is a special market for any type of Nazi and war memorabilia.

Paper dolls are wanted by special collectors. The full-page pictures of dolls or the separate paper-doll books are collected and sell best at either doll shows or with other paper ephemera. Look for the dolls called LETTIE LANE, BETTY BONNET, KEWPIE, and DOLLY DINGLE.

Movie magazines are wanted by many of the buyers of other types of movie memorabilia. (See section on Celebrity Memorabilia.) Collectors are also trying to buy old *TV Guides*

and other television-related magazines. There is also interest in sports and health magazines.

Magazines that have short stories by famous authors are collected by the same people who want old books. Often an author wrote the first version of a story in a magazine. Of special interest are science-fiction magazine stories, which sell best at a Sci Fi show. (See section on Books.)

Girlie magazines or men's magazines are collected, but only the early ones sell for good prices. The collectors want special issues that feature BRIGITTE BARDOT, JANE FONDA, JAYNE MANSFIELD, MARILYN MONROE, or CANDY STARR. *Playboy* generates the most interest. Because each issue includes comic strips, the comic magazine dealers often buy and sell the *Playboy* issues known as "fillers." These are the issues complete except for the centerfold.

Some collectors are searching for old advertisements. Best are the CREAM OF WHEAT ads by famous illustrators and the COCA-COLA ads that appeared on the back cover of *National Geographic* magazine for many years. Small ads from magazines that were published before 1940 are often cut out and sold as individual pictures to collectors, so you might sell car ads to car collectors, food ads to advertising collectors, etc. Each ad must be matted.

There is a special class of magazines known as the "pulps." These are magazines, often printed on poor-quality paper, that published mystery and science-fiction stories. Pulps should never be cut. The value is greater for the complete magazine than for any combination of cut-up illustrations and stories. These magazines are usually wanted by book and comic dealers.

Don't be disappointed if your large stack of *Life* magazines or *National Geographic* is not worth a small fortune. It is rare for a magazine to sell at retail for over $5 unless it is mint, has an interesting cover or story, and is at least pre-1960. Many magazines have no value at all. Still, try to sell your stacks of old magazines, especially *Life, National Geographic, Playboy,* and other similar magazines, decorating magazines like *House Beautiful,* gardening and cooking magazines, sports, movie, TV, automobile, and special-interest magazines. If you have enough, you will find that even at less than $1 each, the value adds up.

See also the section on Books.

Price Books

Blue Book on The Red Cover: Life, *1936–1980,* Robert Lenson (Fondest Memories, 306 Langley Rd., Newton Centre, MA 02159, © 1992).

Collectible Magazines Identification & Price Guide, David K. Henkel (Avon Books, New York, © 1993).

Destiny Reference Guide, Volume I: The Magazine, Bob Chatham and Paul Hugli (Paul Hugli, 9440 Nichols, Bellflower, CA 90706, © 1992).

Maud Humphrey: Her Permanent Imprint on American Illustration, Karen Choppa and Paul Humphrey (Schiffer, Atglen, PA, © 1993).

The Men's Girlie Magazines Price & ID Guide, booklet, Jack C. Denison (TICN, PO Box 1958, Sequim, WA 98382, © 1994).

Old Magazines Price Guide (L-W Book Sales, PO Box 69, Gas City, Indiana, 46933, © 1994).

The Price and Identification Guide to: Pin-Ups & Glamour Art, pamphlet, Denis Jackson (TICN, PO Box 1958, Sequim, WA 98382, © 1992).

The Price & Identification Guide to Maxfield Parrish, 9th edition, booklet, Denis C. Jackson (TICN, PO Box 1958, Sequim, WA 98382, © 1994).

Club & Publications

Playboy Collectors Association, *PCA Newsletter* (NL), PO Box 653, Phillipsburg, MO 65722-0653.

Pulp Collector (MAG), PO Box 3232, Frederick, MD 21705 (annual).

Marble

Marble carvings sell like any other sculpture; the better the artist, the higher the price. Size is also a factor. Busts and small figures sell for hundreds of dollars. Life-sized statues, especially those suitable for a garden, sell for thousands.

The major concern regarding marble is its care and upkeep. Marble should be kept clean. Wipe up any spills as soon as possible or the marble may become etched. If the stain is stubborn, use soap and lukewarm water. Marble should be dusted with a damp cloth and washed with water and a mild detergent about twice a year. You can wax marble with a colorless paste wax, but white marble may appear yellow if waxed.

Minor breaks can be mended with instant epoxy glue. Most marble cutters, cemetery monument makers, tile setters, or windowsill installers have the product. Stains can be removed, but it takes time and requires more information. Check your library or contact a marble worker in your area.

Sometimes a white marble carving will have a strange reappearing stain. This is from dirty water that has soaked into the porous marble. It can't be cured.

Marbles are listed in the Toys section.

Book on Repair

How to Keep Your Marble Beautiful, Marble Institute of America (33505 State Street, Farmington, MI 48024).

Repairs, Parts & Supplies

A. Ludwig Klein & Son, Inc., PO Box 145, Harleysville, PA 19438, 215-256-9004, Tues.–Fri. 10:00 A.M.–5:00 P.M. Marble restoration. Statuary and monuments, appraisals, insurance claims by appointment. Free brochure.

Ceramic Restorations, Inc., Jareth Holub, 161 W. 61st St., Apt. 9F, New York, NY 10023, 212-247-8657, 9:00 A.M.–6:00 P.M. Marble repair and restoration. Free estimates.

Dean's China Restoration, 131 Elmwood Dr., Cheshire, CT 06410, 800-669-1327, Mon.–Fri. 9:00 A.M.–5:00 P.M. Repair and restoration of marble. Mail order worldwide. Free brochure.

Phoenix Restoration Inc., 5305 N. 7th St., Suite C, Phoenix, AZ 85014, 602-263-5178, 800-234-5178; 8:00 A.M.–6:00 P.M.; fax: 602-263-6009. Restoration and conservation of marble.

Pleasant Valley Antique Restoration, Joe Howell, 1725 Reed Rd., Knoxville, MD 21758, 301-432-2721, 9:30 A.M.–9:00 P.M. Restoration of marble.

Talas, Division of Technical Library Service, Inc., 213 W. 35th St., New York, NY 10001, 212-736-7744, Mon.–Fri. 9:00 A.M.–5:00 P.M.; fax: 212-465-8722. Cleaner for marble and stone, archival storage materials and supplies, tools, and other items. Catalog $5.

Venerable Classics, 645 Fourth St., Suite 208, Santa Rosa, CA 95404, 800-531-2891, 9:00 A.M.–5:00 P.M.; fax: 707-575-3626. Restoration of marble and other materials. Specializing in statuary, dolls, lamps, and clocks. Shipping instructions and free brochure available on request.

Medical & Scientific Collectibles

*A*ntique microscopes, telescopes, medical apparatus, and much more are included in scientific collectibles. Of special interest are quack medical machines. These all require special restoration and repair. Sometimes a local expert who works with modern microscopes or telescopes can help. (Scales are listed in their own section.)

The best customers for medical and dental antiques are doctors and dentists. Strange-looking old tools, dental chairs, examining tables, advertising cards, catalogs, medicine bottles, and anything else related to medicine has a market. Dental and barber items like shaving mugs, razors, barbershop signs (the old-time dentist and barber were the same man), extraction tools, and even false teeth are collected, usually by dentists. All early pharmaceutical collectibles can be sold easily. A small local shop or drugstore will often buy pieces for use in window displays. Decorative bottles (see Bottles section), cabinets, and early medicine labels and packets sell easily to general collectors. Quack medicine items like electric-shock machines to cure rheumatism are of special interest to many.

A different group of people will buy any drug-related items.

There are special dealers who conduct mail-order auctions of medical, dental, and drug-related collectibles. You can locate them through the general antiques publications ads. If you have a large collection, it would be profitable to take an ad in a professional magazine of interest to doctors, dentists, or lawyers. Locate these with the help of your local librarian.

There is not much that can be done about the weather, but for centuries people have wanted to know when storms are approaching. The barometer was invented by Evangelista Torricelli in Florence, Italy, in the 1640s. It measures the change in air pressure and helps indicate changes in weather. Many eighteenth- and nineteenth-century barometers still exist and, like all sensitive scientific instruments, often need repair by a specialist. Some are listed here. All early barometers sell for hundreds of dollars.

Price Book

A Collector's Guide to Personal Computers and Pocket Calculators, Dr. Thomas F. Haddock (Books Americana, Florence, AL, © 1993).

Clubs & Publications

Antique Telescope Society, *Journal of the Antique Telescope Society* (MAG), 30 Green Valley Rd., Wallingford, PA 19086.

International Association of Calculator Collectors, *International Calculator Collector* (NL), 10445 Victoria Ave., Riverside, CA 92503.

Medical Collectors Association, *Medical Collectors Association Newsletter* (NL), 1300 Morris Park Ave., Bronx, NY 10461.

Scientific Medical & Mechanical Antiques (MAG), PO Box 412, Taneytown, MD 21787.

Repairs, Parts & Supplies

Barometer World, Quicksilver Barn, Merton, Okehampton, Devon, England EX20 3DS, 08053 443, 8:00 A.M.–5:00 P.M. Barometer restoration, spare parts, books on barometers. Catalog $10 in currency. VISA, MasterCard, and Eurocard accepted. Contact first before sending barometer for repair.

Neville Lewis, HC 68, Box 130-L, Cushing, ME 04563, 207-354-8055, anytime. Complete barometer restoration service. Mercury tubes of all types. New and old parts available.

New York Nautical Instrument & Service Co., 140 W. Broadway, New York, NY 10013, 212-962-4523, 9:00 A.M.–5:00 P.M.; fax: 212-406-8420. Sextants, compasses, ships' clocks, and barometers reconditioned. Brochure.

Tele-Optics, 5514 Lawrence Ave., Chicago, IL 60630, 312-283-7757, 8:00 A.M.–5:00 P.M., fax: 312-283-7757. Service and repairs on all makes and models of binoculars, telescopes, and riflescopes. Aneroid-type barometers repaired. No mercurial (glass tube) type.

Metals & Cloisonné

*E*ighteenth- and nineteenth-century iron, brass, tin, toleware, pewter, and copper utensils have long been popular collectibles and are easily sold to dealers, decorators, and collectors. The fashion for the "country look" has added to the popularity, and any old tool, trivet, or kitchen utensil that can be put on a shelf or hung on a wall is wanted. Fine Early American examples, especially those stamped with a maker's mark, sell for hundreds to thousands of dollars. These early pieces can be sold through mail-order ads, at auction, or to collectors or dealers. They are part of the general merchandise found in most antiques shops. (See section on Kitchen Paraphernalia for additional information.)

Twentieth-century metalwork is sometimes mistakenly sold for low prices at garage sales because the uninformed don't realize that many recent pieces have a great value in the collectors' market. Iron doorstops have sold for over $6,000. An old figural doorstop with original paint is worth $50 or more. Heavy, solid copper cooking pots are also selling well. Price these by comparing them to new ones available in gourmet cooking stores. Art Nouveau and Art Deco pewter, chrome, or copper are in demand. Hammered aluminum from the 1940s and 1950s has some value if it is in very good condition. Of special interest are chrome cocktail shakers, Art Deco pieces with Bakelite (plastic) handles, and Arts and Crafts hammered-copper bookends or vases. Look for these names: pewter, KAYZERZINN, TUDRIC, LIBERTY; copper, NEKRASSOFF, DIRK VAN ERP, HEINTZ ART, ROYCROFT, STICKLEY, CHASE; aluminum, WENDELL AUGUST FORGE, STEDE, FARBERWARE, RODNEY KENT.

Cloisonné is a form of enameled metal. Small strips of wire, or cloisons, are applied to a metal (usually brass) vase. Enamel is then floated between the strips. The finished vase is smoothed until the surface shows the pattern of colored enamels and brass lines. All oriental cloisonné is now selling well. Age

and quality determine the price. Any damage or dent lowers the value as much as 90 percent because repairs are difficult. Good-quality old cloisonné should be sold to a top antiques dealer or by an auction gallery. The new cloisonné is very similar to the old, and it takes an expert to evaluate the piece.

Bronze figures were very important decorative pieces in the 1880–1900 period, but then lost favor. A new-style Art Deco bronze, often set with ivory, became fashionable in the 1920s and 1930s and became popular again in the 1970s. The bronze figure was scorned for many years, so there may be some very valuable ones in your attic or living room. Some of the best bronzes were given to thrift shops or resale stores in the 1950s. They were purchased for a few dollars by far-thinking collectors.

Always try to check the importance of a signed marble or bronze sculpture. Even unsigned figures, if well made, sell for hundreds of dollars today. Fine marble and bronze figures have been re-created in other materials such as spelter or plaster. The most famous of these are the JOHN ROGERS groups, figures made in late nineteenth-century America. They sell quickly if the original painted surface is in good condition.

A bronze can be judged by the quality of the casting, the fame of the artist, and the appeal of the subject. Age is not as important as you might think. Many modern bronzes sell better than antique examples. Western subjects, the animal figures by nineteenth-century French artists, the Art Deco designs of the 1920s, and huge masculine subjects, such as nude males wrestling or warriors on horseback, are now bringing the highest prices. To check on the artist, see *Abage Encyclopedia: Bronzes, Sculptors & Founders* by Harold Berman. Look for names like

FREDERIC REMINGTON, LANCERAY, CHIPARUS, PREISS, CLODION, KAUBA, MOREAU, BARYE, MÉNE, CARRIER-BELLEUSE, or NAM GREB.

A group is probably worth more than a single figure by the same artist. A marble base adds value. Generally the larger the bronze, the greater the value, although miniatures (under six inches) sell for surprisingly high prices. The artist's signature, founder's seal, number, and any other special marks increase the value.

Poor details, crossed eyes, dented noses, repaired fingers, missing parts, or cracks lower the value. If the patina has been removed or damaged, the value is lowered by 50 percent. Recast pieces have low values. If you discover a Remington or any other very famous bronze figure, take it to a qualified appraiser to find out if it is an old or new reproduction. Replicas have been made by using the original statue to make a new mold. The replicas will be slightly smaller than the original. An original Remington bust is worth over $100,000; a recast may sell for as low as a few hundred dollars.

Any auction house, antiques dealer, or art dealer can easily sell a good bronze figure, and you should have no problem selling yours.

REPAIR

Each type of metal requires particular cleaning and care. Some copper, bronze, and brass should be kept polished. Bronze should never be cleaned in any way that might affect the patina. Soap, water, dusting, and even a light waxing are safe for most metal items. There are several tarnish-preventative silicon-based polishes that are safe for metals. Do not use harsh abrasives like scouring powder or steel wool on any metal. Always rinse off all polishes completely. Many polishes are made with acids that continue to "eat" the metal after it has been polished.

Do not keep bronzes in a room that is being cleaned with bleaching powders, disinfectants, or floor-washing products containing chlorine. The chlorine can harm the bronze. Never store bronzes near rubber mats. Some carpet adhesives, paints, and fabrics may contain chemicals that are corrosive.

Once damaged, enamel and cloisonné are very difficult to repair. Dents and chipped enamel require the attention of an expert. The cost of the repair is often more than the value of the piece. Some minor repairs might be done by a local jeweler or metalsmith. Radical changes in temperature can crack enamel, so pieces should never be kept in a sunny window or over heat ducts, or washed in very hot or cold water.

Pewter is very soft and can be damaged easily or melted. Never put a piece of pewter near a burner on a stove. Never mechanically buff a piece of pewter; it will permanently change the color of the piece. Never use harsh scouring powder or steel wool to clean pewter. There are several commercial pewter polishes available at jewelry and grocery stores.

Tin and toleware should be kept dry and free of rust. If tin is rusty, try removing the rust with 0000 steel wool. For painted toleware, just touch up the spot, but never paint more than is necessary.

A redecorated piece of toleware is of value as a new item but not as an antique. Once the tin is repainted it has lost its value to the serious collector, but sometimes repainting is the only solution for a severely damaged piece. Serious toleware decorators often look for old pieces with worn paint to redecorate even though it is possible to get new tinware made in the same manner as the old. Many restored-village museums have tinshops where tin is made and sold. Dents can be removed from tin and toleware by any competent silverworker or metalsmith.

Never wrap metals in plastic or nonventilated materials. Moisture can collect under the wrap, or the plastic may melt and cause damage.

Check in the Yellow Pages of the telephone book under "Plating" to find shops that replate, polish, and restore metal items. See also the section in this book on Silver & Silver Plate.

Price Books

Collectible Aluminum, Everett Grist (Collector Books, Paducah, KY, © 1994).

Hammered Aluminum Hand Wrought Collectibles, Book Two, Dannie A. Woodard (Aluminum Collector's Books, PO Box 1346, Weatherford, TX 76086, © 1993).

Reference Books

Abage Encyclopedia: Bronzes, Sculptors & Founders, Vols. I–III, Harold Berman (Abage Publishers, Chicago, IL, © 1974–© 1977).

Early American Decoration, Esther Stevens Brazer (Pond-Ekberg Company, Springfield, MS, © 1961).

Early American Decoration Made Easy, Edith Cramer (General Publishing, 30 Lesmill Rd., Don Mills, ON M3B 2T6, Canada, © 1985).

IMR Sourcebook (Institute of Metal Repair, 1558 S. Redwood St., Escondido, CA 92025).

Oriental Cloisonné and Other Enamels, Arthur and Grace Chu (Crown Publishers, New York, © 1975).

A Quarter Century of Decorating and Teaching Country Painting, Dorothy Dean Hutchings (Shandling Lithographing Co., Tucson, AZ, © 1975).

Clubs & Publications

American Spoon Collectors, *Spooners Forum* (NP), 4922 State Line, Westwood Hills, KS 66205-1964.

Chase Collectors Society, *Art Deco Reflections* (NL), 2149 W. Jibsail Loop, Mesa, AZ 85202-5524 (Chase Brass & Copper Company).

Cloisonné Collectors Club, *Cloison* (NL), Box 96, Rockport, MA 01966.

Enamelist Society, *Glass on Metal* (MAG), PO Box 243, Winthrop, WA 98862.

Hammered Aluminum Collectors Association, *Aluminist* (NL), PO Box 1346, Weatherford, TX 76086 (hand hammered aluminum).

Pewter Collectors Club of America, *Pewter Bulletin* (NL), *PCCA Newsletter* (NL), Sherwin Herzog, Treasurer, 4635 W. Brummel St., Skokie, IL 60076.

Society of North American Goldsmiths, *Metalsmith* (MAG), 5009 Londonberry Dr., Tampa, FL 33647.

Silver (MAG), PO Box 1243, Whittier, CA 90609.

Spoony Scoop Newsletter (NL), 84 Oak Ave., Shelton, CT 06484.

Repairs, Parts & Supplies

A. Ludwig Klein & Son, Inc., PO Box 145, Harleysville, PA 19438, 215-256-9004, Tues.–Fri. 10:00 A.M.–5:00 P.M. Restoration of brass, bronze, and pewter. Appraisals, insurance claims by appointment. Free brochure.

Abend Metal Repair, Delavan Center, 501 W. Fayette St., Syracuse, NY 13204, 315-478-2749, 9:00 A.M.–3:00 P.M., 315-471-8112 rush orders only. Repair and restoration of brass, bronze, cast iron, steel, stainless steel, and aluminum. Contemporary sculpture repair, patina restoration. Send photos and details prior to call for estimate.

Abercrombie & Co., 9159A Brookeville Rd., Silver Spring, MD 20910, 301-585-2385, anytime; fax: 301-587-5708. Metal repair, plating, and polishing. Custom matching of patinas and oxidized finishes. Specialty services, such as casting, metal spinning, engraving, glass bead blasting, and chemical stripping. Replacement knife blades, combs, and custom-cut beveled glass. Garbage disposal damaged flatware repaired.

Al Bar-Wilmette Platers, 127 Green Bay Rd., Wilmette, IL 60091, 708-251-0187, Mon.–Fri. 8:00 A.M.–5:00 P.M., Sat. 8:00 A.M.–3:00 P.M. Restoration of metal antiques from sterling silver pieces to brass light fixtures. Plating, polishing, repairing, lacquering. Door and window hardware polished and lacquered. Antique door hardware for sale. Will provide quotes from photos sent. Nationwide service. Daily UPS service. Please insure all shipments.

Antique Restoration by Wiebold, 413 Terrace Pl., Terrace Park, OH 45174, 513-831-2541, Mon.–Fri. 9:00 A.M.–5:30 P.M., Sat. 10:00 A.M.–2:00 P.M.; fax: 513-831-2815. Metal plating, repair, buffing, and polishing. Missing parts replaced or duplicated. Free brochure.

Antique Restoration Co., 440 E. Centre Ave., Newtown, PA 18940, 215-958-2343, Tues.–Sat. 9:00 A.M.–5:00 P.M. Furniture stripping, repairs, and refinishing. Faux finishes. Mirror resilvering. Brass and copper polishing, caning, rush, and split weave. Free brochure.

B & G Antique Lighting, 28-05 Broadway (Rt. 4W), Fairlawn, NJ 07410, 201-791-6522, Mon.–Sat. 9:00 A.M.–5:00 P.M.; fax: 201-791-6545. Metal refinishing: door hardware, fireplace equipment, beds, tables, etc. Plating: 24k gold, silver, antique brass, copper, chrome, and pewter. Architectural metal work.

Bailey & Walke Enterprises, PO Box 6037, Shreveport, LA 71136-6037, 318-861-4109, 8:00 A.M.–5:00 P.M. Tarnguard tarnish inhibitor will protect silver, gold, brass, copper, and other metals from tarnish.

Brass & Copper Polishing Shop, Don Reedy, 13 S. Carroll St., Frederick MD 21701, 301-663-4240, Mon.–Fri. 8:00 A.M.–5:00 P.M. Brass, copper,

and silver polishing, repair, and lacquering. Antique and new lamp parts and supplies.

Brass Anvil, Inc., 186 N. DuPont Hwy., Bldg. 30, New Castle, DE 19720, 302-322-7679, 9:00 A.M.–5:00 P.M. Restoration of all nonferrous metals, brass, silver, tin, copper, and pewter. Custom brass railings. Custom tinsmithing.

Broken Art Restoration, Michelle and Bill Marhoefer, 1841 W. Chicago Ave., Chicago, IL 60622, 312-226-8200, Tues.–Fri., 9:00 A.M.–5:00 P.M. Metal, pottery, porcelain, ceramics, wood, ivory, metal, and stone art objects restored. Missing parts replaced, invisible repairs made to almost any art object. Free brochure.

Cambridge Smithy, RR 1, Box 1280, Cambridge, VT 05444, 802-644-5358, 7:00 A.M.–6:00 P.M. Wrought-iron and copper antique restoration.

Carl "Frank" Funes, 57 Maplewood Ave., Hempstead, NY 11550, 516-481-0147, 7:00 P.M.–9:00 P.M. Metalwork. Can weld and fabricate broken pieces on brass, steel, iron, and other metals; polish and replate silver and brass; restore arms, armor, and artifacts; and remove rust from weapons. Free brochure.

Chatree's, 711 Eighth St., SE, Washington, DC 20003, 202-546-4950. Metalwork, polishing, soldering, brazing, welding, casting, cleaning, lacquering. Parts duplicated.

Cole Silver Shop, Barney and Kitty Hays, 107 Third St., Santa Rosa, CA 95401, 707-546-7515, Mon.–Fri. 10:00 A.M.–5:00 P.M., Sat. morning by appointment. Metal repair, polishing, and plating. Silver, gold, brass, and tin plating. Silver, brass, and copper polished. Brass and copper brazing, brass bed parts replaced, knife blades replaced, combs for dresser sets. Garbage-disposal-damaged items repaired. Send SASE for brochure.

Conant Custom Brass, PO Box 1523A, 270 Pine St., Burlington, VT 05402, 802-658-4482, Mon.–Fri. 9:00 A.M.–5:00 P.M., Sat. 10:00 A.M.–5:00 P.M.; fax: 802-864-5914. Repair and restoration of metal antiques, specializing in brass and copper. Custom fabrication. Lamp parts. Free brochure.

Country Accents, PO Box 437, Montoursville, PA 17754, 717-478-4127, 9:00 A.M.–5:00 P.M. Handcrafted pierced metal panels in sixteen different types of metal. Custom work a specialty. Materials for the do-it-yourselfer, including piercing tools, blank metal stock, and patterns. Mail order U.S. and Canada. Catalog $5.

Crowfutt Art Brass, 94 Bethlehem Pike, Philadelphia, PA 19118, 215-242-8818, Tues.–Sat. 10:00 A.M.–6:00 P.M.; fax: 215-242-8846. Antique metal restoration, refinishing, and repairing: brass, copper, iron. Chandeliers and other lighting rewired. Brochure.

Custom Metal Finishing, 6150 Bldg. E, Airline Rd., Fruitport, MI 49415, 616-865-3545, Mon.–Fri. 8:00 A.M.–5:00 P.M.; fax: 616-865-6970. Polishing and buffing, chrome plating, zinc plating: bikes, pedal cars, boats, motorcycles, cars, lamps, pot-bellied stoves, etc.

D & J Glass Clinic, David Jasper, 40658 267th St., Sioux Falls, SD 57106, 605-361-7524, 9:00 A.M.–5:00 P.M.; fax: 605-361-7216. Metal repair, resilvering, brass plating. Free brochure.

Diane Wight, 30 Lafayette St., Randolph, MA 02368, 617-961-1028. Pewter figurines repaired.

Ephraim Forge, Inc., 8300 W. North Ave., Frankfort, IL 60423, fax: 815-464-5656, 9:00 A.M.–6:00 P.M. Restoration amd reproduction of old iron work, cast or forged.

George Basch Company, Inc., PO Box 188, Freeport, NY 11520, 516-378-8100, 9:00 A.M.–3:00 P.M.; fax: 516-378-8140. Nevr-Dull, treated cotton wadding cloth, cleans and polishes metal. Can be used on aluminum, brass, chromium, copper, gold, nickel, pewter, silver, and zinc.

Hiles Plating Company, Inc., 2028 Broadway, Kansas City, MO 64108, 816-421-6450, Mon.–Fri. 9:00 A.M.–5:00 P.M. Restoration of antique sterling silver, silver plate, pewter, copper, and brass. Parts supplied. Plating of silver, gold, copper,

nickel, and brass. Repairs on weighted sterling. Price list available.

I.P.G.R., Inc., PO Box 205, Kulpsville, PA 19443, 800-869-5633 orders only; 215-256-9015, Tues.–Fri. 9:30 A.M.–4:30 P.M., Sat. 9:30 A.M.–1:30 P.M.; fax: 215-256-9644. Complete line of restoration materials. Catalog $3, refundable with first order.

Institute of Metal Repair, 1558 S. Redwood, Escondido, CA 92025, 619-432-8942. Repair, restoration, and consultation on decorative metal, flatware, hollowware, band instruments, bronze art objects, pewter figurines and art objects, and other metal art objects.

J & H China Repairs, 8296 St. George St., Vancouver, BC Canada V5X 3C5, 604-321-1093, 7:30 A.M.–2:00 P.M. Cloisonné restoration.

Kayne & Son Custom Forged Hardware, Steve Kayne, 76 Daniel Ridge Rd., Candler, NC 28715, 704-665-8868, 8:00 A.M.–11:00 P.M.; fax: 704-665-8303. Repair, restoration, and conservation of all metals, including pot metal and cast iron. Furniture hardware recast. Hand-forged hardware made to your design. Oven doors, Blake hardware, locks, parts, and unavailable pieces reproduced. Cast brass colonial hardware; Early American hardware in brass, antique, or black finish. Reproductions catalog $4.

McBuffer's, 20401 Roseland Ave., Euclid, OH 44117, 216-486-6696, Mon.–Fri. 9:00 A.M.–5:00 P.M., Sat. 9:30 A.M.–12:30 P.M. Refinish and repair brass, copper, silver, and other metals. Cleaning, buffing, and polishing. Plate in brass, copper, nickel, chrome, silver, and gold. Specialize in lamp repair. Free brochure.

Meeting House Furniture Restoration, John T. Schechtman, 11 Waterman Hill, Queechee, VT 05059, 802-295-1309, Mon.–Sat. 9:00 A.M.–5:00 P.M., answering machine other times. Brass and metal restoration.

Memphis Plating Works, 682 Madison Ave., Memphis, TN 38103, 901-526-3051, Mon.–Fri. 8:00

A.M.–5:00 P.M., Sat. 8:00 A.M.–noon. Repairing and refinishing of metals. Repair and restoration of fire-damaged brass and silver. Restoration of brass beds and chandeliers. Can weld pot metal statues; do show chrome on automobiles; and gold, silver, copper, brass, nickel, and chrome plating.

Michael J. Dotzel & Son, 402 E. 63rd St., New York, NY 10021, 212-838-2890, 8:00 A.M.–4:00 P.M. Antiques repaired. Missing parts cast; chandeliers rewired and polished; lacquering, silver plating, and chrome plating. Hardware.

Michael's Art Restoration Studio, Michael Scheglov, 8312 Eighth NW, Seattle, WA 98117, 206-789-2900, 11:00 A.M.–5:00 P.M.; fax: 206-778-6963. Restoration of brass art objects.

Mike and Jo Baldwin, 125 Nursery Rd., PO Box 2971, Anderson, IN 46018-2971, 317-643-7065, 9:00 A.M.–10:00 P.M. Tin parts and closures for candy containers. Send SASE for free list.

New England Country Silver, Inc., PO Box 271, 23 Smith Rd., East Haddam, CT 06423, 203-873-1314, 9:00 A.M.–3:00 P.M. Complete restoration service for silver plate, sterling silver, copper, brass, and pewter. New parts made. New knife blades, combs, brushes, and mirrors. Silver, gold, and copper plating. Engraving. Send merchandise insured mail or UPS. Free estimates.

Olde House Lighting, Daniel E. Hodges, 847 17th St., Des Moines, Iowa 50314, 515-288-7304, 5:00 P.M.–10:00 P.M. Brass and copper polishing of fan blades, faucets, door and window hardware, etc.

Orum Silver Company, PO Box 805, 51 S. Vine St., Meriden, CT 06450, 203-237-3037, Mon.–Thurs. 8:00 A.M.–4:30 P.M., Fri. 8:00 A.M.–1:00 P.M. Repairing, refinishing, and replating of old silver and antiques. Pewter, brass, copper, bronze, and aluminum cleaned, buffed, polished, restored, and refinished. Gold, silver, nickel, copper, and brass plating. Parts made and fabricated. Clear-coat lacquering. Free bro-chure.

Paul Trageser, Metalsmith, 10400 Howard Rd., Harrison, OH 45030, 513-367-6226, 9:00 A.M.–5:00

P.M. Silver, pewter, brass, and copper. A last resort for the impossible repair, unavailable part, and unfindable piece of a set. Casting, spinning, sculpting, turning, soldering, etc. Will work from remnants, mates, photo, or drawing. Send for estimate.

Paul's Chrome Plating Inc., 341 Mars-Valencia Rd., Mars, PA 16046, 412-625-3135, Mon.–Fri. 8:00 A.M.–5:00 P.M., plus Wed. 7:00 P.M.–8:30 P.M.; fax: 412-625-3060. Copper, nickel, and chrome plating. Polishing stainless steel and aluminum. Specializing in the restoration of antique car parts, motorcycles, jukeboxes, and brass on boats.

Peninsula Plating Works, 232 Homer Ave., Palo Alto, CA 94301, 415-326-7825, 8:30 A.M.–5:00 P.M.; fax: 415-322-7392. Metal repair, polishing, and replating.

Pleasant Valley Antique Restoration, Joe Howell, 1725 Reed Rd., Knoxville, MD 21758, 301-432-2721, 9:30 A.M.–9:00 P.M. Restoration of metal.

Restoration & Design Studio, Paul Karner, 249 E. 77th St., New York, NY 10021, 212-517-9742, Mon., Tues., Thurs., Fri. 10:00 A.M.–5:00 P.M., Wed. 1:00 P.M.–5:00 P.M. Repair and restoration of silver, silver plate, brass, bronze, copper, pewter, and other metals. Silver, gold, nickel, chrome, and brass plating and polishing. Silver soldering. Flatware blades replaced, missing parts reproduced. Ivory insulators for tea or coffee pots.

Restoration Clinic, Inc., 2801 NW 55th Ct., Bldg. 8 W, Fort Lauderdale, FL 33309, 800-235-OLDY, anytime; fax: 305-486-4988. Antique and art conservation and restoration, including sculpture and other metal objects. By appointment only. Send SASE for free leaflet *What to Do Until the Restorer Comes.*

Restorers of America, RD 4, Box 382, Wynantskill, NY 12189, 407-364-8661, anytime. Restoration of metal ware. Supplies, workshops, and seminars.

Retinning & Copper Repair, Inc., Jamie Gibbons, 525 W. 26th St., New York, NY 10001, 212-244-4896, Mon.–Fri. 9:00 A.M.–5:00 P.M.; fax:

212-695-3058. Retinning of copper cookware and steel cooking utensils. Refinishing and repairing of metal objects, such as brass beds, copper tubs, and lamps. Polishing and laquering of brass, copper, bronze, etc. Can help you find a repair service for a particular item. Free telephone help for the do-it-yourselfer. Pieces accepted via UPS or Parcel Post. Turnaround time generally one week.

Rocco V. DeAngelo, RD 1, Box 187R, Cherry Valley, NY 13320, 607-264-3607, 8:00 A.M.–6:00 P.M. daily. Restoration of antique cast-iron garden furniture, statuary, benches, fountains, fences, gates, and urns. Parts made.

Specialized Repair Service, 2406 W. Bryn Mawr Ave., Chicago, IL 60659, 312-784-2800, Mon.–Fri. 8:30 A.M.–5:00 P.M., Sat. 9:00 A.M.–1:00 P.M. Repair of metal items, including brass, steel, pewter, and aluminum. Some plastic repaired. New parts and castings custom-made to order, zinc die cast, and bronze statues repaired. Chandeliers and lamps repaired.

Speed & Sport Chrome Plating, 404 Broadway, Houston, TX 77012, 713-921-0235, 8:00 A.M.–5:00 P.M. Chrome, nickel, and gold plating jukeboxes, Coke machines, cars, etc. Mail order throughout the U.S.

Stoneledge, Inc., 17 Robert St., Wharton, NJ 07885, 201-989-8800, Mon.–Fri. 9:00 A.M.–5:00 P.M.; fax: 201-361-6574. Conservation and restoration of metals: gold, silver, bronze, brass, aluminum, iron, and corten steel. Bronze sculptures repaired and repatinated. Free brochure.

Thome Silversmiths, 49 W. 37th St., Suite 605, New York, NY 10018, 212-764-5426, 8:30 A.M.–1:00 P.M., 2:30 P.M.–5:30 P.M. Restoration of silver, pewter, copper, brass, and bronze. Gold and silver plating; engraving. Brass, copper, silver, and pewter polished. New velvet backs for picture frames; velvet liners for boxes.

Vermont Plating, Inc., 113 S. Main St., Rutland, VT 05701, 802-775-5759, 7:00 A.M.–4:00 P.M. Metal restoration, plating, cleaning, and polishing. Copper, nickel, and chrome plating. Cadmium plating keeps metal from rusting. Work done on antiques, brass kettles, copper wash boilers, hardware, lamps, tools, toys, vehicle trim, etc. Free brochure.

William Spencer, Inc., 118 Creek Rd., Rancocas Woods, NJ 08054, 609-235-1830, 10:00 A.M.–5:00 pm.; fax: 609-235-8552. Metal refinishing. Lighting restoration and refinishing.

WTC Associates, Inc., 2532 Regency Rd., Lexington, KY 40503, 800-535-4513, 10:00 A.M.–5:30 P.M.; fax: 606-277-5720. Silver plating, sterling repairs, missing parts reproduced. Brass, copper, nickel, and gold plating. Work on pot metal.

Video

Restoring & Preserving Bronze Signs, Markers, & Memorials, **Institute of Metal Repair,** 1558 S. Redword, Escondido, CA 92025, 619-432-8942. 15 minutes, $15.95.

Miniatures & Dollhouses

*T*here are many collectors of dollhouses and miniature dollhouse furniture. The older and more complete the dollhouse, the more valuable. There is also an extra interest in wooden houses with lithographed paper exteriors made by BLISS. The name is often included on the dollhouse. Other important names are McLOUGHLIN BROTHERS, SCHOENHUT, and TOOTSIE-TOY. Doll-houses were made in many sizes. By the 1870s most of them were made on a scale of one inch to one foot. Dollhouses seem to sell best at special auctions; look in the section on Toys to learn where these sales are held. Local dealers can also sell dollhouses. Scale houses sell well, especially those made before 1930. Price new doll-houses at a toy store, and always price yours higher than the comparable new ones. Be sure the dollhouse will fit through a normal door: The price is 50 percent less if it must be dismantled to be moved or set up in a home. Do not attempt to restore or repaint a dollhouse before selling it. Keep all loose pieces, or glue trim back in place, but do nothing major. Most buyers will want to do their own restoration. We have even seen a dollhouse sold in pieces in a plastic bag.

Dollhouse furniture was made to the same scale as the dollhouses and is always the easiest miniature to sell. However, anything in miniature is in demand and can bring surprisingly high prices. Doll-size dishes or dollhouse-size dishes, doll-size chairs or dollhouse-size chairs, and other decorative objects, from tiny needlepoint rugs to silverware and vases of flowers, sell well. A fine 4-inch chair could sell for over $100.

Many antiques dealers have a case filled with what are called "smalls" by the trade. Smalls include all the tiny, expensive, and easy-to-misplace items. Always look for a dealer with dollhouse smalls. If you own a furnished dollhouse or many pieces of furniture, try talking to dealers at a miniature show. These shows are for collectors of old and new dollhouse items and are often listed in your local paper. The national collector groups and collector magazines for miniature enthusiasts have complete show listings printed each month. They often list prices for new miniatures that can help you set a price for yours. Prices for any sort of old dollhouse or furnishings are listed in general price books.

There are clubs and shows for collectors of miniatures in most parts of the country. Craftsmen who make new miniatures can often repair old ones. Also, see the Toys section.

Book
Reproducing Period Furniture and Accessories in Miniature, Virginia Merrill and Susan Merrill Richardson (Crown Publishers, New York, © 1981).

Clubs & Publications
Mini-Phone Exchange, *Telephonically Yours* (NL), 5412 Tilden Rd., Bladensburg, MD 20710 (toy phones, dollhouse phones, and anything depicting a telephone).

Miniature Piano Enthusiast Club, *Musically Yours!* (NL), 5815 N. Sheridan Rd., Suite 202, Chicago, IL 60660.

National Association of Miniature Enthusiasts, *Miniature Gazette* (MAG), PO Box 69, Carmel, IN 46032.

International Dolls' House News (MAG), PO Box 154, Cobham, Surrey England KT11 2YE.

Miniature Collector (MAG), 30595 Eight Mile, Livonia, MI 48152-1798.

Nutshell News (MAG), PO Box 1612, Waukesha, WI 53187.

Mirrors & Picture Frames

An antique mirror consists of a frame and the silvered glass. The value is higher if both parts are original. Unfortunately, old mirrors often lose some of the backing and the reflective qualities are diminished. It is possible to "resilver" the old glass or to replace the glass entirely if you do not wish to live with flawed glass.

An inexpensive way to restore some old mirrors with poor "silvering" is to remove the metallic backing from the old glass and put a new mirror behind the old glass. This saves the old glass, yet gives a mirror that reflects properly. Contact local mirror installers located through the Yellow Pages of your phone book.

A painting or print needs a frame—old, new, or restored. Try to reframe any print or painting with a frame in the same style as the original. It is possible to buy antique frames or copies of antique frames from general antiques shops, modern frame shops, or special firms that deal only in period picture frames.

When reframing a picture, use acid-free archival mountings. The frame shop can tell you about these.

Some of the craftsmen listed in the Furniture section also restore mirrors and picture frames.

Repairs, Parts & Supplies

Antique Restoration Co., 440 E. Centre Ave., Newtown, PA 18940, 215-958-2343, Tues.–Sat. 9:00 A.M.–5:00 P.M. Mirror resilvering. Free brochure.

Antiquities, 5 Ordnance Mews, The Historic Dockyard, Chatham, Kent ME4 4TE United Kingdom, 0634 818866; fax: 0634 818877. Picture frames gilded.

Balboa Art Conservation Center, PO Box 3755, San Diego, CA 92163, 619-236-9702, 8:30 A.M.–5:00 P.M.; fax: 619-236-0141. Conservation of picture frames.

Bardwell Conservation, Ltd., Margaret Bardwell, 11373 Park Dr., Fairfax, VA 22030, 703-385-8451, 9:00 A.M.–6:00 P.M. Restoration of antique frames, including gilding and casting parts.

Chaudron Glass & Mirror Co., Inc., Henry Chaudron, 1801 Lovegrove St., Baltimore, MD 21202, 410-685-1568, Mon.–Fri 8:00 A.M.–5:00 P.M., Thurs. until 8:00 P.M. Resilvering of old mirrors, hand beveling, stone wheel engraving on flat glass.

Dec-Art, Inc., 7731 Long Point Rd., Houston, TX 77055, 713-523-5267. Picture frames and mirrors restored. Damaged or missing pieces remolded or carved. Gold leafing.

Eli Wilner & Co., Inc., Period Frames and Mirrors, 1525 York Ave., New York, NY 10028, 212-744-6521, Mon.–Fri. 9:30 A.M.–5:30 P.M.; fax: 212-628-0264. Period frames, frame restoration, frame replication. Catalog $17.50. Video $33.

Fine Art Conservation Laboratories, PO Box 23557, Santa Barbara, CA 93131, 805-564-3438, Mon.–Fri. 9:00 A.M.–5:00 P.M.; fax: 805-568-1178. Restoration and preservation of frames. Cleaning, gilding, missing pieces replaced, art work mounted into the frame. Free brochure.

FredEric's Frame Studio, Inc., 1230 W. Jackson Blvd., Chicago, IL 60607, 312-243-2950, Mon.–Fri. 8:00 A.M.–5:00 P.M.; fax: 312-243-4673. Restoration of picture frames. Hand-carved reproductions of antique gold leaf frames. Manufacture of wood, metal, and acrylic frames.

Gainsborough Products Co., Ltd., 3545 Mt. Diablo Blvd., Lafayette, CA 94549, 510-283-4187, 800-227-2186. Art restoration supplies, including: frame glazes, glass etching equipment, and products for restoring and cleaning oil paintings. Free catalog.

Gifts From Twopin Cottage, Clifford Birmelin, PO Box 321, Pennsauken, NJ 08110, 609-665-7845, 9:00 A.M.–9:00 P.M. Custom framing and restoration work. Wooden frames repaired, plaster work, gold leaf and antiquing; metal repair; easel backs repaired, velvet or moiré. Ornate French mats; custom-designed mats. Wooden boxes repaired; leather or fabric relining of all types of antique boxes, including lap desks and jewelry boxes. Send SASE for price list.

Gilder's Studio, 24 Burbank St., Sandwich, MA 02563, 508-833-0782, 9:00 A.M.–5:00 P.M. Conservation and restoration of gilded objects: frames and mirrors. Estimates for projects provided in writing. Gilding workshops. Custom-made 22K gilded frames.

Gold Leaf Studios, Inc., PO Box 50156, Washington, DC 20091, 202-638-4660, Mon.–Fri. 9:00 A.M.–5:30 P.M.; fax: 202-347-4569. Conservation of gilded frames. Gilded-frame fabrication.

Guido, 118 Newbury St., Boston, MA 02116, 617-267-0569, Tues.–Sat. 9:30 A.M.–5:30 P.M. Repair and restoration of old and damaged frames. Custom framing, gold leafing. Catalog $15 plus $2 handling.

Harvard Art, Susan B. Jackson, 49 Littleton County Rd., Harvard, MA 01451, 508-456-9050, 9:00 A.M.–5:00 P.M. Gilding conservation and restoration, particularly frames. Missing pieces replaced, gilded, and toned to match.

Hess Restorations, 200 Park Ave. S., New York, NY 10003, 212-260-2255, 10:30 A.M.–4:00 P.M. Restoration of mirrors and picture frames. New velvet easel backs for silver frames. Brochure.

Hoffer Glass, George J. Hoffer, 613 W. College Ave., Appleton, WI 54911, 800-236-2413 (Brian or Glenn), 8:00 A.M.–5:00 P.M.; fax: 414-731-8272. Convex and oval picture frame glass in stock. Send pattern or call with sizes for quote. Free brochure.

Intermuseum Laboratory, 83 N. Main St., Allen Art Building, Oberlin, OH 44074, 216-775-7331, 8:30 A.M.–5:00 P.M.; fax: 216-774-3431. Conservation of frames.

J & H China Repairs, 8296 St. George St., Vancouver, BC, Canada V5X 3C5, 604-321-1093, 7:30 A.M.–2:00 P.M. Picture frames restored.

James M. Muell Company, 628 Fairhaven Rd., Fairhaven, MD 20754, 202-347-1171, 9:00 A.M.–5:00 P.M.; fax: 202-737-2682. Custom frame restoration, gilding, frame design, and fabrication of modern and period frames. Large mural framing.

John Edward Cunningham, 1525 E. Berkeley, Springfield, MO 65804, 417-889-7702, Mon.–Sat. 9:00 A.M.–5:00 P.M. Frames restored. Mail order or by appointment. Send SASE for more information.

Loughlin's Restoration Studio, 749 Indian Beach Circle, Sarasota, FL 34234, 813-355-7318, Mon.–Fri. 9:00 A.M.–5:00 P.M. Frames cleaned and gilded. Missing pieces cast. Brochure.

MAC Enterprises, Martha A. Cleary, Master Restorer, 14851 Jeffrey Rd. #75, Irvine, CA 92720, 714-262-9110, 9:00 A.M.–6:00 P.M. Frames restored. Ship UPS or call for information. Send SASE for brochure.

Michael C. Hinton, RD#2, Box 313, Mertztown, PA 19539, 215-682-7096 anytime. Repairs, restoration, and conservation of frames. Gold, silver, and patient leafing; missing mold details replaced.

Minuteman Furniture Restoration, Jim Gauthier, 115 N. Monroe St., Waterloo, WI 53594, 800-733-1776, 8:00 A.M.–5:00 P.M.; fax: 414-478-3966. Picture frame restoration and mirror resilvering products and kits. Catalog $2.

Museum Shop, Ltd., Richard Kornemann, 20 N. Market St., Frederick, MD 21701, 301-695-0424, Mon.–Thurs. 10:30 A.M.–6:00 P.M., Fri.–Sat. 10:30 A.M.–9:00 P.M., Sun. noon–5:00 P.M.; fax: 301-698-5242. Restoration of antique frames; 23K gold leafing.

Old World Restorations, Inc., 347 Stanley Ave., Cincinnati, OH 45226, 800-878-1911, 513-321-1911, Mon.–Fri. 8:30 A.M.–5:30 P.M.; fax: 513-321-1914. Restoration and conservation of art and antiques, including frames. Free brochure.

Original Woodworks, 360 N. Main St., Stillwater, MN 55082, 612-430-3622, Thurs.–Sat. noon–5:00 P.M. Mirror resilvering.

Paxton Hardware Ltd., PO Box 256, 7818 Bradshaw Rd., Upper Falls, MD 21156, 410-592-8505, 9:00 A.M.–5:00 P.M.; fax: 410-592-2224. Miscellaneous period hardware and framing supplies. Cleaning and restoration products. Free brochure. Catalog $4.

PECO Glass Bending (Pat's Etcetera Co., Inc.), PO Box 777, 810 E. First St., Smithville, TX 78957, 512-237-3600, 10:00 A.M.–3:00 P.M. Convex glass for old picture frames.

R. Wayne Reynolds, Ltd., Wayne Reynolds, 3618 Falls Rd., Baltimore, MD 21211, 410-467-1800, 9:00 A.M.–5:30 P.M.; fax: 410-467-1205. Complete conservation treatment for gilded decorative art objects, picture frames and mirrors.

Raphael's Antique Furniture Restoration, Mark DeVito, owner, 655 Atlantic St., Stamford, CT 06902, 203-348-3079, Mon.–Fri. 8:30 A.M.–4:30 P.M., Sat. 9:00 A.M.–noon. Restoration of antique picture and mirror frames. Gold-leaf application.

RGS Glass & Frame Corp., Ron's Gallery Supply, 159 Duane St., New York, NY 10013, 800-735-7667; fax: 212-587-5957. Restoration of picture frames. Picture-hanging systems.

Sheffield Plains Antiques, Jeff Von Er, PO Box 598, S. Main St., Rt. 7, Sheffield, MA 02157, 413-229-0113, Wed.–Sun. 11:00 A.M.–4:00 P.M.; fax: 413-229-8914. Gold-leaf restoration, burnish gilding, reverse painting, églomisé panels.

Sheild Art & Hobby Shop, Sandra H. Sheild, 4417 Danube Dr., King George, VA 22485-9374, 703-663-3711 anytime, leave message if no answer. Picture frames repaired. Missing carved pieces replaced.

Thome Silversmiths, 49 W. 37th St., Suite 605, New York, NY 10018, 212-764-5426, 8:30 A.M.–1:00 P.M., 2:30 P.M.–5:30 P.M. Restoration of silver, pewter, copper, brass, and bronze. Gold and silver plating; engraving. Brass, copper, silver, and pewter polished. New velvet backs for picture frames; velvet liners for boxes.

Vances' Antique Frame Restoration, Old 69 Hwy., Box 150, Camden, TN 38320, 901-584-8122, weekdays 7:00 A.M.–noon, weekends anytime. Frame restoration and repair. Missing pieces reconstructed. Free estimate with photo and SASE.

Vigues Art Studio, 54 Glanders Rd., Woodbury, CT 06798, 203-263-4088, 10:00 A.M.–5:00 P.M. Conservation and restoration of picture frames. Casting and replacement of missing parts.

Williamstown Regional Art Conservation Laboratory, Inc., 225 South St., Williamstown, MA 01267, 413-458-5741, 8:30 A.M.–5:00 P.M.; fax: 413-458-2314. Conservation of picture frames and gilded objects. Free brochure.

Witherspoon Galleries, 3545 Mt. Diablo Blvd., Lafayette, CA 94549, 510-283-3342, Tues.–Sat. 10:00 A.M.–6:00 P.M. Restoration of frames.

Movie Memorabilia

Movie memorabilia is a large field, ranging from movie films, sound-track albums, comic materials, toys, and dolls representing characters in movies, to ceramics commemorating movie characters and related events. It also includes movie posters, lobby cards, press kits, movie stills, costumes, and memorabilia from the stars, such as Joan Crawford's false eyelashes or Judy Garland's ruby slippers.

All this material is rightly considered movie memorabilia and can be found in any shop or show. Specialists should be familiar with the publications and shows that are devoted exclusively to movies. Special groups like the "Star Trek" enthusiasts or fan clubs of deceased stars hold regular conventions and meetings, exchanging information and memorabilia. Anything pertaining to *Gone With the Wind*, Marilyn Monroe, Elvis Presley, or James Dean has added value.

Anything related to the movie business is in high demand: old props, costumes, lobby cards, still photographs, scripts, publicity packets, promotional giveaways, signs, objects (especially clothing) owned by a star, and of course the movies themselves. Even scrapbooks filled with newspaper clippings or the movie fan magazines are bought and sold.

Although much movie memorabilia is sold through flea markets, antiques shows, and even auctions, these do not represent the major market. Several newspapers are devoted to buying and selling movie material.

Special shows are held during the year, especially in California. There are also several special mail auctions of movie material. Fan clubs want appropriate items. Try to find the movie collectors in your area. If you have a tie that belonged to John Wayne, you can find the proper fan club and contact the members. To locate the star or fan club, look in *The Address Book: How to Reach Anyone Who Is Anyone* by Michael Levine at your library.

It is important to verify the authenticity of your movie memorabilia. Many autographs were not originally signed by the stars. Pictures were often signed by someone on the staff.

REPAIR

Because movie memorabilia is so recent and so abundant, it does not pay to repair any but the greatest rarities. Movie film is a special consideration. The old nitrate film is combustible and dangerous to store and should be copied. Contact the National Center for Film and Video Preservation to learn what to do with old nitrate film. You may phone the center at (213) 856-7637, or write to: National Center for Film and Video Preservation, American Film Institute, 2021 N. Western Ave., Los Angeles, CA 90027.

Also see the sections on Celebrities, Comic Art, Paper, Photographs, Textiles, and Toys.

Clubs & Publications

Lucasfilm Fan Club, *Lucasfilm Magazine* (MAG), PO Box 111000, Aurora, CO 80042.

Marx Brotherhood, *Freedonia Gazette* (MAG), 28 Darien, New Hope, PA 18938-1224 (Marx Brothers).

Roy Rogers/Dale Evans Collectors Association, *Roy Rogers/Dale Evans Collectors Association Newsletter* (NL), PO Box 1166, Portsmouth, OH 45662.

Shirley Temple Collectors By The Sea, *Lollipop News* (NL), PO Box 6203, Oxnard, CA 93031.

Star Trek: The Official Fan Club, *Official Star Trek Magazine* (MAG), PO Box 111000, Aurora, CO 80042.

Westerns & Serials Club, *Westerns & Serials* (MAG), Rt. 1, Box 103, Vernon Center, MN 56090.

Beyond the Rainbow Collector's Exchange (NL), PO Box 31672, St. Louis, MO 63131 (Judy Garland and Wizard of Oz collectibles).

Big Reel (NP), PO Box 1050, Dubuque, IA 52004-1050.

Classic Images (NP), PO Box 809, Muscatine, IA 52761-0809.

Movie Advertising Collector (MAG), PO Box 28587, Philadelphia, PA 19149.

Movie Collector's World (NP), PO Box 309, Fraser, MI 48026.

Silver Bullet (NL), PO Box 553, Forks, WA 98331 (Lone Ranger memorabilia).

Trek Collector: A Newsletter for Star Trek Fans and Collectors (NL), 1324 Palms Blvd., Venice, CA 90291.

Under Western Skies (MAG), Rt. 3, Box 263H, Waynesville, NC 28786 (movie, TV, and radio westerns).

Musical Instruments, Player Pianos & Music Boxes

*E*veryone has heard of the Stradivarius violin that sold for over $1 million. Unfortunately, very few people know that 99.99 percent of the violins labeled Stradivarius are nineteenth- or twentieth-century versions and are worth very little even if labeled inside. Some old musical instruments have great value, but most of them should be priced as secondhand instruments to be used by young musicians. If you have an old violin or other musical instrument, the best way to start determining the value is to take it to a friend who is a competent musician. Don't forget that even the bow might be of value. Very good bows can sell for thousands of dollars. You might price a new violin and bow to get some idea of value. Anyone who plays the violin well will know if your violin is of good quality. If it seems good, take it to a local store that sells used musical instruments. They are listed in the Yellow Pages of the phone book. If it seems very good, you might try to contact a violin appraiser. This type of specialist is often listed in the phone book but is not found in every city. The only other way to sell old violins is through a local auction, through an ad in the newspaper, or even at a flea market. Few antiques dealers buy and sell average-quality musical instruments.

Collectible musical instruments are old, decorative, and often unusual in appearance. Some are no longer made or used but are often playable. These instruments might include a sarrusophone (used in marching bands from the 1860s to the 1920s) or an American harp-guitar (popular from 1800 to 1925). Banjos and mandolins with carvings and mother-of-pearl inlay appeal both to collectors who want something decorative to display and to musicians who are looking for instruments.

Look for the names of major manufacturers such as GIBSON, VEGA, or EPIPHONE. Look at the construction of the instrument. Like fine furniture, it should be well made and have crisp detail. Inlays and carvings are often signs of quality. Collectors pay a premium for instruments in original condition and original cases, but musicians don't seem to mind restorations if it is a fine instrument that can be played.

Because pianos are so large and difficult to move, they present some special problems. Fine pianos with elaborately painted cases are very popular with decorators, especially for large apartments. The decorative value of the piano as a piece of furniture, as well as the quality of the instrument, is considered in determining the price. "Reproducing pianos," a special type of piano that plays automatically, bring high prices. Any top-quality piano will probably sell best at a well-advertised antiques auction. If there is no gallery nearby, it can be sold to a piano store to be resold. An average-quality piano can be sold at a house sale, through an ad in the papers, to a music store, or through an auction. The best method will depend on what is available in your area.

Square pianos, the 1880s type with rosewood case and heavy carved legs, are the most disappointing to sell. The square piano doesn't remain tuned very long. It is not a good instrument for a musician. Most of these pianos are finally sold for a few hundred dollars. The insides are removed and the case is remade into a desk.

Player pianos are wanted for entertainment. If your player piano works, it will sell quickly at a good price. The more attractive the case, the higher the price. Well-finished wood and stained-glass panels add to the price. If the piano does not play, have it checked by a piano restorer. It may not be salable because the repairs are too expensive.

Small musical instruments, like harmonicas and kazoos, sell at flea markets for prices a little lower than the cost of new ones. Unusual designs, extra large or small examples, or other odd features will raise the price.

MUSIC BOXES

All music boxes, from the early cylinder types with bells and dancing figures to a ten-year-old musical powder box, are in demand. However, age, rarity, and the quality of the box are important in pricing it for sale. The nineteenth-century boxes that play using cylinders, teeth, and combs have values from hundreds to thousands of dollars. The REGINA boxes that play flat metal disks are also high priced and easy to sell. Go to a serious music box collector (your town may have an active chapter of the Musical Box Society International) or to your library. There are many books about music boxes that will help you decide if yours is average or special. The price books also price many of the boxes.

Look for anything that moves, like bells or dancers, a selection of tunes, or an elaborate case. Some boxes play paper "rolls." These are old and, if working, should sell well. Very large cylinder boxes (over three feet long) are usually of top quality. Small boxes, twelve inches long or less, were usually made for tourists and often were not as well made. Musical, animated birds are always popular with buyers. Any moving bird sells for hundreds of dollars. Twentieth-century music boxes include carved wooden figures that turn their heads and whistle tunes, musical powder boxes and jewelry cases, even carved chairs that play when you sit on them. Anything that moves and makes noise is popular with collectors.

SHEET MUSIC

Sheet music is collected for many reasons. Some want the music, but most want the old covers to frame as pictures. Others want covers that are celebrity or movie related. So there are several ways to sell the sheet music you might find in a box or a piano bench. A few pieces of sheet music may not have great value, but a pile of the music could add up to considerable money.

There is added value to covers illustrated with an old car, a train, a political event, a Gibson girl, blacks, well-known movie stars, Elvis Presley, or even a war scene. The general rule is the smaller the picture on the title page, the older the sheet music. Only historians want the early pieces. By the 1870s, the cover was a full picture, which was almost always lithographed. Photographs were used by the early 1900s. Sheet music

was printed on pages measuring $13\frac{1}{2} \times 10\frac{1}{2}$ inches before 1917. Most sheet music was published on sheets measuring 12×9 inches after 1920. Collectors like covers made before the 1930s.

The best prices are paid for music with all the pages intact and untrimmed. After 1920 the old music was often cut to fit in the piano bench. Dust the music and carefully erase pencil marks and smudges with an art-gum eraser before you sell. Transparent tape and tears always lower the value, sometimes to a few cents. Dealers in shops and flea markets sell most of the music. It doesn't sell well at auctions.

Collectors and dealers of sheet music advertise in the general antiques publications and the paper ephemera and sheet music publications. There are several dealers who sell music through the mail using monthly lists. They could be your best customers.

REPAIR

Music collectibles range from musical instruments to reproducing pianos. The value of each of these items is in the music it makes, so each piece must be in good working condition. Repairs of mechanical music-making machines are slow. Many of the restorers have two- and three-year waiting lists. If you can fix this type of antique yourself, you can usually make good buys. Be very careful if you buy a machine that needs repairs that you can't do yourself.

All music boxes are delicate, intricate mechanisms that require care. Don't try to repair a music box unless you're an expert—it's a job for a professional. Restorers and parts can be found, but they are rare and expensive. You may be lucky enough to find a local music box devotee who restores; contact the Musical Box

Society International (Route 3, Box 205, Morgantown, IN 46160) for information. Other restorers are listed here, but they have advised us that they are very busy and repairs may take years.

Minor repairs of instruments are possible in some cities, or through dealers or service shops listed in the Yellow Pages under "Musical Instruments—Repairing."

Books on Repair

Compleat Talking Machine, Eric L. Reiss (Vestal Press, PO Box 97, Vestal, NY 13850, © 1986).

Piano Care & Restoration, Eric Smith (Tab Books, Blue Ridge Summit, PA 17214, © 1982).

Piano Servicing Tuning & Rebuilding, Arthur A. Reblitz (Vestal Press, PO Box 97, Vestal, NY 13850, © 1976).

Player Piano Servicing and Rebuilding, Arthur Reblitz, (Vestal Press, PO Box 97, Vestal, NY 13850, © 1985).

Preservation and Restoration of Sound Recordings, Jerry McWilliams (AASLH, 172 Second Ave. N., Suite 102, Nashville, TN 37201, © 1979).

Rebuilding the Player Piano, Larry Givens (Vestal Press, PO Box 97, Vestal, NY 13850, © 1963).

Restoring and Collecting Antique Reed Organs, Horton Presley (Vestal Press, PO Box 97, Vestal, NY 13850, © 1977).

Reference Books

Michel's Organ Atlas, N. E. Michel (8345 Cravell Ave., PO Box 123, Pico Rivera, CA 90660, © 1969).

Pierce Piano Atlas, Bob Pierce (1880 Termino, Long Beach, CA 90815, © 1965). Known as the "Bible of the Piano Business."

Clubs & Publications

American Musical Instrument Society, *AMIS Journal* (MAG) *AMIS Newsletter* (NL), Albert R. Rice, Membership Registrar, 6114 Corbin Ave., Tarzana, CA 91356.

Automatic Musical Instrument Collectors Association, *AMICA Bulletin* (MAG), 919 Lantern Glow Trail, Dayton, OH 45431-2915.

Maple Leaf Club, *Rag Times* (NL), 15522 Ricky Ct., Grass Valley, CA 95949.

Musical Box Society International, *Journal of Mechanical Music* (MAG), *News Bulletin* (MAG), 1062 Alber St., Wabash, IN 46992.

National Sheet Music Society, *Song Sheet* (NL), 1597 Fair Park Ave., Los Angeles, CA 90041.

Reed Organ Society International, *ROS Bulletin* (MAG), c/o James J. Quashnock, 3575 Hwy 258 E., Wichita Falls, TX 76308-7037.

Joslin's Jazz Journal (MAG), Box 213, Parsons, KS 67357.

Remember That Song (NL), 5623 N. 64th Ave., Glendale, AZ 85301 (sheet music).

Sheet Music Exchange (NL), PO Box 2114, Key West, FL 33045.

West Coast Rag (NP), Box 4127, Fresno, CA 93744.

Repairs, Parts & Supplies

Another Time Restorations, PO Box 42013, Portland, OR 97242-0013, 503-656-9757. Restoration and repair of automatic musical instruments. Player piano restoration; band organs and orchestrions repaired; pump and reed organ service. Custom wood and metal work.

Antique Music Box Restoration, Christian Eric, 1825 Placentia Ave., Costa Mesa, CA 92627, 714-548-1542, 8:00 A.M.–7:30 P.M. Restoration and historical research on antique music boxes. They do not repair modern, inexpensive, or toy musical pieces.

Antique Village Museum, Larry Donley, 8512 S. Union Rd., Union, IL 60180, 815-923-9000, anytime; fax: 815-923-2253. Complete parts and repair service for music boxes.

Beehive Reed Organ Studio, PO Box 41, Oak St., Alfred, ME 04002, 207-324-0990, 9:00 A.M.–5:00 P.M. Maintenance and rebuilding of reed organs, including cleaning and tuning reeds, refinishing and repairing organ cases. Replacement reeds. Will answer questions about the reed organ. Catalog $6.

Bryant Stove & Music, Inc., RR 2, Box 2048, Rts. 139 and 220, Thorndike, ME 04986-9657, 207-568-3665, Mon.–Sat. 8:00 A.M.–5:00 P.M. Player pianos rebuilt. Piano rolls for sale. Free brochure.

Carl Rinker, 6226 Waterloo Rd., Box 38, Atwater, OH 44201, 216-947-2268, phone and fax, weekdays 6:00 P.M.–11:00 P.M., Sat. 7:00 A.M.–5:00 P.M. Parts for music boxes made to order from sample or drawing. Mainsprings, gears, and pinions. Repairs. Catalog $3.

Chet Ramsay Antiques, Chester Ramsay, RD #1, Box 383, Coatesville, PA 19320-4342, 610-384-0514, 9:00 A.M.–9:00 P.M. Complete restoration of antique music boxes, cylinder and disc type.

Daniel's Den, John Daniel, 720 Mission St., South Pasadena, CA 91030, 213-682-3557, 10:00 A.M.–4:00 P.M. Restoration of automatic musical instruments. Parts.

Dawson's Antiques, Tom Dawson, 512 N. Ave. B, Washington, IA 52353, 319-653-5043, 9:00 A.M.–5:00 P.M., answering machine other times. Reed organs, player pianos, and nickelodeons restored.

DB Musical Restorations, Carol and David Beck, 75 Waters Edge Ln., Newman, GA 30263, 404-304-9066, Mon.–Sat. 9:00 A.M.–9:00 P.M. Total restorations of antique cylinder and disc music boxes. Combwork, cylinder repinning, gear work, governors repaired or replaced, parts fabrication. Free brochure.

Diane Wight, 30 Lafayette St., Randolph, MA 02368, 617-961-1028. Anri music boxes repaired.

Erb Consulting Engineering, Alan S. Erb, 2318 Tahiti St., Hayward, CA 94545, 510-783-5068, 3:00 P.M.–12:00 P.M. Self-playing mechanical music machines, specializing in carousel organs and roll-playing pianos. Restoration. Free brochure.

Great Canadian Nickelodeon Co. Ltd., RR #4, Mount Forest, ON, Canada N0G 2L0, 519-323-

3582. Mon.–Sat. 9:00 A.M.–6:00 P.M. Complete restoration or repairs of all automated music machines: player pianos, pipe organs, monkey organs, music boxes, nickelodeons, orchestrions, jukeboxes, band and fairground organs, etc. Custom-built parts. Brochure.

Institute of Metal Repair, 1558 S. Redwood, Escondido, CA 92025, 619-432-8942. Repair and restoration of woodwind and brass band instruments.

Inzer Pianos, Inc., John and Hazel Inzer, 2473 Canton Rd., Marietta, GA 30066, 404-422-2664, Mon.–Fri. 10:00 A.M.–5:00 P.M., Sat. 10:00 A.M.–3:00 P.M. Repair and restoration of antique pianos, player pianos, and pump organs. Parts and supplies.

Jandi Goggin, Box 175, Huntington, NY 11743-0175. Complete or partial restoration of singing birdcages, boxes, and cuckoo bellows. Repair kit for do-it-yourselfers. Send LSASE for information.

Johnson Music, 147 N. Main St., Mt. Airy, NC 27030, 919-320-2212. Antique pump organ parts and restoration supplies, including original reeds, stop knobs, stop knob faces, reed organ tops, bellows cloth, pedal straps, keys, and books on pump organ restoration. Reed organ restoration. Mail order bellows recovering. Brochure $2.

K.R. Powers Antique Music Boxes, 28 Alton Cir., Rogers, AR 72756, 501-263-2643, 9:00 A.M.–9:00 P.M. Cylinder and disc music box repair and restoration.

Mechanical Musicologist, Ronald J. Schultz, 420 W. State St., Belle Plaine, MN 56011, 612-873-6704, 7:00 A.M.–9:00 P.M. Antique music box restoration and repair. Any make or type of mechanical movement. Governor work, cylinder pin straightening, tooth and tip replacement, mainspring, general maintenance, case refinishing. Call or write for information.

The Musical Wonder House, 18 High St., PO Box 604, Wiscasset, ME 04578, 800-336-3725, anytime. Repair and restoration of antique and new musical boxes, spring-wound phonographs, and talking machines. Combs retuned. Piano and organ rolls, records, and parts. The Musical Wonder House contains a museum of mechanical musical instruments, open Memorial Day through October 15. Mail order year-round. Telephone orders accepted 24 hours a day. Brochure $1.

Obsolete Electronics, Bill Bickers, 1304 Tenth St., Cochran, GA 31014, 912-934-4900, Mon.–Sat. 9:00 A.M.–6:00 P.M. Repair of tube-type guitar amplifiers.

Oexning Silversmiths, 800 N. Washington Ave., Suite 118, Minneapolis, MN 55401, 612-332-6857, 8:00 A.M.–5:00 P.M., 800-332-6857 outside Minnesota. Musical instrument mouthpieces repaired and replated. Dent removal.

Panchronia Antiquities, Nancy Fratti, PO Box 210, Whitehall, NY 12887-0210, 518-282-9770, 9:00 A.M.–7:00 P.M.; fax: 518-282-9800. Restoration of disc and cylinder musical boxes, restoration supplies, restoration school. Worldwide mail order. Musical box restoration supply catalog $5, refundable with order.

Performing Pianos Plus, Inc., 2726 Dodier, St. Louis, MO 63107, 314-231-0600, 9:00 A.M.–6:00 P.M. Restorations of pianos, player pianos, pump organs, pipe organs, forte pianos, barrel pianos and organs, and all automatic or historic keyboard instruments. Limited number of rebuilding supplies available. Free newsletter.

Phoenix Reed Organ Resurrection, Ned Phoenix, HC 3 Box 28, Townshend, VT 05353, 802-365-7011, 8:00 A.M.–9:00 P.M. Complete restoration of reed organs, specializing in parlor organs and two-manual/pedal instruments. Parts, reeds, and information available. Reed work a specialty: tuning, replacement reeds, voicing, reed repair. Send SASE and specify parts wanted or send sample.

Player Piano Co., Inc., 704 E. Douglas, Wichita, KS 67202, 316-263-3241, Mon.–Fri. 7:30 A.M.–4:30 P.M. Player piano parts and restoration supplies. Tubing, bellows cloth, and hardware for all types of roll-operated instruments, or any

bellows-operated instrument. White or yellowed key-tops, felts, fallboard decals, tuners' tools, and specialized parts. Orchestrion, reed organ, and melodeon parts. Manual reprints, books, and music rolls. Free catalog.

Pump and Pipe Shop, 7698 Kraft Ave., Caledonia, MI 49316, 616-891-8743, 10:00 A.M.–9:00 P.M. Restoration of reed pump organs. Parts. Appraisals. Hours by appointment.

Ragtime Nickelodeons, Bruce Fanzlaw, 2685 SE 35th St., Ocala, FL 32671, 904-732-4006, 9:00 A.M.–5:00 P.M.; fax: 904-694-6970. Restoration and repair of all automatic musical instruments: player pianos, nickelodeons, etc. Brochure.

Tendrup Music Boxes, 7 Ashland Ct., Holtsville, L.I., NY 11742, 515-758-4755, 8:00 A.M.–9:00 P.M. Antique music boxes and automata restored.

Randolph Herr, 111-07 77th Ave., Forest Hills, NY 11375, 718-520-1443, 8:00 A.M.–11:00 P.M. Player pianos and other automatic music items repaired. Free brochure.

Sal Provenzano, PO Box 843, Bronx, NY 10469, 718-655-7021. Singing birdcages, bird boxes, feathering on birds, music boxes, and animated figures repaired.

Paintings

*O*riginal art can be the most valuable and the most complicated antique to sell. You must be able to tell if it is an oil painting, a print, an original Remington sketch, or just a photographic copy. Find a friend who can tell you which pieces look authentic. It might be a local artist, craftsman, or photographer who can recognize quality. Then try to check on the artist before you offer the piece for sale.

If you live in or near a big city, ask whether the local art museum schedules a day for authenticating works of art for the general public. Many museums will tell you the age of the piece and information on the artist, but none will estimate price. Watch for an appraisal day at local auction galleries or at fund-raisers. Take the piece to the appraiser. If it is too big, take a black-and-white photograph.

The work of any artist listed in *Thieme-Becker Lexicon, Dictionnaire des Peintres, Sculpteurs, Dessinateurs et Graveurs* by Benezit, *Dictionary of American Painters, Sculptors and Engravers* by Fielding, or *Mallet's Index of Artists* has a value. Look in the library for copies of these books. Check prices for the past ten years in the price books listed in this section and similar books found at your library, at your local art museum library, or available through some computer networks. You can also write to the National Museum of American Art, The Inventory of American Paintings, to learn about paintings by American artists.

Photograph the piece, write a description, copy down the artist's name, and contact a local or out-of-town auction gallery or any dealer to sell the item.

Before you decide how to sell your artwork, it would be prudent to go to some local auctions and see if the art sells for good prices. Sometimes a small local gallery does not get high prices for good art, because it specializes in furniture, country antiques, or other types of sales.

Valuable paintings are sometimes found in unexpected places. An American tourist in England went to a "boot sale" (flea market) and noticed a painting of two hummingbirds near a nest. He bought the picture for about $5. He vaguely remembered seeing a similar painting so he took the oil to Christie's in London. It was identified as the work of Martin Johnson Heade, one of a group of paintings done after Heade returned from Brazil. The picture was soon sold in the United States at an auction for $96,000.

Over 50 years ago a Boston dowager sent a dusty oil painting the family called "The Old Geezer" to a thrift shop. The store's paintings expert took it to the museum. When it was x-rayed they found it was a painting on a painting. Underneath the Old Geezer was a painting by Bellini. The Museum offered to buy the picture from the thrift store for $20,000, a high price for a painting at that time. The donor approved and the "priceless" painting was sold to the Bostom Museum of Fine Arts where it hangs today.

When you have a piece that seems to be old and authentic, it is always wise to have an appraisal by a qualified art appraiser before you sell it. If you decide to sell it through an auction gallery, no appraisal is needed. The gallery should be able to tell you the approximate value.

It is important to know the history of family pieces. Many good pieces of art "liberated" by soldiers during World War II are now appearing in house sales and estates. Many times, the value is unrecognized by the present owners. Some were obtained illegally and might still belong to an overseas owner, so a gallery might want to check it out.

Age does not always determine the value

of fine art, but condition, quality, and the prestige of the artist do. You may think a painting is ugly, but someone else may pay a significant sum for it. The size of an average-quality painting helps to determine the price. It should fit over a fireplace or sofa. If too high and narrow, it is worth 30 percent less. If the subject matter is unappealing (dead bodies, gored matadors, or unattractive factory views), the picture will not sell as easily as landscapes, seascapes, or still lifes by the same artist. Animals, beautiful women, nudes, sweet children, Jewish subjects, oriental views, and Paris street scenes are good sellers. Historical events, military battles, and Bible subjects are not as popular. If a landscape includes that of a town that can be identified, the value is at least doubled.

A good gold-leaf frame is of added value when selling a large painting. Most buyers plan to hang the picture on a wall, and if they have to spend extra money to restore or frame a painting, it is worth less.

Rips and damage in the main part of the painting (on a face, for example) are considered serious problems. Small tears in the background area are not serious if the painting has value. If the pictures were in the home of an elderly relative, be sure to check under the dust cover paper on the back for hidden money or stock certificates. The labels and writing on the back may provide valuable information about the work's history.

Don't be discouraged if friends tell you what a "bad" painting you have. Beauty is in the eye of the beholder. Respectable copies of famous paintings, decorative subjects, very primitive-looking pictures, and huge pictures (especially of food) that are suitable for restaurant walls will all sell. They are bought and sold, not as great art, but as decorations for boring walls or dark corners. They may even be purchased because the new owners like "kitsch," something that is so bad it has charm.

REPAIR

Oil paintings require special care. Home care should include just a light dusting of the surface once a month or less. Never wash a painting, or try any at-home restoration unless you are trained or care very little about the final results. Never entrust a good oil painting to anyone but a competent restorer or conservator. Many pictures have been completely ruined by overrestoration, too much overpainting or an overzealous cleaning that "skinned" the picture. These procedures may cause problems that can never be rectified.

If you believe that your painting, no matter how dirty, is valuable, take it to your local museum to learn about the artist. Museums will not appraise, but they can tell you if your picture is worth restoring, and may furnish the names of local conservators. In some cities, restorers are listed in the Yellow Pages under "Art Restoration and Conservation" or "Picture Restoring."

We have listed restorers, conservators, and companies using their own descriptions of title, training, and work methods. If you are concerned about the quality of the work or whether the firm is headed by a conservator or a restorer, you must check further. More information can be obtained through the American Institute for Conservation, 1522 K Street NW, #804, Washington, DC 20005.

Price Books

ADEC/International Art Price Annual, annual, ADEC-Production, Paris (available from Dealer's Choice Books, Inc., PO Box 710, Land O'Lakes, FL 34639).

American Artists at Auction (Currier Publications, 241 Main St., Stoneham, MA 02180, © 1994).

Art Price Index International, 2 volumes, annual (Sound View Press, 170 Boston Post Rd., Madison, CT 06443).

Art Sales Index, annual, edited by Richard Hislop (available from Dealer's Choice Books, Inc., PO Box 710, Land O'Lakes, FL 34639).

European Artists at Auction (Currier Publications, 241 Main St., Stoneham, MA 02180, © 1994).

Leonard's Annual Price Index of Art Auctions, annual, edited by Katheryn Acerbo (Auction Index, Inc., 30 Valentine Park, Newton, MA 02165).

Lyle Official Paintings Price Guide, 24th edition, Curtis (Dealer's Choice Books, Inc., PO Box 710, Land O'Lakes, FL 34639, © 1993).

Mayer International Auction Records, annual, compiled by E. Mayer (available from Dealer's Choice Books, Inc., PO Box 710, Land O'Lakes, FL 34639).

Miller's Picture Price Guide, edited by Judith and Martin Miller (Bath Press, Avon, England, © 1992). Values given in British pounds.

Sotheby's Art at Auction, annual (Conran Octopus Ltd., London).

Books on Conservation

A Handbook on the Care of Paintings, Caroline K. Keck (AASLH, 172 Second Ave. N., Suite 102, Nashville, TN 37201, © 1965).

How to Take Care of Your Paintings, Caroline K. Keck (Charles Scribner's Sons, New York, © 1978).

Preservation Guide 3: Paintings, Priscilla O'Reilly (Historic New Orleans Collection, 533 Royal St., New Orleans, LA 70130, © 1986).

Clubs & Publications

International Foundation for Art Research, *IFAR Reports* (MAG), 46 E. 70th St., New York, NY 10021 (reports of stolen, forged, or misattributed art).

American Art Journal (MAG), 730 Fifth Ave., New York, NY 10019.

Apollo Magazine Ltd., The International Magazine of the Arts (MAG), PO Box 47, N. Hollywood, CA 91603-0047.

Westbridge Art Market (NL), 2339 Granville St., Vancouver, BC, Canada V6H 3G4.

Repairs, Restoration & Supplies

Andrea Pitsch Paper Conservation, New York, NY, 212-594-9676, Mon.–Fri. 9:00 A.M.–6:00 P.M.; fax: 212-268-4046. Conservation and restoration of paper-based objects, including oil and acrylic paintings on paper, watercolors and gouaches, and drawings. Consultation on condition of paper collections, prospective purchases, storage, and handling. Brochure $1 and SASE. By appointment only.

Andrew Hurst, 2423 Amber St., Knoxville, TN 37917, 615-523-3498, 8:00 A.M.–7:00 P.M. Conservation and restoration of oil paintings and antique frames. Paintings cleaned.

Antique Restoration by Wiebold, 413 Terrace Pl., Terrace Park, OH 45174, 513-831-2541, Mon.–Fri. 9:00 A.M.–5:30 P.M., Sat. 10:00 A.M.–2:00 P.M.; fax: 513-831-2815. Restoration and conservation of oil paintings and frames. Free brochure.

Antique Restoration Co., 440 E. Centre Ave., Newtown, PA 18940, 215-958-2343, Tues.–Sat. 9:00 A.M.–5:00 P.M. Paintings restored. Free brochure.

Antique Restoring Studio Inc., DBA Trefler & Sons, 99 Cabot St., Needham, MA 02194, 617-444-2685, Mon.–Fri. 9:00 A.M.–5:00 P.M., Sat. 10:00 A.M.–2:00 P.M.; fax: 617-444-0659. Restoration of paintings and frames, paintings on metal and cloisonné, reverse paintings on glass. Cleaning, tears repaired, relining. Free brochure.

Antiquities, 5 Ordnance Mews, The Historic Dockyard, Chatham, Kent ME4 4TE United Kingdom, 0634 818866; fax: 0634 818877. Paintings restored, specializing in the restoration of wall paintings. Free brochure.

Appelbaum & Himmelstein, 444 Central Park W., New York, NY 10025, 212-666-4630, Mon.–Fri. 10:00 A.M.–6:00 P.M. Conservation treatment of paintings, objects, and textiles; collection surveys; consultation on collections care, including lighting, storage, and humidity control. Brochure.

Art Conservation Laboratory, Raymond, NH 03077, 603-895-2639, 9:00 A.M.–5:00 P.M. Conservation and restoration services: insurance claims, institutional and private clients. Both European and American art, specializing in paintings.

Balboa Art Conservation Center, PO Box 3755, San Diego, CA 92163, 619-236-9702, 8:30 A.M.–5:00 P.M.; fax: 619-236-0141. Conservation of paintings, paper, photographs, and frames. Consultations and collection surveys.

Bardwell Conservation, Ltd., Margaret Bardwell, 11373 Park Dr., Fairfax, VA 22030, 703-385-8451, 9:00 A.M.–6:00 P.M. Conservation of oil paintings, including icons.

Chicago Conservation Center, Barry Bauman, Director-Painting Conservator, 730 N. Franklin, Suite 701, Chicago, IL 60610, 312-944-5401, anytime; fax: 312-944-5479. Specializing in the restoration of paintings. Free brochure.

Conservation of Art on Paper, Inc., Christine Smith, 2805 Mount Vernon Ave., Alexandria, VA 22301, 703-836-7757, Mon.–Fri. 9:30 A.M.–6:00 P.M. Conservation of watercolors, drawings, pastels, and other art and historic artifacts on paper. Publications about the care of paper objects. Examination and condition reports for insurance purposes. By appointment.

Fine Art Conservation Laboratories, PO Box 23557, Santa Barbara, CA 93131, 805-564-3438, Mon.–Fri. 9:00 A.M.–5:00 P.M.; fax: 805-568-1178. Fine art restoration and preservation. Analytical services include pigment analysis, infrared and x-radiography. Specializing in the conservation of easel paintings, art on paper, and murals in historic buildings. Free brochure.

Fine Art Restoration, John Squadra, RFD 2, Box 1440, Brooks, ME 04921, 207-722-3464. Conservation and restoration of oil paintings. Mail photo of your painting and size for free written estimate. Upon approval, a foam-lined wooden box will be sent to you for shipping.

Foster Art Restoration, 711 W. 17th St. C-12, Costa Mesa, CA 92627, 800-824-6967, 8:30 A.M.–5:00 P.M., 714-645-9953; fax: 714-645-8381. Restoration of paintings and other art works and collectibles. Free brochure.

FredEric's Frame Studio, Inc., 1230 W. Jackson Blvd., Chicago, IL 60607, 312-243-2950, Mon.–Fri. 8:00 A.M.–5:00 P.M.; fax: 312-243-4673. Restoration of oil paintings and works of art on paper.

George Martin Cunha, 4 Tanglewood Dr., Lexington, KY 40505, 606-293-5703, 8:00 A.M.–5:00 P.M.; fax: 606-233-9425. Repair and restoration of watercolor paintings and other works of art on paper.

Graphic Conservation Co., 329 W. 18th St., Suite 701, Chicago, IL 60616, 312-738-2657, Mon.–Fri. 9:00 A.M.–noon, 1:00 P.M.–5:00 P.M.; fax: 312-738-3125. Conservation of works of art on paper, including watercolors. Dry cleaning, stain reduction, flattening, deacidification, inpainting, and tear repairs and fills. Proposal and examination fee $15 and up.

Guido, 118 Newbury St., Boston, MA 02116, 617-267-0569, Tues.–Sat. 9:30 A.M.–5:30 P.M. Oil paintings restored.

The Icons Conservation and Restoration Company, Tad Sviderskis, 730 Fifth Ave., 9th floor, New York, NY 10019, 212-333-8638, weekdays 9:00 A.M.–5:00 P.M.; fax: 212-333-8720. Restoration of ancient Byzantine, Greek, and Russian icons, old master paintings, polychrome sculpture, egg tempera or oil paintings on wood panel and canvas. Repairing, cleaning, relining, retouching, regilding. Free brochure.

Intermuseum Laboratory, 83 N. Main St., Allen Art Bldg., Oberlin, OH 44074, 216-775-7331, 8:30 A.M.–5:00 P.M.; fax: 216-774-3431. Conservation of paintings in all media, on panel, metal, or canvas.

J. K. Flynn Group, 525 5th St., Brooklyn, NY 11215, 718-768-4726, Mon.–Fri. 9:00 A.M.–5:00 P.M. Restorations of eighteenth- through twentieth-century American and European paintings. Restoration and cleaning of reversible linings and inpainting; varnishing for paintings on both canvas and panel supports.

John Edward Cunningham, 1525 E. Berkeley, Springfield, MO 65804, 417-889-7702, Mon.–Sat. 9:00 A.M.–5:00 P.M. Oil paintings restored. Mail order or by appointment. Send SASE for more information.

Just Enterprises—Art & Antique Restoration, Gary and Susanne Gottfried, 2790 Sherwin Ave., #10, Ventura, CA 93003, 805-644-5837, 10:00 A.M.–noon, 2:00 P.M.–5:00 P.M. Restoration of paintings.

Kramer Gallery, 1012 Nicollet Mall, Minneapolis, MN 55403, 612-338-2911, Mon.–Fri. 10:00 A.M.–6:00 P.M., Sat. 10:00 A.M.–4:00 P.M.; fax: 612-338-2854. Fine art restorations and appraisals.

Leonard E. Sasso, Master Restorer, 23 Krystal Dr., RD 1, Somers, NY 10589, 914-248-8289, 9:00 A.M.–5:00 P.M. Art restoration and conservation. Appraisals.

Liros Gallery, PO Box 946 (Main St.), Blue Hill, ME 04614, 207-374-5370, Mon.–Fri. 9:00 A.M.–5:00 P.M., Sat. 10:00 A.M.–1:00 P.M. Restoration of paintings. Appraisals.

Loughlin's Restoration Studio, 749 Indian Beach Circle, Sarasota, FL 34234, 813-355-7318, Mon.–Fri. 9:00 A.M.–5:00 P.M. Specializing in gold leaf and restoration of oil paintings. Tears mended, cleaning, and canvas stretching. Brochure.

MAC Enterprises, Martha A. Cleary, Master Restorer, 14851 Jeffrey Rd. #75, Irvine, CA 92720, 714-262-9110, 9:00 A.M.–6:00 P.M. Restoration of oil paintings. Call for information. Send SASE for brochure.

Michael C. Hinton, RD #2, Box 313, Mertztown, PA 19539, 215-682-7096, anytime.

Repairs, restoration, and conservation of oil paintings and frames. Watercolors cleaned, defoxed, and deacidified.

Michael F. Robinson & Associates, 1269 First Ave., New York, NY 10021, 212-517-3819; fax: 212-744-9109. Appraisal, advisory, and consulting services in all areas of fine and decorative arts. Specializing in preparing documents for IRS and estate tax purposes. Forensic analysis of paintings. Will advise or conduct negotiations with auction houses.

Michael's Art Restoration Studio, Michael Scheglov, 8312 Eighth NW, Seattle, WA 98117, 206-789-2900, 11:00 A.M.–5:00 P.M.; fax: 206-778-6963. Restoration of oil paintings.

Museum Shop, Ltd., Richard Kornemann, 20 N. Market St., Frederick, MD 21701, 301-695-0424, Mon.–Thurs. 10:30 A.M.–6:00 P.M., Fri.–Sat. 10:30 A.M.–9:00 P.M., Sun. noon–5:00 P.M.; fax: 301-698-5242. Restoration of oil paintings, watercolors, original prints, etchings, lithographs, pen and inks, and anything on paper.

Old World Restorations, Inc., 347 Stanley Ave., Cincinnati, OH 45226, 800-878-1911, 513-321-1911, Mon.–Fri. 8:30 A.M.–5:30 P.M.; fax: 513-321-1914. Restoration and conservation of art and antiques, including paintings. Free brochure.

Phoenix Restoration Inc., 5305 N. 7th St., Suite C, Phoenix, AZ 85014, 602-263-5178, 800-234-5178; 8:00 A.M.–6:00 P.M.; fax: 602-263-6009. Restoration and conservation of paintings.

Peter Kostoulakos, 15 Sayles St., Lowell, MA 01851, 508-453-8888, anytime, answering machine. Cleaning and restoration of oil paintings on canvas and solid supports. Résumé and sample estimate form available.

Restoration Clinic, Inc., 2801 NW 55th Ct., Bldg. 8 W, Fort Lauderdale, FL 33309, 800-235-OLDY, anytime; fax: 305-486-4988. Antique and art conservation and restoration, including paintings. By appointment only. Send SASE for free leaflet, *What to Do Until the Restorer Comes.*

RGS Glass & Frame Corp., Ron's Gallery Supply, 159 Duane St., New York, NY 10013, 800-735-7667; fax: 212-587-5957. Restoration of paintings and picture frames. Picture-hanging systems.

Rikki's Studio Inc., Gilbert Kerry Hall, 2809 Bird Ave., Coconut Grove, FL 33133, 305-446-2022, 305-446-2230, 9:00 A.M.–4:30 P.M.; fax: 305-446-6388. Restoration of paintings. Appraisals.

St. Julian Fishburne, 6 Meadow Rd., New Paltz, NY 12561, 914-255-1042. 9:00 A.M.–9:00 P.M. Conservation of paintings.

Stoneledge, Inc., 17 Robert St., Wharton, NJ 07885, 201-989-8800, Mon.–Fri. 9:00 A.M.–5:00 P.M.; fax: 201-361-6574. Conservation and restoration of oil, tempera, and acrylic paintings on canvas, fresco, and panel. Paintings cleaned, repaired, and inpainted. Free brochure.

Thomas Portue, 639 Silliman St., San Francisco, CA 94134, 510-938-3900, Mon.–Sat. 9:00 A.M.–6:00 P.M. Conservation and restoration of paintings, murals, and decorative objects. Collection survey. Free brochure.

Van Cline & Davenport, Ltd., 792 Franklin Ave., Franklin Lakes, NJ 07417, 201-891-4588, 10:00 A.M.–11:30 A.M. Oil-painting restoration. Appraisals. Brochure.

Vigues Art Studio, 54 Glanders Rd., Woodbury, CT 06798, 203-263-4088, 10:00 A.M.–5:00 P.M. Conservation and restoration of oil paintings and frames.

Williamstown Regional Art Conservation Laboratory, Inc., 225 South St., Williamstown, MA 01267, 413-458-5741, 8:30 A.M.–5:00 P.M.; fax: 413-458-2314. Conservation of fourteenth-through twentieth-century paintings on canvas, wood, glass, and metal and in all media. On-site mural and fresco conservation. Free brochure.

Witherspoon Galleries, 3545 Mt. Diablo Blvd., Lafayette, CA 94549, 510-283-3342, Tues.–Sat. 10:00 A.M.–6:00 P.M. Restoration of oil paintings and frames. Appraisals of art.

Computer Programs

Research & Scholars Center, National Museum of American Art, 8th and G St. NW, MRC 210, Washington, DC 20560, 202-357-2941 (painting), 202-786-2384 (sculpture); fax: 202-633-9351. *Inventory of American Paintings Executed Before 1914* and *Inventory of American Sculpture*, database reference service. Available also through some computer networks, such as Internet and Research Libraries Information Network.

Paper Collectibles & Ephemera

*P*aper collectibles were almost ignored until the 1970s, when the word "ephemera" came into common use. If you have a bookplate that belonged to Charles Dickens, a 1910 gum wrapper, a bill of sale for a slave, or an 1890 menu, it is called ephemera. They were throwaway bits of history.

We seem more aware today that these bits are of historic importance. Several centuries ago, paper was not common and very little ephemera has remained. We have no accurate idea of what the Pilgrims wore on their feet because we have no photographs or personal letters. We can only make educated guesses about many of the everyday activities of the past. The history of the rich and famous remains in paintings and documents, but the everyday ephemera is gone.

Menus, newspapers, maps, ration books from the wars, personal letters, letterheads, diaries, children's lesson books, paper end-labels from bolts of cloth, wallpaper, fabric sample books, and instruction books for obsolete machinery are among the items of interest to the ephemera collector. There are collectors of local-history ephemera in every part of the country. Any paper item with a city or state name can probably be sold, and it will bring the best price near the city named on it.

Old newspapers are not very valuable. The paper is acidic and "self-destructs" after a number of years, becoming brittle and falling apart. Many libraries are selling old newspapers and replacing them with microfilm, so the supply is larger than the demand. Most papers are worthless unless sold as a full-year set. A few special papers reporting interesting events are worth up to $15 to $20.

Sort through boxes of old papers and "junk" you may find in the attic. Try to imagine who would find it useful. The best way to sell many special paper items can be found in the various appropriate sections of this book. Other items can be sold through mail-order ads in the general antiques publications. Ephemera is usually small, lightweight, and easy to mail to a buyer. There is even an international club of ephemera collectors and several newspapers devoted to the subject. Look at the want ads and try to find just the right person for your ephemera.

When all else fails, place a box filled with the papers on a table at a flea market and lightly pencil a low price on each piece.

Guess the value from the subject matter. Single pieces of paper over fifty years old can be worth from 10 cents to a few dollars even if they seem of no consequence to you.

REPAIR

The proper storage, display, and repair of paper collectibles is both difficult and important if you wish to preserve old maps, handwritten documents, sheet music, or other paper items.

For storage, humidity should range between 45 and 65 degrees. If a room is too dry, the paper can become brittle; if it is too wet, various molds and insects can attack. Never glue or paste any paper items. Transparent mending tape can be especially damaging, as it will eventually react with the paper and make a stain. Even so-called removable tape and notes will eventually leave a mark.

Be sure to display printed paper away from strong sunlight or direct heat. The sun will fade paper and the heat will cause damage. Unfortunately, ideal conditions are almost impossible for collectors who wish to hang a Currier & Ives print or an old map as decoration.

Consider the value and the possible damage before framing any paper item. Follow these strict rules: Use acid-free matting available at art supply or framing stores. Always leave a space between the paper and the glass. Seal the back to keep it dust-free.

Instructions for framing and/or storing valuable paper collectibles can be found in most paper preservation books. If your local art supply shop or frame shop is unfamiliar with the proper materials, you can purchase them by mail through the companies listed here.

See also the sections on Advertising, Books, Photographs, and Prints.

Price Books

Collecting Paper: A Collector's Identification & Value Guide, Gene Utz (Books Americana, Florence, AL, © 1993).

Collector's Guide to Trading Cards, Robert Reed (Collector Books, Paducah, KY, © 1993).

The Price and Identification Guide to: Pin-Ups & Glamour Art, pamphlet, Denis Jackson (TICN, PO Box 1958, Sequim, WA 98382, © 1992).

Warman's Paper, Norman E. Martinus and Harry L. Rinker (Wallace-Homestead Book Company, Radnor, PA, © 1994).

Books on Conservation

Curatorial Care of Works of Art on Paper, Anne F. Clapp (Nick Lyons Books, 31 W. 21st St., New York, NY 10010, © 1974).

How to Care for Works of Art on Paper (Museum of Fine Arts, Boston, © 1971).

Procedures for Salvage of Water-Damaged Library Materials, Peter Waters (Library of Congress, Washington, DC, 1975).

Clubs & Publications

American Business Card Club, *Card Talk* (NL), PO Box 460297-K, Aurora, CO 80046-0297.

Arcade Collectors International, *Penny Arcade* (NL), 3621 Silver Spur Ln., Acton, CA 93510 (arcade and exhibit cards).

Association of Map Memorabilia Collectors, *cartomania* (NL), c/o S. Feller, 8 Amherst Rd., Pelham, MA 01002-9746 (maps and anything with maps on it).

Bond & Share Society, *Bond & Share Society Newsletter* (NL), c/o R.M. Smythe & Co., Inc., 26 Broadway, Suite 271, New York, NY 10004.

Ephemera Society of America, Inc., *Ephemera News* (NL), PO Box 37, Schoharie, NY 12157.

Ephemera Society of Canada, *Ephemera Canada* (NL), 36 Macauley Dr., Thornhill, ON, Canada L3T 5S5.

National Association of Paper and Advertising Collectors, *P.A.C.* (NP), PO Box 500, Mount Joy, PA 17552.

Newspaper Collectors Society of America, *Collectible Newspapers* (MAG), PO Box 19134, Lansing, MI 48901. Also *Primer on Collecting Old & Historic Newspapers,* send SASE and $1.

Transport Ticket Society, *Journal of the Transport Ticket Society* (NL), 4 Gladridge Close, Earley, Reading, England RG6 2DL.

Auction Block (NP), PO Box 337, Iola, WI 54945, 715-445-5000; fax: 715-445-4053 (includes mail auctions of paper and ephemera).

Card Times (MAG), 70 Winifred Ln., Aughton, Ormskirk, Lancashire, U.K. L39 5DL (cigarette cards, trading cards, sports and non-sports cards, phone cards, printed ephemera, etc.).

Friends of Financial History (MAG), Museum of American Financial History, 26 Broadway, New York, NY 10004-1763 (stocks and bonds).

Mapline (NL), Hermon Dunlap Smith Center for the History of Cartography, Newberry Library, 60 West Walton St., Chicago, IL 60610-3380.

Non-Sport Update (MAG), PO Box 5858, Harrisburg, PA 17110 (non-sport cards).

Paper Collectors' Marketplace (MAG), PO Box 128, Scandinavia, WI 54977-0128.

Paper Pile Quarterly (NL), PO Box 337, San Anselmo, CA 94979-0337.

Wrapper (NL), 7 Simpson St., Apt. A, Geneva, IL 60134 (non-sports collectibles).

Repairs, Parts & Supplies

Andrea Pitsch Paper Conservation, New York, NY, 212-594-9676, Mon.–Fri. 9:00 A.M.–6:00 P.M.; fax: 212-268-4046. Conservation and restoration of paper-based objects: art, architectural drawings and blueprints, manuscripts and documents, maps, and ephemera. Consultation on condition of paper collections, prospective purchases, storage, and handling. Brochure $1 and SASE. By appointment only.

Antique Restoring Studio Inc., DBA Trefler & Sons, 99 Cabot St., Needham, MA 02194, 617-444-2685, Mon.–Fri. 9:00 A.M.–5:00 P.M., Sat. 10:00 A.M.–2:00 P.M.; fax: 617-444-0659. Restoration of paper. Removal of stains, molds, and foxing; repair tears, paper loss, and folds; restore watercolors. Free brochure.

Archival Conservation Center, Inc., 8225 Daly Rd., Cincinnati, OH 45231, 513-521-9858, 8:30 A.M.–3:30 P.M. Repair and restoration of works of art on paper, including engravings, family Bibles, historical documents, lithographs, maps, newspapers, parchment documents, posters, and prints. Free brochure.

Balboa Art Conservation Center, PO Box 3755, San Diego, CA 92163, 619-236-9702, 8:30 A.M.–5:00 P.M.; fax: 619-236-0141. Conservation of paper. Consultations and collection surveys.

Bernice Masse Rosenthal, 51 McClellan St., Amherst, MA 01002, 413-256-0844, Mon.–Fri. 8:30 A.M.–5:30 P.M. Conservation and restoration of flat-printed paper.

Bill Cole Enterprises, Inc., PO Box 60, Dept. RK1, Randolph, MA 02368-0060, 617-986-2653, 8:00 A.M.–4:00 P.M.; fax: 617-986-2656. Manufacturers and distributors of archival supplies to protect paper documents from turning yellow. Free catalog.

Conservation of Art on Paper, Inc., Christine Smith, 2805 Mount Vernon Ave., Alexandria, VA 22301, 703-836-7757, Mon.–Fri. 9:30A.M.–6:00 P.M. Conservation of art and historic artifacts on paper: drawings, prints, posters, pastels, watercolors, etc. Publications about the care of paper objects. Examination and condition reports for insurance purposes. By appointment.

Fine Art Conservation Services, Ltd., Nancy Wu, 94 Mercer St., New York, NY 10012, 212-966-5513; fax: 212-274-8424. Conservation of works of art on paper and parchment, as well as nineteenth- and twentieth-century photographs. Collection

management and display consulting. Archival matting and framing. Free brochure.

George Martin Cunha, 4 Tanglewood Dr., Lexington, KY 40505, 606-293-5703, 8:00 A.M.–5:00 P.M.; fax: 606-233-9425. Repair and restoration of rare and valuable books, manuscript materials, prints, posters, maps, watercolor paintings, and other works of art on paper. Preservation surveys for books and paper records, prints, posters, maps, and photographic materials, with recommendations for restoration, if required.

Graphic Conservation Co., 329 W. 18th St., Suite 701, Chicago, IL 60616, 312-738-2657, Mon.–Fri. 9:00 A.M.–noon, 1:00 P.M.–5:00 P.M.; fax: 312-738-3125. Conservation of works of art on paper, including maps, prints, posters, historical documents, watercolors, documents, globes, oriental screens, and sports cards and memorabilia. Dry cleaning, stain reduction, flattening, deacidification, inpainting, tear repairs and fills. Proposal and examination fee $15 and up.

Intermuseum Laboratory, 83 N. Main St., Allen Art Bldg., Oberlin, OH 44074, 216-775-7331, 8:30 A.M.–5:00 P.M.; fax: 216-774-3431. Conservation of fine art and historic documents on paper and parchment. Surveys and consultations on preservation planning.

Kathryn Myatt Carey, 24 Emery St., Medford, MA 02155, 617-396-9495, 9:00 A.M.–5:00 P.M. Conservation of works of art on paper, manuscripts, and historic wallpaper. Facility, environmental, and conservation surveys.

Lane Conservation Associates, Nan Lane Terry, Director, 9 Station St., Brookline, MA 02146, 617-738-1126, 10:00 A.M.–6:00 P.M. Conservation of works of art on paper. Consultations on proper storage and display. Collection surveys.

Larry Toth, 163 Varick St., 6th floor, New York, NY 10013-1108, 212-989-4520, Mon.–Fri. 10:00 A.M.–6:00 P.M. Linen mounting and restoration of posters, cleaning, bleaching, and paper replacement.

Museum Shop, Ltd., Richard Kornemann, 20 N. Market St., Frederick, MD 21701, 301-695-0424, Mon.–Thurs. 10:30 A.M.–6:00 P.M., Fri.–Sat. 10:30 A.M.–9:00 P.M., Sun. noon–5:00 P.M.; fax: 301-698-5242. Restoration of anything on paper: watercolors, original prints, etchings, lithographs, engravings, pen and inks, documents, etc.

Northeast Document Conservation Center, 100 Brickstone Sq., Andover, MA 01810-1494, 508-470-1010; fax: 508-475-6021. Nonprofit regional conservation center specializing in treatment of art and artifacts on paper, including books, documents, maps, photographs, posters, prints, and works of art on paper. Treatment of baseball cards, board games, cartoon cels, globes, and very large paper objects. Preservation microfilming, duplication of historical photographs, preservation planning surveys, disaster assistance, technical leaflets. Brochure.

Preservation Emporium, PO Box 226309, Dallas, TX 75222-6309, 214-630-1197, Mon.–Fri. 9:00 A.M.–5:00 P.M., Sat. 9:00 A.M.–4:00 P.M.; fax: 214-630-7805. Acid-free/lignin-free storage materials and conservation chemicals. Full conservation treatments and restoration work on documents and paper ephemera. Document dry cleaning, paper and book deacidification, paper mending and repair.

Restorations, PO Box 2000, Nevada City, CA 95959, 916-477-5527. Mylar bags for storing postcards. Brochure.

Stoneledge, Inc., 17 Robert St., Wharton, NJ 07885, 201-989-8800, Mon.–Fri. 9:00 A.M.–5:00 P.M.; fax: 201-361-6574. Conservation and restoration of works on paper. Free brochure.

Vigues Art Studio, 54 Glanders Rd., Woodbury, CT 06798, 203-263-4088, 10:00 A.M.–5:00 P.M. Conservation and restoration of works of art on paper. Watercolors, etchings, engravings, graphic art, books, and documents cleaned. Fumigation and deacidification.

Wei T'o Associates, Inc., Unit #27, 21750 Main St., Matteson, IL 60443, 708-747-6660, 8:00 A.M.–5:00 P.M.; fax: 708-747-6639. Deacidification sprays and solutions, application equipment, and specialty environmental chambers. Send SASE for catalog.

Williamstown Regional Art Conservation Laboratory, Inc., 225 South St., Williamstown, MA 01267, 413-458-5741, 8:30 A.M.–5:00 P.M.; fax: 413-458-2314. Conservation of prints, drawings, photographs, posters, maps, documents from all periods, and non-Western art such as Japanese woodblock prints and folding screens. Free brochure.

Video

Paperworks: Stabilizing Archival Collections, **American Association for State and Local History,** 530 Church St., Suite 600, Nashville, TN 37219-2325, 615-255-2971; fax: 615-255-2979. Video lending library for members includes *Paperwork: Stabilizing Archival Collections, Basic Deterioration and Preventive Measures for Museum Collections,* and other videos. Write for a current list and prices.

Paperweights

*T*he media is always reporting the high prices of antique French paperweights. For many years, the value was rising so quickly that paperweights were considered a better investment than stocks or real estate.

Unfortunately, few of us will ever discover the rare antique paperweight in fine condition that would sell for over $258,500 (a record price set in 1990). The paperweights we might own could be average-to-good antique French, English, or American weights, modern weights, or Chinese or Italian copies of old weights. They could also be some of the many paperweights that are not all glass: the snow weights, advertising weights, and others.

The Paperweight Collectors Association newsletter had these words for members: "Fortunate indeed is the collector whose heir will enjoy and continue to develop the collection. Many families are faced with the problem of disposing of a collection. One collector told me that he enjoyed his paperweights so much that he was going to take them with him when he went, but he never gave me the secret of how he proposed to do this. Another collector, who has since learned the wisdom of his words, said that he had never seen a U-Haul trailer behind a hearse."

The newsletter continues with good advice: "If you want to sell a collection for the highest dollars, you must find a collector who wants each weight, and sell it directly. Of course, this is time-consuming, if not impossible. Consider donating the weights to a museum and taking the tax deduction. This has been done by several well-known paperweight collectors and the collections can be seen by those who want to learn how to recognize a fine old weight of value.

"Auctions are a good method but don't expect the high prices announced for the best weights. A minor difference in color, design, or any flaws can alter the value. If you have rare weights, the auction, even with the seller's fees and other costs, is a good way to sell. The rare weights are advertised to a worldwide group of collectors with money and an interest in buying more weights. You might want to sell to a paperweight dealer. There are a few who sell old and new weights but many specialize. Some will buy the weights outright, some will take your collection on consignment and send you the money as the weights are sold."

A list of dealers can be found through the *Paperweight Collectors Association Newsletter*. Some advertise in the antiques publications. Modern weights are sold by gift shops as well as antiques dealers, and some of these shops may be willing to sell your weights on consignment.

Chinese and Italian paperweights were made in the twentieth century to look like older, better weights. These can be very confusing for a novice. Ask an expert in paperweights, preferably a dealer, appraiser, or auctioneer who sells fine paperweights. They will be glad to show you what characteristics of the glasswork are important.

In general, if the weight is made of small "canes" that look like hard candy, the canes should be very crisp and clear with no blurring of color or distortion of edges. The clear glass should be perfect, with no bubbles, flaws, or discoloration. The bottom should be ground flat. If there are flowers or animals inside, these too should be made with precision, no blurred edges or blurred color. Flowers and insects should be lifelike. If you remember that each color is made from a single strand of glass that has been worked by hand, you can understand the artistry in a single paperweight.

Advertising weights, small metal figural weights, snow weights, and other collectible but not artistic weights sell through the regular antiques dealers and auction houses, flea markets, and sales. Because weights are small, you can take them to these sales and discreetly try to sell them to dealers who have some others in stock. Remember, the best way to sell any antique or collectible is to find someone who has already shown an interest in and a knowledge of the item. Any dealer who sells an antique has to buy that antique from someone.

REPAIR

A slightly nicked or scratched paperweight can be restored. The glass can be repolished to remove scratches and nicks. Cracks cannot be repaired. It is important to be sure the condition of the paperweight is good. Repolishing scratched glass will not lower the value of the item, but if there is a large nick and removing it changes the overall shape of the weight, the value is lowered.

See also books listed in the Glass section.

Price Books

Collector's Guide to Snow Domes, Helene Guarnaccia (Collector Books, Paducah, KY, © 1994).

Clubs & Publications

Caithness Collectors Club, *Caithness Collectors Newsletter* (NL), *Reflections* (MAG), 141 Lanza Ave., Bldg. 12, Garfield, NJ 07026.

Friends of Degenhart, *Heartbeat* (NL), PO Box 186, 65323 Highland Hills Rd., Cambridge, OH 43725.

International Paperweight Society, *Paperweight News* (NL), 761 Chestnut St., Santa Cruz, CA 95060.

Paperweight Collectors Association, *Paperweight Collectors Association Newsletter* (NL), *Bulletin of the Paperweight Collectors Association* (MAG), PO Box 1059, Easthampton, MA 01027.

Snow Biz, *Snow Biz* (NL), PO Box 53262, Washington, DC 20009 (snow domes).

Roadside Attractions (NL), 7553 W. Norton Ave. #4, West Hollywood, CA 90046 (snowdomes).

Repairs, Parts & Supplies

Andrew H. Dohan, 49 E. Lancaster Ave., Frazer, PA 19355, 215-647-3310, 8:00 A.M.–5:00 P.M.; fax: 215-647-3318. Free appraisals, restoration advice, and auctioneer recommendations for antique and modern quality paperweights. Send focused close-up photo and SASE. If unable to supply photo, send long SASE for preliminary evaluation questionnaire.

Crystal Workshop, Edward D. Poore, PO Box 475, 794 Rt. 6A, Sagamore, MA 02561, 508-888-1621, Mon.–Fri. 8:00 A.M.–5:00 P.M. Restoration of glass paperweights.

George N. Kulles, 13441 Little Creek Dr., Lockport, IL 60441, 708-301-0996, anytime. Glass paperweights restored, paperweight appraisals.

Herb Rabbin, PO Box 421205, Los Angeles, CA 90042, 213-258-1776, 10:00 A.M.–7:00 P.M.; daily. Repairs, restores, and reconstructs broken snowdomes. Glass or plastic; old or new; whole or damaged. Please call first.

Phonographs & Records, Radios & Television Sets

*P*honographs, phonograph records, radios, and even television sets are popular collectibles. Early phonographs are stocked in some shops, but later models are often ignored. The item must be in good working condition to be of value. "Crossover" examples, those wanted by collectors of another type of antique, are worth more than might be suspected and are worth restoring. For instance, Barbie's Vanity Fair record player sold at auction in 1989 for $760. An old Hopalong Cassidy radio can be worth $1,100.

RECORDS

Enrico Caruso was a great opera singer, but in spite of the stories you hear, his records are not all worth thousands of dollars. One very early European record has a high value. The others are only worth a few dollars. Price is determined by demand. Today's collectors are more interested in "My Bonnie" by Tony Sheridan and the Beat Brothers (early Beatles) on the 1961 Decca label than they are in Bing Crosby singing "White Christmas." Probably the rarest record is "Stormy Weather" by the Five Sharps, auctioned for $3,800 in 1977. It might not sell for as much today—just a very few rare records are worth over $1,000 presently.

Sad but true, most 78s (a standard size after 1926, but almost completely replaced by 1957) and strange-looking early records are not of great value. Cylinder discs for the pre-1906 phonographs are usually worth just a few dollars in the shops; flat, one-sided records (made until 1923) are also of very limited interest to collectors. The 33 RPM record was developed in 1930, but was not popular until 1948, the same year the 45 RPM record was introduced. Picture records, those with a picture showing on the plastic record, are collected, but most sell for under $40.

Most records sell for low prices, if they can be sold at all. Condition is important, and any record that has overwhelming surface noises, a label in poor condition, cracks, chips, or deep scratches is not salable to anyone. Records in mint (never played) to very good condition can be sold. Try playing the record before you sell it, unless you are sure it has never been played.

The picture sleeve is important and adds to the value. The value of albums is sometimes determined partially by the picture on the album cover. Even empty albums with important artwork or graphics are sold.

Pricing records can be difficult because it is not just the artist and the song, but also the label, that determine the value. The best price books about records include pictures of the labels, so you have no problem identifying what you have.

The most valued 78 RPM records were made between 1915 and 1935. Unfortunately, if the same record was reissued on a 33 or 45 RPM disc, the earlier record is of less value. Some Enrico Caruso records are now available in reissue with enhanced sound quality, so the 78s do not sell well. Some combinations of artists are treasured but were recorded without listing all the artists' names on the record; some artists are valued highly only on particular labels (Al Jolson on Columbia or Brunswick); and some artists recorded under many names. Many 45s have been bootlegged or illegally copied, and these copies are not of great value. These factors show that it will take real study to know your records and to set a sensible price. The library and the price books will help.

Collectors specialize, so your records can be sold not only by artist and song, but also by type of music: rock, jazz, big band, blues, country and western, etc. If you plan to sell the records yourself at a show or house sale, be sure to sort them into separate boxes to make it easier for people to find the type of music they are interested in.

If you have some rare records, perhaps the best way to sell them is through the dealers who specialize in records. If you just have a pile of old records in poor condition, you may find it doesn't pay to spend the time researching and selling them. Most accumulations of old records found at house sales and rummage sales are of very little, if any, value. They are not even welcomed at some thrift shops.

See also Celebrity Memorabilia and Movie Memorabilia sections.

PHONOGRAPHS

We are constantly asked the value of old phonographs. The early type with the large horn is probably the most valuable. Least desirable are the floor-standing phonographs from the 1910s to 1950s. They may play, but they are not attractive, and the quality of the music from the old records is poor. Phonographs are listed in *Kovels' Antiques & Collectibles Price List* and in several special price lists devoted to phonographs.

The general rule is to check carefully if the machine has an exposed horn or unusual turntable arrangement with obvious pulleys and belts. Lower your expectations for enclosed machines, even if they are floor models. Many of the old phonographs are found with records, and if the records are unusual in size or shape, cylinders or "fat," one-sided, flat records, you probably own an old machine. A collector may want it if it is unusual and still in working condition. Even if it is not working, a collector able to fix your phonograph might be willing to buy it.

RADIOS

The streamlined, colored-plastic creations of the 1930s are the most wanted radios. More recent figural radios, especially those patterned on Disney characters, are selling for high prices. The blue mirror-covered EMERSON or SPARTON is worth money, even if it is not in working order. Brown plastic-cased radios, wooden radios, and large elaborate floor models made after 1935 are of limited value even if they are in working order. Some floor models are considered furniture, and the insides are removed and replaced with a stereo. If your radio is the proper size and shape for this, it has some sale value. Sets with added value are FADA, EMERSON, and CRYSTAL sets.

In the 1990s a new group of collectors started looking for transistor radios. These must work and have an unusual or high-style case to sell.

TELEVISIONS

The very early TV sets, those made before 1950 with screens of two inches or less, are of some interest to collectors. Very fifties-looking TVs with strange modern designs are also bought. Even these do not sell for thousands of dollars, and it is difficult to find the right collector. Unfortunately, your old TV has very little value, especially if it is not working. The earliest sets worked on a chemical battery that requires maintenance.

Do not plug in the radio or TV to test it. You may cause damage or a fire. Just look for obviously missing parts. The serious collector will be able to judge value better than you.

Even the tubes could be of use to repair other sets.

REPAIR

Phonograph repairs can be expensive, slow, and sometimes impossible. If you are able to fix this type of collectible, you can usually make a good buy. Repairs can often cost more than the value of a phonograph in very good condition.

Early phonograph records include many types. There are price books that list thousands of phonograph records, but many record titles are still unlisted. Records cannot be restored and have value only if they are in good playing condition.

Radios have gained in interest since the 1970s. Old tubes and other parts are hard to find, but there are dealers, publications, and clubs that make the search a little easier. Most expensive are the colorful plastic or very Art Deco–styled radios. The slightest crack in the plastic or scratches in the surface will lower the value by over 50 percent. This type of damage cannot be repaired.

Television sets that are wanted are in the most modern styles of the '50s. They include those with round picture tubes above the rectangular set or other unusual designs. These can often be repaired by an old-time TV serviceman, but many of the parts are out of production and difficult to locate.

Price Books

Collector's Guide to Antique Radios, 3rd edition, Marty and Sue Bunis (Collector Books, Paducah, KY, © 1995).

Collector's Guide to Transistor Radios, Marty and Sue Bunis (Collector Books, Paducah, KY, © 1994). First book on transistors.

Evolution of the Radio, Volume 2, edited by Scott Wood (L-W Books, PO Box 69, Gas City, IN 46933, © 1993).

Goldmine's Price Guide to Collectible Jazz Albums 1949–1969, 2nd edition, Neal Umphred (Krause, Iola, WI, © 1994).

Goldmine's Price Guide to Collectible Record Albums 1949–1989, 3rd edition, Neal Umphred (Krause, Iola, WI, © 1993).

Goldmine's Rock 'n' Roll 45 RPM Record Price Guide, 3rd edition, Neal Umphred (Krause, Iola, WI, © 1994).

How to Buy & Sell Used Record Albums, William M. Miller (Loran Publishing, PO Box 1604, Florissant, MO 63031, © 1994).

Official Price Guide to Compact Discs, Jerry Osborne and Paul Bergquist (House of Collectibles, New York, © 1994).

Official Price Guide to Elvis Presley Records and Memorabilia, Jerry Osborne (House of Collectibles, NY, © 1994).

Official Price Guide to Records, Jerry Osborne (House of Collectibles, New York, © 1993).

Picture Discs of the World, Joe Lindsay (BIOdisc, PO Box 8221, Scottsdale, AZ 85251, © 1990).

Poster's Radio & Television Price Guide, 1920–1990, 2nd edition, Harry Poster (Wallace-Homestead, Radnor, PA, © 1994).

Reference Books

Antique Radios; Restoration and Price Guide, David And Betty Johnson (Wallace-Homestead Book Co., Radnor, PA, © 1982).

Collecting Phonographs and Gramophones, Christopher Proudfoot (Mayflower Books, New York, © 1980).

Guide to Old Radios: Pointers, Pictures & Prices, David and Betty Johnson (Chilton Book Company, Radnor, PA 19089, © 1988).

Book on Repair

Antique Radios Restoration Guide, 2nd edition, David & Betty Johnson (Chilton Book Company, Radnor, PA 19089, © 1993).

Clubs & Publications

1950s/1960s American Bandstand, *Bandstand Boogie* (MAG), PO Box 131-A, Adamstown, PA 19501.

Antique Radio Club of America, *Antique Radio Gazette* (MAG), 300 Washington Trails, Washington, PA 15301 (sample copy $3.50).

Antique Wireless Association, Inc., *Old Timer's Bulletin* (MAG), PO Box E, Breesport, NY 14816.

Association for Recorded Sound Collections, *ARSC Journal* (MAG), PO Box 543, Annapolis, MD 21404-0543.

Dark Shadows Fan Club, *Dark Shadows Announcement* (MAG), PO Box 69A04, Dept. K, West Hollywood, CA 90069.

Friends of Old-time Radio, *Hello Again* (NL), Box 4321, Hamden, CT 06514.

International Association of Jazz Record Collectors, *IAJRC Journal* (MAG), PO Box 75155, Tampa, FL 33605.

Memory Lane Records, *Record Finder* (NP), PO Box 1047, Glen Allen, VA 23060.

Michigan Antique Phonograph Society, *In the Groove* (NL), 2609 Devonshire, Lansing, MI 48910.

New England Antique Radio Club, *Escutcheon* (NL), PO Box 474, Pelham, NH 03076.

Puett Electronics, *Antique Radio Topics* (NL), Box 28572, Dallas, TX 75228.

Southern California Antique Radio Society, *SCARS Gazette* (MAG), c/o C. Hill, 6934 Orion Ave., Van Nuys, CA 91406.

Vintage Radio & Phonograph Society, Inc., *Reproducer* (NL), PO Box 165345, Irving, TX 75016.

Antique Phonograph Monthly (MAG), 502 E. 17th St., Brooklyn, NY 11226.

Antique Radio Classified (MAG), PO Box 2-V23, Carlisle, MA 01741.

DISCoveries (NP), PO Box 1050, Dubuque, IA 52004-1050 (records).

Goldmine (MAG), 700 E. State St., Iola, WI 54990 (records).

Horn Speaker (NP), Box 1193, Mabank, TX 75147 (radios).

New Amberola Graphic (MAG), 37 Caledonia St., St. Johnsbury, VT 05819 (old phonographs and records).

POW-WOW (NL), 301 E. Buena Vista Ave., North Augusta, SC 29841 (Straight Arrow radio show and comics).

Record Collector's Monthly (NP), PO Box 75, Mendham, NJ 07945 (1950s and '60s rock & roll, R&B, doo-wop, and rockabilly).

Record Research (MAG), 65 Grand Ave., Brooklyn, NY 11205 (record statistics and information; mail order auction).

Transistor Network (NL), RR 1 Box 36, Bradford, NJ 03221 (transistor radios).

VideoMania (NP), PO Box 47, Princeton, WI 54968-0047.

Repairs, Parts & Supplies

A.M.R. Publishing Company, 3816 168th Pl. NE, Arlington, WA 98223, 206-659-6434, Mon.–Fri. 9:00 A.M.–5:00 P.M.; fax: 206-659-5994. Jukebox service manuals. Books, manuals, and original literature on pinball machines, soda machines, slot machines, player pianos, radios, and phonographs. Mail order worldwide. Free catalog.

Andy's Record Supplies, 48 Colonial Rd., Providence, RI 02906, 401-421-9453, Mon.–Sat. 9:00 A.M.–9:00 P.M. Record sleeves, CD sleeves, jewel boxes, import sleeves. Free shipping in the U.S. Free catalog.

Antique Electronic Supply, 6221 S. Maple Ave., Tempe, AZ 85283, 602-820-5411, 8:30 A.M.–5:00 P.M.; fax: 602-820-4643. Vacuum tubes and parts for antique radio restoration. Crystal set parts, reproduction radio knobs, cabinet restoration supplies. Phonograph parts. Tools, books, reprints of manuals. Free catalog.

Antique Phonograph Supply Company, Rt. 23, Box 123, Davenport Center, NY 13751-0123, 607-278-6218, Mon.–Fri. 10:30 A.M.–4:00 P.M. Products for restoration of mechanical talking machines. All size steel main springs, steel needles, manuals, books, record sleeves, parts, and refinishing supplies. Repair and rebuilding. Canadian and overseas trade welcome. Catalog $3.

Antique Radio Restoration & Repair, Bob Eslinger, 20 Gary School Rd., Pomfret Center, CT 06259, 203-928-2628, Mon.–Sat., 10:00 A.M.–7:00 P.M.; fax: 203-928-2628. Tubes, parts, and repair of antique table radios, consoles, cathedrals, battery sets, automobile radios, phones, amplifiers, and communication receivers. Complete overhauls, cabinet refinishing. Free estimates.

Antique Village Museum, Larry Donley, 8512 S. Union Rd., Union, IL 60180, 815-923-9000, anytime; fax: 815-923-2253. Complete parts and repair service for wind-up phonographs. Steel phonograph needles. Free brochure.

Atom Radio/The Kays, 5 Fiske St., Worcester, MA 01602-2922, 508-755-4880, 8:30 A.M.–11:00 P.M. Antique radios rebuilt. Tube radios repaired, rebuilt, and restored.

Bags Unlimited, 7 Canal St., Rochester, NY 14608, 800-767-BAGS, Mon.–Fri. 8:30 A.M.–5:00 P.M.; fax: 716-328-8526. Collection protection supplies. High clarity, recyclable, 100% polyethylene bags. Three grades of backing boards, several sizes of storage boxes and divider cards. Free brochure.

C & C Electronic Restorations, Enos Crum, 143R Edwards Rd., Johnstown, OH 43031, 614-967-3573, Mon.–Fri. 9:00 A.M.–6:00 P.M., Sat. 10:00 A.M.–5:00 P.M.; fax: 614-967-3573. Service and restoration for phonographs, radios, tape recorders, and televisions.

Cabco Products, PO Box 8212, Columbus, OH 43201, 614-267-8468, 614-263-0284. Record collectors' supplies, including record jackets, sleeves, and protectors; cassette tape boxes; and compact disc jewel boxes, sleeves, and storage boxes. Brochure.

Dan Reed, PO Box 169, Victorville, CA 92392, 619-242-5748, 8:00 A.M.–6:00 P.M. Repairs and parts for hand-wound phonographs, gramophones, and victrolas. Cylinder records, Nipper books, and instruction manuals. Catalog of cylinder records $6.

Dawson's Antiques, Tom Dawson, 512 N. Ave. B, Washington, IA 52353, 319-653-5043, 9:00 A.M.–5:00 P.M., answering machine at other times. Restoration of antique radios and spring-wind phonographs.

DH Distributors, David Headley, PO Box 48623, Wichita, KS 67201, 316-684-0050, Mon.–Sat. 9:00 A.M.–9:00 P.M. Repair and restoration service for tube-type radios, jukeboxes, and other audio equipment. Tubes and capacitors for sale.

George Bursor, 977 Kings R., Schenectady, NY 12303, 518-346-3713, until 11:00 P.M. Antique radio repair.

Jerry Madsen, 4624 W. Woodland Rd., Edina, MN 55424, 612-926-7779. Phonograph reproducers, Edison, Columbia, Zonophone, Pathe, and others. Books, pamphlets, needle tins, and other items having to do with old phonographs. Free catalog.

John Okolowicz, 624 Cedar Hill Rd., Ambler, PA 19002, 215-542-1597, 7:00 P.M.–9:00 P.M. Radio repair service. Reproduction radio grille cloth for Philco, RCA, GE, Westinghouse, Zenith, and Scott radios. Mail order worldwide. Send LSASE for free samples.

Mac's Old Time Radios & Radio Museum, 4335 W. 147th St., Lawndale, CA 90260, 310-675-6017, Tues.–Sat. 11:00 A.M.–5:30 P.M. Old radios restored and repaired. Cabinets restored.

Maurer TV Sales & Service, Donald S. Maurer, 29 S. Fourth St., Lebanon, PA 17042, 717-272-2481,

9:30 A.M.–6:00 P.M. New and old radio and TV tubes. Send tube numbers and large SASE for price quotes and availability. Mail order only.

The Musical Wonder House, 18 High St., PO Box 604, Wiscasset, ME 04578, 800-336-3725, anytime. Repair and restoration of antique and new musical boxes, spring-wound phonographs, and talking machines. Combs retuned. Piano and organ rolls, records, and parts. The Musical Wonder House contains a museum of mechanical musical instruments, open Memorial Day through October 15. Mail order year-round. Telephone orders accepted 24 hours a day. Brochure $1.

Novus, 10425 Hampshire Ave. S., Minneapolis, MN 55438, 800-548-6872, 612-946-0450; fax: 612-944-2542. Novus plastic polish cleans and restores plastic radios; removes scratches and cloudiness.

Obsolete Electronics, Bill Bickers, 1304 Tenth St., Cochran, GA 31014, 912-934-4900, Mon.–Sat. 9:00 A.M.–6:00 P.M. Repair of home audio equipment and car radios, specializing in Corvette radios. Parts, including tubes, capacitors, and transformers.

Olde Tyme Radio Company, 2445 Lyttonsville Rd., Suite 317, Silver Spring, MD 20910, 301-585-8776, 10:00 A.M.–10:00 P.M. Electronic restoration of chassis of all American radios. Parts, including capacitors, resistors, tubes, transformers, dial lamps, etc. Data packages on American radios from 1920 to 1960. A-B-C battery regulated power supply made to order. Send double-stamped LSASE for brochure.

Puett Electronics, Box 28572, Dallas, TX 75228, 214-321-0927, 214-327-8721, 7:00 A.M.–10:00 P.M. Antique radio books, tubes, literature, instruction manuals, etc. Old-time radio programs on cassettes. Technical data and schematic diagrams on almost any older radio. Catalog $5, comes with $6 discount coupon applicable to $25 or larger order.

Randle Pomeroy, 54 12th St., Providence, RI 02906, 401-272-5560, after 5:00 P.M. Antique phonographs cleaned and restored, specializing in reproducer work.

Romney, 615 Hill St., Emlenton, PA 16373, 412-867-0314, anytime. Camera repair books, antique radio repair books, precision tools to repair and refinish cameras, radios, and other collectibles.

Sam Faust, PO Box 94, Changewater, NJ 07831, 908-689-7020, after 5:00 P.M. Tubes, schematics, manuals, and service information for early radios. Send SASE for free brochure.

Simonson Clock Shop, 240 E. Washington St., Medina, OH 44256, 216-725-7056, shop hours Mon., Tues., Fri., Sat. 10:00 A.M.–5:00 P.M.; Thurs. 1:00 P.M.–8:00 P.M., 216-647-5548, home. Phonograph restoration. Free estimates.

Sound Remedy, 331 Virginia Ave., Collingswood, NJ 08108, 609-869-0238, 9:00 A.M.–6:00 P.M. Repair loudspeakers used in antique radios. Free price list.

The Thomas A. Edison Collection, Ralph C. Woodside, 51 W. Main St., Georgetown, MA 01833, 508-352-9830, 10:00 A.M.–5:00 P.M. except Mon. and Thurs. Phonograph repairs, spring replacement, motor replacement, parts, etc.

Tom Hawthorn, 4731 Melvin Dr., Carmichael, CA 95608, 916-973-1106, daytime. Antique phonograph repair, specializing in Edison and other reproducers. Needles, parts, and supplies available. Cylinder records and 78 rpm records for sale; custom taping of old records. Professional appraisals of record and phonograph collections. Research and information on most types of phonographs and records.

University Products, Inc., PO Box 101, S. Canal St., Holyoke, MA 01040, 800-628-1912, 800-336-4847 in Massachusetts; fax: 800-532-9281. Archival supplies and materials for paper, book, and general storage; photograph albums, mounting materials, negative and print storage;

frames and matting supplies; specialized storage for baseball cards, coins, comics, postcards, records, textiles, and other collectibles. Conservation tools and equipment, books and videos. Free catalog.

Victrola Repair Service, Rod Lauman, 19 Cliff St. #2, St. Johnsbury, VT 05819, 802-239-4188, 5:00 P.M.–10:00 P.M. Antique phonograph repairs, parts, mainsprings, service, books, record sleeves, and needles. Send broken parts via UPS for free estimate. Worldwide service. Free brochure.

Vintage TV & Radio, 3498 W. 105th St., Cleveland, OH 44111, 216-671-6712, Tues.–Fri. 10:00 A.M.–4:00 P.M.; fax: 216-251-1617. Tubes, capacitors, parts, reproduction knobs, grille cloth, decals, refinishing supplies, and books on collectible radios and TVs. Mail order. Catalog $2, refundable with order.

Wiesner Radio & Electronics, 149 Hunter Ave., Albany, NY 12206, 518-438-2801, 9:00 A.M.–5:00 P.M. Repair of obsolete electronic equipment, including antique radios.

William Hulbert, Jr., PO Box 151, Adams Center, NY 13606, 315-583-5765, 6:00 P.M.–9:30 P.M. Restoration of auto radios, pretransistor, all makes.

Yesterday Once Again, Box 6773, Huntington Beach, CA 92615, 714-963-2472, Mon.–Fri. 6:00 A.M.–9:30 A.M., 4:30 P.M.–8:30 P.M., Sat. and Sun. after 11:30 A.M.; fax: 714-963-2105, Attn.: Yesterday Once Again. Antique and vintage phonograph repair service. Parts and accessories, mainsprings, reproducers, books, and reprints of instruction manuals. Mail order worldwide. Free catalog.

Photographs & *Photographic Equipment*

CAMERAS

Any old camera has a value. So do stereo viewers and cards, screens, darkroom equipment, most professional photographs, sports photos, and amateur photos taken before 1918 that show everyday life or historic events. Most working old cameras can be sold at your local camera store, which is a better place than an antiques shop to try to sell a camera. An old camera can often be traded in for a new one, and this might be a good way to gain cash value for your collectible.

There are camera and photography clubs in most large cities. The members of these clubs buy many types of cameras, photographs, and photographic equipment. Call some local camera stores or the museum or historical society and ask for information on local camera clubs. Then call a member and describe what you have for sale. Often the members will help you price the items, will offer to buy them, or will tell you about dealers who might want them. Most large cities have camera and photography shows, and you can find customers for all types of photography-related items. Even film boxes, tripods, lenses, slide mounts, darkroom equipment, screens, and other photographica are wanted.

A working 35-mm camera made after 1950 can be sold to most pawnbrokers. More unusual cameras probably cannot. There are publications for the photography collector with interests in cameras, vintage pictures, 3-D, or other related subjects. Most of these publications have buy and sell ads and wanted lists. It is always best to read these for information on prices and possible customers. Cameras and exceptional pictures, daguerreotypes and daguerreotype cases, stereo viewers and stereo pictures (3-D), glass plate slides, and twentieth-century photographs by well-known photographers are often sold by antiques and art auction houses. Fine photographs are often sold in art galleries or at antique auctions.

We have found that information about old cameras and photographs spreads well by word-of-mouth. If you have time to wait to sell your items, try this subtle form of advertising. Go to the flea markets and the shows, and tell your local camera store and friends exactly what you have to offer for sale. Give them a list of the items, including brand names, condition, and identifying numbers. When describing a camera, include the manufacturer's name, serial number, words written near the lens, type and condition of case, and any instruction books, lenses, or other parts that are included. Even the original bill and box are important. The word will be spread to other collectors, and one day you will receive a phone call from an unknown collector searching for just the items you have.

Any camera that seems unusual to you may have a value. Very old cameras, pre-1900, are of special interest. Unusual shapes, even a Mickey Mouse–shaped camera, extra large or extra small cameras, and of course cameras of exceptional quality sell well. Condition is important. Wear, scratches, and minor, repairable problems lower the price by 25 to 50 percent.

PHOTOGRAPHS

Early pictures, daguerreotypes (silver images on glass), ambrotypes (glass negatives backed with dark paper), tintypes (photos printed on black tin), and other pictures that were not printed on paper have a special group of customers. Some want to add to their "country look" decorating. Some want pictures for historical reasons and search for street views, war views, pictures of soldiers, miners, or people in other occupations, children with toys or buggies, or interior shop scenes. Some seek the most artistic photographs by the often nameless but early skilled photographers. All types sell unless they are badly damaged. Restoration is next to impossible.

Cartes de visite (2 × 4-inch photographs on cardstock), cabinet cards (4 × 7-inch photographs on cardstock), album photos of grandparents, and other Victorian pictures also sell, but often for low prices.

Modern art photographs by artists like ANSEL ADAMS or DIANE ARBUS sell for high prices in the galleries. There has been some speculation that the price structure at auctions has been unduly influenced by some preplanned bidding, but whatever the reason for the ups and downs of this market, your picture will have a value if it is an original. Wallace Nutting "prints" are really hand-tinted photographs taken in the early 1900s. They picture views of early homes, landscapes, and interiors. Mr. Nutting sold hundreds of thousands of these pictures, each signed with his name. Collectors rediscovered them in the early 1980s.

Some collectors are interested in the oddities, the photos printed on porcelain dishes or enameled on plaques for tombstones. Stanhopes are tiny pictures seen through peepholes in canes or charms. These and other older oddities also have a market.

EQUIPMENT

*O*nce at a house sale we watched a teenaged friend of our son buy a strange metal and glass object for a quarter. He told us later that he took it to a camera store and sold it for $50. He had recognized the close-up lens for a special make of camera. At the same sale we saw a happy collector buy an old wooden tripod, oak cases for slides, and other 1910 paraphernalia. He wanted it to decorate a room. Anything connected with photography will sell. There is new interest in old magazines and trade catalogs on photography. The collectors will buy it all. Your job is to find the true collector of photographica.

STEREO VIEWS

Stereo view cards are often found in boxes. Sets from the 1920s were often sold with a photograph of the family who bought them. There was one picture of some children, then boxes and boxes of educational scenes. These are of very low value. The stereo card has two almost identical pictures mounted on a piece of cardboard. The cardboard corners were square from 1854 to 1870 and sometimes the cardboard

was colorful. Round corners were favored from 1868 to 1882. The curved cardboard mounts used after 1880 were usually buff, gray, or black. Thin cardboard was introduced about 1900. Colored pictures were made from 1900 to 1929.

Prices vary with age and subject. Views sell best near the area they picture. It may pay to try to sell out-of-state views by mail. Dealers at flea markets and postcard shows, as well as general antiques dealers, sell stereo views, so any of them might buy yours.

REPAIR

Prices of photographs have risen into the thousands of dollars for choice pictures, so that conservation, restoration, and storage have become very important. Many types of photographs can be included in the collector's world. Movies are one special type. The old nitrate film is combustible and it is dangerous to store. If you are fortunate enough to find or own some early movies, have them copied on modern film. The American Film Institute at the Kennedy Center for the Performing Arts, Washington, DC 20566, can help you with this problem.

Walt Disney original art done on celluloid for cartoon features, or what the collectors call "cels," is also collected and requires careful framing or flat storage. These too can be restored.

All types of photographs, from daguerreotypes and glass-plate slides to stereopticon slides, *cartes de visite,* and modern pictures, are important as art as well as history. Do not try a home-remedy restoration. Many old pictures can be saved if the work is done by an expert.

Old cameras can be restored, but once again expertise is required. Sometimes a local camera shop can have the camera repaired, but most old cameras need special parts that are no longer available. There are often modern photography club members who are interested in antique cameras and photographic equipment, and it is helpful to check with a local professional photographer to see if there is someone in your area who likes to work with old cameras.

See also the sections on Comic Art, Movie Memorabilia, and Paper Collectibles.

Price Books

Hove International Blue Book Guide Prices for Classic and Collectable Cameras 1992–1993, edited by Douglas St Denny (Hove Foto Books, Sussex, England, distributed by Chilton Book Co., Radnor, PA, © 1992).

Leonard's Annual Price Index of Prints, Posters & Photographs, annual, edited by Katheryn Acerbo (Auction Index, 30 Valentine Park, Newton, MA 02165).

The Price and Identification Guide to: Pin-Ups & Glamour Art, Denis Jackson (TICN, PO Box 1958, Sequim, WA 98382, © 1992).

Prints, Posters & Photos Identification and Price Guide, Susan Theran (Avon Books, New York, © 1993).

Book on Repair

Care of Photographs, Siegfried Rempel (Nick Lyons Books, 31 W. 21st St., New York, NY 10010, © 1987).

Clubs & Publications

American Photographic Historical Society, *Photographica* (MAG), 1150 Ave. of the Americas, New York, NY 10036 (cameras and accessories).

Leica Historical Society of America, *Viewfinder* (MAG), 7611 Dornoch Ln., Dallas, TX 75248-2327.

Magic Lantern Society of U.S. & Canada, *Magic Lantern Gazette* (MAG), 445 Burr Rd., San Antonio, TX 78209.

National Stereoscopic Association, Inc., *Stereo World* (MAG), PO Box 14801, Columbus, OH 43214 (Stereoscope, Viewmasters and anything 3-D).

Nikon Historical Society, *Nikon Journal* (MAG), PO Box 3213, Munster, IN 46321.

Photographic Historical Society of Canada, *Photographic Canadiana* (MAG), Box 54620, 1712 Avenue Rd., Toronto, ON, Canada M5M 4N5.

Photographic Historical Society of New England, Inc., *New England Journal of Photographic History* (MAG), PO Box 189, W. Newton Station, Boston, MA 02165 (cameras and images).

Wallace Nutting Collectors Club, *Wallace Nutting Collectors Club Newsletter* (NL), 186 Mountain Ave., North Caldwell, NJ 07006-4006.

Western Photographic Collectors Association, *Photographist* (MAG), PO Box 4294, Whittier, CA 90607.

Zeiss Historica Society, *Zeiss Historica* (MAG), PO Box 631, Clifton, NJ 07012 (Zeiss cameras and binoculars).

CameraShopper (MAG), PO Box 1086, New Canaan, CT 06840 (buy-sell-trade photographic equipment and images).

Military Images (MAG), RD 1, Box 99A, Henryville, PA 18332 (military photographs, 1839–1900).

Repairs, Parts & Supplies

Balboa Art Conservation Center, PO Box 3755, San Diego, CA 92163, 619-236-9702, 8:30 A.M.–5:00 P.M.; fax: 619-236-0141. Conservation of photographs and frames. Consultations and collection surveys.

Elbinger Laboratories, Inc., 220 Albert St., East Lansing, MI 48823, 800-332-0302, 9:00 A.M.–5:00 P.M.; fax: 517-332-3227. Restoration and preservation of old photographs; copies made. Free brochure.

Eugene R. Groves, PO Box 2471, Baton Rouge, LA 70821-2471, 504-387-3221, 8:00 A.M.–5:00 P.M.; fax: 504-346-8049. Minor repairs of daguerreotypes. Referral to qualified conservator where needed. Free appraisals.

Exposures, 41 S. Main St., Norwalk, CT 06854, 800-222-4947, 203-854-1610 in CT; fax: 414-231-6942. Archival supplies, albums, frames, and boxes.

Fine Art Conservation Services, Ltd., Nancy Wu, 94 Mercer St., New York, NY 10012, 212-966-5513; fax: 212-274-8424. Conservation of nineteenth- and twentieth-century photographs and works of art on paper and parchment. Collection management and display consulting. Archival matting and framing. Free brochure.

George Martin Cunha, 4 Tanglewood Dr., Lexington, KY 40505, 606-293-5703, 8:00 A.M.– 5:00 P.M.; fax: 606-233-9425. Repair and restoration of works of art on paper. Preservation surveys for photographic materials, with recommendations for restoration, if required.

James Macdonald Company, Inc., Jacques Desmonts, 25 Van Zant St., East Norwalk, CT 06855, 203-853-6076, 7:30 A.M.–4:30 P.M. Restoration of daguerreotype frames.

Light Impressions, PO Box 940, Rochester, NY 14603-0940, 800-828-6216, 800-828-9629 in NY; fax: 800-828-5539. Archival albums, paper and plastic pages, boxes, display cases, envelopes, papers, and tissues. Home storage systems for photos, negatives, and slides. Free catalog.

Museum Shop, Ltd., Richard Kornemann, 20 N. Market St., Frederick, MD 21701, 301-695-0424, Mon.–Thurs. 10:30 A.M.–6:00 P.M., Fri.–Sat. 10:30 A.M.–9:00 P.M., Sun. noon–5:00 P.M.; fax: 301-698-5242. Old photographs airbrushed, restored, and copied.

Northeast Document Conservation Center, 100 Brickstone Sq., Andover, MA 01810-1494, 508-470-1010; fax: 508-475-6021. Nonprofit regional conservation center specializing in treatment of art and artifacts on paper, including photographs. Preservation microfilming, duplication of historical photographs, preservation planning surveys, disaster assistance, technical leaflets. Brochure.

Painted Light Photos, Barbara Dusinberre Laing, 5301 N. Clark St., Chicago, IL 60640, 312-728-5301 or 312-275-4121. Restoration and duplication of old photographs. Hand-colorizing and sepia-toning. Custom framing, glass replacement, etc. Free estimates. Deposit required before specific work is done. Send SASE for brochure.

Preservation Emporium, PO Box 226309, Dallas, TX 75222-6309, 214-630-1197, Mon.–Fri. 9:00 A.M.–5:00 P.M., Sat. 9:00 A.M.–4:00 P.M.; fax: 214-630-7805. Acid-free/lignin-free storage materials and conservation chemicals. Full conservation treatments and restoration work on photographs. Chemical treatment of tintypes to stop corrosion, photos unstuck from glass, removal of adhesive tapes, pictures mounted in archival albums, preservation of old albums.

RGS Glass & Frame Corp., Ron's Gallery Supply, 159 Duane St., New York, NY 10013, 800-735-667; fax: 212-587-5957. Restoration of photographs.

Rochester Institute of Technology, Image Permanence Institute, 70 Lomb Memorial Dr., Rochester, NY 14623-5604, 716-475-5199; fax: 716-475-7230. Nonprofit research laboratory. Technical information on image stability and preservation. Books on conservation, preservation, and identification of photographs and film.

Romney, 615 Hill St., Emlenton, PA 16373, 412-867-0314, anytime. Camera repair books, precision tools to repair and refinish cameras and other collectibles.

University Products, Inc., PO Box 101, S. Canal St., Holyoke, MA 01040, 800-628-1912, 800-336-4847 in Massachusetts; fax: 800-532-9281. Archival supplies and repair materials for books, documents, negatives, paper, photographs, prints, and slides. Acid-free board and papers, adhesives, albums, tapes, pens, labels, tools, microfilm and microfiche materials, deacidification materials. Specialized storage for collectibles. Free catalog.

*P*lastic

*O*bjects made of all types of plastics, from Parkesine to Lucite, are now being collected. Plastic is fragile, and a scratched or cracked piece is lower in value. Some types of plastic fade in sunlight, scorch if overheated, or are stained by alcohol or other materials. Plastic should be washed with a solution of soap and warm water and a soft cloth. Very hot water and detergents may remove the shine. Never use scouring powder or any form of abrasive. Do not put plastic dishes in the dishwasher unless they are marked "dishwasher safe." They will eventually become dull and, if decorated, may lose the color in the decoration.

Removing the old adhesive from price-tag labels can be a problem. Use turpentine but not alcohol, acetone (nail polish remover), or lighter fluid. Novus II is a plastic cleaner that can be found in some stores.

Plastic that is cracked or badly scratched or stained cannot be restored. It is often best to replace the part.

A word of warning: Celluloid is flammable and must be stored in a well-ventilated area where the temperature is never over 120 degrees Fahrenheit. If the celluloid in a favored old toy is decomposing, it may help to soak it in washing soda (sodium carbon-

ate). After it is dry, coat the item with clear nail polish.

Plastic pieces are listed in this book by form. See the sections on Advertising & Country Store Collectibles, Dolls, Furniture, Jewelry, Kitchen Paraphernalia, Lamps & Lighting Devices, and Toys.

Price Books

Everyday Elegance, Holly Wahlberg (Schiffer, Atglen, PA, © 1994). Plastic housewares and furniture, 1945–1960.

Plastic Toys: Dimestore Dreams of the '40s and '50s, Bill Hanlon (Schiffer, Atglen, PA, © 1993).

Helpful Books

Art Plastic Designed for Living, Siegfried Rempel (Abbeville Press, New York, © 1984). Short chapter on care.

Wallace-Homestead Price Guide to Plastic Collectibles, Lyndi Stewart McNulty (Wallace-Homestead Book Co., Radnor, PA, © 1987). Chapter on care and cleaning.

*P*olitical *M*emorabilia

*E*very fourth year, when a presidential race is filling the minds and newspapers of Americans, the price of political ephemera rises. The political buttons, banners, and oddities are suddenly discovered by a new group of collectors. Of course, there are many serious collectors who seek political items every year. The hobby has a national club, publication, shows, and a built-in publicity possibility that encourages new collectors and higher prices regularly. To a collector there are two kinds of political memorabilia: authentic items and "brummagems." The brummagems are the tourist-trap pieces, made because they will sell. Most of the buttons with off-color or insulting slogans were made to be sold by hucksters, and they are not true political pieces.

In the back of the drawer at grandfather's house you found a treasure trove that includes some John Kennedy campaign buttons, a cake of soap shaped like a baby but labeled McKinley, a pencil that says "Win with Willkie," "I Like Ike" cigarettes, a newspaper telling about the "election of Dewey," and a Teddy Roosevelt bandanna. Are they really political items? Are they rare and valuable?

The record price for a campaign button, set in 1991, was $49,700 for a Cox-Roosevelt metal pinback button. It is one of only four known. It is a type known to the trade as a "jugate." In general, a jugate or picture button is of much more value than a button with just the names of the candidates. A button for two candidates is priced higher than a button for a single candidate. Buttons promoting a candidate for mayor or senator are of interest locally, but if your candidate eventually ran for president, the button may be high priced. Buttons for candidates for the smaller parties are often high priced because they are rare. Buttons that promote both a local candidate for Senate or Congress and a national candidate for president also have a good value. Foreign-language buttons are scarce and sell well.

There are many books about political memorabilia. They include a set of three books on buttons, one on textiles, and several on the general subject. Most of these books include prices. Unfortunately, since the general price guides do not have room for complete descriptions and pictures, they are of limited use. The buttons are priced differently for slightly different print style, color, size, photo, or other feature. The American Political Items Collectors, whose membership represents the serious political buyers in the country, publishes material on real and fake political pieces. If you have rarities, their members are your best prospective customers.

Buttons are small and easy to store, so most collectors have many. Other items are often rarer and bring high prices. Political bandannas, jewelry, knives, cigars, trays, dishes, dolls, umbrellas, canes, and posters are all collected. Anything that pictures a candidate running for office is salable. Anything that pictures an elected president or vice-president is in demand among regular political collectors and other groups of collectors. In recent years there has been active interest in campaign material for women who ran for office or the wives of elected officials. Older items are usually of more value than the newer ones. Never discard anything that mentions a politician. It can be sold.

Kleenex had a national promotion in the 1970s that included reproductions of many old campaign buttons. Several other similar promotions have offered repros since then. These buttons are marked on the edge with information about the reproduction year and company. Even these are now worth a few dollars.

But what about grandfather's treasures? The Kennedy button and the Willkie pencil and Ike cigarettes are probably worth under $10; the baby-shaped soap with the original box is worth over $75; the bandanna is worth $60. The newspaper about Dewey's "election" is worth about $200.

REPAIR

The purist collector only saves buttons and other items that were made for an actual campaign and not those produced for a gift or novelty shop afterward. The American Political Items Collectors (APIC), Box 340339, San Antonio, TX 78234, carefully documents actual campaign material each year in the publications sent to its members. Reproductions have been made of many early campaign items. It does not pay to restore the reproductions. Check in other sections for restorers of political memorabilia made of glass, metals, or textiles.

Clubs & Publications

American Political Items Collectors, *Keynoter* (MAG), *Political Bandwagon* (NP), Box 340339, San Antonio, TX 78234. (There are several subgroups that specialize in particular presidents. Contact the APIC for more information.)

White House Collectors Club, Barbara Martin, 4N301 Foxfield Dr., St. Charles, IL 60174.

Political Collector (NP), PO Box 5171, York, PA 17405.

Postcards

*T*he first postal card with a printed stamp was issued in Austria in 1869. The idea proved to be so profitable for the government that it was quickly copied by many other countries. The United States used its first government postcard in May 1873. (A card dated May 12 or 13, 1873, would be a very high-priced rarity.) These early cards had printed messages. Personal messages were charged first-class rates. It was not until May 19, 1898, that private postcards were charged at a lower rate. A postal card has a preprinted stamp. A postcard has a space for an adhesive stamp.

It seems as if everyone's elderly aunts saved boxes of picture postcards sent to them by friends and relatives. A card can sell for anywhere from 5 cents to over $500. It pays to study before you take an offer for the whole box. First examine the stamps and check on the value of any unusual ones. The postmark and amount of postage will help to date the card. Look for any strange stickers. Christmas seals, parcel post stamps, TB or Red Cross stickers, Easter seals, and other can add to the value of your card. There are collectors who want just stickers.

There are seven periods of postcards for a

collector. *The Pioneer Era Cards* (1893–1898) are the oldest available and bring high prices. *Private Mailing Cards* (1898–1901) have the words "Private Mailing Card—Authorized by Act of Congress" printed on the back. These cards also sell for premium prices. *The Undivided Back* period is from 1902 to 1907. These cards were printed so that only the name and address, no message, could be written on the back. Next was *The Divided Back* era (1907–1915). *The White Border* period (1915–1930) had many printed cards of poor quality with white borders. *Linen Cards* (1920–1950) were printed on paper with linen-textured surface. These were often bright colored cards with cartoons or jokes. *The Photochrome Cards* (1939 to present) are those seen today. Color film was available for these glossy cards. Cards made before 1900 were often drawn by an artist. Color lithographed cards were popular until about 1914. Photographs or pictures printed in black and white or sepia were used on cards in the early 1900s. Prices are high for any types of cards made before 1915.

Some collectors seek postcards made of unusual materials. Birch bark, woven silk, leather, feathers, fur, peat moss, mother-of-pearl, celluloid, real hair, fabrics, wood, and paper were used for cards. Some cards, called "mechanicals," were made with a metal spring to produce some action. A donkey tail might wag or a head nod. A few double cards were made that squeaked when pressed. Foldout, see-through, hold-to-light, and puzzle cards were made. All these novelty cards should be priced higher than a regular card made after 1915. Condition for these cards and all others is very important. A very worn card is of little value.

Manufacturers and artists with famous names add to the value of your cards. Look for RAPHAEL TUCK, ELLEN CLAPSADDLE, BERTHA CORBETT, HOWARD CHANDLER CHRISTY, LOUIS WAIN, HARRISON FISHER, LANCE THACKEREY, GENE CARR, and FRANCES BRUNDAGE. Add to your price if the card pictures coins, stamps, famous or infamous people, kewpies, blacks, advertising, disasters, animals dressed like people, fruits or vegetables that look like people, World's Fairs, expositions, or holidays. The best holidays are Halloween and Christmas, especially any card that includes a full-length picture of Santa Claus. All types of patriotic cards, including those featuring Fourth of July and political events, are in demand. Early planes, early autos, fire equipment, and other types of transportation are always wanted. The larger the picture of the car, the better; the largest are the so-called "close-up" transportation cards. Photograph cards of the streets filled with stores, advertising, people, ads, or special events are collected. Extra-large cards or sets of cards bring a premium. Unpopular cards include views of woods, parks, rivers, mountains, churches, residential street scenes, and other scenery with few buildings or people.

After you have some idea of the value of the postcards, you have several options for selling them. A private collector may want your cards. Expect to get 50 to 75 percent of the published retail value. If private collectors were to pay 100 percent, they could buy it retail from any dealer's stock. If you sell just a few to a collector, you may find you are left with a relatively unsalable collection.

There are many postcard shows. Collectors and dealers usually pay well for rare cards. Go to a show and mention your collections. Decide if you want to sell single cards or the whole box. Make that decision before you sell the best ten items and then find that no one wants the rest. If you have time, you can sell the ordinary cards at any flea market or house sale. They can often be sold from a box labeled "All cards one price." Dealers tell us to use the prices 5 cents, 10 cents, 25 cents, 50 cents, etc. Never price at $1.25. There is a psychology to pricing merchandise, and for some reason, postcards sell best for one coin or bill; 45¢ or $1.25 are just not good prices.

Most serious dealers sort the cards by subject and state and display them in boxes or plastic mounts. Most collectors only want a special type of card and won't look through too big a pile.

If you don't want to work at selling each postcard, offer them as a lot to a dealer. There is a rule of thumb. A dealer can usually pay you 50 to 75 percent of the retail value of a card worth $1 or more, but can pay only 25 percent or less for the less expensive cards. The work involved in mounting, showing, and carrying is the same and most dealers prefer selling the better cards.

You might send the postcards to a mail-order auction that specializes in postcards. These auctions sell the best cards individually and the others in groups or lots. You will be paid for the lots that are sold and all the unsold items will be returned. It can take from three to six months to get your money after you send the collection to a mail-order auction. There is usually a 20 to 30 percent fee charged. The postcard publications list many possible places to sell cards.

The best advice we've heard regarding the pricing of cards came from a dealer who said, "Ask yourself, which would the customer prefer to have in his pocket, the card or the money?" The value is not like the value of gold or silver; it is a matter of demand. The value is in the eye of the buyer. Look at the price books, but they are only guides.

REPAIR

Most postcards are made of paper and have all of the storage and care problems of any other paper collectibles. They should be kept out of the heat, away from the strong sunlight and damp air, and most of all, they should never be glued or taped. Slight soil can be cleaned off postcards with an art-gum eraser. Bent cards can sometimes be ironed flat. (See Paper Collectibles & Ephemera.) If postcards are glued into an album, it may be possible to soak them free. This requires care and time.

Price Books

The Artist-Signed Postcard Price Guide, J. L. Mashburn (WorldComm Press, 65 Macedonia Rd., Alexander, NC 28701, © 1993).

The Encyclopedia of Antique Postcards, Susan Brown Nicholson (Wallace-Homestead Book Company, Radnor, PA, © 1994).

The Official 1995 Price Guide of United States Postage Stamps, 17th edition, Marc Hudgeons (Random House, New York, © 1994).

The Postcard Price Guide, 2nd edition, J. L. Mashburn (PO Box 609, Enka, NC 28728, © 1995).

Archives

Curt Teich Postcard Archives at The Lake County Museum, *Image File* (MAG), Lakewood Forest Preserve, Wauconda, IL 60084. 708-526-8638.

Clubs & Publications

Deltiologists of America, *Postcard Classics* (MAG), PO Box 8, Norwood, PA 19074.

Postcard History Society, *Postcard History Society Bulletin* (NL), PO Box 1765, Manassas, VA 22110.

Barr's Postcard News (NP), 70 S. Sixth St., Lansing, IA 52151.

The Encyclopedia of Antique Postcards, Susan Brown Nicholson (Wallace-Homestead Book Company, Radnor, PA, © 1994).

Gloria's Corner (NL), PO Box 507, Denison, TX 75021-0507.

Picture Postcard Monthly (MAG), 15 Debdale Ln., Keyworth, Nottinghamshire, England NG12 5HT.

Postcard Collector (MAG), PO Box 1050, Dubuque, IA 52004.

Repairs, Parts & Supplies

Russell Norton, PO Box 1070, New Haven, CT 06504-1070, 203-562-7800, 11:00 A.M.–8:00 P.M., daily. Archival polypropylene sleeves for postcards and other collectibles. Send SASE for sample.

Shiloh Postcards, Main St., PO Box 728, Clayton, GA 30525, 706-782-4100, Mon., Tues., Thurs., Fri. 9:00 A.M.–5:00 P.M. Archival supplies for the preservation of paper collectibles, specializing in postcard supplies. Mail order worldwide. Catalog $1.

Videos

Auto Advertising on Postcards; Collecting Postcards and Related Ephemera; What Is This Postcard Worth? **Advision Incorporated,** 3100 Arrowwood Ln., Boulder, Co 80303-2419, 800-876-2320. Each video is 60 minutes long and sells for $29.95 plus $4 shipping and handling. Write for complete list of videos available.

Pottery & Porcelain

An aunt left you her household belongings representing fifty or more years of accumulation, including figurines, lamps, kitchen mixing bowls, pottery crocks that held pickles, flower vases, dresser sets, ashtrays, three sets of dishes, and serving pieces. How would you sell everything for the best total price? Age and quality of ceramics do influence price, but a 1950 Hall pottery pitcher could be worth more than an 1850 German bowl. The whims of collectors determine the value, and sometimes the fashion of the day makes originally inexpensive pieces more important. The stoneware crocks that were cheap food-storage containers during the 1800s, yellowware, the Art Deco dishes of the 1920s, the nineteenth-century R. S. Prussia pieces decorated with voluptuous women, and some recent art pottery and California studio pottery sell for higher prices than fine wares from the eighteenth and early nineteenth centuries.

If you are fortunate enough to have a close friend who understands antiques and collecting, ask for help. Few collectors are experts in everything, but many of them can make good guesses about what might have value. A collector has been to the shops and shows and absorbs much information about what sells.

If the task of identification seems overwhelming, you might want to send the contents to a consignment shop. These shops sell good-quality items and usually charge about 25 to 35 percent commission. The shop knows the highest retail price to ask, and even if a few things do not sell, you will have most of your money in a few months with very little work on your part. If you consign your dishes, be sure the shop has insurance. Get a signed contract describing the items (including any damage) and stating the terms of sale and the commission you will be charged.

You could also sell your items through your own house or garage sale, or through an ad in the local paper. If you are offering the items through an ad, be sure to follow the sensible rules of safety: Never admit a stranger when you are alone in the house, take only cash and not checks, and watch for theft when strangers are inside. It might be wise to put all "for sale" items in the garage and let no one enter your house.

If you sell most of the items to an antiques shop, you face the problem of what price to ask. To decide, you need a knowledgeable friend, a book like *Kovels' New Dictionary of Marks—Pottery & Porcelain*, a few good price books, and a working idea of the going prices in the gift and china shops. A simple rule of thumb is to compare your prices against those for similar pieces of new china. Most buyers will never pay more than 50 percent of china store prices and usually pay only 30 percent of retail prices. Many new sets of dishes can now be purchased for less than retail at discount stores.

Antiques dealers are interested in what sells quickly, so they want attractive, undamaged figurines, lamps, vases, and the currently "hot" items like FIESTA (bright-colored pot-

tery of the 1930s) and CALIFORNIA figurines of the 1950s, country-look crocks and bowls, cookie jars and marked art pottery.

The auction house offers another way to sell a house filled with ceramics. It is a good method if you can't take the time to separate the good from the bad. The good pieces will be sold separately. The best pieces may even be pictured and described in a brochure or catalog. There is a charge to have your piece pictured in the catalog. Sets of dishes sell, but for low prices. Odd dishes can be placed into box lots and sold, but prices will be low. The auction house pays within three to six months, and its employees do all the work. Be sure to get a signed contract before leaving your merchandise. Have a written description of the items, including damage and repairs, and all terms of the sale.

Sets of dishes can be sold to a matching service. There are many dealers throughout the country who make a living by selling matching pieces for sets of dishes, silver, or glassware. Most are listed in this book, and many advertise in antiques publications and decorating magazines. These dealers always have customers waiting for dishes, and if your set is a popular pattern that is in demand you can sell the set for a good price. The price a matching service is willing to pay is often better than an auction price. Send a description and a photograph or photocopy of a plate, front and back, and indicate the colors. Offer your set for sale. Be sure to include a self-addressed, stamped envelope.

Modern dishes like FIESTA sell easily through newspaper ads, garage sales, and flea markets, or to dealers. Only perfect pieces can be sold. Chips and scratches make a difference. If the piece of pottery is twentieth century and common, a chip lowers the value by 90 percent. If the piece is rare (a Rookwood vase decorated with an Indian), a chip lowers the value only 10 to 20 percent. Prices are easy to find in the general price guides. AUTUMN LEAF pattern, WILLOW WARE, and LENOX china also sell easily. Anything by CLARICE CLIFF brings high prices.

Lamps are always hard to sell. If the ceramic base is not by a well-known art pottery or a name artist, it will sell simply as secondhand furniture.

Figurines of top quality from the eighteenth and early nineteenth centuries sell well, but perhaps not as high as you may hope. Look for the crossed swords mark of MEISSEN, the anchor of CHELSEA, or other symbols. Art Deco figures are popular now. Names worth extra money are WEINER WERKSTATTE, GOLDSCHEIDER, and ROBJ. Staffordshire figurines of dogs or unidentifiable people, romantic bisque Victorian men and women, and copies of eighteenth-century pieces also sell for less than most people think. We often hear descriptions like "I know it is of value because every fingernail can be seen." This is not always true. You can often see every fingernail on a poor-quality figurine. The very best figures do sell for hundreds of thousands of dollars, however, and it might pay to take a clear picture or the actual figures to an auction house, dealer, or appraiser to learn the value.

"Country look" pieces are the most confusing to a novice. Grandmother's yellow-ware mixing bowl or blue spatter butter jar can be worth hundreds of dollars to the right collector or dealer. You must go to the shows and see the types of wares that are now popular and high priced. Stoneware crocks get publicity because examples with cobalt blue decorations of birds, people, or animals sell for thousands of dollars. Plain crocks are not expensive. The modern-shaped, bright red, cream, or blue pottery dishes made during the 1940s to store water or leftovers in the refrigerator sell well. So do some of the salt and pepper sets, cookie jars, and canister sets of the 1920s to the 1980s.

Ashtrays don't sell well unless marked with a famous maker's name. Plain bowls, trays, and candy dishes sell for low prices unless they are by big makers. Beer steins of any type sell well; best are those by METT-LACH. Novelty items, like figurines with nodding heads, open-mouthed monsters that are toothpick holders, fairings, and trinket boxes, GOSS souvenirs, small figurines of blacks, and "pink pig with green basket" figures, are all in demand.

How do you tell if you own a piece by an important factory in high demand by collectors? Look in the general price guides under the names you might find on your dishes. For example, R. S. PRUSSIA, NIPPON, ROYAL DOULTON, WEDGWOOD, SUSIE COOPER, HALL, HULL, McCOY, ROSEVILLE, WELLER, ROYAL BAY-REUTH, HAVILAND, MINTON, LOTUS, NORITAKE, ROYAL COPENHAGEN, and many others are listed by name. If the factory is listed by name, the collectors are buying it. Some types are listed but not marked, so look at the shows and in the books until you can recognize SATSUMA, BANKO, SUMIDA GAWA, CHINESE EXPORT PORCELAIN, STAFFORDSHIRE, GOUDA, YELLOW-WARE, SPATTERWARE, STONEWARE, IRONSTONE, PÂTE-SUR-PÂTE, and MAJOLICA. The collectors also look for the names of countries, such as OCCUPIED JAPAN and CZECHOSLOVAKIA.

Art pottery from the United States and England has become popular since the 1970s. Prices are steadily rising. The best of

ROOKWOOD can sell for thousands of dollars. Record price in 1991 was $198,000 for a Rookwood vase with an electroplated copper fish swimming under a sea green glaze. It was made in 1900 by Kataro Shirayamadani. There are many books about art pottery, including *Kovels' American Art Pottery,* that list names, patterns, and marks. The art pottery that many collect today was the florist's flower container of yesterday. A vase, filled with chicken wire so it could hold flowers, may still be in your mother's basement. Books have now made the dealers and collectors experts, and they are willing to pay top prices for good pieces. If the original cover for an art pottery or other type of ceramic jar is noticeably missing (some jars are made to be complete in appearance without a cover), deduct 50 percent. If a vase is decorated with, or shaped like, a pig or a snake, add 25 to 100 percent. The ROYAL DOULTON and HUMMEL figurine craze has cooled since the 1980s. Prices may not be as high as you hope. Royal Doulton dinnerwares sell like any other sets of dishes. They sell quickly to dealers or at auction. The Royal Doulton price books give retail prices, so you can easily price figures and jugs by name or HN number. Anything marked "Goebel Hummel" sells, although collectors prefer pieces with the old marks. If two figurines look exactly alike, the value may be different because of the small black V and Bee on the bottom. Marks, figurines, plates, and values are easy to find in the general price books.

Limited editions include many types of newer collectibles. The designation "limited edition" first became popular during the 1960s, even though the first dated plate produced for one year was the Bing & Grondahl Christmas plate of 1895. Many types of porcelains and silver were made in limited quanti-ties, but the idea of stating the limits before offering the collectible was new. Some pieces are limited to an announced number, some to the number made before a special date. Limited editions can include plates, figurines, eggs, bells, forks, spoons, plaques, boxes, steins, mugs, urns, Christmas ornaments, paperweights, bottles, thimbles and more.

It is very difficult to sell limited edition plates, figurines, etc., at a profit. Many of them were made and sold. There is a small resale market for most of them. A few have gained in value. There are a few dealers who list plates. (They buy at a certain percent less than their selling price.) Advertising for limited editions often stressed the "investment" potential. In the real world, there is almost never a gain in dollar value to the retail buyer. When reselling a limited piece, it is necessary to have the original box and certifying paper to get a good price. Because of the demand for the original box, some dealers will gladly pay for the rare, empty box. Look in the plate magazines for prices and dealers who buy plates. Talk to the local gift shops that sell plates or to those that handle what is known as the "secondary market" plates. Go to the shows. There is a huge swap meet at each national convention; if you can't sell your plates, perhaps you can trade them.

Anything oriental sells. If the marks are Chinese or Japanese characters, they are a mystery to most of us. They are not only hard to read but were often copied and put on the bottom of later porcelain pieces. It is said that 80 percent of the Chinese porcelains have "retrospective" marks (for example, an eighteenth-century copy with a sixteenth-century mark). An unmarked piece is usually of more value than a piece with an earlier, but retrospective, mark. The very old pieces (old is over 250 years old) sell to museums and serious collectors. This type of porcelain should be sold through a major auction house or top-priced dealer. Only experts can recognize the difference between old and more recent oriental pieces. Since the 1970s, quantities of average-quality blue and white nineteenth-century china have been shipped from China and Hong Kong for sale to collectors. These pieces are salable as decorative items, and they should be priced accordingly.

Chinese Export porcelain includes the dishes not only made in China in the eighteenth and nineteenth centuries to be sold in America and Europe, but also twentieth-century pieces. Some of the early dishes can be very valuable. Their gray-blue color can be easily recognized. Important tureens or platters with elaborate decorations or with a famous owner's initials can sell for thousands of dollars. A plain cup and saucer could be worth at least $100. If you have any export dishes, have them appraised before offering them for sale. Other oriental wares are also popular. The early, sophisticated Satsuma, the cruder, twentieth-century Satsuma pieces made in Occupied Japan after World War II, and almost any other oriental porcelains sell quickly and for more money than comparable English or American pieces. Try to find someone to identify your pieces, and then check the prices in the general guides.

Blue and white dishes seem to be a favorite of collectors. Staffordshire "flow blue" was made in many patterns. Look for pieces without the word "England." They are usually older and should be worth more. If the center design is an American or Canadian architectural or historical scene, it is part of what collectors call "historic blue," and it can be worth a high price. The more common, fanciful oriental scenes, flowers, or other center designs are on the average-priced pieces. Platters, pitchers, and service bowls sell well because so few can be found. A soup tureen with an American view would be the best of all. It would sell for thousands of dollars. There are auctions and dealers who handle historic Staffordshire exclusively.

ROWLAND AND MARSELLUS made a similar twentieth-century blue and white ware that is gaining in value. They made "rolled edge" plates with views of towns and cities for the local tourist trade. Collectors want all of the hundreds of different examples. Other popular blue and white patterns are IVANHOE, GIBSON GIRL, and the special plates made for colleges and universities by WEDGWOOD.

If you have a few dishes, spend a little time and do the research to be sure that you are not selling a treasure for 50 cents at your garage sale. If you have a houseful of dishes, you may have to sell them through a dealer or auction gallery and hope to get the best price for everything. Even the experts miss a few of the best items at times.

REPAIR

Dishes, figurines, lamp bases, flowerpots, crocks, and garden ornaments may be made of ceramics—pottery or porcelain. To care for and repair them properly, it is necessary to have some idea of the difference between pottery and porcelain.

Pottery is usually heavier than porcelain. It is opaque and chips more easily. Because it is more porous, it may become stained by dark-colored food or dirt. Porcelain is translucent; if it is held in front of a strong light, the light will show through. If it is chipped, the break will be shell-like in shape. Pottery usually cracks on a line. Porcelain is thinner, lighter, more durable, and usually more expensive than pottery. The names stoneware, delft, bone china, majolica, and ironstone all refer to either pottery, porcelain, or similar wares with similar problems.

If your pottery or porcelain dishes are stained, as a last resort it is possible to bleach them using household laundry bleach. If dishes are cracked or chipped, repairs are possible. Invisible waterproof glues are available in most hardware, art-supply, drug, and building-supply stores. For a simple break, glue is the best method of repair. If there is further damage and a hole or crack must be filled or if repainting is required, it can still be a do-it-yourself job, but special equipment and instructions are necessary.

Many old sets of dishes have, say, only eleven dinner plates, ten cups and saucers, and twelve of everything else. It is possible to buy the same pattern of old dishes to fill in the set. Haviland, Castleton, Franciscan, Lenox, Noritake, Oxford, Syracuse, Wedgwood, and other makes are sold through matching services, which are described and listed in Part II. To order from a service, you must know the pattern of the dish. There are hundreds of patterns listed in books at your library. Many of the patterns have names included on the back as part of the mark. Identify the pattern name from this information or use this easy method: Place a plate face down on a photocopying machine and copy the front and the back. Indicate the colors that appear on the plate and send the photocopies to one of the matching services listed in this book.

To properly identify makers, it may be necessary to check the marks in a special book of marks. For example, "H & Co" is one the marks used by the Haviland Company that can be matched through services. Some patterns are still being made and can be replaced through special orders.

Firms such as Wedgwood, Royal Doulton, Spode, and Royal Worcester offer this service for a limited number of their patterns.

Here are a few quick clues for dating your dishes. If the name of the country of origin appears, such as "Spode, England," the dishes were probably made after 1891. Since about World War I, the words "made in England" or "made in France" have been favored. The term "Ltd." as part of a company name for English companies was used after 1880. "RD" in a diamond-shaped cartouche was used in England from 1842 to 1883. The letters "RD" followed by numbers were in use after 1884. The words "22 carat gold" and "ovenproof" were used after the 1930s. "Microwave safe" first appeared in the 1970s. "Made in Occupied Japan" was used only from 1945 to 1952.

Repairs to limited editions are almost useless if you are concerned with value. The slightest chip, crack, or imperfection lowers the value considerably and almost any repair will cost more than the value of the repaired piece. The only exception might be for very rare figurines. Hummels and Royal Doultons are sometimes repaired.

Price Books

1992–93 Who's Who in Limited Editions and Reference Guide by Collector's Mart Magazine (WEB Publications, PO Box 12830, Wichita, KS 67277, © 1992).

American Bisque, Mary Jane Ciacomini (Schiffer Publishing, Atglen, PA, © 1994).

American Pottery and Porcelain Identification and Price Guide, William C. Ketchum, Jr. (Avon Books, Mineola, NY, © 1994).

Bergesen's British Ceramics Price Guide, Victoria Bergesen (Barrie & Jenkins, London, © 1992). Each item valued in British pounds.

British Ceramic Art 1870–1940, John A. Bartlett (Schiffer, Atglen, PA 19310, © 1993).

Camark Pottery, Letitia Landers (Colony Publishing, PO Box 203, Camden, AR 71701, © 1994).

Ceramic Arts Studio Identification and Price Guide, Mike Schneider (Schiffer, Atglen, PA 19310, © 1994).

Ceramics Price Guide: Pottery & Porcelain, Kyle Husfloen (Antique Trader Books, PO Box 1050, Dubuque, IA 52004, © 1994).

The Character Jug Collectors Handbook, Kevin Pearson (Kevin Francis Publishing, London, England, © 1992).

Charlton Catalogue of Royal Doulton Figurines, 3rd edition, Jean Dale (Charlton Press, 2010 Yonge St., Toronto, Ontario, Canada M4S 1Z9, © 1993).

The Charlton Standard Catalogue of Royal Doulton Jugs, 2nd edition, Jean Dale (The Charlton Press, 2010 Yonge St., Toronto, Ontario, Canada M4S 1Z9, © 1993).

Collectible Vernon Kilns, Maxine Feek Nelson (Collector Books, Paducah, KY, © 1994).

Collector's Books of Egg Cups, Pat Stott (180 Bigelow St., Port Perry, ON, Canada, L9L 1L6, © 1993).

Collector's Encyclopedia of Colorado Pottery, Carol and Jim Carlton (Collector Books, Paducah, KY, © 1994).

Collector's Encyclopedia of Cookie Jars, Book II, Fred Roerig and Joyce Herndon Roerig (Collector Books, Paducah, KY, © 1994).

Collector's Encyclopedia of Cowan Pottery, Tim and Jamie Saloff (Collector Books, Paducah, KY, © 1994).

Collector's Encyclopedia of Flow Blue China, second series Mary Frank Gaston (Collector Books, Paducah, KY, © 1994).

The Collector's Encyclopedia of Hall China, second edition, Margaret and Kenn Whitmyer (Collector Books, Paducah, KY, © 1994).

The Collector's Encyclopedia of Homer Laughlin China, Joanne Jasper (Collector Books, Paducah, KY, © 1993).

The Collector's Encyclopedia of Majolica, Mariann Katz-Marks (Collector Books, Paducah, KY, © 1992, values updated 1994).

The Collector's Encyclopedia of Niloak Pottery, David Edwin Gifford (PO Box 7617, Little Rock, AR 72217, © 1993).

The Collector's Encyclopedia of Nippon Porcelain Price Guide No. 3, Joan Van Patten. Revised edition of price guide companion to items pictured in Van Patten's *The Collector's Encyclopedia of Nippon Porcelain* © 1988. (Collector Books, Paducah, KY, © 1994.)

The Collector's Encyclopedia of Noritake, Joan Van Patten. Updated version of 1984 edition (Collector Books, Paducah, KY, © 1994).

The Collector's Encyclopedia of Roseville Pottery, Sharon and Bob Huxford (Collector Books, Paducah, KY, © 1993).

Collector's Encyclopedia of R.S. Prussia, 3rd series, Mary Frank Gaston (Collector Books, Paducah, KY, © 1994).

Collector's Encyclopedia of Van Briggle Art Pottery: An Identification & Value Guide, Richard Sasicki and Josie Fania (Collector Books, Paducah, KY, © 1993).

The Collector's Guide to Harker Pottery, Neva W. Colbert (Collector Books, Paducah, KY, © 1993).

Collector's Guide to Made in Japan Ceramics, Carole Bess White (Collector Books, Paducah, KY, © 1994).

Collector's Guide to Wall Pockets, Affordable & Other$, Marvin and Joy Gibson (L-W Book Sales, PO Box 69, Gas City, IN 46933, © 1994).

Collecting Yellow Ware, Lisa S. McAllister and John L. Michel (Collector Books, Paducah, KY, © 1993).

Colourful World of Clarice Cliff, Howard and Pat Watson (Kevin Francis Publishing, 32246 Oakview, Warren, MI 48092, © 1992).

The Complete Salt and Pepper Shaker Book, Mike Schneider (Schiffer, Atglen, PA, © 1993).

The David Winter Cottages Handbook 1992–93, John Hughes (Kevin Francis Publishing, London, England, © 1992).

The Doulton Figure Collectors Handbook, 3rd edition, Kevin Pearson (Kevin Francis Publishing, London, England, © 1993).

Flow Blue: A Collector's Guide to Pattern, History, and Values, Jeffrey B. Snyder (Schiffer, Atglen, PA, © 1992).

Goebel Salt & Pepper Shakers: Identification and Value Guide, Hubert and Clara McHugh (Vintage Machinery Co., 1850 W. Main St., Stroudsburg, PA 18360, © 1992).

Hull Shirt Pocket Price List, Joan Gray Hull (1376 Nevada SW, Huron SD 57350, © 1994).

An Illustrated Value Guide to Cookie Jars, Book II, Ernagene Westfall (Collector Books, Paducah, KY, © 1993).

Knowles, Taylor & Knowles American Bone China, Timothy J. Kearns (Schiffer Publishing, Atglen, PA, © 1994).

Lenox Collectibles, Richard E. Morin (A & J Printing, PO Box 518, Highway 160 N., Nixa, MO 65714, © 1993).

Lowell Davis Official Secondary Market Price Guide, 4th edition, edited by Rosie Wells. Black-and-white illustrations (RR #1, Canton, Il 61520, © 1992).

Luckey's Hummel Figurines & Plates, 10th edition, Carl F. Luckey (Books Americana, Florence, AL, © 1994).

Made in Czechoslovakia, Book 2, Ruth A. Forsythe (Antique Publications, PO Box 553, Marietta, OH 45750, © 1993).

The Mettlach Book, Gary Kirsner (Glentiques, Ltd., PO Box 8807, Coral Springs, FL 33075, © 1994).

Official Club Directory and Price Guide to Limited Edition Collectibles, Susan K. Elliott and J. Kevin Samara (House of Collectibles, New York, © 1994).

The Official Lladró Collection Identification Catalog and Price Guide, Dr. Glenn S. Johnson (Lladró Collectors Society, 43 W. 57th St., New York, NY 10019, © 1993).

Official Price Guide to American Stoneware, George Sullivan (House of Collectibles, NY, © 1993).

A Price Guide to Rookwood, edited by L-W Book Sales (PO Box 69, Gas City, IN 46933, © 1993).

Purinton Pottery: An Identification and Value Guide, Susan Morris (Purinton Pottery, PO Box 708, Mason City, IA 50402, © 1994).

Roberts' Ultimate Encyclopedia of Hull Pottery and *The Companion Guide to Roberts' Ultimate Encyclopedia of Hull Pottery,* Brenda Roberts (Walsworth Publishing Co., Marceline, MO, © 1992).

Salt and Pepper Shakers Identification and Price Guide, Gideon Bosker and Lena Lencer (Avon Books, New York, © 1994).

Shawnee Pottery, Jim and Bev Mangus (Collector Books, Paducah, KY, © 1994).

Stangl and Pennsbury Birds Identification & Price Guide, Mike Schneider (Schiffer Publishing, Atglen, PA, © 1994).

Stangl Pottery, Harvey Duke (Wallace-Homestead, Radnor, PA, © 1993).

Stoneware in the Blue and White, M.H. Alexander (PO Box 34309, Pensacola, FL 32507, © 1993).

Toothpick Holders: China, Glass and Metal, The National Toothpick Holder Collector's Society (Antique Publications, Marietta, OH, © 1992).

Watt Pottery, Dennis Thompson and W. Bryce Watt (Schiffer Publishing, Atglen, PA, © 1994).

Watt Pottery: An Identification and Value Guide, Sue and Dave Morris (Collector Books, Paducah, KY, © 1993).

World of Head Vase Planters, Mike Posgay and Ian Warner (Antique Publications, PO Box 553, Marietta, OH 45750, © 1992).

Identification

Collectors Catalogue, Vol. I & II (Lladró Collectors Society, 43 W. 57th St., New York, NY 10019, © 1991, supplements 1993, 1994).

Books on Repair

How to Mend Your Treasures, Laurence Adams Malone (Phaedra Inc., 49 Park Ave., New York, NY 10016, © 1972).

Repairing and Restoring China and Glass, The Klein Method, William Karl Klein (Harper & Row, New York, © 1962).

Repairing Old China and Ceramic Tiles, Jeff Oliver (Little, Brown, Boston, © 1985).

Restorer's Handbook of Ceramics and Glass, Jean-Michel Andre (Van Nostrand Reinhold, New York, © 1976).

Two Sisters' Guide to Antique Restoration & China Repair, Jean Myers and Judy Myers Denson (2622 North Dobson Road, Chandler, AZ 85224).

Clubs & Publications

Abingdon Pottery Collectors, *Abingdon Pottery Collectors Newsletter* (NL), c/o Elaine Westover, 210 Knox Hwy. 5, Abingdon, IL 61410.

American Art Pottery Association, *Journal of the American Art Pottery Association* (MAG), 125 E. Rose, Webster Groves, MO 63119.

American Ceramic Circle, *American Ceramic Circle Journal and Newsletter* (NL), 888 17th St. NW, Suite 508, Washington, DC 20006.

Belleek Collectors' International Society, *Belleek Collector* (NL), Belleek Ireland, Inc., 9893 Georgetown, Suite 525, Great Falls, VA 22066.

Beswick Collectors Circle, *Beswick Collectors Circle* (NL), PO Box 1793, Gerrards Cross, Bucks., England SL9 7YN.

Blair Museum of Lithophanes & Carved Waxes, c/o City of Toledo, Dept. of Natural Resources, 2201 Ottawa Pkwy., Toledo, OH 43606.

Blue & White Pottery Club, *Blue & White Pottery Club* (NL), 224 12th St. NW, Cedar Rapids, IA 52405.

Butter Pats International Collectors' Club, *Butter Pats International Collectors' Newsletter* (NL), 38 Acton St., Maynard, MA 01754.

Collector's Corner, *Wade Watch* (NL), 8199 Pierson Ct., Arvada, CO 80005.

Collectors of Illinois Pottery and Stoneware, *Collectors of Illinois Pottery and Stoneware Newsletter* (NL), 1527 E. Converse St., Springfield, IL 62702.

Cookie Jar Collector's Club, *Cookie Jar Collector's Club Newsletter* (NL), 595 Cross River Rd., Katonah, NY 10536.

Dedham Pottery Collectors Society, *Dedham Pottery Collectors Society Newsletter* (NL), 248 Highland St., Dedham, MA 02026.

Duncan Royale Collector's Club, *Royale Courier* (NL), 1141 S. Acacia Ave., Fullerton, CA 92631.

ENESCO Precious Moments Collectors' Club, *Goodnewsletter* (NL), PO Box 1466, One Enesco Plaza, Elk Grove Village, IL 60009-1466.

Flow Blue International Collectors' Club, *Blue-Berry Notes* (NL), PO Box 205, Rockford, IL 61105.

Franciscan Collectors Club, *Franciscan Newsletter* (NL), 8412 5th Avenue NE, Seattle, WA 98115.

Goss Collectors' Club, *Goss Hawk* (NL), 4 Khasiaberry, Walnut Tree, Milton Keynes, U.K. MK7 7DP.

Haviland Collectors Internationale Foundation, *Haviland Collectors Internationale Quarterly Newsletter* (NL), PO Box 423, Boone, IA 50036.

Heartland Doulton Collectors, *Doulton Beat* (NL), PO Box 2434, Joliet, IL 60434.

Hummel Collector's Club, *Hummel Collector's Club, Inc.* (NL), 1261 University Dr., P.O. Box 257, Yardley, PA 19067.

International Association of R.S. Prussia Collectors, Inc., *International Association of R.S. Prussia Collectors* (NL), 22 Canterbury Dr., Danville, IN 46122.

International Nippon Collectors Club, *INCC Newsletter* (NL), 112 Ascot, Southlake, TX 76092.

International Plate Collectors Guild, *Platter Patter* (NL), PO Box 487, Artesia, CA 90701.

International Willow Collectors, PO Box 13382, Arlington, TX 76094-0382.

Lladró Collectors Society, *Expressions* (MAG), *Lladró Antique News* (NL), 43 W. 57th St., New York, NY 10019.

M. I. Hummel Club, *Insights* (NL), PO Box 11, Pennington, NJ 08534-0011.

Majolica International Society, *Majolica Matters* (NL), 1275 First Ave., Suite 103, New York, NY 10021.

Mid-America Doulton Collectors, *Madcap* (NL), PO Box 483, McHenry, IL 60050.

National Autumn Leaf Collectors Club, *Autumn Leaf Newsletter* (NL), PO Box 1, Mira Loma, CA 91752-0001.

National Shelley China Club, *Shelley News* (NL), PO Box 18121, Portland, OR 97218.

National Toothpick Holder Collectors Society, *Toothpick Bulletin* (NL), Red Arrow Hwy., Box 246, Sawyer, MI 49125.

North American Torquay Society, *Torquay Collector* (MAG), PO Box 397, Dalton, GA 30722.

North Dakota Pottery Collectors Society, *North Dakota Pottery Collectors Society Newsletter* (NL), Box 14, Beach, ND 58621.

O. J. Club, *Upside Down World of an O. J. Collector* (NL), 29 Freeborn St., Newport, RI 02840-1821 (Occupied Japan collectibles).

Old Sleepy Eye Collectors Club of America, Inc., *Sleepy Eye Newsletter* (NL), PO Box 12, Monmouth, IL 61462.

Phoenix-Bird Collectors of America, *Phoenix-Bird Discoveries* (NL), 685 S. Washington, Constantine, MI 49042.

Pickard Collector's Club, *Pickard Collector's Club* (NL), 300 E. Grove St., Bloomington, IL 61701.

Precious Moments Collectibles, *Precious Collectibles* (MAG), RR #1, Box 255, Canton, IL 61520-9730.

Red Wing Collectors Society, *Red Wing Collectors Newsletter* (NL), PO Box 184, Galesburg, IL 61402.

Roseville's of the Past, *Roseville's of the Past Newsletter* (NL), PO Box 681117, Orlando, FL 32868-1117.

Royal Bayreuth International Collectors' Society, *Royal Bayreuth International Collectors' Society Newsletter* (NL), PO Box 325, Orrville, OH 44667.

Royal Copley Collectors, *The Copley Connection* (NL), 4213 Sandhurst Dr., Orlando, FL 32817.

Royal Doulton International Collectors Club, *Gallery* (MAG), *Royal Doulton International Collectors Club Newsletter* (NL), 700 Cottontail Ln., Somerset, NJ 08873.

Sebastian Miniatures Collectors Society, *Sebastian Exchange Quarterly* (NL), *Sebastian Miniatures Collectors Society News* (NL), 321 Central St., Hudson, MA 01749.

Shawnee Pottery Collector's Club, *Exclusively Shawnee* (NL), PO Box 713, New Smyrna Beach, FL 32170-0713.

Shelley Group, *Shelley Group Newsletter* (NL), 12 Lilleshall Rd., Clayton, Newcastle-Under-Lyme, Staffordshire, England ST5 3BX.

Southern Folk Pottery Collectors Society, *Southern Folk Pottery Collectors Society Newsletter* (NL), 1828 N. Howard Mill Rd., Robins, NC 27325.

Stein Collectors International, *Prosit* (MAG), PO Box 2675, Meriden, CT 06450.

Studio Potter Network, *Studio Potter Network Newsletter* (NL), 69 High St., Exeter, NH 03833.

Susie Cooper Collectors' Club, PO Box 48, Beeston, Nottinghamshire, England NG9 2RN.

Tea Leaf Club International, *Tea Leaf Readings* (NL), 324 Powderhorn Dr., Houghton Lake, MI 48629.

Tile Heritage Foundation, *Tile Heritage: A Review of American Tile History* (MAG), *Flash Point* (NL), PO Box 1850, Healdsburg, CA 95448.

Tiles & Architectural Ceramics Society, *Glazed Expressions* (MAG), Reabrook Lodge, 8 Sutton Rd., Shrewsbury, England SY2 6DD.

Torquay Pottery Collectors Society, *US/Canada News* (MAG), Box 373, Schoolcraft, MI 49087-0373.

Uhl Collectors Society, *Uhl Family Happenings* (NL), 233 E. Timberlin Ln., Huntingburg, IN 47542.

Watt Collectors Association, *Watt's News* (NL), PO Box 708, Mason City, IA 50402 (Watt pottery).

Watt Pottery Collectors USA, *Spoutings* (NL), Box 26067, Fairview Park, OH 44126.

Wedgwood Society of New York, *Ars Ceramica* (MAG), 5 Dogwood Ct., Glen Head, NY 11545.

Antique Souvenir Collector (NL), PO Box 562, Great Barrington, MA 01230 (old "view" souvenir china, postcards, souvenir spoons, old photographs, etc., glass).

Beer Stein Journal (MAG), Glentiques, Ltd., PO Box 8807, Coral Springs, FL 33075.

California Pottery Trader (NL), PO Box 844, Cambria, CA 93428.

Collectibles Canada (MAG), 103 Lakeshore Rd., Suite 202, St. Catharines, ON, Canada L2N 2T6 (limited editions).

Collecting Doulton (MAG), B.B.R. Publishing, 5 Ironworks Row, Elsecar Project, Wath Rd., Elsecar, Barnsley, South Yorkshire, England S74 8HJ.

Collectors' Bulletin (MAG), RR #1, Box 255, Canton, IL 61520 (Precious Moments and other collectibles).

Collector's mart magazine (MAG), 700 E. State St., Iola, WI 54990-0001 (limited editions).

Cookie Jar Collectors Express (NL), Box 221, Mayview, MO 64071.

Cookie Jarrin' (NL), RR #2, Box 504, Walterboro, SC 29488.

Copley Connection (NL), 4213 Sandhurst Dr., Orlando, FL 32817 (Royal Copley china).

Dorothy Kamm's Porcelain Collector's Companion (NL), PO Box 7460, Port St. Lucie, FL 34985-7460.

Doulton Divvy (MAG), PO Box 2434, Joliet, IL 60434.

Eggcup Collectors' Corner (NL), 67 Stevens Ave., Old Bridge, NJ 08857.

Elegance of Old Ivory (NL), PO Box 1004, Wilsonville, OR 97070 (Old Ivory china made by Hermann Ohme).

Fiesta Collector's Quarterly (NL), 19238 Dorchester Circle, Strongsville, OH 44136.

Gonder Collector's Newsletter (NL), PO Box 4263, N. Myrtle Beach, SC 29597.

Head Hunters Newsletter (NL), Box 83 H, Scarsdale, NY 10583 (lady head vases).

Hull Pottery News (NL), 466 Foreston Pl., St. Louis, MO 63119.

Laughlin Eagle (NL), 1270 63rd Terrace S., St. Petersburg, FL 33705.

Majolica Market (NL), 2720 N 45 Rd., Manton, MI 49663.

National Blue Ridge Newsletter (NL), 144 Highland Dr., Blountville, TN 37617-5404.

NM Express (NL), 3081 Rock Creek Dr., Broomfield, CO 80020 (McCoy pottery).

Noritake News (NL), 1237 Federal Ave. E., Seattle, WA 98102 (excluding dinnerware).

Our McCoy Matters (NL), PO Box 14255, Parkville, MO 64152.

Tea Talk (NL), PO Box 860, Sausalito,, CA 94966.

U.S. Pottery News (MAG), PO Box 14255, Parkville, MO 64152.

Vernon Views (NL), PO Box 945, Scottsdale, AZ 85252.

Victorian Times (NL), PO Box 245, Elk Grove Village, IL 60009-0245 (Maud Humphrey Bogart figurines).

Willow Word (MAG), PO Box 13382, Arlington, TX 76094-0382.

Work of Art (MAG), 12 Legion Dr., Valhalla, NY 10595 (Lladró secondary market).

Repairs, Parts & Supplies

A. Ludwig Klein & Son, Inc., PO Box 145, Harleysville, PA 19438, 215-256-9004, Tues.–Fri. 10:00 A.M.–5:00 P.M. Restoration of porcelain, dolls, and more. Appraisals, insurance claims by appointment. Free brochure.

Allan B. Mittelmark, 366 Clinton Ave., Cedarhurst, NY 11516, 516-569-2000, 8:00

A.M.–9:00 P.M.; 516-569-2001. Porcelain restoration, including Boehm, Lladró, Goebel, and other manufacturers.

Andrew Hurst, 2423 Amber St., Knoxville, TN 37917, 615-523-3498, 8:00 A.M.–7:00 P.M. Conservation and restoration of porcelain.

Antique Porcelain Restoration, Gregory A. Ehler, 4786 Lee Highway, Arlington, VA 22207, 703-525-2470, Mon.–Sat. 10:00 A.M.–5:00 P.M. Restoration of porcelain, pottery, and enamels. Nationwide. By appointment.

Antique Restoration by Wiebold, 413 Terrace Pl., Terrace Park, OH 45174, 513-831-2541, Mon.–Fri. 9:00 A.M.–5:30 P.M., Sat. 10:00 A.M.–2:00 P.M.; fax: 513-831-2815. Invisible restoration and conservation of art pottery, ceramics, and porcelain. Free brochure.

Antique Restoring Studio Inc., DBA Trefler & Sons, 99 Cabot St., Needham, MA 02194, 617-444-2685, Mon.–Fri. 9:00 A.M.–5:00 P.M., Sat. 10:00 A.M.–2:00 P.M.; fax: 617-444-0659. Restoration of art objects, including porcelain, ceramics, and sculpture. Can reassemble broken parts and make missing pieces. Free brochure.

Barbara J. Spector Restorations, 206 E. 85th St., #3E, New York, NY 10028, 212-535-7643, 212-737-6564. Porcelain, china, and pottery restoration; also *objets d'art.* Replacement of missing parts. Pieces can be left for a free estimate at Louis J. Nathanson Antique Shop, 219 E. 85th St., New York, NY 10028. Phone 212-249-3235. Open noon-6:00 P.M.

Belle Haven Clay Works, Dona Danziger and John E. Nichols, PO Box 178, Belle Haven Rd., Belle Haven, VA 23306, 804-442-5964, Mon.–Sat. 9:00 A.M.–5:00 P.M. Restoration of Hummels, Roseville, Royal Doulton, and other porcelain objects. Missing parts made. Free estimates. Free brochure.

Broken Art Restoration, Michelle and Bill Marhoefer, 1841 W. Chicago Ave., Chicago, IL 60622, 312-226-8200, Tues.–Fri. 9:00 A.M.–5:00 P.M. Pottery, porcelain, ceramics, wood, ivory, metal, and stone art objects restored. Missing parts replaced, invisible repairs made to almost any art object. Free brochure.

Butterfly Shoppe, 637 Livernois, Ferndale, MI 48220, 313-541-2858, Mon.–Wed. 10:30 A.M.–4:00 P.M., Thurs. until 7:00 P.M. Hummels, Lladrós, and all other porcelain and ceramics repaired. Mail UPS for estimate.

Ceramic Restorations of Westchester, Inc., 81 Water St., Ossining, NY 10562, 914-762-1719, 11:00 A.M.–5:00 P.M.; fax: 914-762-1719. Repair and restoration of ceramic and porcelain figurines, sculptures, collectibles, art objects, and antiques. Re-creation of missing parts. Free estimates. Mail order. Free brochure.

Ceramic Restorations, Inc., Jareth Holub, 161 W. 61st St., Apt. 9F, New York, NY 10023, 212-247-8657, 9:00 A.M.–6:00 P.M. Specializing in the repair of pottery and porcelain. Invisible repairs, replacement of missing elements, and reglazing for antique and contemporary ceramics. Free estimates.

Chatree's, 711 Eighth St., SE, Washington, DC 20003, 202-546-4950. Pottery and porcelain repaired.

Coulter's China Repair & Restoration, HC 83, Box 715, Crosslake, MN 56442, 218-543-4006, 8:00 A.M.–5:00 P.M., answering machine 24 hours. Repairs; missing pieces restored on bone china, porcelain, ceramics, and pottery. Specializing in Lladró, Hummel, Boehm, and R. S. Prussia. No charge for estimates.

Crystal Medic, Jon Kurtz & Carol Jasper, 3126 Fairview Street, Davenport, IA 52802, 319-322-5512. Conservators of pottery and porcelain, bisque, dolls, etc. By appointment only.

D & J Glass Clinic, David Jasper, 40658 267th St., Sioux Falls, SD 57106, 605-361-7524, 9:00 A.M.–5:00 P.M.; fax: 605-361-7216. Restoration of porcelain, dolls, figurines, porcelain, and bisque. Hummel repair. Multiple breaks, chips, and discoloration restored. Missing parts of figurines, such as hands, fingers, legs, and arms, rebuilt and replaced. Free brochure.

Dean's China Restoration, 131 Elmwood Dr., Cheshire, CT 06410, 800-669-1327, Mon.–Fri. 9:00 A.M.–5:00 P.M. Repair and restoration of china, figurines, and dolls. Invisible repairs. Mail order worldwide. Free brochure.

Diane Wight, 30 Lafayette St., Randolph, MA 02368, 617-961-1028. Figurines repaired, including Hummels, Lowell Davis, Broder Fine Arts, Dresden, Lilliput Lane, and David Winter cottages repaired.

Dunhill Restoration, c/o Lee Upholstery, 2309 Lee Rd., Cleveland Heights, OH 44118, 216-921-2932, Mon.–Sat. 9:00 A.M.–5:00 P.M. Conservators of antiques and collectibles, specializing in the repair of Hummels, Doultons, Lladrós, lamps, china, porcelain, and pottery. Replacement of missing parts, such as finials, handles, fingers, toes, etc.

The Finishing Touch, Ned Guyette, 5128 W. Center St., Milwaukee, WI 53210, 414-444-4557. Repair and restoration of pottery and porcelain, including figurines and statues. Cracks and chips repaired, missing parts reproduced.

Foster Art Restoration, 711 W. 17th St. C-12, Costa Mesa, CA 92627, 800-824-6967, 8:30 A.M.–5:00 P.M., 714-645-9953; fax: 714-645-8381. Repair of broken or otherwise damaged porcelains, ceramics, figurines, and other art works and collectibles. Missing pieces duplicated. Specializing in Lladró, Boehm, Cybis, Hummel, Royal Doulton, and other manufacturers. Free brochure.

Gerlinde Kornmesser, 1804½ Glenview Road, Glenview, IL 60025, 708-724-3059. Pottery and porcelain restoration classes, summer only, Lawrence University, Appleton, WI.

Glass Restoration by Dianne, 54 Hartford Turnpike, Piccadilly Square, Vernon, CT 06066, 203-647-7074, Tues.–Sat. 10:00 A.M.–5:30 P.M. Restoration of china and porcelain. Brochure.

Grady Stewart—Expert Porcelain Restoration, 2019 Sanson St., Philadelphia, PA 19103, 215-567-2888, Tues. and Wed. noon–3:00 P.M. Restoration of fine antique or contemporary ceramic works of art. Pack very well and ship only via UPS.

Harry A. Eberhardt & Son, Inc., 2010 Walnut St., Philadelphia, PA 19103, 215-568-4144, Mon.–Fri. 9:00 A.M.–5:00 P.M. Restoration of porcelains, Satsuma, glass, cloisonné, and other objects of art.

Hess Restorations, 200 Park Ave. S., New York, NY 10003, 212-260-2255, 10:30 A.M.–4:00 P.M. Restoration of china and porcelain. Chips filled in. Brochure.

I.P.G.R., Inc., PO Box 205, Kulpsville, PA 19443, 800-869-5633, orders only; 215-256-9015, Tues.–Fri. 9:30 A.M.–4:30 P.M., Sat. 9:30 A.M.–1:30 P.M.; fax: 215-256-9644. Restoration materials for porcelain, dolls, glass, jade, ivory, and metals. Catalog $3, refundable with first order.

International Doll Restoration Artists Association, Lavonne Lutterman, Rt. 2, Box 6, Worthington, MN 56187, 507-372-2717, anytime. Workshops for those who are interested in the restoration of ceramic ware as a career. Taught on an individual basis only. Workshops concentrate on porcelain from dolls to dinnerware, but include the restoration of earthenware and stoneware. Applicants must be interested in restoration as a career. Interview and arrangements by telephone only.

J & H China Repairs, 8296 St. George St., Vancouver, BC, Canada V5X 3C5, 604-321-1093, 7:30 A.M.–2:00 P.M. Restoration of porcelain, ceramics, figurines, sculptures, and dolls.

J & K Curios, 4868 SW Southwind Ct., Dunnellon, FL 34431, 904-465-0756, Mon.–Fri. 9:00 A.M.–9:00 P.M. Restoration and preservation of pottery and porcelain. Custom-made lids, handles, and finials. Colors enhanced. Porcelain clock housings and dials restored. Porcelain dolls restored. Free estimates.

John Edward Cunningham, 1525 E. Berkeley, Springfield, MO 65804, 417-889-7702, Mon.–Sat. 9:00 A.M.–5:00 P.M. Porcelains restored. Missing parts sculpted. Mail order or by appointment. Send SASE for more information.

Jonathan Mark Gershen, 1463 Pennington Rd., Ewing Township, NJ 08618, 609-882-9417, Mon.–Fri. 10:00 A.M.–4:00 P.M. Repair and restoration of porcelain and pottery. Missing parts fabricated, shattered pieces restored, historically accurate reconstruction of decorative art objects. Send for information on how to ship your items to the studio for evaualion. Worldwide service.

Just Enterprises—Art & Antique Restoration, Gary and Susanne Gottfried, 2790 Sherwin Ave., #10, Ventura, CA 93003, 805-644-5837, 10:00 A.M.–noon, 2:00 P.M.–5:00 P.M. Restoration of porcelain, including dolls' heads and figurines. Missing parts manufactured when necessary.

Lid Lady, Charles Bodiker, 7790 E. Ross Rd., New Carlisle, OH 45344, 513-845-1266. Lids for antique and new items, china to zinc. Send SASE for a reply.

Lladró Collectors Society, 43 W. 53rd St., New York, NY 10019, 201-807-0018, Mon.–Fri. 8:00 A.M.–4:45 P.M. Replacement parts for Lladró figures: parasols, flowers, fans, swords, etc. Call for list and prices. List of restorers.

Loughlin's Restoration Studio, 749 Indian Beach Circle, Sarasota, FL 34234, 813-355-7318, Mon.–Fri. 9:00 A.M.–5:00 P.M. Restorers of fine porcelain, including Meissen, Royal Worcester, Royal Doulton, Cybis, and Hummels; ivory; and jade. Edward Marshall Boehm porcelains are their specialty. Beginner's guide, *The Art of Restoration of Fine Porcelain,* $12; videotape on restoration, $17 (see following Video section). Brochure.

MAC Enterprises, Martha A. Cleary, Master Restorer, 14851 Jeffrey Rd. #75, Irvine, CA 92720, 714-262-9110, 9:00 A.M.–6:00 P.M. Restore porcelain, ceramics, pottery, frames, oil paintings, and collectibles. Registered Hummel restorer. Ship UPS or call for information. Send SASE for brochure.

Meeting House Furniture Restoration, John T. Schechtman, 11 Waterman Hill, Queechee, VT 05059, 802-295-1309, Mon.–Sat. 9:00 A.M.–5:00 P.M., answering machine other times. Porcelain and china repair.

Michael's Art Restoration Studio, Michael Scheglov, 8312 Eighth NW, Seattle, WA 98117, 206-789-2900, 11:00 A.M.–5:00 P.M.; fax: 206-778-6963. Restoration of fine porcelain and china art objects, including Boehm, Belleek, and Hummel.

Mike Meshenberg, 2571 Edgewood Rd., Beachwood, OH 44122, 216-464-2084, 9:00 A.M.–9:00 P.M. Restoration of porcelain figurines and art work, including Lladró.

Nelson Dale, Restoration Services, 621 Main St., #3, Waltham, MA 02154, 617-647-9470, 9:00 A.M.–5:00 P.M. Restoration of porcelain, pottery, sculpture, and small objects of all kinds. Free brochure.

Old China Patterns Limited, 1560 Brimley Rd., Scarborough, ON, Canada, M1P 3G9, 416-299-8880; fax: 416-299-4721. Quilted cotton storage pouches with acrylic felt inserts for chinaware. Custom sizes available.

Old World Restorations, Inc., 347 Stanley Ave., Cincinnati, OH 45226, 800-878-1911, 513-321-1911, Mon.–Fri. 8:30 A.M.–5:30 P.M.; fax: 513-321-1914. Restoration and conservation of art and antiques, including pottery, porcelain, and sculpture. Free brochure.

Peter's Antiques, 4113 Oechsli Ave., Louisville, KY 40207, 502-893-8498, business; 502-458-8498, residence. China and porcelain repaired and restored. Missing pieces replaced.

Phoenix Restoration Inc., 5305 N. 7th St., Suite C, Phoenix, AZ 85014, 602-263-5178, 800-234-5178; 8:00 A.M.–6:00 P.M.; fax: 602-263-6009. Restoration and conservation of porcelain and ceramics. Conservator and restorer of Lladró and Belleek.

Pleasant Valley Antique Restoration, Joe Howell, 1725 Reed Rd., Knoxville, MD 21758, 301-432-2721, 9:30 A.M.–9:00 P.M. Restoration of porcelain. Custom color matching and airbrush work. Previous restorations detected and verified.

Professional Restoration, R. DiCarlo, PO Box 616222, Orlando, FL 32861, 407-886-7423, anytime. Restoration of porcelain, china, pottery, and related items.

Restoration Tile Co., 3511 Interlake N., Seattle, WA 98103, 206-633-4866, 9:00 A.M.–5:00 P.M. On-site restoration of tile installations. Reproduction of Arts & Crafts tiles and Victorian tiles. Specializing in reproductions of Batchelder, Claycraft, Grueby, and Fulper. Catalog $5.

Restorations by Dudley, Inc., Box 345, West Orange, NJ 07052, 201-731-4449, 10:00 A.M.–5:00 P.M. Restoration of Hummel, Lladró, and all figurines.

Restorations By Linda, Linda M. Peet, 1759 Hemlock St., Fairfield, CA 94533, 707-422-6497. Restoration of porcelain and china objects, including Hummel, Boehm, and Lladró. Free estimates.

Restorers of America, RD 4, Box 382, Wynantskill, NY 12189, 407-364-8661, anytime. Restoration of fine porcelains, collectibles, and sculptures. Supplies, workshops, and seminars.

Restorite Systems, PO Box 7096-A, West Trenton, NJ 08628, 609-530-1526. Products for restoring ceramics. Repair kit for broken or chipped china includes supplies necessary to mend dozens of pieces and illustrated instruction book. Mail order only. Free brochure.

Rikki's Studio Inc., Gilbert Kerry Hall, 2809 Bird Ave., Coconut Grove, FL 33133, 305-446-2022, 305-446-2230, 9:00 A.M.–4:30 P.M.; fax: 305-446-6388. Restoration of porcelain and ceramics. Appraisals.

Sano Studio, 767 Lexington Ave. at 60th St., New York, NY 10021, 212-759-6131, 10:00 A.M.–5:00 P.M. Restoration of antique pottery, porcelain, tortoiseshell, and ivory.

Sharon Smith Abbott, Fine Wares Restoration, PO Box 753, Bridgton, ME 04009, 207-647-2093, 8:00 A.M.–5:00 P.M., answering machine after hours. Ceramic conservation services for museum and private collections. Treatments include cleaning, bonding, gapfilling, and replacement by casting with appropriate resins. Written estimates and suggested treatment provided at no cost.

T. S. Restoration, J. M. Denson, 2622 N. Dobson Rd., Chandler, AZ 85224. Restoration of antique and modern collectibles, by appointment. Boehm, Cybis, Lladró, Royal Doulton, Hummels, David Winter, and other modern collectibles. Antique porcelain, ceramics, stoneware, ivory, natural stone, cloisonné, plaster, wax, and papier-mâché. Books on restoration. Mail order. Send LSASE for information.

Venerable Classics, 645 Fourth St., Suite 208, Santa Rosa, CA 95404, 800-531-2891, 9:00 A.M.–5:00 P.M.; fax: 707-575-3626. Restoration of porcelain, including Lladró and Boehm. Specializing in statuary, dolls, lamps, and clocks. Shipping instructions and free brochure available on request.

Vigues Art Studio, 54 Glanders Rd., Woodbury, CT 06798, 203-263-4088, 10:00 A.M.–5:00 P.M. Conservation and restoration of porcelain and china. Reconstruction of missing parts, matching design and glaze.

Yolanda Studio, Yolanda DiSalvo, 228 Washington Ave., Elmwood Park, NJ 07407, 201-791-8611, Mon.–Fri. 9:00 A.M.–5:00 P.M. Restoration of porcelain and china. Specializing in Hummel, Lladró, and antiques.

Videos

Porcelain Restoration Basics, **Antique & Collectible Restoration Services,** 1417 Third St., Webster City, IA 50595.

Majolica, adapted from the book *Majolica* by Nicholas M. Dawes, helps identify Majolica, 35 minutes. *Rookwood Pottery,* adapted from the book *Rookwood Pottery: The Glorious Gamble* by Anita J. Ellis, helps identify Majolica. 45 minutes. **Award Video & Film Distributors, Inc.,** 4857 Primrose Path, Sarasota, FL 34242, 813-955-1818; fax: 813-346-2583.

Passport to Antiques (restoration of fine porcelains), **Loughlin's Restoration Studio,** 749 Indian Beach Circle, Sarasota, FL 34234, 813-355-7318. $15 plus $2 shipping and handling.

The Magic of a Name, Vol. One & Vol. Two, **Quill Productions,** 166 Elmdon Ln., Marston Green, Birmingham, England B377EB, 021-779-3140. Royal Doulton figurines and jugs. Free leaflet on request.

Kovels' American Art Pottery I and *Kovels' American Art Pottery II.* **40 minutes each. $39.95 each. Ralph and Terry Kovel, PO Box 22900, Beachwood, OH 44122, 216-752-2252; fax: 216-752-3115.**

Celebrating 150 Years of Haviland China (1842–1992), **Wisconsin Antiques Dealers Association Educational Film Committee,** c/o Sharron Cypher, 135 N. Main, Hartford, WI 53027, 414-673-2751. 60 minutes.

Prints, Woodcuts, Posters & Calendar Art

*I*t is difficult to sell black-and-white prints, etchings, and engravings. They are not popular now, and only very special prints in excellent condition by known artists will bring good money. Many prints that are attractive if framed have no antiques value. Some are just pages taken from old books. It takes an art expert to evaluate art prints. Your local museum may be able to help you identify the artist and age. The research needed to determine how to price the print is the same as the research needed to price a fine painting. (See Paintings section.)

There are many terms that have meaning only to an expert. You don't need to know the difference between first strike, restrike, foxing, edition, steel engraving, etc., unless you plan to go into the business of selling prints. The subtleties of these terms are very difficult to learn.

Japanese woodblock prints are popular and sell quickly. Some old, rare prints were available immediately after World War II for only a few dollars each, and many soldiers brought them home. Today, some of the old prints in fine condition are worth thousands of dollars. The colors should be bright, the paper untorn and without stains. If the print has been glued to a backing, it has lost its value. Several books are available to help you identify these prints, but once again it takes an expert to know whether the woodblock print is worth a few hundred or a few thousand dollars. If you have had the prints for over thirty years, it would be wise to have an appraisal by an expert.

Other types of pictures can be more easily priced for sale. Movie, travel, and other posters are listed in price books and are easier to identify. The only hazards are the reproductions. Many old posters have been reissued and reproduced. There are clues, especially for movie posters, and research in the library will help.

Travel posters and circus posters sell at highest prices as decorative pictures. Large colorful posters with interesting subjects sell quickly if in very good condition. Torn, faded posters do not sell. French posters by well-known artists, advertising posters, and posters printed by important companies are bought by specialists who will pay more than the average poster price. Check the value in a general price book or look in the catalogs sent out by the mail-order poster dealers. These dealers also have to buy more posters, so they could be your customers.

Calendar art, the pictures printed for the tops of wall-hung, paper calendars, is a new area of collecting. Pinup girl prints by PETTY, VARGAS, and other artists working after 1940 are in demand. Sentimental pictures of children by early 1900s artists like BESSIE PEASE GUTMANN or ROSE O'NEILL sell well. Landscapes by R. ATKINSON FOX or Art Deco prints by MAXFIELD PARRISH are also desirable.

Old CURRIER & IVES prints have always been popular. Action scenes and outdoor scenes are priced the highest; religious subjects, vases of flowers, and portraits of children are priced low. Be careful, because there have been many reproductions. Look in *Currier & Ives Prints: An Illustrated Check List* for the exact size of the original of your print. Then look up the value in the general price books.

Hand-colored bird prints by JOHN GOULD or JOHN JAMES AUDUBON, botanical prints, interior room views, architectural drawings, military scenes, and many other prints removed from nineteenth-century books are sold by special dealers at most large antiques shows. These may be the dealers who will buy your prints.

See also the Paper Collectibles section.

REPAIR

Restoration of any type of paper is very difficult. It is possible to carefully clean dust from a print by using wallpaper cleaner, wadded fresh white bread, or an art-gum eraser. Creases can be carefully ironed out with a very cool iron. More ambitious repairs should always be done by a restorer. Do not tape or glue any paper item: The acids in the adhesive will eventually cause damage. Marks from old tape can sometimes be removed by a restorer.

Price Books

American and European Prints at Auction, William P. Carl, edited by William T. Currier (Currier Publications, 241 Main St., Stoneham, MA 02180, © 1994).

Art Price Index International, 2 volumes, annual (Sound View Press, 170 Boston Post Rd., Madison, CT 06443).

The Collectible Maxfield Parrish, William Holland and Douglas Congdon-Martin (Schiffer, Atglen, PA, © 1993).

Currier & Ives Prints, Robert Kipp (Currier Publications, 241 Main St., Stoneham, MA 02180, © 1994).

Leonard's Annual Price Index of Prints, Posters & Photos, edited by Katheryn Acerbo (Auction Index, 30 Valentine Park, Newton, MA 02165, © 1993).

Maxfield Parrish: A Price Guide, Stephanie Lane (L-W Books, PO Box 69, Gas City, IN 46933, © 1993).

More Wonderful Yard-Long Prints, Book II, Keagy and Rhoden (PO Box 106, Bloomfield, IN 47424, © 1992).

Posters Identification and Price Guide, 2nd edition, Tony Fusco (Avon Books, New York, © 1994).

The Price & Identification Guide to Maxfield Parrish, 9th edition, Denis C. Jackson (TICN, PO Box 1958, Sequim, WA 98382, © 1994).

Print Price Index, annual, Mehren and Gordon (Dealer's Choice Books, Inc., PO Box 710, Land O'Lakes, FL 34639, © 1993).

Prints, Posters & Photos Identification and Price Guide, Susan Theran (Avon Books, New York, © 1993).

Clubs & Publications

American Historical Print Collectors Society, *Imprint* (MAG and NL), PO Box 201, Fairfield, CT 06430.

Gutmann Collectors Club, *Gutmann Collectors Club Newsletter* (NL), 1353 Elm Ave., Lancaster, PA 17603 (products featuring Bessie Pease Guttman art, including plates and figurines).

Journal of the Print World (NP), 1008 Winona Rd., Meredith, NH 03253-9599.

Print Collector's Newsletter (NL), 119 E. 79th St., New York, NY 10021.

Repairs, Parts & Supplies

Andrea Pitsch Paper Conservation, New York, NY, 212-594-9676, Mon.–Fri. 9:00 A.M.–6:00 P.M.; fax: 212-268-4046. Conservation and restoration of paper-based objects, including posters and prints. Consultation on condition of paper collections, prospective purchases, storage, and handling. By appointment only.

Antique Prints & Restorations, Robert P. Kipp, 16 Wedgemer Rd., Beverly, MA 01915-1435, 508-922-6852, 8:00 A.M.–5:00 P.M.. Print restorations. Specializing in the cleaning and restoration of hand-colored prints, especially Currier & Ives. Serving the entire U.S. Free information sheet sent upon request.

Archival Conservation Center, Inc., 8225 Daly Rd., Cincinnati, OH 45231, 513-521-9858, 8:30 A.M.–3:30 P.M. Repair and restoration of prints and other works of art on paper. Prints cleaned. Free brochure.

Conservation of Art on Paper, Inc., Christine Smith, 2805 Mount Vernon Ave., Alexandria, VA 22301, 703-836-7757, Mon.–Fri. 9:30A.M.–6:00 P.M. Conservation of prints, posters, and other art and historic artifacts on paper. Publications about the care of paper objects. Examination and condition reports for insurance purposes. By appointment.

George Martin Cunha, 4 Tanglewood Dr., Lexington, KY 40505, 606-293-5703, 8:00 A.M.–5:00 P.M.; fax: 606-233-9425. Repair and restoration of prints, posters, and other works of art on paper. Preservation surveys with recommendations for restoration, if required.

Graphic Conservation Co., 329 W. 18th St., Suite 701, Chicago, IL 60616, 312-738-2657, Mon.–Fri. 9:00 A.M.–noon, 1:00 P.M.–5:00 P.M.; fax: 312-738-3125. Conservation of works of art on paper, including prints. Dry cleaning, stain reduction, flattening, deacidification, inpainting, and tear repairs and fills. Proposal and examination fee $15 and up.

Michael C. Hinton, RD #2, Box 313, Mertztown, PA 19539, 215-682-7096, anytime. Prints cleaned, de-foxed, and de-acidified.

Museum Shop, Ltd., Richard Kornemann, 20 North Market St., Frederick, MD 21701, 301-695-0424, Mon.–Thurs. 10:30 A.M.–6:00 P.M., Fri.–Sat. 10:30 A.M.–9:00 P.M., Sun. noon–5:00 P.M.; fax: 301-698-5242. Restoration of original prints, etchings, lithographs, engravings, pen and inks, and anything on paper.

Northeast Document Conservation Center, 100 Brickstone Sq., Andover, MA 01810-1494, 508-470-1010; fax: 508-475-6021. Nonprofit regional conservation center specializing in treatment of art and artifacts on paper, including posters, prints, and works of art on paper. Preservation microfilming, preservation planning surveys, disaster assistance, technical leaflets. Brochure.

Poster Plus, David A. Gartler, 210 S. Michigan Ave., Chicago, IL 60604, 312-461-9277, Mon.–Fri. 10:00 A.M.–6:00 P.M.; fax: 312-461-9084. Poster restoration, conservation, mounting, and retouching. Linen backing and framing. Free brochure.

Preservation Emporium, PO Box 226309, Dallas, TX 75222-6309, 214-630-1197, Mon.–Fri. 9:00 A.M.–5:00 P.M., Sat. 9:00 A.M.–4:00 P.M.; fax: 214-630-7805. Conservation of prints. Acid-free mounting and matting materials, ultraviolet filtering light ray plexiglass.

Robert L. Searjeant, PO Box 23942, Rochester, NY 14692. Restoration of Currier & Ives prints. Books and literature on prints.

Appraiser

The Oriental Corner, 280 Main St., Los Altos, CA 94022, 415-941-3207, Tues.-Sat. 10:30 A.M.-5:00 P.M.; fax: 415-941-3297. Appraisals of oriental antiques and art, including woodblock prints.

Rugs

Everyone knows that oriental rugs have value, but it is almost impossible to determine the value unless you are a rug expert. If you inherit a large, old oriental, have it appraised by a rug dealer or sold through an auction gallery. Never ask a rug dealer to "make an offer." If you were in the business of selling old rugs, wouldn't you offer as little as possible so that you could make a larger profit? The actual worth of the rug and the offer may have little in common. It is better to pay for an appraisal from a competent person and then try to sell it elsewhere. If you sell it as part of a house sale, be sure to learn the proper name for the rug, and be sure you have an expert set the price. Many things affect rug prices: the condition (no worn spots, stains, or missing fringe), the color (unfaded), the number of knots to the inch, the material (silk or wool are best), and the design and overall quality. Size is also important. Room-sized rugs and stair runners sell quickly. Very large rugs, 18 × 30 feet or larger, can only bring good prices at a well-advertised auction or from a major rug dealer.

Chinese rugs, especially those with Art Deco designs and pleasing colors (purple and chartreuse are hard to sell), any type of pictorial rag rug, needlepoints, dhurries, Navajo rugs, and almost any other type of usable floor coverings sell for good prices. If you have no guidelines and your rug is in good condition, measure it, determine the number of square yards, and price it at a little more than good new carpeting.

R E P A I R

Oriental rugs should always be kept clean and in good repair. Repairs should be done by a professional, although some minor work can be accomplished at home. A worn spot can be covered temporarily by coloring the exposed beige backing with crayon or colored ink. A full fringe adds to the value of a rug and should never be trimmed or replaced unless absolutely necessary. There are rug dealers in large department stores or in shops in large cities who can do repairs. If a local restorer is not available, a rug can be shipped to another city. See also Textiles.

Book on Repair

Oriental Rugs Care and Repair, Majid Amini (Van Nostrand Reinhold Co., New York, © 1981).

Clubs & Publications

Decorative Rug (MAG), PO Box 709, Meredith, NH 03253 (oriental rugs).

Oriental Rug Review (MAG), PO Box 709, Meredith, NH 03253.

Repairs, Parts & Supplies

Chevalier Conservation, 500 West Ave., Stamford, CT 06902, 203-969-1980; fax: 203-969-1988. Cleaning, restoration, and conservation of antique and contemporary tapestries, rugs, carpets, and textiles. Free brochure.

David Zahirpour, 4918 Wisconsin Ave. NW, Washington, DC 20016, 202-338-4141, 9:00 A.M.–6:00 P.M.; fax: 202-244-1800. Restoration of

handmade rugs; hand washing, stain removal. Appraisals.

Hooked Rug Restoration, Charles J.P. Quigley, 72 Rt. 28, Suite 28, West Harwich, MA 02671-1114, 508-432-0897, 10:00 A.M.–6:00 P.M. Restoration of hooked rugs. Edges bound or replaced as in original, without binding, filling in missing areas. Placement of tapis sleeves for wall hanging. Full backings where required. Free brochure.

Koko Boodakian & Sons, Steve Boodakian, 1026 Main St., Winchester, MA 01890, 617-729-5566, Tues.–Sat. 9:30 A.M.–5:00 P.M., Wed. and Thurs. until 9:00 P.M.; fax: 617-729-5595. Restoration of oriental rugs. Cleaning and repair services performed at their facility.

Linda Eliason, Box 542, Manchester, VT 05254, 802-325-3026. Hooked rug restoration. Free estimates.

M. Finkel & Daughter, Morris and Amy Finkel, 936 Pine St., Philadelphia, PA 19107, 215-627-7797, 10:00 A.M.–5:00 P.M.; fax: 215-627-8199. Restoration and conservation of hooked rugs. By appointment.

Persian Rug Cleaning Co., Robert Ouzounian, 2118 Temple St., Los Angeles, CA 90026, 213-413-6373, weekdays 8:00 A.M.–5:00 P.M. Navajo rug and blanket cleaning and removal of color runs or color bleeding. Navajo rug and blanket repairs.

Sanford Restoration Works, Emily Sanford, 2102 Speyer Ln., Redondo Beach, CA 90278, 213-374-7412, Mon.–Sat. 9:00 A.M.–6:00 P.M.; fax: 310-798-2792. Restoration, repair, and conservation of antique rugs and textiles, including oriental rugs, tribal rugs and flatweaves, Navaho weavings, and hooked rugs. Custom spinning and dyeing to match original materials. Specializing in village and nomadic weaving. Reweaving, cleaning, custom mounting. Teaching.

Serunian & Sons, Inc., Oriental Rug Specialists, PO Box 1916, Greensboro, NC 27402, 919-272-2294, 9:00 A.M.–5:00 P.M. Cleaning, repairing, restoring, and reweaving oriental rugs.

Appraisals. Located at 1311 Grove St., Greensboro, NC 27403.

Shallcross & Lorraine, Holly L. Smith, State House, PO Box 133, Boston, MA 02133, 617-720-2133, 9:00 A.M.–6:00 P.M. Invisible restoration, conservation, and maintenance of oriental rugs, tapestries, and Native American textiles. Hand-spun and custom-dyed wools used.

Sylvia J. Dole, Sugarwood Rd., Plainfield, VT 05667, 802-454-7184. Hooked rug repairs.

Thomas J. Dwyer Ltd., Fine Oriental Rugs, 304 East Genesee St., Fayetteville, NY 13066, 315-637-4988, Tues.–Fri. 9:00 A.M.–5:00 P.M., Sat. 10:00 A.M.–4:00 P.M.; fax: 315-637-0771. Cleaning and repair of new and antique oriental rugs. Free estimates on repair and cleaning, mothproofing. Free brochure.

Video

Consumer's Guide to Old Decorative Oriental Rugs, **Concept Videos,** PO Box 30408, Bethesda, MD 20824, 800-333-8252. 60 minutes, $39.95.

Scales

*A*ll types of scales are collected, from nineteenth-century balance scales used to weigh gold or letters or drugs, to twentieth-century drugstore scales. Old ones are of value, but

there are few experts who can help you. However, there is a scale collectors' society with a very informative newsletter and the club may be able to help you. Twentieth-century drugstore scales in working order sell for hundreds to thousands of dollars. The large figural cast iron Mr. Peanut scale is worth over $15,000.

REPAIR

Information about repair of scales is scarce. There are a few books and articles to help you solve problems with early scales. Sometimes a large, spring-operated scale can be repaired by a local shop that fixes scales for grocery stores and commercial businesses. Search for these through the "Business to Business" Yellow Pages if that is how your phone books are divided, or look under "Scales" in the regular Yellow Pages.

Club & Publication

International Society of Antique Scale Collectors, *Equilibrium* (NL), 76 W. Adams St., Suite 1706, Chicago, IL 60603.

Silver & Silver Plate

*A*n old sterling silver teaspoon is never worth less than its meltdown value, which is the weight of the spoon multiplied by the going price of silver bullion. The number is reported in the daily newspapers on the stock quotation pages. If a dime is old enough to be made of a silver alloy, it could be worth more than 10 cents in meltdown value based on the price of silver.

Most antique silver is worth more than the meltdown value, but the value is often calculated from that figure. Some appraisers weigh old silver and multiply the result by two to four times the meltdown; some use other formulas. Jewelry stores, coin shops, and "Gold, Silver, and Platinum Dealers" are listed in the phone book, and they will weigh and buy for the meltdown value. This is actually the lowest price you should receive for your pieces. Don't forget that some pieces of old silver, especially candlesticks, are "weighted." There is a heavy material in the base that keeps the candlestick from tipping. The meltdown buyers are interested in what the thin sterling shell weighs after the weight is removed.

"Coin," "Sterling," and "925" are all indications of solid silver. The number 925 means 925 parts silver for every 1,000 parts of metal. It is marked on what is called "sterling silver." The word "coin" is stamped on nineteenth-century pieces that were made from melted coins. The silver content varies from 800 to 925 parts of silver. Many European silver pieces are marked 800. All these pieces are wanted for meltdown.

Silver plate, A1, EPNS, triple plate, and other similar terms mean that the piece is made of a base metal and is covered with a thin layer of silver. The word "Sheffield" has several meanings. If it is stamped on the bottom of your piece, you probably have an item that is silver plated. None of the plated pieces have a good meltdown value.

Makers' names and hallmarks are very important in determining value. The names GEORG JENSEN, TIFFANY, MARTELÉ, LIBERTY, and (PAUL) REVERE, or the initials of the famous English silversmiths, like PAUL STORR or PAUL DE LAMERIE, add to the value of a piece of silver. The English hallmark system of four or five small marks looks like this ⊕⊠◔Ⓐ. If the king's head looks to the right, the piece was made before 1850 and probably has added value. Queen Victoria's head faces left. Queen Elizabeth II's head faces left. The lion is an indication of sterling quality.

The showiest pieces of silver, such as the tea sets, punch bowls, epergnes, and large candelabra, always have a good resale value. Elaborate English pieces dating from 1850 to 1900 are usually "ballpark" priced from five to seven times the meltdown value. If the work is exceptional, if the silversmith is well known, or if the history ties the silver to a famous family or event, it could be worth ten to twelve times the meltdown price or more. The condition is always important. There should be no dents, broken handles, or alterations.

Tea sets of any description usually can be sold, even in poor condition. Twentieth-century plated or sterling sets should be priced at less than half the modern department store prices. Sterling sets must be priced with the weight considered. Earlier sets are worth more than modern sets. The price is determined by age, artistic value, and the maker. Silver tea services sell best at important house sales. Contact local house sale managers to see if you can have it sold by them at someone else's house. Silver-plated trays, small dishes, and flatware have a very low resale value, especially if they are not in mint condition.

Ordinary silver made after 1900 usually sells for about twice the meltdown price. If the decorations are lavish or if the piece is a very desirable shape, such as a punch bowl, it might sell for four times the meltdown. Very large or very decorative pieces can bring up to ten times meltdown. Pieces with a special meaning, such as Jewish religious items or historic pieces, sell for even more. Commemorative silver medals and modern limited edition sets usually sell for meltdown.

Very ornate Victorian silver is back in fashion and "more is better" when it comes to pricing. All sterling serving spoons, forks, asparagus servers, fish servers, grape shears, and other large serving pieces sell at prices comparable to modern examples. Very small pieces, like nut picks or pickle forks, do not sell as well. Pieces with elaborate, crisp, bright-cut designs sell well. Those with worn bright cutting are not in much demand. Figural napkin rings, picture frames, and souvenir spoons have a special value to collectors, so the meltdown value is in no way related to the price.

Sterling silver flatware in good condition is always worth more than meltdown. Sell it through an auction or offer it at a house sale at a price from 30 to 50 percent less than the department store price for a similar set. It can also be sold to a silver matching service. (To find matching services, visit large antiques shows or look in publications listed below or the Matching Service section in Part II.) Send a photocopy of the front and back of a spoon or fork if you don't know the pattern name. Include a list of pieces and a stamped, self-addressed envelope.

A monogram will lower the value on a set of silver less than 100 years old, but a crest or elaborate monogram on eighteenth-century or early nineteenth-century silver adds to the value. You do not have to remove a monogram; doing so is expensive and can cause damage. The market for silver flatware is many-leveled. If the retailer, department store, or gift shop gets $5,000 for a new set of silver, a discount store might get 25 percent less or $3,750. The antiques shop or auction gallery would probably ask 50 percent of retail, or $2,500, for a used set. The meltdown would be half of that, $1,250 or even less. You determine your price by where you plan to sell the set. Silver-plated flatware is also collected and can be matched but sells for low prices.

Early Sheffield plated silver, made before 1840 by rolling a thin layer of silver on a copper base, has a special value for collectors. Good pieces are worth thousands of dollars. If the copper shows because the top layer of silver is worn, the value is at least 50 percent less. If a piece of early rolled Sheffield is replated, deduct 90 percent.

If a piece of electroplated silver made after 1840 needs resilvering, deduct 50 percent. If a piece of electroplated silver has been replated, deduct 5 percent. If the handle of a piece has been replaced, the feet redone, or any other part totally replaced, deduct 75 percent. If the piece has been reworked (a stein made from a vase), the result is worth meltdown value plus about 10 percent.

REPAIR

Silver should be kept clean. Use any good commercial polish, and if you keep the silver on display, use a tarnish-retarding polish. For storage, tarnish-retarding cloths and papers are also available.

Never use household scouring powder or instant silver polish on your silver. Never store silver in a nonporous plastic wrap, because the wrap may melt or moisture may collect between the silver and the wrap. Never wrap with rubber bands. Silver will tarnish more quickly if displayed on latex-painted shelves, in oak furniture, or near oak trees. If you use camphor (mothballs) to prevent tarnish, don't let the camphor touch the silver.

Knife blades may separate from hollow handles if they are stored in a hot attic or washed in a dishwasher. They can be repaired by using a nonmelting filler. An expert should do this.

Silver that is kept on display and never used for eating, such as a large candelabrum, can be lacquered. This will keep the piece clean almost indefinitely. Any good plating company can lacquer a piece.

Antique plated silver may "bleed" (the copper underneath shows through the silver). This is not totally objectionable. Resilvering may lower the value, so check on the age and type of silver plate before you replate. Very early "rolled-on" silver on copper Sheffield pieces should rarely be replated. Late nineteenth- and twentieth-century plated silver that was originally electroplated can be replated with no loss of value. These pieces are usually marked "silver plate." The handles and feet were often made of Britannia metal and will appear black when the silver plate wears off. Local platers are listed in the Yellow Pages under "Plating."

There is a new product on the market that adds a thin layer of silver to worn pieces. The silver liquid is applied with a cloth. This is a temporary "repair" but it does improve the appearance of worn silver plate.

For information about silver flatware, see the Matching Services list in Part II.

See also Metals in this book.

Price Books

1830's–1990's American Sterling Silver Flatware: A Collector's Identification & Value Guide, Maryanne Dolan (Books Americana, Florence, AL, © 1993).

Spoons from Around the World, Dorothy T. Rainwater and Donna H. Felger (Schiffer, Atglen, PA, © 1992).

Toothpick Holders: China, Glass and Metal, The National Toothpick Holder Collector's Society (Antique Publications, Marietta, OH, © 1992).

Publication

Silver (MAG), PO Box 9690, Rancho Santa Fe, CA 92067.

Repairs, Parts & Supplies

Al Bar-Wilmette Platers, 127 Green Bay Rd., Wilmette, IL 60091, 708-251-0187, Mon.–Fri. 8:00 A.M.–5:00 P.M., Sat. 8:00 A.M.–3:00 P.M. Restoration of metal antiques from sterling silver pieces to brass light fixtures. Plating, polishing, repairing, lacquering. Door and window hardware polished and lacquered. Antique door hardware for sale. Will provide quotes from photos sent. Nationwide service. Daily UPS service. Be sure to insure shipments.

Blue Crystal (Glass) Ltd., Unit 6-8, 21 Wren St., London, England WC1X 0HF, +44 71 578 0142, 8:15 A.M.–4:45 P.M. Blue glass inserts for antique silver. Reproduction crystal tableware cut to match or as specified. Bottles for cruet stands, claret bottles for silver mount, etc. Mail order worldwide.

Cole Silver Shop, Barney and Kitty Hays, 107 Third St., Santa Rosa, CA 95401, 707-546-7515, Mon.–Fri. 10:00 A.M.–5:00 P.M., Sat. morning by appointment. Repairs, polishing, and plating. Silver soldering, knife blades replaced, combs for dresser sets. Garbage-disposal-damaged items repaired. Send SASE for brochure.

Fletcher Silversmiths, Inc., 12744 Ventura Blvd., Studio City, CA 91604, 818-762-5625. Restoration of antique silver hollowware and flatware, specializing in sterling. Replating of silver and gold plate.

Hess Restorations, 200 Park Ave. S., New York, NY 10003, 212-260-2255, 10:30 A.M.–4:00 P.M. Restoration of silver; silver plating. Specializing in the restoration of old silver dresser sets, removing dents, replacing worn brushes, combs, and mirrors; polishing and lacquering the silver. Blue glass liners for silver salt dishes, sugar baskets, and condiment holders; new velvet easel backs for silver frames; linings for fine boxes. Brochure.

Hiles Plating Company, Inc., 2028 Broadway, Kansas City, MO 64108, 816-421-6450, Mon.–Fri. 9:00 A.M.–5:00 P.M. Restoration of antique sterling silver, silver plate, pewter, copper, and brass. Parts supplied. Plating of silver, gold, copper, nickel, and brass. Repairs on weighted sterling. Price list available.

Institute of Metal Repair, 1558 S. Redwood, Escondido, CA 92025, 619-432-8942. Silver plating. Repair, restoration, and consultation on flatware, hollowware, and metal art objects.

Jeffrey Herman, PO Box 3599, Cranston, RI 02910, 401-461-3156; fax: 401-461-3196. Restoration, conservation, and refinishing of sterling and pewter hollowware and flatware. Dents and monograms removed, disposal-damaged flatware refurbished, silver soldering, rebuilding, knife blades installed, etc. Hand finishing a specialty. Price list and museum references available.

Jerry Propst, PO Box 45, Janesville, WI 53547-0045, 608-752-2816. Repairs silver-back hair brushes. Repair or replacement of hair, military, cloth, hat, infant hair, or infant military brush pads. Combs, buffs, whisks, mirrors, files, and shaving brushes. Remounting and polishing; dents removed. Send SASE for list.

Michael J. Dotzel & Son, 402 East 63rd St., New York, NY 10021, 212-838-2890, 8:00 A.M.–4:00 P.M. Silver plating.

Michael's Art Restoration Studio, Michael Scheglov, 8312 Eighth NW, Seattle, WA 98117,

206-789-2900, 11:00 A.M.–5:00 P.M.; fax: 206-778-6963. Restoration of silver art objects.

MidweSterling Flatware, Thomas J. Ridley, 4311 NE Vivion Rd., Kansas City, MO 64119-2890, 816-454-1990; fax: 816-454-1605. Sterling silver flatware repaired, garbage disposal damage fixed, knife blades replaced, professional polishing.

New England Country Silver, Inc., PO Box 271, 23 Smith Rd., East Haddam, CT 06423, 203-873-1314, 9:00 A.M.–3:00 P.M. Complete restoration service for silver plate, sterling silver, copper, brass, and pewter. New parts made. New knife blades, combs, brushes, and mirrors. Silver, gold, and copper plating. Engraving. Send merchandise insured mail or UPS. Free estimates.

New Orleans Silversmiths, 600 Chartres St., New Orleans, LA 70130, 504-522-8333, 9:30 A.M.–4:30 P.M. Repair and replating of sterling and silver plate. Replacement blades, handles, insulators, and other parts.

Oexning Silversmiths, 800 N. Washington Ave., Suite 118, Minneapolis, MN 55401, 612-332-6857, 8:00 A.M.–5:00 P.M., 800-332-6857 outside Minnesota. Antique and contemporary silver plating and repair. Sterling repair and refinishing. Pewter, brass, and copper refinishing; copper plating, gold plating. Dent removal. Missing parts cast, including feet, handles, and ornate work. New brushes and combs; steel blades, meat forks, knife sharpeners, nail sets, and letter openers. New insulators for coffee sets. Can repair or replate musical instrument mouthpieces and church altar ware.

Old China Patterns Limited, 1560 Brimley Rd., Scarborough, ON, Canada M1P 3G9, 416-299-8880; fax: 416-299-4721. Flannel cotton storage pouches for silverware. Custom sizes available.

Orum Silver Company, PO Box 805, 51 S. Vine St., Meriden, CT 06450, 203-237-3037, Mon.–Thurs. 8:00 A.M.–4:30 P.M., Fri. 8:00 A.M.–1:00 P.M. Repairing, refinishing, and replating of old silver and antiques. Pewter, brass, copper, bronze, and aluminum cleaned, buffed, polished, restored, and refinished. Gold, silver, nickel, copper, and brass plating. Parts made and fabricated. Clear coat lacquering.

Pairpoint Crystal Co., 851 Sandwich Rd., PO Box 515, Sagamore, MA 02561, 800-899-0953, 508-888-2344, Mon.–Fri. 8:30 A.M.–6:00 P.M.; fax: 508-888-3537. Handcrafted full lead crystal liners for silver salts, vases, and more. Cobalt, amethyst, and ruby. Custom work available. Call for details. Will ship anywhere in the U.S. Reproduction catalog $4.

Peninsula Plating Works, 232 Homer Ave., Palo Alto, CA 94301, 415-326-7825, 8:30 A.M.–5:00 P.M.; fax: 415-322-7392. Repair, polishing, and replating of silver hollowware.

Peter's Antiques, 4113 Oechsli Ave., Louisville, KY 40207, 502-893-8498, business; 502-458-8498, residence. Silver repaired and replated.

R & K Weenike Antiques, Roy H. Weenike, Rt. 7, Box 140, Ottumwa, IA 52501, 515-934-5427. Silver plated frames repaired.

Restoration & Design Studio, Paul Karner, 249 E. 77th St., New York, NY 10021, 212-517-9742, Mon., Tues., Thurs., Fri. 10:00 A.M.–5:00 P.M., Wed. 1:00 P.M.–5:00 P.M. Repair and restoration of silver, silver plate, brass, bronze, copper, pewter, and other metals. Silver, gold, nickel, chrome, and brass plating and polishing. Silver soldering. Flatware blades replaced, missing parts reproduced. Ivory insulators for tea or coffee pots.

Thome Silversmiths, 49 W. 37th St., Suite 605, New York, NY 10018, 212-764-5426, 8:30 A.M.–1:00 P.M., 2:30 P.M.–5:30 P.M. Restoration of silver; silver plating, polishing, and engraving. New velvet backs for picture frames; velvet liners for boxes.

Vroman's Silver Shop, 442A Fleetwood Place, Glendora, CA 91740, 818-824-5174, Tues.–Fri. 9:30 A.M.–5:00 P.M., Sat. 10:00 A.M.–2:00 P.M.; fax: 818-963-1402. Silver restoration, including replating and knife reblading. Mail order worldwide.

Pieces for restoration should be sent well wrapped and insured. Matching service. Send SASE and pattern name for list.

Walter Drake Silver Exchange, Drake Building, Colorado Springs, CO 80915-9988, 800-525-9291, 7:30 A.M.–5:00 P.M. Sterling silver flatware repaired. Machine buffing and polishing, dents and monograms removed, knife blades replaced.

WTC Associates, Inc., 2532 Regency Rd., Lexington, KY 40503, 800-535-4513, 10:00 A.M.–5:30 P.M.; fax: 606-277-5720. Silver plating, sterling repairs, missing parts reproduced. Brass, copper, nickel, and gold plating. Work on pot metal.

Smoking Collectibles

*T*obacco, like beer, seems to be a popular collecting area for men. Anything that has a picture of tobacco or that has held tobacco has a market. Labels, ads, tobacco cards, felts, tins, pipes, tags, and other smoking memorabilia sell well to general antiques dealers or in any of the usual ways one sells antiques. (Look in the sections on Advertising and Labels for some special suggestions.) A large collection of tobacco-related material might do well at auction. A small collection could be sold quickly at flea markets and shows.

A nonsmoker is amazed that old pipes sell for high prices to men who want to use them or display them. Lighters, cigar clippers, tobacco stamps, and cigar and cigarette cases are wanted for use and display. Only ashtrays seem unpopular. Prices can be found in the general price books. These are items that also sell well to friends who are smokers.

Cigarette and cigar lighters have been made since the late nineteenth century, but collectors search for the unusual pocket lighters made since the 1940s and the large electric-spark or kerosene cigar lighters that were kept on the store counter. The store lighters should be sold to those interested in advertising and country store materials. (See section on Advertising.)

Remember those silver-plated Ronson lighters that everyone received as a wedding gift in the 1950s? They were unsalable until about 1985, when the fifties room was being revived by avant-garde collectors, and the lighter was needed as a table ornament. Now all types of figural lighters are in demand. The bartender-behind-the-bar lighter of the 1930s, the Coca-Cola bottle lighter of the 1950s, or the dueling-pistol lighter of the 1960s all sell well. Any lighter with an ad or an unusual shape will usually sell to a collector or flea market dealer. This is an international market with many buyers from Europe and Japan.

The common urn-shaped Ronson table lighters do not sell well because there are so many of them. Silver and gold pocket lighters, some with precious jewels, should be sold like jewelry. Look for RONSON, figurals, the Kool cigarettes' plastic penguin, and large, figural, cigar-store lighters.

REPAIR

It is now possible to have old lighters repaired. Matchbooks should be stored in scrapbooks, but first carefully remove the staple and the matches. The staple may rust and the matches are a fire hazard. Pipes can be restored by any dealer in modern pipes. You will probably want a new, unused stem if you plan to smoke the pipe.

Price Books

Cigarette Card Values, Martin Murray (Imperial Collections International, PO Box 10814, Lynchburg, VA 24506, © 1994). Value in British pounds.

Collecting Cigarette Lighters, A Price Guide, Neil S. Wood (L-W Books, PO Box 69, Gas City, IN 46933, © 1994).

The Matchcover Collector's Price Guide, Bill Retskin (American Matchcover Collecting Club, PO Box 18481, Asheville, NC 28814-0481, © 1993).

Official Price Guide of Cigar Label Art, edited by Nancy French (American Antique Graphics Society Press, PO Box 66, Sharon Center, OH 44274, © 1992).

Ronson Wick Lighters 1913–1966, Urban K. Cummings (Bird Dog Books, PO Box 1482, Palo Alto, CA 94302, © 1992).

Smoking Collectibles, A Price Guide, Neil Wood (L-W Book Sales, Gas City, IN, © 1994).

Clubs & Publications

American Matchcover Collecting Club, *Front Striker Bulletin* (NL), PO Box 18481, Asheville, NC 28814 (matchcovers).

Ashtray Collectors Club, *Ashtray Journal* (NL), PO Box 11652, Houston, TX 77293.

Cartophilic Society of Great Britain, *Cartophilic Notes & News* (NL), 116 Hillview Rd., Ensbury Park, Bournemouth, Dorset, England, BH10 5BJ (cigarette cards).

Cigar Label Collectors International, *Stone-Press* (NL), 14761 Pearl Rd. #154, Strongsville, OH 44136.

Cigarette Pack Collectors Association, *Brandstand* (NL), 61 Searle St., Georgetown, MA 01833.

Clay Pipe Collectors Circle, CPCC-International Newsletter/Catalog (NL), c/o Mr. Piet J. G. Tengnagel, NL-1200 BH Hilversum, The Netherlands. Subscription fee deducted from purchase.

International Seal, Label & Cigar Band Society, *International Seal, Label & Cigar Band Society News Bulletin* (NL), 8915 E. Bellevue St., Tucson, AZ 85715.

Long Beach Matchcover Club, *Matchcover Beachcomber* (NL), 2501 W. Sunflower, H-5, Santa Ana, CA 92704.

On the LIGHTER Side, International Lighter Collectors, *On the LIGHTER Side* (NL), 136 Circle Dr., Quitman, TX 75783 (lighters).

Pipe Collectors International, *Tobak News and Views* (NL), 1715 Promenade Ctr., Richardson, TX 75080.

Pocket Lighter Preservation Guild, *Flint & Flame* (NL), 11220 W. Florissant, Suite 400, Florissant, MO 63033.

Rathkamp Matchcover Society, *R.M.S. Bulletin* (NL), 25 Huntsman's Horn, Dept. KA, The Woodlands, TX 77380-0938.

Society of Tobacco Jar Collectors, *Tobacco Jar Newsletter* (NL), 3011 Falstaff Rd., #307, Baltimore, MD 21209.

Universal Coterie of Pipe Smokers, *Pipe Smoker's Ephemeris* (NL), 20-37 120th St., College Point, NY 11356-2128.

Windy City Matchcover Club, *Windy City Matchcover News* (NL), 3104 W. Fargo Ave., Chicago, IL 60645-1110. (Meetings include auctions. Send LSASE for information and free leaflet, *So What Are They Worth?/So What Have They Sold For?*)

Card Times (MAG), 70 Winifred Ln., Aughton, Ormskirk, Lancashire, U.K. L39 5DL (cigarette cards, trading cards, sports and non-sports cards, phone cards, printed ephemera, etc.).

Cigarette Card News & Trade Card Chronicle (NL), London Cigarette Card Co. Ltd., Sutton Rd., Somerton, Somerset, England TA11 6QP.

Tobacco Antiques & Collectibles Market (NL), Chuck Thompson, Box 11652, Houston, TX 77293 (buy-sell-trade ads for tobacco-related collectibles).

Repairs, Parts & Supplies

Authorized Repair Service, 30 W. 57th St., New York, NY 10019, 212-586-0947, Mon.–Fri. 9:00 A.M.–5:00 P.M.; fax: 212-586-1296. Restoration of antique cigarette lighters, specializing in lighters from manufacturers no longer in business. Obsolete parts in stock. No charge for estimate of repairs.

Von Erck's Pipe & Repair, PO Box 425, 259 Kawbawgam Rd., Marquette, MI 49855, 906-249-1567, 8:00 A.M.–5:00 P.M. Pipe repair.

Sports Collectibles

*B*aseball cards and other sports cards have been collected since they were first distributed in the 1880s. The first cards were placed in packs of cigarettes or tobacco as free advertising promotion pieces. From 1910 to 1915 the cards were made by the millions; then only a few were made until the 1930s. The second period of baseball cards came with their use by candy and gum companies. The modern baseball card really started in 1933 with the Goudey Gum Company. World War II caused paper shortages and baseball cards were not made. In 1948 the Bowman and Leaf companies made cards. Topps Gum Company cards were introduced in 1951.

Baseball cards are the favorites of collectors, but there are cards for other sports such as hockey or basketball. Value is determined by condition, rarity, and the popularity of the player pictured. Collectors also save gum wrappers, Dixie cup lids, and other paper items that picture sports stars. They even save the empty boxes that held the gum packs in the store.

There are special shows and publications for sports card collectors. Most major cities have card shows on a regular basis. Ask anyone you see selling cards where the nearest shows will be held. They are often not announced in general publications.

There are many price books and publications for collectors. Most are available in public libraries and bookstores because baseball card collecting is a popular pastime for millions. Our son first entered the world of collecting when he was in second grade. He started saving baseball cards. His cards were traded, carried in a cramped pocket, "flipped" in a then-popular game, and finally stored in a shoebox. When one of his friends moved to Australia, he was given the treasure trove of baseball cards that belonged to the friend and his older brothers. A few years ago we rediscovered the cards, which had been stored in our attic. Many are rare, but they are all in poor condition with scuffed pictures and ragged edges, and their value is low.

Sort your cards by date and manufacturer. Match up the sets and put the cards in numerical order. Look at a current price book from your bookstore or library, and make a list of the cards you own and their approximate value. Always consider the condition when pricing a card. Note which sets are complete. Watch for error cards. The price books will comment on these. If you find a card that does not seem to be in the price book, look again. You may be looking in the gum card section and have cards that came with breakfast cereal.

There are several strange pricing truths. The earlier in a player's career the card was printed, the more it is worth. That means the rookie cards for famous players are high priced. Cards sell for more on the two coasts than in the middle of the country (so do many other collectibles). Cards sell best near the hometown of the team or player. Cards were numbered as they were printed, the high numbers released late in the season. Although for most antiques the lowest or earliest numbers are most wanted, for baseball cards it is the opposite. The high numbers bring the highest prices. This is because there were usually fewer of the high-numbered cards. Another odd pricing fact: if you add the price book prices for each card in a set, the total is less than the listed price for the complete set. This is probably because buyers are more interested in completing a set than in buying a full one. Buyers will pay extra for a single card if they need it. Take your list to a local baseball card show. They are easy to find in all parts of the country. If you can't find one, check the ads that can be found in the publications listed here.

Talk to the dealers. Show your inventory list and the cards. Be careful not to give a box of cards to a dealer and offer to sell a part of them. Hold out for an offer for all of them unless you want to set up your own booth to sell the collection individually.

Good cards sell quickly. The others are worth very little and can be difficult to sell. Remember that a dealer is trying to sell and not just buy at a show. The rules of etiquette say you must never try to start selling your items to a busy dealer. Don't interrupt any ongoing conversations in a booth—wait until the dealer is free. You will find that stories spread quickly, and dealers and collectors will soon look for you and the possible treasure that might be in your baseball card collection. Expect to get less than half the price book value for a card, and remember to judge the condition accurately. If you are unsure, examine other cards. Never throw out a baseball card. Give it to a young friend.

Anything that looks like a baseball card or pictures a ballplayer or sports figure has a value. This includes cigarette cards (often from England), as well as small felt or silk pictures of players, candy boxes, bread wrappers, labels, plastic cups with a player and an ad, ads cut from comic pages and many other items. Some of these strange collectibles sell for good prices, over $100 for the right empty box, over $500 for a cardboard sign advertising a cigarette and picturing a ballplayer. Most of the cards sell for under $2 each, but a box of hundreds has enough value to make it worth the effort. The dream of every collector is to find an old box with the fabled Honus Wagner card. (But be careful about finding the card of your dreams; the Wagner card has been faked in recent years.)

SPORTS OTHER THAN BASEBALL

Don't overlook the other sports-related items. Football, golf, tennis, Olympic events, soccer, and many other sports have serious collecting fans. Anything that pictures a sports activity, is used to play a sport (golf clubs or tennis rackets), is associated with an important player or winning team (photos, autographed footballs, Olympic medals, programs), or even uniforms, children's games, and toys are wanted by the right collector. The baseball enthusiasts gather at the baseball card shows. Football cards and other sports cards can also be found there. The specialty auction offering sports items developed in the 1980s. There are sales that include wooden-handled golf clubs, odd-shaped gut-strung tennis rackets, and even cricket bats. They also include boxing gloves, dishes picturing sports, figural whiskey bottles that are sports related, and oddities like nodding dolls with team logos, or plastic figurines of players. Some of these auctions are advertised in the general antiques publications, while some are part of the auction schedule of the major auction galleries. Ask a collector of any of the sports materials to suggest how to find these auctions. Every item offered for sale belonged to someone like you who wanted cash instead of an old football. Other potential buyers of sports memorabilia are local sports enthusiasts and members of the sports-related collecting clubs.

Don't forget the importance of college sports. The pennants, programs, and souvenirs are cherished by many alumni. Talk to the university librarian or coaches to see if they have any sort of sports trophy display. One family found their father's autographed baseball from a 1914 university team. Instead of including it in the house sale after his death, they gave it to the school sports department. It is displayed in the case with an appropriate tag mentioning their father, the winning pitcher. They also got a tax deduction for the estate.

REPAIR

Cards should be stored so that they will be dirt and insect free. Plastic holders made to hold the cards are sold through shows and publications. Little can be done to restore cards, except for dusting or a simple cleaning with an art-gum eraser. Very rare cards can be restored by a conservation expert, but this is expensive. Condition is very important in determining price. Bent corners might be ironed straight; use a cool iron and protect the card with a thin piece of fabric.

If you want to fix a tennis racket, see a pro at a tennis shop. You may have trouble getting old materials such as gut for stringing, but it can be done.

See section on Paper.

Repair sources for decoys may be found in the Folk Art section.

Price Books

Baseball Card Price Guide 1995, Allan Kaye and Michael McKeever (Avon Books, New York, © 1994).

Boxing Memorabilia, Bill Cayton and Robert Obojski (Sterling, New York, © 1992).

Collectible Golfing Novelties, Beverly Robb (Schiffer, Atglen, PA, © 1992).

The Complete Guide to Baseball Memorabilia, Mark K. Larson (Krause Publications, Iola, WI, © 1992).

The Confident Collector: Baseball Card Price Guide 1995, Allan Kaye and Michael McKeever (Avon Books, New York, © 1994).

The Confident Collector: Basketball Card Price Guide 1995, Allan Kaye and Michael McKeever (Avon Books, New York, © 1994).

The Confident Collector: Football Card Price Guide 1995, Allan Kaye and Michael McKeever (Avon Books, New York, © 1994).

The Confident Collector: Hockey Card Price Guide 1995, Allan Kaye and Michael McKeever (Avon Books, New York, © 1994).

Florence's Standard Baseball Card Price Guide, 6th edition, Gene Florence (Collector Books, Paducah, KY, © 1994).

Golf Antiques & Other Treasures of the Game, John M. Olman and Morton W. Olman (Market Street Press, 325 W. Fifth St., Cincinnati, OH 45202, © 1993).

Hager's Comprehensive Price Guide to Rare Baseball Cards: 1886 to Present, Alan Hager (AHG Inc., PO Box 245, Norfolk, CT 06058, © 1993).

The 1994 Sanders Price Guide to Sports Autographs, George Sanders, Helen Sanders, and Ralph Roberts (Scott Publishing, 911 Vandemark Rd., Sidney, OH 45365, © 1993).

Official 1995 Price Guide to Baseball Cards, Dr. James Beckett (House of Collectibles, New York, © 1994).

Official 1994 Price Guide to Basketball Cards, 3rd edition, Dr. James Beckett (House of Collectibles, New York, © 1993).

Official Price Guide: Football Cards, 12th edition, James Beckett (House of Collectibles, New York, © 1992).

Official Price Guide: Hockey Cards, 2nd edition, James Beckett (House of Collectibles, New York, © 1992).

Sanchez Third Annual Basketball Card Price Guide 1993, Greg and Virginia Sanchez (PO Box 5419, 2216 Bernina, Frazier Park, CA 93222, © 1993).

Sport Americana Price Guide to the Non-Sports Cards, No. 4, Christopher Benjamin (Edgewater Book Co., PO Box 40238, Cleveland, OH 44140, © 1992).

Sports Collectors Digest Baseball Card Price Guide, annual (Krause, Iola, WI)

Sports Collectors Digest Football, Basketball & Hockey Price Guide, 2nd edition (Krause, Iola, WI, © 1994).

Vintage Baseball Glove Pocket Price Guide, Dave Bushing and Joe Phillips (The Glove Collector, 14057 Rolling Hills Ln., Dallas, TX 75240-3807, © 1994).

Clubs & Publications

American Fish Decoy Association, *American Fish Decoy Forum* (NL), 624 Merritt, Fife Lake, MI 49633.

Antique Snowmobile Club of America, *Iron Dog Tracks* (NL), 1804 Hall St., Redgranite, WI 54970.

Callmakers & Collectors Association of America, *National Callmakers & Collectors Newsletter* (NL), 303 Murfreesboro Rd., Nashville, TN 37210.

Collector's Edge Collector Club, *Leading Edge* (NL), PO Box 9010, Denver, CO 80209-0010 (limited edition "durable" sports cards).

Ducks Unlimited, Inc., *Ducks Unlimited Magazine* (MAG), One Waterfowl Way, Memphis, TN 38120.

Golf Club Collectors Association, *Golf Club Collectors Association* (NL), 640 E. Liberty St., Girard, OH 44420-2308.

Golf Collectors' Society, *Bulletin* (NL), PO Box 20546, Dayton, OH 45420.

Great Lakes Fish Decoy Collectors & Carvers Association, *Thru the Shanty Hole* (NL), 35824 W. Chicago, Livonia, MI 48150.

National Fishing Lure Collectors Club, *N.F.L.C.C. Gazette* (MAG), PO Box 619, Honor, MI 49640.

National Rifle Association of America, *American Rifleman* (MAG), 11250 Waples Mill Rd., Fairfax, VA 22030.

The 1996 Olympic Games Pin Society, *Pin Points* (NL), PO Box 4496, Maple Plain, MN 55592-4496. 800-PINS-4-96.

North American Trap Collectors Association, *Traps* (NL), PO Box 94, Galloway, OH 43119.

Old Reel Collectors Association, *Old Reel Collectors Association Newsletter* (NL), c/o Edwin

E. Corwin, 200 St. Rd. 206 E., St. Augustine, FL 32086 (old fishing reels).

Olympin Collector's Club, *Olympin Collector's Club Newsletter* (NL), 1386 Fifth St., Schenectady, NY 12303.

Tennis Collectors, *Tennis Collector* (MAG), Guildhall, Great Bromley, Colchester, Essex England CO7 7TU.

Vintage Snowmobile Club of America, *Vintage Snowmobiler* (NL), PO Box 1111, Concord, MA 01742.

Baseball Card Investment Report (NL), PO Box 3745, Dana Point, CA 92629 (baseball, basketball, football, and hockey cards).

Beckett Baseball Card Monthly (MAG), *Beckett Basketball Monthly* (MAG), *Beckett Focus on Future Stars* (MAG), *Beckett Football Card Monthly* (MAG), *Beckett Hockey Monthly* (MAG), 15850 Dallas Parkway, Dallas, TX 75248. (*Future Stars* features minor league and college athletes.)

Bill Nelson Newsletter (NL), PO Box 41630, Tucson, AZ 85717-1630 (Olympic pins, sports items; trivia and treasures).

Black Ball News: The Journal of Negro Leagues Baseball History (MAG), PO Box 160591, Nashville, TN 37216-0591.

Bobby Mintz's Rookie Report (NL), 4615 Southwest Freeway, Suite 950, Houston, TX 77027.

Boxing Collector's News (NL), 3316 Luallen Dr., Carrollton, TX 75007.

Canadian Sports Card News (NP), 103 Lakeshore Rd., Suite 202, St. Catharines, ON, Canada L2N 2T6.

Card & Comic Trader (MAG) 410 Ware Blvd., Suite 406, Tampa, FL, 33619 (free publication distributed at Florida card and comic shows).

Card Times (MAG), 70 Winifred Ln., Aughton, Ormskirk, Lancashire, U.K. L39 5DL (cigarette cards, trading cards, sports and non-sports cards, phone cards, printed ephemera, etc.).

Collector's Sportslook, 151 Wells Ave., Congers, NY 10920.

Decoy Hunter Magazine (MAG), 901 N. 9th St., Clinton, IN 47842.

Decoy Magazine (MAG), PO Box 277, Burtonsville, MD 20866.

The Diamond (MAG), PO Box 8396, Scottsdale, AZ 85252-8396.

Diamond Duds (NL), PO Box 10153, Silver Spring, MD 20904-0153.

Fistic Fever: The Boxing Memorabilia Magazine (MAG), PO Box 24111, Oakland, CA 94623-1111.

Global Golflore (NP), PO Drawer 1209, West Fork, AR 72774.

Glove Collector Newsletter (NL), 14057 Rolling Hills Ln., Dallas, TX 75240-3807 (baseball gloves).

Kovels Sports Collectibles (NL), PO Box 420026, Palm Coast, FL 32142-0026.

Legends Sports Memorabilia (MAG), 15801 Graham St., Huntington Beach, CA 92649.

Low and Inside (MAG), PO Box 290228, Minneapolis, MN 55429.

Malloy's Sports Cards and Collectibles (MAG), PO Box 569, Ridgefield, CT 06877.

On Target! The Newsletter for Collectors of Target Balls (NL), 20135 Evergreen Meadows, Southfield, MI 48076-4222.

Right on Schedules (NL), 204 N. Charro Ave., Thousand Oaks, CA 91320 (sports schedules).

Sked Notebook (NL), 8 Fillmore Pl., Lawrenceville, NJ 08648 (sports schedules).

Sporting Collector's Monthly (NL), PO Box 305, Camden, DE 19934.

Sports Card Price Guide Monthly (MAG), 700 E. State St., Iola, WI 54990.

Sports Card Trader (MAG), PO Box 360, Mt. Morris, IL 61054-0360.

Sports Cards (MAG), 700 E. State St., Iola, WI 54990.

Sports Collectors Digest (NP), 700 E. State St., Iola, WI 54990.

Stadium Newsletter (NL), 213 Lilac St., Elburn, IL 60119.

Trading Cards (MAG), PO Box 341, Mt. Morris, IL 61054-9840.

Tuff Stuff (MAG), PO Box 1637, Glen Allen, VA 23060 (baseball, basketball, football, and hockey cards and memorabilia).

USA Today Baseball Weekly (NP), PO Box 4500, Silver Spring, MD 20914.

Repairs, Parts & Supplies

G. Schoepfer Inc., 138 W. 31st St., New York, NY 10001, 203-250-7794, 9:00 A.M.–5:00 P.M.; fax: 203-250-7796. Glass and plastic eyes for decoys.

Graphic Conservation Co., 329 W. 18th St., Suite 701, Chicago, IL 60616, 312-738-2657, Mon.–Fri. 9:00 A.M.–noon, 1:00 P.M.–5:00 P.M.; fax: 312-738-3125. Conservation of works of art on paper, including sports cards and memorabilia. Dry cleaning, stain reduction, flattening, deacidification, inpainting, and tear repairs and fills. Proposal and examination fee $15 and up.

Lin Terry, 59 E. Madison Ave., Dumont, NJ 07628, 201-385-4706; fax: 201-385-0306. Baseball card binders, acrylic cases, pennant covers, custom cases for displaying sports collectibles, and books.

Northeast Document Conservation Center, 100 Brickstone Sq., Andover, MA 01810-1494, 508-470-1010; fax: 508-475-6021. Nonprofit regional conservation center specializing in treatment of art and artifacts on paper, including baseball cards. Preservation microfilming, preservation planning surveys, disaster assistance, technical leaflets. Brochure.

Restorations, PO Box 2000, 323 Clay St., Nevada City, CA 95959, 800-959-5309. Restoration supplies for repairing baseball cards. Baseball card corner repair kit, ink sets, stain removal system, video on how to restore baseball cards. Mylar bags. Brochure.

Russell Norton, PO Box 1070, New Haven, CT 06504-1070, 203-562-7800, 11:00 A.M.–8:00 P.M., daily. Archival polypropylene sleeves for baseball cards and other collectibles. Send SASE for sample.

Seitz and Co., 1772 Selby Ave., St. Paul, MN 55104-6030, 612-646-3659. Stadium box seat chairs refinished. Touch-up kits, stands, and felt pads.

Wood 'n Wildlife, 9922 Bostwick Park Rd., Montrose, CO 81401, 303-249-5863, before 9:00 P.M. Restoration of decoys and other objects. Send SASE for more information.

Video

Baseball Card Restoration Video Training Program, **Restorations,** PO Box 2000, 323 Clay St., Nevada City, CA 95959, 800-959-5309. Complete restoration techniques for baseball cards. 60 minutes, $65.

Computer Program

Baseball Checklist, **Noodleware Software Co.,** PO Box 83, Lindenhurst, NY 11757-0083, 516-321-9776, Mon.–Fri. 10:00 A.M.–6:00 P.M. Baseball card inventory program for IBM compatibles, manages unlimited number of items. DOS 2.1 or greater, 3.5-in. disk. Hard drive required. Manual included.

Stamps & Related Material

*T*here have been stamp collectors since 1840, when the first postage stamp was intro- duced by Sir Rowland Hill of England. It is a very specialized field. Stamps should be examined by a dealer in stamps or an auction house that knows that market. A large, serious collection requires an expert.

Condition, rarity, and demand determine the prices. A stamp should have its original bright color, a centered design, and wide margins. There should be no defects, full gum on the back, no hinge marks, and only a light, clear cancellation mark if used. It should have no tears, dirt, creases, pinholes, or uneven perforations. The average child's collection is rarely very valuable, but it should always be checked.

The post office sells corner blocks of stamps to collectors every day. These have been put away as an investment by many casual collectors who have little understanding of the market. Most of the blocks under thirty years old only sell for their face value or less. Check with a stamp dealer. If they have no value to collectors, then use them on letters. Many sheets of commemoratives are equally unsalable for more than the face value. If you have blocks or sheets or sets of stamps, be sure you determine the value before you split them up or use them.

Don't ignore the stamps on old postcards and letters. Even printed stamps on postal cards could give extra value to the card. First-day covers have a special value, and the stamp should not be removed. The cover is printed with a special drawing and is used the first day of issue of the stamp. Sell the entire envelope. Envelopes with stamps post-marked before 1900 should be checked for value. Those dating from before the Civil War should be appraised by an expert. Letters mailed without stamps for special reasons (during the Civil War) can be very valuable. Never remove a stamp from an envelope to sell it. Sell the envelope and stamp together.

Dealers are listed in the Yellow Pages of the telephone book. Clubs and publications are listed below. The best way to value or to sell stamps is with the help of experts. You may want a formal appraisal before you decide whether the collection should be auctioned or sold to a dealer. It is rarely a good idea to break up a collection and sell the stamps yourself unless you are a serious collector who has purchased through clubs and shows. The stamps are too small and too fragile to be handled over and over.

Sometimes the stamp is more valuable as part of a "cover" (the special stamped envelope). Unusual cancellation marks, postal marks, written information, handstamps, or decorations on the envelope make a cover valuable. First-day covers should always be left intact.

REPAIR AND STORAGE

Stamp collectors know that condition and storage are important considerations. Most stamps are kept in albums and mounted with either hinges or mounts. Never tape or glue a stamp into an album. Inexpensive or used stamps may be "hinged" using the special stamp hinges made with gum that will not harm the stamps. High-priced and mint, unused stamps should be mounted with stamp mounts, small corners that hold the stamp in place. Hinges, mounts, and albums can be found at your local stamp stores or though the mail-order companies listed in stamp publications.

Sometimes you will want to soak a stamp off an envelope. If the envelope is colored or there is ink writing or heavy postmarks, you must test to be sure nothing will fade or run. Brightly colored envelopes from Christmas cards should not be soaked; the color could run and ruin the stamps. Soak white envelopes with stamps in a large dish of warm (room-temperature), not hot, water. Stir gently. The stamps will float away from the paper. Sometimes a drop of detergent should be added to the water. Gently rub the back of the stamp with your fingers to remove any remaining glue.

Never leave a stamp in the water for more than an hour. Dry the stamps on white absorbent paper, newspaper, or terry-cloth towels. When almost dry, press the stamps flat under a heavy weight or place them in a drying book made of blotters. Let the stamps dry at least four days before you mount them as part of your collection.

There are products that remove marks from tape or adhesives, ink, grease, and other disfiguring blotches. There are also experts who restore stamps, but only rare and valuable stamps make the expenditure worthwhile.

Store stamps in a dry, not too warm place, out of direct sunlight. Do not remove the selvage edge around a mint or used stamp. Especially important is a selvage with plate numbers and markings. Don't tear stamp groups apart. Blocks and sets are collected in a different way than single stamps. Check your local library for books on stamps. Many contain information on care and conservation.

Price Books

Specialized Catalogue of U.S. Stamps, annual (Scott Publishing Co., Sidney, OH).

Standard Postage Stamp Catalogue, annual (Scott Publishing Co., Sidney, OH).

Clubs & Publications

Aerophilatelic Federation of the Americas, *Jack Knight Air Log & AFA News* (MAG), PO Box 1239,

Elgin, IL 60121-1239. (There are several specialty groups, some of which are the Amelia Earhart Collectors Club, Charles A. Lindbergh Collectors Club, Jack Knight Air Mail Society, and the Zeppelin Collectors Club.)

American Philatelic Society, *American Philatelist* (MAG), PO Box 8000, State College, PA 16803-8000.

American Topical Association, *Topical Time* (MAG), PO Box 630, Johnstown, PA 15907-0630.

Bureau Issues Association, *United States Specialist* (MAG), PO Box 23707, Belleville, IL 62223.

Carto-Philatelists, *Carto-Philatelist* (MAG), L.W. Kent, Treasurer, 1171 Main St., Leominster, MA 01453-1765 (maps on stamps).

Christmas Philatelic Club, *Yule Log* (NL), 6900 W. Quincy Ave., 9E, Littleton, CO 80123.

Collectors of Religion on Stamps Society, *COROS Chronicle* (MAG), 425 N. Linwood Ave., #110, Appleton, WI 54914-3433.

Confederate Stamp Alliance, *Confederate Philatelist* (MAG), *Alliance Bulletin* (NL), PO Box 1816, Kernersville, NC 27285.

Dogs on Stamps Study Unit, *DOSSU Journal* (NL), 3208 Hana Rd., Edison, NJ 08817-2552.

Junior Philatelists of America, *Philatelic Observer* (NL), PO Box 850, Boalsburg, PA 16827-0850 (information on stamp collecting for young people).

Korea Stamp Society, Inc., *Korean Philately* (NL), PO Box 15306, Columbus, OH 43215.

Liechtenstudy USA, *Liechtenstudy* (NL), 100 Elizabeth St. #112, Duluth, MN 55803.

Post Mark Collectors Club, *PMCC Bulletin* (NL), 23381 Greenleaf Blvd., Elkhart, IN 46514-4504.

Society of Philatelists and Numismatists (SPAN), *Ex-SPAN-sion* (NL), 1929 Millis St., Montebello, CA 90640-4533 (specializing in philatelic-numismatic combinations).

Tonga/Tin Can Mail Study Circle, *Tin Canner* (NL), 36975 S. Highway 213, Mount Angel, OR 97362.

Universal Ship Cancellation Society, *USCS Log* (MAG), 14416 Lake Winds Way, Gaithersburg, MD 20878.

Canadian Stamp News (NP), 103 Lakeshore Rd., Suite 202, St. Catharines, ON, Canada L2N 2T6.

Linn's Stamp News (NP), PO Box 29, Sidney, OH 45365.

Mekeel's Weekly Stamp News (NP), Box 5050, White Plains, NY 10602.

Scott Stamp Monthly (MAG), PO Box 828, Sidney, OH 45365.

Stamp Collector (NP), Box 10, Albany, OR 97321.

Stamp Wholesaler (NP), Box 706, Albany, OR 97321.

Stocks & Bonds

*I*t seems that everyone who survived the stock market crash of 1929 had some stocks or bonds that, although worthless, were saved. Today there are two possible values for these old stocks. A few might have value due to a merger or acquisition. The worthless company or mine may have merged, been sold, found gold, or become part of a valuable company in some other way. To learn if you own stocks or bonds of value, first try your library. Look in *The Directory of Obsolete Securities* (Financial Information, Inc.), *The Capital Changes Reporter* (Commerce Clearing

House), or even try tracking mergers through the *Standard & Poor's* or *Moody's* directories. It is also possible to find a company that will research your stock for a fee.

If your stocks have no value as part of a company, they still have a value for collectors who specialize in the scripophily market. (That's the formal name for the collecting of stocks and bonds.) Old certificates were decorated with elaborately engraved vignettes. Some were fanciful pictures of Liberty or other symbols, some pictured the industry with oil wells or smokestacks, while others were a combination of these. These certificates are sometimes framed and sold as gifts to collectors. For example, a picture of an oil well may intrigue a car collector. Railroads, mines, airplanes, and automobiles are favored. If the certificate is signed by a famous person, such as Thomas Edison or John D. Rockefeller, the price is higher. Some certificates have revenue stamps, and rare ones are purchased by stamp collectors.

Condition is always important; clean, crisp certificates are worth more than creased, worn examples. Hole-punched cancel marks lower the value. Other fiscal paper, such as mortgages, checks, and legal documents, may also have value. (See Paper Collectibles & Ephemera section.)

REPAIR

Take care of your stocks and bonds like other paper items. Never use glue or tape to mount the paper unless you feel the item is of minimal value. Old stock certificates used to paper walls can rarely be removed and sold. See Paper Collectibles & Ephemera.

Club & Publications

Bond & Share Society, Bond & Share Society Newsletter (NL), c/o R.M. Smythe & Co., Inc., 26 Broadway, Suite 271, New York, NY 10004.

Friends of Financial History (MAG), Museum of American Financial History, 26 Broadway, New York, NY 10004-1763 (stocks and bonds).

Research

Annual Reports Library, PO Box 2006, San Francisco, CA 99133, 415-956-8665, 10:00 A.M.–4:00 P.M.; fax: 415-421-2544. Corporate reports from all types of firms, including nonprofits, banks, foundations, partnerships, and governments. The library currently has reports dating from 1968 to 1994. There is a charge for information based on time required and materials provided. Call, fax, or write for more information.

Stock Search International Inc., Micheline Masse, 10855 N. Glen Abbey Dr., Tucson, AZ 85737, 800-537-4523, 602-544-2490, 8:30 A.M.–4:30 P.M.; fax: 602-544-9395. Researches stocks and bonds issued by companies no longer listed and helps recover the funds. Any stock or bond issued anywhere in the world since 1850 can be traced and evaluated. Free brochure. Appraisals.

Stoves

Antique cooking and heating stoves have gained popularity in recent years and all types can be sold. The problem is they are large and heavy. Try to sell them through an ad in your local paper. Be sure that your stove, as well as your chimney, is in safe working condition if you plan to use it. Old parts are available through many of the dealers who sell antique stoves. New parts can be purchased or made for most old stoves.

An amateur should never restore or install an old stove that is to be used. Many communities have strict fire code laws that require permits plus an inspection of any working stove after installation. Local workmen can safely install your stove; their addresses can be found in the Yellow Pages of your phone directory.

Club & Publications

Antique Stove Association, *Stove Parts Needed* (NL), 417 N. Main St., Monticello, IN 47960.

Antique Stove Exchange (NL), Box 43, Pacific Junction, IA 51561 (all buy-sell-trade ads).

Repairs, Parts & Supplies

Antique Stove Information Clearinghouse, 417 N. Main St., Monticello, IN 47960, 219-583-6465, anytime. The Clearinghouse puts buyers and sellers of stove parts together, and offers restoration consultation, catalogs, and books on antique stoves. Manufacturers' original catalogs bought, sold, located, and reprinted.

Barnstable Stove Shop, Inc., Box 472, Rt. 149, W. Barnstable, MA 02668, 508-362-9913, 9:00 A.M.–5:00 P.M. Antique wood, coal, and gas stoves restored. Large parts inventory, mostly coal and wood stoves. Catalog $1.

Brunelle Enterprises, Inc., 203 Union Rd., Wales, MA 01081, 413-245-7396, 8:00 A.M.–6:00 P.M. Restoration of antique coal and wood kitchen and parlor stoves. Brochure $2.

Bryant Stove & Music, Inc., RR 2, Box 2048, Rts. 139 and 220, Thorndike, ME 04986-9657, 207-568-3665, Mon.–Sat. 8:00 A.M.–5:00 P.M. Restoration of antique stoves, specializing in nickel plating, kitchen, parlor, Franklin, wood/gas combination, wood/electric combination, electric, and gas stoves. Stove parts for sale. Free brochure.

Johnny's Appliances & Classic Ranges, 17549 Sonoma Hwy., PO Box 1407, Sonoma, CA 95476-1407, 707-996-9730, 10:00 A.M.–5:00 P.M. Restoration and parts for classic ranges, 1900–1960. Thermostats recalibrated, safety valves tested or installed, porcelain panels redone, nickel and chrome replated. Wednesday-Saturday; call first to be sure they are open. Send SASE for free brochure.

Keokuk Stove Works, 1201 High St., Keokuk, IA 52632, 319-524-6202, Mon.–Sat. 8:00 A.M.–5:00 P.M.; fax: 319-524-7388. Antique stoves restored. Hard coal to gas conversions. Free brochure.

Larry Havel, 1680 E. 4th Street, Colby, KS 67701, 913-462-7617, anytime. Restoration of antique heating and cooking stoves, 1880–1920. Brass, copper, and nickel plating. Brass and copper polishing.

Lehman Hardware, PO Box 41, 4779 Kidron Rd., Kidron, OH 44603-0041, 216-857-5441, Mon.–Sat. 7:00 A.M.–5:30 P.M., Thurs. 7:00 A.M.–9:00 P.M.; fax: 216-857-5785. Stove paint, stove door gaskets, tools, and more. Catalog $2.

Macy's Texas Stove Works, 5515 Almeda Rd., Houston, TX 77004-7443, 713-521-0934, Mon.–Fri. 10:00 A.M.–6:30 P.M., Sat. 10:00 A.M.–2:00 P.M.; fax: 713-521-0889. Parts and services for classic ranges and space heaters, gas, electric, and wood burning. Clay radiants, valves, thermostats, knobs, etc. Ranges and heaters cleaned and reconditioned. Timers replaced or rebuilt. Porcelain finishes repaired or replaced with new porcelain. Service technician available for in-home service. Catalog $3.50.

Tomahawk Foundry, Inc., 2337 29th St., Rice Lake, WI 54868, 715-234-4498, 7:30 A.M.–10:00 A.M. Castings for old stoves reproduced in cast iron from a good or broken part. Catalog $2.

Van Dyke's, Box 278, Woonsocket, SD 57385, 605-796-4425, 800-843-3320, orders only, 8:00 A.M.–6:00 P.M.; fax: 605-796-4085. Isinglass sheets for stove doors. Catalog $1.

*T*elephone *C*ollectibles

*I*f you have anything old that has the word "telephone" or the familiar bell symbol, it can be sold. Everything from telephone booths to telephones to telephone insulators is collected. The highest-priced phones are those that look old and that can be altered to actually work on today's phone lines. Blue glass paperweights, banks, enameled signs, and anything else marked with the Bell Telephone logo are purchased. Prices can be found in the general price books.

Telephone insulators are the glass, dome-shaped objects found at the top of telephone poles. Most insulators are found by digging in dumps or near old poles; selling is usually done at special shows for insulators or at bottle shows. Only unusual or rare insulators in perfect condition sell for over a few dollars. Insulators are priced in many general price books, but it takes some special knowledge to recognize a treasure. If you have a basket of old insulators, take them to a show and talk to the collectors. They will tell you what the insulators are worth, and the show is the best place for you to dispose of them.

REPAIR

Many types of old telephones can be repaired and used. Old dial phones can even be converted to push-button phones through the addition of an extra box or by another method. Contact your local phone company for exact information about the types of equipment that will work.

Old phones often require more power to ring the bell, and sometimes too many phones on one line can keep all of them from working. We learned about this the hard way when we tried to install an answering machine. A normal house line can handle "five ringers," we were told; some new phones are only half ringers, but old phones can be more than one ringer. Reproduction phones and phone parts are available.

Price Book
Telephone Collecting: Seven Decades of Design, Kate E. Dooner (Schiffer, Atglen, PA, © 1993).

Clubs & Publications
Antique Telephone Collectors Association, *ATCA Newsletter* (NL), PO Box 94, Abilene, KS 67410.

Telephone Collectors International, *Singing Wires* (NL), PO Box 124, Newark, IL 60541.

Repairs, Parts & Supplies
Billiard's Old Telephones, 21710 Regnart Rd., Cupertino, CA 95014, 408-252-2104, 7:30 A.M.–8:00 P.M. Restoration of old telephones. Repair parts. Conversion to modern touch-tone system. Mail order. Free consultations on phone repairs. Appraisals.

Chicago Old Telephone Co., PO Box 189, Lemon Springs, NC 28355, 800-843-1320, 9:00 A.M.–5:00 P.M.; fax: 919-774-7666. Restoration of old telephones; new parts for old telephones. Catalog and video tapes available.

Farmerstown Hardware & Supplies, Junior and Robert Hershberger, 3155 S.R. 557, Dept. K, Baltic, OH 43804, 216-893-2464, Mon.–Fri. 8:00 A.M.–5:00 P.M. Antique telephone parts. Wholesale catalog $2.

House of Telephones, 15 East Ave. D, San Angelo, TX 76903, 915-655-4174; fax: 915-655-4177, 8:00 A.M.–4:30 P.M. Antique telephone parts and supplies. Restoration and refinishing. Reproduction cloth cords. Mail order worldwide. Free catalog.

Mahantango Manor Inc., PO Box 170K, Dalmatia, PA 17017, 800-642-3966 or 717-758-8000, Mon.–Thurs. 7:00 A.M.–5:00 P.M.; fax: 717-758-6000. Replacement parts for antique telephones. Parts for wooden wall phones, candlestick phones, cradle phones, and modern wooden decorator wall phones with handsets. Mouthpieces, receivers, cords, crank handles, door locks, books, and more. Catalog $2, with coupon for $2 off next purchase.

Phone Wizard, PO Box 70, Leesburg, VA 22075-0070, 703-777-0000, 10:00 A.M.–10:00 P.M.; fax: 703-777-1233. Repair and restoration of antique telephones. Conversions. Antique telephone parts and supplies. Mail order worldwide. Catalog $3.

Phoneco, PO Box 70, 207 E. Mill Rd., Galesburg, WI 54630, 608-582-4124, daily 8:00 A.M.–9:00 P.M.; fax: 608-582-4593. Telephone repair and restoration. Original and reproduction parts.

Wiesner Radio & Electronics, 149 Hunter Ave., Albany, NY 12206, 518-438-2801, 9:00 A.M.–5:00 P.M. Repair of obsolete electronic equipment, including telephones.

Textiles

The women's movement sparked an interest in the work of women from past centuries. That seems to have started the amazing rise in the price of old quilts, woven coverlets, samplers, and other examples of feminine handiwork from the past. The country decorating magazines added to the interest, and it wasn't long before collectors wanted open shelves piled high with examples of quilts and homespun cloth. Quilts are hung like huge pictures on the walls behind beds heaped with white work pillows and covers. Paisley shawls have become tablecloths. All of this means that any type of old textile that exhibits some handiwork can be sold.

People who collect fabrics also buy Stevengraphs and other silk woven fabric pictures, good examples of needlepoint and Berlin work, and the many tools used in sewing, lacework, and other needlework. If you find an old, filled sewing basket, you have a treasure. There are buyers for thimbles, tape measures, buttons, trim, half-finished embroideries, and even the sewing basket.

SAMPLERS

The sampler originated in England. It was literally a sample of needlework done by a young girl. Every well-to-do girl was expected to weave and sew enough for her future home. It was considered an important part of her dowry. Hand-loomed sheets, covers, towels, and underclothes were expensive. In the legal accountings after a death, the linens were among the most valuable items in an eighteenth-century home. Each item was embroidered with letters and numbers as part of an inventory system. Samplers had the alphabet, numbers, some symbolic pictures, and perhaps a motto or favorite saying. It was then proudly signed and dated by the girl who had stitched it.

Samplers were made on homespun fabric, and the thread was often home-dyed. These materials discolor and fade, so condition is very important. A sampler with clear colors and a light background is worth from five to ten times as much as a similar sampler that is brown and faded. American and Canadian samplers are priced higher than English examples. You can sometimes identify the country of origin from the wording and designs. Crowns usually indicate an English sampler.

Seventeenth-century samplers are long and thin. In the eighteenth century, the sampler became more rectangular. Nineteenth-century samplers have pictorial and memorial designs. Some "darning" samplers were made. Holes were cut and then darned. These were often from Holland. Italian samplers were frequently fringed instead of hemmed, and they often featured religious motifs. German samplers favored very small designs, often made with wool thread. Spanish samplers were almost always square, with a center design and borders. American samplers from the 1920s to the 1950s usually had a motto and lots of white space. These have decorative value only.

Age can influence the price. The older, the better, provided the condition is good. Repairs lower the value of a sampler, and you should never repair an old one before selling it. Leave that to an expert. The history of the family of the maker always adds to the value. If your sampler was made by a distant relative, write down all the information you know, including the name, birthplace, and birthdate of the maker. Attach the history to the back of the frame. The sampler would be even more valuable if your great-great-aunt had been part of a presidential family or had roomed with Nellie Bly. Any verifiable facts that connect the sampler to local or national history add to the price.

Eighteenth-century American samplers sell for very high prices. If you are selling, try to have an appraisal by an expert before setting the price. Early nineteenth-century samplers are also high priced; the handiwork of a 1920s child, however, is of a limited value.

QUILTS

*I*f you can call it a quilt, you can sell it. The newspapers often report sales of quilts for thousands of dollars, but these quilts are exceptional. Record price in 1991 was $264,000 for an appliquéd quilt dated November 18, 1867, depicting the reconciliation between the North and South. Age influences the price, but the most important factor is skill. The better the quilt design and stitching, the higher the price. Quilts are judged like fine paintings. Experts look for good design, originality, and unusual fabrics.

There are several kinds of quilts. Some are pieced with many small patches stitched together. This large composite piece is then used as the top layer of a sandwich with a plainer bottom layer and a cotton filling. The three layers are then quilted together into one useful covering. Small stitches and attractive curved patterns in the almost invisible quilting are the key to a top-quality quilt. The very late or very simple quilt "sandwiches" may only be held together with knotted threads placed at intervals.

Machine-stitched quilts were made in the late nineteenth century and after. The earliest quilts had a large center design. By the Civil War, it had become fashionable to use overall repetitive designs that are known by names like Four-Patch, Log Cabin, Pineapple, and Sunburst.

Many fine quilts can still be found today in attic trunks. The mountain areas of West Virginia and Kentucky seem to furnish an endless quantity to the "pickers" who supply the best shops with antiques. The Amish from all areas made quilts of geometric blocks and dark colors; these quilts have become fashionable and expensive. Beware, as there are still skilled needleworkers making Amish and other quilts. The fabrics are probably the best guide to age, although old fabrics are being used in some new quilts.

The libraries are filled with books about quilts and quilt values. Quilts are considered "folk art" and sell quickly. There will be quilts of all qualities at almost every antiques show. We went to a tailgate show in Indiana one weekend, and a single dealer had 150 quilts hanging on a fence.

The supply seems endless, but there is a real shortage of top-quality pieces. They sell well everywhere, but sell for the most money at the trendy New York shops. If you find twenty quilts made over eighty years ago by a very talented relative, it might pay to take them to New York.

COVERLETS AND HOMESPUN

*E*arly fabrics were often completely handmade, from the growing of the cotton or flax to the cleaning, clipping, spinning, dyeing, and weaving of the finished thread. Homespun cloth was usually made in subdued shades of blue, green, brown, or red. Checked or striped patterns gained in favor and price during the 1980s when the faded, country look was "in." Modern copies of the fabrics are being made, but collectors will always pay a premium for the real thing. Prices are standard and are easy to determine from a careful look at an antiques show. If your homespun is of similar size and condition, it should sell to a dealer for about half the retail price asked at a show.

Coverlets are more complicated to price because the condition, design, and maker's signature are equally important. Many coverlets have a name and date woven into the corner. These names can be checked in *Checklist of American Coverlet Weavers* by John W. Heisey, published in 1978 by Williamsburg, Virginia: Colonial Williamsburg Foundation, Abby Aldrich Rockefeller Folk Art Center, P.O. Box C, Williamsburg, Va. 23185. Coverlets by some weavers and coverlets with special borders, like a train, boat, or building design, are popular and expensive. Check in the price books and at the shows to learn more about their value; books list coverlets by maker pattern. Coverlets sell well at shows and auctions or to private collectors.

PRINTED TEXTILES

*P*rinted textiles sell to a very small group of collectors. An old textile, such as a piece of drape, bedspread, or valance that is over 100 years old, is sometimes valuable because the print is historically interesting. Scenes of the death of Washington, fabrics used in political campaigns, World's Fair mementos, or important, early, roller-printed fabrics are high priced. They sell best in pieces that can be framed and hung as pictures or used to make pillows. The entire repeat of the pattern should be included.

Some newer fabrics are in demand for use as upholstery materials for curtains or pillows. Art Deco and Art Nouveau designs, the free-form patterns of the 1950s, or bright Hawaiian Deco prints sell to the right person. The fabrics probably have low value if there is not sufficient yardage for at least one chair.

Some collectors want historical handkerchiefs to frame for pictures. A good fabric "picture" is worth hundreds of dollars. Look in the library for books that picture old roller-printed fabrics. Many modern reproductions have been made, but if you are selling fabric found in an old attic trunk, you probably know if it is old or new. The dealer buying it will certainly know. Just remember, don't throw away any fabrics before you try to sell them.

LACE

There are probably fewer experts on old lace than in almost any field of collecting. Pieces of very old lace, such as collars, cuffs, or bits of trim, sell for thousands of dollars in Europe, where lace has been recognized and appreciated. There are few collectors or dealers in the United States who are interested in lace of that quality. Only the museums seem to be knowledgeable.

If you have a box of your mother's old lace, chances are it is not over fifty years old and is of value only in the places where vintage clothing is bought and sold. If your mother made lace, or came from Europe and possibly saved the lace from her or her grandmother's wedding dress, you might have some valuable pieces. Take the lace to be appraised by an auction gallery if possible. Ask if they sell much lace and what prices they seem to get. If they can't identify old lace, ask for the expert at your local museum. The museum can't give a price, but an expert can tell you if it is old, handmade, and rare.

Large lace pieces might sell for good prices to the vintage clothing shops that sell elaborate, redesigned, lace blouses or wedding dresses. If you have lace that a museum identifies as made before 1750, contact a major auction gallery.

We have tried to understand lace for years. We are able to tell handmade from machine-made and good from bad, but we still are not able to distinguish great from good. It takes an expert with experience. Pricing is even more difficult, so if you have any suspicion that your lace treasures are old and handmade, take them to an expert dealer, appraiser, museum curator, or auction gallery for an opinion.

REPAIR

Textiles include everything from rugs, coverlets, and quilts to lace and needlework. Care is especially important for all of these, as they are perishable. The greatest harm to a fabric can come from strong sunlight and dirt.

A small piece of fabric can be successfully displayed if it is washed and stitched to unbleached muslin with unbleached pure cotton thread. It should be mounted on acid-free backing and framed under glass. Never hang it in full sunlight.

It is often safer to wash or clean a quilt than to store it as found. Proper washing and hanging are important if you plan to display the quilt on a wall. Be sure that the quilt is hung from a rod held by a tunnel of cloth that supports the entire weight of the quilt and does not cause tears. The Abby Aldrich Rockefeller Folk Art Center, P.O. Box 1776, Williamsburg, VA 23187, identifies quilts and sells books about their care and display.

It is possible to do an almost undetectable restoration on a quilt if you can find the proper fabric. If you have some minor damage on a quilt, you might check on the cost and quality of repairs before you sell. The usual rule for antiques is never to repair before you sell, but if the quilt is to be sold at auction, it will probably pay to have it in usable condition.

Many modern quilt makers will repair old quilts. Some even have supplies of old fabrics. Sources of the many types of supplies needed are listed in the book *Considerations for the Care of Textiles and Costumes* by Harold Maitland (Indianapolis: Indianapolis Museum of Art, 1980). If not in your local library, it should be available through interlibrary loan.

Rugs can also be hung from rods. Instructions for this type of display can be found in how-to books.

Lace should be laundered, stretched, repaired, and either used or framed. Stores that sell old clothing may be able to help with repairs.

Cleaning a rug or quilt requires care and the proper supplies. Use Orvus WA Paste (found at stores that have supplies for horses and farm animals) or Woolite. Always test the colors first to be sure that they will not run. Rinse thoroughly, dry, and either use or store on rolls. This is not too difficult a project for the careful amateur, but be sure to follow directions.

Most rug dealers also clean and repair rugs, so you may be able to find a local expert by checking the Yellow Pages of your local telephone book.

Price Books

Collecting Antique Linens & Lace Needlework: Identification, Restoration and Prices, Frances Johnson (Wallace-Homestead Book Company, Radnor, PA, © 1991).

Identification and Price Guide: Quilts, Liz Greenbacker and Kathleen Barach (Avon Books, New York, © 1992).

Legacy of Lace: Identifying, Collecting and Preserving American Lace, Kathleen Warneick and Shirley Nilsson (Crown Publishers, New York, © 1988).

Books on Repair

The American Quilt, a History of Cloth and Comfort 1750–1950, Roderick Kiracofe (Crown, New York, © 1993).

Art of Crewel Embroidery, Mildred J. Davis (Crown Publishers, New York, © 1962).

Collecting Costume: The Care and Display of Clothes and Accessories, Naomi Tarrant (Allen & Unwin, Winchester, MA, © 1983).

Considerations for the Care of Textiles and Costumes, Harold F. Mailand (Indianapolis Museum of Art, 1200 West 38th Street, Indianapolis, IN 46208, © 1980).

Encyclopedia of Embroidery Stitches Including Crewel, Marion Nichols (Dover Publications, New York, © 1974).

How to Wet-Clean Undyed Cotton and Linen, No. 478, Maureen Collins McHugh (Smithsonian Institution, Washington, DC, © 1967).

Legacy of Lace, Kathleen Warnick and Shirley Nilsson (Crown Publishers, New York, © 1988).

Clubs & Publications

Colonial Coverlet Guild of America, *Colonial Coverlet Guild of America* (NL), 5617 Blackstone, LaGrange, IL 60525.

Stevengraph Collectors' Association, *Stevengraph Collectors' Association Newsletter* (NL), 2829 Arbutus Rd., #2103, Victoria, BC, Canada V8N 5X5.

Thimble Collectors International, *TCI Bulletin* (NL), 6411 Montego Bay Rd., Louisville, KY 40228-1241 (nonprofit organization; will help antique thimble and sewing tool collectors with information and research).

Lill's News Gazette on Vintage Clothing (NL), 19 Jamestown Dr., Cincinnati, OH 45241.

Textile Museum Bulletin (NL), Textile Museum, 2320 S St. NW, Washington, DC 20008.

Thimbletter (NL), 93 Walnut Hill Rd., Newton Highlands, MA 02161-1836.

Repairs, Parts & Supplies

Appelbaum & Himmelstein, 444 Central Park W., New York, NY 10025, 212-666-4630, Mon.–Fri. 10:00 A.M.–6:00 P.M. Conservation treatment of paintings, objects, and textiles; collection surveys; consultation on collections care, including lighting, storage, and humidity control. Brochure.

Chevalier Conservation, 500 West Ave., Stamford, CT 06902, 203-969-1980; fax: 203-969-1988. Cleaning, restoration, and conservation of antique and contemporary tapestries, rugs, carpets, and textiles. Free brochure.

Chicago Conservation Center, Barry Bauman, Director-Painting Conservator, 730 N. Franklin, Suite 701, Chicago, IL 60610, 312-944-5401, anytime; fax: 312-944-5479. Specializing in the restoration of textiles. Free brochure.

Country Patchworks, Beth Eckert, PO Box 811, Middlebury, VT 05753, 802-388-6510. Antique quilt restoration services; specializing in highly damaged quilts and hole repair through all three layers. Backing and quilting of antique quilt tops. Free brochure.

Tina Kane, 8 Big Island Rd., Warwick, NY 10990, 914-986-8522, evenings; fax: 914-986-8522. Tapestry restoration.

Key Tassels, 1314 21st St. NW, Washington, DC 20036, 202-775-9460, 10:00 A.M.–8:00 P.M. Handmade cotton tassels. Mail order.

Lane Conservation Associates, Nan Lane Terry, Director, 9 Station St., Brookline, MA 02146, 617-738-1126, 10:00 A.M.–6:00 P.M. Conservation of textiles and costumes. Specializing in samplers and painted needlework pictures. Consultations on proper storage and display. Collection surveys.

The Laundry at Linens Limited, Inc., 240 N. Milwaukee St., Milwaukee, WI 53202, 800-637-6334, 414-223-1123, Mon.–Fri. 8:00 A.M.–4:00 P.M.; fax: 414-223-1126. Laundering and restoration of bed, bath, and table linens; wedding dresses, christening gowns, and other clothing; needlepoint and some other special items. Free brochure.

M. Finkel & Daughter, Morris and Amy Finkel, 936 Pine St., Philadelphia, PA 19107, 215-627-7797, 10:00 A.M.–5:00 P.M.; fax: 215-627-8199. Restoration and conservation of samplers, needlework, quilts, and hooked rugs. By appointment.

Mary Ann Senatro Textile Restorations, 28 Swan Ave., Bedford, NH 03110, 603-627-6276, 8:30 A.M.–5:00 P.M. Textile restoration service. Oriental rugs, hooked rugs, and needlework. Call for appointment or information about shipping textiles for estimate.

Museum of American Textile History, 800 Massachusetts Ave., North Andover, MA 01845, 508-686-0191, 9:00 A.M.–5:00 P.M.; fax: 508-686-8567. Laboratory conservation services, including cleaning, stabilization, display systems, and documentation. On-site examinations and treatments. Lectures, workshops, and consultations. Free brochure. Call or write for additional information before sending textiles.

Persian Rug Cleaning Co., Robert Ouzounian, 2118 Temple St., Los Angeles, CA 90026, 213-413-6373, weekdays 8:00 A.M.–5:00 P.M. Navajo blanket and rug cleaning and removal of color runs or color bleeding. Navajo blanket and rug repairs.

Rumplestiltskin Designs, 1714 Rees Rd., San Marcos, CA 92069, 619-743-5541, Mon.–Sat. 9:00 A.M.–6:00 P.M.; fax: 619-480-5539. Hand-beaded fringe in assorted patterns and colors. All glass or glass and plastic mix. Heavy rayon fringe. Antique metallic guimpe (braid) in bolts. Brochure $1 and SASE. Please include resale number, letterhead, or business card and phone number for wholesale prices.

Sanford Restoration Works, Emily Sanford, 2102 Speyer Ln., Redondo Beach, CA 90278, 213-374-7412, Mon.–Sat. 9:00 A.M.–6:00 P.M.; fax: 310-798-2792. Restoration, repair, and conservation of antique textiles, including Navajo weavings, tapestries, embroideries, needlepoint, and quilts. Custom spinning and dyeing to match original materials. Specializing in village and nomadic weaving. Reweaving, cleaning, custom mounting. Teaching.

Shallcross & Lorraine, Holly L. Smith, State House, PO Box 133, Boston, MA 02133, 617-720-2133, 9:00 A.M.–6:00 P.M. Invisible restoration, conservation, and maintenance of oriental rugs, tapestries, and Native American textiles. Hand-spun and custom-dyed wools used.

Textile Conservation, Sarah Lowengard, PO Box 6611, New York, NY 10128, 212-860-2386, leave message. Art conservation, specializing in textiles, particularly embroidery and nonwoven. Analysis, cleaning, repair, housing. Will develop special storage systems and prepare textiles for storage.

Textile Conservation Center/Museum of American Textile History, 800 Massachusetts Ave., North Andover, MA 01845, 508-686-0191, Mon.–Fri. 9:00 A.M.–5:00 P.M.; fax: 508-686-8567. Preservation assistance and laboratory conservation of historic and modern textiles. Stabilization, cleaning, and mounting for display. Lectures and workshops on textile preservation. On-site examination and remedial treatment of textiles too large or too fragile to travel. Emergency and first-aid services. Advice on disaster preparedness. Free brochure.

Textile Conservation Workshop, Patsy Orlofsky, Main St., South Salem, NY 10590, 914-763-5805, 9:30 A.M.–5:00 P.M. Conservation and restoration of antique textiles: archeological and ethnographic, needlework, laces, quilts, coverlets, samplers, tapestries, flags and banners, costumes and accessories, rugs, ethnic and ecclesiastical textiles, Judaica, antique household and domestic textiles, and political memorabilia. Free brochure and newsletter.

Thanewold Associates, PO Box 104, Zieglerville, PA 19492, 215-287-9158, anytime. Restoration of samplers and decorative needlework.

Unique Art Lace Cleaners, 5926 Delmar Blvd., St. Louis, MO 63112, 314-725-2900, 9:00 A.M.–4:00 P.M. Cleaning and repairing of fine table linens, wedding veils, wedding gowns, antique clothing, tapestries, and samplers. Send items for price quotation and consultation. Fee $25, applied to bill if work is performed.

Tools

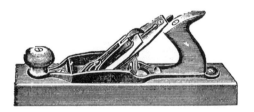

A few tools hung on the wall as sculptural decorations are often seen in the decorating magazines. Old tools can be sold to any friend or antiques dealer. There are also many serious tool collectors who specialize in one type of tool, such as wrenches or planes, or who have large general collections. If you have a toolbox filled with old hand tools, it would pay to try to find the dealers who specialize in tools or to contact the members of a tool-collecting club. There are some auction houses that have special tool sales a few times a year. If you have only one item, it is probably best to sell it locally. Many old-looking tools have minimal value, but some special tools are worth hundreds or even thousands of dollars.

Look for the name STANLEY. It adds to the value, and there are several special price books for Stanley tools. Also look for KEEN KUTTER, WINCHESTER, and stamped names and locations that were sometimes put on the early handmade tools by the makers. The most popular tools seem to be axes, planes, and rulers.

There is a disagreement among collectors about the desired condition of tools. Some clean and wax the wood and clean the metal. Others will not buy a tool that has been newly waxed or varnished. It won't hurt to remove the major dirt with a quick washing, but don't wax, scour, or use rust remover. Let the new owner make that decision. If you do it, you are taking a chance of losing a sale.

REPAIR

The restoration of tools requires the knowledge of a woodworker, a metalworker, and an expert on tools. Local shops dealing with tools may be able to help, but many antique tools are beyond the skill and knowledge of the modern toolworker.

Tools should be kept clean and in working condition. Metal parts should be rust-free and usually require oil or another preservative.

Price Books

Antique & Collectible Stanley Tools Guide to Identity and Value, annual, John Walter. *Stanley Tool Pocket Guides* (The Tool Merchant at the Old Tool Shop, 208 Front St., Marietta, OH 45750).

A Price Guide to Keen Kutter Tools (L-W Books, PO Box 69, Gas City, IN 46933, © 1993).

Town-Country Old Tools With Prices, Jack Wood (L-W Books, PO Box 69, Gas City, IN 46933, © 1992).

Clubs & Publications

American Precision Museum Association, Inc., *Tools & Technology* (NL), PO Box 679, Windsor, VT 05089 (machine tools and their products).

Early American Industries Association, Inc., c/o John S. Watson, *Chronicle* (MAG), *Shavings* (NL), Cultural Education Center, PO Box 2128, Empire State Plaza Station, Albany, NY 12220.

Mid-West Tool Collectors Association, *Gristmill* (MAG), c/o William Rigler, RR 2, Box 152, Wartrace, TN 37183.

Ohio Tool Collectors Association, *Ohio Tool Box* (NL), PO Box 261, London, OH 43140.

Tool and Trades History Society, *Tools and Trades* (NL), 60 Swanley Ln., Swanley, Kent, U.K. BR8 7JG.

Tool Group of Canada, *Yesterday's Tools* (NL), 7 Tottenham Rd., Don Mills, ON, Canada M3C 2J3.

Fine Tool Journal (NL), Iron Horse Antiques, Inc., PO Box 4001, Pittsford, VT 05763.

Plumb Line (NL), 10023 St. Clair's Retreat, Fort Wayne, IN 46825.

Stanley Tool Collector News (NL), The Tool Merchant, 208 Front St., Marietta, OH 45750.

Tool Ads (NP), Box 33, Hamilton, MT 59840.

*T*oys

*D*on't discard any old toys. Even a Barbie doll's girdle has value to a collector. The best-selling toys are antique dolls, teddy bears, nineteenth-century iron toys, robot and space toys, pedal cars, and scale model autos and trains. Dollhouses and dollhouse furnishings, dolls from the 1930s to the 1960s, including Barbie and her accessories, banks, and lithographed tin toys are valuable. Games, game boards, celebrity items, and farm toys are good sellers. Any toy that is out of production and mint-in-the-box has a resale value to collectors.

Any old toy in good condition has value. The only toy that can be tattered and torn and still worth big money is a teddy bear over fifty years old; collectors seem to think it proves the bear was "loved." Other badly worn toys are of little value except for use as parts for repairs.

There are special antique toy and doll shows. They are the best places to sell old toys. Dealers at these shows sell for the highest prices and can usually afford to pay the highest prices.

Doll hospitals are listed in the Yellow Pages of the telephone book, and the owners often buy dolls and doll parts. General antiques dealers buy many types of toys. Look around in the shops and offer your toys to the dealer with toys like yours.

It may be embarrassing to think that your childhood toys are antiques, but age is not the only factor determining value. The most desirable robots, space toys, and Barbie dolls from the 1960s sell for hundreds of dollars. Big isn't necessarily better. Size doesn't determine the value. All types of miniatures and dollhouse items are in demand. Lead and even plastic soldiers also sell well if they are rare and in good condition. Look for the name BRITAINS.

MODEL TRAINS AND CARS

*B*ig is better for electric model trains. The most valued are the Standard Gauge (two inches between the rails), then 0 gauge (half as big as Standard Gauge). There are special train collector shows in many cities and they provide the best place to sell an old train and its accessories. Even the houses, lampposts, trees, and figures made for elaborate train landscapes are selling well. Names that add value to trains and accessories include LIONEL, AMERICAN FLYER, CARLISLE

AND FINCH, DORFAN, REVELL INC., MECCANO, and PLASTICVILLE.

All sorts of small and large automotive toys are wanted, from miniatures to pedal cars large enough for a child to ride. Look for the names: BUDDY L, TOOTSIETOY, DINKY TOY, CORGI, HUBLEY GREY, KENTON, MANOIL, and ARCADE.

Some very well known toy makers produced a great variety of toys for many years: wooden, iron, battery-operated, tin, slush-cast models, and windups. Collectors recognize the most famous of these companies and sometimes specialize in their products. This means there is added value to early toys marked MARX, BING, CHEIN, FISHER-PRICE, IVES, LINEOL, LEHMANN, MARKLIN, SCHUCO, STRAUSS, and STEPHENS AND BROWN.

Don't repaint, restore, or redress an old toy before you sell it. You could destroy all the value for a collector. If an iron or tin toy is repainted, deduct 75 percent. If a small piece is missing, such as a driver of a wagon, the wheel of a car, or an arm from a figure in the Dogpatch band, deduct only 20 percent. These missing pieces can be found.

BANKS

*B*ank collectors search for old mechanical banks and iron still (nonmechanical) banks. A mechanical bank usually moves when a lever is pressed. Many of these have been reproduced and some have the words "Book of Knowledge" on the bottom. Other reproductions are unmarked. Even the reproduction can be sold, but for a low price. There are books that tell which banks have been made recently, how to tell a fake by checking the bottom marking, and other clues.

If there are indications that your bank has been altered on the bottom, it is probably a recent copy. "Recent" means after 1930. The "age of mechanical banks" was from the late 1890s to World War I. Mechanical banks have sold for hundreds to thousands of dollars since the 1970s, so collectors have now started to buy iron still banks. Several special price books picture and price hundreds of these banks. Repainted banks are worth much less than examples with old, worn paint. New paint might even hide identification marks of a recent copy.

TEDDY BEARS

*C*ondition is important when selling old toys, games, or dolls, but collectors do not seem to mind how worn or tattered a teddy bear may be. Poor condition lowers value a little, but not as much as it does for any other type of antique. We have seen teddy bears with no eyes, worn "fur," and arms torn off and hanging sell at auction to a dealer for over $300.

The first teddy bear was made in 1902. Early teddy bears often have longer noses than the new ones have. Some have added features like electrically lit eyes or internal music boxes. There seems to be no explanation for the teddy bear mania of today. Any bear made before 1950 is worth over $100. Some are worth thousands.

There has been so much interest in teddy bears that there are clubs, calendars, contests, newspapers, magazines, and books on the subject. If you have an old bear, everyone will want to buy it. Try to find a trusted collector friend or a qualified appraiser who will know if you own a fortune or just a nice bear. Look for the name STEIFF (and a tag in the ear), for long noses, and for unfamiliar types of fur.

GAMES

Games have a special appeal for collectors. If you are lucky enough to have a very early baseball game, it may be of more value to a baseball memorabilia collector than to a game collector. The Lindbergh games based on his airplane flight, the games with ads for products like Coca-Cola, and the celebrity or TV-related games like "Star Trek" sell for more money to the specialist than to the game collector. If Little Orphan Annie, Jack Armstrong, Charlie Chaplin, or Disney characters are on the game or box, you have a high-priced item.

Collectors divide games into types. "Name Games" are those that are collected for their association with well-known events, people, places, or collecting areas. The theme of the game is important. Remember, the collector is not buying the game to play it, but rather to display it. The graphics of the board, the box, and the shape of the playing pieces add to the value. Look for anything that includes pictures of airplanes, animals, automobiles, bicycles, blacks, cartoons, circus themes, fortune-tellers, motorcycles, movies, political themes, radios, Santa Claus, sports, the Statue of Liberty, TV, and war battles.

Game collectors also want what one expert calls "Game Games." These games are collected for their graphics, their parts, or their historic value. Unless early (pre-1910) or exceptionally decorated, "Game Games" do not sell as well as "Name Games." The companies that made these games are important. Those marked MILTON BRADLEY, McLOUGHLIN BROTHERS, IVES, PARKER BROTHERS, SELCHOW & RIGHTER, BLISS, E. I. HORSMAN, CLARK & SOWDON, and WEST & LEE are popular and usually high priced.

The first board game, "Mansion of Happiness" was manufactured in 1843 by W. & S. B. Ives. Other "Mansion of Happiness" games were made by Parker Brothers in 1894 and by McLoughlin in 1895, but they are not as valuable as the Ives example. A very rare game may not be more valuable, because collectors prefer games by well-known companies.

Games were bought for children. They were usually loved, used, abused, and eventually damaged. Condition is important; a pristine game is always more valuable. A large piece torn from the graphics on the front of a box can lower the value by 30 percent. With the exception of the very rare and the very early, metal games are worth more than lithographed paper and wooden games. Wood is worth more than cardboard. A few games have playing pieces made of metal, Bakelite or other plastics, ceramics, or even ivory. Pewter pieces are worth more than wooden pieces. Modern plastic is of no extra value.

Sometimes the playing pieces are of special interest because they are small toys or marbles that have a resale value even when separated from the game board. Unusual spinners, ivory dice, play money, and uncommon designs on the playing cards add value. Unusual playing cards over fifty years old have special buyers and clubs.

All these are just hints. The market for games is strictly supply and demand. A collector eager for everything ever made about the Dionne quintuplets will pay a premium for the right game picturing the babies. You must price your games with this intangible in mind. It is often not the age or beauty alone that determines the price of a game. In the late 1970s, the country-look decorating magazines began to show rooms with checkerboards and backgammon boards hung like rare paintings. Today, no old, wooden game board is too shabby or too crude to demand a high price as "folk art." Don't discard any type of game board; it will sell.

Another toy that has found favor as folk art is the wooden sled. The best example we have seen sold brought over $30,000 at auction. Most ordinary sleds sell for under $100. It pays to check the market. Old sleds should have hand-wrought iron runners and painted wooden bodies. A date as part of the decoration is a plus. Other toys that have gained in value from the "folk art" tag are decorated drums, whirligigs, painted wooden toys, rag dolls, especially black and Amish examples, and doll quilts.

There are specialists who want almost every type of toy or game. Try to find the right dealers, collectors, and clubs. Marbles, sports-related toys, celebrity toys, puzzles, magic tricks, cars, military toys, farm toys, even toys in special shapes, like dogs, cats, or particular breeds, are bought by these specialists.

It is difficult to discuss toy sales, because absolutely every toy older than five years is wanted by someone. Even the early computer-type games are collected. (They have to work.) Tin windup toys are wanted, but prices are 75 to 90 percent lower if they have a broken spring. If you have boxes of toys in the attic, be sure to check carefully on their possible value before you sell.

See also the sections on Dolls and Music.

REPAIR

It is not advisable for the amateur to make many types of repairs on toys. Remember, too, that many toys have been reproduced. Be sure you understand the differences between old and new toys before you spend money on repairs. Libraries are filled with books on this subject.

Never repaint or restore a metal toy if there is any way to avoid it. It is now possible to find reproduced parts for old toys, especially cars and trucks. Decals, wheels, and other parts are available. An old toy that is missing its paint is usually worth more than a toy from the same period that has been repainted. The exception to this rule seems to be pedal cars. Collectors of these, just like collectors of full-sized cars, seem to prefer a "new" look. A fine restoration will add to the value.

If you want a cast-iron bank that looks like a new one, buy a reproduction, but don't paint an old one. The working parts of old toys are very difficult to replace unless you are mechanically inclined. Key-wind mechanisms and power sources for trains are complicated and must often be replaced.

The battery-driven mechanical toys of the 1950s that featured a cigarette-smoking bartender or monkey can be made to smoke again if you add a drop of oil.

Price Books

Antique & Collectible Toys 1870–1950, David Longest (Collector Books, Paducah, KY, © 1994).

A Penny Saved: Still and Mechanical Banks, Don Duer (Schiffer, Atglen, PA, © 1993).

Aurora History and Price Guide, Bill Bruegman (30 Merriman Rd., Akron, OH 44303, © 1992).

Baby Boomer Toys and Collectibles, Carol Turpen (Schiffer, Atglen, PA, © 1993).

Bear Memorabilia: Reference & Price Guide, Dee Hockenberry (Hobby House, Cumberland, MD, © 1992).

Board Games of the 50's, 60's & 70's, Stephanie Lane and David Dilley (L-W Book Sales, PO Box 69, Gas City, IN 46933, © 1994).

Collecting Battery Toys, Don Hultzman (Books Americana, Florence, AL 35630, © 1994).

Collecting Toy Cars & Trucks, Richard O'Brien (Books Americana, Florence, AL 35630, © 1994).

Collecting Toys, No. 6, Richard O'Brien (Books Americana, Florence, AL, © 1993).

Collector's Encyclopedia of Children's Dishes, Margaret and Kenn Whitmyer (Collector Books, Paducah, KY, © 1993).

Collector's Guide to Miniature Teddy Bears, Cynthia Powell (Collector Books, Paducah, KY, © 1994).

Collector's Guide to Tonka Trucks, Don and Barb DeSalle (L-W Books, PO Box 69, Gas City, IN 46933, © 1994).

The Confident Collector: Toy Soldiers Identification and Price Guide, Bertel Bruun (Avon Books, New York, © 1994).

Evolution of the Bicycle, Vol. 2, David Devon Killey (L-W Book Sales, PO Box 69, Gas City, IN 46933, © 1994).

Evolution of the Pedal Car, Vol. 4, Neil S. Wood (L-W Books, PO Box 69, Gas City, IN 46933, © 1993).

Games: American Boxed Games and Their Makers 1822–1992, With Values, Bruce Whitehill (Wallace-Homestead, Radnor, PA, © 1992).

Greenberg's Guide to Cadillac Models and Toys, Jeffrey C. Gurski (Kalmbach Publishing, PO Box 1612, Waukesha, WI 53187, © 1992).

Greenberg's Guide to Gilbert Erector Sets, Vol. 1: 1913–1932, William M. Bean and Al M. Sternagle (Greenberg Publishing Co., 7566 Main St., Sykesville, MD 21784, © 1993).

Greenberg's Guide to Ives Trains, Vol. II, Bruce C. Greenberg (Greenberg Publishing Co., 7566 Main St., Sykesville, MD, 21784, © 1992).

Greenberg's Guide to Tootsietoys: 1945–1969, Raymond R. Klein (Kalmbach Publishing Co., 21027 Crossroads Circle, Waukesha, WI 53187, © 1993).

The Hess Toy Collector and *The Toy Truck Collectors Quick Reference & Price Guide,* Michael V. (F.S.B.O. Inc., PO Box 712, Far Hills, NJ 07931, © 1991, price guide © 1993).

Lesney's Matchbox Toys: Regular Wheel Years, 1947–1969, Charlie Mack (Schiffer, Atglen, PA, © 1992).

Matchbox Toys 1948 to 1993, Dana Johnson (Collector Books, Paducah, KY, © 1994).

McElwee's Collector's Guide #9, Structo 1912–1976, Neil McElwee (40 Fornof Lane, Pittsburgh, PA, 15212, © 1993).

McElwee's Collector's Guide #10, Postwar Big Metal Classics, Neil McElwee (40 Fornof Lane, Pittsburgh, PA, 15212, © 1994).

Metal Toys from Nuremberg, Gerhard G. Walter (Schiffer, Atglen, PA, © 1992).

Occupied Japan Toys With Prices, David C. Gould and Donna Crevar-Donaldson (L-W Books, PO Box 69, Gas City, IN 46933, © 1993).

Plastic Toys: Dimestore Dreams of the '40s & '50s, Bill Hanlon (Schiffer, Atglen, PA, © 1993).

Plasticville: An Illustrated Price Guide, 3rd edition, edited by Frank C. Hare (Iron Horse Productions, PO Box 13269, Pittsburgh, PA 15243, © 1993).

Playtime Kitchen Items and Table Accessories, Lorraine May Punchard (8201 Pleasant Ave., S., Bloomington, MN 55420, © 1993).

Profits from PEZ, Dean F.V. Du Vall (Du Vall Press Financial Publications, Box 14, Williamston, MI 48895, © 1993).

Renewal, World's Finest Toys, Vol. 1, Charles Donovan Jr. (11877 U.S. Highway 431, Ohatchee, AL 36271, © 1994).

Riding Toys With Price Guide (L-W Books, PO Box 69, Gas City, IN 46933, © 1992).

Schroeder's Collectible Toys, Antique to Modern, edited by Sharon and Bob Huxford (Collector Books, Paducah, KY, © 1995).

Solido Toys, Dr. Edward Force (Schiffer, Atglen, PA 19310, © 1993).

Tomart's Price Guide to Hot Wheels, Michael Thomas Strauss (Tomart Productions, 3300 Encrete Lane, Dayton, OH 45439, © 1993).

Toy Auction Price Guide, Vols. I and II (Beowulf Fine Art Ltd., PO Box 6020-466, Spring, TX 77391, © 1992 and 1993).

Toy Auction Price Guide Volume III for 1994 (Beowulf Fine Art Ltd., PO Box 6020-466, Spring, TX 77391, © 1993).

Toys and Miniature Sewing Machines, Glenda Thomas (Collector Books, Paducah, KY, © 1995).

Toy Soldiers Identification and Price Guide, Bertel Bruun (Avon Books, New York, © 1994).

The Toy Truck Collectors Quick Reference & Price Guide, annual, Michael V. Harwood (Toy Truck Collector, 314 Stuyvesant Ave., Lyndhurst, NJ 07071).

Troll Identification & Price Guide, Debra Clark (Hobby House Press, Cumberland, MD 21502, © 1993).

Universal's Matchbox Toys, Charlie Mack (Schiffer, Atglen, PA, © 1993).

Other Helpful Books

Collectable Machine-Made Marbles, Castle and Marlow Peterson (Utah Marble Connection, P.O. Box 1857, Ogden, UT 84402).

Greenberg's American Flyer Factory Manual, Richard D. Smith and I.D. Smith (Greenberg Publishing Co., Sykesville, MD, © 1988).

Greenberg's Guide to Lionel Postwar Parts, Alan T. Weaver (Greenberg Publishing Co., Sykesville, MD, 1989).

Mechanical Toys, Athelstan and Kathleen Spilhaus (Crown Publishers, New York, © 1989).

Teddy Bear Catalog, Peggy and Alan Bialosky (Workman Publishing Co., New York, © 1980).

Archives

National Bicycle History Archives, PO Box 28242, Santa Ana, CA 92799, 714-647-1949.

Clubs & Publications

52 Plus Joker—The American Antique Deck Collectors Club, *Clear the Decks* (MAG), PO Box 1002, Westerville, OH 43081 (playing card decks).

A.C. Gilbert Heritage Society, *A.C. Gilbert Heritage Society Newsletter* (NL), 594 Front St., Marion, MA 02738.

Action Toy Collectors Club, *Action Toys* (NL), 2908 2nd Ave. N, Billings, MT 59101.

American Flyer Collectors Club, *Collector* (MAG), PO Box 13269, Pittsburgh, PA 15243.

American Game Collectors Association, *Game Researchers' Notes* (NL), *Game Times* (NL), 49 Brooks Ave., Lewiston, ME 04240.

American-International-Matchbox, *A.I.M.* (NL), 532 Chestnut St., Lynn, MA 01904-2717.

Antique Engine, Tractor & Toy Club, Inc., *Antique Engine, Tractor & Toy Club, Inc. Quarterly Newsletter* (NL), 5731 Paradise Rd., Slatington, PA 18080.

Canadian Marble Collectors Association, *Swirls* (NL), c/o Craig Gamische, 59 Mill St., Milton, ON, Canada L9T 1R8.

Chicago Playing Card Collectors Inc., *Chicago Playing Card Collectors Inc.* (NL), 1559 W. Pratt Blvd., Chicago, IL 60626.

Classic Bicycle & Whizzer Club, *Coaster* (NL), 35892 Parkdale, Livonia, MI 48150.

Club of Anchor Friends, *MLB* (MAG), c/o George Hardy, 1670 Hawkwood Ct., Charlottesville, VA 22901 (Richter's Anchor Stone building sets).

CTM Farm Toy & Collectors Club, *CTM Tractor Classics* (MAG), Box 489, Rocanville, SK, Canada S0A 3L0.

English Playing Card Society, *English Playing Card Society Newsletter* (NL), 11 Pierrepont St., Bath, Avon, England BA1 1LA.

Fisher-Price Collector's Club, *Gabby Goose* (NL), 1442 North Ogden, Mesa, AZ 85205.

G.I. Joe Collectors Club, *G.I. Joe Collectors Club*

Newsletter (NL), 150 S. Glenoaks Blvd., #9204, Burbank, CA 91510.

Ideal Collector's Club, *Ideal Collector's Newsletter* (NL), PO Box 623, Lexington, MA 02173.

International Figure Kit Club, *Kitbuilders Magazine* (MAG), Box 201, Sharon Center, OH 44274-0201.

International Playing Card Society, *Playing Card* (MAG), *Playing Card World* (NL), c/o Barbara Clark, 3570 Delaware Common, Indianapolis, IN 46220.

Lionel Collectors Club of America, *Lion Roars* (NL), PO Box 479, La Salle, IL 61301.

Lionel Operating Train Society, *Switcher* (MAG), 6832 Meadowdale Circle, Cincinnati, OH 45243.

Marble Collectors Society of America, *Marble Mania* (NL), PO Box 222, Trumbull, CT 06611.

Marble Collectors Unlimited, *Marble Mart/ Newsletter* (NL), PO Box 206, Northboro, MA 01532.

Marble Connection Club, *The Marble Connection Newsletter* (NL), PO Box 132, Norton, MA 02766

Marklin Club, *Telex* (MAG), PO Box 51559, New Berlin, WI 53151-0559.

Matchbox International Collectors Association, *MICA* (MAG), PO Box 28072, Waterloo, ON, Canada N2L 6J8.

Mechanical Bank Collectors of America, *Banker* (NL), PO Box 128, Allegan, MI 49010 (publication for members only).

National Marble Club of America, *National Marble Club of America Newsletter* (NL), 440 Eaton Rd., Drexel Hill, PA 19026.

National Model Railroad Association, Inc., *NMRA Bulletin* (MAG), 4121 Cromwell Rd., Chattanooga, TN 37421.

Pennsylvania Matchbox Collector's Club, *Pennsylvania Matchbox Collector's Club Newsletter* (NL), c/o Lindia Murra, Kiddie Kar Kollectibles, 1161 Perry St., Reading, PA 19604-2308.

Schoenhut Collectors' Club, *Schoenhut Newsletter* (NL), 1003 W. Huron, Ann Arbor, MI 48103.

Still Bank Collectors Club, *Penny Bank Post* (NL), 4175 Millersville Rd., Indianapolis, IN 46205.

Toy Gun Collectors of America, *Toy Gun Collectors of America Newsletter* (NL), 175 Cornell St., Windsor, CA 95492.

Toy Store's Collectors Club of Steiff, *Collectors Life* (NL), PO Box 798, Holland, OH 43528.

Toy Train Collectors Society, *New Century Limited* (NL), 109 Howedale Dr., Rochester, NY 14616.

Toy Train Operating Society, *Toy Train Operating Society (T.T.O.S.) Bulletin* (MAG), *TTOS Order Board* (MAG), 25 W. Walnut St., Suite 308, Pasadena, CA 91103 (all ads).

Train Collectors Association, *Train Collectors Quarterly* (MAG), 300 Paradise Ln., Strasburg, PA 17579; *National Headquarters News* (NL), Box 248, Strasburg, PA 17579.

Wheelmen, *Wheelmen* (MAG), 55 Bucknell Ave., Trenton, NJ 08619.

Action Figure News & Toy Review (MAG), 556 Monroe Turnpike, Monroe, CT 06468.

Antique Toy World (MAG), PO Box 34509, Chicago, IL 60634.

Classic Bicycle & Whizzer News (NL), PO Box 765, Huntington Beach, CA 92648 (bicycles from 1920–1965).

Classic Toy Trains (MAG), PO Box 1612, Waukesha, WI 53187.

Collectible Toys & Values (MAG), PO Box 569, Ridgefield, CT 06877.

Collecting Toys (MAG), PO Box 1612, Waukesha, WI 53187-9951.

Collectors Gazette (NP), 200 Nuncargate Rd., Kirkby-in-Ashfield, Nottinghamshire, England NG17 9AG.

Die Cast & Tin Toy Report (MAG), PO Box 501, Williamsburg, VA 23187-0501.

Headquarters Quarterly™ (MAG), G.I. Joe Nostalgia Co., 62 McKinley Ave., Kenmore, NY 14217 (G.I. Joe dolls and accessories).

Hot Wheels Newsletter, 26 Madera Ave., San Carlos, CA 94070.

Kit Collector's Clearinghouse (MAG), 3213 Hardy Dr., Edmond, OK 73013.

Master Collector (NL), 12513 Birchfalls Dr., Raleigh, NC 27614-9675 (all ads: toys, dolls, trains, reader services).

Matchbox U.S.A. (NL), 62 Saw Mill Rd., Durham, CT 06422.

Model & Toy Collector (NL), PO Box 347240, Cleveland, OH 44134-9998.

O Gauge Railroading (MAG), PO Box 239, Nazareth, PA 18064.

Old Toy Soldier Newsletter (MAG), 209 N. Lombard, Oak Park, IL 60302.

Plane News (MAG), PO Box 845, Greenwich, CT 06836 (aviation toys and models).

Plastic Fanatic (MAG), 19088 Santa Maria Ave., Castro Valley, CA 94546 (model cars).

Plastic Figure & Playset Collector (MAG), PO Box 1355, LaCrosse, WI 54602-1355 (model cars).

Plastic Warrior (MAG), c/o Stad's, 905 Harrison St., Allentown, PA 18103 (54mm plastic figures).

The Replica (NL), The Ertl Company, PO Box 500, Dyersville, IA 52040-0500.

S Gaugian (MAG), 7236 W. Madison St., Forest Park, IL 60310.

Spin-offs (NL), Toy Museum, 533 Milwaukee Ave., Burlington, WI 53105 (tops, yo-yos, gyroscopes, etc.).

Tomart's Action Figure Digest (MAG), 3300 Encrete Ln., Dayton, OH 45439-1944.

Toy Collector and Price Guide (MAG), 700 E. State St., Iola, WI 54990-0001.

Toy Farmer (MAG), 7496 106th Ave. SE, LaMoure, ND 58458.

Toy Shop (NP), 700 E. State St., Iola, WI 54990-0001.

Toy Soldier Review (MAG), 127-74th St., North Bergen, NJ 07047.

Toy Tractor Times (MAG), PO Box 156, Osage, IA 50462.

Toy Trader (MAG), PO Box 1050, Dubuque, IA 52004-9969.

Toy Trucker & Contractor (MAG), 7496 106th Ave. SE, LaMoure, ND 58458-9404.

Toybox Magazine (MAG), 8393 E. Holly Rd., Holly, MI 48442.

Traders' Horn (NL), 1903 Schoettler Valley Dr., Chesterfield, MO 63017 (all ads for model vehicles).

Trainmaster (NL), PO Box 1499, Gainesville, FL 32602.

Turtle River Toy News (NL), *Oliver Collector's News* (NL), RR 1, Box 44, Manvel, ND 58256-9763 (toy tractors and farm toys).

U.S. Toy Collector (MAG), PO Box 4244, Missoula, MT 59806.

Wheel Goods Trader (NL), PO Box 435, Fraser, MI 48026-0435 (pedal cars, bicycles, etc.).

Repairs, Parts & Supplies

American Game Collectors Association, 49 Brooks Ave., Lewiston, ME 04240. Dedicated to the collection, preservation, and research of the history of games in America. The club newsletter, *Game Times,* includes classified ads for missing parts wanted or available. Members may obtain copies of game rules and catalogs from the archives.

Arnie Prince, 23 N. Houston Ln., Lodi, CA 95240, 209-334-6101, 6:00 A.M.–10:00 P.M. Repair and restoration of cast-iron toy cars, trucks, airplanes, trains, mechanical banks, etc. Parts fabricated, paint matched. Buys broken toys.

Barap Specialties, 835 Bellows, Frankfort, MI 49635, 800-322-7273, 9:00 A.M.–5:00 P.M. Wooden toy parts, whirligigs, tools, finishing materials, etc. Catalog $1.

Buddy K Toys, RD 9, Box 322, Bingen Rd., Bethlehem, PA 18015, 610-838-6505, anytime. Repair and restoration of large pressed-steel toys of the 1920s through 1940s. Decals, parts, and accessories available. Showroom open by appointment. Insured UPS delivery and COD orders. Catalog $5.

Cabin Toys & Parts, Howard and Glenda Andrew, 31874 Tappers Corner Rd., Cordova, MD 21625, 410-364-5490, Mon.–Sat. 8:00 A.M.–8:00 P.M. Farm toy parts. Restoration parts for 1/16th and pedal tractors. Customized parts for 1/16th and 1/64th tractors. Mail order worldwide. Catalog $4.

Charlie's Trains, PO Box 158-N, Hubertus, WI 53033, 414-628-1544, 8:00 A.M.–8:00 P.M.; fax: 414-628-2651. Toy train restoration. Repair parts and supplies. Wire, light bulbs, parts, and supplies for older Lionel trains. Mail order worldwide. Wholesale and retail. Send large double-stamped envelope for catalog.

Chrome-Tech USA, Robert D. Shebilske, 2314 Ravenswood Rd., Madison, WI 53711, 608-274-9811, 9:00 A.M.–9:00 P.M. Chrome plating of plastic for the hobbyist and collector. Will chrome-plate your plastic model car parts. Call or write for more information.

Classic Tin Toy Co., PO Box 193, Sheboygan, WI 53082, 414-693-3371, 9:00 A.M.–6:00 P.M.; fax: 414-693-8211. Repair and restoration of tin toys; also pressed-steel toys, aluminum trucks and toys, tricycles, pedal cars, and toy trains. Replacement parts for toys and trains.

Collector Auto Services Co., Bob Gerrity, 28048 13th Ave. S., Kent, WA 98032, 206-941-6055, 8:30 A.M.–6:00 P.M. Reproduction decals, ¼ inch to 18 inches, for toys or gas pump restoration. Mobil gas curved gas pump glass, Chevron globes and ad panels. Send a large triple-stamped SASE and $2 for photocopy of all decals in full size, color photo, and order sheet.

CTM Parts, Box 489, Rocanville, SK, Canada S0A 3L0, 306-645-4566. 10:00 A.M.–10:00 P.M.; fax: 306-645-4566. Farm toy restoration and parts. Mail order or in-store service. Parts catalog $3.

Daniel's Den, John Daniel, 720 Mission St., South Pasadena, CA 91030, 213-682-3557, 10:00 A.M.–4:00 P.M. Restoration of Baranger window displays, using original parts.

David or Debbie Sharp, 6449 W. 12th St., Indianapolis, IN 46214, 317-243-3172, day and early evening. Tonka replacement parts and decals for regular Tonka, 1950–1970. Original Tonka decals, 1970 and after, for various sizes. No phone orders, but you can call with questions. Catalog $1.

Dean Hile, 2411 Sheridan Blvd., Lincoln, NE 68502, 402-435-0406. Parts for pedal cars. Bearings, bodies, bumpers, chassis parts, cow catchers, cranks, decals, dump boxes, frames, grills, hood ornaments, horns, kick plates, ladders, latches, lights, pedal rubber, steering wheels, windshields, and more. Send SASE for free brochure.

Der Alt Mann of Auto's, Dwight E. Mauer, 4524 LuAnn Ave., Toledo, OH 43623, 419-474-8750, 9:00 A.M.–9:00 P.M. Parts for Arcade, A.C. Williams, Dinky, Champion, and other toys. Original parts for Yesteryear and Hubley. Some repair work. Brochure $2.

Diversified Associates Inc., PO Box 45, Mason, MI 48854, 517-676-9670, 9:00 A.M.–11:00 A.M., 1:00 P.M.–5:00 P.M. Pedal car, gas pump, and toy restorations. Pedal car parts.

Doll Hospital, 419 Gentry Street #102, Spring, TX 77373, 713-350-6722, Tues.–Sat. 10:00 A.M.–5:00 P.M.; Sun. 1:00 P.M.–6:00 P.M.; fax: 713-446-3353. Toy repair. Wicker doll furniture and doll trunks repaired.

Donald R. Walters, W2490 City Highway A, Curtiss, WI 54422, 715-654-5440. Metal toys repaired and repainted. Farms toys, pedal cars, and pedal tractors. Send SASE for information.

Eccles Brothers, Ltd., RR 1, Box 253-D, Burlington, IA 52601, 319-752-3840. Repair parts and accessories for Barclay, Manoil, Jones, and other toy soldiers. Arms, heads, legs, helmets, guns, tents, antennas, propellers, paints, and supplies. Catalog $3.

Edinburgh Imports, Inc., Elke and Ron Block, PO Box 722, Woodland Hills, CA 91365-0722,

818-591-3800, 8:30 A.M.–5:00 P.M.; fax: 818-591-3806. Supplies for making and repairing teddy bears and soft sculpture art. Mohair, alpaca, and wool plush; joint parts, glass and safety eyes, books, patterns, and kits. Worldwide mail order. Brochure.

Egli Toy Salvage, 1750 Udall Ave., Manson, IA 50563, 712-469-3949, before 9:00 A.M. or evenings. New and used parts for toy farm tractors and implements. Complete restoration of farm toys. Mail order worldwide. Send double-stamped SASE for brochure.

G. Schoepfer Inc., 138 W. 31st St., New York, NY 10001, 203-250-7794, 9:00 A.M.–5:00 P.M.; fax: 203-250-7796. Glass and plastic eyes for dolls, teddy bears, mechanical banks, etc.

George's Classic Cyclery, 712 Morrison St., Fremont, OH 43420, 419-334-7844. Repair and restoration of antique and classic bicycles. Old parts; no reproduction parts. Send name and address on a postcard for a free list of parts available.

Hobby Surplus Sales, 287 Main St., PO Box 2170, New Britain, CT 06051, 203-223-0600, Mon.–Fri. 10:00 A.M.–5:00 P.M. Repair parts for Lionel and American Flyer trains. Reproduction stickers for American Flyer. Repair manuals. Mail order worldwide. Catalog $3.

J & K Curios, 4868 SW Southwind Ct., Dunnellon, FL 34431, 904-465-0756, Mon.–Fri. 9:00 A.M.–9:00 P.M. Restoration of mechanical characters, but not the mechanism. Free estimates.

J. Neumann, 88-15 Union Turnpike, Glendale, NY 11385, 718-847-1715 Mon.–Sat. after 6 P.M. Restoration, mechanical, electrical and custom painting on all prewar and postwar standard gauge, O gauge, and scale rolling stock, motive power and accessories. Send SASE with wants.

Jim Coustier, 64 Terry Lane, Suisun City, CA 94585, 707-427-2175, 8:00 A.M.–10:00 P.M. Repair and restoration of old toy trains, specializing in American Flyer, Marx, and Lionel. Electronic devices made for large gauge trains. Mail order. Custom layouts and displays.

Jim Newark, 1730 LaPorte, Whiting, IN 46394, 219-659-6576, after 6:00 P.M. Toys and pedal cars repaired.

K & D Creation and Preservation, PO Box 344, Centerport, NY 11721-0344, 516-351-0982, evenings and weekends. Restoration of old toys, specializing in Schoenhut.

Locomotive Repair Co., 23 Monroe St., North Haven, CT 06473. Toy train repair; engines, operating cars, accessories, and transformers. Prompt turnaround. Send SASE for information.

Log Cabin Train Shop, Bill Trushel, 600 Rochester Rd., Pittsburgh, PA 15237-1704, 412-366-7060. Repair, parts, and supplies for Lionel trains. Lionel-type flat cable and light bulbs, liquid smoke, train lubricants, track cleaner. Mail order nationwide. Free repair estimates. For repair service, send items insured. Catalog $1.

Louis Bernier, 6443 Bl. Galeries D'Anjou, Local #9, Anjou, QU, Canada, H1M 1W1, 514-354-9121, anytime; cellular: 514-945-1148. Chrome and gold vacuum plating for plastic and metal parts for model cars. Cast resin parts for restoration of old model car kits and promotional models. Detail items and tools for model car building. Free brochure.

Marc Olimpio's Antique Toy Restoration Center, Marc Olimpio, PO Box 1505, Wolfeboro, NH 03894, 603-569-6739, 9:00 A.M.–5:00 P.M. Restoration of Early American tin toys c. 1840–1900: mechanical banks, still banks, and other hand-painted toys of the period.

Marion Designs, Bill and Judy Harrison, 594 Front St., Marion, MA 02738, 508-748-2540, daily 9:00 A.M.–9:00 P.M. Erector set parts and restoration. Electroplating and painting. Mail order worldwide.

Michael Sabatelle, Box 040136, Brooklyn, NY 11204-0006, 718-236-1278, 10:00 A.M.–10:00 P.M.

Lionel train repair and restoration. Original and reproduction parts from the 1930s to the present. Water decals, lamps. Repair newsletter. Mail order worldwide. Phone calls welcome. Send double-stamped SASE for catalog.

New York Doll Hospital, Inc., 787 Lexington Ave., New York, NY 10021, 212-838-7527, 10:00 A.M.–6:00 P.M., except Sunday. Mechanical toys repaired. Repairs, restorations, and appraisals of dolls, teddy bears, and other animals. Send item for estimate.

New-Era Quality Toys, Marvin Silverstein and Avi Jerchower, PO Box 10, Lambertville, NJ 08530, 609-397-2113, 908-788-0587. Restoration of pressed-steel vehicles and pedal cars.

Northeast Document Conservation Center, 100 Brickstone Sq., Andover, MA 01810-1494, 508-470-1010; fax: 508-475-6021. Nonprofit regional conservation center specializing in treatment of art and artifacts on paper, including board games. Preservation microfilming, preservation planning surveys, disaster assistance, technical leaflets. Brochure.

Old Father Time/Toy Expert, 5384 Boundary Rd., Carlsbad Springs, ON, Canada K0A 1K0, 613-822-7474, 613-822-7407, anytime. Toy repairs; specializing in battery-operated toys. Original and custom-made replacement parts, including gears, springs, shafts, bellows, etc.; available or can be located on request.

Parts Shop, 9 Bunting Pl., Elmira, ON, Canada N3B 3G7, 519-669-5079, 9:00 A.M.–8:00 P.M. Ertl farm toy parts and decals. Brochure $1.

Paul Fideler, Dept. KOV, Box 1591, Waltham, MA 02254. Toy, soldier, airplane spare parts, decals, figures, tires, kits, bulldozer and tank treads, and miscellaneous parts for Dinky, Corgi, Britains, Matchbox, Minic, Tekno, Tootsietoy, Shackleton, etc. Send a double-stamped LSASE and $1 (refundable) for listing of 3,000 items.

Pedal Car Graphics by Robert, 1207 Charter Oak Dr., Taylors, SC 29687, 803-244-4308, anytime. Pedal car decals, pedal car reference books. Catalog $4.

Portell Restorations, PO Box 91, Hematite, MO 63047, 314-937-8192, 9:00 A.M.–10:00 P.M. Complete restorations and parts for American-made pedal cars. Catalog $3.

Puppetry Guild of Greater Kansas City, Diane Houk, 11711 Markham Rd., Independence, MO 64052, 816-252-7248. Parts for Hazelle puppets, including heads, wood parts, clothing, and accessories.

Quarterhorse Investments, Inc., Sally L. Craig, 336 W. High St., Elizabethtown, PA 17022. Tanned horsehair tails for rocking horse restorations. Send SASE for brochure.

Randy's Toy Shop, 13106 River Ave., Carmel, IN 46033, 317-843-1998, 8:00 A.M.–4:00 P.M.; fax: 317-843-1998. Antique toy restoration. Reproduction parts for tin, celluloid, and plastic toys; paint touch-up; mechanisms repaired. Can match parts for most American, German, and Japanese toys. Box restoration. Mail order or UPS shipment. Brochure $4.

Restoration Train Parts, RD 1, Queensboro Manor, Box 390, Gloversville, NY 12078, 518-725-4446, 9:00 A.M.–1:00 P.M. only. Reproduction model train parts and model ignition engine parts for Lionel, American Flyer, AMT, Ives, Marx, Buddy L, Voltamp, Kasner, and others. Stampings, metal and plastic castings. Parts for prewar and postwar trains. Mail order worldwide. Catalog $15.

RF Giardina Co., Box 562, Oyster Bay, NY 11771, 516-922-1364 10:30 A.M.–4:30 P.M. American Flyer parts, silk screening and plastic molding for all restoration parts. Catalog $2.

Robert McCumber, 201 Carriage Dr., Glastonbury, CT 06033, 203-633-4984, 8:00 A.M.–10:00 P.M. Mechanical and still banks repaired; books on banks. Book list $3.

Rockinghorse Antiques, Bette Jeane

Rutkowski, 111 St. Helena Ave., Dundalk, MD 21222, 410-285-0280, 8:00 A.M.–11:00 P.M. Restoration of rocking horses and antique wicker carriages. Appraisals, identification and value. Free brochure.

Rogay, Inc., 4937 Wyaconda Rd., Rockville, MD 20852, 301-770-1700, Mon.–Fri. 7:30 A.M.–4:30 P.M.; fax: 301-468-1032. Repairing of antique ship models. Molding and casting of miscellaneous parts in epoxy resin.

Russ Harrington Antique Toys, 1805 Wilson Point Rd., Baltimore, MD 21220, 410-687-8596, 9:00 A.M.–10:00 P.M. Restoration of iron toys and mechanical banks. Replacement parts for cast-iron toys and banks. Parts available in iron, brass, bronze, aluminum, and lead.

Specialty Castings, Walter Allen, 15 Revere St., Gloucester, MA 01930, 508-283-2988, 10:00 A.M.–8:00 P.M. Replicas of cast iron, bronze, and aluminum parts. Sand casting and investment casting. Shrinkage compensation. Mold making. Plastic and rubber parts. New complete piece made from broken pieces. Call, write, send samples, photos, or drawings of part needed.

Stan Orr, Box 97, Stormville, NY 12582-0097, 914-221-7738, 9:00 A.M.–9:00 P.M. Lionel train repair part. Catalog $2 plus LSASE.

Sy Schreckinger, PO Box 104, East Rockaway, NY 11518, 516-536-4154, 9:00 A.M.–9:00 P.M. Invisible repairs made on mechanical banks and toys; restoration, repainting, cleaning. Repairs made in all metals. No welding or brazing.

Teddy Bear Doctor, Dick Roenspies, 100 S. 4th St., Stoughton, WI 53589, 608-873-3083, 7:00 A.M.–6:00 P.M. Restoration of teddy bears and stuffed animals, specializing in Steiff and Schuco. Limbs and other parts replaced, faces reconstructed, mechanicals repaired, electric-eye bears rewired. Work completed using materials appropriate to the age and condition of the toy. Invisible stitching on repairs. Cleaning.

References available. Nationwide service via UPS and U.S. mail.

Thomas Toy, Inc., Julian Thomas, PO Box 405, Fenton, MI 48430, 313-629-8707. Custom reproduction parts and tires for old toys. Catalog $5.

Tim Oei, 241 Rowayton Ave., Rowayton, CT 06853, 203-866-2470, anytime; fax: 203-866-1758. Restoration of old toys: cars, trucks, planes, boats, soldiers, trains, etc.

Tin Toy Works, Joe Freeman, 1313 N. 15th St., Allentown, PA 18102, 215-439-8268, Mon.–Sat. 8:30 A.M.–5:00 P.M.; fax: 215-439-1288. Antique tin toys restored, missing parts manufactured, mechanisms repaired. Tin and composition figures, life boats, masts, go-rounds, etc.

Tony Orlando, 6661 Norborne, Dearborn Heights, MI 48127-2076, 313-561-5072, business hours. Conservation and restoration of wooden rocking horses.

Toy Doctor, RR 1, Box 202, Eades Rd., Red Creek, NY 13143, 315-754-8846, anytime. Repair of battery-operated toys. Robots and space toys a specialty. If they can't repair your toy, they pay UPS ground shipping, both ways.

Toy Surgeon, Gerald D. Shook, 6528 Cedar Brook Dr., New Albany, OH 43054, 614-855-7796, phone, fax, and answering machine, anytime. Manufacturer of plastic replacement parts for robots, cars, animals, and other toys. Cocktail glass and shaker for bartender and Weaver, belly button for Chief Robot Man, replacement hose for bubblers, crank for High-Jinx Circus, hood emblem for Mercedes, and many other unique parts. Toy repair. Send LSASE plus $2 for parts list.

Train Works, 251F Hurricane Shoals Rd., Lawrenceville, GA 30245, 800-964-8724, Mon.–Fri. 11:00 A.M.–7:00 P.M., Sat. 10:00 A.M.–8:00 P.M., Sun. noon–5:00 P.M.; fax: 404-339-4417. Collectible toy trains repaired. Complete Lionel and American Flyer replacement parts list available with your SASE. Mail order worldwide.

Vod Varka Springs, US Rt. 30, PO Box 170, Clinton, PA 15026-0170, 412-695-3268, 8:45 A.M.–4:30 P.M.; fax: 412-695-3268. Custom-made springs for toys, cars, antiques, anything made out of wire. Flat-type springs for clocks and windup toys. Made to order per print or sample.

Walt's Carmine Caboose, 49137 County Rd. 14, Caldwell, OH 43724, 614-732-5065, evenings until 11:00 P.M. Restoration of toy trains, specializing in tin plate and die-cast engines.

WEJ Sales, Bill Johnson, 1107 N. Blackhawk Blvd., Rockton, IL 61072, 815-624-4204, 10:00 A.M.–3:00 P.M.; fax: 815-624-4540. Repair and restringing of wooden toys, specializing in Schoenhut. Dyed-to-match leather repair parts, including elephant ears, goat beards or tails, and alligator feet; rope tails and other parts. Send SASE for cost sheet.

West Virginia Railroad Co., 118 Chestnut Hill Rd., Hanover, PA 17331, 717-359-8392, 8:00 P.M.–11:00 P.M. Toy train repair and restoration. Lionel, Flyer, and Marx tin-plate parts. Glass bead blasting. Free train list with SASE.

Wood 'n Wildlife, 9922 Bostwick Park Rd., Montrose, CO 81401, 303-249-5863, before 9:00 P.M. Restoration of papier-mâché toys, dolls, and other objects. Send SASE for more information.

Video

Part I: An Introduction to Marble Collecting, **Marble Collectors Society of America,** PO Box 222, Trumbul, CT 06611. 120 minutes, $15 for MCSA contributors, $25 for noncontributors.

Computer Program

Toy Collector, **Noodleware Software Co.,** PO Box 83, Lindenhurst, NY 11757-0083, 516-321-9776, Mon.–Fri. 10:00 A.M.–6:00 P.M. Toy inventory program for IBM compatibles, manages unlimited number of items. DOS 2.1 or greater, 3.5-in. disk. Hard drive required. Manual included.

Appraiser

Continental Hobby, PO Box 193, Sheboygan, WI, 53082 414-693-3371; fax: 414-693-8211. Appraisals.

....

Transportation

*T*he larger an antique, the harder it is to sell to an out-of-town customer. That is the general rule, but for cars the rule does not hold. A car in working condition can be driven or hauled to its new home with a minimum of problems. This means that antique and classic automobiles have a national market. To get the best price for a car, first check the guides used by automobile dealers and wholesalers when they make an offer on your secondhand car. After you have established these prices, get a copy of *Hemmings Motor News,* the newspaper for car collectors, and check further.

There are car swap meets and sales in every area of the country. Any old-car owner near you can tell you how to find these rallies. This is the best place to sell a car if you know the value. If you don't, it may pay to visit a rally and ask for some opinions from collectors. They are always happy to help.

An ad in the local paper sells classic autos just as well as it sells used cars. If you own a desirable antique auto or an expensive classic, it will sell well at an antique car auction. They are listed in *Hemmings* or in the other car publications found in your library.

In 1839, when roads were rough and the way long, a Scottish blacksmith named Kirkpatrick MacMillan invented the bicycle. It weighed 57 pounds and sported a carved horsehead at its front. The years have seen many improvements, steering, rubber tires, and motors. Collectors of vintage motorcycles and bicycles often ride the antique models. Parts can be found in commercial bicycle and motorcycle shops and at huge automobile flea markets. There are special clubs and publications for motorcycle collectors and some crossover with the car-collecting organizations.

Railroads have a charm that never fades. Collectors are interested in toy railroads (see Toys) as well as real ones. You can buy dining-car silverware or dishes or even whole train cars if you wish. Full-sized trains, and airplanes, boats, and farm machinery present problems. They are huge, difficult to transport, and of limited interest. Sometimes they can be sold to a town restoration, a large outdoor village museum, or an amusement park. An ad in the antiques papers, a specialized publication, or even a local newspaper might bring results. The best customer for you is someone who has previously purchased a full-sized vehicle.

There are meets for owners of farm equipment, especially steam-powered equipment, and for train, boat, motorcycle, firefighting, and airplane enthusiasts. Locate the meets, attend (if possible), and explain what you have to sell.

The smaller transportation collectibles, such as light bulbs, paint, floor mats, hubcaps, hood ornaments, instruction books, or anything else needed for a car, sell well through the regular antiques dealers and shows, as well as at the special car meets. A car meet usually has tables for dealers or collectors who want to swap or sell parts. You can sell your items at the meet to dealers or collectors. Don't forget old license plates and gasoline station memorabilia like gas pump globes or even full-sized gas pumps.

The lure of the sea remains as romantic today as it has for centuries. Many collectors search for memorabilia about whaling, steamships, famous sinkings, sailboats, fishing, and other specialties. All these are included in maritime antiques. The Ivory section in this book includes information on scrimshaw.

Transportation memorabilia like railroad bells, uniforms, menus, china, replicas of trains, ads, boating brochures, spark plugs, motors, makers' nameplates, and farm machinery parts, especially cast-iron seats, are easily sold if you locate the right collectors. Toys related to all these collections also sell well through the meets and publications and through the regular toy shows. The same rules apply for large horse-drawn carriages, sleighs, popcorn wagons, or any of the oversized riding antiques.

Horse-drawn vehicles, like carriages and sleds, are collected by a small, earnest group with space and, probably, horses. To learn more about horse-drawn vehicles, read the special publications on the subject. Meets, restoration problems, and history are discussed. There are still a few working wheelwrights in rural America who can put an iron band on a wooden wheel and do other repairs. To locate one requires ingenuity and determination. Try calling a local farm paper and ask if they can help. Talk to the stables and riding schools in your area. We met a Midwestern wheelwright doing demonstrations at a local "living history" fair.

REPAIR

There are many collectors of old automobiles, automobile parts, instruction books, and memorabilia. Many professional restorers work in all parts of the country. Local collectors can tell you about nearby restoration shops. Parts can be found through ads in automobile-related publications or your local newspaper. Word-of-mouth advertising through other collectors and dealers is also successful. Huge auto collectors' flea markets are held throughout the country. Almost every type of part—old or reproduction—can be found. Collectors often go to shows looking like walking billboards with lists of wants written in large letters on a shirt or sign. After a day of walking through miles of dealers' and collectors' booths and asking questions, you will probably get the answer about where to find your car part. Check at your library for more information about local clubs and events.

Price Books

Antique Classic Marque Car Keys, 2nd edition, Don Stewart (Key Collectors International, PO Box 9397, Phoenix, AZ 85068, © 1993).

Railroad Switch Keys & Padlocks, 2nd edition, Don Stewart (Key Collectors International, PO Box 9397, Phoenix, AZ 85068, © 1993).

Book on Repair

The Restoration of Vintage & Thoroughbred Motorcycles, Jeff Clew (Motorsport, 550 Honey Locust Rd., Jonesburg, MO 63351).

Clubs & Publications

American Aviation Historical Society, *AAHS Journal* (MAG), *Newsletter* (NL), 2333 Otis St., Santa Ana, CA 92704.

American Driving Society, *Whip* (MAG), (NL), PO Box 160, Metamora, MI 48455 (horse-drawn vehicles).

Antique & Classic Boat Society, Inc., *Rusty Rudder* (NL), 715 Mary St., Clayton, NY 13624.

Antique Airplane Association, Inc., *Antique Airplane News & Digest* (MAG), Rt. 2, Box 172, Ottumwa, IA 52501.

Antique Automobile Club of America, Inc., *Antique Automobile* (MAG), 501 W. Governor Rd., Hershey, PA 17033.

Antique Motorcycle Club of America, *Antique Motorcycle* (MAG), PO Box 333, Sweetser, IN 46987.

Antique Truck Club of America, Inc., *Double Clutch* (MAG), PO Box 291, Hershey, PA 17033.

Automobile License Plate Collectors Association, Inc., *ALPCA Newsletter* (NL), Box 77, Horner, WV 26372.

Carriage Association of America Inc., *Carriage Journal* (MAG), 177 Pointers Auburn Rd., Salem, NJ 08079 (horse-drawn carriages, driving, restoration).

Cast Iron Seat Collectors Association, *Newsletter of Cast Iron Seat Collectors Association* (NL), RR #2, Box 40, Le Center, MN 56067.

Chesapeake & Ohio Historical Society, Inc., *Chesapeake & Ohio Historical Magazine* (MAG), PO Box 79, Clifton Forge, VA 24422.

Chris Craft Antique Boat Club, Inc., *Brass Bell* (NL), 217 S. Adams St., Tallahassee, FL 32301-1708 (Chris Craft and other antique and classic boats).

Contemporary Historical Vehicle Association Inc., *Action Era Vehicle* (MAG), PO Box 98, Tecumseh, KS 66542-0098.

Cushman Club of America, *Cushman Club of America Magazine* (MAG), PO Box 661, Union Springs, AL 36089 (Cushman motor scooters).

Historical Construction Equipment Association, *Equipment Echoes* (NL), PO Box 328, Grand Rapids, OH 43522.

International Bus Collectors Club, *International Bus Collectors Club* (MAG), *IBC News* (NL), 1518 "C" Trailee Dr., Charleston, SC 29407 (buses and bus collectibles, badges, pins, buckles, timetables, models; books and historic videos).

International Hart-Parr/Oliver Collectors Association, *Hart-Parr/Oliver Collector* (MAG), PO Box 685, Charles City, IA 50616 (tractors).

International Harvester Collector, *Harvester Highlights* (NL), RR 2, Box 286, Winamac, IN 46996.

Milestone Car Society, *Mile Post* (MAG), PO Box 24612, Speedway, IN 46224 (postwar cars, 1945–1970, and other certified milestone cars unique in engineering or styling).

Model "A" Restorers Club, *Model "A" News* (MAG), 24800 Michigan Ave., Dearborn, MI 48124.

Mustang Club of America, Inc., *Mustang Times* (MAG), PO Box 447, Lithonia, GA 30058-0447.

Nautical Research Guild, *Nautical Research Journal* (MAG), 19 Pleasant St., Everett, MA 02149 (research on large vessels for builders of model ships).

New York Central System Historical Society Inc., *Central Headlight* (MAG), PO Box 24817, Lyndhurst, OH 44124-0817.

Oceanic Navigation Research Society, Inc., *Ship to Shore* (MAG), PO Box 8005, Universal City, CA 91608-0005.

Railroadiana Collectors Association, Inc., *Railroadiana Express* (MAG), 795 Aspen Dr., Buffalo Grove, IL 60089-1359.

Route 66 Association of Illinois, *The 66 News!* (NL), PO Box 8262, Rolling Meadows, IL 60008.

Spark Plug Collectors of America, *Ignitor* (NL), *Hot Sheet* (NL), 3401 NE Riverside, Pendleton, OR 97801.

Steamship Historical Society of America, Inc., *Steamboat Bill* (MAG), 300 Ray Dr., Suite #4, Providence, RI 02906.

Texas Date Nail Collectors Association, *Nailer News* (NL), 501 W. Horton, Brenham, TX 77833.

Threaded Hubcap Collectors Club Int., *Hubcapper* (NL), PO Box 54, 504 E. North, Buckley, MI 49620 (screw-on hubcaps, used on wooden spoke wheels).

Titanic Historical Society, Inc., *Titanic Commutator* (MAG), 1053 Indian Orchard, MA 01151-0053.

Titanic International, Inc., *Voyage* (MAG), PO Box 7007, Freehold, NJ 07728.

Tucker Automobile Club of America, *Tucker Topics* (NL), 311 W. 18th St., Tifton, GA 31794.

Veteran Motor Car Club of America, *Bulb Horn* (MAG), PO Box 360788, Strongsville, OH 44136.

World War I Aeroplanes, Inc., *Skyways* (MAG), *WW I Aero* (MAG), 15 Crescent Rd., Poughkeepsie, NY 12601. (*Skyways* is about 1920–1940 airplanes.)

Zeppelin Collectors Club, *Zeppelin Collector* (NL), PO Box A3843, Chicago, IL 60690-3843 (aerophilatelic).

American Neptune: The Journal of Maritime History (MAG), Peabody Essex Museum, East India Square, Salem, MA 01970.

Antique Power (MAG), Antique Power, Inc., PO Box 838, Yellow Springs, OH 45387 (antique tractors; antique tractor pulling; antique and classic truck restoration, pre-1980).

Automobile Quarterly (MAG), PO Box 348, 15040 Kutztown Rd., Kutztown, PA 19530-0348.

Belt Pulley (MAG), PO Box 83, Nokomis, IL 62075 (tractors and other farm equipment).

British Bike Magazine (MAG), *Classic Bike* (MAG), *Classic Motor Cycle* (MAG), *Classic Racer* (MAG), 550 Honey Locust Rd., Jonesburg, MO 63351-9600.

Car Collector & Car Classics (MAG), 1241 Canton St., Atlanta, GA 30075.

Cars & Parts (MAG), *Collectible Trucks* (MAG), *Collectible Car Annual* (MAG), PO Box 482, Sidney, OH 45365.

Check The Oil! (NL), PO Box 937, Powell, OH 43065-0937.

Classic Boating Magazine (MAG), 280 Lac La Belle Dr., Oconomowoc, WI 53066-1648.

Collectible Automobile (MAG), 7373 N. Cicero, Lincolnwood, IL 60646 (includes a section on scale models).

Convertible Magazine (MAG), PO Box 1011, San Mateo, CA 94403.

du Pont Registry (MAG), 2325 Ulmerton Rd., Suite 16, Clearwater, FL 34622 (cars, all ads).

Farm Antiques News (NL), 812 N. Third St., Tarkio, MO 64491 (news, events, and prices for collectors of farm and rural antiques and collectibles of all types).

Gas Engine Magazine (MAG), PO Box 328, Lancaster, PA 17608 (gasoline engine tractors and stationary engines).

Green Magazine (MAG), PO Box 7, Bee, NE 68314 (John Deere tractors and collectibles).

Hemmings Motor News (MAG), Box 100, Bennington, VT 05201.

Iron-Men Album Magazine (MAG), PO Box 328, Lancaster, PA 17608 (steam traction engines, tractors, and threshers).

Key, Lock and Lantern (MAG), 3400 Ridge Rd. W., #266, Rochester, NY 14626 (railroad, railroad-related collectibles, anthracite coal collectibles).

Locomotive & Railway Preservation (MAG), PO Box 246, Richmond, VT 05477.

Mobilia (NL), PO Box 575, Middlebury, VT 05753.

Model A & Model T Ford Monthly (MAG), Rt. 3, Box 425, Jasper, FL 32052.

Monthly Old Bike Mart (NP), PO Box 99, Horncastle, Lincolnshire, U.K. LN9 6LZ (motorcycles).

Motorcycle Collector (MAG), 30011 Ivy Glen Dr., #114, Laguna Niguel, CA 92677.

Motorcycle Shopper (MAG), 1353 Herndon Ave., Deltona, FL 32725-9046.

Nautical Brass (NL), PO Box 3966, N. Fort Myers, FL 33918-3966.

Nautical Collector: The Journal of Nautical Antiques, Collectibles & Nostalgia (MAG), PO Box 16734, Alexandria, VA 22302-0734.

Old Bike Journal (MAG), PO Box 391, Mt. Morris, IL 61054 (motorcycles).

Old Car Price Guide (MAG), *Old Cars News & Marketplace* (NP), 700 E. State St., Iola, WI 54990

(cars/parts for sale).

Oliver Collector's News (NL), RR 1, Box 44, Manvel, ND 58256 (tractors, full scale and models).

Red Power (MAG), Box 277, Battle Creek, IA 51008 (International Harvester, full scale and models).

Rumely Collector's News (MAG), 12109 Mennonite Church Rd., Tremont, IL 61568 (Rumely, Advance Rumely, Aultman-Taylor, and Gaar-Scott tractors and equipment).

Rusty Iron Monthly (NL), Box 342, Sandwich, IL 60548 (old iron tractors, engines, and equipment).

Signpost (NL), PO Box 41381, St. Petersburg, FL 33743 (highway signs and markers).

Vintage Truck and Fire Engine Monthly (MAG), Rt. 3, Box 425, Jasper, FL 32052.

Walneck's Classic Cycle—Trader (MAG), 7923 Janes Ave., Woodridge, IL 60517 (buy-sell-trade ads for antique and classic motorcycles).

Repairs, Parts & Supplies

American Marine Model Gallery, Inc., 12 Derby Sq., Salem, MA 01970-3704, 508-745-5777, 9:00 A.M.–4:30 P.M.; 508-745-5778. Restoration of marine models. Display cases. Appraisals.

Brass 'n Bounty, Richard Dermody and Maryanne Baiakian, 68 Front St., Marblehead, MA 01945, 617-631-3864. Restoration of marine antiques, including navigational instruments, models, dioramas, ship lights, clocks, and miscellaneous gear. Will search for customer's wants.

Eagle Restoration, Sherman Langell, HCR 9547, Keaau, HI 96749-9317, 808-966-4648, anytime. Reproduction rubber step pads for antique boats. Replacement engine mounts for antique marine engines.

Little Century, H. Thomas and Patricia Laun, 215 Paul Ave., Syracuse, NY 13206, 315-437-4156, summer residence 315-654-3244. Fire department antiques and collectibles repaired. Parts made.

Old Wheels, 4846 W. Earll Dr., Phoenix, AZ

85031, 602-278-0520, 8:00 A.M.–8:00 P.M. Manufacturers of fiberglass replica horn tanks for popular classic bicycles. Send LSASE for price list and model availability.

Paul's Chrome Plating Inc., 341 Mars-Valencia Rd., Mars, PA 16046, 412-625-3135, Mon.–Fri. 8:00 A.M.–5:00 P.M., plus Wed. 7:00 P.M.–8:30 P.M.; fax: 412-625-3060. Copper, nickel, and chrome plating, polishing stainless steel and aluminum. Specializing in the restoration of antique car parts, motorcycles, and brass on boats.

Time Passages, Ltd., Scott Anderson, PO Box 65596, West Des Moines, IA 50265, 515-223-5105, 8:30 A.M.–5:30 P.M.; fax: 515-223-5149. Antique gasoline pumps, globes, signs, oil cans, restoration parts, and supplies. Mail order. Consulting and appraisals. Catalog $4.

Vod Varka Springs, US Route 30, PO Box 170, Clinton, PA 15026-0170, 412-695-3268, 8:45 A.M.–4:30 P.M.; fax: 412-695-3268. Custom-made springs for cars. Made to order per print or sample.

William Hulbert, Jr., PO Box 151, Adams Center, NY 13606, 315-583-5765, 6:00 P.M.–9:30 P.M. Restoration of all makes of auto radios, pre-transistor. Chevrolet parts, 1928–1932.

Video

How, Why and When to Buy a Collector Car, by Mitchell Kruse, **Advision Incorporated,** 3100 Arrowwood Ln., Boulder, Co 80303-2419, 800-876-2320. Tips on how to buy and restore collector cars. 30 minutes, $29.95.

*T*runks

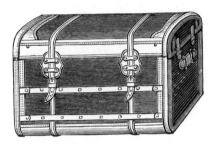

*N*ineteenth-century trunks sell to people who want to use them as tables or toy chests. All kinds sell—humpback, flat, leather-covered, or wooden. In bad condition, the price is low, but since many people want to restore the trunk as a do-it-yourself project, almost any trunk sells. In the 1990s old alligator doctor bags, twentieth-century hard-sided suitcases, and steamer trunks started to sell. These must be in good condition. Watch for any by VUITTON. These sell for hundreds of dollars.

REPAIR

Old trunks should be restored to their original condition. If they are in very poor condition, they can be refinished in some decorative manner, but this will change the piece from an old trunk to a decorative accessory. There are many books about modern decorations for trunks, but very few on correct restoration. Parts, including hardware, leather handles, and trim, are available by mail.

One major problem with old trunks is that they may smell musty. To remove the odor, wash the interior of the trunk and let it dry in a sunny spot. If the odor persists, try storing some charcoal, crumpled newspaper, or other absorbent material in the trunk for a few days.

Repairs, Parts & Supplies

Antique Trunk Supply Co., 3706 W. 169th St., Cleveland, OH 44111, 216-941-8618, 9:30 A.M.–5:30 P.M. Trunk parts, including corners, coverings, handles, locks, nails, straps, repair books, plans, and more. Catalog $1.

C & H Supply, 5431 Mountville Rd., Adamstown, MD 21710, 301-663-1812, Mon.–Fri. 9:00 A.M.–5:00 P.M.; fax: 301-874-2524. Replacement trunk parts. Veneers, paint and varnish removers, stains and lacquers. Most orders shipped within 24 hours. Catalog $4.

Charlotte Ford Trunks, Box 536, Spearman, TX 79081, 806-659-3027, 800-553-2649 for orders, 9:00 A.M.–4:00 P.M. Trunk repair supplies. Locks, hinges, drawbolts, handles, nails, leather straps, and more. *Trunk Talk* shows how to clean, repair, and decorate any style trunk, $7.50. Quarterly newsletter contains restoration information, $15 a year.

House of Antique Trunks, 753B Northport Dr., PO Box 508K, West Sacramento, CA 95691, 916-372-8228, Tues.–Fri. 9:00 A.M.–4:00 P.M., Sat. 9:00 A.M.–2:00 P.M., 916-371-4979 other times. Antique trunk restoration, parts, and accessories. Iron, brass, tin, nickel-plated, and brass-plated hardware: straps, handles, doll trunk supplies, prints for lids, linings; rust remover, adhesives, and decorative supplies. Parts catalog, $2.50. *Art of Trunk Restoration,* $6.

Joyce's Choices, Rt. 1, Box 89F, White Point Rd., Leonardtown, MD 20650, 301-475-7279, 9:00 A.M.–5:00 P.M. Trunk restoration and parts. Booklet *Practical Trunk Restoration,* $4.95 plus 50 cents postage. Catalog, $2.50 plus 50 cents postage. Both for $8.

Just Trunks, Peter A. Comeau, Sr., 110 Sugarberry Dr., New Castle, DE 19720, 302-834-8408, Mon.–Sat. 9:00 A.M.–5:00 P.M. Trunk restorations, parts, and supplies. Catalog $2.

Original Woodworks, 360 North Main Street, Stillwater, MN 55082, 612-430-3622, Thurs.–Sat. noon–5:00 P.M. Trunk restorations. Restoration hardware.

Phyllis Kennedy, 9256 Holyoke Ct., Indianapolis, IN 46268, 317-872-6366, 10:00 A.M.–5:00 P.M. Trunk hardware, leather handles, and leather straps. Store located at 10663 Andrade Drive, Zionsville, IN 46077. Catalog $3.

Trunks by Paul, Paul Berkowitz, 14 Park Ave., Gaithersburg, MD 20877, 301-840-0920, 9:00 A.M.–8:00 P.M. Restoration and refinishing of antique trunks. Trunk hardware. Mail order.

Van Dyke's, Box 278, Woonsocket, SD 57385, 605-796-4425, 800-843-3320, orders only, 8:00 A.M.–6:00 P.M.; fax: 605-796-4085. Brass hardware of all kinds, including trunk parts. Tools, stains, varnishes, brushes, modeling compounds. Special parts designed to duplicate the original pieces. Mail order worldwide. Catalog $1.

Western Artifacts, "Cowboys & Indians"

*A*nything representative of the Old West is very easily sold. Spurs, saddles, photographs, carvings, furniture, snowshoes, even old boots sell well. All Indian-made pieces are in demand, both old and new. This includes blankets, rugs, beadwork, pottery, baskets, clothing and special crafts like quill work.

There are a few restrictions on the sale of Indian pieces. Anything using an eagle feather cannot be sold because of the endangered species act. Sometimes the feathers appear on kachina dolls or ceremonial head pieces. A few animal furs may also cause trouble. Mexican Indian pieces of importance are, by law, kept in Mexico, and smuggled items will be confiscated in both the United States and Mexico. Religious items may be reclaimed by the Indian tribe so these are not sold through an open auction or show. Discreet conversations with dealers in Indian items may make it possible for you to donate the piece to a museum or to quietly sell it to another private collector. But remember, this may be illegal.

Many baskets, dolls, and beaded pieces were made by the Indians to sell to tourists in the early 1900s. These all sell quickly at reasonable prices, and you can learn the values through the general price books. It is the unusual, a carved figure or ceremonial pipe, that is very valuable.

Arrowheads dug up on your farm should be sold to nearby specialists. Any Indian item sells best closest to its point of origin, if that is known. If you have a collection of baskets, clothing, or carvings assembled from many sources, you should contact a Southwestern or major Eastern dealer or gallery. A large collection or an important piece should be appraised by a competent expert on Indian art, a rarity in most cities. It will be of no help to go to the average appraiser of fine arts for values. Ask for references and be sure the appraiser has appraised Indian art before.

Look in *The Indian Trader* or other publications about Indian art. Dealers and shows will be listed, and if you live far away, you can offer your pieces by mail with pictures. Rarity, artistic value, condition, and age determine the price of an Indian artifact.

Indian objects, including tourist baskets, cow-horn chairs, and Navajo rugs, as well as cowboy equipment, including elaborate boots and belts, and prints, paintings, and bronzes depicting horses and horsemen of the West, all came into favor in the 1960s and prices have continued rising. Don't underestimate the value of any collectible that pictures a cowboy or Western scene. Even a child's wastebasket picturing a horse will sell. It is difficult to sell good Western art for the best possible prices in the East or South, but it can be done with a little study and effort.

The best place to sell Western pieces is in the West, where the decorators search for the unusual. If you live in another section of the country, you may have to sell your pieces at a lower price to a dealer who goes to the Western shows. Top quality, authentic, old pieces sell well at auction houses in any part of the country.

REPAIR

Perfect pieces of American Indian pottery are so rare that the slightly damaged and repaired piece is in demand. If you break a piece of cut glass in half, then glue it together, the resale value drops to about 10 percent of the original value. If you repair a broken piece of American Indian pottery, the resale value is from 50 to 75 percent of the original value. So if you drop your Maria vase, save the pieces and have the vase professionally restored.

Many Western pieces are listed in other sections of this book, so be sure to look in the chapters on barbed wire, dolls, jewelry, wicker, rattan and basketry, clothing, pottery and porcelain, textiles, folk art, rugs, scrimshaw, and firearms.

Price Books

Collector's Guide to Hopalong Cassidy Memorabilia, Joseph J. Caro (L-W Books, PO Box 69, Gas City, IN 46933, © 1993).

Cowboy Culture: The Last Frontier of American Antiques, Michael Friendman (Schiffer, Atglen, PA, © 1992).

Indian Artifacts of the Midwest, Book II, Lar Hothem (Collector Books, Paducah, KY, © 1995).

North American Indian Artifacts, 5th edition, Lar Hothem (Books Americana, Florence, AL, © 1994).

Official Price Guide to Old West Collectibles, R.C. House (House of Collectibles, New York, © 1994).

The Overstreet Indian Arrowheads Identification and Price Guide, 4th edition, Robert M. Overstreet and Howard Peake (Avon Books, New York, © 1995).

Western Memorabilia Identification and Price Guide, William C. Ketchum (Avon Books, New York, © 1993).

Club & Publications

National Bit, Spur & Saddle Collectors Association, *Bit, Spur & Saddle* (NL), 3604 Galley Rd., Suite 120, Colorado Springs, CO 80909.

Indian Trader (MAG), PO Box 1421, Gallup, NM 87305.

Southwest Art (MAG), 460535, Houston, TX 77056.

Yippy-Yi-Yea (MAG), 8393 E. Holly Rd., Holly, MI 48442.

Conservator & Restorer

Wood 'N Wildlife, 9922 Bostwick Park Rd., Montrose, CO 81401, 303-249-5863, before 9:00 P.M. Restoration of Indian artifacts: broken stone tips and bone objects repaired and replaced. Send SASE for more information.

See also the sections on Folk Art, Jewelry, Pottery & Porcelain, Textiles, and Wicker, Rattan & Basketry.

Wicker, Rattan & Basketry

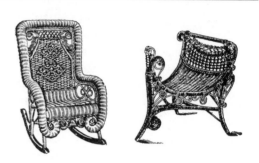

All baskets, from Indian and Nantucket baskets to Chinese sewing baskets, are popular. The price is determined by quality, design, maker, variety, and condition. Miniatures under two inches high and the very large baskets always command premium prices. Amateurs have a hard time pricing baskets. New African, Chinese, Filipino, South American, Korean, Taiwanese, and other baskets are often made as exact replicas of old baskets. Since natural materials are used, the design is copied exactly, and the work is by hand. It takes great knowledge to tell the old from the new. As a seller, you are only worried about getting as much as possible. If you know the basket has been in your family for fifty years, you know it is old, so you can price it accordingly. If you bought it at a house sale last year, you may not have a valuable basket, and pricing could be difficult. Dealers in baskets and good auction houses can tell the difference. Rather than price your baskets too low, take them to an expert.

Prices are often listed by the maker in general price books. The most desirable baskets are by the Shakers, American Indians, or the Nantucket lightship makers. Added features like potato-stamp designs, feathers or beads incorporated in the basket, or a strong history of maker and ownership will add to the price. Remember, baskets are of many shapes and sizes, from laundry baskets to toys, to oriental flower containers.

REPAIR

Wicker and rattan baskets, furniture, and other objects should be kept away from direct heat and sunny windows. Pieces should be washed occasionally or wiped with a damp sponge. Moisture will keep wicker from becoming dry and brittle. Repairs can be made. There are several books that include pictures and simple descriptions of how to fix a leg or mend a bit of snagged wicker.

See also Furniture.

Books on Repair

Caner's Handbook, Bruce W. Miller and Jim Widess (Van Nostrand Reinhold Co., New York, © 1983).

Old New England Splint Baskets, John E. McGuire (Schiffer Publishing Co., West Chester, PA, © 1985).

Successful Restoration Shop, Thomas Duncan (Sylvan Books, P.O. Box 481, Syracuse, IN 46567, © 1985).

Techniques of Basketry, Virginia I. Harvey (Van Nostrand Reinhold Co., New York, © 1974).

Wicker Furniture, A Guide to Restoring & Collecting, Richard Saunders (Crown Publishers, New York, © 1990).

Publication

Martha Wetherbee Basket Shop News (NL), HCR 69 Box 171, Sanbornton, NJ 03269.

Repairs, Parts & Supplies

Able to Cane, 439 Main St., PO Box 429, Warren, ME 04864, 207-273-3747, anytime. Caning and basketry supplies, restoration of antique furniture. Catalog $1.

Cane & Basket Supply Company, 1238 S. Cochran Ave., Los Angeles, CA 90019, 213-939-9644; fax: 213-939-7237. Chair caning and basketry supplies. Raffia cloth, rattan, bamboo, willow, rush, seagrass, splint, hand-weaving cane, hoops and handles, pressed-fiber replacement seats, rubber webbing for modern chairs, Shaker tape, books, tools, and supplies. Mail order worldwide. Catalog $2.

Canecraft, Lilian Cummings, RD 1 Box 126-A, Andreas, PA 18211, 717-386-2441, Mon.–Sat. 9:00 A.M.–6:00 P.M. Chair seat weaving and basketry supplies. Instruction books for caning, rush and splint weaving, and basketry work. Wicker repair. Send SASE (#10 envelope) for catalog.

Caning Shop, 926 Gilman St., Dept. KOV, Berkeley, CA 94710-1494, 510-527-5010, Tues.–Fri. 10:00 A.M.–6:00 P.M., Sat. 10:00 A.M.–2:00 P.M., answering machine after hours. Complete line of basketry and chair caning supplies, including cane, splint, reed, rush, sea grass, Shaker tape, pressed-fiber seats, books, and tools. Catalog $1, refundable with purchase.

Carolina Caning Supply, PO Box 2179, Smithfield, NC 27577, 800-346-0142, 919-934-3469, anytime. Various types of materials for caning and wicker repair. Mail order. Send SASE for free catalog.

Connecticut Cane & Reed Co., PO Box 762, Manchester, CT 06040, 203-646-6586, Mon.–Fri. 9:00 A.M.–5:00 P.M.; fax: 203-649-2221. Chair seating and wicker repair materials. Mail order. Send sample to be matched. Free catalog.

Dotty McDaniel, 1900 Stoney Ridge Rd., Cumming, GA 30131, 404-887-8518, anytime. Wicker restoration and repair. Chair caning. Laced cane, pressed cane, split oak, binder cane, fiber rush, natural rush, seagrass, Shaker tape, and Danish cord.

Frank's Cane & Rush Supply, 7244 Heil Ave., Huntington Beach, CA 92647, 714-847-0707, 8:00 A.M.–5:00 P.M.; fax: 714-843-5645. Canes, cane webbing, reed spline, fibers, oriental sea grass, wicker braids and knobs, reeds, upholstery supplies, wood parts, basketry kits and supplies, seat weaving kits, brass hardware, wood hoops and handles, natural weaving supplies, rattan and bamboo poles, wheat straw, waxed linen, rawhide strips, cotton cordage, tools, books, and other supplies. Free brochure.

Furniture Restoration Supply Co., 5498 Rt. 34, Oswego, IL 60543, 800-432-2745, 708-554-2745, Mon.–Fri. 8:00 A.M.–5:00 P.M., Sat .8:00 A.M.–noon; fax: 708-554-1545, anytime. Upholstery supplies, caning and wicker repair supplies, stripping and refinishing supplies. Catalog $2, refundable with first purchase.

Gundula's & Peerless Rattan at the Wrap n Post, 624 S. Burnett Rd., Springfield, OH 45505, 513-323-0003, 513-323-7353. Retail and wholesale basket and chair caning supplies. Hours: Mon.–Fri. 8:30 A.M.–5:30 P.M.; Sat. 8:30 A.M.–2:30 P.M. Orders may be left on answering machine. Phone orders shipped promptly. Free price list.

H. H. Perkins Co., 20 S. Bradley Rd., Woodbridge, CT 06525, 800-462-6660, Mon.–Fri. 9:00 A.M.–5:00 P.M., Sat. 9:00 A.M.–noon; fax: 203-389-4011. Basketry and seat weaving supplies: cane, rush, splint, Shaker tape, reeds, Hong Kong grass, handles, tools, literature, and how-to videos. Mail order. Free catalog.

Original Woodworks, 360 N. Main St., Stillwater, MN 55082, 612-430-3622, Thurs.–Sat. noon–5:00 P.M. Cane, rush, splint, leather seats, and supplies.

Price House Antiques, 137 Cabot St., Beverly, MA 01915, 508-927-5595, 10:00 A.M.–5:00 P.M. daily. Restoration of antique and other wicker furnishings. Caning, porch weave seats, natural and fiber rush seat replacements. Furniture refinishing.

Rockinghorse Antiques, Bette Jeane Rutkowski, 111 St. Helena Ave., Dundalk, MD 21222, 410-285-0280, 8:00 A.M.–11:00 P.M. Restoration of antique wicker carriages. Appraisals, identification, and value.

Wicker Fixer & Chair Caning, Cheri and Mike Russell, Rt. 1, Box 349, Ozark, MO 65721, 417-485-6148, 8:00 A.M.–8:00 P.M., leave message. Wicker repairs and restoration, minor to major surgery, painting, seats recaned. Will ship anywhere in U.S. Tip sheet on wicker, $3 plus LSASE.

The Wicker Woman, 531 Main St., PO Box 61, Zumbro Falls, MN 55991, 507-753-2006. Wicker restoration, chair caning, seat weaving.

Wicker Workshop, Larry Cryderman and Shoshana Enosh, 18744 Parthenia St. #1, Northridge, CA 91324, 818-886-4524, anytime; fax: 818-886-0115. Restoration and repair of wicker, caning, rushing, split reed, hickory, and splint. Spindles for chairs and rockers. Upholstering.

Writing Utensils

*P*ens, automatic pencils, ink bottles, inkwells, typewriters, and many other devices connected with writing are being collected. In the 1980s, early pens and the plastic-cased pens of the 1920s through the 1950s became of interest to collectors. The problems associated with old fountain pens are stiff or leaky ink sacs or dirty pen points, which can be fixed carefully at home if the proper parts are purchased. There are also some specialists in pen repairs listed in this chapter.

Typewriters have been difficult to sell unless they are very old and unusual, but a new group of collectors has emerged in the 1990s.

See also Glass and Pottery & Porcelain.

Price Books

The Book of Fountain Pens and Pencils, Stuart Schneider and George Fischler (Schiffer, Atglen, PA, © 1992).

The Illustrated Guide to Antique Writing Instruments, Stuart Schneider and George Fischler (Schiffer Publishing, Atglen, PA, © 1994).

Reference Books

Fountain Pens, 2nd edition, Cliff Lawrence (Pen Fancier's Club, 1169 Overcash Dr., Dunedin, FL 34698, © 1985).

Fountain Pens and Pencils: The Golden Age of Writing Instruments, George Fischler and Stuart Schneider (Schiffer, Atglen, PA, © 1990).

What You Need to Know About Collecting Fountain Pens, Judson Bell (World Publications, 2240 Northpark Dr., Kingwood, TX 77339, © 1989).

Clubs & Publications

American Pencil Collectors Society, *Pencil Collector* (NL), 7853 W Co. Rd. 100 N., Greensburg, IN 47240 (pens and pencils).

Early Typewriter Collectors Association, *ETCetera* (MAG), 2591 Military Ave., Los Angeles, CA 90064.

Society of Inkwell Collectors, *Stained Finger* (NL), 5136 Thomas Ave. S., Minneapolis, MN 55410.

Pen World Magazine (MAG), PO Box 6007, Kingwood, TX 77325.

PenFinder (NL), PO Box 6007, Kingwood, TX 77325 (buy-sell-trade ads).

Ribbon Tin News (NL), 28 The Green, Watertown, CT 06795 (typewriter ribbon tins).

Typewriter Exchange (NL), 2125 Mount Vernon St., Philadelphia, PA 19130.

Repairs, Parts & Supplies

Authorized Repair Service, 30 W. 57th St., New York, NY 10019, 212-586-0947, Mon.–Fri. 9:00 A.M.–5:00 P.M.; fax: 212-586-1296. Restoration of antique pens. No charge for estimate of repairs.

Classic Fountain Pens, PO Box 46723, Los Angeles, CA 90046, 213-655-2641, 8:30 A.M.–5:00 P.M.; 213-651-0265. All gold fountain pen nib repairs: retipping any size nib, repairs to nib cracks and splits.

Fountain Pen Hospital, 10 Warren St., New York, NY 10007, 212-964-0580, 7:30 A.M.–6:00 P.M.; fax: 212-227-5916. Antique pens repaired. Supplies, including pen sacs, Sac-Glue, fountain pen polish, and books on pens. Free brochure.

Geoffrey Berliner, 327 W. 18th St., No. 3F, New York, NY 10011, 212-243-7014, Mon.–Fri. 9:00 A.M.–5:00 P.M.; fax: 212-243-1328. Repair and restoration of vintage fountain pens, all makes and models. Special request, nib repair, and lathe work done.

Howard Levy, 2567 Sherwood Rd., Bexley, OH 43209, 614-236-6057, Mon.–Fri. 6:00 P.M.–10:00 P.M., weekends 9:00 A.M.–10:00 P.M.; fax: 614-529-0344. Repair and restoration of fountain pens, antique, and modern.

Pen Fancier's Club, 1169 Overcash Dr., Dunedin, FL 34698, 813-734-4742, 10:00 A.M.–10:00 P.M. Ink sacs (bladders); repair manuals for fountain pens and mechanical pencils.

Pen Store Inc., 404 Zack St., Tampa, FL 33602, 813-223-3865, Mon.–Fri. 9:00 A.M.–5:00 P.M.; fax: 813-228-9460. Repair and restoration of antique and modern pens. Engraving and calligraphy service.

Society of Inkwell Collectors, 5136 Thomas Ave. S., Minneapolis, MN 55410. Handcrafted glass inkwell inserts made to order. Size chart available.

Vintage Fountain Pens, PO Box 8212, Columbus, OH 43201, 614-267-8468. Pen restoration, full service.

....

*A*ll the *R*est

*O*ver twenty-five years ago we wrote: "There is a time in everyone's life when you must decide what to do with an attic, basement, or even a drawer full of odd bits of small 'junk.' Don't throw anything away. More good antiques have been lost because of overeager housekeeping than by all other ways combined. Open all boxes and sort the contents. Stop for a moment and think, study, read, and ask lots of questions. There is a collector for almost anything. We have known of individuals and organizations that want matchboxes, playing cards, racetrack betting tickets, theater ticket stubs, theater programs, postmarks, Masonic items, erotica, gambling chips, trunks, Christmas seals, funeral invitations, old valentines and greeting cards, ads, trading cards, military insignia, railroad passes, coffin markers, newspapers, sheet music, comic books, magazines, almost anything (including the box it came in). Be patient! No item loses value

with age. If, after looking around, you can find no value for the items, give them to a collector, historical society, or even a neighbor's young child. It will go into another box of 'junk' to be saved for another generation of collectors. Maybe in twenty-five years it will have a value, and for the next twenty-five it will give joy to the child who received it."

The advice was good then and is still. Notice that many of the things we mentioned then that were considered worthless, such as greeting cards, ads, and comic books, are valued today, some even worth thousands of dollars. It's impossible to mention everything you might have that could be sold through the antiques market. We have tried to discuss selling most types of collectibles. A few other specialized collecting interests that are important enough to have created a club or publication include animal license tags, lightning rods, badges, barbed wire, bells, buttons, buckles, fans, flags, ships in bottles, the Statue of Liberty, miniature key chain tags, fireworks, Boy Scout memorabilia, and World's Fair and exposition items.

One word of pessimism: There are a few things that are poor sellers. They are often not worth the time required to find a buyer. These include most old Bibles, encyclopedias and dictionaries, flags, sewing machines (unless very old), and swizzle sticks (usually traded). In our book written over twenty-five years ago we had a list of things the country store collectors ignored. Included were brooms, turkey-feather dusters, and soapstone foot warmers—all still not very easy to sell. But we wish we had the rest of the list: bathtubs, candy-making tools, early electrical equipment, egg carriers, eggbeaters, flour sifters, gas mantels, glass rolling pins, graniteware (enamel on metal dishes), ice boxes, ice-cream makers, ice-cream scoops, needle cases, peanut butter pails, and pencil sharpeners.

Our last bit of advice about selling is the "Damn Fool Theory": "REMEMBER, IF I WAS DAMN FOOL ENOUGH TO BUY THIS ANTIQUE, SOMEWHERE THERE IS ANOTHER DAMN FOOL WHO WILL BUY IT FOR MORE MONEY." So don't throw anything away. A buyer is out there somewhere; it just takes time.

Price Books

Avon & C.P.C. Collector's Encyclopedia, 13th edition, Bud Hastin (Bud Hastin, PO Box 9868, Kansas City, MO 64134, © 1994).

Black Memorabilia Around the House, Jan Lindenberger (Schiffer, Atglen, PA, © 1993).

British Royalty Commemoratives, Douglas H. Flynn, and Alan H. Bolton (Schiffer, Atglen, PA, © 1994).

Collecting the Space Race, Stuart Schneider (Schiffer, Atglen, PA, © 1993).

Complete Gillette Collector's Handbook, Phillip L. Krumholz (PO Box 4050, Bartonville, IL 61607, © 1992).

The Complete Salt and Pepper Shaker Book, Mike Schneider (Schiffer, Atglen, PA, © 1993).

Firehouse Memorabilia Identification and Price Guide, James Piatti (Avon Books, New York, © 1994).

Gambling Collectibles: A Sure Winner, Leonard Schneir (Schiffer, Atglen, PA, © 1993).

Hot Stuff! Firefighting Collectibles, Andrew G. Gurka (L-W Books, PO Box 69, Gas City, IN 46933, © 1994).

Illustrated Encyclopedia of Metal Lunch Boxes, Allen Woodall and Sean Brickell (Schiffer, Atglen, PA, © 1992).

Lenny's Lottery Ticket Price Guide, Lenny (Lenny's 1024 Borgert Ave., N., St. Cloud, MN 56303, © 1994).

Naughties, Nudies & Bathing Beauties, Sharon Hope Weintraub (Hobby House Press, Cumberland, MD, © 1993). Small bisque figurines of nude women made © 1880–1915.

1904 St. Louis World's Fair Mementos and Memorabilia, Robert L. Hendershott (Kurt R. Krueger Publishing, 160 N. Washington, Iola, WI 54945-0275, © 1994).

Salt and Pepper Shakers Identification and Price Guide, Gideon Bosker and Lena Lencer (Avon Books, New York, © 1994).

School Collectibles of the Past, Lar & Sue Hothem (Hothem House, PO Box 458, Lancaster, OH 43130-0458, © 1993).

Clubs & Publications

Aeronautica & Air Label Collectors Club, *Aeronautica & Air Label Collectors Club* (NL), PO Box 1239, Elgin, IL 60121 (airline baggage labels, schedules, emblems, and other memorabilia).

Air Horn & Steam Whistle Enthusiasts, *Horn & Whistle* (NL), 1043 Richwood Ave., Cincinnati, OH 45208.

American Bell Association, *Bell Tower* (NL), PO Box 19443, Indianapolis, IN 46219.

American Fan Collector Association, *Fan Collector Newsletter* (NL), PO Box 804, South Bend, IN 46624 (electric fans).

American Scouting Traders Association Inc., *ASTAReport* (NL), PO Box 210013, San Francisco, CA 94121.

Angel Collectors' Club of America, *Halo Everybody!* (NL), 16342 W. 54th Ave., Golden, CO 80403.

Black Memorabilia Collectors Association, *Collecting Our Culture* (NL), 2482 Devoe Terr., Bronx, NY 10468.

Brewster Society, *News Scope* (NL), Studio B, 9020 McDonald Dr., Bethesda, MD 20817 (kaleidoscopes).

Canine Collectibles Club of America, *Canine Collectibles Club of America Quarterly Newsletter* (NL), 736 N. Western Ave., Suite 314, Lake Forest, IL 60045.

Cat Collectors, *Cat Talk* (NL), 33161 Wendy Dr., Sterling Heights, MI 48310.

Circus Fans Association of America, *White Tops* (MAG), PO Box 59710, Potomac, MD 20859-9710.

Cow Observers Worldwide (C.O.W.), *MOOsletter* (NL), 240 Wahl Ave., Evans City, PA 16033 (cow collectibles).

Cream Separator Collectors Association, *Cream Separator & Dairy Newsletter* (NL), Rt. 3, Arcadia, WI 54612.

Doorstop Collectors Club of America, *Doorstopper* (NL), 2413 Madison Ave., Vineland, NJ 08360.

Firemark Circle of the Americas, *FMCA Journal* (NL), *FMCA Newsletter* (NL), 2859 Marlin Dr., Chamblee, GA 30341-5119.

Flag Research Center, *Flag Bulletin* (MAG), PO Box 580, Winchester, MA 01890.

Flashlight Collectors of America, *Flashlight Collectors Newsletter* (NL), PO Box 3572, Downey, CA 90242.

Historical Society of Early American Decoration, Inc., *Decorator* (MAG), PO Box 300, Norwell, MA 02061.

Holly Hobbie Club of America, *Holly Hobbie Club of America* (NL), PO Box 397, Butler, MO 64730-0397.

International Bossons Collectors Society, *Bossons Briefs* (NL), 21-C John Maddox Dr., Rome, GA 30165 (Bossons artware, plaster wall masks and figures).

International Brick Collectors Association, *Journal of the International Brick Collectors Association* (MAG), 1743 Lindenhall Dr., Loveland, OH 45140.

International Society of Animal License Collectors, *Paw Prints* (NL), 2778 Amad Dr., York, PA 17403.

International Wood Collectors Society, *World of Wood* (MAG), 5900 Chestnut Ridge Rd., Riner, VA 24149-1808.

Lawrence L. Lee Scouting Museum, *Scout Memorabilia* (MAG), PO Box 1121, Manchester, NH 03105-1121.

Lottery Collector's Club, *Lottery Collector's Newsletter* (NL), Richard Bertrand, 4 E. Main St., Brookside, NJ 07926-0419.

Maytag Collector's Club, *Maytag Collector's Club* (NL), 960 Reynolds Ave., Ripon, CA 95366.

National Association of Soda Jerks, *Fiz Biz* (NL), PO Box 115, Omaha, NE 68101-0115.

National Scouting Collectors Society, *Scouting Collectors Quarterly* (MAG), 806 E. Scott St., Tuscola, IL 61953.

Netsuke Kenkyukai Society, *Netsuke Kenkyukai Study Journal* (MAG), PO Box 31595, Oakland, CA 94604-7595.

Novelty Salt and Pepper Shakers Club, *Novelty Salt and Pepper Shakers Club Newsletter* (NL), 581 Joy Rd., Battle Creek, MI 49017.

Nutcracker Collectors' Club, *Nutcracker Collectors' Newsletter* (NL), 12204 Fox Run Dr., Chesterland, OH 44026.

Rogers Group, *Minutes, News & Bits* (NL), 4932 Prince George Ave., Beltsville, MD 20705.

Rose Bowl Collectors, *Rose Bowl Collectors* (NL), 5214 Rt. 309, Center Valley, PA 18034.

Ships in Bottles Association of America, *Bottle Shipwright* (NL), PO Box 180550, Coronado, CA 92178.

Society for Industrial Archeology, *Society for Industrial Archeology Newsletter* (NL), Room 5014, MRC 629 Smithsonian Institution, Washington, DC 20560 (study and preservation of industrial sites and structures, such as buildings, canals, railroads, water wheels, steam engines, etc.).

Souvenir Building Collectors Society, *Souvenir Building Collector* (NL), 25 Falls Rd., Roxbury, CT 06783 (collectors of building replicas).

Statue of Liberty Collectors' Club, *Statue of Liberty Collectors' Club* (NL), 26601 Bernwood Rd., Cleveland, OH 44122.

Strawberry Shortcake Collectors Club, *Berri-Bits* (NL), 1409 72nd St., North Bergen, NJ 07047 (dolls and other collectibles based on the American Greetings Corp. character).

Sugar Packet Collectors Club, *Sugar Packet* (NL), 15601 Burkhart Blvd., Orrville, OH 44667.

Wee Scots, *Scottie Sampler* (NP), PO Box 1512, Dept. 93-17, Columbus, IN 47202-1512 (Scottie dog collectibles).

World's Fair Collectors' Society, Inc., *Fair News* (NL), PO Box 20806, Sarasota, FL 34276-3806.

Antique Souvenir Collector (NL), PO Box 562, Great Barrington, MA 01230 (old "view" souvenir china, postcards, souvenir spoons, old photographs, glass, etc.).

Baby Boomer Collectibles: The Pop Culture Magazine (MAG), PO Box 1050, Dubuque, IA 52004 (toys, records, TV and movie memorabilia, etc.).

Bridal-Wedding Collectors' Roster (NL), PO Box 105, Amherst, NH 03031.

Classified K-9 (NL), 28828 207th Ave. SE, Kent, WA 98042-6802.

Crown Point Magazine (MAG), 2615 Echo Lane, Ortonville, MI 48462 (lightning rods, balls, and other lightning protection items).

Gone With the Wind Collector's Newsletter (NL), PO Box 2072, Dublin, GA 31040-2072.

Honey Pot's International (NL), 4455 Nevada St., Salem, OR 97305 (collectibles related to bees, bears, and honey, including honey pots, honey comb dishes, etc.).

Ice Screamer (NL), Box 465, Warrington, PA 18976 (ice cream and soda fountain collectibles).

Keychain Tag & Mini License Plate Collectors Newsletter (NL), 888 Eighth Ave., New York, NY 10019 (mini license keychains and tags only).

Paileontologist's Retort (NL), PO Box 3255, Burbank, CA 91508 (lunch boxes).

Pig Tales and Hogwash Newsletter (NL), Rt. 1, Box 711, Audubon, MN 56511.

Positively PEZ (NL), 3851 Gable Lane Dr. #513, Indianapolis, IN 46208.

Pyro-Fax (MAG), PO Box 2010, Saratoga, CA 95070 (fireworks).

Ribbit, Ribbit (NL), PO Box 193, Beech Grove, IN 46107 (frog-related items).

Spinning Wheel Sleuth (NL), PO Box 422, Andover, MA 01810.

Western & Eastern Treasures (MAG), PO Box 1095, 5440 Ericson Way, Arcata, CA 95521 (coins, relics, gold, bottles, collectibles).

Will's Safety-Razor & Safety-Razor-Blade Newsletter (NL), PO Box 522, Crescent City, CA 95531.

Windmillers' Gazette (MAG), PO Box 507, Rio Vista, TX 76093-0507 (windmills).

World's Fair (NL), PO Box 339-ABK, Corte Madera, CA 94976-0339.

Repairs, Parts & Supplies

A-One Electric Company, Bud Stasa, 3925 Pine Knot Ct., Wichita, KS 67208, 316-685-5295, 8:00 A.M.–8:00 P.M. Restoration of antique fans and any other antique mechanical apparatus.

Adele Bishop, PO Box 3349, Kinston, NC 28502, 800-334-4186, Mon.–Thurs. 7:00 A.M.–5:30 P.M.; fax: 919-527-4189. Creative stencils and supplies. Decorative stencils, paints, brushes, and how-to books. Mail order. Catalog $4.

Decorative Arts Studio, RR 1, Box 136, Rt. 30, Dorset, VT 05251, 802-867-5915, 9:00 A.M.–5:00 P.M. Stencils and related products. Historic restoration as well as contemporary designs. Seminars. Brochure $2.

The Fan Man, 1914 Abrams Pky., Dallas, TX 75214, 214-826-7700, Mon.–Fri. 9:00 A.M.–6:00 P.M., Sat. 10:00 A.M.–4:00 P.M. Parts and restoration services for ceiling, pedestal, and oscillating fans from 1890 to the present. Retail and mail order. Catalog $2.

Graphic Conservation Co., 329 W. 18th St., Suite 701, Chicago, IL 60616, 312-738-2657, Mon.–Fri. 9:00 A.M.–noon, 1:00 P.M.–5:00 P.M.; fax: 312-738-3125. Conservation of works of art on paper, including maps, historical documents, globes, and oriental screens. Dry cleaning, stain reduction, flattening, deacidification, inpainting, tear repairs and fills. Proposal and examination fee $15 and up.

Hand-Stenciled Interiors, Pamela S. Friend, 590 King St., Hanover, MA 02339, 617-878-7596, 9:00 A.M.–9:00 P.M. Wall stencils and supplies; antique, antique reproductions, and custom designs. Restorations, sponge texturing, decorative painting, and hand stenciling on ceilings, floors, walls, furniture, and fabrics. Catalog $3.

Jacquelyn Sage, Handpainted Walls, Floors, Cloths & Furniture, 2272 W. 29th Pl., Los Angeles, CA 90018, 213-733-5459, 11:00 A.M.–2:00 P.M. and 4:00 P.M.–6:00 P.M. Hand-stenciled floors, wall borders, cabinets, floor cloths, and tile designs.

Nagel and Sproesser Stencils, Gerri Sproesser, PO Box 832, Richboro, PA 18954, 215-322-7823, answering service, anytime. Mylar wall stencils. Reproductions of New England designs, children's stencils, Victorian, and original designs. Catalog $4.50.

Rasa Arbas Design, 306 22nd St., Santa Monica, CA 90402. Stencil designs with an emphasis on botanicals. Send SASE for price sheet.

The Simple Machine, Cathy and Stephen Racine, 18 Masonic Home Rd., Rt. 31, Charlton, MA 01507, 508-248-6632, 9:00 A.M.–7:00 P.M. Repair and restoration of sewing machines; instruction manuals, needles, bobbins, bobbin cases, leather treadle belts, etc.

Appraiser

The Oriental Corner, 280 Main St., Los Altos, CA 94022, 415-941-3207, Tues.–Sat. 10:30 A.M.–5:00 P.M.; fax: 415-941-3297. Appraisers of netsuke and other oriental antiques and art.

PART II

General Information & Source Lists

General Books for Collectors

Many books list prices of antiques and collectibles. These range from general books like *Kovels' Antiques & Collectibles Price List*, with 50,000 prices and more than 500 photos and drawings, to specialized small pamphlets that picture and price Uhl pottery, Popeye collectibles, or key-wind coffee tins. Specialized price books are listed in each chapter.

Many of the small specialized books are not found in the average bookstore or library. They can be ordered with the information listed here. Privately printed books include a complete address. Books that are listed here without the address can be located at your library or bookstore through Books in Print.

The most current price information is found in our monthly newsletter, available to subscribers and at many libraries. For information, send a double-stamped envelope to *Kovels on Antiques and Collectibles*, PO Box 22200, Beachwood, OH 44122.

Price Guides

Antique Trader Antiques & Collectibles Price Guide, annual, edited by Kyle Husfloen (The Antique Trader, PO Box 1050, Dubuque, IA 52004).

Art Deco Identification and Price Guide, 2nd edition, Tony Fusco (Avon Books, New York, © 1993).

The Care of Antiques & Historical Collections, 2nd edition (AASLH 172 Second Avenue North, Suite 102, Nashville, TN 37201).

Collectibles Market Guide & Price Index, annual, *Collectibles Price Guide*, annual, Collectors' Information Bureau (Collectors' Information Bureau, 2420 Burton S.E., Grand Rapids, MI 49546, © 1994). Limited edition collectibles.

Collectibles Price Guide, annual, Collectors' Information Bureau (Collectors' Information Bureau, 2420 Burton S.E., Grand Rapids, MI 49546, © 1994). Limited edition collectibles.

Collecting the '50s & '60s: A Handbook & Price Guide, Jan Lindenberger (Schiffer, Atglen, PA, © 1993).

The Collectors' Connection & Registry Buyer & Seller Dictionary, annual (505-1 S. St., Hwy. 49, #269, Jackson, CA 95642).

Collectors' Information Bureau's Collectibles Market Guide & Price Index, Tenth Anniversary Edition (Wallace-Homestead, Radnor, PA, © 1993).

Early American Antique Country Furnishings, George C. Neumann (L-W Books, PO Box 69, Gas City, IN 46933, © 1993).

Flea Market Trader, 9th edition, edited by Sharon and Bob Huxford (Collector Books, Paducah, KY, © 1993).

'40s and '50s Designs & Memorabilia Identification and *Price Guide, and '60s and '70s Designs*

and Memorabilia and Identification, Anne Gilbert (Avon Books, New York, © 1994).

Garage Sale & Flea Market Annual (Nostalgia Publishing Co., PO Box 277, La Center, KY 42056).

The Great Antiques Treasure Hunt, Paul Atterbury (Harry N. Abrams, New York, © 1993).

Kovels' Antiques & Collectibles Price List, annual, Ralph and Terry Kovel (Crown, New York).

Limited Edition Collectibles: The Official Club Directory and Price Guide, Susan K. Elliott and J. Kevin Samara (House of Collectibles, New York, © 1994).

The Lyle Official Antiques Review 1995, Anthony Curtis. (Perigee Books, New York, © 1994).

The Lyle Price Guide to Collectibles and Memorabilia, Vol. 3, Anthony Curtis (Perigree Books, New York, © 1994).

The Official Club Directory & Price Guide to Limited Edition Collectibles, Susan K. Elliott and J. Kevin Samara (House of Collectibles, New York, © 1994).

Official Price Guide to Antiques and Collectibles, annual, David P. Lindquist (House of Collectibles, New York).

Official Price Guide to Arts and Crafts, 2nd edition, Bruce Johnson (House of Collectibles, NY, © 1992).

Price Guide to American Country Antiques, 12th edition, Don and Carol Raycraft (Wallace-Homestead, Radnor, PA © 1993).

Price Guide to Flea Market Treasures, 2nd edition, Harry L. Rinker Jr. (Wallace-Homestead, Radnor, PA, © 1993).

Roycroft Collectibles, Charles F. Hamilton (SPS, PO Box 769, Tavares, FL 32778, © 1992).

Salt and Pepper Shakers Identification and Price Guide, Gideon Bosker and Lena Lencer (Avon Books, New York, © 1994).

Schroeder's Antiques Price Guide, annual, edited by Sharon and Bob Huxford (Collector Books, Paducah, KY).

Wallace-Homestead Price Guide to American

Country Antiques, 12th edition, Don and Carol Raycraft (Wallace-Homestead, Radnor, PA, © 1993).

Warman's Antiques and Their Prices, 26th edition, edited by Harry L. Rinker (Wallace-Homestead, Radnor, PA, © 1992).

Warman's Country Antiques & Collectibles, Dana Gehman Morykan and Harry L. Rinker (Wallace-Homestead, Radnor, PA, © 1992).

General Clubs, Publications & Computer Programs

Clubs

Antiquarian & Landmarks Society, Inc., *Landmark* (MAG), 394 Main St., Hartford, CT 06078 (museum publication about Connecticut antiques).

Art Deco Society of Boston, *Motif* (NL), 1 Murdock Terr., Brighton, MA 02135.

Art Deco Society of California, 100 Bush St., Suite 511, San Francisco, CA 94104.

Art Deco Society of Cleveland, *Newsreel* (NL), PO Box 210134, South Euclid, OH 44121-7134.

Art Deco Society of Los Angeles, *The Exposition,* PO Box 972, Hollywood, CA 90078.

Art Deco Society of New York, *Art Deco Society of New York* (NL), 385 Fifth Ave., New York, NY 10016.

Art Deco Society of Northern Ohio, 3439 W. Brainard Rd., #260, Woodmere, OH 44122.

Art Deco Society of the Palm Beaches, *Streamline* (NL), 325 SW 29th Ave., Delray Beach, FL 33445

Chase Collectors Society, *Art Deco Reflections* (NL), 2149 W. Jibsail Loop, Mesa, AZ 85202-5524.

Chicago Art Deco Society, *Chicago Art Deco Society Magazine* (MAG), 400 Skokie, #270, Northbrook, IL 60052.

Collectors Connection and Registry, *Collectors Connection and Registry* (NL), 505-1 S. State Hwy. 49, #269, Jackson, CA 95642.

Craftsman Homeowner Club, *Craftsman Homeowner Club Newsletter* (NL), 31 S. Grove St., East Aurora, NY 14052.

Franklin Mint Collectors Society, *Almanac* (MAG), Franklin Mint, Franklin Center, PA 19091.

National Coalition of Art Deco Societies, 1 Murdock Terr., Brighton, MA 02135.

National Trust for Historic Preservation, *Historic Preservation* (MAG), 1785 Massachusetts Ave. NW, Washington, DC 20036.

Ohio Historical Society, *Timeline* (MAG), 1982 Velma Ave., Columbus, OH 43211-2497.

Roycrofters-At-Large Association, *Roycroft Campus Chronicle* (NL), PO Box 417, East Aurora, NY 14052.

Sacramento Art Deco Society, *Moderne Times* (NL), PO Box 162836, Sacramento, CA 95816-2836.

Publications

American Bungalow (MAG), *American Bungalow News* (NL), PO Box 756, Sierra Madre, CA 91025.

American Collectors' Classified (MAG), PO Box 686, Southfield, MI 48037.

American Collector's Journal (NP), Box 407, Kewanee, IL 61443.

American Country Collectibles (MAG), 1700 Broadway, New York, NY 10019.

American Heritage (MAG), PO Box 5022, Harlan, IA 51593-0522.

Antique & Collectables (NP), PO Box 1565, 1000 Pioneer Way, El Cajon, CA 92022.

Antique & Collectible News (NP), PO Box 529, Anna, IL 62906-0529.

Antique & Collector's Guide (NP), 8510 Frazier Dr., Beaumont, TX 77707 (Guide to Texas and Louisiana).

Antique & Collectors Reproduction Newsletter (NL), PO Box 71174, Des Moines, IA 50325-0174.

Antique Collecting (MAG), Antique Collectors' Club, 5 Church St., Woodbridge, Suffolk, England 1P12 1DS.

Antique Collector (MAG), Orphens Publications Ltd., PO Box 648, Harrow, Middlesex, England HA1 2NW.

Antique Dealer & Collectors Guide (MAG), Collectors' Guide Publications Expediting Inc., 200 Meacham Ave., Elmont, NY 11003.

Antique Gazette (NP), 6949 Charlotte Pike, Suite 106, Nashville, TN 37209.

Antique Markets Quarterly (MAG), PO Box 219K, Western Springs, IL 60558 (antiques and collectibles markets and shows).

Antique Press (NP), 12403 N. Florida Ave., Tampa, FL 33612.

Antique Review (NP), Box 538, Worthington, OH 43085.

Antique Shoppe (NP), PO Box 2175, Keystone Heights, FL 32656.

Antique Showcase (MAG), 103 Lakeshore Rd., ON, Canada L2N 2T6.

Antique Traveler (NP), PO Box 656, 115 S. Johnson, Mineola, TX 75773.

Antiques & Art Around Florida (MAG), PO Box 2481, Fort Lauderdale, FL 33303-2481.

Antiques & Auction News (NP), PO Box 500, Mount Joy, PA 17552.

Antiques & Collectibles Magazine (NP), Box 33, Westbury, NY 11590.

Antiques & Collecting (MAG), 1006 S. Michigan Ave., Chicago, IL 60605.

Antiques & The Arts Weekly (NP), Newtown Bee Publishing Co., PO Box 5503, Newtown, CT 06470-5503.

Antiques Today (NP), 977 Lehigh Cir., Carson City, NV 89705.

Antiques West (NP), 3315 Sacramento St., #618, San Francisco, CA 94118.

AntiqueWeek (NP), PO Box 90, Knightstown, IN 46148.

Arizona Antique News & Southwest Antiques Journal (NP), PO Box 26536, Phoenix, AZ 85068.

Art & Antiques (MAG), 2100 Powers Ferry Rd., Atlanta, GA 30339.

Art & Auction (MAG), PO Box 11344, Des Moines, IA 50340-1344.

Art, Antiques & Collectibles Monthly (MAG), PO Box 750895, Petaluma, CA 94975-0895.

Auction World (NP), 417 W. Stanton, PO Box 745, Fergus Falls, MN 56538.

Buckeye Marketeer (NP), PO Box 954, Westerville, OH 43086.

Collector (NP), PO Box 148, Heyworth, IL 61745.

Collector Editions (MAG), 170 Fifth Ave., New York, NY 10010.

Collector Magazine (MAG), 436 W. 4th St., #222, Pomona, CA 91766.

Collector Magazine & Price Guide (MAG), PO Box 1050, Dubuque, IA 52004.

Collector's Marketplace (NP), PO Box 25, Stewartsville, NJ 08886.

Collectors Journal (NP), PO Box 601, Vinton, IA 52349.

Collectors News & The Antique Reporter (MAG), PO Box 156, 506 Second St., Grundy Center, IA 50638.

Collectors' Classified (NL), PO Box 347, Holbrook, MA 02343-0347.

Collectors' Showcase (MAG), 4099 McEwen, Suite 350, Dallas, TX 75244-5039.

Cotton & Quail Antique Trail (NP), PO Box 326, 205 E. Washington St., Monticello, FL 32345.

Country & Americana Collectibles (MAG), 1700 Broadway, New York, NY 10019.

Country Collectibles (MAG), 1115 Broadway, New York, NY 10010.

Country Folk Art (MAG), 8393 E. Holly Rd., Holly, MI 48442.

Early American Life (MAG), PO Box 1620, Mt. Morris, PA 61054.

Farm and Dairy (NP), PO Box 38, Salem, OH 44460 (Antique Collector and Auction Guide section).

Farm Antiques News (NL), 812 N. Third St., Tarkio, MO 64491 (news, events, prices, for collectors of farm and rural antiques and collectibles of all types).

Indiana Antique Buyers News (NP), PO Box 213, Silver Lake, IN 46982.

Inside Collector (MAG), 225 Main St., Suite 300, Northport, NY 11768.

Journal of Decorative and Propaganda Arts, 2399 NE Second Ave., Miami, FL 33137 (covers the period 1875–1945).

Journal of Early Southern Decorative Arts (MAG), PO Box 10310, Winston-Salem, NC 27108-0310.

Keystone Country Peddler (NP), PO Box 467, Richmond, IL 60071 (covering northern Illinois-southern Wisconsin).

Kovels' on Antiques and Collectibles **(NL), PO Box 420347, Palm Coast, FL 32142-0347.**

Magazine Antiques (MAG), PO Box 10547, Des Moines, IA 50340.

Maine Antique Digest (NP), Box 1429, Waldoboro, ME 04572-1429.

MassBay Antiques (NP), Box 192, Ipswich, MA 01938.

Michigan Antiques Trading Post (NP), 132 S. Putnam, Williamston, MI 48895.

MidAtlantic Antiques (NP), PO Box 908, Henderson, NC 27536.

Mountain States Collector (NP), PO Box 2525, Evergreen, CO 80439.

National Hobby News (NP), PO Box 612, New Philadelphia, OH 44663-0612.

New England Antiques Journal (NP), PO Box 120, Ware, MA 01082.

New York Antique Almanac (NP), PO Box 335, Lawrence, NY 11559.

New York-Pennsylvania Collector (NP), PO Box C, Fishers, NY 14453.

Ohio Collectors' Magazine (MAG), PO Box 66, Mogadore, OH 44260.

Old-House Journal (MAG), *Old-House Interiors* (MAG), 2 Main St., Gloucester, MA 01930.

Old News Is Good News Antiques Gazette (NP), PO Box 65292, Baton Rouge, LA 70896.

Old Stuff (NP), PO Box 1084, McMinnville, OR 97128.

Orientalia Journal (NL), PO Box 94, Little Neck, NY 11363.

Orientations (MAG), 14th Floor, 200 Lockhart Rd., Hong Kong.

Renninger's Antique Guide (NP), PO Box 495, Lafayette Hill, PA 19444.

Shaker Messenger (MAG), PO Box 1645, Holland, MI 49422-1645.

Smithsonian (MAG), Smithsonian Institution, PO Box 55593, Boulder, CO 80322-5593.

Southeastern Antiques and Collectibles Monthly (NP), Rt. 1, Box 88, Whittle Rd., Macon, GA 31210.

Southern Antiques (NP), PO Drawer 1107, Decatur, GA 30031-1107.

Style 1900 (MAG), 9 S. Main St., Lambertville, NJ 08530 (Arts & Crafts movement).

Today's Collector (NP), 700 E. State St., Iola, WI 54990-0001.

Treasure Chest (NP), 2112 Broadway, Suite 414, New York, NY 10023.

Upper Canadian (NP), PO Box 653, Smiths Falls, ON, Canada K7A 4T6.

Victoria (MAG), PO Box 7147, Red Oak, IA 51591-4147.

Victorian Homes (MAG), PO Box 61, Millers Falls, MA 01349.

West Coast Peddler (NP), PO Box 5134, Whittier, CA 90607.

World of Interiors (MAG), International Subscription Services, 30 Montgomery St., Seventh Floor, Jersey City, NJ 07302.

Yesteryear (NP), PO Box 2, Princeton, WI 54968.

Computer Programs

Artfact, **Artfact, Inc.,** 1130 Ten Rod Rd., Suite E104, North Kingstown, RI 02852, 401-295-2656, 9:00 A.M.–5:30 P.M., answering machine other times; fax: 401-295-2629. CD-ROM data base of auction catalog transactions. Antiques, collectibles, and fine arts. Full catalog listings. Results via fax, mail, or telephone. Mail order worldwide.

Centrox Art Price Index, **Centrox Corporation,** 145 E. 57th St., New York, NY 10022, 212-319-4800, 9:00 A.M.–5:00 P.M.; fax: 212-319-4620. Complete auction house records available on-line via computer on CD-ROM or via fax. Records updated daily.

Mercury Trade Online, **Mercury,** One Corporate Dr., Suite 119, Clearwater, FL 34622, 800-736-0122. International data network and information system for antiques and collectibles. Computer access to a wide variety of services, including an international directory and schedule of events, library of information and services, buy-sell marketplace, auction preview monitor, and special-features forum with experts.

ORGANIZE! Your Collection for Windows, **HomeCraft,** PO Box 974, 20676 SW Elk Horn Ct., Suite 200, Tualatin, OR 97062, 503-692-3732, 9:00 A.M.–5:00 P.M.; fax: 503-692-0382. Inventory program for collectors; runs on Windows 3.1.

Reports Galore, **Sleepy Hollow Software,** 56 Sleepy Hollow Rd., Andover, NJ 07820, 201-786-6578, 9:00 A.M.–9:00 P.M. Inventory programs for antique collectors and dealers. Special version available for glass collectors and dealers. Send SASE for brochure.

Selling Through Auction Houses

Most antiques can be sold through an auction gallery. It is best to show the actual antique to the gallery, but if distance makes that impossible, the mail will help. Write a letter about the antique, giving its size and a description of all its flaws. Copy any markings as closely as possible. It is necessary to send a clear photograph for most items. Black-and-white pictures show the details best when you are selling paintings. Some things like plates, fabrics, books, and other flat objects can be placed on the glass of a photocopy machine and "pictured" in this way. Be sure to describe the colors if you are sending a black-and-white image, and include a stamped self-addressed envelope and a letter explaining where you live, how many items you wish to sell, and any history of the antique.

Ask for a contract from the gallery outlining their sales policies and charges. Ask if the money from any sale will be kept in an escrow account. Reread the advice in the Introduction of this book before you sign a contract. Never ship merchandise without a contract. All items should be sent by mail or a delivery service with insurance and a return receipt request. If you are shipping a large piece of furniture by truck, be sure you have insurance and a receipt that states the value and includes a full description, including condition. Remember, the antique is yours until you have proof it has been received by the auction house. If it is lost or damaged on the way to the sale, your insurance is expected to pay the claim. We once shipped a large sideboard with gilt-bronze ormolu and a porcelain plaque on the front cabinet door. The porcelain was removed by the movers, and packed separately. When the piece arrived, the two small gold-headed screws that held the plaque in place were missing. The movers paid the claim of over $100 for these small items because we could prove that the replacements had to be exact, or the value of the sideboard would be lowered.

There are many regional auction houses. Those listed here advertise nationally and offer catalogs and sale results through the mail. We have seen the advertising and catalogs from these auction galleries and have attended many of their sales. Do not take inclusion in this list as any form of endorsement. To those who may have been omitted, we apologize: The lack of listing is an oversight and is not a lack of endorsement.

Most of these auction houses sell all types of antiques and collectibles during the year. A few sell just specialty items, such as coins or dolls. We have indicated some of these.

A. Lerman Galleries, 172 Sunrise Hwy., Rockville Centre, NY 11570, 516-766-1234. Military memorabilia. Mail and phone bids accepted. No buyer's premium. Catalogs $1 per auction. Appraisals.

AAG Militaria Mail Auction, 20 Grandview Ave., Wilkes-Barre, PA 18702, 717-822-5300; fax: 717-822-9992. Mail order auctions of militaria from 1700–1976. Buyer's premium 15%. By subscription only, $35 for 3 catalogs. Prices realized mailed after auction. Appraisals.

Alderfer Auction Company, 501 Fairgrounds Rd., Hatfield, PA 19440, 215-997-5100; fax: 215-368-9055. Pennsylvania art and antiques. Mail and phone bids accepted. No buyer's premium. Catalogs $65 per year, 4 catalogs. Prices realized mailed after cataloged auctions. Appraisals.

America West Archives, PO Box 100, Cedar

City, UT 84721, 801-586-9497; 801-586-7323; fax: 801-586-6227. Historical documents, letters, autographs, photographs, and papers from the Old West. Mail and phone bids accepted. Buyer's premium 10%. Catalogs $15 for 5 issues. Prices realized printed in next catalog. Appraisals.

Andre Ammelounx, PO Box 136, Palatine, IL 60078, 708-991-5927; fax: 708-991-5947. Steins and related items. Mail and phone bids accepted. Buyer's premium 10%. Catalog $25. Prices realized mailed after auction. Appraisals.

Anderson Auction, PO Box 644, Troy, OH 45373, 513-339-0850; fax: 513-339-8620. Mail order historical Americana, political, and advertising auctions. No buyer's premium. Mail and phone bids accepted. Catalog subscription $20 for 3 issues. Prices realized mailed after auction. Appraisals.

Apple Tree Auction Center, 1616 W. Church St., Newark, OH 43055, 614-344-9449; fax: 614-344-3673. Heisey auctions. Monthly antique sales, as well as several specialty auctions per year: toys, trains, dolls, advertising and country store items. Mail bids accepted. No buyer's premium. Catalogs and prices realized, $15 per year. Appraisals.

Arthur Auctioneering, Auctioneer, RR. 2, Box 155, Hughesville, PA 17737, 717-584-3697. Stoneware. Mail bids accepted. Buyer's premium 10%. Catalog $12. Prices realized mailed after auction. Appraisals.

Auction Team Koln, Postfach 501168, D-5000 Koln 50 Germany, 077-49-227-387049; fax: 077-49-227-374878. Specialties include cameras, office equipment, small appliances, and other twentieth-century technology. Mail and phone bids accepted, minimum bid $500. Buyer's premium and tax 20%. Catalog subscription $50, includes list of prices realized. Appraisals, restoration, and conservation.

Baltimore Book Co. Inc., 2114 N. Charles St., Baltimore, MD 21218, 301-659-0550. Books, prints, autographs, photographs. Mail or phone

bids prior to sale. Buyer's premium 10%. Catalog subscription, $25 for 7 issues, includes list of prices realized after auction. Appraisals.

Barridoff Galleries, PO Box 9715, Portland, ME 04104, 207-772-5011.

Barry S. Slosberg, Inc., 232 N. 2nd St., Philadelphia, PA 19106; 215-925-8020. Antiques, estates, bankruptcies, liquidations, and real estate auctions. Mail and phone bids accepted. Buyer's premium 10% for certain sales. Appraisals.

BBR, 5 Ironworks Row, Elsecar Project, Wath Rd., Elsecar, Barnsley, S. Yorkshire UK S74 8HJ, 0226 745156. Bottles, pot lids, and antique advertising auctions. Buyer's premium 10%. Mail, phone, and fax bids accepted. Single catalog overseas, $15.

Bill Ballor Auction Service, PO Drawer 249, 201 N. First St., Linwood, MI 48634, 517-697-4212, 800-225-4212; fax: 517-697-3355. Antiques and estates. Mail and phone bids accepted. No buyer's premium. Catalogs, $20 yearly subscription. Appraisals.

Bill Bertoia, 2413 Madison Ave., Vineland, NJ 08360, 609-692-4092; fax: 609-692-TOYS. Antique toys and banks. Mail and phone bids accepted. Buyer's premium 10%. Catalogs $30. Prices realized mailed after auction. Appraisals, restoration, and conservation.

Block's Box, PO Box 51, Trumbull, CT 06611, 203-261-3223, 203-775-0138. Marbles. Mail and phone bids accepted. Buyer's premium 5%. Catalogs $15-$20, yearly subscription $80. Prices realized mailed after auction. Appraisals.

Bob & Sallie Connelly, 666 Chenango St., Binghamton, NY 13901, 607-722-9593; fax: 607-722-1266. Christmas items, clocks. Mail and phone bids accepted. No buyer's premium. Prices realized mailed after auction. Appraisals.

Bob Kay, 216 N. Batavia Ave., Batavia, IL 60510, 708-879-6214; fax: 708-879-0308, Bob Kay. Mail auctions of beer labels. Bid by mail, phone, or fax. No buyer's premium. Catalogs $7;

$14 per year. Catalogs include *Collectors Corner* with news and tips on collecting labels, how to arrange and display, conservation, etc.

Bonhams Knightsbridge, Montpelier St., Knightsbridge, London, England SW7 1HH, 071-584-9161; fax: 071-589-4072. Fine art auctioneers and valuers. Mail and phone bids accepted. Buyer's premium 10%. Prices realized mailed upon request. Appraisals. Can provide restoration and conservation information.

Bowers & Merena, Box 1224, Wolfeboro, NH 03894, 603-569-5095; 800-222-5993; fax: 603-569-5319. Coins. Auction catalogs, *Rare Coin Review* magazine, price lists, subscription $79 per year.

Butterfield & Butterfield, 220 San Bruno Ave. at 15th St., San Francisco, CA 94103, 415-861-7500; fax: 415-861-8951. Buyer's premium 15%, except wine and firearms 10%. Mail and phone bids accepted. Prices realized mailed to catalog subscribers. Appraisals.

Butterfield & Butterfield, 7601 Sunset Blvd., Los Angeles, CA 90046, 213-850-7500; fax: 218-850-5843. Fine art, antiques, entertainment memorabilia, firearms. Mail and phone bids accepted. Buyer's premium 15%; 10% for guns, stamps, coins, and wine. Prices realized mailed after auction. Appraisals.

C. E. Guarino, Box 49, Denmark, ME 04022, 207-452-2123. Mail order auctions of Americana arts and American Indian arts. Specialties are antique maps, prints, historical ephemera, early photography, and American Indian arts. Buyer's premium 10%. Catalogs $20 per year. Prices realized, SASE. Appraisals.

C. G. Sloan & Co. Inc., 4920 Wyaconda Rd., Rockville, MD 20852, 301-468-4911; fax: 301-468-9182. Fine art and antiques. Mail and phone bids accepted. Buyer's premium 10%. Catalogs $25; by U.S. mail $28. List of prices realized $2. Appraisals.

C. S. & S. Mail Order Auction House, PO Box 4037, Middletown, RI 02840, 404-849-5012.

Historical Staffordshire, English ceramics, paperweights, Early American Glass. Mail and phone bids accepted. Buyer's premium 10%. Prices realized mailed after auction. Restoration and conservation services.

Cardamone's Riverfront Auction, 60 S. River St., Coxsackie, NY 12051, 518-731-6040; fax: 518-731-6300. Specialty auctions and collections. Mail and phone bids accepted. Buyer's premium 10%. Catalog $3. Prices realized mailed if requested. Appraisals.

Castner Auction & Appraisal Service, 6 Wantage Ave., Branchville, NJ 07826, 201-948-3868; fax: 201-948-3919. Estates auctions. Buyer's premium 10% in gallery; no buyer's premium on site. Catalogs $10. Appraisals. Expert witness testimony, appraisal reviews, claims, unusual or difficult problems.

Cedarburg Auction Co., 235 N. Main St., Thiensville, WI 53092, 414-242-7911; 414-377-4444. Mail and phone bids accepted. Catalog $4.50. Appraisals.

Cerebro, PO Box 327, East Prospect, PA 17317, 717-252-2400, 800-69-LABEL; fax: 717-252-3685. Antique advertising labels. Mail and phone bids accepted. No buyer's premium. Catalog $5. Prices realized mailed after auction. Appraisals.

Charles E. Kirtley, PO Box 2273, Elizabeth City, NC 27096, 919-335-1262; 800-525-3399; fax: 919-335-4441. Specializes in political, medallic art, exonumia, world's fairs, Civil War material, antique advertising, etc. Mail and phone bids accepted. Buyer's premium 10%. Catalogs $20. Prices realized $2, free to subscribers. Appraisals.

Chicago Art Gallery, 5039 Oakton St., Skokie, IL 60077, 708-677-6080; 708-677-6081. Estate auctions. Absentee bids must be accompanied by a 25% deposit. No phone bids. Buyer's premium 10%. Catalog $5. Personal property appraisals.

Christie's, 502 Park Ave., New York, NY 10022,

212-546-1000; fax: 212-980-8163. Full-service international auction house. Mail and phone bids accepted. Buyer's premium 15% up to and including $50,000; 10% on the amount above $50,000. Prices realized mailed after auction. Appraisals.

Christie's East, 219 East 67th St., New York, NY 10021, 212-606-0543. Auction Results 212-546-1199; fax: 212-737-6076, Mail and phone bids accepted. Buyer's premium 15% of the final bid up to and including $50,000, 10% of the excess. Prices realized mailed after auction.

Chuck de Luca Maritime Antiques, PO Box 322, York, ME 03909-0322, 207-363-4247; fax: 207-363-1416. Nautical and fire department antiques and auctions. Mail and phone bids accepted. Buyer's premium 10%. Catalog $17.50. Prices realized available after auction.

Christie's London, 8 King St., St. James, London, England SW1Y 6QT, 071 839 9060; fax: 071 839 1611. Fine art auctioneers. Mail and phone bids accepted. Buyer's premium 15% of the first £L30,000, 10% of the excess. Cost of catalogs vary. Prices realized mailed to subscribers. Valuation services.

Cincinnati Art Galleries, Michele and Randy Sandler, 635 Main St., Cincinnati, OH 45202, 513-381-2128; fax: 513-381-7527, Rookwood pottery auctions. Mail and phone bids accepted. Buyer's premium 10%. Catalog prices vary, $30-$45. Prices realized mailed after auction. Appraisals.

Clinton-Ivankovich Auction Company, PO Box 29, Ottsville, PA 18942, 215-847-5432; fax: 215-847-2536. Clocks, Wallace-Nutting, household estates. Buyer's premium 10% on specialty auctions only. Specialty auction subscription $12. Prices realized sent if catalog is ordered. Appraisals; restoration and conservation.

Cobb's Doll Auctions, 1909 Harrison Rd. N., Johnstown, OH 43031-9539, 614-964-0444. Doll auctions. Contemporary and antique dolls and accessories. Catalogs for antique doll auctions.

Mail and phone bids accepted. No buyer's premium. Catalog $22, $28 outside of U.S. Prices realized mailed after auction. Appraisals.

Collectors Auction Services, RR 2, Box 431, Oakwood Rd., Oil City, PA 16301-9426, 814-677-6070; fax: 814-677-6166. Mail auction of oil and gas memorabilia. Buyer's premium 10%. Catalogs $30 each. Prices realized mailed after sale. Appraisals.

Conestoga Auction Co., Inc., 768 Graystone Rd., Manheim, PA 17545, 717-898-7284; fax: 717-898-6628. Monthly antique sales, firearms, toys, Indian relics. Mail and phone bids accepted. Buyer's premium 10%. Catalog subscription $10. Prices realized mailed after auction. Appraisals.

Connecticut Book Auction Gallery, 251 Carroll Rd., Fairfield, CT 06430, 203-259-1997. Mail and phone bids accepted. Buyer's premium 10%. Free catalogs and price lists. Prices realized mailed to all bidders. Appraisals.

Copake Country Auction, Old Rt. 22, Box H, Copake, NY 12516, 518-329-1142. Specialty bicycle auction (1850–1950), Americana, estate sales. Mail and phone bids accepted. Buyer's premium 10%. Catalogs $4-$15. Prices realized mailed after auction. Appraisals; fine furniture restoration.

Crittenden Schmitt Archives, Court House, PO Box 4253, Rockville, MD 20849. Video auctions of ammunition and explosive ordnance; reference material about the subjects. Mail and phone bids accepted. Catalogs $24.95 each. Appraisals.

Dave Beck, PO Box 435, Mediapolis, IA 52637, 319-394-3943. Mail order auctions of advertising mirrors, fobs, pinbacks, and radio premiums. Mail and phone bids accepted. No buyer's premium. Catalog subscription $12 for 4 issues. Prices realized mailed after auction.

David Frent, PO Box 455, Oakhurst, NJ 07755, 908-922-0768; fax: 908-922-6488. Mail order political Americana auctions. Mail and phone bids accepted. No buyer's premium. Catalogs $12 for 3 issues, sample $4. Prices realized listed in next auction catalog. Appraisals.

David Rago, 17 S. Main St., Lambertville, NJ 08530, 609-397-9374; fax: 609-397-9377. Specializing in the Arts & Crafts movement. Mail and phone bids accepted. Buyer's premium 10%. Catalogs $25, subscription $90 for 6 auctions per year. Prices realized mailed after auction. Appraisals.

Decoys Unlimited, 2320 Main St., W. Barnstable, MA 02668, 508-362-2766. Specializing in antique decoys. Americana and other items are also auctioned. Mail and phone bids accepted. Buyer's premium 10%. Catalogs about $22 each. Prices realized mailed after auction. Appraisals, restoration, and conservation.

DeFina Auctions, 1591 State Rt. 45, Austinburg, OH 44010, 216-275-6674; fax: 216-275-2028. Mail and phone bids accepted. No buyer's premium. Catalog prices vary. Prices realized mailed upon request.

The Depot Attic, 377 Ashford Ave., Dobbs Ferry, NY 10522, 914-693-5858. Railroad items. No buyer's premium. Mail and phone bids accepted. Catalog $7. Appraisals.

Col. Doug Allard, PO Box 460, St. Ignatius, MT 59865, 406-745-2951; fax: 406-745-2961. Indian artifacts. Mail and phone bids accepted. Buyer's premium 10%. Catalogs $10-$25. Prices realized mailed after auction. Appraisals.

Douglas Auctioneers, Rt. 5, South Deerfield, MA 01373, 413-665-2877; fax; 413-665-2877. Antique and real estate auctions. Mail and phone bids accepted. Buyer's premium 10%. Catalog subscription $20 per year. Appraisals.

DuMouchelles Art Galleries Co., 409 E. Jefferson Ave., Detroit, MI 48226, 313-963-6255; 313-963-0248; fax: 313-963-8199. Mail and phone bids accepted, 25% deposit required. Buyer's premium 10%. Catalog subscription $65, prices realized mailed after auction.

Dunbar Gallery, 76 Haven St., Milford, MA 01757, 508-634-TOYS (8697, 8097), 508-634-8698. Mail, phone, fax auction. Buyer's premium

0-10%. Catalogs $15-$25. Prices realized mailed after auction. Appraisals. Limited restoration and conservation.

Dunning's Auction Service Inc., 755 Church Rd., Elgin, IL 60123, 708-741-3483; fax: 708-741-3589. Mail and phone bids accepted. Buyer's premium 15% on first $50,000, 10% of excess. Prices realized mailed to purchasers of catalog. Appraisals.

Early Auction Co., 123 Main St., Milford, OH 45150, 513-831-4833; fax: 513-831-1441. Art glass, antiques, and general auctions. Mail and phone bids accepted. Buyer's premium 10% on major sales only. Catalog subscription $54. Prices realized mailed after auction. Appraisals.

F. O. Bailey Co., 141 Middle St., Portland, ME 04141, 207-774-1479; fax: 207-774-7914. General estates auctions. Mail and phone bids accepted. Buyer's premium 10%. Catalog subscription $10 a year. Prices realized for cataloged sales. Appraisals.

FDC Publishing Co., PO Box 206, Stewartsville, NJ 08886, 908-479-4614; fax: 908-479-6158. Mail auctions of first day covers. Mail and phone bids accepted. No buyer's premium. Catalogs, $1 for 3 issues. Prices realized sent after auction. Appraisals.

F.T.S. Inc., 416 Throop St., North Babylon, NY 11704, 516-669-7232. Regularly scheduled stein auctions.

Fink's Off the Wall Auctions, 108 E. 7th St., Lansdale, PA 19446-2622, 215-855-9732. Mail auctions of breweriana. Catalog $12. Prices realized mailed after auction.

Frank H. Boos Gallery, 420 Enterprise Ct., Bloomfield Hills, MI 48302, 810-332-1500; fax: 810-332-6370. Mail and phone bids accepted. Buyer's premium 10%. Catalog subscription $90 domestic, $130 foreign. Prices realized mailed to subscribers. Appraisals.

Frasher's, Rt. 1 Box 142, Oak Grove, MO 64075, 816-625-3786; fax: 816-625-6079.

Auctions of dolls and related items. Mail and phone bids accepted. Buyer's premium 5%. Catalog $25 per issue. Prices realized mailed after auction. Appraisals.

Freeman Fine Arts of Philadelphia, 1808 Chestnut St., Philadelphia, PA 19103, 215-563-9275; fax: 215-563-8236. Americana and fine art. Mail and phone bids accepted. Buyer's premium 10%. Catalog subscription $110. Prices realized mailed after auction. Appraisals.

G. Ray Hawkins Gallery, 910 Colorado Ave., Santa Monica, CA 90401, 310-394-5558; fax: 310-576-2468. Photography, contemporary and vintage. Mail and phone bids accepted. Buyer's premium 10%. Catalogs $30 per year. Appraisals.

Garth's, 2690 Stratford Rd., PO Box 369, Delaware, OH 43015, 614-362-4771; fax: 614-363-0164. Mail and phone bids accepted. Buyer's premium 10%. Catalog subscription $85 per year. Prices realized mailed after auction. Appraisals.

Gary Metz's Muddy River Trading Co., 4803 Lange Ln. SW, Roanoke, VA 24018, 703-989-0475. Antique advertising, specializing in soda pop collectibles and signs of all kinds. Mail and phone bids accepted. Buyer's premium 10%. Catalog, usually $15. Prices realized mailed after auction. Appraisals.

Gene Harris Family Antique Auction Center, 203 S. 18th Ave., PO Box 476, Marshalltown, IA 50158, 515-752-0600, 515-753-0226. Buyer's premium 10%. Minimum bid and 50% deposit required on mail and phone bids.

George & Florence Theriault, The Dollmasters, PO Box 151, 2148 Renard Ct., Annapolis, MD 21404, 800-638-0422; 410-224-3655; fax: 410-224-2515. Dolls. Mail and phone bids accepted. No buyer's premium at catalogued auctions. Subscription $159 yearly, 10 catalogs. Prices realized mailed after auction. Appraisals.

Glass-Works Auctions, PO Box 180, East Greenville, PA 18041, 215-679-5849; fax: 215-679-3068. Bottles and glass, barbershop memorabilia.

Mail and phone bids accepted. Buyer's premium 10%. Catalog subscription $70 for 4 catalogs. Small video auctions. Prices realized mailed after auction.

Glasses, Mugs & Steins Auction, PO Box 207, Sun Prairie, WI 53590; fax: 608-837-4818. Mail auction of glasses, mugs, steins, and related items. Mail and phone bids accepted. Buyer's premium, none up to $100, 5% for $101-$200, 10% over $200. Catalog $8, subscription $21. Prices realized with subscription. Appraisals for subscribers.

Great Gatsby's, 5070 Peachtree Industrial Blvd., Atlanta, GA 30341, 800-428-7297, 404-457-1905; fax: 404-457-7250. Auctions of architectural items, chandeliers, stained glass windows, statues, fountains, and period furniture. Mail and phone bids accepted. Buyer's premium 10%. Free catalogs. Appraisals.

Green Valley Auctions Inc., Rt. 2, Box 320, Mt. Crawford, VA 22841, 703-434-4260; fax: 703-434-0309. Antiques and fine furnishings; book, paper, and other specialty auctions. Mail or phone bids accepted. No buyer's premium. Listings for specialty auctions; free brochure. Appraisals.

Greenberg Auctions, 7566 Main St., Sykesville, MD 21784, 410-795-7447; fax: 410-549-2553. Lionel, American Flyer, LGB, and other toy trains. Mail and phone bids accepted. Buyer's premium 10%. Catalog $10 plus $3 postage and handling. Prices realized mailed after auction.

Green Dragon, 128 N. Main St., St. Albans, VT 05478, 802-524-6427. Fine arts, erotica, books, ephemera. Mail and phone bids accepted. No buyer's premium. Fully illustrated catalogs. Write to be put on mailing list. Prices realized mailed after auction. Appraisals. Restoration of paper and painting.

Greg Manning Auctions Inc., 115 Main Rd., Montville, NJ 07045, 201-299-1800; fax: 201-299-9026. Entire collections and stocks of stamps; sports cards. Mail, phone and fax bids accepted. Buyer's premium 10%. Minimum bids. Stamp catalogs $3, prices realized sent after auction. Sports catalog free. Appraisals.

Grogan & Company, 890 Commonwealth Ave., Boston, MA 02215, 617-566-4100; fax: 617-566-7715. Full service auctions: paintings, sculpture, prints, jewelry, silver, oriental rugs, furniture, and decorative arts. Mail and phone bids accepted. Buyer's premium 10%. Catalog subscription $225 a year, includes list of prices realized. Appraisals.

Guernsey's, 108 East 73rd St., New York, NY 10021, 212-794-2280, 212-744-3638. Carousels, posters, vintage automobiles. Mail and phone bids accepted. Buyer's premium 10%. Prices realized available after auction. Appraisals.

H. R. Harmer Inc., 14 E. 33rd St., New York, NY 10016, 212-532-3700; fax: 212-447-5625. Stamps, philatelic literature. Mail and phone bids accepted. Buyer's premium 10%. Catalogs $20 bulk, $30 first class, $60 overseas. Prices realized mailed after auction. Appraisals.

Hake's Americana & Collectibles, PO Box 1444, York, PA 17405, 717-848-1333. Mail auction. Nostalgia and character collectibles, twentieth-century popular culture, political Americana. Mail, phone, or fax bids accepted. No buyer's premium. Catalogs $7.50, $30 for 5 issues a year. Prices realized mailed upon request. Appraisals.

Hanzel Galleries Inc., 1120 S. Michigan Ave., Chicago, IL 60605, 312-922-6234; fax: 312-922-6972. Fine art, antiques, decorative arts. Mail and phone bids accepted. Buyer's premium 15% up to and including $50,000, 10% on excess. Prices realized mailed after auction. Appraisals. Will refer to restoration and conservation sources.

Harmer Rooke Galleries, 32 E. 57th St., New York, NY 10022, 212-751-1900; fax: 212-758-1713. Early American glass and stoneware, advertising pot lids, Americana, bottles, classical antiquities, collectibles, and coins. Primarily mail and phone bid auctions. Buyer's premium 10%. Minimum bids. Catalog prices vary. Prices realized. Appraisals.

Harris Auction Galleries, Inc., 875 N. Howard St., Baltimore, MD 21201, 410-728-7040; fax: 410-728-0449. Absentee bids accepted. Buyer's premium 10%. Catalog subscription $35 per year. Appraisals.

Hart Galleries, 2301 S. Voss Rd., Houston, TX 77057, 713-266-3500; fax: 713-266-3500. Eighteenth- and nineteenth-century English furniture, fine art, objects of art, and oriental rugs. Mail and phone bids must be set up 24 hours in advance. Buyer's premium 10%. Brochures $20 annually. Referrals on appraisal, restoration, and conservation.

Herman Darvick Autograph Auctions, PO Box 467, Rockville Centre, NY 11571-0467, 516-766-0289; fax: 516-766-7456. Mail bids accepted, 25% deposit or references required. Buyer's premium 10%. Prices realized mailed after auction.

High Noon Western Collectibles, 9929 Venice Blvd., Los Angeles, CA 90034, 310-202-9010; fax: 310-202-1340. Cowboy collectibles. Buyer's premium 10%. Mail and phone bids accepted. Catalog $15 U.S., $20 foreign. Prices realized mailed after auction. Appraisals.

The Holiday Auction, 4027 Brooks Hill Rd., Brooks, KY 40109, 502-955-9238; fax: 502-957-5027. Mail auctions of holiday memorabilia; specializing in antique Christmas. Mail and fax bids accepted. No buyer's premium. Catalogs $6 per year; prices realized in next catalog.

Howard Lowery, 3810 W. Magnolia Blvd., Burbank, CA 91505, 818-972-9080; fax: 818-972-3910. Animation art. Mail and phone bids accepted. Buyer's premium 10%. Catalog $55 a year, or about $15 each. Prices realized mailed after auction. Appraisals.

Howard Parzow, 5 Bostwick Ct., Gaithersburg, MD 20878, 301-977-6741; fax: 301-208-8947. Apothecary, drug store, country store, advertising, and soda fountain–related items. Mail and phone bids accepted. Buyer's premium 10%. Appraisals.

Illustration House, 96 Spring St., New York,

NY 10012, 212-966-9444; fax: 212-966-9425. Cartoon art and illustration original art. Mail and phone bids accepted. Buyer's premium 13%. Catalog $15 in U.S., $21 elsewhere. Prices realized mailed after auction. Appraisals, restoration, and conservation.

Ivy, Shreve & Mader, 32 E. 57th Street, New York, NY 10022, 212-486-1222; fax: 212-486-0676. Individual rare stamps are auctioned. Mail, phone, and fax bids accepted. Buyer's premium 10%. Catalogs usually $10. Prices realized sent after auction. Appraisals.

J. W. Auction Co., 11 Chestnut St., Rochester, NH 03867, 603-332-0192. Toys, toy trains, railroad, sports, and advertising memorabilia. Mail and phone bids accepted. Buyer's premium 10%. Descriptive list, graded, $3. Prices realized mailed after auction. Appraisals, restoration, and conservation.

Jackson's Auction Gallery, 5330 Pendleton Ave., Anderson, IN 46011, 317-642-7563; fax: 317-640-9485. Indiana art, St. Clair glass, antiques, and estates. Mail and phone bids accepted. No buyer's premium. Catalogs, $25 per year, 4 auctions. Art price list mailed after auction.

James D. Julia, RFD #1 Box 91 Route #201, Skowhegan Rd., Fairfield, ME 04937, 207-453-7125 207-453-9493; fax: 207-453-2502. Toys, advertising, guns, dolls, lamps and glass, Americana, and Victoriana. Mail and phone bids accepted. Buyer's premium 10%. Catalogs, various prices. Prices realized mailed after auction. Appraisals.

Jim Depew Galleries, 1860 Piedmont Rd. NE, Atlanta, GA 30324, 404-874-2286. Mail and phone bids accepted. Buyer's premium 10%, on designated sales. Unillustrated catalogs available prior to sale by request. Appraisals.

Joy Luke Fine Arts Brokers, Auctioneers & Appraisers, 300 E. Grove St., Bloomington, IL 61701, 309-828-5533; fax: 309-829-2266. Fine arts and antiques. Mail and phone bids accepted. No buyer's premium. Prices realized mailed after auction. Appraisals.

Kirsner's Auctions, PO Box 8807, Coral Springs, FL 33075, 305-344-9856; fax: 305-344-4421. Steins and Hummels. Mail and phone bids taken before auction. Buyer's premium 10%. Stein catalogs $30 a year; Hummel $5 per auction. Prices realized mailed after auction. Appraisals.

Kruse International, 5400 County Rd. 11A, PO Box 190, Auburn, IN 46706, 219-925-5600, 219-925-5467. Cars. Mail and phone bids by prior arrangement. Buyer's premium 10% on antiques and collectibles, 3% on cars. Free catalog. Appraisals.

Lincoln Galleries, 225 Scotland Rd., Orange, NJ 07050, 207-729-3053; fax: 201-677-1176. American, Continental, and oriental antique furniture; porcelains, silver, collectibles, paintings, oriental rugs, coins, stamps, etc. Mail and phone bids accepted. Buyer's premium 10%. Catalog $2. Appraisals, restoration, and conservation.

L. A. Landry Antiques, 164 Main St., Essex, MA 01929, 508-768-6233; fax: 508-768-6233. General auctions. Mail and phone bids accepted. Buyer's premium 10%. Catalog prices vary. Appraisals, restoration, and conservation.

L. H. Selman Ltd., 761 Chestnut St., Santa Cruz, CA 95060, 800-538-0766; fax: 408-427-0111. Paperweights. Mail, telephone, and fax bids accepted. Buyer's premium 10%. Catalogs $25 each or $60 for 3 issues. Prices realized mailed after auction. Appraisals, restoration, and conservation.

Lang's Fishing Tackle Auctions, 31R Turtle Cove, Raymond, ME 04071, 207-655-4265. Fishing tackle, advertising, and sporting collectibles. Mail and phone bids accepted. Buyer's premium 10%. Catalog $25, includes list of prices realized. Appraisals.

Larry Gottheim Fine Early Photographs, 33 Orton Ave., Binghamton, NY 13905, 607-797-1685; fax: 607-797-4775. Mail auctions, specializing in unusual nineteenth- and early twentieth-century photographic images. Mail and phone bids. No buyer's premium. Catalogs $25 for 2 issues plus supplement. Prices realized mailed after auction. Appraisals.

Lelands, 245 Fifth Ave., Suite 202, New York, NY 10016, 212-545-0800; fax: 212-545-0713. Sports memorabilia and vintage baseball cards. Mail and telephone bids accepted. Buyer's premium 10%. Appraisals.

Leslie Hindman Auctioneers, 215 W. Ohio St., Chicago, IL 60610, 312-670-0010; fax: 312-670-4248. Auctions of English, American, and Continental furniture and decorative arts. Mail and phone bids accepted. Buyer's premium 15% up to $50,000; 10% after $50,000. Catalog subscription $150 domestic, $200 international. Appraisals, restoration, conservation.

LFK Art & Antiques, 2840 Roe Ln., Kansas City, KS 66103, 913-262-7860; fax: 913-262-9689. General fine arts, decorative arts, American furniture. Mail and phone bids accepted. Buyer's premium 10%. Catalog $20. Prices realized mailed after auction.

Lloyd Ralston, 173 Post Rd., Fairfield, CT 06432, 203-255-1233; 203-366-3399; fax: 203-256-9094. Mail and fax bids accepted. No phone bids day of sale. Buyer's premium 10% to 13%. Catalog $17. Prices realized mailed after auction. Appraisals.

The Local, PO Box 159, Kennedale, TX 76060, 817-535-6283; fax: 817-535-6283. Mail auctions of political buttons and campaign memorabilia of all sorts. Catalog $10. Prices realized sent to winning bidders. Appraisals.

Lynn Geyer's Advertising Auctions, 300 Trail Ridge, Silver City, NM 88061, 505-538-2341. Advertising. Mail and phone bids accepted. No buyer's premium. Catalog $20. Prices realized mailed after auction. Appraisals.

Mail Bid Auction, PO Box 414, Yucca Valley, CA 92286; fax: 619-365-9668. Mail order collectibles. Fax and mail bids only. Catalog $2. List of prices realized sent to successful bidders.

Majolica Auctions, PO Box 332, Wolcottville,

IN 46795, 219-854-2895; fax: 214-854-3979. Majolica. Mail bids accepted. Buyer's premium 10%. Prices realized $5. Appraisals.

Manion's International Mail Order Auction House, Box 12214, Kansas City, KS 66112. Militaria. Mail and phone bids accepted. Buyer's premium 15%. Catalogs $35 for 6 issues. Prices realized mailed upon request, $2. Appraisals.

Mark Vail Auction Co., Kelly Ave., PO Box 956, Pine Brush, NY 12566, 914-744-2120; fax: 914-744-2450. Antiques, collectibles, and estate auctions. Mail and phone bids accepted. Buyer's premium 10%. Free list. Appraisals.

Marlin Denlinger Auctions, RR. 3, Box 3775, Morrisville, VT 05661, 802-888-2774. Stoneware, antique/blue decorated. Mail and phone bids accepted. Buyer's premium 10%. Catalog $12. Prices realized mailed after auction. Appraisals.

Martin Auction Co. Inc., PO Box 343, Clinton, IL 61727, 217-935-3245; fax: 717-768-7714. Horse-drawn items. Mail and phone bids accepted. No buyer's premium. Catalog subscription $60, 3 auction catalogs and post auction price lists. Appraisals.

Martone's Gallery, 699 New London Turnpike., W. Greenwich, RI 02817; fax: 401-885-3880. Mail and phone bids accepted. Catalogs $3 at the door. Buyer's premium 10%. Appraisals.

McAllister Auction Service, 958 Maynard Rd., Portland, MI 48875, 517-647-7482; 517-647-4852; fax: 517-647-7482. Art pottery. Mail and phone bids accepted. Catalog $10. Prices realized mailed after auction. Appraisals.

McClintock PC Sales, PO Box 1765, Manassas, VA 22110, 703-368-2757. Postcard mail auctions. Send 52-cent stamped, self-addressed #10 envelope for illustrated catalog. Prices realized and next catalog sent to successful bidders. Others may send SASE for list. No buyer's premium. Appraisals.

McMasters Doll Auctions, PO Box 1755, Cambridge, OH 43725, 800-842-3526, 614-432-

4419; fax: 614-432-3191. Dolls. Cataloged auctions, mail and phone bids accepted, catalogs $25, 4 for $65. Specialty auctions, mini-catalogs $15 each. No buyer's premium. Prices realized mailed after auction. Appraisals. Restoration and conservation available.

Michael Bennett Auctions, RFD #3, Pickering Rd., Dover, NH 03820, 603-742-9955; fax: 603-742-2992. Paper and ephemera, estates, large and small antiques. Buyer's premium 0-10%. Mail and phone bids accepted. Catalog $10-$15, includes list of prices realized after auction. Appraisals.

Michael Henry, 1456 Carston Ct., Homewood, IL 60430, 708-798-7508. Still and mechanical banks. Mail only. Buyer's premium 10%. Catalogs $20–$25. Appraisals.

Mid-Hudson Galleries, One Idlewind Ave., Cornwall-on-Hudson, NY 12520, 914-534-7828; fax: 914-534-4802. Estate and specialty auctions. Mail and phone bids accepted. Buyer's premium 10%. Auction fliers $25 a year, includes free catalog at gallery. Prices realized mailed after specialty auctions. Appraisals.

Mohawk Arms Inc., PO Box 399, Utica, NY 13503, 315-724-1234. Militaria. Mail and phone bids accepted. Buyer's premium, sliding scale 15% to 5%. Catalogs $15 each, $45 per year. Prices realized mailed after auction. Appraisals.

Monson & Baer, 310 Maple Ave. W., Suite #270, Vienna, VA 22183; fax: 703-938-2129. Catalogued auctions of perfume bottles. Buyer's premium 10%. Mail bids accepted. Oral appraisals only. Catalog $28, includes list of prices realized.

Morton M. Goldberg Auction Galleries, 547 Baronne St., New Orleans, LA 70113, 504-592-2300; fax: 504-592-2311. Mail and phone bids accepted. Buyer's premium 10%. Prices realized mailed on request. Appraisals, restoration, and conservation.

Neal Auction Company, 4038 Magazine St., New Orleans, LA 70115, 504-899-5329; fax: 504-

897-3808. Mail and phone bids accepted. Buyer's premium 10%. Catalogs $25-$28, $100 annually. Prices realized mailed after auction. Appraisals.

New England Auction Gallery, Box 2273, W. Peabody, MA 01960, 508-535-3140; fax: 508-535-7522. Toys, character collectibles, and games. Mail and phone bids accepted. No buyer's premium. Catalogs $8; $30 per year, $40 international. Prices realized mailed after auction. Appraisals.

New Hampshire Book Auctions, PO Box 460, Weare, NH 03281, 603-529-7432. Books, maps, prints, ephemera. Mail and phone bids accepted, but not during the auction. Buyer's premium 10%. Yearly subscription to catalogs $20 U.S. $30 Canada and overseas. Prices realized mailed to subscribers. Appraisals.

Noel Barrett Antiques & Auctions Ltd., Carversville Rd., Carversville, PA 18913, 215-297-5109. Antique toys and advertising. Mail and phone bids accepted. Buyer's premium 10%. Catalogs $25-$30 each. Prices realized mailed after auction. Appraisals.

Norman C. Heckler & Co., Bradford Corner Rd., Woodstock Valley, CT 06282, 203-974-1634; fax: 203-974-2003. Bottles, flasks, and early glass. Mail and phone bids accepted. Buyer's premium 10%. Catalog $23. Prices realized mailed after auction. Appraisals.

Nostalgia Publications Inc., Allan Petretti, 21 S. Lake Dr., Hackensack, NJ 07601, 201-488-4536, evenings. Mail auction of Coca-Cola and other soda-pop advertising items. No buyer's premium. Catalogs $8 for 3 auctions. Prices realized printed in next auction catalog. Appraisals..

Nutmeg Auction Service, 661 Washington St., Woodbury, CT 06798, 203-263-5599; fax: 203-264-6160. Estate fresh goods and collections. Fine arts, antiques, specialty auctions including sports, books, Americana, ephemera, etc. Mail and phone bids accepted. Buyer's premium 10%. Prices realized mailed after some sales. Appraisals.

O'Gallerie Inc., 228 NE 7th St., Portland,

OR 97232, 503-238-0202; fax: 503-236-8211. Mail and phone bids accepted. Buyer's premium 10%. Catalogs $83 per year, 10 illustrated catalogs with estimates and prices realized. Appraisals, restoration, and conservation.

Oakland Galleries, PO Box 40, Saginaw, MO 64864, 417-782-4400. Antique and estates. Mail bids with deposit. No buyer's premium. Free catalogs. Appraisals.

Pacific Book Auction Galleries, 139 Townsend St., Suite 305, San Francisco, CA 94107, 415-896-2665; fax: 415-896-1664. Fine and rare books and manuscripts. Mail and phone bids accepted. Buyer's premium 10%. Full catalog subscription $160. Specialty subscriptions less. Prices realized. Appraisals, advice and recommendation on restoration services. Newsletter.

Paul McInnis, 356 Exeter Rd., Hampton Falls, NH 03844, 603-778-8989; fax: 603-772-7452. Antiques and estate sales. Mail and phone bids accepted. Buyer's premium 10%. Catalogs $10-$25 per auction. Prices realized mailed after auction. Appraisals.

Paul J. Dias, 30 E. Washington St., Route 58, Hanson, MA 02341, 617-447-9057; fax: 617-447-0432. Militaria. Mail and phone bids accepted. Buyer's premium 10%. Appraisals.

Pennypacker-Andrews Auction Centre Inc., PO Box 558, Shillington, PA 19607, 610-777-6121, 610-777-5890; fax: 610-777-3751. Mail and phone bids with deposit. Buyer's premium 10%. Free notification of auctions. No prices realized mailed after auction. Appraisals.

Pettigrew's, 1645 S. Tejon St., Colorado Springs, CO 80906, 719-633-7963; fax: 719-633-5035. Estate auctions, nineteenth- and early twentieth-century American furniture and decorations. Mail and phone bids welcome, 25% deposit required. Buyer's premium 10%. Catalogs and prices realized $40 per year. Appraisals, limited restoration and conservation.

Phillips, 406 E. 79th St., New York, NY 10021,

800-825-ART1, 212-570-4830; fax: 212-570-2207. Jewelry, modern and antique. Other antiques sold through their European auctions. Buyer's premium 15% of the first $50,000, 10% of the excess. Catalogs and prices realized. Appraisals, specializing in jewelry, paintings, prints, and stamps.

Political Gallery, 1325 W. 86 St., Indianapolis, IN 46260, 317-257-0863; fax: 317-254-9167. Political and sports memorabilia. Mail and phone bids accepted. Catalog subscription, political $20 for 4 issues, sports $15 for 4 issues. Prices realized published in following auction catalog. Appraisals.

Pook & Pook, Inc., 463 E. Lancaster Ave., Downingtown, PA 19353, 215-269-0695; fax: 215-269-9274. Mail and phone bids accepted. Buyer's premium 10%. Prices realized mailed after auction. Appraisals.

Pop Shoppe Video Connection, Jim Millar, 2180 Ellery Ave., Clovis, CA 93611-0652, 209-298-7531, 6:00 P.M.–9:00 P.M. Video auctions featuring ACL (painted label) sodas, go-withs, and advertising. Phone-in bids only. Free auction catalog. Video $15, includes list of prices realized.

Postcards International, PO Box 2309, New Haven, CT 06515-0030, 203-865-0814; fax: 203-495-8005. Vintage picture postcards. Mail and phone bids accepted. No buyer's premium. Catalog subscription $15; prices realized published in following catalog. Mail approval service.

Poster Mail Auction Co., Box 133, #2 Patrick St., Waterford, VA 22190, 703-882-3574; fax: 703-882-4765. Mail and phone auctions of vintage posters of all types. Buyer's premium 10%. Catalogs $12 for 4 issues.

QRS Music Rolls Inc., 1026 Niagara St., Buffalo, NY 14213, 716-885-0250; fax: 716-885-7510. Mail auctions of old player piano rolls. Catalog free to bidders. No buyer's premium. Prices realized for specific items requested.

Riba Auctions, PO Box 53 Main St., South Glastonbury, CT 06073, 203-633-3076. American history, Civil War, autographs, early photography. Mail and phone bids. Buyer's premium 10%. Catalogs $18 each; $48 per year, 3 auctions. Prices realized mailed after auction.

Richard Crane Auctions, 63 Poor Farm Rd., Hillsboro, NH 03244, 603-478-5723. Monthly tool auctions. No buyer's premium. Catalogs $12, yearly subscription $10. Appraisals.

Richard Opfer Auctioneering Inc., 1919 Greenspring Dr., Timonium, MD 21093, 410-252-5035; fax: 410-252-5863. Advertising, toys, and general antiques. Mail and phone bids accepted with 20% deposit. Call for further information. Buyer's premium 10%. Catalog purchase includes list of prices realized mailed after auction.

Richard W. Withington Inc., Hillsboro, NH 03244, 603-464-3232. Doll auctions and estate auctions. No mail or phone bids. Buyer's premium 10%. Doll auction catalog subscription $105. Prices realized mailed after auction. Appraisals. Conservation of paintings only.

Richard Wolffers Auctions, Inc., 133 Kearny St., Suite 400, San Francisco, CA 94108, 415-781-5127; fax: 415-956-0483. Sports, stamps, rock-and-roll, manuscripts. Catalog prices vary. Mail, phone, and fax bids; prearrange to bid live by phone during auction; bid on floor during sale. Buyer's premium 15%. Prices realized mailed upon request. Appraisals.

Roan Auctions, Box 118 RD #3, Cogan Station, PA 17728, 717-494-0170; fax: 717-494-1911. Estates, firearms, miniature lamps. Mail and phone bids accepted. Buyer's premium 10%. Catalogs and prices realized available for some auctions. Appraisals.

Robert C. Eldred Co., Inc., PO Box 796, 1483 Rt. 6A, East Dennis, MA 02641, 508-385-3116; fax: 508-385-7201. Antiques and fine art. Mail and phone bids, deposit required. Buyer's premium 10%. Catalog subscriptions vary; mail list $6 per year. Prices realized mailed for all illustrated catalogs. Appraisals.

Robert Edward Auctions, PO Box 1923, Hoboken, NJ 07030, 201-792-9324. Baseball collectibles. Mail and phone bids accepted. Send self-addressed manila envelope with $1 postage for catalog. List of prices realized after auction. Appraisals.

Rocky Mountain Brewery Collectibles, PO Box 242, Winter Park, CO 80482, 303-726-5035; fax: 303-726-9346. Breweriana, advertising, and other auctions. Mail, phone, and fax bids welcome. No buyer's premium. Catalogs $10 each, 3 issues per year. Prices realized mailed after auction. Appraisals.

Roger S. Steffen Historical Militaria, 14 Murnan Rd., Cold Spring, KY 41076, 606-431-4499; fax: 606-431-3113. Mail order auctions, specializing in militaria, arms, and armor. Mail and phone bids accepted. Buyer's premium 15%. Catalogs $54.95 for 4 issues. Prices realized mailed after auction. Appraisals.

Running Rabbit Video Auctions, PO Box 210992, Nashville, TN 37221, 615-952-3699. Mail order marble and button auctions. Mail and phone bids accepted. No buyer's premium. Video catalog $15, includes list of prices realized after auction. Appraisals.

Russ Carlsen, Rt. 32, Ingalside Rd., Greenville, NY 12083, 518-966-5068; fax: 518-634-2465. Antiques and estate merchandise. Buyer's premium 10%. Appraisals. (No list of prices realized mailed.)

Ryan's Auction Services, PO Box 3225, N. Attleboro, MA 02761, 508-695-6464; fax: 508-695-3758. Estates. Expertise in the areas of period and Victorian furniture; toys; pre-1900 glass, china, and pottery; military items; and ephemera. Mail and phone bids accepted. Buyer's premium 10%. Free catalogs, prices realized sent on request.

Samuel Cottone Auctions, 15 Genesee, Mt. Morris, NY 14510, 716-658-3180; fax: 716-658-3152. Fine Americana and art. Mail and phone bids accepted. Buyer's premium 10%. Catalog

$15; free brochure. Prices realized with catalogs. Appraisals.

Samuel Yudkin & Associates, A-232 Woodner, Box A117, Washington, DC 20010, 202-232-6249, 202-234-0786. Books, prints, maps, and paper. Mail and phone bids accepted. Buyer's premium 10%. Catalogs $20 a year; $30 with lists of prices realized. Free lists for smaller auctions. Appraisals.

Sandy Rosnick, 73 Washington St. Suite 33, Salem, MA 01970, 508-741-1130; fax: 508-741-1132. Mail auctions of antique advertising and country store auctions. Mail and phone bids only. No buyer's premium. Catalog $25. Prices realized mailed after auction. Appraisals.

Savoia's Auction Inc., Rt. 23, S. Cairo, NY 12482, 518-622-8000; fax: 518-622-9453. American arts and crafts, twentieth-century design, sports memorabilia, estate, and other specialty auctions. Mail and phone bids accepted. Buyer's premium 10%. Catalog $20. Prices realized mailed after auction. Appraisals.

Schmidt's Antiques, 5138 W. Michigan Ave., Ypsilanti, MI 48197, 313-434-2660; fax: 313-434-5366. Mail and phone bids accepted. Buyer's premium 10%. Catalogs $24 a year. Prices realized mailed after auction. Appraisals, restoration, and conservation.

Schrager Auction Galleries Ltd., PO Box 10390, Milwaukee, WI 53210, 414-873-3738; fax: 414-873-5229. Art and antiques. Mail and phone bids accepted. No buyer's premium. Fine arts catalogs $12. Prices realized mailed if requested. Appraisals.

Selkirk's, 4166 Olive St., St. Louis, MO 63108, 314-533-1700; fax: 314-533-1704. Antique furniture, decorative arts, paintings, sculpture, bronzes, oriental rugs, Americana, toys, jewelry, collectibles. Mail and phone bids accepted with deposit. Buyer's premium 15% on first $50,000; 10% on remainder. Appraisals for estate taxes.

Shine Gallery, 16133 Ventura Blvd., Penthouse

E, Encino, CA 91436, 818-783-3640; fax: 818-990-3519. Disney and cartoon memorabilia. Mail and phone bids accepted. Buyer's premium 10%. Mailing list, periodic catalogs. Prices mailed after auction. Appraisals.

Skinner Inc., The Heritage on the Garden, 63 Park Plaza, Boston, MA 02116, 617-350-5400; fax: 617-350-5429. Mail and phone bids. Buyer's premium 10% over $50,000, 15% all other purchases. Catalogs, yearly subscription, $755. Prices realized included for all but Discovery Auctions. Appraisals.

Smith House Toy Sales, Herb & Barb Smith, 26 Adlington Rd., Eliot, ME 03903, 207-439-4614; fax: 207-439-4614. Toys, 1890–1960. Mail and phone bids accepted. No buyer's premium. Catalogs $8, $30 yearly. Prices realized sent after auction. Appraisals.

Soldiers Trunk, 60 Craigs Rd., Windsor, CT 06095, 203-687-1900; fax: 203-688-0580. Military items, American and foreign. Mail and phone bids accepted. Buyer's premium 12%. Catalog $20, includes list of prices realized. Four issues, 3,000–4,000 items each. Appraisals.

Sotheby's, 1334 York Ave., New York, NY 10021, 212-606-7000, Sales Results 212-606-7901. Mail and phone bids accepted. Buyer's premium 15% up to and including $50,000, 10% of the excess. Prices realized mailed after auction.

Sotheby's London, 34-35 New Bond St., London, England W1A 2AA, 071 693 0080; fax: 071 409 3100. Fine art auctioneers. Mail and phone bids accepted. Buyer's premium 15% up to £30,000; 10% thereafter. Catalog prices vary. Prices realized mailed after auction. Appraisals, restoration, and conservation.

South Bay Auctions Inc., 485 Montauk Hwy., East Moriches, NY 11940, 516-878-2909; fax: 516-878-1863. Antiques, fine arts, sporting collectibles, furniture, silver, porcelains, paintings, bronzes, oriental rugs. Mail and phone bids accepted. Buyer's premium 10%. Appraisals.

Sports Collectors Store, 1040 S. LaGrange Rd.,

LaGrange, IL 60525, 708-354-7970, fax: 708-354-7972. Sports cards and memorabilia. Mail auction, mail and phone bids accepted. Catalog $3. Prices on various lots available upon request. Appraisals.

Superior Galleries, 9478 West Olympic Boulevard, Beverly Hills, CA 90212, 800-421-0754; fax: 213-203-0496. Coins, stamps, sports, space and Hollywood memorabilia, animation art, manuscripts, fine arts, antiques, estate sales. Mail, fax, and phone bids accepted. Buyer's premium 10%. Catalog subscription, Kovel special, $175. Prices realized. Appraisals.

Swann Galleries, 104 East 25th St., New York, NY 10010, 212-254-4710; fax: 212-979-1017. Rare books, autographs, photographs, Judaica, works of art on paper. Mail and phone bids accepted. Buyer's premium 15% up to and including $50,000; 10% of amount over $50,000. Catalogs singly or by subscription. Appraisals.

Thomas Historical Militaria Auction Service, PO Box 1792, Santa Ana, CA 92702, 714-558-0328; fax: 714-558-1536. Military collectibles. Mail, phone, and fax bids accepted. Buyer's premium 15% under $1,000; 10% over. Catalogs $20 for 4; sample on request. Prices realized mailed after auction. Appraisals.

Tim Unterholzner Auctions & Appraisals, PO Box 930216, Verona, WI 53593, 608-833-6384. Antique and estate auctions. Mail and phone bids accepted. No buyer's premium, except 10% for large oriental rug auctions. Catalog prices vary. Appraisals.

'Tiques Auction, 7 Rittner Ln., Old Bridge, NJ 08857, 908-679-8212; fax: 908-679-1090. Mail and phone auctions of esoteric items, specializing in early Disney, comic and fairy tale characters, rock-and-roll memorabilia, Western, baby-boomer, TV, space, sports, and other collectibles. Catalog $8, $20 for 3. Appraisals.

Tony Hyman, Box 3028, Shell Beach, CA 93448, 805-776-6777; fax: 805-773-0117. Tobacciana auctions. Mail and phone bids only.

Buyer's premium 10%. Prices realized mailed after auction. Catalogs and list of prices realized. Free appraisal of tobacco-related items. Send photo or photocopy, description of condition, and SASE.

Toomey Gallery, 818 North Blvd., Oak Park, IL 60301, 708-383-5234; fax: 708-383-4828. Specializing in twentieth-century design. Mail and phone bids accepted. Buyer's premium 10%. Catalogs $30, yearly subscription $125. Prices realized mailed after auction. Appraisals.

Treadway Gallery, Inc., 2029 Madison Rd., Cincinnati, OH 45208, 513-321-6742; fax: 513-871-7722. Twentieth-century American and European decorative arts, including Rookwood pottery, mission furniture, Italian glass, and 1950s and modern design. Mail and phone bids accepted. Buyer's premium 10%. Catalog $30. Prices realized mailed. Appraisals.

U. I. Chick Harris, Box 20614, St. Louis, MO 63139, 314-352-8623. Mail auction of historical Americana. Prices realized mailed after auction. Appraisals.

U-Grade It Video Auction, 4411 Bazetta Rd., Cortland, OH 44410, 216-637-0357. Two video auctions per year, usually March and September. Specializing in Coca-Cola memorabilia. Mail and phone bids only. No buyer's premium. Video/booklet combination $25 for each auction. Prices realized are sent after auction.

Victorian Images, PO Box 284, Marlton, NJ 08053, 609-985-7711; fax: 609-985-8513. Mail and phone auctions of trade cards, nineteenth–century ephemera, and advertising. Buyer's premium 10%. Catalogs $12, $60 per year, 6 auctions. Prices realized mailed after auction. Appraisals.

W. E. Channing & Co., 53 Old Santa Fe Trail, Santa Fe, NM 87501, 505-988-1078; fax: 505-988-3879. American Indian, ethnographic, and Western Americana. Mail and phone bids accepted. Buyer's premium 15%. Catalogs approximately $35. Prices realized mailed after auction. Appraisals.

Waverly Auctions, Inc., 4931 Cordell Ave., Bethesda, MD 20814, 301-951-8883; fax: 301-718-8375. Graphic art, books, paper ephemera, autographs, and maps. Mail and phone bids accepted. Buyer's premium 10%. Catalogs $35. Prices realized mailed after auction. Appraisals.

Weschler's, 905 E St. NW., Washington, DC 20004, 202-628-1281; 800-331-1430; fax: 202-628-2366. American, English, and Continental furniture and decorations, twentieth-century decorative art, orientalia, jewelry, coins, paintings, sculpture. Mail and phone bids accepted. Buyer's premium 10%. Catalog subscription $360. Prices realized. Appraisals.

William Doyle Galleries, 175 East 87th St., New York, NY 10128, 212-427-2730; fax: 212-369-0892. Fine art and antiques; American, English, and Continental furniture and decorations, paintings, prints, books, jewelry. Mail and phone bids accepted. Buyer's premium 15% on first $50,000, 10% on excess. Prices realized mailed after auction. Appraisal.

William J. Jenack Auctioneers & Appraisers, 18 Hambletonian Ave., Chester, NY 10918, 914-469-9095; fax: 914-469-7129. Fine arts, antiques, decorative accessories. Mail and phone bids accepted. Buyer's premium 10%. Individual catalogs $5. Prices realized mailed upon request. Appraisals.

Willis Henry Auctions, 22 Main St., Marshfield, MA 02050, 617-834-7774; fax: 617-826-3520. Mail and phone bids accepted. Buyer's premium 10%. Catalog $20. Prices realized for illustrated catalogs mailed after auction. Appraisals. Referrals to restoration and conservation services.

Winter Associates, 21 Cooke St., Plainville, CT 06062-0823, 203-793-0288; fax: 203-793-8288. Estate liquidation, antiques and fine art. Mail and phone bids accepted. Catalogs available at sales and previews only. Prices realized sent to catalog buyers. Buyer's premium 10%. Appraisals.

Witherell's, PO Box 804, Healdsburg, CA 95448, 707-433-8950. Victorian furniture, vintage gambling, advertising, Western decor. Mail and phone bids accepted. Buyer's premium 10%. Catalogs $20 each. List of prices realized mailed after auction. Appraisals, restoration, and conservation.

Wm. A. Smith Inc., Plainfield, NH 03781, 603-675-2549; fax: 603-675-2549. Mail and phone bids accepted. Buyer's premium 10%. Free catalogs. Prices realized mailed after auction. Appraisals.

Wolf's, Michael Wolf, 1239 W. 6th St., Cleveland, OH 44113, 216-575-9653, 800-526-1991; fax: 216-621-8011. Mail and phone bids accepted. Buyer's premium 10%. Prices realized mailed after auction.

Woody Auction, PO Box 618, Douglass, KS 67039, 316-747-2694; fax: 316-746-2145. Carnival glass, R. S. Prussia, and general antiques. Mail auction of antiques. No buyer's premium. Free catalogs. Prices realized mailed upon request, $5. Appraisals.

Worldwide Amusement Auctioneers, 50 W. Pearl, Coldwater, MI 49036, 517-279-9063; fax: 517-279-9191. Specialty auctions: museums, tourist attractions, theme parks, unique collections. No mail or phone bids. Catalog $10 domestic, $25 foreign. Prices realized mailed after auction. Appraisals.

Young Fine Art Auctions Inc., PO Box 313, North Berwick, ME 03906, 207-676-3104; fax: 207-676-3105. Paintings. Mail and phone bids accepted. Buyer's premium 10%. Catalog subscription $20 for 5 auctions. Prices realized mailed after auction.

Appraisal Groups

*T*he major antiques appraisal associations are listed below. Most have lists of members and will send you a complete list or the names of local appraisers. Many appraisers include their membership information in their advertising in the Yellow Pages of the telephone book. Many appraisers are noted in the preceding section on auction houses.

American Society of Appraisers, PO Box 17265, Washington, DC 20041, 800-ASA-VALU, 703-478-2228; fax: 703-742-8471. Call for appraiser member in your area. *Directory of Accredited Personal Property Appraisers* lists tested and accredited members, geographically, in the U.S. and abroad. *Information on the Appraisal Profession,* questions and answers about appraising. Single copy free.

Antique Appraisal Association of America, 11361 Garden Grove Blvd., Garden Grove, CA 92643, 714-530-7090.

Appraisers Association of America, 386 Park Ave. South, Suite 2000, New York, NY 10016, 212-889-5404. Free referral service of personal property appraisers. Membership directory available, $14.95. Video tapes of lectures; newsletter, *The Appraiser.*

Appraisers National Association, 120 S. Bradford Ave., Placentia, CA 92670, 714-579-1082. Standardized educational requirements for certification of members.

Art Dealers Association of America, 575 Madison Ave., New York, NY 10022, 212-940-8590, Mon.–Fri. 9:30 A.M.–5:30 P.M.; fax: 212-940-7013. Appraisal of works of fine art, paintings, drawings, sculpture, and graphics, when they are being donated to a museum or other nonprofit organization and where an appraisal is required for income tax purposes. Free membership list.

International Society of Appraisers, 16040 Christensen Rd., Suite 320, Seattle, WA 98188, 206-241-0359; fax: 206-241-0436.291

Mid-Am Antique Appraisers Association, PO Box 9681, Springfield, MO 65801, 415-865-7269, 10:00 A.M.–4:00 P.M.; fax: 417-865-7269. Membership roster lists appraisers by specialty and by locality, $3.75.

New England Appraisers Association, 5 Gill Terrace, Ludlow, VT 05149, 802-228-7444, 9:00 A.M.–5:00 P.M. Referral service. Publication, *The Appraisers Standard,* available by subscription, $20 per year. Information package with application available free upon request.

*C*onservation, *R*estoration & *P*reservation *S*upplies

*T*he best place to start looking for supplies is at your local hardware or art store. These are products that can be used to clean chandeliers still in place on the ceiling, tarnish-proof silver, replate silver, or remove candle wax from tabletops. Ask at the store. All types of metal polishes, battery-powered picture lights, felt pads to keep lamp bottoms from scratching the furniture, polishes to match any shade of wood, marble polish, dry cleaners to remove stains on cloth, linen wash that whitens old damask napkins, and even special cleaners to remove crayon or paint marks can be found. Dozens of new types of "instant" glue and solder are available. Some are clear for use on glass.

Some supplies needed for the proper care of antiques are difficult to locate, including such products as acid-free paper backing materials, special soaps, and special waxes. These are used primarily by the professional restorer or conservator, but collectors often need them as well. A list of these part and supply sources follows. Some of these companies sell only to wholesale accounts and will not sell to individuals, but will direct you to the store or dealer nearest you that carries the products. **Special items for use with one**

type of antique, such as clock parts or doll eyes, are listed in the appropriate sections.

There are stores where you can rent mail boxes that also pack and ship antiques. Check your local phone book.

Abatron, Inc., 33 Center Dr., Gilberts, IL 60136, 800-445-1754; 708-426-2200, 7:00 A.M.–6:00 P.M.; fax: 708-426-5966. Wood restoration products. LiquidWood penetrates deteriorated wood and restores structural strength. WoodEpox replaces missing sections of wood. Decorative elements such as finials, moldings, and capitals can be re-created using MasterMold 12-3 flexible mold-making compound. Free brochures.

Albert Constantine & Son, Inc., 2050 Eastchester Rd., Bronx, NY 10461, 800-223-8087, 8:00 A.M.–6:00 P.M.; fax: 718-792-2110. Veneers, hardwoods, finishing and refinishing supplies, cane and rush for seats, reproduction hardware, moldings and decorative carvings, clock movements, upholstery supplies, gold leaf, metal finishes, tools, how-to books and videos. Genuine mother-of-pearl inlay blanks; gold-colored natural mother-of-pearl; "just like real mother of pearl" cast polyester in large size sheets; genuine green abalone; alternative ivory cast polyester. Catalog $1.

Allied Resin Corp., Weymouth Industrial Park, East Weymouth, MA 02189, 617-337-6070, 8:30 A.M.–5.00 P.M.; fax: 617-340-1431. Resin systems for restoration. Epoxies, polyesters, silicone rubber, casting compounds, and other products. Free brochure.

Antique & Collectible Restoration Services, 1417 Third St., Webster City, IA 50595, 800-832-3828, anytime. Restoration materials, including hard-to-find cold cure glass and fillers. Antique and collectible restoration service. Restoration classes; instructional video: *Porcelain Restoration Basics.* Mail order worldwide. Free brochure.

Art Essentials of New York Ltd., 3 Cross St., Suffern, NY 10901-4601, 914-368-1100, 800-283-

5323; 416-787-7331 in Canada. Gold-leaf supplies, brushes, books, and videos.

Broadnax Refinishing Products, Inc., 112 Carolina Forest, Chapel Hill, NC 27516, 919-967-1011; fax: 919-942-4686. Furniture care and refinishing products, including furniture refinisher, wood preservative, and furniture and household cleaners. Free flyer.

Collector Items, PO Box 55511, Seattle, WA 98155, 206-365-1188; fax: 206-367-1188. Nylon and poly bubble wrap, reclosable bags, archival and inert page inserts, foam plate jackets, display cases, dealer show supplies. Custom-made nylon bubble-wrap bags made to any size. Free brochure.

Colophon Book Arts Supply, 3046 Hobum Bay Rd. NE, Olympia, WA 98516, 206-459-2940, 24 hours a day, answering machine; fax: 206-459-2945. Supplies for hand bookbinding, book repair, and restoration. Restorative leather cream. Supplies for hand-marbling paper, including tools, colors, chemicals, and technical assistance. Mail order worldwide. Catalog $2.

Competition Chemicals, Inc., PO Box 820, Iowa Falls, IA 50126, 515-648-5121, Mon.–Fri. 8:00 A.M.–5:00 P.M. Distributor of metal polish. Free brochure.

Conservation Materials Ltd., PO Box 2884, Sparks, NV 89432, 800-733-5283, 702-331-0582, 8:00 A.M.–4:00 P.M.; fax: 702-331-0588. Over 3,000 products for the conservator, including adhesives, brushes, chemicals, consolidants, and tools. Supplies for bookbinding, gilding, paper, textile, painting, and furniture conservation. Quake-Wax™ and Museum Mounting Wax for securing art and artifacts. Catalog $4.

Conservation Resources International, 8000 H Forbes Pl., Springfield, VA 22151, 703-321-7730, 8:30 A.M.–5:00 P.M.; fax: 703-321-0629. Archival materials for long-term storage of collections. Free catalog available.

Craftsman Wood Service Company, 1735 West Cortland Corut, Addison, IL 60101, 708-629-3100,

8:30 A.M.–5:00 P.M.; fax: 708-629-8292 for information; 800-543-9367 for orders. Over 4,000 items for the wood hobbyist, including domestic and imported hardwoods, veneers, kits, plans, cane and upholstery supplies, tools, finishes, and hard-to-find hardware. Mail order worldwide. Catalog $1.

D. A. Culpepper Mother of Pearl Company, PO Box 445, Franklin, NC 28734, 704-524-6842, 9:00 A.M.–5:00 P.M.; fax: 704-369-7809. Bone parts for cutlery repair. Mother-of-pearl for inlay and repair. Abalone, samme, shagreen, and horn. Brochure $2 and long SASE.

Daly's Wood Finishing Products, 3525 Stone Way N., Seattle, WA 98103, 800-735-7019, 206-633-4200, Mon.–Fri. 8:00 A.M.–5:00 P.M.; fax: 206-632-2565. Line of wood finishing and refinishing products, including some water-based polyurethanes. Will ship COD, or call for the name of dealer in your area. Free brochure.

Darworth Company, PO Box 639, 3 Mill Pond Ln., Simsbury, CT 06070-0639, 800-624-7767, 8:00 A.M.–5:00 P.M.; fax: 800-227-6095. Manufacturer of wood-patching compounds and putty sticks to repair holes, gouges, and scratches in wood surfaces. Call for name of dealer in your area.

Easy Time Wood Refinishing Products Corp., 1208 Lisle Pl., Lisle, IL 60532, 708-515-1160; fax: 708-515-1165. Wood refinishing products: Easy Gun Heat Gun, wood refinisher, tung oil, and lemon oil. Open 8:00 A.M.–5:00 P.M. Free brochure.

Environsafe Cleaning Products, PO Box 620356, Woodside, CA 94062, 800-227-9744, 415-369-3711, Mon.–Fri. 9:00 A.M.–5:00 P.M.; fax: 415-369-3713. Environmentally safe products, including T.L.C. Stripper, T.L.C. Wax, Envirosafe Metal Cleaner/Polish, Envirosafe Totally Awesome for carpet and fabrics, products for cleaning glass, marble, wood, and stone. Paint remover and stripper.

Epoxy Technology, Inc. 14 Fortune Dr., Billerica, MA 01821, 800-227-2201, 508-667-3805, 8:30 A.M.–P.M.; fax: 508-663-9782. Transparent, low viscosity epoxies for repair of glass or porcelain and impregnating wooden objects. General, pastelike epoxies for bonding and repair of broken objects. Brochure.

Exposures, 41 S. Main St., Norwalk, CT 06854, 800-222-4947, 203-854-1610 in CT; fax: 414-231-6942. Archival supplies, albums, frames, and boxes.

Finishing Products, 8165 Big Bend, St. Louis, MO 63119, 314-962-7575, Mon.–Sat. 9:00 A.M.–5:00 P.M.; fax: 314-962-7785. Aniline stains, custom lacquers and coatings, strippers, heat guns, crackle paint, graining tools, glazes. Furniture hardware and caning supplies. Catalog.

Floyd J. Rosini, Rt. 22 North, Millerton, NY 12546, 518-789-3582, 9:00 A.M.–5:00 P.M.; fax: 518-789-6386. Furniture repaired, restored, and reconditioned. French polishing. Furniture care products, including Rosini's Furniture Preservative & Rejuvenator, Briwax, Simichrome metal polish, touch-up markers, and other supplies.

G. Schoepfer Inc., 138 W. 31st Street, New York, NY 10001, 203-250-7794, 9:00 A.M.–5:00 P.M.; fax: 203-250-7796. Glass and plastic eyes for dolls, teddy bears, figurines, taxidermy, or umbrella handles, mechanical banks, decoys, etc.

Garrett Wade Company, 161 Avenue of the Americas, New York, NY 10013, 212-807-1155, anytime; fax: 212-255-8552. Woodworking tools, books, and supplies. Mail order worldwide. Catalog $4.

Gaylord Bros., Box 4901, Syracuse, NY 13221-4901, 800-448-6160, orders, 8:00 A.M.-7:00 P.M.; 800-634-6307, customer service; fax: 800-272-3412, 24 hours a day. Archival storage materials and conservation supplies. Postcard protectors, storage boxes, card file boxes, artifact storage cartons, trays, record storage cartons, map and print folders, map and newspaper envelopes, photo albums, archival mounting corner, *cartes de visite* storage, deacidification spray. Catalog.

George Basch Company, Inc., PO Box 188, Freeport, NY 11520, 516-378-8100, 9:00 A.M.–3:00 P.M.; fax: 516-378-8140. Nevr-Dull, treated cotton wadding cloth, cleans and polishes metal. Used on aluminum, brass, chromium, copper, gold nickel, pewter, silver, and zinc.

H. F. Staples & Co., Inc., Webb Dr., Box 956, Merrimack, NH 03054, 603-889-8600, 9:00 A.M.–5:00 P.M.; fax: 603-883-9409. Wood care and repair products, Staples wax, paint stripper, ladder mitts, and other products.

Hollinger Corporation, PO Box 8360, Fredericksburg, VA 22404, 800-634-0491, 8:30 A.M.–5:00 P.M.; fax: 800-947-8814. Archival print boxes, photographic storage materials, acid-free papers, document containers. Free brochure.

Homestead Paint & Finishes, 111 Mulpus Rd., PO Box 1668, Lunenburg, MA 01462, 508-582-6426, Mon.–Fri. 9:00 A.M.–5:00 P.M. Milk paint, crackle finish, extra bonding agent, clear coat. Retail and wholesale. Send SASE for free brochure.

Hope Co., Inc. PO Box 749, 12777 Pennridge Drive, Bridgeton, MO 63044, 314-739-7254, 8:00 A.M.–4:00 P.M.; fax: 314-739-7786. Hope's Furniture Refinisher, Tung Oil, Tung Oil Varnish, and Lemon Oil. Free brochure.

Howard Products, Inc., 411 W. Maple Ave., Monrovia, CA 91016, 818-357-9545, 800-266-9545, 7:30 A.M.–4:30 P.M.; fax 818-359-6440. Wood care products: Restor-A-Finish restores existing finish; Feed-N-Wax feeds wood, Orange Oil cleans and polishes wood. Silver polish, copper and brass polish, and jewelry cleaner. Free information pack.

I.P.G.R., Inc., PO Box 205, Kulpsville, PA 19443, 800-869-5633 orders only; 215-256-9015, Tues.–Fri. 9:30 A.M.–4:30 P.M., Sat. 9:30 A.M.–1:30 P.M.; fax: 215-256-9644. Restoration materials for glass, porcelain, jade, ivory, metals, and dolls, including adhesives, brushes, cleaners, fillers, glazes, stains, tools, and books. Catalog $3, refundable with first order.

John Sand, 1 N. Federal Highway, Dania, FL 33004, 305-925-0856, 11:00 A.M.–4:30 P.M. Gold-testing kits.

Lee Valley Tools, Ltd., 1080 Morrison Dr., Ottawa, ON Canada K2H 8K7, 613-596-0350, Mon.–Fri. 8:00 A.M.–6:00 P.M.; fax: 613-596-6030. Woodworking and finishing tools, products for restoration and fine woodworking. Catalog $5, refundable with first purchase.

Liberon/star Supplies, PO Box 86, Mendocino, CA 95460, 707-937-0375, 8:00 A.M.–5:00 P.M.; fax: 707-877-3566. Liberon/star supplies, wood finishes, refinishing, Touch-Up, and restoration materials. Brushes, steel wool, burnishing cream, furniture waxes, polishing materials; pearl hide, rabbit skin, and instant glues; gilt creams, varnishes, and fillers; flake shellacs and other hard-to-find wood-finishing supplies. Free catalog.

Light Impressions, PO Box 940, Rochester, NY 14603-0940, 800-828-6216, 800-828-9629 in NY; fax: 800-828-5539. Archival albums, paper and plastic pages, boxes, display cases, envelopes, papers, and tissues. Home storage systems for photos, negatives, and slices. Free catalog.

M. Swift & Sons, Inc., 10 Love Ln., PO Box 150, Hartford, CT 06141, 800-628-0380, 203-522-1181, Mon.–Fri. 8:00 A.M.–4:30 P.M.; fax: 203-249-5934. Manufacturers of gold leaf; metal leaf made of silver, copper, aluminum, palladium, and composition. Adjustable gilding wheels for roll gold. Free leaflet, a guide to genuine gold-leaf application.

Marshall Imports, 816 N. Seltzer St., Crestline, OH 44827, 800-992-1503, 9:00 A.M.–5:00 P.M., fax: 419-638-1258. Importer and distributor of Antiquax waxes and polishes. Mail order. Free brochure.

Masters Magic Products Inc., PO Box 31, Perry, TX 76677, 800-548-6583, Mon.–Fri. 8:00 A.M.–5:00 P.M.; fax: 817-896-2023. Restoration chemicals, including strippers, stains, lacquers, and thinners. Touch-up products, chair canes, hardware, veneers, glues, etc. Classes in restoration. Catalog $3.

mdi, inc., James Hong, 2058 Wright Ave., LaVerne, CA 91750, 909-596-2380, 9:00 A.M.–5:00 P.M.; fax: 909-596-2248. Self-adhesive, acid-free, polypropylene bags for comic books, jewelry, magazines, newspapers, postcards, sheet music, and other collectibles. Plastic sleeves, flexible and rigid. Will manufacutre plastic items to specifications. Call or write for information and free sample.

Mini-Magic, 3675 Reed Rd., Columbus, OH 43220, 614-457-3687, Mon.–Fri., 1:00 P.M.–5:00 P.M. Acid free tissue and boxes, museum washing paste, oxygen bleach for fabric restoration and conservation. Old-type silks, wools, cottons for costume restoration. Silk ribbons and trims, laces, nets, tulle, etc. Duplication of antique clothing. Will answer questions by phone, or by letter if an SASE is enclosed.

Mylan Enterprises, Inc., PO Box 194, Dept. K, Morris Plains, NJ 07950, 201-538-6186, 9:00 A.M.–7:00 P.M.; fax: 201-538-6154, 24 hours a day. Wrapping pads, bubble pack, and bubble bags for packing antiques and fragile items. Free brochure.

Nielsen & Bainbridge, 40 Eisenhower Dr., Paramus, NJ 07652. Framing materials. Alphamat conservation mat board also available through retail custom picture framing locations. Check the Yellow Pages.

Novus, 10425 Hampshire Ave. S., Minneapolis, MN 55438, 800-548-6872, 612-946-0450; fax: 612-944-2542. Novus plastic polish cleans and restores plastics; removes scratches and cloudiness from plastic toys, fountain pens, jukeboxes, purses, radios, telephone parts, and other items.

Origina Luster, Box 2092, Dept. K, Wilkes-Barre, PA 18703, 717-693-3624. Portable ultraviolet black light; Origina Luster restores transparency to sick glass. Mail order worldwide. Free brochure.

Packaging Store Inc., 5675 DTC Blvd., Suite 280, Englewood, CO 80111, 800-344-3528, anytime; fax: 303-741-6653. Packer and shipper specializing in large, awkward, fragile, and valuable items. Pack, crate, and ship anything from 1 to 1,000 pounds. Antiques, art, furniture, electronics. Sell tape, boxes, and packing materials. Free brochure lists store locations nationwide.

Paper Technologies, Inc., 929 Calle Negocio #D, San Clemente, CA 92673, 714-366-8799, 9:00 A.M.–5:00 P.M.; fax: 714-366-8798. Archival quality papers and products for the conservation, storage, and restoration of museum and library materials.

Paxton Hardware Ltd., PO Box 256, 7818 Bradshaw Rd., Upper Falls, MD 21156, 410-592-8505, 9:00 A.M.–5:00 P.M.; fax: 410-592-2224. Cleaning, restoration products, including Antiquing Solution, metal polish, furniture wax, and wood touch-up kit. Period brass furniture hardware, ice box and Hoosier hardware, miscellaneous hardware, framing supplies, lamp parts. Free brochure. Catalog $4.

Poxywood, Inc., Ronald W. England, PO Box 4231, Martinsville, VA 24115. Wood repair putty. Poxywood is a patented super putty wood paste. Looks, stains, and finishes like wood. Free brochure.

Q.R.B. Industries, 3139 US 31 North, Niles, MI 49120, 616-683-7903, 9:00 A.M.–5:00 P.M.; fax: 616-471-3887. Q.R.B. Refinishing Kit includes Paint & Varnish Remover, Instant Finish, Match-a-Color Stain, Scratch Remover, and audio cassette. Ultimate Cleaner, an all-purpose cleaner, and Clear Cost, which restores dull finishes on fiberglass, vinyl, and Formica. Mail order. Free brochure.

QH&F, Box 23927, Cola, SC 29224, 800-421-7961, 8:30 A.M.–5:00 P.M.; fax: 803-736-4731. Faux finishing, restoration and sign supplies, gold-leaf supplies. Mail order worldwide. Catalog $5.

Restoration Technology, 319 N. Tampa Ave.,

Orlando, FL 32805, 407-423-5480, 9:00 A.M.–7:00 P.M.; fax: 407-648-8511. Products for restoration of antiques, fiberglass, marble, metals, mica, plastic, porcelain, and wood. Stripper for painted surfaces, wood and metal; metal cleaner, wax that cleans, seals, and protects wood and metals, all-purpose cleaner for fabrics, carpets, windows, etc. Free brochure. Advice.

Restorations, PO Box 2000, Nevada City, CA 95959, 916-477-5527. Mylar bags. Standard sizes or custom made. Restoration supplies for repairing baseball cards and comic books. Brochure.

Russell Norton, PO Box 1070, New Haven, CT 06504-1070, 203-562-7800, 11:00 A.M.–8:00 P.M., daily. Archival polypropylene sleeves for baseball cards, postcards, and other collectibles. Send SASE for sample. Appraisals.

Solar Screen, 53-11 105th St., Corona, NY 11368, 718-592-8222; fax: 718-271-0891. Products that prevent fading caused by ultraviolet rays and help control glare and heat include Kool Vue window shades made of Mylar, Solar-Screen Transparent Sun Shades, transparent window covering material in sheets, E-Z Bond film for direct use on glass, and fluorescent bulb jackets. Free brochures.

Stroblite Co., Inc., 430 W. 14th St., Suite 500, New York, NY 10014, 212-929-3778, 9:00 A.M.–4:30 P.M. Ultraviolet black lights for examining objects and documents to detect repairs. Free brochure.

T-Distributing, Inc., 24 St. Henry Court, St. Charles, MO 63301, 314-724-1065, 9:00 A.M.–6:00 P.M. only. Manufacturers of Kwik Poly, a combination filler, coating, and bonding agent that can be used to fix deteriorating and rotten wood; fill holes, deter rust, and repair damaged surfaces on metal objects; and repair and restore other materials. It can be sanded, drilled, sawed, nailed, cut, and worked like hard wood; machined, turned, shaped, ground, and polished like aluminum. Free brochure.

Talas, Division of Technical Library Service, Inc., 213 W. 35th St., New York, NY 10001, 212-736-7744, Mon.–Fri. 9:00 A.M.–5:00 P.M.; fax: 212-465-8722. Archival storage materials and supplies, including acid-free paper, boxes, and adhesives. Waxes for furniture and wood paneling, cleaner for marble and stone, detergent for washing fabrics, leather dressing, Vellum for lamp shades, tools, and other items. Catalog $5.

University Products, Inc., PO Box 101, S. Canal St., Holyoke, MA 01040, 800-628-1912, 800-336-4847 in Massachusetts; fax: 800-532-9281. Archival supplies and repair materials for books, documents, negatives, paper, photographs, prints, and slides. Acid-free board and papers, adhesives, albums, tapes, pens, labels, tools, microfilm and microfiche materials, deacidification materials. Specialized storage for stamps, comics, records, postcards, baseball cards, and other collectibles. Free catalog.

Van Dyke's, Box 278, Woonsocket, SD 57385, 605-796-4425, 800-843-3320, orders only, 8:00 A.M.–6:00 P.M.; fax: 605-796-4085. Lamp replacement parts, furniture components, brass hardware of all kinds; curved glass china cabinet parts, isinglass for stove doors, trunk parts, pie-safe tins, clock parts, cane, reed, veneer, upholstery supplies, tools, stains, varnishes, brushes, modeling compounds. Special parts designed to duplicate the original pieces. Mail order. Catalog $1.

Wei T'o Associates, Inc., Unit #27, 21750 Main St., Matteson, IL 60443, 708-747-6660, 8:00 A.M.–5:00 P.M.; fax: 708-747-6639. Manufactures and sells deacidification sprays and solutions for paper, etc., application equipment, and specialty environmental chambers. Send SASE for catalog.

William Zinsser & Co., 39 Belmont Dr., Somerset, NJ 08875, 908-469-8100, 8:30 A.M.–4:30 P.M.; fax: 908-563-9774. Bulls Eye Shellac: finish and sealer, fast-drying, nonyellowing. Zinsser also manufactures primers and wall-covering specialty items. Free catalog.

Conservators & Restorers

Listed here are restorers and conservators who work on a variety of objects; and though others are listed in the appropriate sections of this book, this is only a partial listing of the conservators in America. For a more complete list, contact the American Institute for Conservation, listed below. They publish a list of conservators and have a referral service: You can call or write and tell them what you need and they will send you a list of conservators in your geographical area who specialize in your problem.

We have not seen the work done by many of the conservators listed here. Therefore this listing does not represent a recommendation of quality.

Be sure to check further if you decide to hire someone to restore a valuable work of art. Get a written receipt that includes work to be done, time, price, and details of insurance coverge. You may want to check your own insurance to be sure your valuable is properly insured against loss or damage. We sent an antique chair to be refinished and reupholstered. When the upholstery shop burned to the ground, a legal battle ensued to determine who would pay—the decorator, the department store, the upholsterer, or our insurance company.

A. Ludwig Klein & Son, **Inc.,** PO Box 145, Harleysville, PA 19438, 215-256-9004, Tues.–Fri. 10:00 A.M.–5:00 P.M. Restoration of glass, jade, porcelain, ivory, dolls, brass, bronze, pewter, marble, and more. Statuary and monuments, appraisals, insurance claims by appointment. Free brochure.

All-Star Celebrity Collectibles, 248 E. Main St., Ventura, CA 93001, 805-643-9224, 9:00 A.M.–10:00 P.M.; fax: 805-659-5107. Specializing in sports figures. Missing parts replaced. Free estimates.

American Institute for Conservation, 1717 K St. NW, Suite 301, Washington, DC 20006, 202-452-9545, 8:00 A.M.–5:00 P.M.; fax: 202-452-9328. Free conservation services referral system. In response to your inquiry, a computer-generated list of conservators will be compiled and grouped geographically, by specialization and by type of service requested. Free brochures include *Guidelines for Selecting a Conservator* and *Caring for Your Treasures: Books to Help You.*

Andrew Hurst, 2423 Amber St., Knoxville, TN 37917, 615-523-3498, 8:00 A.M.–7:00 P.M. Conservation and restoration of porcelain, leather books, oil paintings, antique frames, and encapsulation of documents. Can stabilize red rot of leather. Paintings cleaned.

Antique & Collectible Restoration Services, 1417 Third St., Webster City, IA 50595, 800-832-3828, anytime. Complete antique and collectible restoration service. Restoration materials, including hard-to-find cold-cure glass and fillers. Restoration classes; instructional video; *Porcelain Restoration Basics.* Mail order worldwide. Free brochure.

Antique Restoration by Wiebold, 413 Terrace Pl., Terrace Park, OH 45174, 513-831-2541, Mon.–Fri. 9:00 A.M.–5:30 P.M., Sat. 10:00 A.M.–2:00 P.M.; fax: 513-831-2815. Invisible restoration and conservation of art pottery, ceramics, porcelain, crystal, glass, ivory, oil paintings, frames, mirrors, gold leaf, silver, bronze, brass, copper, pewter, lead, chandeliers, and more. Free brochure.

Antique Restoring Studio Inc., DBA Trefler & Sons, 99 Cabot St., Needham, MA 02194, 617-444-2685, Mon.–Fri. 9:00 A.M.–5:00 P.M., Sat. 10:00 A.M.–2:00 P.M.; fax: 617-444-0659. Restoration of art objects, including porcelain, ceramics, glass, ivory, jade, Lucite, marble, metals, paper, paintings, photographs, Plexiglas, sculpture, frames, and furniture. Free brochure.

Appelbaum & Himmelstein, 444 Central Park W., New York, NY 10025, 212-666-4630, Mon.–Fri. 10:00 A.M.–6:00 P.M. Conservation treatment of paintings, objects, and textiles; collection surveys; consultation on collections care, including lighting, storage, and humidity control. Brochure.

Archival Conservation Center, Inc., 8225 Daly Rd., Cincinnati, OH 45231, 513-521-9858, 8:30 A.M.–3:30 P.M. Repair and restoration of works of art on paper, including engravings, family Bibles, historical documents, lithographs, maps, newspapers, parchment documents, posters, and prints. Free brochure.

Broken Art Restoration, Michelle and Bill Marhoefer, 1841 W. Chicago Ave., Chicago, IL 60622, 312-226-8200, Tues.–Fri., 9:00 A.M.–5:00 P.M. Pottery, porcelain, ceramics, wood, ivory, metal, and stone art objects restored. Missing parts replaced, invisible repairs made to almost any art object. Free brochure.

Carl "Frank" Funes, 57 Maplewood Ave., Hempstead, NY 11550, 516-481-0147, 7:00 P.M.–9:00 P.M. Restoration of arms, armor, artifacts, brass, bronze, cast iron, ivory, marble, metalwork, *objets de vertu,* paintings, terra-cotta, silver, weapons, and wood carvings. Free brochure.

Ceramic Restorations, Inc., Jareth Holub, 161 W. 61st St., Apt. 9F, New York, NY 10023, 212-247-8657, 9:00 A.M.–6:00 P.M. Specializing in the repair of pottery and porcelain. Invisible repairs, replacement of missing elements, and reglazing of antique and contemporary ceramics. Will also repair marble, jade, ivory, enamel, tortoiseshell, and cloisonné. Free estimates.

Chatree's, 711 Eighth St., SE, Washington, DC 20003, 202-546-4950. Restoration, conservation, and repair of architectural forms, bronze, dolls, frames, furniture, glass, ivory, lamps, marble, mother-of-pearl, oil paintings, oriental art objects, paper, porcelain, and other materials.

Chicago Conservation Center, Barry Bauman, Director-Painting Conservator, 730 N. Franklin, Suite 701, Chicago, IL 60610, 312-944-5401, anytime; fax: 312-944-5479. Specializing in the restoration of paintings, sculptures, and textiles. Free brochure.

D & J Glass Clinic, David Jasper, 40658 267th St., Sioux Falls, SD 57106, 605-361-7524, 9:00 A.M.–5:00 P.M.; fax: 605-361-7216. Glass and crystal repair. Restoration of dolls, figurines, porcelain, bisque, ivory, oil paintings, frames, and other objects of art. Breaks, chips, and discoloration restored. Lamp repair, metal repair, resilvering, brass plating. Free brochure.

Dean's China Restoration, 131 Elmwood Dr., Cheshire, CT 06410, 800-669-1327, Mon.–Fri. 9:00 A.M.–5:00 P.M. Repair and restoration of bisque, bronze, china, clocks, cloisonné, dolls, enamel, ivory, jade, lamps, marble, metal, paperweights, etc. Invisible repairs. Mail order. Free brochure.

Dunhill Restoration, c/o Lee Upholstery, 2309 Lee Rd., Cleveland Heights, OH 44118, 216-921-2932, Mon.–Sat. 9:00 A.M.–5:00 P.M. Specializing in the repair of Hummels, Doultons, Lladrós, lamps, china, porcelain, and pottery. Replacement of missing parts, finials, handles, fingers, toes, etc. Chipped and broken glass repaired. Jewelry repaired.

Foster Art Restoration, 711 W. 17th St. C-12, Costa Mesa, CA 92627, 800-824-6967, 8:30 A.M.–5:00 P.M., 714-645-9953; fax: 714-645-8381. Repair of broken or damaged porcelains, ceramics, figurines, crystal, paintings, and other art works and collectibles. Missing pieces duplicated. Specializing in Lladró, Boehm, Cybis, Hummel, Royal Doulton, and other manufacturers. Free brochure.

Harry A. Eberhardt & Son, Inc., 2010 Walnut St., Philadelphia, PA 19103, 215-568-4144, Mon.–Fri. 9:00 A.M.–5:00 P.M. Restoration of porcelains, glass, cloisonné, Satsuma, and other objects of art.

Hess Restorations, 200 Park Ave. S., New York, NY 10003, 212-260-2255, 10:30 A.M.–4:00 P.M.

Restoration of alabaster, antiques, boxes, brass, bric-a-brac, bronze, candelabra, carvings, china, crystal, cut glass, cutlery, decanters, dresser sets, epergnes, figurines, glassware, handbags, ivory, jade, keepsakes, lamps, miniatures, mirrors, onyx, pewter, picture frames, porcelain, pottery, quartz, reed, screens, sculpture, silver, silver plating, tableware, tortoiseshell, urns, vacuum bottles, vases, wood, and wrought iron. Brochure.

The Icons Conservation and Restoration Company, Tad Sviderskis, 730 Fifth Ave., 9th floor, New York, NY 10019, 212-333-8638, weekdays 9:00 A.M.–5:00 P.M.; fax: 212-333-8720. Restoration of ancient Byzantine, Greek, and Russian icons, old master paintings, polychrome sculpture, egg tempera or oil paintings on wood panel and canvas. Repairing, cleaning, relining, retouching, regilding. Research, attribution, and appraisals. Free brochure.

Image Maintenance Assurance, Inc., David Kummerow, PO Box 8407, Bartlett, IL 60103, 708-830-7965, 8:00 A.M.–7:00 P.M.; fax: 708-830-1458. Repair and restoration. Refabrication of parts, including glass, metal, and marble. Figurine repair. Appraiser of art, furniture, household goods. Makes house calls.

Intermuseum Laboratory, 83 N. Main St., Allen Art Bldg., Oberlin, OH 44074, 216-775-7331, 8:30 A.M.–5:00 P.M.; fax: 216-774-3431. Conservation of paintings in all media, on panel, metal, or canvas; fine art and historic documents on paper and parchment; ceramics, glass, metals, stone, and wooden objects; surveys and consultations on preservation planning.

J & H China Repairs, 8296 St. George St., Vancouver, BC, Canada V5X 3C5, 604-321-1093, 7:30 A.M.–2:00 P.M. Restoration of porcelain, ceramics, figurines, sculptures, dolls, stone, enamel, cloisonné, and picture frames.

John Edward Cunningham, 1525 E. Berkeley, Springfield, MO 65804, 417-889-7702, Mon.–Sat. 9:00 A.M.–5:00 P.M. Porcelains, ivory, jade, gold leaf, oil paintings, and frames restored. Missing parts replaced. Mail order or by appointment. Appraisals. Send SASE for more information.

Just Enterprises—Art & Antique Restoration, Gary and Susanne Gottfried, 2790 Sherwin Ave., # 10, Ventura, CA 93003, 805-644-5837, 10:00 A.M.–noon, 2:00 P.M.–5:00 P.M. Restoration of porcelain (including dolls' heads), paintings, jade, ivory, cloisonné, glass, and *objets d'art*. Missing parts manufactured when necessary. Also work on alabaster, boxes, brass, bronze, cameo glass, carvings, clock cases, crystal, cutlery, decanters, dresser sets, enamel ware, epergnes, figurines, furniture hardware, inlay repair, jewelry, keepsakes, lamps, marble, metal polishing, metal smithing, miniatures, perfume bottles, pewter, picture frames, pre-Columbian artifacts, quartz, screens, sculpture, sterling silver, silver plating tableware, tortoiseshell, urns, vases, and wood.

MAC Enterprises, Martha A. Cleary, Master Restorer, 14851 Jeffrey Rd. #75, Irvine, CA 92720, 714-262-9110, 9:00 A.M.–6:00 P.M. Restore porcelain, ceramics, pottery, frames, oil paintings, and collectibles. Registered Hummel restorer. Ship UPS or call for information. Send SASE for brochure.

Michael's Art Restoration Studio, Michael Scheglov, 8312 Eighth NW, Seattle, WA 98117, 206-789-2900, 11:00 A.M.–5:00 P.M.; fax: 206-778-6963. Restoration of fine art objects, including porcelain, china, oil paintings, brass or silver art objects.

Nelson Dale, Restoration Services, 621 Main St., #3, Waltham, MA 02154, 617-647-9470, 9:00 A.M.–5:00 P.M. Restoration of porcelain, pottery, lacquer, tortoiseshell, sculpture, and small objects of all kinds. Glass reconstruction, cracks and missing pieces. Furniture conservation: finishes, veneer, marquetry, gilding. Free brochure.

New York Conservation Center, Inc., 519 W. 26 St., New York, NY 10001, 212-714-0620, 9:00 A.M.–6:00 P.M.; fax: 212-714-0149. Consulting and hands-on restoration. Cleaning and preservation of painted, unpainted, or patinated surfaces;

inpainting, revarnishing, repatination; structural and surface repairs. Outdoor, architectural, and monumental sculpture conservation. Condition examinations, surveys, and reports. Brochure.

Old World Restorations, Inc., 347 Stanley Ave., Cincinnati, OH 45226, 800-878-1911, 513-321-1911, Mon.–Fri. 8:30 A.M.–5:30 P.M.; fax: 513-321-1914. Restoration and conservation of art and antiques, including paintings, frames, porcelain, glass, sculpture, murals, gold leaf, and much more. Microscopic examination, X-ray and paint analysis, lectures, and consultations. Free brochure.

Phoenix Restoration Inc., 5305 N. 7th St., Suite C, Phoenix, AZ 85014, 602-263-5178, 800-234-5178; 8:00 A.M.–6:00 P.M.; fax: 602-263-6009. Restoration and conservation of paintings, porcelain, ceramics, ivory, marble, and jade. Conservator and restorer of Lladró and Belleek.

Pleasant Valley Antique Restoration, Joe Howell, 1725 Reed Road, Knoxville, MD 21758, 301-432-2721, 9:30 A.M.–9:00 P.M. Restoration of glass, porcelain, marble, plaster, wood, and metal. Custom color matching and airbrush work. Previous restorations detected and verified.

Preservation Emporium, PO Box 226309, Dallas, TX 75222-6309, 214-630-1197, Mon.–Fri. 9:00 A.M.–5:00 P.M., Sat. 9:00 A.M.–4:00 P.M.; fax: 214-630-7805. Acid-free/lignin-free storage materials and conservation chemicals. Full conservation treatments and restoration work on documents, photographs, bookbinding, paper ephemera, etc.

Restoration Clinic, Inc., 2801 NW 55th Court, Bldg. 8 W, Fort Lauderdale, FL 33309, 800-235-OLDY, anytime; fax: 305-486-4988. Antique and art conservation and restoration. Paintings, sculpture, metals, wood, stone, glass, paper, books, leather, architectural, and archeological. Antique Champagne preservative. By appointment only. Send SASE for free leaflet, *What to Do Until the Restorer Comes.*

Rikki's Studio Inc., Gilbert Kerry Hall, 2809 Bird Ave., Coconut Grove, FL 33133, 305-446-

2022, 305-446-2230, 9:00 A.M.–4:30 P.M.; fax: 305-446-6388. Restoration of porcelain, paintings, crystal (including grinding and polishing), and ceramics. Lamps restored and rewired. Chandeliers repaired. Appraisals of art work, antiques, collectible automobiles, and personal items.

Senders Galerie Nouvelle, 23500-C Mercantile Rd., Beachwood, OH 44122, 216-595-0000, anytime; fax: 216-595-1111. Repair and restoration of art and antiques.

Society of Gilders, Inc., PO Box 50179, Washington, DC 20091, 202-347-1171, 9:00 A.M.–5:00 P.M.; fax: 908-290-9342. Devoted to the craft of gilding; representing conservators, restorers, artists, framers, manuscript illuminators, sign makers, suppliers, and venders of gilt objects. Can supply a list of names of people who do gilding.

Sotheby's Restorations, 1425 York Ave., New York, NY 10021, 212-860-5446. Restoration of decorative arts. Include black-and-white photo and measurements of object to be restored. Workshops for collectors, dealers, and artisans. Video *Caring for Antiques.*

SPNEA Conservation Center, 185 Lyman St., Waltham, MA 02154, 617-891-1985, Mon.–Fri. 9:00 A.M.–5:00 P.M.; fax: 617-893-7832. Furniture and upholstery conservation; architectural conservation; preservation carpentry. Traditional repairs, cross-section analysis, nonabrasive hardware cleaning, collections surveys, lectures on collections care. Free brochure.

Stoneledge, Inc., 17 Robert St., Wharton, NJ 07885, 201-989-8800, Mon.–Fri. 9:00 A.M.–5:00 P.M.; fax: 201-361-6574. Conservation and restoration of fine arts and antiques; decorative objects, paintings, metal, sculpture, wood, works on paper. Collection and facilities surveys; environmental control design; pre-purchase examination. Free brochure.

Strong Museum, Richard W. Sherin, Director of Conservation, One Manhattan Sq., Rochester, NY 14607, 716-263-2700, ext. 281, 10:00 A.M.–4:30

P.M.; fax: 716-263-2493. Conservation (preservation) consultancies and collection surveys.

T. S. Restoration, J. M. Denson, 2622 N. Dobson Rd., Chandler, AZ 85224. Restoration of antique and modern collectibles, by appointment. Boehm, Cybis, Lladró, Royal Doulton, Hummel, David Winter, and other modern collectibles. Antique porcelain, ceramics, stoneware, ivory, natural stone, cloisonné, plaster, wax, and papier-mâché. Books on restoration. Mail order. Send LSASE for information.

Venerable Classics, 645 Fourth St., Suite 208, Santa Rosa, CA 95404, 800-531-2891, 9:00 A.M.–5:00 P.M.; fax: 707-575-3626. Restoration of porcelain, marble, crystal, jade, ivory, bronze, etc. Specializing in statuary, dolls, lamps, and clocks. Shipping instructions and free brochure available on request.

Victor von Reventlow, 13 Bergen Street, Brooklyn, NY 11201, 718-858-0721, 1:00 P.M.–midnight. Conservation and restoration of wooden objects, wood structure problems of panel paintings, furniture and inlays. Collection conservation surveys. Send SASE for flyer listing services.

Williamstown Regional Art Conservation Laboratory, Inc., 225 South St., Williamstown, MA 01267, 413-458-5741, 8:30 A.M.–5:00 P.M.; fax: 413-458-2314. Nonprofit regional conservation center specializing in the treatment of paintings, objects, sculpture, furniture, frames, and works on paper. Free brochure.

Wood 'n Wildlife, 9922 Bostwick Park Rd., Montrose, CO 81401, 303-249-5863, before 9:00 P.M. Restoration of decoys, cigar store figures, carousel horses, papier-mâché dolls and toys, and other objects. Restoration of Indian artifacts: broken stone tips and bone objects repaired and replaced. Send SASE for more information.

Video

Caring for Antiques, **Sotheby's Restorations,** 1425 York Ave., New York, NY 10021, 212-860-5446. 75 minutes, $49.

Ideas for Displaying Your Collection

There are some special problems in displaying antiques properly. Rough porcelain or glass bases should not scratch furniture tops, picture hooks should be strong enough, and collectibles should be displayed to their greatest advantage.

Many display items can be purchased at local giftware, hardware, and art supply stores, but we have listed items that are not always found with ease. Other supplies can be found in the section Conservation, Restoration & Preservation Supplies.

Carv/Craft Carousel Animal Stands, Ray Jones, 417 Valley Rd., Madison, WI 53714, 608-222-1100, 8:00 A.M.–4:00 P.M. Cast-iron carousel animal display stands. Send SASE for brochure.

The Collectors Choice Display Case Co., Rt. 2 Box 73, Fremont, NE 68025, 402-721-4765. Clear, soft plastic display cases for small collectibles. Cases are 9 × 12½ × 1⅜ inches and are divided into compartments or pockets. Pocket sizes to fit buttons, figurines, jewelry, marbles, pens, thimbles, toy cars, and many other items.

Collectors Supply Company, 8415 G St., Omaha, NE 68127, 402-597-3727, Mon.–Fri. 10:00 A.M.–6:00 P.M., Sat. 10:00 A.M.–5:00 P.M.; fax: 402-592-9015. Display materials, Riker mounts, album pages, coin holders, postcard and magazine boxes, special products and books for collectors of Boy Scout memorabilia. Catalog $1, refundable with order.

Display Case Co., Box 880, Exmore, VA 23350, 804-442-7777, 8:30 A.M.–4:30 P.M.; fax: 804-442-6513. Protective Lucite vitrines. Custom sizes available. Doll stands and cases. Call for free price quote. Send name and address for free catalog.

Items of Value, Inc., 818 Elaine Ct., Alexandria,

VA 22308, 703-360-3114. Velcro strips and Velcro panels for hanging textiles, including carpets, quilts, and tapestries.

J-Mounts/Militaire Promotions, 6427 W. Irving Park Rd., Suite 160, Chicago, IL 60634, 312-777-0499, 9:00 A.M.–5:00 P.M.; fax: 312-777-4017. Glass-top display frames and cases, both cardboard and wood. Various sizes for jewelry, medals, pocket knives, watches, and other small collectibles. Send SASE for free brochure.

Lin Terry, 59 E. Madison Ave., Dumont, NJ 07628, 201-385-4706; fax: 201-385-0306. Coin and sports collectibles supplies, including acrylic showcases, binders, bags, baseball bat tubes, pennant covers, custom cases, coin mounts, currency holders, and books.

Morris Caroussell Works, Terri-Lee Morris, PO Box 786, Philadelphia, PA 19105, 215-383-1655. Wooden bases for carousel animals. Catalog $2.

Museum Shop, Ltd., Richard Kornemann, 20 N. Market St., Frederick, MD 21701, 301-695-0424, Mon.–Thurs. 10:30 A.M.–6:00 P.M., Fri.–Sat. 10:30 A.M.–9:00 P.M., Sun. noon–5:00 P.M.; fax: 301-698-5242. Special preservation cases designed and fabricated for the storage and display of documents, memorabilia, and collections.

Perfect Passementeries, 314 Keyes Ave., Watertown, NY 13601, 315-788-1854. Picture hangers. Braided picture cord with rosette and tassel. Brochure $1.

Roberts Colonial House, 570 W. 167th St., PO Box 308, South Holland, IL 60473, 708-331-6233, 8:00 A.M.–4:30 P.M.; fax: 708-331-0538. Easels, plate hangers, dinnerware stands, risers, jewelry displays, glass domes. Christmas ornament holders and display stands. Free catalog and brochure.

Shiloh Postcards, Main Street, PO Box 728, Clayton, GA 30525, 706-782-4100, Mon., Tues., Thurs., Fri. 9:00 A.M.–5:00 P.M. Supplies for displaying paper collectibles, specializing in postcard supplies. Acrylic frames and holders; albums. Mail order. Catalog $1.

Matching Services

*L*isted here are matching services for china, silver, and crystal patterns. When writing, include the name of your pattern and a clear photograph, photocopy, or sketch showing the design and any markings. It is important to include the manufacturer's name, if it appears. Do not send a piece of the china, silver, or crystal: You can obtain a usable image by placing a spoon or plate on a photocopy machine.

List the pieces you want, and be sure to include a stamped, self-addressed envelope for a reply. If you want to know that the service received your request, include a stamped, self-addressed post card, too. Remember that your order may be kept on file for months until a matching piece is found. If you ask more than one service to search for a piece, let the others know if another service finds it.

Manufacturers that are still in business, such as Waterford or Spode, sometimes take special orders for discontinued patterns. These orders are filled about once a year.

The dealers listed below have a general replacement line unless a specialty is indicated. The list is not an endorsement of any kind. It includes those services that sent us the requested information. There are probably many others we have not yet discovered. If you can suggest any additions, please let us know.

China Matching Services

A & A Dinnerware Locators, PO Box 50222, Austin, TX 78763, 512-264-1054 (Castleton, Denby, Franciscan, Lenox, Mikasa, Noritake, Royal Doulton, Spode, Syracuse, Wedgwood, and other major manufacturers).

A Wedgewood China Cupboard, 740 N. Honey Creek Pkwy., Milwaukee, WI 53213, 414-259-1025 (Wedgwood, Adams, Coalport, Midwinter).

Abby's Attic, PO Box 1041, Picayune, MS 39466, 601-798-5309, 601-255-2799.

Aberdeen Crockery Co., 511 S. Main St., Aberdeen, SD 57401 (Noritake).

Ackerman Antiques, Box 2310, Athens, OH 45701, 614-593-7681 (Warwick).

B.R. Barn, Mary & Ray Farley, 1379 W. Commerce, Lewisburg, TN 37091, 615-359-2906 (Blue Ridge matching).

Betty's Crystal & China, PO Box 433, Lawrence, KS 66044, 913-842-8054.

Bygone China Match, 1225 W. 34th N., Wichita, KS 67204, 316-838-6010 (Castleton, Dansk, Denby, Fitz & Floyd, Flintridge, Franciscan, Gorham, Haviland, Lenox, Metlox, Mikasa, Noritake, Royal Doulton, Sango, Syracuse, Wedgwood).

Cee Cee China, 3904 Parsons Rd., Chevy Chase, MD 20815, 301-652-6226 (Lenox, Oxford, Syracuse).

China & Crystal Matchers Inc., 2379 John Glenn Dr., Suite 108-A, Chamblee, GA 30341, 404-455-1162; fax: 404-452-8616.

China & Crystal Matching, 141 Sedgwick Rd., Dept. RTK, Syracuse, NY 13203, 315-472-6834.

China & Crystal Replacements, PO Box 187, 5613 Manitou Rd., Excelsior, MN 55331, 612-474-2144 (Adams, Aynsley, Castleton, Coalport, Cuthbertson, Denby, Fostoria, Franciscan, Gorham, Johnson Bros., Lenox, Oxford, Minton, Mikasa, Noritake, Oxford, Pickard, Royal Crown Derby, Royal Worcester).

China and Crystal Match, 72 Longacre Rd., Rochester, NY 14621, 716-338-3781 (Fitz & Floyd, Royal Doulton, Royal Worcester, Spode, Wedgwood).

China and Crystal Replacements, 2263 Williams Creek Rd., High Ridge, MO 63049, 800-562-2655; fax: 314-376-6319 (discontinued patterns).

China by Pattern, PO Box 129, Farmington, CT 06034, 203-678-7079. (All china patterns and makers. Adams, Aynsley, Blue Ridge, Castleton, Coalport, Crown Ducal, Doulton, Franciscan, Lenox, Hutschenreuther, Rosenthal, Syracuse, etc. Active and discontinued patterns.)

China Cabinet, PO Box 426, Clearwater, SC 29822, 803-593-9655.

China Chasers, Inc., 3280 Peachtree Corners Circle, Norcross, GA 30092, 404-441-9146 (Castleton, Franciscan, Franconia, Gorham, Heinrich, Hutschenreuther, Johnson Bros., Lenox, Minton, Noritake, Oxford, Pickard, Royal Copenhagen, Royal Doulton, Royal Worcester, Spode, Syracuse).

China Connection, Box 972, 329 Main St., Pineville, NC 28134, 800-421-9719, 704-889-8198 (discontinued Noritake, Haviland, Lenox, Spode;. appraisals).

China Crystal Exchange, PO Box 95, Kennesaw, GA 30144, 800-326-MATCH, 404-516-5956.

China House, 801 W. Eldorado, Decatur, IL 62522, 217-428-7212 or 217-864-2938 (French and American Haviland).

China Matching Service, 56 Meadowbrook, Ballwin, MO 63011, 314-227-3444 (German, Bavarian, Austrian, and Czechoslovakian china; Lenox and other American dinnerware).

China Matching, Inc., 420 Belle Grove Rd., Middletown, VA 22645, 703-869-1261 (Castleton, Haviland, Lenox, Wedgwood).

China Teacup, 112 N. MacArthur Blvd., Dept. K, Irving, TX 75061, 214-254-1713.

China Trade Ltd., 2133 Birchwood Ave., Wilmette, IL 60091, 708-256-7414 (discontinued patterns).

China Traders, PO Box 302, Simi Valley, CA 93062, 805-527-5440.

CK's China Trace, Box A-5297, Ocala, FL 34478, 904-622-4077. (Buy, sell, and match Mikasa and Royal Jackson. SASE requested. For matching Royal Jackson, send photocopy of pattern.)

C.L. Egelston, PO Box 12331, Homewood, IL 60430 (Noritake).

Classic Tableware, PO Box 4265, Dept. KG, Stockton, CA 95204, 209-956-4645. (Large stock on hand. Most manufacturers of china and earthenware. Shop located at 1868 Country Club Blvd.)

Clintsman International, 20855 Watertown Rd., Waukesha, WI 53186, 414-798-0440.

Conner Architectural Antiques, 701 P St., Lincoln Haymarket, Lincoln, NE 60508 (American Haviland and late French Haviland patterns).

Country Oaks Antiques, 3325 Bailey Creek Cove N., Collierville, TN 38017 (flow blue).

Crystal Corner, PO Box 756, 317 Dyar Blvd., Boaz, AL 35957, 205-593-6169, 205-593-2102.

D & J Locations, PO Box 1587, Tarboro, NC 27886, 919-823-1408.

David N. Reichard—Haviland Matching Service, 150 S. Glenoaks Blvd., Suite 9245, Burbank, CA 91510, 818-848-5087, evenings preferred (Haviland).

Dining Elegance, Ltd., PO Box 4203, St. Louis, MO 63163 (Haviland, Lenox, Oxford, Raynaud-Ceralene, English and Bavarian manufacturers).

Ettleman's Discontinued China & Crystal, PO Box 6491 KOV, Corpus Christi, TX 78466, 512-888-8391 (Castleton, Flintridge, Franciscan, Haviland, Lenox, Oxford, Syracuse).

Ferne & Davi Stephenson, 730 N. Fifth St., Hamburg, PA 19526, 215-562-4967 (Noritake Azalea).

Fiesta Plus, 380 Hawkins Crawford Rd., Cookeville, TN 38501, 615-372-8333 (Fiesta, Harlequin, Riviera, and other Homer Laughlin. patterns; Franciscan, LuRay, Metlox, Russel Wright, Vistosa).

5th Generation Antiques, 124 W. 8th Ave., Chico, CA 95926, 916-895-0813 (all manufacturers of china).

Finders Keepers, China Lady, 3118 Magazine St., New Orleans, LA 70115, 504-895-2702, 504-455-1530 (Doulton, Lenox, Oxford, Minton, Noritake, Pickard, Spode, Wedgwood; appraisals).

Fostoria Registry and China Replacements, 1060 Crestline Dr., Crete, NE 68333, 402-826-2622.

Franciscan Dinnerware Matching Service, 323 E. Matilija, Suite 112, Ojai, CA 93023 (Franciscan and earthenware).

Galerie de Porcelaine, PO Box 293, Elmhurst, IL 60126, 708-858-9494 (old French and American Haviland; by appointment only).

Garbo, PO Box 41197, Los Angeles, CA 90041 (Belora [USA]. Flintridge, Franciscan/Interpace/Independence, Metlox Poppytrail, Mikasa, Noritake, Vernonware)

Glass Lady @ Kaleidoscope, 7501 Iron Bridge Rd., Richmond, VA 23237, 804-743-9846; fax: 804-743-5540.

Grace Graves—Haviland Matching Service, Ltd., 3959 N. Harcourt Pl., Milwaukee, WI 53211, 414-964-9180; fax: 414-964-4453 (French and American Haviland).

Grandview Fine Tableware, PO Box 12461, Columbus, OH 43212, 614-486-3509 (American and English china).

Harners Gift Shop Inc., 218 N. Main St., Pontiac, IL 61764, 815-844-7333 (Fiesta, Fostoria, Mikasa, Noritake, Pfalzgraff, Pickard).

Heirloom Completions Division, Don's Antiques & Gifts, 1620 Venice St., Granite City, IL 62040, 618-931-4333.

Heirloom Crystal & China, PO Box 149, Mt. Vernon, MO 65712, 417-466-3818.

House of Serendipity, 645 Main St., Montevallo, AL 35115, 205-665-7996 (American dinnerware and china).

International Association of Dinnerware Matchers, 112 N. MacArthur Blvd., Irving, TX 75061 (list of dinnerware matchers).

Irene DeLengyel, 215 Federal Rd., Englishtown, NJ 07726, 908-446-0499 (Stangl).

Jacquelyn B. Hall, 10629 Baxter Ave., Suite K, Los Altos, CA 94024, 408-739-4876 (Lenox only).

Jacquelynn's China Matching Service, 219 N. Milwaukee St., Milwaukee, WI 53202, 414-272-8880 (Castleton, Coalport, Flintridge, Franciscan, Gorham, Johnson Bros., Lenox, Minton, Pickard, Royal Copenhagen, Royal Crown Derby, Royal Doulton, Royal Worcester, Spode, Wedgwood).

J.B. and ME, 3576 Clairmont Rd., Atlanta, GA 30319, 404-634-1194 (Johnson Brothers only).

Jo's Antiques & Collectibles, 2318 61st St., Lubbock, TX 79412, 806-792-2557 (Lenox).

Joanne Cone Matching Service, 34 Silverwood, Irvine, CA 92714, 714-551-3173 (Mikasa, Castleton, Denby, Franciscan, Johnson, Lenox, Metlox, Noritake, Royal Doulton, Spode, Syracuse, Wedgwood).

Judy Giangiuli, R.D. 6, Box 292, New Castle, PA 16101, 412-652-5806, 800-669-5806 (Castle-ton).

Judy's House of Hope, 1400 Third Ave., West Point, GA 31833-1297, 404-643-7181 (specializing in Wedgwood and Royal Doulton, but has stock in all manufacturers; send SASE please).

Larry Hamm, 2265 Hamilton-Middletown Rd., Hamilton, OH 45011, 513-892-0803 (French and American Haviland).

Laura's China & Crystal, 2625 W. Britton Rd., Oklahoma City, OK 73120, 405-755-0582 (Castleton, Franciscan, Haviland, Lenox, Oxford, Royal Doulton, Spode, Syracuse and Wedgwood).

Lillian Johnson Antiques, PO Box 1207, 405 Third St., San Juan Bautista, CA 95045, 408-623-4381 (Haviland of many periods).

Linda Skuba, Box 7400, Edmonton, AB, Canada T5E 6C8 (British patterns).

Linda's Collectibles, PO Box 864, Fairburn, GA 30213, 800-346-3296 (Johnson Brothers, Mason's, and Franciscan).

Locator's Inc., 908 Rock St., Little Rock, AR 72202, 800-367-9690, 501-371-0858; fax: 501-372-4006.

Louise Donoghue McKay, PO Box 8561, Mobile, AL 36689, 205-344-8124 (Haviland).

Louise's Old Things, 163 W. Main St., Kutztown, PA 19530, 610-683-8370, 610-683-6388 (flow blue and willow, including blue willow).

Marfine Antiques, PO Box 3618, Boone, NC 28607, 704-262-3441 (Johnson Brothers dinnerware replacement service).

Maricia Cornelius, 5615 Sprucewood, Cincinnati, OH 45239. (Buy, sell, and match discontinued Noritake; send SASE for reply.)

Marjann's Tabletops, PO Box 06255, Columbus, OH 43206, 614-444-1694, 614-878-4792 (discontinued china: Lenox, Royal Doulton, Spode, Syracuse, Wedgwood).

Marv's Memories, 1914 W. Carriage Dr., Santa Ana, CA 92704, 714-751-2463 (Franciscan and Mikasa).

Matchers, 181 Belle Meade, Memphis, TN 38117, 901-683-1337, anytime; fax: 901-529-8520 (Noritake specialists, other name-brand china).

Matchmakers, 1718 Airport Ct., Placerville, CA 95667, 916-626-5672 (Haviland, Noritake).

Miki's Crystal & China, Inc., 100 Bridge Ave., Delano, MN 55328, 612-972-6885, 800-628-9394 (Noritake).

Nora Travis, PO Box 6008, 13337 E. South St., Suite 161, Cerritos, CA 90701, 714-521-9283 (French and American Haviland).

Old China Patterns Limited, 1560 Brimley Rd., Scarborough, ON, Canada M1P 3G9, 416-299-8880; fax: 416-299-4721 (English and American discontinued china patterns, no charge for services).

Old China Patterns Limited, PO Box 290-K, Fineview, NY 13640-0290, 800-724-5576 or 315-482-3829; fax: 800-724-5530, 315-482-5827. (Buy and sell patterns of various manufacturers; named and numbered Haviland patterns, Aynsley, Castleton, Coalport, Franciscan, Gorham, Lenox, Minton, Royal Worcester, Spode, Syracuse, etc. Appraisals.)

Old Toll Gate Antiques, 600 North Ave., Milan, IL 61264, 309-787-2392. (For French

Haviland, send Schleiger number; for American and Johann Haviland, send photocopy of front and back of plate.)

Out of the Blue Antiques, PO Box 397, 2801 Churchville Rd., Churchville, MD 21028, 410-734-7436 (flow blue).

Past & Presents, Alice Korman, 65-07 Fitchett St., Rego Park, NY 11374, 718-897-5515 (Adams, Aynsley, Coalport, Denby, Franciscan, Gorham, Johnson Brothers, Lenox, Mikasa, Minton, Noritake, Oxford, Royal Doulton, Royal Worcester, Spode, Wedgwood, and others).

Pattern Finders, PO Box 206, Port Jefferson Station, NY 11776, 516-928-5158; fax: 516-928-5170 (Denby, Lenox, Noritake, Oxford, Rosenthal, Royal Doulton, Royal Worcester, Spode, Wedgwood, and others).

Patterns Unlimited International, PO Box 15238, Seattle, WA 98115, 206-523-9710 (American, English, French manufacturers).

Paul Church, 1415 Michigan Ave., St. Cloud, FL 34769, 800-222-7357, 407-957-1719 (Lenox, Oxford, Franciscan, Castleton).

Peggy's Matching Service, PO Box 476, Ocala, FL 34478, 904-629-3954 (Noritake).

Popkorn, PO Box 1057, 4 Mine St., Flemington, NJ 08822, 908-782-9631 (Fiesta, Hall, Russel Wright, Stangl, blue willow).

Presence of the Past, 488 Main St., Old Saybrook, CT 06475, 203-388-9021 (Haviland and Theodore Haviland, Noritake).

Proper Setting Discontinued Patterns, PO Box 3113, Covina, CA 91722-9113.

Ralph Clifford, PO Box 5403, Berkeley, CA 94705, 510-843-9336 (Franciscan, Russel Wright, Luray, California ceramics).

Replacements, Ltd., PO Box 26029, 1089 Knox Rd., Greensboro, NC 27420-6029, 800-562-4462.

Roseville Pottery Mart, PO Box 6382, Ventura, CA 93006, 805-659-4733 (Roseville pottery; send SASE for list).

Roundhill's Patterns Unlimited International, PO Box 15238 KO, Seattle, WA 98115-0238, 206-523-9710. (Buy and sell discontinued patterns of English, French, and American china. Appraise all tabletop items, $40 per pattern.)

Royal Court Ltd., Dick & Rosemarie Lewis, 6166 Tower Top, Columbia, MD 21045, 410-997-2952 (Syracuse).

Sara's China Closet, 7749 E. Luke Ln., Scottscale, AZ 85250, 602-946-9145 (discontinued American, Bavarian, and English patterns).

Scott's Haviland Matching Service, 1911 Leland Ave., Des Moines, IA 50315, 515-285-2739, 800-952-7857; fax: 515-287-4811 (French, American, and Johann Haviland).

Shirley Stamen Matching Service, 9601 Arby Dr., Beverly Hills, CA 90210, 310-278-4040; fax: 310-552-3828 (buy and sell china).

Side Door, 103 Main St., Box 573, Dennisport, MA 02639, 508-394-7715 (flow blue, mulberryware).

Silver & China Exchange, PO Box 4601, Dept. K, Stamford, CT 06907, 203-322-5963 (discontinued Lenox and Oxford patterns).

Silver Lane Antiques, PO Box 322, San Leandro, CA 94577, 415-483-0632 (Castleton, Flintridge, Franciscan, Lenox, Minton, Royal Doulton, Royal Worcester, Spode, Syracuse, Wedgwood).

Table Toppers, PO Box 148471, Chicago, IL 60614-8471 (search service for china and pottery; will answer questions regarding tabletop items).

Tabletop Matching Service & Collectors Items, Mrs. Betty H. Allen, PO Box 205, Cookeville, TN 38501, 615-526-4303 (Coalport, Oxford, Syracuse, Stangl dinnerware, German china, and named Haviland patterns).

Tea Leaf China, 209 W. Main, Norman, OK 73069, 405-360-1015, 405-321-0889 (Tea Leaf).

Unique Antiques, PO Box 15815, San Diego, CA 92175-5815, 619-281-8650; fax: 619-281-8407 (French and American Haviland, Lenox).

Van Ness China Company, Waynesboro Outlet Village, 601 Shenandoah Village Dr., 7D,

Waynesboro, VA 22980, 703-942-2827 (discontinued china: Aynsley, Coalport, Minton, Royal Doulton, Royal Worcester, Spode, Wedgwood).

Varner's Matching Service, 1439 NE 13th Ave., Rochester, MN 55906, 507-289-2938 (French and American Haviland).

Vintage Patterns Unlimited, 3571 Crestnoll Dr., Dept. K, Cincinnati, OH 45211 (Rosenthal, mail order only).

Vintage Wedgwood Patterns, Rosemary Evans, 9303 McKinney Rd., Loveland, OH 45140, 513-489-6247 (Adams, Coalport, Wedgwood).

Walker's Haviland China, PO Box 357, Athens, OH 45701, 614-593-5631 (French and American Haviland).

Walter Drake Silver & China Exchange, Drake Building, Colorado Springs, CO 80940, 800-525-9291, 7:30 A.M.–5:00 P.M. (Aynsley, Castleton, Franciscan, Haviland, Lenox, Minton, Noritake, Royal Doulton, Spode, Syracuse, Wedgwood).

Warwick China Matching Service, PO Box 2310, Athens, OH 45701, 614-593-7681 (War-wick).

Westerling, 5311 St. Charles Rd., Berkeley, IL 60163, 312-547-8488 (specializing in Easterland and Westmoreland).

White's Collectibles & Fine China, PO Box 680, 616 E. First, Newberg, OR 97132, 800-618-2782, 503-538-7421 (Castleton, Denby, Franciscan, Lenox, Minton, Oxford, Royal Doulton, Royal Worcester, Spode, Syracuse, Wedgwood).

Willow Wood Antiques, Box 380, Valentine, NE 69201, 402-376-2622 (French Haviland).

Crystal Matching Services

A Wedgewood China Cupboard, 740 N. Honey Creek Pkwy., Milwaukee, WI 53213, 414-259-1025 (Wedgwood crystal and Waterford crystal ornaments only).

Abby's Attic, PO Box 1041, Picayune, MS 39466, 601-798-5309, 601-255-2799.

Ackerman Antiques, Box 2310, Athens, OH 45701, 614-593-7681 (Candlewick).

Betty's Crystal & China, PO Box 433, Lawrence, KS 66044, 913-842-8054.

Bygone China Match, 1225 W. 34th N., Wichita, KS 67204, 316-838-6010 (Cambridge, Denby, Fostoria, Gorham, Imperial, Lenox, Mikasa, Noritake, Tiffin).

Candlewick (by Imperial) Matching Service, PO Box 2310, Athens, OH 45701, 614-593-7681 (Candlewick).

China & Crystal Matchers Inc., 2379 John Glenn Dr., Suite 108-A, Chamblee, GA 30341, 404-455-1162; fax: 404-452-8616.

China & Crystal Matching, 141 Sedgwick Rd., Dept. RTK, Syracuse, NY 13203, 315-472-6834.

China & Crystal Replacements, PO Box 187, 5613 Manitou Rd., Excelsior, MN 55331, 612-474-2144 (Gorham, Lenox, Mikasa, Noritake, Royal Doulton, Schott, Tiffin, Wedgwood).

China and Crystal Match, 72 Longacre Rd., Rochester, NY 14621, 716-338-3781 (Fostoria, Gorham, Lenox, Noritake, Mikasa).

China and Crystal Replacements, 2263 Williams Creek Rd., High Ridge, MO 63049, 800-562-2655; fax: 314-376-6319 (discontinued crystal).

China by Pattern, PO Box 129, Farmington, CT 06034, 203-678-7079 (active and discontinued crystal of all makes, including Cambridge, Fostoria, Hawkes, Heisey, Candlewick, Steuben, Tiffin, Waterford, etc.).

China Cabinet, PO Box 426, Clearwater, SC 29822, 803-593-9655.

China Crystal Exchange, PO Box 95, Kennesaw, GA 30144, 800-326-MATCH, 404-516-5956.

China Matching, Inc., 420 Belle Grove Rd., Middletown, VA 22645, 703-869-1261 (Fostoria and Lenox).

China Teacup, 112 N. MacArthur Blvd., Dept. K, Irving, TX 75061, 214-254-1713.

Classic Tableware, PO Box 4265, Dept. KG, Stockton, CA 95204, 209-956-4645. (Large stock on hand. Shop located at 1868 Country Club Blvd.)

Clintsman International, 20855 Watertown Rd., Waukesha, WI 53186, 414-798-0440.

Conner's Architectural Antiques, 701 P Street, Lincoln, NE 68508, 402-435-3338 (Fostoria stemware and serving pieces).

Crystal Connection, Nancy A. Skaja, 8661 West Midland Dr., Greendale, WI 53129, 414-425-1321 (discontinued stemware patterns of Lenox and Fostoria crystal).

Crystal Corner, PO Box 756, 317 Dyar Blvd., Boaz, AL 35957, 205-593-6169, 205-593-2102.

D & J Locations, PO Box 1587, Tarboro, NC 27886, 919-823-1408.

Dining Elegance, Ltd., PO Box 4203, St. Louis, MO 63163, 314-865-1408 (Franciscan, Gorham, Josair, Lenox, Lotus, Royal Brierly, Royal Leerdam, St. Louis, Seneca, Stuart, Tiffin, Val St. Lambert).

EAPG Inc., 1220 Monroe NE, Albuquerque, NM 87110. (Computer search for early American pressed glass, $3 for a specific piece or $15 for pattern-wide search. Inventories of other dealers are listed in their computer.)

Ettleman's Discontinued China & Crystal, PO Box 6491 KOV, Corpus Christi, TX 78466, 512-888-8391 (Cambridge, Duncan, Fostoria, Heisey, Lenox, Tiffin).

5th Generation Antiques, 124 W. 8th Ave., Chico, CA 95926, 916-895-0813 (all manufacturers of crystal).

Fostoria Registry and China Replacements, 1060 Crestline Dr., Crete, NE 68333, 402-826-2622 (Fostoria).

Fran Jay, 10 Church St., Lambertville, NJ 08530, 609-397-1571 (Cambridge, Fenton, Fostoria, Heisey, Morgantown, Tiffin, and Depression glass).

Glass Lady @ Kaleidoscope, 7501 Iron Bridge Rd., Richmond, VA 23237, 804-743-9846; fax: 804-743-5540.

Glass Urn, 456 W. Main St., Mesa, AZ 85201, 602-833-2702, 602-838-5936 (Cambridge, Fostoria, Heisey, Tiffin, and other American-made glass).

Hawkes Hunter, 5384 Pennock Point Rd., Jupiter, FL 33458, 407-746-6382 (Hawkes).

Hazel Rawls, 2117 Monterrey, Orange, TX 77630 (pattern glass).

Heirloom Completions Division, Don's Antiques & Gifts, 1620 Venice St., Granite City, IL 62040, 618-931-4333.

Heirloom Crystal & China, PO Box 149, Mt. Vernon, MO 65712, 417-466-3818.

House of Serendipity, 645 Main St., Montevallo, AL 35115, 205-665-7996 (American crystal).

Jacquelyn B. Hall, 10629 Baxter Ave., Suite K, Los Altos, CA 94024, 408-739-4876 (Lenox crystal only).

Jerry Gallagher, Red Horse Inn, 420 1st Ave. NW, Plainview, MN 55964, 507-534-3511 (Cambridge, Duncan, Fostoria, Heisey, Old Morgantown, Tiffin, and other American glass).

Joanne Cone Matching Service, 34 Silverwood, Irvine, CA 92714, 714-551-3173 (Mikasa, Cambridge, Fostoria, Gorham, Heisey, Imperial, Tiffin, Franciscan, Towle, Lenox).

Jo's Antiques & Collectibles, 2318 61st St., Lubbock, TX 79412, 806-792-2557 (Lenox).

Judy Giangiuli, RD No. 6, Box 292, New Castle, PA 16101, 412-652-5806, 800-669-5806 (Fostoria).

Judy's House of Hope, 1400 Third Ave., West Point, GA 31833-1297, 404-643-7181 (Fostoria and all other manufacturers; send SASE for reply).

Laura's China & Crystal, 2625 W. Britton Rd., Oklahoma City, OK 73120, 405-755-0582 (Cambridge, Duncan, Fostoria, Heisey, Imperial, Lenox, Rock Sharpe, and Tiffin).

Locator's Inc., 908 Rock St., Little Rock, AR 72202, 800-367-9690, 501-371-0858; fax: 501-372-4006.

Margaret Lane Antiques, 2 E. Main St., New Concord, OH 43762, 614-826-7414 (Cambridge, Fenton, Fostoria, Heisey).

Matchers, 181 Belle Meade, Memphis, TN 38117, 901-683-1337, anytime; fax: 901-529-8520 (Fostoria, Lenox, Noritake, and other stemware).

Miki's Crystal & China, Inc., 100 Bridge Ave., Delano, MN 55328, 612-972-6885, 800-628-9394 (Fostoria).

Milbra's Crystal Matching, PO Box 363, Rio Vista, TX 76093, 817-645-6066 (Cambridge, Fostoria, Heisey, Imperial, Lenox, Tiffin).

Nadine Pankow, 207 S. Oakwood, Willow Springs, IL 60480, 708-839-5231 (Cambridge, Depression glass, Duncan Miller, Fostoria, Heisey).

Old China Patterns Limited, 1560 Brimley Rd., Scarborough, ON, Canada M1P 3G9, 416-299-8880; fax: 416-299-4721.

Past & Presents, Alice Korman, 65-07 Fitchett St., Rego Park, NY 11374, 718-897-5515.

Pattern Finders, PO Box 206, Port Jefferson Station, NY 11776, 516-928-5158; fax: 516-928-5170 (stemware).

Paul Church, 1415 Michigan Ave., St. Cloud, FL 34769, 800-222-7357, 407-957-1719 (Lenox and Fostoria).

Popkorn, PO Box 1057, 4 Mine St., Flemington, NJ 08822, 908-782-9631 (Cambridge, Fostoria, Imperial, Depression glass, and kitchen glassware).

Replacements, Ltd., PO Box 26029, 1089 Knox Rd., Greensboro, NC 27420-6029, 800-562-4462.

Silver Lane Antiques, PO Box 322, San Leandro, CA 94577, 415-483-0632.

Table Toppers, PO Box 148471, Chicago, IL 60614-8471 (search service for crystal; will answer questions regarding tabletop items).

Tabletop Matching Service & Collectors Items, Mrs. Betty H. Allen, PO Box 205, Cookeville, TN 38501, 615-526-4303 (Duncan, Fostoria, Imperial, Tiffin).

Unique Antiques, PO Box 15815, San Diego, CA 92175-5815, 619-281-8650; fax: 619-282-8407 (Lenox).

Varner's Matching Service, 1439 NE 13th Ave., Rochester, MN 55906, 507-289-2938 (Heisey).

Vintage Patterns Unlimited, 3571 Crestnoll Dr., Dept. K, Cincinnati, OH 45211 (Rosenthal, mail order only).

Westerling, 5311 St. Charles Rd., Berkeley, IL 60163, 312-547-8488 (specializing in Easterling).

William Ashley Ltd., 50 Bloor St. W., Toronto, ON, Canada M4W 3L8, 800-268-1122, 416-964-2900 (discontinued crystal patterns).

Silver Matching Services

Aaron's Antiques, 576 Fifth Ave., New York, NY 10036, 800-447-5868, 212-764-7929; fax: 212-764-7931 (sterling flatware, including Tiffany and Georg Jensen).

Alice Korman, Past & Presents, 65-07 Fitchett St., Rego Park, NY 11374, 718-897-5515.

Anita Aames, A Nationwide Network, 206-984-0701, weekday afternoons, always ask for Lisa (discontinued sterling, stainless, and silverplate; pewter, Dirilyte, insurance appraisals).

Apple Tree Antiques, 301 N. Harrison St., Bldg. B, #375, Princeton, NJ 08540 (sterling and silverplated flatware).

Arlene's Silverplate Matching Service, N 109 W 15426 Lyle Ln., Germantown, WI 53022, 414-255-3889 (silverplate only; send SASE with request).

As You Like It Silver Shop, 3025 Magazine St., New Orleans, LA 70115, 800-828-2311, 504-897-6915 (sterling flatware: active, inactive, obsolete; hollowware).

Beverly Bremer Silver Shop, 3164 Peachtree Rd. NE, Atlanta, GA 30305, 404-261-4009 (sterling flatware, hollowware).

C. H. McCarthy, PO Box 11278, Oakland, CA 94611-0278, 510-530-3216 (sterling flatware).

Carman's Collectables, PO Box 238, Levittown, PA 19059, 215-946-9315 (silver plate).

Cecil F. Skillin, 111 Caribbean Rd., Naples, FL 33963-3404, 813-597-3676; fax: 813-597-3676 (sterling, silver plate, stainless, sterling II, pewter, Dirilyte, Dirigold).

Cherishables—Sally A. Peelen, 1214 Matanzas Way, Santa Rosa, CA 95405, 707-579-2475 evenings and weekends (silverplate).

China Chasers, Inc., 3280 Peachtree Corners Circle, Norcross, GA 30092, 404-441-9146 (stainless flatware. Oneida, Gorham, Reed & Barton).

China Crystal Exchange, PO Box 95, Kennesaw, GA 30144, 800-326-MATCH, 404-516-5956 (discontinued silver flatware).

China Teacup, 112 N. MacArthur Blvd., Dept. K, Irving, TX 75061, 214-254-1713 (stainless).

Classic Tableware, PO Box 4265, Dept. KG, Stockton, CA 95204, 209-956-4645 (large stock on hand; shop located at 1868 Country Club Blvd.).

Clintsman International, 20855 Watertown Rd., Waukesha, WI 53186, 414-798-0440 (silverplate, stainless, sterling).

Coinways, 136 Cedarhurst Ave., Cedarhurst, NY 11516, 800-645-2102, 516-374-1970 (sterling).

Colonial Silver Shoppe, 20-D Gaylan Ct., Montgomery, AL 36109, 800-675-4837, 205-272-7282 (sterling: active, inactive, obsolete).

Cookson, 1111 Union St., Alameda, CA 94501, 510-523-4106; message only 510-523-1993 (silverplate).

Coronado Coins, PO Box 181440, 942 Orange Ave., Coronado, CA 92178-1440, 619-437-1435 (sterling).

Crystal Corner, PO Box 756, 317 Dyar Blvd., Boaz, AL 35957, 205-593-6169, 205-593-2102 (stainless).

Gebelein Silversmiths Inc., PO Box 157, East Arlington, VT 05252, 802-375-6307 (buy, sell, and match nineteenth- and twentieth-century sterling, coin silver).

Graham Silver, PO Box 6021, Omaha, NE 68106, 800-228-2294 (sterling: active, inactive, and obsolete American patterns).

Grandview Fine Tableware, PO Box 12461, Columbus, OH 43212, 614-486-3509 (American and English silver-plated flatware).

Heirloom Completions Division, Don's Antiques & Gifts, 1620 Venice St., Granite City, IL 62040, 618-931-4333 (American sterling and silverplate, stainless, Dirilyte).

Helen Lawler's Silverplate Matching Service, 5400 E. County Rd. #2, Blytheville, AR 72315, 314-720-8502 (silver-plated flatware by mail only; free lists of individual patterns sent on request with SASE).

Heritage Gallery of Antiques, PO Box 3474, Champaign, IL 61826-3474.

Imagination Unlimited, 4302 Alton Rd., Suite 820, Miami Beach, FL 33140, 305-534-5870, 305-538-0914 (Georg Jensen and other Danish silversmiths).

Jane Rosenow, Rt. 1, Box 177-AA, Galva, IL 61434, 309-932-3953 (sterling, silver plate).

Joanne Cone Matching Service, 34 Silverwood, Irvine, CA 92714, 714-551-3173 (stainless steel, sterling silver, silver plate; Oneida and other manufacturers).

John F. Kingston, Silver Merchant, PO Box 6037, Syracuse, NY 13217, 315-446-0630 (silver plate and sterling; appraisals, fee dependent on distance traveled and number of pieces involved).

Kinzie's, PO Box 522, Turlock, CA 95380, 209-634-4880 (sterling and silver plate).

Lampost Silver Co., 13012 E. 21st St., Tulsa, OK 74134, 918-835-3686 (sterling, silver plate, and stainless, old and new).

Lee and Helen Dunkel Collectibles, 222 Belle Ave., Boalsburg, PA 16827, 814-466-6494 (sterling and silver-plated flatware).

Littman's, 151 Granby St., Norfolk, VA 23510, 800-FOUND-IT, 804-622-6989 (sterling).

Locator's Inc., 908 Rock St., Little Rock, AR 72202, 800-367-9690, 501-371-0858; fax: 501-372-4006 (sterling: active, inactive, and obsolete patterns).

Margaret & Joseph Martines, Martines' Antiques, 516 E. Washington, Chagrin Falls,

OH 44022, 216-247-6421 (flatware matching; appraisals of silver).

Margaret Lane Antiques, 2 E. Main St., New Concord, OH 43762, 614-826-7414 (silver plate).

Martin M. Fleisher, Silversmith, PO Box 305, Copiague, NY 11726 (sterling flatware: active, inactive, obsolete, antique).

Mary S. Butler, 2518 Taylor, Dept. RTK, Commerce, TX 75428, 903-886-7289 (silver plate).

Matchmaker of Iowa, PO Box 43, Waterloo, IA 50704, 319-233-0578 (flatware: pewter, stainless steel, and gold electroplated).

MidweSterling—Silverware Division, 4311 NE Vivion Rd., Kansas City, MO 64119-2890, 816-454-1990; fax: 816-454-1605 (sterling: matching, repair, polishing, and blade replacement; buying sterling flatware and hollow ware).

Overtons Sterling Matching, 200 Avenida Santa Margarita, San Clemente, CA 92672, 714-498-5330 (sterling, specializing in discontinued and obsolete patterns).

R. S. Goldberg, 67 Beverly Rd., Hawthorne, NJ 07506, 800-252-6655, 201-427-6555 (sterling).

Ren's Antiques, 14 S. State St., Newtown, PA 18940, 215-968-5511 (sterling and silver plate).

Replacements, Ltd., PO Box 26029, 1089 Knox Rd., Greensboro, NC 27420-6029, 800-562-4462.

Robert D. Biggs, 1155 E. 58, Chicago, IL 60637, 312-702-9540; fax: 312-702-9853 (sterling and silver-plated flatware).

Shirley Stamen Matching Service, 9601 Arby Dr., Beverly Hills, CA 90210, 310-278-4040; fax: 310-552-3828.

Silver & China Exchange, PO Box 4601, Dept. K, Stamford, CT 06907, 203-322-5963 (discontinued sterling flatware replacements).

Silver Antiquities, PO Box 6137, Leawood, KS 66206, 816-753-5589. (Not a matching service, but they stock some popular patterns, specializing in ornate sterling, 1840–1910, by Durgin, Gorham, Kirk, Stieff, Tiffany, and others.)

The Silver Girls Silverplated Matching, 168

Riverview Rd. SW, Eatonton, GA 31024, 912-968-5225 (silver-plated flatware).

Silver Lane Antiques, PO Box 322, San Leandro, CA 94577, 415-483-0632 (sterling: active, inactive, and obsolete).

Silver Queen Inc., 730 N. Indian Rocks Rd., Belleair Bluffs, FL 34640, 813-581-6827, 800-262-3134 (sterling).

Silver Sails, 8 Manor Oak Dr., Amherst, NY 14228, 716-691-8802 (silver-plated flatware).

Silver Season, PO Box 1136, Norwalk, CT 06850, 203-847-8217 (American silver plate only; free lists available).

Silver Service, Ted Rickard, 708-256-5900 (discontinued patterns of American and English sterling silver flatware).

Silver Shop, 2348 Bissonnet St., Houston, TX 77005, 713-526-7256; fax: 713-526-3119 (sterling flatware, hollowware).

Silver Smiths, PO Box 5118, Fresno, CA 93755, 209-431-1611 (sterling).

Silver Talent—Donna Young, PO Box 9182, Norfolk, VA 23505, 804-587-9016 (sterling, silver plate, coin silver; active, inactive, obsolete).

Sterling & Collectables Inc., PO Box 1665, 453 Lexington Ave., Mansfield, OH 44907, 800-537-5783; in Ohio 419-756-8800; fax: 419-756-2990 (new and restored sterling, silver plate, stainless).

Sterling Shop, PO Box 595, Silverton, OR 97381, 503-873-6315 (sterling, silver plate, hollow ware).

Table Toppers, PO Box 148471, Chicago, IL 60614-8471 (search service for silver; will answer questions regarding tabletop items).

Tabletop Matching Service & Collectors Items, Mrs. Betty H. Allen, PO Box 205, Cookeville, TN 38501, 615-526-4303 (silver plate, specializing in 1847 Rogers).

Tere Hagan, PO Box 25487, Tempe, AZ 85285, 800-528-7425; in greater Phoenix, 602-966-8838 (sterling, silver plate, Dirilyte flatware).

Thurber's, 2256 Dabney Rd., Richmond,

VA 23230, 804-278-9080, 800-848-7237; fax: 804-278-9480 (flatware).

Vi Walker, PO Box 88377, Indianapolis, IN 46208, 317-283-3753 (sterling and silver plate, specializing in American silver and rare serving pieces).

Vintage Silver, 33 LeMay Ct., Williamsville, NY 14221, 716-631-0419 (silver-plated flatware, all patterns active, inactive, obsolete, and individual items).

Vroman's Silver Shop, 442A Fleetwood Pl., Glendora, CA 91740, 800-824-5174; fax: 818-963-1402 (flatware matching, specializing in discontinued patterns of sterling and silver plate; send SASE and pattern name for list).

Walter Drake Silver and China Exchange, Drake Building, Colorado Springs, CO 80940, 800-525-9291, 7:30 A.M.-5:00 P.M. (sterling and silverplated flatware).

Westerling, 5311 St. Charles Rd., Berkeley, IL 60163, 312-547-8488 (specializing in Easterling and Westmoreland).

Wilma Saxton, Inc., PO Box 395, 37 Clementon Rd., Berlin, NJ 08009, 609-767-8640 (sterling, silver plate, stainless, Dirilyte, pewter: active, inactive, and obsolete patterns).

Woodland Antiques, PO Box 3793, Mansfield, OH 44907-3793, 419-756-7831 (sterling, silver-plated, stainless, and flatware).

PART III

Loving Care
for Your Collectibles

CARING FOR YOUR COLLECTIONS

A good housekeeper usually washes the dishes, makes the bed, sweeps the floor, and dusts each day, or so we are told. That rule only applies if the housekeeper is not a collector. There are special housekeeping rules for collections and antiques. Placement of the antiques is one of the most important. To the extent possible, efforts should be made to keep most collectibles out of strong sunlight, extremes of heat or cold (attics or unheated porches), areas with very high or low humidity (basements and attics), or areas too close to working fireplaces. Even the smoke from cigarettes will eventually damage some items.

Don't be too clean. Furniture should be lightly dusted and polish should be used in small amounts only when needed. Wax and dust can eventually build into a dark layer that must be carefully removed with cleaner or the appropriate detergent-and-water treatment.

If you ever find sawdust, rodent or insect droppings, or small flying insects in your house, call an expert to help you look for the source. Old furniture can harbor eggs from wood-eating insects and worms that might infect other furniture in the house. Fabrics, even foods, can harbor eggs that hatch into moths or carpet beetles.

If you have cats or dogs (or even pet cheetahs) that gnaw on wood, find a way to keep them away from the legs of old tables and chairs. There are several products on the market that discourage animals, or try rubbing hot pepper sauce on the wood.

Sometimes dishwasher damage creates hazardous dinnerware. Badly crazed pieces should not be used to serve food, because glasslike slivers could be ingested. Gold trim on fifties cocktail glasses that has turned gray indicates lead, and the glasses should be discarded.

Silver and pewter should be kept clean. Any commercial polish is good, but you can also protect the shine with an antitarnish polish that will save you from frequent cleanings. Never ever use harsh abrasives such as scouring powder or steel wool.

Fabrics are the only collectibles that should be cleaned often. Dirt can do more damage than cleaning. Washable fabrics should be laundered with the proper soap or special detergent. Rinse thoroughly. Soap causes damage, too.

To store fabrics, roll them; do not fold. Old quilts, coverlets, curtains, and pillows can be used, but always remember that the threads are fragile and easy to damage. Rugs should be swept or vacuumed and occasionally cleaned. Always protect fabrics from extremes of heat and light. Store woolens and other insect-attracting fabrics with cedar wood or moth balls.

Books should be dusted regularly. If the climate is damp, be sure to protect against insects. All paper collectibles attract small insects and fungus that will cause damage. Keep paper items in an environment that is not too humid, too hot, or too bright. Handle paper (except books) as seldom as possible, and never fold or tape it. Even the new removable self-stick notes leave some bits of glue that will eventually show up as a discoloration on the page. This problem becomes serious if you leave one of the markers on glossy-finished paper, such as that used in expensive auction catalogs. Never use cellophane tape or regular household glue on paper collectibles.

Be sure to have fire alarms and fire extinguishers handy, and check them at regular intervals. A burglar alarm is a good investment, and if your collection is valuable, carry special insurance. A fire, hurricane, or earthquake can destroy anything.

The sections that follow contain more detailed information about home care of furniture, silver, other metals, paper, and textiles.

CARE OF FURNITURE

The grimy, dirty, scratched, and even slightly marred, old chest you just found has waited for a new finish for more than fifty years. The waiting has been important. If the old patina (appearance of aging) were not desirable, total stripping and refinishing would be the solution to all refinishing problems. But the old color and patina are the most important

features on an antique piece of furniture. Always try to restore the finish. Remove the finish or sandpaper and restain the piece only as a last resort. Restoring a finish is easier than total refinishing, and the results are more worthwhile from the view of the collector and the decorator.

Refinishing

Do not try to refinish antiques to look like new pieces. If you prefer the high-gloss, unscarred look, buy new furniture or paint old, but not antique, pieces. A few minor imperfections can be cured without refinishing. Small scratches can be covered using a commercial stain polish and scratch remover, or try shoe polish, which often works just as well.

Repairing

All noticeable repairs should be made before you begin restoring or stripping the paint or other finish. Clean off all old glue, glue any wobbly legs, remove dents, and fill holes; reglue and clamp all of the stretchers, spindles, dovetail joints, and other spots that may be loose; and replace all missing pieces with new ones. For more detailed information, see one of the books listed in the Furniture section.

Stick shellac can be heated and pressed into large holes. After the first refinishing coat is on, you can patch with any good plastic-wood filler. Wax-type scratch removers are used on a completed finish. Dents sometimes can be removed by pressing over them with a damp wool strip and a hot iron. The warm, moist air frequently will cause the wood to swell.

If the surface is painted, *do not* remove the old paint unless the piece is so hopeless you could not give it house room. Frequently, most of the value of an old painted piece is removed with the paint. Even faded old designs are more desirable than repainted new ones. If you prefer a freshly painted chair, buy a reproduction.

Stripping

*T*here are many excellent methods of stripping old paint, varnish, or shellac from a piece of furniture that is to be refinished. These safety rules apply to all methods of stripping. Most of the paint removers are quite strong, so wear gloves and old clothes and do the work in a well-ventilated room or garage. Protect the floor by covering it with papers. Have all the needed chemicals, removers, rags, burlap, newspapers, tools, steel wool, sandpaper, brushes, scrapers, small sticks, and toothbrushes available and keep them handy. It is frustrating to have to stop while working and search for something. Keep a large wastebasket handy. *Do not smoke,* as many of the removers are flammable. Do not eat near the work, since there may be lead dust in the air. Wash your hands before eating.

A screwdriver, pliers, and hammer will be helpful, too. Remove all hardware before you start. Be sure to save all of the screws, nuts, and bolts that go with the hardware in a box kept nearby to hold small items. Remove drawers and all doors that can be easily removed from their hinges. Refinish each of the drawers separately. Mark the location of each screw, bolt, door, or drawer so it can go back to exactly the same place.

Commercial Strippers

*P*ut the piece to be stripped on several layers of newspaper in a well-ventilated room. You must work on a cool day because the remover will dry too quickly on a very hot day. After you have removed all the hardware, read the directions on the can or remover. Pour some of the remover into an old can, and flow it on the wood with an old brush. Work on only a small section of the piece at a time, using short strokes in one direction, with the wood grain. Let the remover stand ten to twenty minutes until the finish softens. *Do not stir or rebrush the remover once it is on.* This just speeds the evaporation and slows down the work of the remover. Scrape the finish off with a very dull knife or a scraper and steel wool.

If you are stripping a chair, keep an empty tuna-fish can handy. The chair leg can be set in the can, and the remover that drips down can be rebrushed on the chair leg.

Carvings can best be cleaned with removers and steel wool pads, a stiff brush, or a toothbrush. Scraping tools should be dull with rounded edges, so they do not make any scratches. When working on a large tabletop, you may find it handy to scrape the sludge directly into an old coffee can.

If the finish is not completely removed, repeat the process. After all of the old finish is removed, wash the piece with water, lacquer thinner, or turpentine, whichever the directions suggest, then wipe the piece, let it dry, and rub very lightly with 0000 steel wool and very fine sandpaper. When you think you have steel-wooled or sanded enough, sand one more time.

The used rags are highly flammable. If

you are going to reuse them, they should be washed or placed in a safe, well-ventilated place. Wash your hands after all of this, and use a hand cream to prevent chapping. These chemicals are strong.

Finishes

*I*f the table or chair to be refinished is stripped to its naked glory and several types of wood appear, we suggest you find an artistic friend who can match color, and paint it. Or you can decide to live with the several shades in the finished piece. We have no objections to variation in shades, and believe it adds interest. However, some purists feel that it shows the refinishing was the work of an amateur. Anyone with a good eye for color can rub stain into the offending wood until a good match is obtained.

If you wish to stain the wood, buy any commercial penetrating oil stain or stain sealer, and follow the directions on the can. Colored stains also can be used.

Some woods need a sealer coat to ensure that the color will be uniformly absorbed. Test a small area where it won't show. If the color of the wood is blotchy, seal the wood first. Use a diluted coat of whatever clear finish you plan to use, either varnish or shellac. Mix the varnish with an equal amount of turpentine, or mix the shellac with eight times as much denatured alcohol. Brush the sealer on the wood, let dry fifteen minutes, wipe off with a dry cloth, and let it dry thoroughly for about twenty-four hours. Rub with 0000 steel wool, dust with a cloth, and then apply the stain.

Shellac is easy to use and easy to polish, but it does chip and is not good for tabletops where wet glasses may leave a ring. Do not use old shellac. Use white shellac on any wood, orange shellac on dark wood. Before starting to shellac, be sure the room is free of dust. Buy as much denatured alcohol as you do shellac. Thin the shellac with an equal amount of alcohol, or until the shellac flows from the brush like water.

The process of putting shellac on wood is simple, if you remember two things: Never work in a damp room or the finished piece will turn white; and never try to rebrush the shellac after it has been applied. Place the piece to be shellacked so that the surface is horizontal. It may mean a few more hours of work, but the result and lack of errors will be well worth the trouble.

When you do the top of a chest, let it dry for at least four hours. Then rub the piece with 0000 steel wool or very find sandpaper. Coat it again with shellac, let dry, and again rub with steel wool. Then wipe it clean with a rag. Four coats give the best finish, but two will be satisfactory for most pieces. If the wood is very porous, more coats may be needed. After the final coat has been applied, steel wool or sand again, and wax the entire piece.

The directions for using varnish are very similar to those for shellac. Varnish is much harder and more durable, and is a better finish for tabletops. Applying varnish is slow and a bit tricky. Always apply varnish in a room with a temperature around 70 degrees. If it is too cold or too hot, the finish might be streaky and bumpy. *Do not use spar varnish.*

Apply the varnish with the grain, flowing it on by brush in a light coat. Do not overlap the brushstrokes. Let the varnish dry at least twenty-four hours, or better yet, a week. Rub down with dampened 6-0 waterproof garnet paper, or with wet 500-A sandpaper. Wash with a wet chamois, then wax, if you wish.

Rottenstone and oil can be used for the final polish.

Lacquer is applied in much the same manner as shellac. It is tricky to use, and most beginners do not succeed. Prepare the furniture as before, by sanding and coloring. Buy a good-quality lacquer. Use it full strength, brushing it on quickly. Let it dry, and sand with no. 360 sandpaper and turpentine. The turpentine softens the finish slightly and helps create a smooth surface. Another method is to thin the lacquer with equal parts of lacquer thinner. Brush it on, then wipe off the excess with a dry cloth. After an hour, rub with 0000 steel wool. Dust, and brush on a coat of full-strength lacquer.

The finished piece may be waxed. Lacquer is for strength, not shine, and if gloss is the desired finish, use shellac.

The most famous and difficult, but probably the finest, finish for choice antiques is the method known as French polishing. Be sure the piece has been sanded and is clean and dry before you begin.

Cut a piece of cheesecloth about 2 × 5 inches. Fold in the loose ends to make a pad about half that size. For large areas, cut a piece of cheesecloth a yard square and fold in the loose ends. Hold the pad with your index finger folded behind it for pressure. Grasp the pad with the thumb and other fingers. It is possible to buy a commercial product called French polish. It will give good results. The other method is to dip the pad into boiled linseed oil, wring it dry, then dip it into shellac and rub in small circles. Add more oil, more shellac, and do more rubbing until a finish has been built up. This takes time and skill. It is best to experiment on a piece of unimportant wood because too much shellac, too long a wait, too much oil, or not enough pressure will cause trouble.

If you really feel brave enough to try this finish on a large piece, read any of the many books about refinishing that devote several chapters to this technique. The finished piece will be smooth, glossy, and well worth the trouble.

Waxing and Polishing

The finished piece, now sanded and dry, probably needs a coat of wax or polish for added gloss and protection. Just wax on wood isn't always good enough, because it will wear off quickly. However, maple, cherry, or other close-grained hardwoods sometimes seem satisfactory with a wax finish.

Use a carnauba-base paste furniture wax. Apply with a soft, lint-free cloth, pretending that you are shining shoes. Apply a thin coat of wax, and rub. Remember, the more you rub, the better the shine.

Cleaning

It is often best to simply wipe furniture with a clean, dry cloth to remove marks and smudges. Too much wax and weekly spray-dusting with the newer products frequently causes the buildup of a layer of dirt and oil that can hide the beauty of the wood. Paste wax is best. Apply using a pad with a thin layer of wax, and rub to a polish. Liquid wax is a paste wax dissolved in a solvent. Shake the bottle, and apply with a damp, soft cloth. Polish with another damp, soft cloth.

Keep furniture out of direct sun, if possible, and keep old wood in a room with proper humidity (plants help). Never use a self-polishing floor wax on furniture; it destroys the finish.

CARE OF PAPER

Centuries have passed since Ts'ai Lun, a Chinese eunuch, accidentally mixed some woven scraps with water, then poured them on a bamboo screen where they dried into paper. During the past centuries, paper has been made with chemicals and it no longer ages as well as older paper. Chemical additives like alum create a more acidic paper that dissolves and disintegrates.

To avoid any problems, handle paper antiques with special care:

1. Use clean hands to handle books and pictures.
2. Use two hands to lift matted or unmatted pictures to prevent bending, creasing, or tearing.
3. Unmatted pictures should never be stacked directly on top of each other. They should be separated by a smooth, nonacid, cover tissue.
4. Valuable pictures should be matted rather than left loose. They may be stored in acid-free folders or envelopes.
5. Be careful not to drag anything across the surface of a picture.
6. Handle with care pictures glued on old cardboard or wood.
7. Always open a mat by the outer edge, not by the window on the inner edge.
8. Pictures in mats or folders should be stored in drawers or a solander box (a special box built to hold books). Airtight metal boxes are not recommended, as they condense moisture and will quickly transmit heat in case of fire.
9. To carry, mail, or ship loose pictures, pack them between two heavy pieces of cardboard. Rolling a good picture could cause it to crack.

Storage and Display Environment

The best environment for your treasured prints, newspapers, and documents should have the following features:

Humidity should be about 55 percent: no less than 45 percent, no more than 60. Excessive moisture encourages mold.

Beware, especially, of dampness on outside walls in stone houses and in basements and cellars. Houses that are closed up for any extended time can become very humid.

If you live near the ocean, or in a damp climate, use an air conditioner to keep humidity under the dangerous 70 percent level. Silica gel can be used as a dehumidifying agent in airtight containers. Small sachets or dishes of thymol crystals can be put around as a preventative.

Mold growth often shows up as dull rusty patches that discolor the sheet of paper. "Foxing" is caused by the chemical action of the mold on the colorless iron salts present in the paper. It feeds on sizing and paper fibers, and thereby weakens the sheet.

Protection from light. Sunlight and ultraviolet light tend to cause brittleness, fading, and rapid oxidation. Fluorescent lights can also accelerate the destruction of paper. Allow only enough light for good viewing. To avoid excess light, never place pictures on a wall directly opposite a sunny window.

Translucent curtains and louvered blinds will provide protection. Plastic sleeves on the fixture will protect against ultraviolet light from fluorescent lights. Plexiglas sheets will filter ultraviolet light and may be substituted for glass in a picture frame. Additionally, there is a protective film that can be permanently applied to very sunny windows.

Heat is another destructive agent. Never

hang pictures or put books over a radiator, heat register, or air duct. Be doubly wary of that spot above the fireplace. Not only is the heat from the fireplace destructive, the soot and gummy residues produced by the fire stick to anything.

Air pollution, including cigarette smoke, also threatens paper. It causes discoloration and eventual disintegration of paper fibers. The sulfur dioxide in the air is absorbed by the paper, and converted into sulfuric acid. This may cause severe brown stains on pictures lacking a backing, and can cause leather book bindings to turn to powder.

To prevent this kind of damage, an air conditioner and air filter can be installed. Rag-board mat in front and back of the picture provides some protection.

Insects are another danger to paper valuables. Paper should be kept off the floor and out of the damp, warm, dark places preferred by insects. Paper should be kept out of basements and attics. Insect spray, sodium fluoride, or moth crystals are recommended as protections. Clean and inspect the dark spaces behind and beneath books to avoid this problem. Beware of silverfish (silvery, pearl-gray insects). They will cut through a large picture to get at the flour paste and glue sizing. They move so quickly they can cause considerable damage before they are noticed. Cockroaches can cause damage to parchment, leather, paper, and glues. Termites and wood worms also do damage.

Framing and Matting

*P*roper framing and matting provide the best protection for pictures. Never use glue. The chemicals can be destructive. Pressure-sensitive tapes cause permanent stains.

Staples and pins cause rust stains and tears. Acidic pastes cause deterioration, and rubber cements cause permanent stains. Gummed brown wrapping tape is also damaging.

Never use wood-pulp matting board. Its highly acidic composition disintegrates, leaving stains on the picture and weakening the paper.

"Museum board" is composed of a high-grade cellulose from cotton fibers. It is the only safe matting material. Its one-sixteenth-inch thickness provides an adequate depth to allow for minor buckling, as well as sufficient breathing space between the glass and the picture. Be sure to provide this space, since moisture condenses and may cause mold growth.

There is also the possibility of the picture adhering to the glass. Even if a mat is not desirable, a narrow strip of mat board should be cut and hidden beneath the inner edge of the frame. If for some reason (for example, an artist's signature) a wood-pulp mat must be saved, it can be placed on top of an all-rag board.

Never spray cleaner on the surface of the glass or covering of a picture. Liquid may run down the inside of the frame and stain the mat. Spray the cloth, then wipe the glass.

Pictures and paintings should be hung to allow air to circulate behind the frame. Use "hangers" or small pads on the lower corners of the frame back. Be sure the picture wire is secure.

Specific Problems That May Have Already Occurred

*C*andle wax. Scrape with an artist's spatula; carefully remove the rest with mineral spirits or paint thinner.

Buckling. Excessive buckling suggests too much pressure on the edges of the picture by either the mat or the frame; this can be corrected by a framer. Localized puckering may be caused by the presence of old tape, patches, or glue on the back of the picture. In that case, the picture should be taken to a restorer. Never paste down a picture to remove a few waves of slight buckling. Stains and weakening of the paper will eventually result.

Water-soaked documents. If you have a number of documents that are water-soaked, place them in the freezer. This will stop any further water damage. They can be defrosted and ironed or treated at a later time.

CARE OF TEXTILES

Textiles are among the most perishable antiques. Old clothing, draperies, linens, samplers, and tapestries have usually seen a lot of wear. They may be disintegrating from careless handling, vigorous washing, or use of the wrong cleaning solvent. Textiles are subject to the fading and weakening effects of natural or artificial light, direct or reflected, and to the corrosive effects of city air. They may be destroyed by moths, insects, fungus, or mold. Temperature and humidity variations, stains, and tears also cause damage.

First decide what type of fiber was used in the fabric. In general, natural fibers are from animal sources (wool and silk) or vegetable sources (cotton and linen). Animal fibers will shrink and lose their luster when washed in hot water or chlorine bleach. They are more sensitive to rubbing, and in great danger from insects and fungi.

There is a simple test to determine animal from vegetable fibers: Take a few threads from the article and burn them in a dish. Animal fibers burn slowly, producing a bead and an odor of burning feathers. Vegetable fibers burn more quickly, producing a soft ash and an odor of burning paper. Synthetics melt like cotton candy.

Repair

First take care of any rips or holes in the fabric, however small, before they become larger. Cigarette burns can be stitched around the hole, then cross-stitched, as in darning. Large rips should be caught up immediately with thread, and then mended by a professional. Never use tape, as it is difficult to remove.

Patching old fabrics with contemporary ones will probably be conspicuous, unless reproductions of period patterns are used. Even these need to be washed, bleached, and sunned first to take out the "newness." Appropriate patching material may often be found at rummage sales and in thrift stores.

Cleaning

Cleaning should begin with the removal of loose dirt. Use a hand vacuum on low suction through a piece of nylon screen to protect delicate fabrics or embroidery.

Old textiles can be safely washed if they are strong enough to be creased without breaking the fibers. This generally means they should be washed in water only if they are in very good condition. If possible, spot washing is preferable to washing the entire piece. Before trying to wash an article, test each color for fastness by placing the fabric between two pieces of clean, white blotting paper, and using an eye dropper to apply a few drops of water to each color. If a color does not appear on the paper, it's safe to proceed. Embroidery or hand painting may also run if washed. Always check the linings.

Some general rules for washing:

1. If you use a washing machine, be sure to use the gentle cycle and cold water, and always put the fabric in a net bag.
2. Never use commercial detergents. Bleaches and additives may damage fabrics. Ivory Flakes, Lux, or special museum-preferred soaps can be used on cotton or linen; Woolite is all right for colorfast woolens. Special silk-washing liquids can be used.
3. Use only soft water; add softener to hard water.
4. Use only cold or lukewarm water. Hot water hardens wool and shrinks wool and linen.
5. Use distilled water for rinsing in order to avoid rust flecks from iron traces in tap water.
6. Don't rub old fabrics during washing. Dirt, if not removed by soaking, can be dislodged by gentle agitation. Water may be forced through sturdy pieces, such as quilts, by the careful use of a plunger.
7. Avoid using chlorine bleaches; they will eventually weaken the fabric. Don't use an alkaline bleach on wool or silk. If an alkaline bleach is used, add vinegar to the rinse water to neutralize it.

Generally, the effect of washing is to expand fibers; that of drying, to contract them. The ability of fibers to bear up under the strain should be taken into account. Quilted pieces have the added stress of the swelling of filler material.

Washing protects the fabric from moths and other insects. Eggs can thrive in the smallest amount of dirt. Fabrics should not be put away dirty. Damage from insects and mold may well exceed any harm that could come to the fabric during careful washing.

Some special cases. If a material has a special finish to give it a glaze or a sheen, such as watered silk or moiré, the finish is probably water soluble and will be ruined by washing. Canvas has often been treated with sizing; if washed, it may go limp, and could possibly shrink.

Fabrics are much heavier when wet, so their weight must be supported during washing. Support the fabric with a large piece of nylon net; otherwise, the added weight may cause the fabric to tear or weaken. Quilts, in particular, should be washed between two pieces of net stitched together.

An hour's soaking in cold water should remove most dirt. The water should be changed several times, or whenever it looks dirty. If a small piece of fabric is strong enough to be agitated, it can be washed in a two-gallon jar by rocking the jar gently back and forth. Drain and rinse in clear water. If, after an hour, the fabric still appears dirty or greasy, it can be washed with mild soap in a diluted solution.

Rinse the fabric thoroughly. Any soap residue not rinsed out may cause a brown stain during ironing. Quilts must be rinsed several times to remove all residue. Put the fabric in a large towel. Roll it up in the towel and let it sit until damp dry. Spread it out onto another towel, or onto blotting paper, to remove the remaining moisture. Pin the piece into shape, using stainless-steel pins to avoid rust spots. Smooth out all folds and wrinkles; shape lace and ruffles by hand. Folds and creases cause undue stress in the fabric.

Let the fabric dry naturally at average temperature and humidity. In general, don't hang fabrics, as this will cause unnecessary strain. Don't use direct heat or hot-air blowers, and don't expose old fabrics to direct sunlight. White cottons and linens may not yellow if given a brief exposure to the sun, but be careful, as a long exposure could weaken them.

Iron fabrics carefully and slowly, always making sure to control the heat. When ironing embroidery, use a well-padded ironing board and cover the fabric with sheeting. Never iron quilts.

Lace can be dry-cleaned by sprinkling powdered French chalk (powdered soapstone) over the lace, then brushing it off with a camel's-hair paintbrush. If it must be washed in water, first try soaking it in distilled water. If necessary, wash it in warm water with a few drops of detergent and rinse in warm water. Lay the lace on white blotting paper and pin into shape to dry.

If your textile can't be washed, but is in obvious need of cleaning, then try dry cleaning. Stain removal is a highly sophisticated science. The use of the wrong solvent, or too much of the right one, can be disastrous.

Even if done by professionals, dry cleaning of old textiles should be attempted only after testing has shown that the solvent won't damage the fabric or the dyes, and that the fabric is strong enough to handle the process. Solvents tend to have less effect on the material than water, but they can have greater effect on the dyes. Each color should be tested individually with minute amounts of solvent and blotting paper. Don't forget the lining. Often, several different solvents will have to be tried before the correct one is found.

Stain Removal

There are many different types of stains, each with its appropriate solvent. Charts are provided in many books found in your local library. It may be necessary to test several different solvents on long-standing stains, using a tiny amount and carefully observing the effect. Once the right solvent is found, use as small an amount as possible. A little bit on a cotton swab may be enough. Apply the solvent and lift the stain off—don't rub the solvent in. For larger stains, stretch the fabric, stain side down, over a white blotter. Use an eyedropper to drop the solvent in a ring around the stain. This will allow the solvent to work inward toward the stain, rather than spreading it. Fresh stains should be taken care of as quickly as possible, preferably before the stain has a chance to dry.

Before treating old stains with a solvent, it's useful to soak the fabric overnight in cold water. When grease spots are fresh, they can often be removed with soap, warm water, and persistence. Older grease spots can be dusted with talc or Fuller's earth and left to set for twenty-four hours.

Storage

Old fabrics should be stored in the dark, at a controlled temperature and humidity. Small closet humidifiers or dehumidifiers are good for this purpose. Stored textiles need air. Storage in zippered bags, trunks, or other tightly sealed containers may trap moisture and invite mold. Don't put fabrics away dirty; dirt provides a breeding ground for moths, silverfish, beetles, or other insects. Rolling fabrics around a tube is preferable to folding them; folds and creases cause strain. If a cardboard tube is used, cover it with acid-free tissue. If folding is the only alternative, pad the folds with tissue. Periodically unfold the fabric and refold along different lines. To prevent yellowing, wrap whites in blue sulfite-free tissue, available from most dry cleaners. Don't allow cottons and linens to come into direct contact with wood, which is acidic. It's better to use old towels or undyed sheeting to wrap textiles than to use paper or tissue that isn't acid-free. Wooden hangers can also discolor the fabric.

Stored textiles should be rolled or folded, wrapped, and packed loosely to allow for air circulation.

Index